UK 2005

The Official Yearbook of the
United Kingdom of Great Britain
and Northern Ireland

Prepared by the Office for National Statistics

London: TSO

Contact points
We welcome comments and suggestions on this publication:
email   uk.yearbook@ons.gov.uk
telephone +44 (0)20 7533 5778
or write to The Editor, UK Yearbook,
Office for National Statistics, Room B5/02,
1 Drummond Gate, London SW1V 2QQ

For general enquiries, contact the
National Statistics Customer Contact Centre:
email   info@statistics.gov.uk
telephone 0845 601 3034
                 (UK local rate)
                 +44 (0)1633 812973
                 (International)
                 01633 812399
                 (Minicom number for the Deaf)
fax   +44 (0)1633 652747

or write to
The Customer Contact Centre,
Office for National Statistics,
Room 1015,
Government Buildings,
Cardiff Road,
Newport NP10 8XG

You can find National Statistics on the Internet
www.statistics.gov.uk

The UK Yearbook is also available on the
National Statistics website
www.statistics.gov.uk/yearbook

About the Office for National Statistics
The Office for National Statistics (ONS) is the government agency responsible for compiling, analysing and disseminating many of the United Kingdom's economic, social and demographic statistics, including the retail prices index, trade figures and labour market data, as well as the periodic census of the population and health statistics. It is also the agency that administers the statutory registration of births, marriages and deaths in England and Wales. The Director of ONS is the National Statistician and the Registrar General for England and Wales.

A National Statistics publication
National Statistics are produced to high professional standards set out in the National Statistics Code of Practice. They undergo regular quality assurance reviews to ensure they meet customer needs. They are produced free from any political influence.

Contents

Contributors

UK 2005 was researched, written and edited by a combination of in-house and freelance authors.

Authors Lisa Almqvist
Anthony Beachey
Louise Bell
Ben Bradford
Siân Bradford
Mary Brailey
Simon Burtenshaw
Richard German
David Harper
Steve Howell
Joyce Huddleston
Henry Langley
Kylie Lovell
Alex Praill
Matthew Richardson
Bernadeta Tendyra
Linda Zealey

Obituaries John Collis

Data support and review Lola Akinrodoye
Carl Bird
John Chrzczonowicz
Ercilia Dini
David Gardener
Caroline Hall
Shiva Satkunam
Sarah Sullivan
Steve Whyman

Cover James Twist

Colour pages Michelle Franco

Maps Alistair Dent
Ray Martin

Index Richard German

Picture research Suzanne Bosman

Production Mario Alemanno
Sharon Adhikari
Joseph Goldstein

Proof readers Richard German
Rosemary Hamilton
Jane Howard
Geoff Potter
Jeff Probst

Charts and typesetting Spire Origination, Norwich

Editors Carol Summerfield
Jill Barelli
Linda Zealey
David Harper

Acknowledgements

UK 2005 has been compiled with the help of over 200 organisations, including many government departments and agencies. The editors would like to thank all the people from these organisations who have taken so much time and care to ensure that the book's high standards of accuracy have been maintained. Their contributions and comments have been extremely valuable.

Cover picture © Jay Syverson/Corbis

Preface

Transport and travel is the theme running through *UK 2005*, as well as being the subject of chapter 21. Although this theme was inspired by a number of notable events, records and anniversaries, the movement of people and goods occurs on such a scale it has profound consequences for every aspect of life, including the environment, work and leisure, as well as the economy.

The majority of people in employment travel to work by car or van (62 per cent in England and Wales in 2001). Far fewer commuters use public transport (14 per cent) and 13 per cent either walk or cycle. Over half of workers (58 per cent) travel less than 10 kilometres to their place of work, and only 5 per cent travel 40 kilometres or more. Chapter 11 provides an overview of the labour market.

The way children travel to school has changed greatly over the past decade, with fewer walking and more being driven. The average length of the school journey has also increased from the early 1990s, from 2.0 to 2.6 kilometres for primary schoolchildren, and from 4.5 to 4.8 kilometres for children at secondary schools. Education and training are key areas of government policy, which are outlined in chapter 10.

More generally, travel by car, van or taxi is by far the most common means of transport in the United Kingdom, accounting for 85 per cent of passenger mileage in Great Britain. In 2003, nearly three quarters of households in the United Kingdom had access to at least one car, while over a quarter had access to two or more.

The first toll motorway, the M6 Toll, opened in December 2003 to ease motorway congestion in the West Midlands. The 43-kilometre expressway cuts journey times around Birmingham by an estimated 45 minutes. By August 2004 it had reached its landmark 10 millionth customer, triggering the end to introductory discounted toll rates.

Vehicle-related thefts have fallen in recent years, partly because of the more sophisticated security measures now fitted to new cars. Vehicles aged between 11 and 15 years are more likely to be stolen than cars aged 3 years or less. Crime and justice is covered in more depth in chapter 14. In January 1904 the *Motor Car Act* brought in the registration of vehicles, the number plate and the driving licence. A hundred years later, the Government introduced a ban on the use of mobile phones while driving.

The rapid increase in the use of mobile phones was one of the reasons why the Royal National Lifeboat Institution (RNLI) had its busiest year in 2003. Lifeboats were launched a record 8,901 times and 7,987 people were rescued. The increase is also a result of changing patterns of sea use by the public and improved search and rescue techniques. In addition, the long hot summer of 2003 was the fifth warmest in much of the United Kingdom since records began in 1659. The climate and physical geography of the United Kingdom is covered in chapter 1 , while the work of charities and volunteers are two of the many issues covered in chapter 9.

Transport contributes about 25 per cent of carbon dioxide (CO_2) emissions in the United Kingdom, with road transport accounting for 85 per cent of this. Cars are responsible for about half of all transport emissions. Between 1970 and 2002 road traffic increased by 142 per cent and CO_2 emissions attributable to road transport were 130 per cent higher in 2001 than in 1970. Chapter 19 looks at the UK environment and covers issues concerning land and water, as well as air quality and the atmosphere.

In the 2004 Public Spending Review the Government introduced a number of measures aimed at improving the efficiency of the transport system while safeguarding the environment (see chapter 23). Alternative forms of transport are also being explored and the first UK fuel cell bus began service in 2004. It runs on hydrogen and its only emission is water vapour.

The first century of powered flight was celebrated at the Royal Air Force Museum in Hendon with the *Milestones of Flight* exhibition. Among the exhibits were a Hawker Tempest V from the 1940s, a Harrier GR3 from the 1960s, and a Eurofighter Typhoon, which came into service in 2003.

Passenger-kilometres flown from UK airports have more than doubled in recent years. The Department for Transport forecasts that over the next decade the number of air passengers will grow by around 4 per cent a year and that freight will grow by 7 per cent a year. UK airports handled 2.2 million tonnes of freight in 2003, over half of which went through Heathrow.

The fastest commercial passenger aircraft, Concorde, made its last passenger flight in November 2003. Meanwhile, the longest established air route in the United Kingdom, between Southampton and Jersey, celebrated its 70th year in 2004. Southampton was also the site of the launch of *Queen Mary 2*, the world's biggest and most expensive cruise liner, which set sail on her maiden voyage to Fort Lauderdale in the United States in January 2004. With 14 decks, 1,310 cabins, 14, bars and a brewery, she can carry 2,620 passengers.

Several railway anniversaries were celebrated during 2004, the centrepiece being Railfest, a nine-day festival at the National Railway Museum in York. Pride of place was taken by the *Flying Scotsman*, the first steam engine to achieve 100 mph (161 km/h), which the Railway Museum had bought earlier in the year.

Many transport companies offer online booking services and in 2002–03 over half of people shopping online brought goods and services connected with travel, accommodation or holidays. Chapter 17 gives more information on the Internet, communications and the media.

Mobile libraries are being upgraded to provide computer and Internet access. Many people without easy access to transport, especially in isolated rural communities, rely on these to borrow books and obtain information. There are over 660 mobile libraries in the United Kingdom, each serving many local communities on a weekly, fortnightly or monthly basis. A mobile library carries about 3,500 items, including books and videos for loan. Chapter 16 gives information on libraries and archives, as well as some of the cultural highlights of the past year.

In April 2004 The Queen made her fourth state visit to France to mark the centenary of the signing of the *Entente Cordiale*, which settled historic disputes and paved the way for diplomatic and military co-operation between the United Kingdom and France at the beginning of the 20th century. The Queen returned to France in June, to join world leaders and thousands of veterans in commemorating the 60th anniversary of D-Day, when allied troops landed in France to start the successful liberation of Europe. Chapter 7 covers international relations, while chapter 8 looks at defence.

Members of the Royal Family carry out about 3,000 official engagements a year in the United Kingdom and overseas. Their expenditure on travel in 2003/04 was £4.7 million. In the same period, the Royal Train made 18 journeys, while RAF aircraft were used for 334 hours for Royal flying and helicopters for 389 hours. Chapter 6 gives information on the UK Government and the Monarchy, while the devolved administrations are outlined in chapters 2 to 5.

A special form of travel associated with religion (covered in chapter 15) is the pilgrimage. Each year about 20,000 British Muslims travel to Makka (Mecca) to perform the Hajj. Since 2000 a British Hajj Delegation has travelled with them to provide consular, pastoral and medical assistance. Back in the United Kingdom, Walsingham, a place of pilgrimage for both Anglicans and Catholics, was voted the nation's most spiritual place in 2003.

During 2003–04 several transport records were broken. Balloonist David Hempleman-Adams, who was partly the inspiration for our front cover, he soared to over 40,000 feet (12,192 metres), breaking the existing record of 35,626 feet (10,859 metres). Richard Branson broke the record for crossing the English Channel in an amphibious vehicle, reaching Calais in 1 hour 40 minutes and 6 seconds. The UK rail speed record was broken in July 2003 when Eurostar reached 208 mph (335 km/h).

As well as transport, *UK 2005* outlines government policy and provides facts and figures on all aspects of life in the United Kingdom, from the economy (chapters 22 to 29) to social and cultural affairs; and from housing, planning and regeneration (chapter 20) to science and technology (chapter 25) and sport (chapter 18). *UK 2005* is also available on *www.statistics.gov.uk/yearbook*.

Notes and definitions

1. Figures given in tables and charts may not always sum to the totals shown because of rounding.

2. The full title of the United Kingdom is 'the United Kingdom of Great Britain and Northern Ireland'. 'Great Britain' comprises England, Wales and Scotland.

3. Statistics in this book apply to the United Kingdom as a whole wherever possible. However, data are not always available on a comparable basis, so in some areas information has been given for one or more of the component parts of the United Kingdom. Geographical coverage is clearly indicated.

4. Every effort is made to ensure that the information given in *UK 2005* is accurate at the time of going to press. The text is generally based on information available up to the end of August 2004. Data for the most recent year may be provisional or estimated.

5. Mid year population estimates for 2003 and revised 2001 and 2002 estimates (published on 9 September 2004) have been included in this edition. However, due to publication deadlines, it has not been possible to include the latest projections (published on 30 September 2004) or the revised estimates for 1992 to 2000 (published on 7 October 2004). In addition, we have not been able to include the resulting revisions to the Labour Force Survey estimates that were published in the national, country and regional labour market statistics First Releases on 13 October 2004.

6. The data from the New Earnings Survey in chapters 9 and 11 are being replaced from October 2004 with the Annual Survey of Hours and Earnings.

7. Any information about named companies has been taken from company reports and news releases, or from other publicly available sources. No information about individual companies has been taken from returns submitted in response to ONS statistical inquiries – these remain entirely confidential.

8. Many of the data sources given at the foot of tables and charts and the publications quoted in the further reading lists are available in full on their relevant websites.

Symbols and conventions

1 billion = 1,000 million

1 trillion = 1,000 billion

Financial and academic years are shown as 2003/04

Data covering more than one year such as
2001, 2002 and 2003 are shown as 2001–03

The following symbols have been used in tables:
n/a   not available
.   not applicable
–   negligible (less than half the final digit shown)
0   nil
EU-15   The European Union of 15 members before
        enlargement in May 2004
EU-25   The European Union of 25 members after
        enlargement in May 2004

Units of measurement
Area
1 hectare (ha) = 10,000 sq metres = 2.4711 acres
1 square kilometre (sq km) = 100 hectares
= 0.3861 square miles

Length
1 centimetre (cm) = 10 millimetres (mm)
= 0.3937 inches
1 metre (m) = 1,000 millimetres = 3.2808 feet (ft)
1 kilometre (km) = 1,000 metres = 0.6214 miles

Mass
1 kilogram (kg) = 2.2046 pounds (lb)
1 tonne (t) = 1,000 kilograms = 0.9842 long tons (UK)

Volume
1 litre (l) = 1.7598 UK pints = 0.2200 UK gallons
1 cubic metre = 1,000 litres

SI prefixes
hecto (h)   = 100   = 10^2
kilo (k)   = 1,000   = 10^3
mega (M)   = 1 million   = 10^6
giga (G)   = 1 billion   = 10^9
tera (T)   = 1 thousand billion   = 10^{12}

1 The United Kingdom

The United Kingdom of Great Britain and Northern Ireland (UK) was created by the *Act of Union 1800* and constitutes the greater part of the British Isles, a group of islands lying off the north-west coast of Europe. The largest of the islands is Great Britain, which comprises England, Wales and Scotland. The next largest is Ireland, comprising Northern Ireland, which is part of the United Kingdom, and, in the south, the Republic of Ireland.

North-west Scotland is fringed by two large island chains, the Inner and Outer Hebrides. To the north of the Scottish mainland are the Orkney and Shetland Islands. These, along with the Isle of Wight, Anglesey and the Isles of Scilly, have administrative ties with the mainland. The Isle of Man and the Channel Islands are not part of the United Kingdom (see page 7).

Physical features

The oldest rocks, dating back 2.6 billion years, are found in the Scottish Highlands and Outer Hebrides. Metamorphic and igneous rocks are widespread in Wales, the Lake District and southern Scotland.

Devonian and Carboniferous strata in south-west England have been intruded by granite. The largest granite area is Dartmoor. Carboniferous limestone forms the Mendip Hills, and part of the Pennine chain in the Peak District and around Malham Tarn in North Yorkshire. Deep valleys, such as the Avon gorge, have cut into the limestone and rivers commonly disappear underground where cave networks have developed. The overlying millstone grit of the Upper Carboniferous age makes up much of the Pennines, with coal measures forming the lower ground flanking the Pennine Hills. Coal seams are also widespread in the Midlands, South Wales and around Bristol.

Permian and Triassic rocks stretch from Devon to north-west and north-east England, but are at their widest across the Midlands, where the sandstones are a major aquifer.[1] Jurassic rocks are dominated by limestone layers, extending from the World Heritage coastline in Dorset, through the Cotswolds and Northamptonshire into Lincolnshire and Yorkshire. Many prominent buildings in London, such as those in Whitehall, are constructed from Jurassic limestone quarried in Dorset.

Cretaceous chalk strata cover wide areas of southern England, such as the South Downs, where they are exposed in white cliffs at Beachy Head and Dover. Younger strata, mainly soft sandstones and clays, are found in east and south-east England and are associated with fertile farmland.

On the Antrim coast in Northern Ireland is the Giants Causeway. At this World Heritage site there are almost 40,000 massive polygonal basalt columns, formed around 60 million years ago from slowly cooling volcanic rock intruded into the surrounding chalk.

About 2 million years ago, ice sheets covered much of the United Kingdom north of a line roughly between the Bristol Channel and London. Glacial erosion shaped landscapes in North Wales, Cumbria, and much of upland Scotland. As the glaciers melted, extensive areas of clay, sand and gravel were deposited, almost entirely obscuring the underlying bedrock of much of East Anglia.

England

England covers about two-thirds of the island of Great Britain. It is mostly low hills and plains, forming meadowlands and pastures. Uplands

---

1 A layer of rock that is able to hold or transmit large quantities of water.

include the Pennine chain, known as the 'backbone of England', which splits northern England into western and eastern sectors. The highest point is Scafell Pike (977 metres) in the north west. The north east includes the rugged landscape of the Yorkshire moors, while the south west has the upland moors of Dartmoor and Exmoor.

Wales

Wales is on the western side of Great Britain. It is mountainous – around one-quarter is above 305 metres and in the north its highest peak, Snowdon (*Yr Wyddfa*), rises to 1,085 metres. The Cambrian Mountains run from north to south and to the south are the Brecon Beacons, with flat, grassy summits, and the steep-sided South Wales Valleys. The Welsh coastline varies from estuaries to sheltered bays, high cliffs, peninsulas, and marsh and low-tide sandbanks.

Scotland

Scotland is located in the north of Great Britain. The Scottish Lowlands and Borders are largely areas of gentle hills and woodland, contrasting dramatically with the rugged landscape of the Highlands to the north. A striking physical feature is the Great Glen, a geological fault, which cuts across the central Highlands from Fort William on the west coast for 97 kilometres north-east to Inverness on the east coast. A string of lochs in deep narrow basins is set between steep-sided mountains that rise past forested foothills to high moors and remote rocky mountains. Ben Nevis, at 1,343 metres, is the highest point in the United Kingdom. Scotland has about 790 islands, of which some 130 are inhabited.

Northern Ireland

Northern Ireland's north-east coast is separated from Scotland by a stretch of water – the North Channel – only 21 kilometres wide at its nearest point. It has a 488-kilometre border with the Republic of Ireland, forming the only UK land boundary with another Member State of the European Union. The landscape is mainly low hill country. There are three mountainous areas: the Mournes in the south east with Northern Ireland's highest point, Slieve Donard (852 metres); the Sperrins in the north west; and the Antrim Plateau, parallel to the north-east coast. Lough Neagh is the largest freshwater lake in the United Kingdom and one of the largest in Europe.

Physical geography

Length and breadth: just under 1,000 kilometres from south to north, and just under 500 kilometres across at the widest point

Highest mountain: Ben Nevis, in the Highlands of Scotland, 1,343 metres

Longest river: the Severn, 354 kilometres, rises in Wales and flows through Shrewsbury, Worcester and Gloucester in England to the Bristol Channel

Largest lake: Lough Neagh, Northern Ireland, 382 square kilometres

Highest waterfall: Eas a'Chual Aluinn, from Glas Bheinn, in Scotland, with a drop of 200 metres

Deepest cave: Ogof Ffynnon Ddu, Powys, Wales, 308 metres deep

Most northerly point on the British mainland: Dunnet Head, north-east Scotland

Most southerly point on the British mainland: Lizard Point, Cornwall, England

Climate

The climate is generally mild and temperate. Prevailing weather systems move in from the Atlantic, and the weather is mainly influenced by depressions and their associated fronts moving eastwards, punctuated by fine, settled, anticyclonic periods lasting from a few days to several weeks. The temperature rarely rises above 32°C or falls below –10°C. The hottest day in 2003 was 10 August, with temperatures at Brogdale, near Faversham, Kent, reaching a record 38.5°C. The coldest night in 2003 was on 7/8 January, when Aviemore in the Scottish Highlands recorded a minimum of –18.6°C. There are four distinct seasons: spring (roughly March to May); summer (June to August); autumn (September to November) and winter (December to February).

Rainfall is greatest in western and upland areas, where the annual average exceeds 1,100 millimetres; the highest mountain areas receive

The Met Office was set up in June 1854 to provide information about the weather and sea currents to the Royal Navy and the UK maritime community. From its origins as a small department in the former Board of Trade, it has grown into a government agency employing 1,800 staff at over 40 UK locations and overseas. It is also one of two World Area Forecast Centres, providing weather information for all international flights from the eastern North Atlantic area to central Australia.

In 2004 the Met Office completed its move to new headquarters in Exeter. The £80 million building won Major Project of the Year and Best Office Building of the Year in awards organised by *Building Services Journal* and the *Electrical and Mechanical Contractor* in June 2004.

more than 2,000 millimetres. Over much of lowland central England, annual rainfall ranges from 700 to 850 millimetres. Parts of East Anglia and the south east have the lowest rainfall, just 550 millimetres. Rain is fairly well distributed throughout the year.

The length of the day varies throughout the year. The relatively high latitude of Scotland means that winter days there are very short, while summer days are long, with an extended twilight. On the longest day, 21 June, there is no complete darkness in the north of Scotland and Lerwick, Shetland, has about four hours more daylight (including twilight) than London.

During May, June and July (the months of longest daylight) the mean daily duration of sunshine varies from five hours in northern Scotland to eight hours in the Isle of Wight. During the months of shortest daylight (November, December and January) sunshine is at a minimum, with an average of an hour a day in northern Scotland and two hours a day on the south coast of England.

Population

The population of the United Kingdom at mid-2003 was 59.6 million (Table 1.1). Official projections, based on 2002 population estimates, suggest that the population will reach 64.8 million by 2031. Longer term projections suggest that the population will peak around 2050 at over 65 million and then begin to fall (see page 100).

The population grew by 5.7 per cent between 1991 and 2003, partly a result of a greater number of births than deaths, with migration an increasing factor from the late 1990s (see page 103).

There are more people in the United Kingdom aged over 60 (12.4 million) than there are children under 16 (11.7 million). Northern Ireland has the youngest population, with children under 16

Table 1.1 Population and area, June 2003, UK

	England	Wales	Scotland	Northern Ireland	United Kingdom
Population (thousands)	49,856	2,938	5,057	1,703	59,554
% population aged:					
under 5	5.7	5.4	5.2	6.5	5.7
5–15	14.0	14.2	13.4	16.3	14.0
16 to pension age[1]	61.9	60.1	62.4	61.3	61.8
above pension age[1]	18.4	20.3	18.9	15.9	18.5
Area (sq km)	130,281	20,732	77,925	13,576	242,514
Population density (people per sq km)	383	142	65	125	246
% population change 1991–2003	6.5	4.4	−2.4	10.3	5.7
Live births per 1,000 population	11.8	10.7	10.4	12.7	11.7
Deaths per 1,000 population	10.1	11.5	11.6	8.5	10.3

1 Pension age is currrently 65 for males and 60 for females.
Source: Office for National Statistics; National Assembly for Wales; General Register Office for Scotland; Northern Ireland Statistics and Research Agency

representing 23 per cent of the population, compared with 20 per cent in the United Kingdom as a whole in 2003.

The United Kingdom has one of the largest populations in the European Union (EU), accounting for 13 per cent of the total.

History of government

Major events in the development of government in the United Kingdom, together with a brief review of early history, are described below. There is a list of significant dates in appendix B (page 496).

'Britain' derives from Greek and Latin words that probably stem from a Celtic original. Although in the prehistoric timescale the Celts were relatively late arrivals in the British Isles, UK recorded history began with them. The term 'Celtic' is often used rather generally to distinguish the early inhabitants of the British Isles from the later Anglo-Saxon invaders.

After two expeditions by Julius Caesar in 55 and 54 BC, contact between Great Britain and the Roman world grew, culminating in the Roman invasion of AD 43. Roman rule, which lasted until about 409, gradually extended from south-east England to Wales and, for a time, the lowlands of Scotland.

England

When the Romans withdrew from Great Britain, the lowland regions were invaded and settled by Angles, Saxons and Jutes (tribes from what is now north-western Germany), England takes its name from the Angles. The Anglo-Saxon kingdoms were small and numerous, but in time fewer, larger areas of control developed. Eventually the southern kingdom of Wessex became dominant, mainly because of its leading role in resisting the Viking invasions in the ninth century. Athelstan (reigned 924–39) used the title 'King of all Britain', and from 954 there was a single kingdom of England.

The last successful invasion of England took place in 1066. Duke William of Normandy defeated the English at the Battle of Hastings and became King William I, known as 'William the Conqueror'. Many Normans and others from France came to settle; French became the language of the ruling classes for the next three centuries; and the legal

and social structures were influenced by those across the Channel.

When Henry II, originally from Anjou, was king (1154–89), his 'Angevin empire' stretched from the river Tweed on the Scottish border, through much of France to the Pyrénées. However, almost all of the English Crown's possessions in France were lost during the late Middle Ages (*c*.1300–1400).

In 1215 a group of barons demanded a charter of liberties as a safeguard against the arbitrary behaviour of King John. The rebels captured London and the King eventually agreed to their demands. The resulting royal grant was the *Magna Carta*. Among other things, the charter promised that 'To no one will we sell, to no one deny or delay right or justice'. It established the important constitutional principle that the power of the king could be limited.

The Hundred Years War between England and France began in 1337, leading to a period of high taxation. In 1381 the introduction of a poll tax led to the Peasants' Revolt, the most significant popular revolt in English history. The peasants marched on London, executed ministers and won promises of concessions, including the abolition of serfdom, although Richard II went back on these promises once the peasants had dispersed.

In 1485 Henry Tudor defeated Richard III at the Battle of Bosworth Field and became Henry VII. His son, Henry VIII, broke away from the Catholic Church and founded the Church of England. During his reign England and Wales were united. The last of the Tudors, Elizabeth I, was childless. She named James VI of Scotland as her successor, thus uniting the monarchies of Scotland, England and Wales when she died in 1603.

Civil War broke out in 1642. The capture and execution of Charles I in 1649 changed the balance of power between Monarch and Parliament. A leading parliamentarian in the civil war was Oliver Cromwell. He declared England a republic in 1649. Appointed Lord Protector of the Commonwealth from late 1653 until his death in 1658, Cromwell had supreme legislative and executive power in association with Parliament and the Council of State; he was the only non-royal to hold this position. The Monarchy was restored when Charles II ascended the throne in 1660. In 1707 the *Acts of Union* united the English and Scottish Parliaments and the *Act of Union 1800* united

Great Britain and Northern Ireland. Parliamentary reform was a recurrent issue in the 18th and 19th centuries. The 1832 *Reform Act* began dismantling the old parliamentary system and extending the franchise. The *Reform Acts* of 1867 and 1884 gave the vote to a gradually wider section of the population. During the 20th century, the *Representation of the People Acts* took the process further. In 1918, women aged 30 or over who were householders, householders' wives or graduates were enfranchised and in 1928 the *Equal Franchise Act* extended the franchise to women aged 21 or over, giving them the same voting rights as men. Universal suffrage for all eligible people over 18 was granted in 1969 (see page 40).

Wales

Wales was a Celtic stronghold ruled by sovereign princes under the influence of England after the Romans left around 409. In 1282 Edward I brought Wales under English rule; the castles he built in the north remain among the finest UK historic monuments. Edward I's eldest son – later Edward II – was born at Caernarvon in 1284 and became the first English Prince of Wales in 1301. The eldest son of the reigning monarch continues to bear this title; Prince Charles was made Prince of Wales in 1969.

At the beginning of the 15th century Welsh resentment of unjust English laws and administration, and widespread economic discontent, resulted in the nationalist leader Owain Glyndŵr leading an unsuccessful revolt against the English (see page 20). The Tudor dynasty, which was of Welsh ancestry, ruled England from 1485 to 1603 and during this period the *Acts of Union* (1536 and 1542) united England and Wales administratively, politically and legally.

This situation prevailed until July 1999, when devolution created a National Assembly for Wales with specific powers to make secondary legislation to meet distinctive Welsh needs (see page 18).

Scotland

Evidence of human settlement in what is now Scotland dates from about the third millennium BC. By the time the Romans invaded Britain, many tribes were living in the region and despite a number of attempts to control them, Roman rule never permanently extended to most of Scotland.

Great Black Britons

Mary Seacole, a veteran nurse in the Crimean War (see page 92), came first in an Internet poll of the 100 Great Black Britons. The poll highlighted the contribution that Black people have made to UK society since Roman times. The website for the poll received more than 1 million hits and 10,000 people voted.

Born in 1805 in Jamaica to a Scottish father and Jamaican mother, Mary Seacole came to England in the 1850s. As a nurse, she volunteered to help in the Crimean war. She was turned down, but went to the Crimea independently and was awarded a Crimean medal for her work.

Wilfred Wood, the first Black bishop, came second in the poll. He was followed by Mary Prince, the first Black female author to be published; Olaudah Equiano, a former slave and political activist; and Queen Philippa, the wife of Edward III. George of Lydda, who became St George, the patron saint of England, came 24th.

By the fifth century AD, the Scots, a Celtic people from Ireland, had settled on the north-west coast of Great Britain and a century later had formed the kingdom of Dalriada. The political connection with Ireland remained until the Battle of Mag Rath in 637. The kingdom of Dalriada lasted until the ninth century when Kenneth Mac Alpin imposed authority over the Scots and their neighbours and rivals, the Picts, to form a single kingdom. He and his successors expanded into traditionally independent territories and the kingdom of Scotland was formed during the ninth and tenth centuries.

The kingdoms of England and Scotland were frequently at war during the Middle Ages (c.1000–1400). When Edward I tried to impose direct English rule over Scotland in 1296, a revolt for independence broke out, which ended in 1328 when Edward III recognised its leader, Robert the Bruce, as King Robert I of Scotland.

The English and Scottish crowns were united in 1603 when James VI of Scotland succeeded Elizabeth I. He became James I of England and was the first of the Stuart kings. In 1745 Charles Edward Stuart (also known as 'Bonnie Prince Charlie' or 'The Young Pretender') attempted to retake the throne for the Stuarts (it had passed to the House of Hanover in 1714). He was eventually defeated at the Battle of Culloden, north-east of Inverness, in April 1746.

Politically, England and Scotland remained separate during the 17th century, apart from a period of union forced on them by Oliver Cromwell in the 1650s. It was not until 1707 that the English and Scottish Parliaments agreed on a single Parliament for Great Britain to sit at Westminster in London. Nearly 300 years later, in July 1999, devolution meant that power to administer Scottish affairs was returned to a new Scottish Parliament (see page 25).

Northern Ireland

Henry II of England invaded Ireland in 1169. He had been made overlord of Ireland by the English Pope Adrian IV. Although Anglo-Norman noblemen controlled part of the country during the Middle Ages (c.1000–1400), little direct authority came from England.

During the reign of Elizabeth I (1558–1603) there were several rebellions, particularly in the northern province of Ulster. In 1607, after the rebel leaders had been defeated, Protestant immigrants from Scotland and England settled there.

The English civil war (1642–51) coincided with uprisings in Ireland, which Oliver Cromwell suppressed. More fighting took place after the overthrow of James II, a Roman Catholic, in 1688. At the Battle of the Boyne in 1690, the Protestant William of Orange (later William III) defeated James II, who was trying to regain the English throne from his base in Ireland.

In 1782 the Government in London gave the Irish Parliament power to legislate on Irish affairs. Only the Anglo-Irish minority were represented in this Parliament. Following the unsuccessful rebellion of Wolfe Tone's United Irishmen movement in 1798, Great Britain took back control of Ireland under the *Act of Union 1800*. The Irish Parliament was abolished in 1801; Irish interests were represented by members sitting in both Houses of the Westminster Parliament.

The question of 'Home Rule' for Ireland remained one of the major issues of British politics. By 1910 the Liberal Government in London depended for its political survival on support from the Irish Parliamentary Party. The conflict deepened as some unionists and nationalists in Ireland formed private armies. In 1914 Home Rule was approved in the *Government of Ireland Act* but implementation was suspended because of the First World War.

In 1916 a nationalist uprising in Dublin was put down and its leaders executed. Two years later the nationalist Sinn Féin party won a large majority of the Irish seats in the General Election to the Westminster Parliament. Its members refused to attend the House of Commons and instead formed their own assembly – the Dáil Éireann – in Dublin. In 1919 the Irish Republican Army (IRA) began operations against the UK administration.

In 1920 a new *Government of Ireland Act* provided for separate Parliaments in Northern and Southern Ireland, subordinate to Westminster. The Act was implemented in Northern Ireland in 1921, giving six of the nine counties of the province of Ulster their own Parliament with powers to manage internal affairs. However, the Act was not accepted in the South and the 26 counties of Southern Ireland left the United Kingdom in 1922.

From 1921 until 1972 Northern Ireland had its own Parliament. The unionists, primarily representing the Protestant community, held a permanent majority and formed the regional government. The nationalist minority was effectively excluded from political office and influence. In the late 1960s and early 1970s, the civil rights movement and reactions to it resulted in serious inter-communal rioting. The UK Army was sent in to help the police keep law and order in 1969.

Terrorism and violence continued to increase. In 1972, the UK Government decided to take back direct responsibility for law and order. The Northern Ireland Unionist Government resigned in protest, the regional government was abolished and direct rule from Westminster began; this was to last until devolved powers were given back to a Northern Ireland Assembly in December 1999 (see page 32). The Northern Ireland Assembly and the Executive has been suspended on a number of occasions since 1999. The latest suspension was in October 2002, because the UK Government considered that it was not possible to hold together an inclusive power-sharing Executive, since the confidence within the community necessary to underpin it had broken down.

Channel Islands and Isle of Man

The Channel Islands (Jersey, Guernsey, Alderney and Sark being the largest in the group) were part of the Duchy of Normandy in the 10th and 11th centuries and remained subject to the English Crown after the loss of mainland Normandy to the French in 1204. The Isle of Man was under the nominal sovereignty of Norway until 1266, and eventually came under the direct administration of the British Crown in 1765, when it was bought for £70,000.

Today these territories each have their own legislative assemblies and systems of law, and their own taxation systems. The UK Government is responsible for their international relations and external defence. The Isle of Man Parliament, Tynwald, was established more than 1,000 years ago and is the oldest legislature in continuous existence in the world. It also has the distinction of having three chambers: the House of Keys; the Legislative Council; and the Tynwald Court, when the House of Keys and the Legislative Council sit together as a single chamber.

The United Kingdom is a member of the European Union (EU – see page 67) but the Channel Islands and Isle of Man are neither EU Member States in their own right nor part of the UK Member State. EU rules on the free movement of goods and the Common Agricultural Policy broadly apply to the Islands, but not those on the free movement of services or persons. Islanders benefit from the latter only if they have close ties with the United Kingdom.

Further reading

Appendix B on page 496 lists significant dates in UK history.

Annual Abstract of Statistics (annual publication). Office for National Statistics. The Stationery Office.

Population Trends (quarterly publication). Office for National Statistics. The Stationery Office.

Regional Trends (annual publication). Office for National Statistics. The Stationery Office.

Social Trends (annual publication). Office for National Statistics. The Stationery Office.

Websites
British Geological Survey
www.bgs.ac.uk

The Met Office
www.metoffice.com

The National Archives
www.nationalarchives.gov.uk

Office for National Statistics
www.statistics.gov.uk

WWW.

2 England

Population

England's population in 2003 was 49.9 million
(Table 2.1), about 84 per cent of the population
of the United Kingdom. The most densely
populated areas are the major cities and
metropolitan areas of London and the South
East, South and West Yorkshire, Greater
Manchester and Merseyside, the West Midlands,
and the conurbations on the rivers Tyne, Wear
and Tees. London has the highest population
density with 4,699 people per square kilometre,
and the South West the lowest (210 people per
square kilometre).

Between 1991 and 2003 the population grew by
4.1 per cent. There were big variations between the
regions; the population in the North East fell by
1.8 per cent between 1991 and 2003, while the
population in London rose by 8.2 per cent during
the same period.

Table 2.1 Population and population change by region,[1] June 2003, England

	Population (thousands)	Change in Population 1991–2003 (%)
North East	2,539	−1.8
North West	6,805	−0.6
Yorkshire and the Humber	5,009	1.5
East Midlands	4,252	6.0
West Midlands	5,320	1.7
East of England	5,463	6.7
London	7,388	8.2
South East	8,080	5.9
South West	4,999	6.6
England	**49,856**	**4.1**

1 These are the areas covered by the Government Offices – see map
  on page 13.
Source: Office for National Statistics

Representation at Westminster and in Europe

There are 529 English parliamentary
constituencies represented in the House of
Commons (Table 2.2). The Labour Party holds the
majority of seats and forms the Government. Its
traditional support comes mainly from the big
cities and areas associated with heavy industry,
but it also holds many seats that were once 'safe'
Conservative constituencies. The Conservative
Party holds the second largest number of seats and
is the official Opposition. Conservative support is
traditionally strong in suburban and rural areas,
and the party has a large number of seats in
southern England. The Liberal Democrats,
traditionally strong in the South West, now have
over a third of their English seats in Greater
London and the South East.

In contrast to Wales, Scotland and Northern
Ireland (see chapters 3, 4 and 5), England has no
separate elected national body exclusively
responsible for its central administration. Instead
a number of government departments look after

Table 2.2 Electoral representation, July 2004, England

	UK Parliament (MPs)	European Parliament (MEPs)
Labour	320	15
Conservative	164	24
Liberal Democrats	43	11
UK Independence Party	0	12
Green Party	0	2
Others	2	0
Total seats	**529**	**64**

**Source: House of Commons Information Office; European
Parliament London Office**

England's day-to-day administrative affairs (see appendix A, page 481) and there is a network of nine Government Offices for the Regions (GOs, see page 12). However, in the longer term, the Government is committed to providing for directly elected regional assemblies in those regions that want them (see page 13).

The House of Commons has a Standing Committee[1] on Regional Affairs, consisting of 13 Members of Parliament (MPs) from English constituencies, reflecting party representation in the House. Any other MP representing an English constituency may take part in its proceedings, but they may not make a motion, vote or be counted in the quorum.

European Parliament elections

England is represented by 64 Members of the European Parliament (MEPs), seven fewer MEPs than before the enlargement of the European Union in May 2004. In the European parliamentary elections held in June 2004, 14.5 million people in England, 39 per cent of the electorate, voted for an MEP (see Table 2.2). All-postal voting was piloted in four of the English regions: North East; North West; Yorkshire and the Humber; and East Midlands (see page 41). Turnout in all four regions was over 40 per cent, the highest being the East Midlands (43.9 per cent) and the lowest the West Midlands (36.6 per cent). Voting is by the d'Hondt system of proportional representation (see glossary).

Local government

The structure of local government in England includes shire areas, which have a two-tier council system, and metropolitan districts, unitary authorities and London boroughs, which all have a single-tier system (see map on page 10). London boroughs, shire district councils, unitary authorities and metropolitan districts are broken down into electoral wards.

Shire counties

Most of England is organised into shire areas with two main tiers of local authority – 34 shire county councils and 238 shire district councils covering 272 out of the 389 elected authorities. The county councils are responsible for large-scale services in their areas including education, strategic planning, transport, highways, social services, fire services, libraries and waste disposal. Each county council area is subdivided into a number of district councils, which are responsible for more local matters including environmental health, housing, local planning applications, local taxation, waste collection, and leisure. Both tiers have powers to provide facilities such as museums, art galleries and parks; these arrangements depend on local agreement. Shire areas also have a police authority, made up of local councillors, magistrates and independent members. Police authorities may cover one or more counties.

Metropolitan district councils

The six metropolitan county areas in England – Greater Manchester, Merseyside, South Yorkshire, Tyne and Wear, West Midlands and West Yorkshire – have 36 district councils[2] but no county councils. The district councils are responsible for all services in their areas apart from those that have a statutory authority over areas wider than the individual district. For example, the fire and police services, public transport, and in some areas, waste disposal services, are run by joint authorities that include elected councillors nominated by each district council.

Unitary authorities

There are 47 unitary authorities where the county and district responsibilities are carried out by a single tier of government. Unitary authorities include some of the larger cities, the County of Herefordshire, the Isle of Wight and the Isles of Scilly. Unitary authorities do not have responsibility for the police or the fire and rescue services. These are administered by a police authority and a fire authority usually made up of local councillors, magistrates and independent members, and covering a larger area than the unitary authority.

---

1 See page 49 for an explanation of Standing Committees.

2 District councils in Metropolitan areas sometimes call themselves boroughs or city councils.

Map 2.3 Local government areas, England

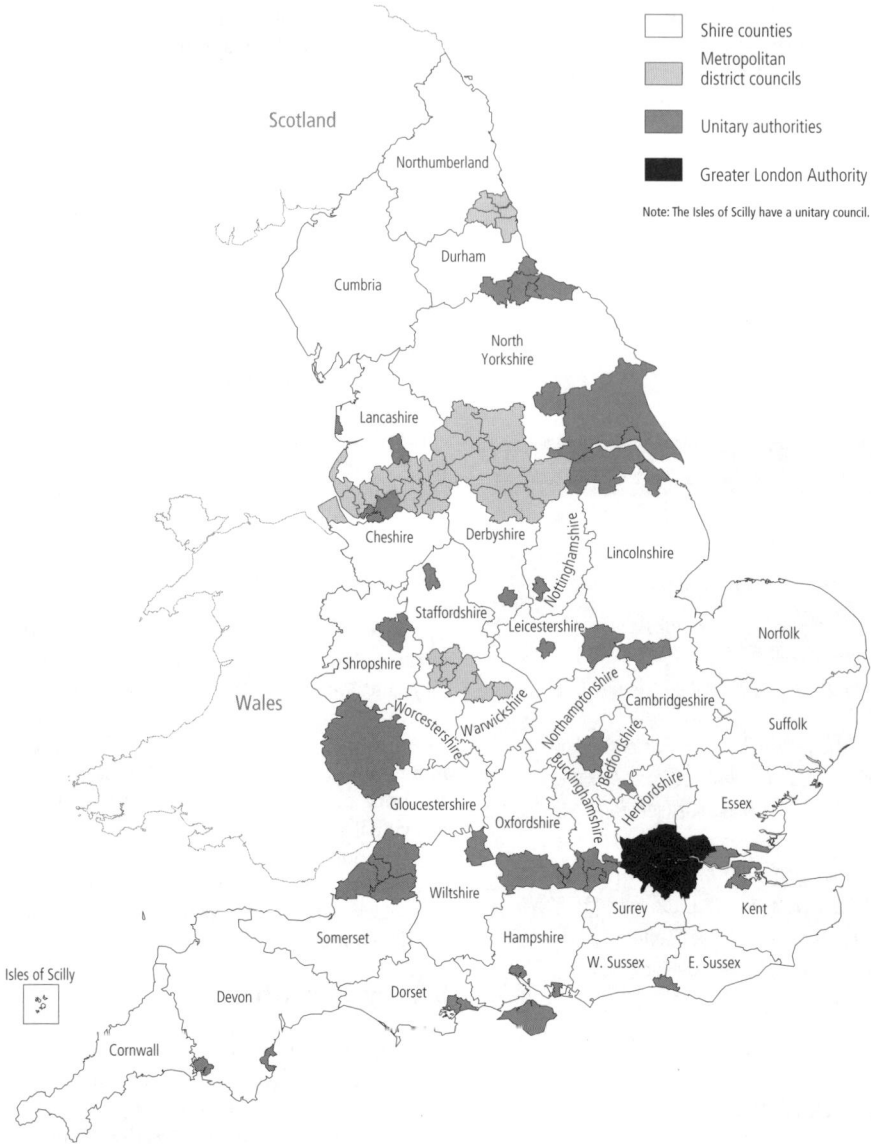

Shire counties

Metropolitan district councils

Unitary authorities

Greater London Authority

Note: The Isles of Scilly have a unitary council.

Greater London

Greater London is made up of 32 boroughs and the City of London, each with a council responsible for most services in its area. The strategic government of London is the responsibility of the Greater London Authority (GLA). This is made up of a directly elected Mayor of London,[3] a separately elected London Assembly, and four functional bodies: the Metropolitan Police Authority (MPA); the London Fire and Emergency Planning Authority (LFEPA); Transport for London (TfL); and the London Development Agency (LDA). In 2004/05 the budget for the GLA and its four functional bodies was £8.8 billion: £5.1 billion for TfL; £2.9 billion for the MPA; £442 million for the LFEPA; £343 million for the LDA; and £73 million for the GLA.

---

3 Not to be confused with the Lord Mayor of London, who is the head of the Corporation of London, the local authority for the 'City', also known as the 'Square Mile'.

The Mayor of London sets key strategies on a range of London-wide issues, such as transport, economic development, strategic and spatial development and the environment. The London Assembly scrutinises both the activities of the Mayor and issues of concern to Londoners.

The first elections for the Mayor and the London Assembly were held in May 2000. Subsequent elections take place every four years (see box). If there are three or more candidates, the Mayor is elected using a system called Supplementary Vote where voters can cast a first and second choice vote. If there are two candidates, the Mayor is elected by the first past the post system. There are 25 members of the London Assembly: the London boroughs are divided into 14 constituencies and each elects a Member on a first past the post basis. A further 11 London-wide Members are elected using the Additional Member System (see glossary).

Greater London elections

The second elections for the London Assembly and the Mayor of London were held on 10 June 2004. Turnout was 36 per cent in both the Assembly and the Mayoral elections. The Mayor of London (Labour) was re-elected on a slightly reduced share of the vote. In the Assembly, the Conservative Party became the largest party, winning nine seats.

Electoral wards/divisions

Metropolitan and shire districts, unitary authorities and the London boroughs are divided into electoral wards (or divisions in the Isle of Wight), each having an average 23 wards/divisions. These are the areas represented in local government by the locally elected councillors, with two or three councillors representing each ward. The exception is the Isles of Scilly, which has its own council but no electoral zoning. The shire county councils use larger units, called electoral divisions, to elect councillors.

Parishes

The smallest type of administrative area in England is the parish. Parishes are confined within local authority boundaries but are not contiguous

Future of local government in England

The Government published *The Future of Local Government: Developing a Ten-Year Vision* in July 2004. The paper sets out four broad themes for debate: leadership; citizen engagement; service delivery; and the relationship between central, regional and local government. As part of the ten-year strategy, the Government published *Local Area Agreements: A Prospectus* in July, which sets out proposals to pilot local area agreements. These include simplifying funding, coordinating public services, devolving decision-making, and reducing bureaucracy.

with electoral wards. In April 2003 there were 10,397 parishes in England.

Parish councils (sometimes called town councils) represent community views and deliver local services. They can provide facilities such as village halls, war memorials, cemeteries, leisure facilities and playgrounds. They maintain public footpaths and may also spend money on cultural projects, community transport initiatives and crime prevention equipment. In addition they must be notified of all planning applications and consulted on the making of certain by-laws.

Not all parishes have a council – if there are fewer than 200 parishioners, or if the parishioners do not want one, decisions can instead be taken at parish meetings. In some cases small parishes may come together to elect a joint council.

Elections

Councillors are elected for four-year terms. Whole council elections are held every four years in all shire county councils in England, borough councils in London, parish and town councils, and the majority of shire district councils and unitary authorities. The different categories of councils hold these elections in different years of the four-year cycle. Most of the remaining local authorities, including the metropolitan districts, elect one-third of their councillors in each of the three years when county council elections are not held. However, a few shire district councils and metropolitan districts have started to hold biennial elections with half of the councillors elected every two years.

Local government elections

In June 2004, local elections were held in 144 local authorities in England with 59 being for whole council, 79 being for one-third of the council, and 6 for half the council. The Labour Party won 1,773 seats, a net loss of 412 seats. The Conservative Party won 1,605 seats, making net gains of 248 seats, and the Liberal Democrats won 1,131 seats, a net gain of 98 seats. Other parties won 301 seats, a net gain of 15. All-postal voting was piloted (see page 41) in four English regions: North East; North West; Yorkshire and the Humber; and East Midlands. Turnout in these regions was higher than at previous local elections.

Finance

Local authorities spent £98 billion in 2001/02. About 65 per cent of their income came from central government and the remainder from local sources, see page 61. Both revenue and capital expenditure per head were highest in the north and lowest in the south, with the exception of London. Much of the variation in revenue expenditure is due to different levels of spending on social services and police. London spent 53 per cent above the average for social services and 79 per cent above the average for police.

The regions of England

Nine Government Offices (GOs) are responsible for coordinating central government programmes at a regional level. They bring together the English regional services for ten government departments: the Office of the Deputy Prime Minister (ODPM); Department of Trade and Industry (DTI); Department for Education and Skills (DfES); Department for Work and Pensions; Department of Health; Department for Transport; Home Office; Department for Culture, Media and Sport (DCMS); the Department for Environment, Food and Rural Affairs (Defra); and the Cabinet Office. The GOs also work with regional partners, including local authorities and Regional Development Agencies (RDAs – see page 13).

Distinctive facts about England

National day: 23 April, St George's Day

National emblem: rose

National flag: the cross of St George, a red Greek cross on a white background

English law comprises 'common law' (ancient custom and previous rulings in similar cases), 'statute law' (parliamentary and EC legislation) and 'equity' (general principles of justice correcting or adding to common or statute law).

The Church of England broke away from the Roman Catholic Church in the 16th century.

There are some 500,000 listed buildings, 11 World Heritage Sites, 17,700 scheduled monuments and 8,500 conservation areas in England.

England has seven National Parks plus the Norfolk and Suffolk Broads, which have equivalent status. There are also 37 Areas of Outstanding Natural Beauty covering some 15 per cent of England (see chapter 19).

The GOs directly manage spending programmes on behalf of these departments. In 2002/03 they were responsible for spending around £9 billion. They oversee budgets and contracts delegated to regional organisations, carry out regulatory functions and sponsor the RDAs. The Regional Coordination Unit manages the network of GOs and represents them in Whitehall, ensuring that regional interests are taken into account in the development and evaluation of policy in central government.

Voluntary, multiparty regional chambers have been established in each of the eight English regions outside London. All of the chambers have adopted the title 'assembly', although their constitutions vary. They are primarily responsible for scrutinising the work of the RDAs and, as the designated regional planning bodies, for drawing up regional spatial strategies.

Representatives of local authorities constitute up to 70 per cent of the members of each regional chamber. The remainder are people who work in higher and further education, and representatives from the Confederation of British Industry, the

Trades Union Congress, Chambers of Commerce, small business, parish and town councils, the National Health Service, rural and environment groups, and other regional stakeholders.

Map 2.4 The regions of England covered by the GOs and RDAs

Regional Development Agencies

There are nine RDAs in England – one for each government region. They are accountable to the Government, and are monitored by the GOs and the voluntary regional chamber. Each RDA has five statutory purposes:

- to further economic development and regeneration;
- to promote business efficiency, investment and competitiveness;
- to promote employment;
- to enhance the development and application of skills relevant to employment; and
- to contribute to sustainable development.

RDAs are financed by money from five contributing departments – DTI (the lead sponsoring department), ODPM, DfES, Defra and DCMS. This money is available to spend as the RDAs see fit, to achieve the regional priorities in their economic strategies and the targets in their corporate plans. RDA funding is tied to a framework of targets and the GO monitors progress every six months.

Funding is through a single funding programme, known as the 'single pot'. In 2004/05 the pot was

£1.8 billion. In the 2004 Spending Review, the Government announced a package of measures to promote economic development in the English regions. Additional funds will be transferred to the pot from the contributing government departments and the RDAs' budget will reach £2.3 billion in 2007/08.

The increased funding will enable RDAs to take on additional functions, including responsibility for delivering Business Link services (see page 355) from April 2005, and new responsibilities for awarding research and development grants, and promoting inward investment and collaborative research between business and universities.

Proposals for devolution to the English regions

The Government's proposals for elected regional assemblies for all English regions outside London were set out in the White Paper, *Your Region, Your Choice: Revitalising the English Regions*, published in 2002. Elected assemblies would be broadly similar to the Greater London Authority (see page 10) and would carry out functions largely drawn

Sustainable communities

In July 2003 the Government announced the first of a series of updates to the *Sustainable Communities: Building for the Future* plan that was launched in February 2003. *Making it Happen – Thames Gateway and the Growth Areas* set out proposals for sustainable growth and housing supply in the wider South East over the next 15 years. The Thames Gateway is one of four priority areas for the development of new residential communities to help relieve housing shortages in the South East.

In February 2004 the Government announced proposals to improve infrastructure and regenerate city areas to create jobs and economic growth across the North of England and to reduce disparities between the North and South. *Making it Happen – The Northern Way* plans to work with RDAs and regional planning bodies to open up a 'Northern Growth Corridor' that will include cities like Leeds, Liverpool, Manchester, Newcastle and Sheffield.

Proposed responsibilities of elected regional assemblies

A draft bill on the proposed powers and responsibilities of regional assemblies was published in July 2004. These included:

- taking charge of the RDAs (see page 13);
- working with local training organisations;
- taking over much of the housing and planning work carried out by the Housing Corporation and the voluntary regional chamber, and ensuring this was coordinated with economic development and regeneration strategies;
- advising the Government on funding needed for local transport, so that it can be integrated with housing and planning developments;
- setting the agenda for cultural activities by taking charge of the regional cultural consortium; and
- promoting improved public health and agreeing long-term action for sustainable development in the region.

The assemblies would also take responsibility for new regional fire authorities that are intended to be large enough to deal with large-scale terrorist incidents and environmental disasters.

The English language

Modern English derives primarily from one of the dialects of Old English (or Anglo-Saxon), itself made up of several Western Germanic dialects brought to Britain in the early fifth century. It has been greatly influenced by other languages, particularly Latin and, following the Norman conquest, by French. It has also borrowed much from other English-speaking countries, particularly the United States and the Commonwealth countries (see page 71). The 14th century saw the first major English literature since Anglo-Saxon days, with works such as *Piers Plowman* by William Langland and the *Canterbury Tales* by Geoffrey Chaucer.

There are about 375 million people speaking English as their first language, with a similar number speaking it as a second language. It is the official language of air traffic control and maritime communications; the leading language of science, technology, commerce and computing (the British Council estimate that 80 per cent of the world's electronically stored information is in English); and a major medium of education, international negotiation, publishing, pop music and advertising.

from central government bodies such as the GOs, and a number of public bodies that are already operating in the regions.

The assemblies would represent geographical areas based on the existing administrative boundaries used by the GOs and RDAs. Assemblies would have a membership of between 25 and 35, depending on the size of the region. The assembly members would appoint a leader and an executive.

Elections to the assembly would take place on a proportional representation basis using the Additional Member System (see glossary). This should ensure that the overall composition broadly reflects the votes cast for the different parties.

Most of each assembly's money would come through a single block grant from central government, with the assembly deciding how it should be spent to address regional priorities.

An elected assembly can only be established if a majority of people in a region vote for one in a referendum. The *Regional Assemblies (Preparations) Act 2003* gave the Government the power to hold referendums in regions that register sufficient interest. Following the first soundings exercise held between December 2002 and June 2003, sufficient interest was registered in three regions: North East; North West; and Yorkshire and the Humber.

The Government directed the Boundary Commission for England to carry out local government reviews in these three regions. The two-tier local authorities in regions that vote for a regional assembly must be restructured into unitary authorities to simplify relationships between government at the local and regional level. People in two-tier areas will be able to vote on which option of unitary local government they prefer.

The reviews were completed by the end of May 2004. Once at least one region has voted for an elected assembly, further legislation will be introduced to provide for an assembly to be set up. The first referendum is planned for the North East in autumn 2004 and will be an all-postal ballot.

Economy

Some 25.0 million people were economically active in England in spring 2004 of whom 23.9 million were in employment. The unemployment rate for England was 4.7 per cent, varying from 3.3 per cent in the South West to 6.8 per cent in London.

Table 2.5 Regional gross value added (GVA) 2002,[1] England[2]

	£ billion GVA	£ thousand GVA per head
North East	30	11.8
North West	93	13.8
Yorkshire and the Humber	66	13.2
East Midlands	59	14.0
West Midlands	73	13.8
East of England	91	16.8
London	147	20.0
South East	148	18.4
South West	69	13.9
England	775	15.6

1 At current basic prices.
2 Excludes compensation of employees and gross operating surplus (which cannot be assigned to regions) and statistical discrepancy.
Source: Office for National Statistics

Estimates of gross value added (GVA, see glossary, Table 2.5, and Table 22.12, page 357 for UK GVA) at current prices in 2002 increased in all English regions. The rate of increase varied from the South West, where GVA was 6.0 per cent higher than in 2001, to London, where it was 4.4 per cent higher. Overall GVA growth in 2002 was 5.1 per cent in England, the same as for the United Kingdom as a whole. London had the highest GVA per head in 2002, at £20,000, while the North East had the lowest at £11,800.

The North East has the smallest population of the English regions. Over half the area is rural. Economic activity is centred on the estuaries of three rivers, the Tyne, the Wear and the Tees, and was traditionally based on coal, steel and shipbuilding. Manufacturing remains important and accounted for 22 per cent of GVA in 2001. The regional economy has diversified into

microelectronics, biotechnology and the automotive industry, and there is a growing service sector, which accounted for 67 per cent of GVA in 2001.

The North West has the largest production centre for film and television outside London. Traditional economic activities include shipping, textiles and engineering, with manufacturing accounting for 22 per cent of GVA in 2001. New sectors include biotechnology, chemicals, aerospace and information and communications technology. The service sector accounted for 69 per cent of GVA in 2001.

Yorkshire and the Humber's traditional industries of coal mining, steel, engineering and textiles have generally declined, although manufacturing accounted for 22 per cent of GVA in 2001. This decline has been partly offset by a growth in financial, legal and telephone-based services. Service industries accounted for 68 per cent of GVA in 2001.

Over 90 per cent rural, the East Midlands is the second smallest region by population. Agriculture and food processing remain important in the local economy, while the manufacturing industries in the former coalfield areas to the north of the region are in decline. In 2001, manufacturing accounted for 24 per cent of GVA. Areas of growth include a diverse and growing service sector that accounted for 65 per cent of GVA in 2001.

The West Midlands has large conurbations in Birmingham, Solihull, Coventry and Stoke-on-Trent, although about 80 per cent of the region is rural. The service sector is growing, and accounted for 67 per cent of GVA in 2001. Manufacturing accounted for 23 per cent of GVA in 2001.

The East of England region's businesses include food and drink, biotechnology, pharmaceuticals and the film industry. The region has the leading UK science parks in and around Cambridge, with many businesses engaged in high-technology manufacturing and computer-aided design. Service industries accounted for 75 per cent of GVA in 2001, while manufacturing accounted for 15 per cent.

In many ways, London is the most successful region. It is the capital city and a major economy, and its GVA per head in 2002 was almost 31 per cent higher than the UK average. However, London is also a city divided between extremes of wealth and deprivation, with 20 per cent of its wards among the 10 per cent most deprived in England.

Economic activity in the South East is closely linked with London and the region's proximity to mainland Europe. At £148 billion, it had the largest GVA in England in 2002. There is a strong service sector, accounting for 78 per cent of the region's GVA in 2001, 30 per cent of which came from real estate, renting and business activities. Manufacturing accounted for 14 per cent of GVA.

The South West's economy is varied. Alongside the traditional areas of agriculture and fishing, food and drink, and tourism, has been a growth in the financial and business services sectors and multimedia. Many manufacturing, telecommunications and electronics industries are situated in the M4/M5 corridor, the area around two motorways linking the South West with London/Birmingham and the North. The service sector accounted for 71 per cent of the region's GVA in 2001, while manufacturing accounted for 18 per cent.

Between 2000 and 2006 three areas of England qualified for EU Objective 1 funding (see page 358). Cornwall and the Isles of Scilly qualified for £321 million, Merseyside £860 million and South Yorkshire £757 million. All of the English regions benefited from Objective 2 funding, totalling over £2 billion. After 2006, Cornwall and the Isles of Scilly will be the only part of England that qualifies for Objective 1 funding.

International trade in goods

In 2003 exports of goods from England were £141 billion, while imports were £199 billion, giving an international trade deficit in goods of £58 billion. The largest overseas trade partner group was the EU for both imports and exports (Figure 2.6), with North America the second largest destination for exports, and Asia and Oceania the second largest source of imports. The largest sector was machinery and transport (45 per cent of exports and 42 per cent of imports), followed by chemicals (19 per cent of exports and 12 per cent of imports), and miscellaneous manufactures (13 per cent and 18 per cent respectively).

Further reading

Regional Trends (annual publication), Office for National Statistics. The Stationery Office.

Social Trends (annual publication), Office for National Statistics. The Stationery Office.

Economic Trends (monthly publication), Office for National Statistics. The Stationery Office.

Your Region, Your Choice: Revitalising the English Regions. Cm 5511. The Stationery Office, 2002.

Figure 2.6 Distribution of international trade in goods, 2003, England

£ billion

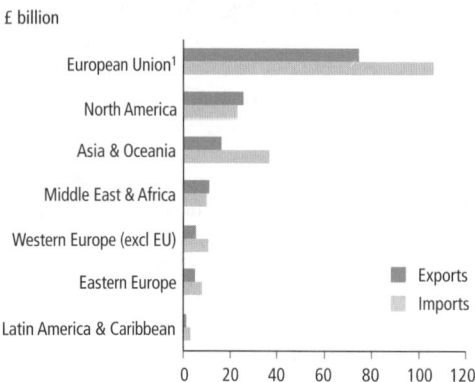

1 Excludes the ten countries that joined the EU in 2004.
Source: *UK Regional Trade in Goods Statistics*, HM Customs and Excise

Websites

Department of Trade and Industry
www.dti.gov.uk

Greater London Authority
www.london.gov.uk

HM Revenue & Customs
www.hmce.gov.uk

Office of the Deputy Prime Minister
www.odpm.gov.uk

Office for National Statistics
www.statistics.gov.uk

United Kingdom Parliament
www.parliament.uk

3   Wales

Population

Wales (*Cymru* in Welsh) had a population of just over 2.9 million in 2003 (Table 3.1), 4.9 per cent of the total for the United Kingdom. The population increased by 2.3 per cent between 1991 and 2003 with the Ceredigion local authority area having the greatest increase (17 per cent). Merthyr Tydfil had the largest population fall, losing 7 per cent.

About two-thirds of the population live in the southern valleys and the lower-lying coastal areas. The highest population density was in Cardiff, the capital, with 2,269 people per square kilometre. Cardiff grew in the 19th century as a coal exporting port. The two other large ports, Swansea and Newport, also depended for their prosperity on the surrounding mining and metal production during the Industrial Revolution (1760s to 1830s). They are still among the most densely populated areas today. The least densely populated area in 2003 was Powys, with 25 people per square kilometre.

An increasing proportion of residents in Wales comes from outside its borders (a quarter in 2001), while 22 per cent of the 2.8 million people in the United Kingdom who were born in Wales were living in other parts of the United Kingdom in 2001.

Representation at Westminster and in Europe

Wales returns 40 Members of Parliament (MPs) to the House of Commons at Westminster (see Table 3.2). All MPs for Welsh constituencies and up to five others who may be added from time to time

Table 3.1 Population and population change by local authority, June 2003, Wales

	Population in 2003 (thousands)	Change in population 1991–2003 (%)
Blaenau Gwent	69	−5.1
Bridgend (Pen-y-bont ar Ogwr)[1]	130	0.3
Caerphilly (Caerffili)	170	−0.2
Cardiff (Caerdydd)	315	6.1
Carmarthenshire (Sir Gaerfyrddin)	176	3.7
Ceredigion (Sir Ceredigion)	77	17.0
Conwy	111	2.7
Denbighshire (Sir Ddinbych)	95	6.1
Flintshire (Sir y Fflint)	149	5.2
Gwynedd	118	2.2
Isle of Anglesey (Sir Ynys Môn)	68	−1.1
Merthyr Tydfil (Merthyr Tudful)	55	−7.1
Monmouthshire (Sir Fynwy)	86	7.5
Neath Port Talbot (Castell-nedd Port Talbot)	135	−2.5
Newport (Casnewydd)	139	2.8
Pembrokeshire (Sir Benfro)	116	3.4
Powys	129	8.0
Rhondda, Cynon, Taff (Rhondda, Cynon, Taf)	232	−1.4
Swansea (Abertawe)	225	−2.2
Torfaen (Tor-faen)	91	−0.3
The Vale of Glamorgan (Bro Morgannwg)	121	2.7
Wrexham (Wrecsam)	130	4.5
Wales (Cymru)	**2,938**	**2.3**

1 Welsh-language local authority names are given in parenthesis if there are differences between the English and Welsh names.
Source: Office for National Statistics; National Assembly for Wales

Table 3.2 Electoral representation, June 2004, Wales

	National Assembly			UK Parliament	European Parliament
	Constituency seats	Regional seats	Total seats AMs	MPs	MEPs
Labour	30	0	30	34	2
Plaid Cymru – the Party of Wales	5	7	12	4	1
Conservative	1	10	11	0	1
Liberal Democrats	3	3	6	2	0
Independent	1	0	1	0	0
Total seats	**40**	**20**	**60**	**40**	**4**

Source: UK Parliament; European Parliament

are members of the House of Commons Welsh Grand Committee. Its role is to consider Bills referred to it at second reading stage, questions tabled for oral answer, ministerial statements, and other matters relating exclusively to Wales.

Following devolution in 1998, the UK Government retains responsibility for certain matters in Wales, including foreign affairs, defence, the Constitution and overall economic policy (for more details see appendix A, page 481).

Welsh interests are represented in the UK Cabinet and the House of Commons by the Secretary of State for Wales, who currently combines this role with that of Leader of the House of Commons. The Secretary of State for Wales also represents the UK Government in Wales.

The Secretary of State ensures that the devolution settlement operates in the best interests of Wales, and brings forward primary legislation, deals with constitutional issues, bids for the Assembly's budget and liaises with the Assembly. The Welsh Budget is voted for by the UK Parliament and for 2004/05 is £11.9 billion, an increase of 6 per cent on the previous year.

Ministers in the Wales Office sit on 27 Cabinet committees and on the Joint Ministerial Committee, allowing Welsh interests to be represented at a detailed level within Government. They also liaise regularly with members of the Assembly Cabinet. The Wales Office is situated in the Department for Constitutional Affairs.

The Public Audit (Wales) Bill, introduced in November 2003, proposed to devolve powers to scrutinise public spending in Wales. This was the third all-Wales Bill since the establishment of the National Assembly.

European Parliament elections

Wales forms a single constituency in the European Parliament (see page 65). Following the enlargement of the European Union (EU, see page 71) in 2004, the number of Members of the European Parliament (MEPs) representing Wales was reduced from five to four.

In the European parliamentary elections on 10 June 2004, 928,775 people, 41.9 per cent of the electorate in Wales, voted for an MEP (Table 3.2). The Labour Party won two seats, and Plaid Cymru – the Party of Wales and the Conservative Party won one seat each. Voting is by the d'Hondt system of proportional representation (see glossary).

National Assembly for Wales and Welsh Assembly Government

Proposals to devolve certain powers and responsibilities to a National Assembly were narrowly endorsed by the Welsh people in 1997; of those who voted, 50.3 per cent were in favour. First elections for the National Assembly for Wales were held in May 1999 and it began functioning as a devolved administration two months later.

The National Assembly for Wales has powers to make secondary legislation (see page 51) to meet distinctive Welsh needs on issues that have been devolved (see appendix A, page 491). Primary legislation on Welsh affairs continues to be made in the UK Parliament at Westminster (see page 48).

The National Assembly for Wales debates and approves legislation. Its debating chamber and members are located at Cardiff Bay. The Assembly is also responsible for over 50 public bodies. The Welsh Assembly Government develops and implements policy. It is accountable to the National Assembly and is primarily located in Cathays Park, Cardiff.

There are plans to move a number of Assembly jobs out of Cardiff to spread the economic benefits of working for the Assembly across Wales. The location strategy will be put in place over a number of years. The first new offices are planned for Merthyr Tydfil, to be opened in early 2006. The North Wales Office should be opened in spring 2007 and the Mid Wales Office by the end of 2007.

The Assembly sits for a four-year term and elections for the second term were held in May 2003. The Labour Party again secured the highest share of the vote and the highest number of seats. As a result, it abandoned the coalition with the Liberal Democrats that had been in place since 2000.

The overall turnout across regions and constituencies in 2003 was 38.2 per cent, down 8 percentage points compared with the 1999 elections. Turnout was generally higher in Mid and West Wales than in South Wales. Following the 2003 elections, the National Assembly is believed to be the first legislative body in the world where there are an equal number of male and female members.

2004 Spending Review – Wales

In the 2004 Spending Review announced in July 2004, spending in Wales is set to grow by an average annual rate of over 4 per cent in real terms over the next three years. In 2004/05 the Welsh departmental expenditure limit (DEL, see page 366) was £11.0 billion, rising to £11.8 billion in 2005/06, £12.8 billion in 2006/07 and £13.6 billion in 2007/08. There is also £106 million for Objective 1 funding (see pages 22 and 358) in 2004/05 and 2005/06.

There are 60 elected Assembly Members (AMs): 40 from local constituencies (with the same boundaries as those for Welsh seats in the House of Commons) and 20 regional members. The Assembly is elected by the Additional Member System of proportional representation. Under this system, electors have two votes: one for a constituency AM elected by the traditional first-past-the-post system, and one to elect four AMs for each of the five electoral regions using the d'Hondt system (see glossary).

The Assembly Members delegate their executive powers to the First Minister, who is elected by the whole Assembly. The First Minister in turn delegates responsibility for delivering executive functions to a

The Richard Commission

The Richard Commission was set up in 2002 to look at whether the Assembly has sufficient powers to operate effectively and if its method of election was suitable to the task. The main recommendations of the Commission's report, published in March 2004, were that:

- the Assembly be given primary law-making powers in devolved areas such as education and health, along the lines of the powers of the Scottish Parliament (see pages 25–27);

- if these law-making powers were granted, the number of AMs should be increased from 60 to 80;

- powers should continue to be devolved from Westminster; and

- the existing closed party list system for selecting AMs needed to be reformed.

The Assembly was considering these recommendations and consulting with political parties and the general public before holding a debate at the start of the autumn 2004 session. If the recommendations are accepted a new draft Government of Wales Bill would need to be introduced to the UK Parliament. Once this was passed a referendum would have to be held before the extra law-making powers could be granted. If there was a yes vote in the referendum, the Boundary Commission would need to carry out constituency reviews for the new AMs. The earliest the new system could be put in place would be in time for the 2011 Assembly elections.

A long tradition

The first Welsh Parliament was held by Owain Glyndŵr in Machynlleth 600 years ago in 1404. Glyndŵr was the first Welsh leader to unite the people of Wales to oppose the harsh English rule of the time. By the end of 1403 he controlled most of Wales. However, the English fought back and by 1409 Harlech Castle, home to Glyndŵr's family, surrendered. Glyndŵr remained elusive, retreating into his heartland in central Wales. He was never captured.

Cabinet of eight ministers, also Assembly Members. The Ministers have responsibility for: finance, local government and public services; government business; social justice and regeneration; health and social services; economic development and transport; education and lifelong learning; environment, planning and the countryside; and culture, the Welsh language and sport. In autumn 2004, the Assembly will gain increased powers over animal health and welfare. A new Veterinary Policy Unit will be based in the Environment, Planning and the Countryside Department.

Local government

The 22 Welsh unitary (single-tier) authorities (see map below) had collective responsibility for spending £3.4 billion, 31 per cent of the National Assembly's DEL (see Spending Review box on page 19) in 2004/05. The Assembly sets the policy framework and makes the secondary legislation within which local government operates. The Assembly also has a responsibility to ensure that local decision-making reflects the requirements of the law and, where appropriate, priorities fixed by

Map 3.3 Unitary authorities, Wales

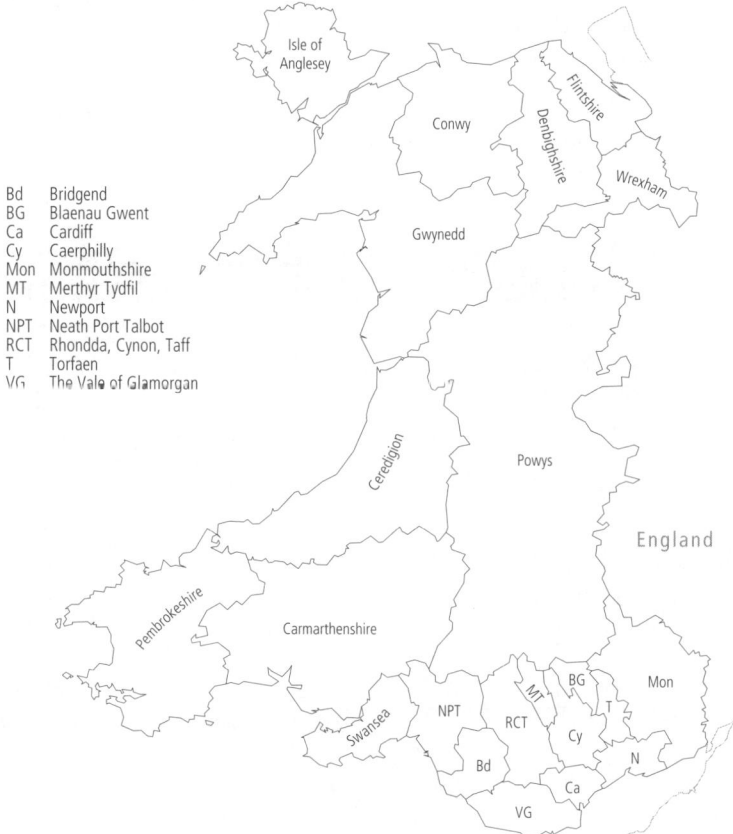

Bd   Bridgend
BG   Blaenau Gwent
Ca   Cardiff
Cy   Caerphilly
Mon   Monmouthshire
MT   Merthyr Tydfil
N   Newport
NPT   Neath Port Talbot
RCT   Rhondda, Cynon, Taff
T   Torfaen
VG   The Vale of Glamorgan

the Assembly. Whole council elections are held every fourth year, with the next due in 2008.

In 2003/04 local government was broadly financed by government grants (53 per cent), a share of non-domestic rates (14 per cent), rents and charges (13 per cent), council tax (10 per cent), and borrowing (8 per cent). Under the provisions of the *Local Government Act 2003* local authorities will have greater freedom over the management of their finances. The Act applies to Wales, as well as to England, and the National Assembly was closely involved with its drafting.

Local authorities spend about 40 per cent of resources on education; 20 per cent on housing; 15 per cent on social services; 9 per cent on the police; and 5 per cent on transport. The remaining 11 per cent of resources are spent on waste management; the fire services; libraries and archives, museums and art galleries; consumer protection; environmental health; planning and economic development; leisure and parks; and environmental services.

As required by the *Government of Wales Act*, the Assembly has set up a Partnership Council to advise it on the exercise of any of its functions and to make representations on matters affecting, or of

Local government elections 2004

Local councillors in Wales normally hold office for four years and all unitary authorities elect their members at the same time. However, local government elections were put back a year from May 2003 to May 2004 so that local government elections and National Assembly elections were not held at the same time. The National Assembly later moved the revised date from May to June 2004 so that local government elections were held on the same day as the European parliamentary elections.

In the June 2004 elections the Labour Party won 478 seats, suffering a net loss of 64 seats. Plaid Cymru – The Party of Wales won 172 seats, a net loss of 28, while the Liberal Democrats and the Conservative Party won 148 and 109 seats respectively, making net gains of 37 and 40 seats. The net gains and losses do not take into account boundary changes.

Distinctive facts about Wales

National day: 1 March, St David's Day

National emblems: daffodil and leek

National flag: red dragon (*Y Ddraig Goch*) on a background of white over green

The Millennium Stadium in Cardiff has a seating capacity of 72,500 and a roof that can be fully opened or closed within 20 minutes, making it an all-weather venue for a variety of premier sporting events, concerts, shows and exhibitions.

Rugby union is regarded as the Welsh national game, although football has more participants and a similarly high profile. Wales is well known for its music, particularly choral singing, and has a long tradition of literature. Special festivals, known as *eisteddfodau*, encourage both literature and music (see chapter 16).

The National Museum & Galleries (NMGW) claims the finest collection of Impressionist and Post-Impressionist paintings outside France. The six NMGW sites across Wales attracted over 1.2 million visitors in 2003–04.

About 25 per cent of the land in Wales is in one of the three National Parks or four Areas of Outstanding Natural Beauty (AONB). In addition, Wales has over 1,000 Sites of Special Scientific Interest and a number of internationally important nature conservation sites (see chapter 19).

concern to, local government. It comprises locally elected representatives – including those from the unitary authorities, National Parks, police and fire authorities, and community councils (see below) – and selected members of the Assembly. The Council also assists the Assembly in preparing guidance and advice to local councils.

Communities and community councils

Welsh unitary authorities are subdivided into smaller areas called communities. There are 868 communities, and over 700 have community councils. These community councils have similar powers and functions to parish councils in England (see page 11), and may also choose to call

The Welsh language

Welsh is a Celtic language closely related to Cornish and Breton. The language spoken today comes from Early Welsh, which emerged as a distinct tongue around the sixth century. The National Assembly is committed to revitalising the Welsh language and creating a bilingual Wales.

The 2001 Census revealed that 21 per cent of the population of Wales aged three or over said they could speak at least some Welsh, with similar proportions able to read (20 per cent) and write (18 per cent) Welsh, and 16 per cent revealing that they had all these skills. For the first time, the Census asked respondents about understanding spoken Welsh; 24 per cent said they could. The proportion of people with Welsh language skills varied greatly by age, with the highest proportions in the young (aged under 20) and the old (aged over 75).

Welsh is a compulsory subject for all pupils between the ages of 5 and 16 in mainstream schools in Wales (see chapter 10) and 41 per cent of children aged 5–15 years are able to speak Welsh. Around 20 per cent of primary pupils and 14 per cent of secondary pupils are taught in classes where Welsh is the medium of instruction for all or part of the day. BBC Wales' Welsh language website encourages learning Welsh through a combination of soap episodes from BBC Radio Wales, videos of the week's news, and online lessons and help with grammar. In spring 2004, a computer magazine named it the best online language teaching site on the Internet.

One of the best known Welsh language novelists, Islwyn Ffowc Elis, died in Carmarthen in January 2004. His novels included *Cysgod Y Cryman* (*Shadow of the Sickle*), published in 1953, which was chosen as Welsh-language book of the 20th century by the Arts Council of Wales.

themselves town councils. Community councillors are unpaid. They have no statutory duties or powers, but they have the statutory right to be consulted on local planning issues and on council decentralisation schemes.

Economy

The Welsh economy, which traditionally relied on coal and steel, experienced major changes during the 20th century. In recent years, Wales has attracted a range of manufacturing industries, with a significant number of investments by overseas companies including many at the forefront of technology.

There were 1.4 million people economically active in Wales in spring 2004, of whom 1.3 million were in employment. Unemployment, at 4.6 per cent, was just below the UK rate of 4.8 per cent.

Gross value added (GVA, see glossary and Table 22.12, page 357 for UK GVA) at current prices in Wales was £35.1 billion in 2002, 3.9 per cent of UK GVA. GVA per head was £12,000, lower than the UK GVA per head of £15,300. Manufacturing accounted for 23 per cent of Welsh GVA in 2001, while the service sector accounted for 67 per cent.

The Welsh Assembly Government's national economic development strategy, *A Winning Wales*, is a ten-year agenda to increase prosperity in Wales so that it matches that of the United Kingdom as a whole, and is evenly spread and sustainable. The strategy is coordinated by the Economic Development and Transport Department (EDT). EDT administers schemes giving grants direct to business in the form of Regional Selective Assistance (see page 357) and the Assembly Investment Grant, which both offer small grants to small and medium-sized enterprises. It also provides international trade support and advice through WalesTrade International, which was established in 2000. EDT works closely with the Welsh Development Agency (WDA), the Wales Tourist Board (WTB), and other public and voluntary bodies.

The WDA was set up in 1976 to promote economic development in Wales. In July 2004 it was announced that the WDA is to be abolished and its functions absorbed into those of the Welsh Assembly Government. It has offices around the world, and aims to attract companies to invest in Wales. It also works with local communities to encourage prosperity and is accountable to the Welsh Assembly Government.

Wales has been allocated almost £1.5 billion of funding from the EU for the period 2000–2006. With matched funding from a range of public, private and voluntary sources, the Structural Funds Programmes are worth over £3.2 billion. The largest of the programmes in Wales is the £1.3 billion Objective 1 programme (see page 358) covering West Wales, the south Wales valleys and parts of north west Wales. This funding is designed to promote growth in regions where GDP is less than 75 per cent of the EU average. In East Wales, Objective 2 funding aims to lift the economy of rural areas and those hit by industrial decline, and Objective 3 funding operates in all areas outside of Objective 1, and aims to improve systems for training and employment. By December 2003, some 1,700 projects had been approved.

The WTB was set up under the *Development of Tourism Act 1969* to promote Wales as a tourist destination and to encourage and support the development of tourist facilities and amenities. It markets Wales throughout the United Kingdom and in key overseas markets such as France, Germany, The Netherlands, the Republic of Ireland and the United States. Like the WDA, it is accountable to the Welsh Assembly Government.

The WTB also provides business support services and grant assistance for tourism businesses, utilising EU Objective 1 funding in eligible areas. During 2003/04, 279 projects received £15.6 million in grants across Wales from various WTB schemes. A further £3 million of Objective 1 funds have been approved for 2004–06. In addition, the WTB received Objective 1 funds worth £9 million for marketing projects, and further funding worth £11 million has been approved for 2004–06.

International trade in goods

In 2003, exports from Wales totalled £7.2 billion and imports £5.5 billion. The largest overseas trading partner was the EU (Figure 3.4). The three largest sectors were machinery and transport (42 per cent of exports and 43 per cent of imports), chemicals (20 per cent of exports and 12 per cent of imports), and manufactured goods (19 per cent and 21 per cent respectively).

Figure 3.4 Distribution of international trade in goods, 2003, Wales

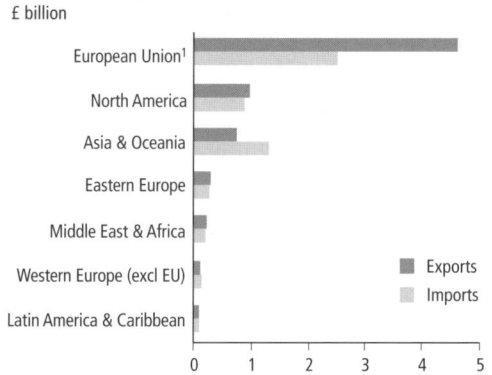

£ billion

1 Excludes the ten countries that joined the EU in 2004.
Source: *UK Regional Trade in Goods Statistics*, HM Customs and Excise

Further reading

Wales Office Departmental Report 2004: The Government's Expenditure Plans 2004–05 to 2006–07. Cm 6228. The Stationery Office, 2004.

Iaith Pawb – A National Action Plan for a bilingual Wales. Welsh Assembly Government, 2003.

Creative Future: Cymru Greadigol – A Culture Strategy for Wales. Welsh Assembly Government, 2002.

Focus on Wales. Office for National Statistics, 2004.

Websites

National Assembly for Wales and Welsh Assembly Government
www.wales.gov.uk

Wales Office
www.walesoffice.gov.uk

Welsh Development Agency (WDA)
www.wda.co.uk

Wales Tourist Board
www.visitwales.com

WalesTrade International
www.walestrade.com

4 Scotland

Population

In mid-2003 the population of Scotland was 5.1 million, 8.5 per cent of the population of the United Kingdom. The population density in Scotland is the lowest in the United Kingdom, averaging 65 people per square kilometre in 2003. There is a wide difference between Scotland's area of highest population density, Glasgow City at 3,288 people per square kilometre, and the lowest in the Eilean Siar and Highland council areas at 8 people per square kilometre. Three-quarters of Scotland's population live in the central lowlands, where the two largest cities are situated: the capital, Edinburgh (population 448,000) in the east, and Glasgow (population 577,000) in the west.

There has been a 0.5 per cent decline in population over the past 12 years (Table 4.1), although there was a slight rise in 2003. This was a result of more people migrating to Scotland than moving away. West Lothian had the largest proportional increase, at 11.0 per cent, while Eilean Siar had the largest decrease, falling by 11.0 per cent. In February 2004 the Scottish Executive launched the Fresh Talent strategy (*Scotlandistheplace.com*) to reverse the population decline by retaining native Scots and attracting fresh talent from overseas. This includes:

- granting visa extensions for overseas students wishing to stay in Scotland after graduation;

- prioritising work permit requests from Scottish firms;

- supporting universities to coordinate recruitment of overseas students;

- granting scholarships to combine postgraduate study with work experience for overseas students; and

- a Relocation Advice Service to be operational from October 2004.

Table 4.1 Population and population change by council area, June 2003, Scotland

	Population (thousands)	Change in population 1991–2003 (%)
Aberdeen City	207	−3.5
Aberdeenshire	229	6.2
Angus	108	−0.8
Argyll and Bute	91	−2.4
Clackmannanshire	48	−0.9
Dumfries and Galloway	147	0.0
Dundee City	143	−8.0
East Ayrshire	120	−3.6
East Dumbartonshire	107	−2.9
East Lothian	91	7.9
East Renfrewshire	90	4.6
Edinburgh, City of	448	2.8
Eilean Siar[1]	26	−11.0
Falkirk	146	2.4
Fife	352	1.3
Glasgow City	577	−8.3
Highland	209	2.6
Inverclyde	83	−9.1
Midlothian	80	0.2
Moray	87	4.1
North Ayrshire	136	−1.5
North Lanarkshire	322	−1.6
Orkney Islands	19	−1.1
Perth and Kinross	136	6.8
Renfrewshire	171	−2.7
Scottish Borders	108	4.3
Shetland Islands	22	−2.9
South Ayrshire	112	−1.4
South Lanarkshire	303	0.2
Stirling	86	6.7
West Dumbartonshire	92	−5.1
West Lothian	161	11.0
Scotland	**5,057**	**−0.5**

1 Formerly Western Isles.
Source: Office for National Statistics; General Register Office for Scotland

Representation at Westminster and in Europe

Scottish constituencies are represented by 72 of the 659 seats in the House of Commons at Westminster. However, the *Scotland Act 1998*, which established the Scottish Parliament and Executive (see below), removed the statutory minimum of 71 Scottish seats at Westminster and required the Boundary Commission for Scotland to determine the level of Scottish representation by applying the same electoral quota as in England. Currently, there are about 55,000 electors in a constituency in Scotland and about 70,000 in England.

The Commission began its review of constituencies in Scotland in 2001. Following consultation and public inquiries, it published its recommendations in December 2003 to reduce the number of Scottish parliamentary constituencies to 59. The Commission is required to make its final report by December 2006. The *Scottish Parliament (Constituencies) Act 2004* was passed in July. This removes the link between the constituencies for the Scottish Parliament and those for the House of Commons and allows the existing constituencies to be retained for the Scottish Parliament when the number of Scottish seats at Westminster is cut.

Following devolution the UK Parliament retained exclusive jurisdiction over a number of issues as 'reserved matters' under the *Scotland Act 1998*. These include foreign affairs, defence, the Constitution and economic policy (for a more detailed list see appendix A, page 481).

Scottish interests are represented in the UK Cabinet and the House of Commons by the Secretary of State for Scotland, who currently combines this role with that of Secretary of State for Transport. The Secretary of State is supported by the Scotland Office, a distinct entity within the Department for Constitutional Affairs (DCA). The DCA also includes the Offices of the Advocate General, who exercises statutory functions under the *Scotland Act 1998* and is the principal legal adviser to the UK Government on Scots Law. Scotland Office ministers are questioned regularly in the House of Commons by Members of Parliament (MPs) at Scottish questions.

The Scottish Affairs Committee[1] is appointed by the House of Commons to examine the

expenditure, administration and policy of the Scotland Office, including relations with the Scottish Parliament. Its 11 members come from all the parties that have Members in the House of Commons representing Scottish constituencies.

All MPs for Scottish constituencies are members of the House of Commons Scottish Grand Committee, which may be convened in Scotland as well as at Westminster. Its business includes questions tabled for oral answer, ministerial statements, and debates that are referred to it.

European Parliament elections

Scotland forms a single constituency in the European Parliament (see page 65). Following the enlargement of the European Union (EU, see page 71) in 2004, the number of Members of the European Parliament (MEPs) representing Scotland was reduced from eight to seven. In the European parliamentary elections in June 2004, 1.18 million people, 31 per cent of the electorate in Scotland, voted for an MEP (see Table 4.2) using the d'Hondt system of proportional representation (see glossary). The Scottish Labour Party gained 26 per cent of the votes cast, the Scottish National Party 20 per cent, the Scottish Conservative and Unionist Party 18 per cent and the Scottish Liberal Democrats 13 per cent.

The Scottish Executive has an office in Brussels that helps to promote Scotland's interests within the EU.

The Scottish Parliament and Scottish Executive

The first Scottish Parliament since 1707 was elected in 1999. This followed a referendum in 1997, in which 74 per cent of those who voted endorsed the UK Government's proposals to establish a Scottish Parliament and Executive to administer Scottish affairs in areas to be devolved to it. On a second question – whether to give the new Parliament limited tax-varying powers – 64 per cent of those who voted were in favour. The following November the *Scotland Act 1998* passed into law. The first Scottish Parliamentary elections were held in May 1999 and the Parliament and Executive took up their full powers on 1 July 1999.

---

1 For information on select committees, see page 47.

Table 4.2 Electoral representation, June 2004, Scotland

	Scottish Parliament			UK Parliament (MPs)	European Parliament (MEPs)
	Constituency seats (MSPs)	Additional seats (MSPs)	Total seats (MSPs)		
Scottish Labour Party	46	4	50	55	2
Scottish National Party	9	18	27	5	2
Scottish Conservative and Unionist Party	3	15	18	1	2
Scottish Liberal Democrats	13	4	17	10	1
Scottish Greens	0	7	7	0	0
Scottish Socialist Party	0	6	6	0	0
Scottish Senior Citizens Unity Party	0	1	1	0	0
Independents	2	1	3	0	0
Speaker of the House of Commons	.	.	.	1	.
Total seats	**73**	**56**	**129**	**72**	**7**

Source: Scottish Parliament; UK Parliament

The Scottish Parliament was initially based at the Church of Scotland Assembly Hall in Edinburgh while a new Parliament building, designed by Enric Miralles, was built. This is based at Holyrood, in the Royal Mile, where the Scottish Parliament met from 1640 to 1707. Staff started moving into the new building in August 2004 and were joined by Members of the Scottish Parliament (MSPs) in September, after the summer recess. The Queen is due to perform the official opening of the new building in October.

The Holyrood building was some three-and-a-half years behind schedule and its estimated final cost was £431 million, more then £320 million over budget. An independent inquiry into the delays and the cost, held under Lord Fraser of Carmyllie, reported in September 2004. The Executive accepted all the recommendations in the report.

The Scotland Act 1998 devolves to the Scottish Parliament and ministers any matter not reserved to the UK Parliament under Schedule 5 of the Act. The Scottish Parliament can legislate in areas that include: education, most health issues and most aspects of home affairs, (see appendix A, page 491). In all devolved areas the Scottish Parliament can amend or repeal existing Acts of the UK Parliament as they apply in Scotland and pass new legislation. During the 1999–2003 session, 62 Acts were passed by the Scottish Parliament.

Unlike the Westminster Parliament, the Scottish Parliament does not have a second chamber to revise legislation that comes before it. Detailed scrutiny of Bills is carried out in committees, which take evidence from a variety of outside sources, including interest groups and experts.

The Scottish Parliament's 129 members (MSPs) are elected for a fixed four-year term. The 73 single-member constituency seats are elected under the first-past-the-post system. A further seven MSPs are returned for each of eight Scottish Parliament regions using the Additional Member System, a type of proportional representation (see glossary).

Elections for the second Scottish Parliament were held in May 2003. The turnout across regions and constituencies was 49 per cent, compared with 59 per cent in the 1999 elections. The Scottish Labour Party was again the largest single party in the Scottish Parliament (Table 4.2).

As no party has an overall majority, the Scottish Executive is formed by a coalition between the Scottish Labour Party and the Scottish Liberal Democrats. The latter has three ministers in the Cabinet, including the position of Deputy First Minister.

The Scottish Executive is the executive branch of the devolved institutions and is accountable to the Scottish Parliament. The devolved government is led by the First Minister, an MSP who is nominated by the Parliament. The First Minister appoints the 11 Cabinet Ministers (see appendix A).

Finance

Most of the funding for the Scottish Parliament comes from the UK Parliament's block grant.

The Scots Makar

Scotland's first national poet, Professor Edwin Morgan, was appointed in February 2004 by Scottish ministers. The national poet will be known as the Scots Makar, a term dating back to Scottish poets in the 15th century, and will represent and promote Scots poetry. The 83-year-old writer was appointed for a three-year period. Future Makars will be selected by an independent committee.

Gaelic language and culture

Scottish Gaelic, a Celtic language related to Irish, was introduced into Scotland in about AD 500. According to the 2001 Census 1.2 per cent of the population spoke Gaelic. In the Eilean Siar Council Area, the number was as high as 60 per cent.

The Royal National Mod, Scotland's premier Gaelic festival, is held each October, attracting visitors and participants from around the world. The *Fèisean nan Gaidheal* also celebrates Gaelic culture. *Fèis,* pronounced faysh (plural *Fèisean*), is Gaelic for a festival or feast. The *Fèis* movement started in 1981 on Barra. By 2004 there were 37 *Fèisean* in which almost 4,000 young people participate. The Hebridean Celtic Festival, staged in the grounds of Lews Castle, Stornoway in mid-July, promotes Gaelic language and culture within an international music programme. With Glasgow's Celtic Connections, the festival brings Gaelic music to a wider audience. Stornoway is also home to *Proiseact Nan Ealan* *(www.gaelic-arts.com)*, a development agency for the Gaelic arts in Scotland. Gaelic festivals and cultural events contributed more than £40 million to the economy in 2003.

Other sources of revenue include income from business rates. The Scottish Parliament is solely responsible for the allocation of the total Scottish budget.

Under the Spending Review announced by the UK Government in July 2004, the Scottish Executive's departmental expenditure limit (DEL, see page 366) is set to rise from £21.3 billion in 2004/05 to £22.7 billion in 2005/06, and to £25.5 billion in 2007/08. The increases ensure that Scotland receives a population-based share of changes in comparable spending in England. Detailed spending proposals for 2005/06 will be announced in autumn 2004.

The Scottish Parliament has the power to increase or decrease the basic rate of income tax in Scotland – 22 pence in the pound – by a maximum of 3 pence. The Parliament did not exercise its right to vary income tax in its first session.

Local government

Scotland's 32 unitary (single-tier) authorities (see map on page 28) are responsible for the full range of local government services, including education, social work, police and fire services, roads, public transport, local planning, urban development, housing, libraries, leisure and recreation. They can either provide these services themselves or buy them in. The planned budget for local government for 2004/05 is £8 billion.

Although local authorities are independent and manage their own day-to-day business, Scotland's First Minister has powers to oversee their work in areas such as finance, town and country planning, transport and housing.

Local councillors in Scotland hold office for four years. Whole council elections in all 32 unitary authorities are held at the same time. The last local elections were held in May 2003 when 49 per cent of the electorate voted. Local elections have traditionally used the first-past-the-post system. However, under the *Local Governance (Scotland) Act 2004* the single transferable vote system (see glossary) of proportional representation will be used in future local government elections. The Act also lowers the age at which people can stand as a councillor from 21 to 18; removes some of the political restrictions on council employees standing for local authority elections; and establishes an independent remuneration committee to advise on a new system for allowances paid to councillors.

There are eight police authorities and eight fire brigades. In both cases six of these cover more than one local authority and are administered by joint boards appointed by the authorities in their areas. These boards appoint their own chief

Map 4.3 Unitary council areas, Scotland

1	Inverclyde
2	West Dunbartonshire
3	Renfrewshire
4	East Renfrewshire
5	Glasgow City
6	East Dunbartonshire
7	North Lanarkshire
8	Falkirk
9	West Lothian
10	Edinburgh, City of
11	Clackmannanshire
12	Dundee City
13	Aberdeen City

constables and firemasters who are responsible for day-to-day operations.

Communities and community councils

Scotland is divided into about 1,350 communities, which fit into and change in line with council areas. Some 1,150 of these have community councils, run by volunteers. Many receive local authority funding for running costs, but they are not always regarded as a tier of local government, even though legally they can have that role.

Community councils act as a channel through which communities can speak and act on issues they have identified locally. Although they have no statutory powers, they do have a right to be consulted on local planning issues. The *Local Government in Scotland Act 2003* provides a framework for community planning to ensure effective partnership between communities and local authorities and other public and private bodies to improve service delivery and link national and local priorities.

Economy

The service sector and high-technology industries, particularly electronics, have largely taken the place of the traditional Scottish industries of coal mining, steel production and shipbuilding. In 2001 the service sector accounted for 70 per cent of Scotland' gross value added (GVA, see glossary), while manufacturing accounted for 18 per cent.

Fair Isle

In 2004 the National Trust for Scotland celebrated the 50th anniversary of its purchase of Fair Isle from Dr George Waterston. The island, lying halfway between Orkney and Shetland, is one of the most isolated inhabited islands in the United Kingdom. It is 5 kilometres long and 3 kilometres wide. The population of about 70 people are involved in projects on wildlife tourism, wind power, and sustainable management of the environment. Fair Isle is home to large sea bird colonies and its bird observatory is a centre of ornithology. Fair Isle's intricate, colourful knitwear takes its name from the island and is sold worldwide.

Distinctive facts about Scotland

National day: 30 November, St Andrew's Day

National emblem: thistle

National flag: white diagonal cross on blue background (St Andrew's Cross, known as the Saltire)

Scotland has distinctive educational and legal systems compared with other parts of the United Kingdom (see chapters 10 and 14).

Scotland has several major collections of the fine and applied arts. These include the National Galleries of Scotland, which have five Edinburgh-based galleries and two outstations, one in the north and the other in the south of Scotland, and the Glasgow Museums, which include the Burrell Collection and the Kelvingrove Art Gallery and Museum.

The annual Edinburgh Festival is the largest arts event in the United Kingdom and brings an estimated £100 million into the local economy and a further £76 million into the Scottish economy.

In 2002, GVA at current prices in Scotland was £73 billion, 8.1 per cent of the UK total (see Table 22.12, page 357 for UK GVA). GVA per head was £14,400, compared with £15,300 for the United Kingdom as a whole. There were 2.57 million economically active people in Scotland in spring 2004, of whom 2.41 million were in employment. Unemployment, at 6.1 per cent, was above the UK rate of 4.8 per cent.

According to the *Scottish Economic Report* published in March 2004, Scotland is the sixth largest equity management centre in Europe and 15th in the world. Banking accounted for nearly half of all financial service activity, with output in banking rising by about 6 per cent in 2003.

Offshore oil and gas has made a significant contribution to the UK economy since the first full year of production in 1976. Many of the offshore oilfields are to the east of the Shetland and Orkney Islands or off the east coast of mainland Scotland. The oilfields are expected to remain productive until at least 2020 (see also chapter 28).

Scotland's software sector has nearly 1,400 companies specialising in software design for engineering and manufacturing, science, neural networks, telecommunications and multimedia. Companies involved in developing computer games had an estimated turnover of £20 million in 2003 and there is an annual Edinburgh International Games Festival. The Scottish Technology and Collaboration (Stac) initiative aims to assist collaboration between companies, linking the expertise of small software companies with the strength of multinationals.

Rural areas are under-represented in the growth areas of the Scottish economy: banking and finance, high-technology manufacturing, information and communication technology (ICT) services, and research and development. *A New Approach: The Way Forward for Rural Scotland* was unveiled by the Scottish Executive in May 2004. This was backed by £780,000 from the European Commission to improve rural transport.

The Scottish Executive's second progress report on the three-year Scottish Tourism Framework for Action was published in June 2004. It estimates that tourists spent £4.5 billion in Scotland in 2002/03 and that tourism accounts for 215,000 jobs.

Forests cover 16 per cent of Scotland's land area (see page 420). Scotland accounts for around 60 per cent of the British conifer harvest and Scottish sawmills produce 42 per cent of lumber production in Great Britain. New markets are developing with biomass power generation using sawmill residues.

The Scottish Executive's Enterprise, Transport and Lifelong Learning Department provides direct grant assistance to a wide range of businesses. Its objectives are promoted in collaboration with Scottish Enterprise and Highlands and Islands Enterprise, the lead economic development agencies in lowland and highland Scotland respectively, which manage domestic support for industry and commerce. Scottish Development International encourages inward investment.

The Highlands and Islands qualified for EU regeneration funding between 2000 and 2006 under a special transitional programme worth around £200 million as the region is below average EU development. It was negotiated following the loss of the region's former Objective 1 status (see page 358). The funding is managed by the Highlands and Islands Partnership Programme.

International trade in goods

In 2003, exports from Scotland were worth £13.2 billion and imports £8.2 billion. The EU was the largest partner group (Figure 4.4). North America was the second largest export market, while Asia and Oceania were the second largest source of imports. The three largest sectors were machinery and transport, accounting for 43 per cent of exports and 55 per cent of imports; beverages and tobacco, 13 per cent of exports although only 3 per cent of imports; and manufactured goods, 11 per cent of both exports and imports. The second largest import sector was miscellaneous manufactures, accounting for 15 per cent.

Natural attractions

Scotland has 40 National Scenic Areas that are conserved as part of the natural heritage, four World Heritage Sites and two National Parks, Loch Lomond and the Trossachs, and the Cairngorms. As well as Ben Nevis, at 1,343 metres the highest mountain in the United Kingdom, Scotland has the Munros (284 summits over 914 metres), and the Corbetts (221 hills between 762 and 914 metres).

Scotland's longest walk, the Southern Upland Way, celebrated its 20th anniversary in 2004. The walk stretches about 340 kilometres coast to coast from Cockburnspath in the east to Portpatrick in the west.

Figure 4.4 Distribution of international trade in goods, 2003, Scotland

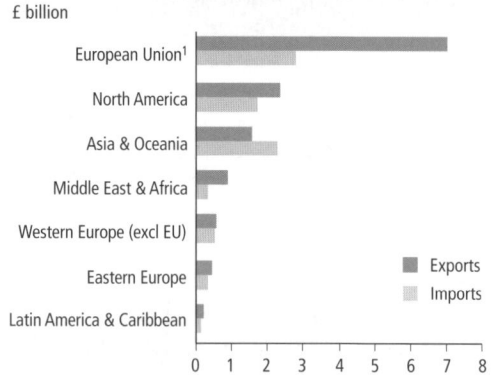

1 Excludes the ten countries that joined the EU in 2004.
Source: *UK Regional Trade in Goods Statistics*, HM Customs and Excise

Further reading

Scottish Economic Report. The Scottish Executive. March 2004.

The Scottish Budget 2004/05. Scottish Executive, 2004.

Scotland Office Departmental Report 2004: The Government's Expenditure Plans 2004–05 to 2005–06. Cm 6227. The Stationery Office, 2004.

Websites

Scottish Executive
www.scotland.gov.uk

Scotland Office
www.scottishsecretary.gov.uk

Scottish Parliament
www.scottish.parliament.uk

Convention of Scottish Local Authorities
www.cosla.gov.uk

Scottish Development International
www.scottishdevelopmentinternational.com

Scottish Tourist Board
www.visitscotland.com

5 Northern Ireland

Population

Northern Ireland's population in mid-2003 was 1.7 million (Table 5.1), 2.9 per cent of the population of the United Kingdom. The population increased by 5.9 per cent between 1991 and 2003. About 39 per cent lived in the area covered by the Eastern Health and Social Services Board, at the centre of which is the capital, Belfast. Population density in 2003 was highest in the district council area of Belfast (at 2,500 people per square kilometre) and lowest in Moyle (at only 33 people per square kilometre). Just under 36 per cent of the population was aged under 25 in 2003, a higher proportion than England, Wales or Scotland.

In the 2001 Census, 40 per cent of the Northern Ireland population said that their religion was Catholic; 21 per cent were Presbyterian; 15 per cent Church of Ireland; 4 per cent Methodist; 6 per cent belonged to other Christian religions; and 0.3 per cent of the population belonged to other (non-Christian) religions. The remainder either had no religion, or did not state their religion.

Representation at Westminster and in Europe

For UK Parliament general elections (see page 39), Northern Ireland is divided into 18 single-seat constituencies. Members of Parliament (MPs) are elected by the 'first-past-the-post' electoral system (see Table 5.2). The four MPs from Sinn Féin would not take the oath of allegiance to The Queen and have therefore not taken their seats in the House of Commons. However, since January 2002 they have had access to facilities there.

The Secretary of State for Northern Ireland is a Cabinet Minister and head of the Northern Ireland Office (NIO), whose main function is to

Table 5.1 Population and population change by board[1] and district council, June 2003, Northern Ireland

	Population (thousands)	Change in population 1991–2003 (%)
Eastern	664	1.7
Ards	74	14.0
Belfast	272	−7.3
Castlereagh	66	7.4
Down	65	11.2
Lisburn	110	8.5
North Down	77	5.2
Northern	433	8.1
Antrim	49	8.0
Ballymena	60	5.0
Ballymoney	28	14.8
Carrickfergus	39	16.0
Coleraine	56	6.6
Cookstown	33	7.1
Larne	31	4.5
Magherafelt	41	12.3
Moyle	16	9.8
Newtonabbey	80	5.5
Southern	319	9.9
Armagh	55	6.1
Banbridge	43	28.3
Craigavon	82	8.9
Dungannon	49	7.1
Newry and Mourne	90	7.2
Western	287	8.7
Derry	106	9.1
Fermanagh	59	7.4
Limavady	34	13.4
Omagh	50	7.9
Strabane	39	6.6
Northern Ireland	**1,703**	**5.9**

1 Health and Social Services Board areas.
Source: Northern Ireland Statistics and Research Agency and Office for National Statistics

ensure that the devolution settlement in Northern Ireland works satisfactorily. Following the decision to suspend devolved government in Northern Ireland in October 2002, the Secretary of State has overall responsibility for the government of Northern Ireland (see appendix A, page 493).

The NIO has policy responsibility for matters not devolved to the Northern Ireland Assembly. These include upholding law, order and security, and running the criminal justice system.

In the 2004 Spending Review announced by the UK Government in July, spending plans for the Northern Ireland Office are set to rise from £1.16 billion in 2004/05 to £1.21 billion in 2005/06 before falling to £1.16 billion in 2006/07 and £1.15 billion in 2007/08. The settlement will support the delivery of the Patten police reforms (see page 34), the modernisation of the criminal justice system (see page 225) and investment in the prison service.

The UK Parliament has a Northern Ireland Grand Committee to consider matters relating to Northern Ireland. It also provides for oral questions to NIO ministers and ministerial statements. The Grand Committee includes all sitting Northern Ireland MPs and up to 25 other MPs.

There is also a Northern Ireland Affairs Select Committee,[1] made up of 13 MPs from around the

---

1 For an explanation of select committees see chapter 6, page 47.

United Kingdom. This examines the expenditure, policy and administration of the NIO. A sub-committee was set up in January 2004 to scrutinise devolved issues that would have come under the remit of the Northern Ireland Assembly when it is sitting. All members of the Northern Ireland Affairs Select Committee are eligible to participate in the sub-committee's inquiries, the first being an investigation into housing in Northern Ireland that started in February 2004.

Northern Ireland Assembly and Executive

Northern Ireland was governed by direct rule from Westminster between 1972 and 1999 (see page 6) but this was never intended to be permanent. Over the years, successive UK and Irish Governments worked closely to try to bring lasting peace to Northern Ireland, recognising the need for new political arrangements that were acceptable to both sides of the community.

In April 1998 multiparty talks concluded with the Belfast (Good Friday) Agreement. Referendums were held in both parts of Ireland in May 1998 and the Agreement received a clear endorsement. Northern Ireland voted 71 per cent in favour and 29 per cent against, while in the Republic of Ireland the result was 94 per cent and 6 per cent respectively. The new Northern Ireland Assembly was elected in June 1998.

Table 5.2 Electoral representation, Northern Ireland

	House of Commons (MPs)[1]	European Parliament (MEPs)[2]	Northern Ireland Assembly (MLAs)[3]
Democratic Unionist Party	5[4]	1	30[5]
Ulster Unionist Party	6[4]	1	27[5]
Sinn Féin	4	1	24
Social Democratic and Labour Party	3	0	18
Alliance Party of Northern Ireland	0	0	6
Independent	0	0	1
Progressive Unionist Party	0	0	1
United Kingdom Unionist	0	0	1
Total	**18**	**3**	**108**

1 General Election June 2001.
2 European Parliament elections June 2004.
3 Northern Ireland Assembly suspended 2002; elections held November 2003.
4 One MP elected for the UUP has moved to DUP, bringing DUP seats to 6 and UUP seats to 5. Three UUP MPs resigned the party whip and became Independent Ulster Unionists, but have since returned to the UUP.
5 Three of the MLAs elected to the Assembly for the UUP later moved to the DUP bringing DUP seats to 33 and UUP seats to 24.
Source: UK Parliament; Northern Ireland Assembly

Physical features

Orkney Islands

Shetland Islands

Land 400 metres and over
Land 100 – 399 metres
Land 0 – 99 metres
Land below sea level
Peaks
Rivers
National borders

Scotland

Cape Wrath
Dunnet Head
Lewis
Clisham 799 m
St Kilda
Harris
Skye
Outer Hebrides
Inner Hebrides
Ben Hope 927 m
Ben More Assynt 998 m
Morven 705 m
Ben Dearg 1081 m
Ben Wyvis 1045 m
Moray Firth
Cuillin Hills 1009 m
Càrn Eige 1182 m
Loch Ness
Cairn Gorm 1245 m
Ben Macdhui 1311 m
R. Dee
Lochnagar 1154 m
Ben Nevis 1343 m
Loch Morar
Grampians
Schiehallion 1081 m
Mull
Ben More 966 m
Ben Lawers 1014 m
Loch Lomond
R. Tay
Firth of Tay
Islay
Atlantic Ocean
Bute
Goat Fell 874 m
Arran
SCOTLAND
R. Clyde
R. Tweed
Holy I.
Firth of Forth
R. Forth
Southern Uplands
Merrick 843 m
The Cheviot 816 m

Northern Ireland / Republic of Ireland

NORTHERN IRELAND
Mountains of Antrim
R. Foyle
Sperrin Mountains
Trostan 554 m
Lough Neagh
Sawel 683 m
R. Bann
Lower Lough Erne
Upper Lough Erne
Strangford Lough
Mourne Mountains
Slieve Donard 852 m
REPUBLIC OF IRELAND
Lough Ree
Lough Derg
North Channel
Solway Firth
Cumbrian Mountains
Scafell Pikes 978 m
Cross Fell 893 m
R. Eden
R. Tyne
North Sea
Isle of Man
Snaefell 620 m
Whernside 737 m
North Yorkshire Moors 454 m
Flamborough Head
Morecambe Bay
R. Ribble
R. Lune
Pennines
R. Swale
R. Ure
Yorkshire Wolds
Spurn Head
Irish Sea

England / Wales

Anglesey
R. Mersey
Cheshire Plain
R. Dee
The Peak 636 m
Lincolnshire Wolds
R. Trent
R. Aire
Snowdon 1085 m
Cader Idris 892 m
Cambrian Mountains
Plynlimon 752 m
Cardigan Bay
WALES
ENGLAND
East Anglia
The Wash
The Fens
The Broads
R. Ouse
R. Nene
R. Welland
Gog Magog Hills
Cleeve Cloud 330 m
Cotswolds
Chiltern Hills
Brecon Beacons 886 m
R. Severn
R. Wye
R. Usk
R. Avon
Berkshire Downs
R. Thames
North Foreland
Bristol Channel
Lundy I.
Hartland Point
Exmoor
Dunkery Beacon 520 m
High Willhays 621 m
Brown Willy 419 m
Bodmin Moor
Dartmoor
R. Exe
Mendip Hills
Salisbury Plain
North Dorset Downs
Hampshire Downs
North Downs
South Downs
The Weald
R. Medway
Strait of Dover
Beachy Head
Lyme Bay
Portland Bill
Isle of Wight
Channel
English Channel
Land's End
Lizard Point
Scilly Isles
Celtic Sea
St. George's Channel
Channel Islands
Greenwich Meridian 0° longitude
FRANCE
R. Seine

0 40 80 120 km
0 20 40 60 80 miles

Passenger railway network

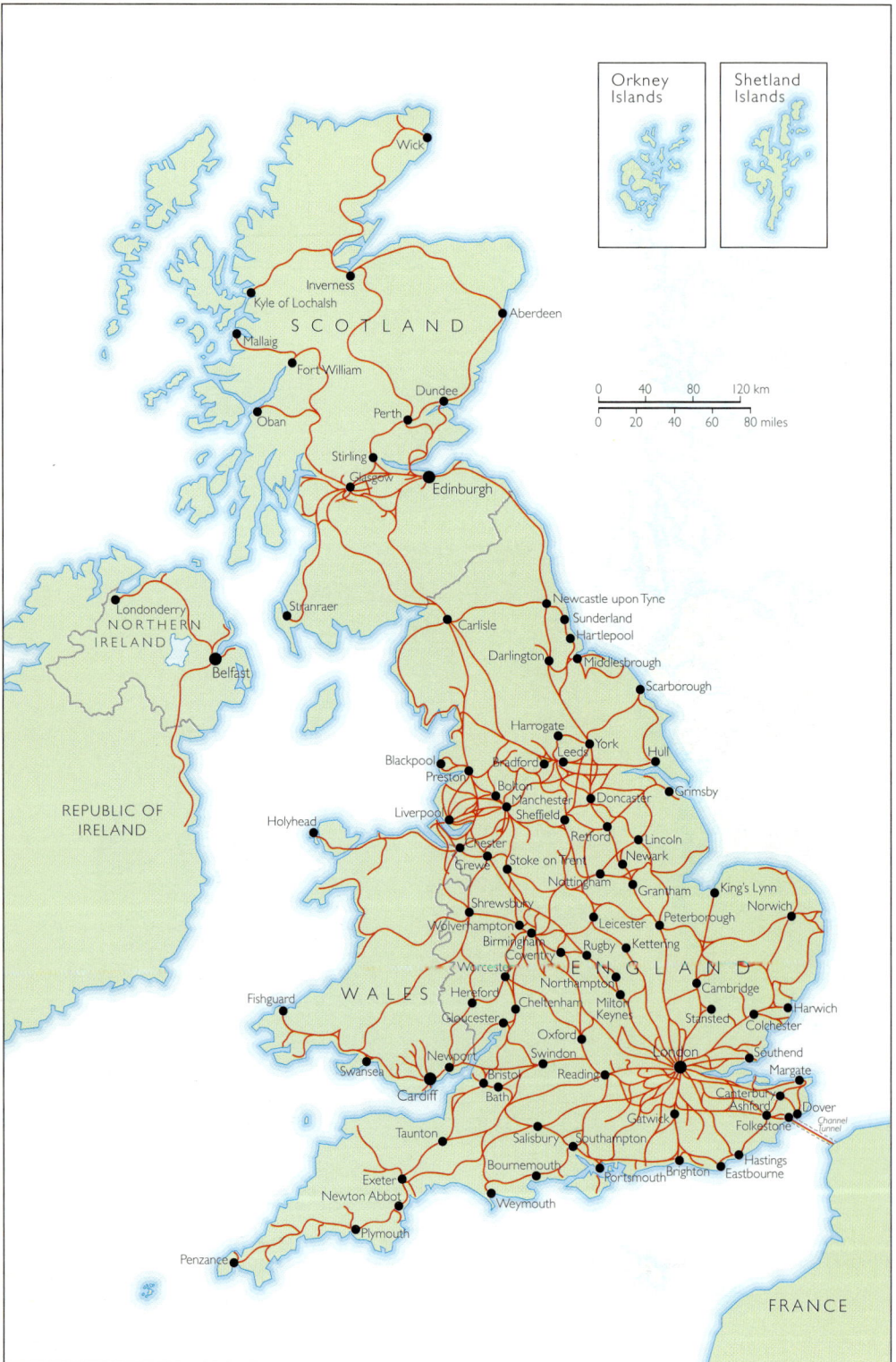

Orkney Islands

Shetland Islands

| 0 | 40 | 80 | 120 km |
| 0 | 20 | 40 | 60 | 80 miles |

Wick

Inverness
Kyle of Lochalsh
S C O T L A N D
Aberdeen
Mallaig
Fort William
Dundee
Oban
Perth
Stirling
Glasgow
Edinburgh

Londonderry
N O R T H E R N
I R E L A N D
Belfast

Stranraer
Carlisle

Newcastle upon Tyne
Sunderland
Hartlepool
Darlington
Middlesbrough
Scarborough

Harrogate
Leeds York
Blackpool Bradford Hull
Preston
Bolton
Manchester Doncaster Grimsby
Liverpool Sheffield
Holyhead Chester Retford Lincoln
Crewe Newark
Stoke on Trent
Nottingham Grantham King's Lynn
Shrewsbury Norwich
Wolverhampton Leicester Peterborough
Birmingham Rugby Kettering
Coventry
Worcester E N G L A N D
Hereford Northampton Cambridge
Fishguard Cheltenham Milton Harwich
W A L E S Gloucester Keynes Stansted Colchester
Oxford
Newport Swindon London Southend
Swansea Bristol Reading Margate
Cardiff Bath Canterbury
Ashford Dover
Gatwick Folkestone Channel Tunnel
Taunton Salisbury Southampton
Bournemouth Hastings
Exeter Brighton Eastbourne
Newton Abbot Portsmouth
Weymouth
Plymouth

Penzance

REPUBLIC OF
IRELAND

FRANCE

Motorways and major roads

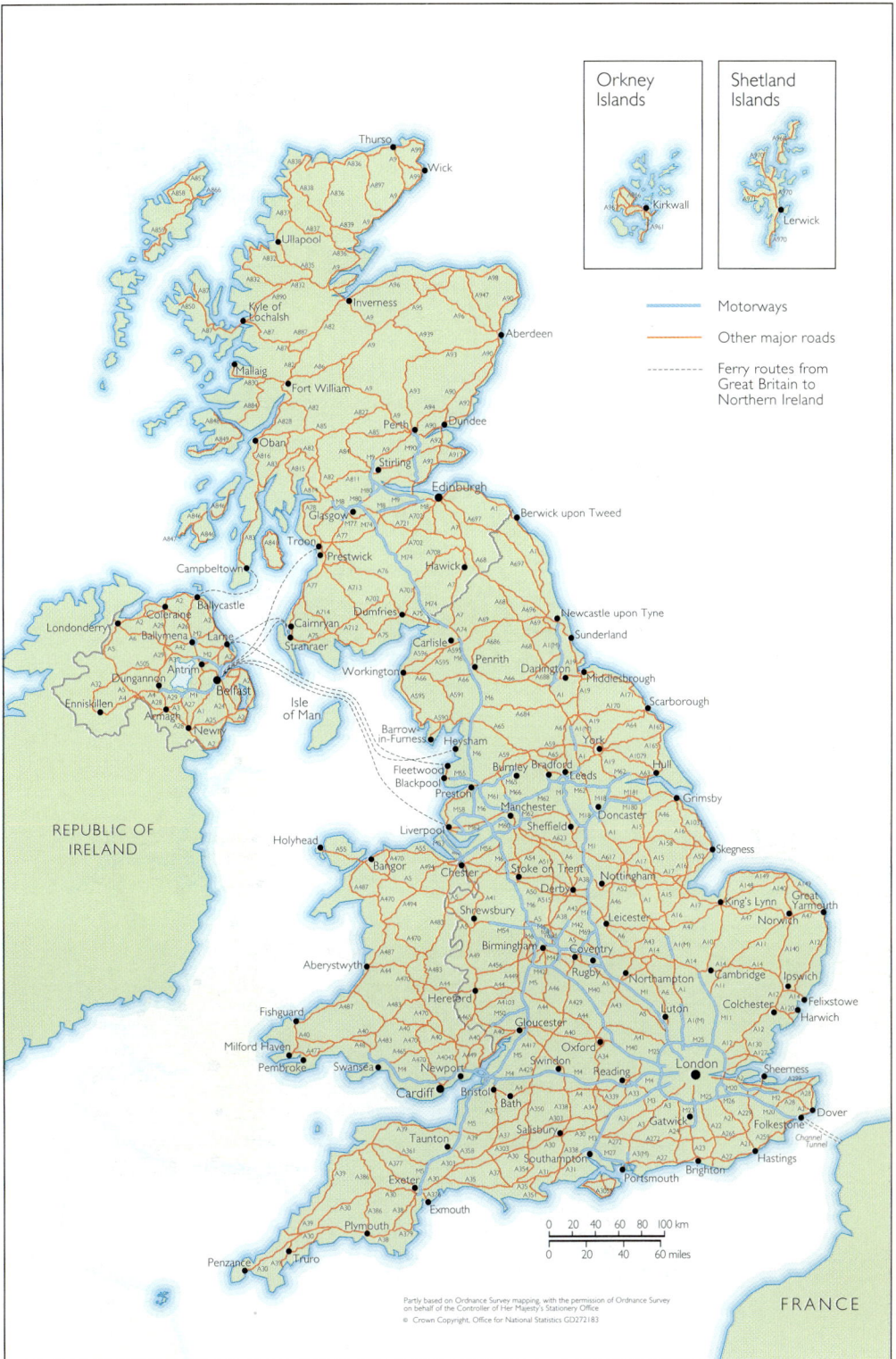

Orkney Islands

Shetland Islands

Kirkwall

Lerwick

Motorways

Other major roads

Ferry routes from Great Britain to Northern Ireland

Thurso
Wick
Ullapool
Kyle of Lochalsh
Inverness
Aberdeen
Mallaig
Fort William
Perth
Dundee
Oban
Stirling
Edinburgh
Glasgow
Berwick upon Tweed
Troon
Prestwick
Hawick
Campbeltown
Dumfries
Newcastle upon Tyne
Ballycastle
Coleraine
Ballymena
Cairnryan
Larne
Stranraer
Carlisle
Sunderland
Londonderry
Antrim
Penrith
Darlington
Middlesbrough
Dungannon
Belfast
Workington
Scarborough
Enniskillen
Armagh
Newry
Isle of Man
Barrow-in-Furness
Heysham
York
Hull
Fleetwood
Blackpool
Burnley Bradford
Leeds
Grimsby
Preston
Liverpool
Manchester
Doncaster
Holyhead
Sheffield
Skegness
Bangor
Chester
Stoke on Trent
Nottingham
King's Lynn
Great Yarmouth
Derby
Leicester
Norwich
REPUBLIC OF IRELAND
Aberystwyth
Shrewsbury
Birmingham
Coventry
Cambridge
Ipswich
Rugby
Northampton
Colchester
Felixstowe
Fishguard
Hereford
Luton
Harwich
Milford Haven
Gloucester
Pembroke
Swansea
Newport
Oxford
Swindon
Reading
London
Sheerness
Cardiff
Bristol
Bath
Salisbury
Gatwick
Dover
Folkestone
Channel Tunnel
Taunton
Southampton
Brighton
Hastings
Portsmouth
Exeter
Exmouth
Plymouth
Truro
Penzance

FRANCE

0 20 40 60 80 100 km
0   20   40   60 miles

Major conservation and recreation areas

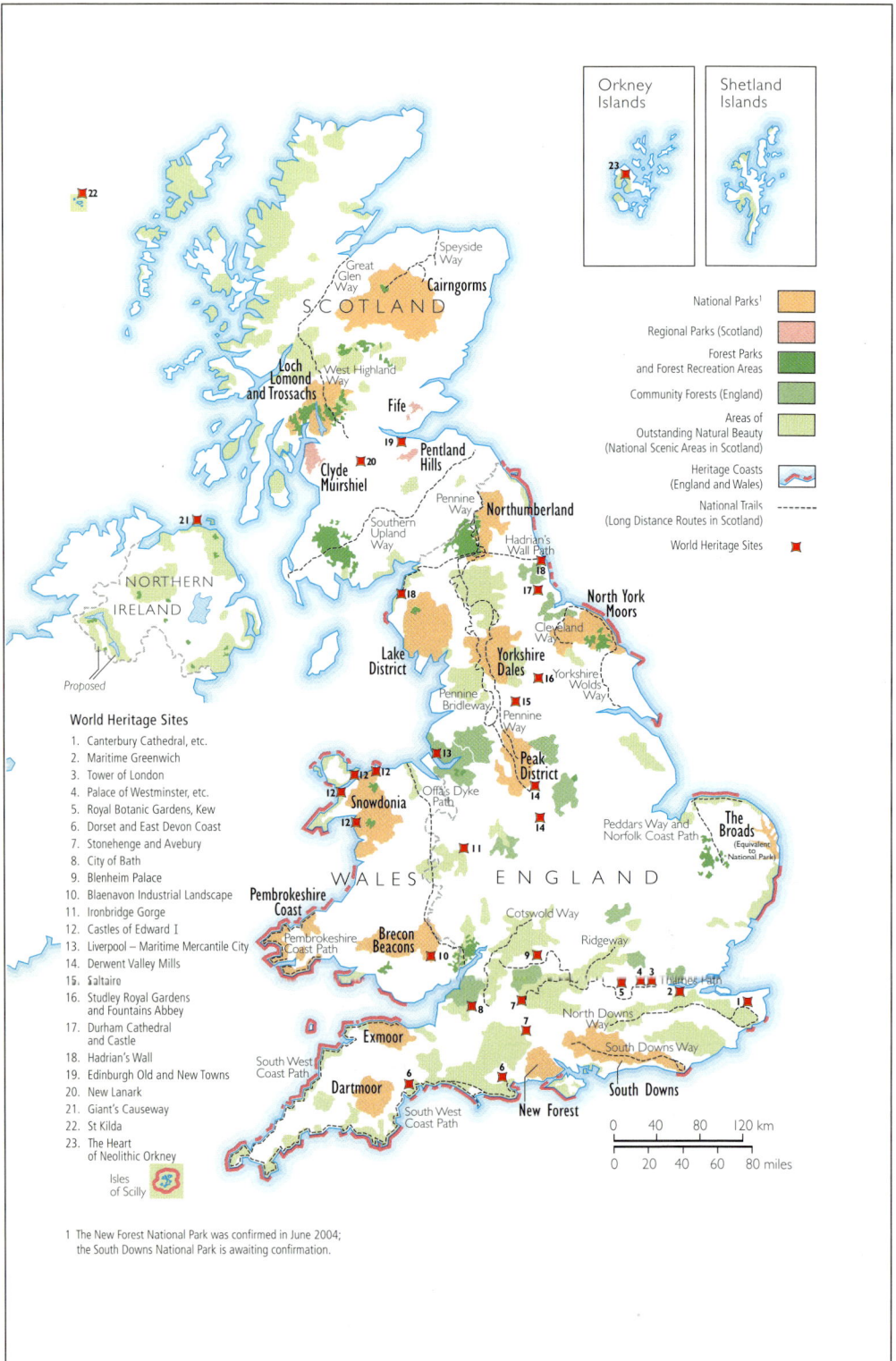

Orkney Islands

Shetland Islands

Legend:
- National Parks[1]
- Regional Parks (Scotland)
- Forest Parks and Forest Recreation Areas
- Community Forests (England)
- Areas of Outstanding Natural Beauty (National Scenic Areas in Scotland)
- Heritage Coasts (England and Wales)
- National Trails (Long Distance Routes in Scotland)
- World Heritage Sites

SCOTLAND

Cairngorms
Speyside Way
Great Glen Way
Loch Lomond and Trossachs
West Highland Way
Fife
19 Pentland Hills
Clyde Muirshiel 20
22

NORTHERN IRELAND

21

Proposed

Southern Upland Way
Pennine Way
Northumberland
Hadrian's Wall Path
18
17
North York Moors
18
Cleveland Way
Lake District
Yorkshire Dales
Yorkshire Wolds Way 16
Pennine Bridleway
15
Pennine Way
Snowdonia
12 12
12
12
Offa's Dyke Path
Peak District
13
14
14
11
Peddars Way and Norfolk Coast Path
The Broads (Equivalent to National Park)

WALES   **ENGLAND**

Pembrokeshire Coast
Pembrokeshire Coast Path
Brecon Beacons
10
Cotswold Way
Ridgeway
9
4 3
5
2
Thames Path
1
North Downs Way
8
7
7
South Downs Way
Exmoor
South West Coast Path
6
6
South Downs
Dartmoor
South West Coast Path
New Forest

Isles of Scilly

World Heritage Sites

1. Canterbury Cathedral, etc.
2. Maritime Greenwich
3. Tower of London
4. Palace of Westminster, etc.
5. Royal Botanic Gardens, Kew
6. Dorset and East Devon Coast
7. Stonehenge and Avebury
8. City of Bath
9. Blenheim Palace
10. Blaenavon Industrial Landscape
11. Ironbridge Gorge
12. Castles of Edward I
13. Liverpool – Maritime Mercantile City
14. Derwent Valley Mills
15. Saltaire
16. Studley Royal Gardens and Fountains Abbey
17. Durham Cathedral and Castle
18. Hadrian's Wall
19. Edinburgh Old and New Towns
20. New Lanark
21. Giant's Causeway
22. St Kilda
23. The Heart of Neolithic Orkney

Scale:
0   40   80   120 km
0   20   40   60   80 miles

1 The New Forest National Park was confirmed in June 2004; the South Downs National Park is awaiting confirmation.

European Parliament elections

Northern Ireland forms a single constituency in the European Parliament (see page 65) and is represented by three Members of the European Parliament (MEPs, Table 5.2). As with local and Assembly elections, the single transferable vote form of proportional representation is used. In the European parliamentary elections held on 10 June 2004, 554,744 people, 52 per cent of the electorate, voted for an MEP. There were seven candidates for the three seats. Sinn Féin won a seat for the first time, at the expense of the Social Democratic and Labour Party.

At the end of 1999 power to run most domestic affairs was devolved to the Assembly and its Executive Committee of Ministers under the *Northern Ireland Act 1998* (see appendix A, page 494 for details about devolved powers). When in session, the Northern Ireland Assembly meets in Parliament Buildings at Stormont, Belfast.

Elections to the Northern Ireland Assembly use the single transferable vote system of proportional representation (see glossary). The 18 constituencies are the same as those for the UK Parliament, but each returns six Members of the Legislative Assembly (MLAs), giving a total of 108 Members.

One of the first actions of a new Assembly is to elect a First Minister and a Deputy First Minister on a cross-community basis. It must also appoint ministers for the ten Northern Ireland departments (see appendix A); this is done using the d'Hondt system (see glossary) and is in proportion to each party's size in the Assembly. These 12 ministers form the Executive.

The Northern Ireland Assembly has ten statutory committees, each of which shadows a department in the devolved administration. Membership of committees is in broad proportion to party strength. Each statutory committee has a scrutiny, policy development and consultation role in relation to its department, and a role in the initiation of legislation. The Committee of the Centre, a standing committee, fulfils a similar role with respect to the Office of the First Minister and Deputy First Minister.

Suspension of the devolved administration

The Northern Ireland Assembly and the Executive has been suspended on a number of occasions since 1999. The latest suspension was in October 2002. The UK Government considered that it was not for the time being possible to hold together an inclusive power-sharing Executive, since the confidence within the community necessary to underpin it had broken down.

The Northern Ireland Assembly (Elections and Periods of Suspension) Act 2003 postponed the Assembly elections from May until November 2003. In the November elections, the Democratic Unionist Party (DUP) gained 25.6 per cent of the vote share (Table 5.2). Sinn Féin came second in terms of votes, with 23.5 per cent of the vote. The Ulster Unionist Party (UUP), gained 22.7 per cent of the vote. Three of the MLAs elected for the UUP subsequently defected to the DUP, increasing DUP seats to 33 and decreasing UUP seats to 24. The Social Democratic and Labour Party got 17.0 per cent of the vote share and seats, losing five.

Following the November 2003 elections, power was not immediately restored to the Assembly; the UK Government considered that there was still not enough confidence and trust necessary for the formation of a new Executive. A review into the workings of the Belfast (Good Friday) Agreement began in February 2004.

A programme of government is decided on each year within an agreed budget. This programme is subject to approval by the Assembly on a cross-community basis. While the Assembly is suspended, the Northern Ireland departments work directly to the Secretary of State for Northern Ireland (see page 31).

North/South Ministerial Council

The North/South Ministerial Council was established in December 1999 following the Belfast (Good Friday) Agreement. It seeks to develop consultation, co-operation and action within the island of Ireland. It directs the work of

Spending plans for Northern Ireland in areas of devolved responsibility, announced by the UK Government in July, are set to rise by an annual average rate of about 3 per cent in real terms over the next three years. In 2007/08 the departmental expenditure limit (DEL, see page 366) will be £1.3 billion higher than in 2004/05 with the budget rising from £7.0 billion to £8.3 billion.

the North/South Implementation Bodies that were set up under the Agreement to deal with special EU programmes, food safety, inland waterways, language, marine matters, and trade and business development. It also oversees cross-border co-operation in agriculture, education, environment, health, tourism, and transport.

The North/South Ministerial Council is unable to meet during suspension. In devolution it meets in plenary format once a year, with Northern Ireland representation led by the First Minister and Deputy First Minister. Sectoral meetings are held on a more frequent basis.

The British–Irish Council

The British–Irish Council was set up under the Belfast (Good Friday) Agreement in 1998 to 'promote the harmonious and mutually beneficial development of the totality of relationships among the peoples of these islands'. It has representatives from the UK and Irish Governments, the devolved institutions in Northern Ireland, Scotland and Wales, as well as from Jersey, Guernsey and the Isle of Man. Summit meetings normally take place twice a year. Northern Ireland interests are represented by the First Minister and the Deputy First Minister. The Council also meets regularly in sectoral format. During the suspension of devolution NIO Ministers represent Northern Ireland interests.

Security policy

The UK Government seeks to secure lasting peace based on the Belfast (Good Friday) Agreement 1998 in which the rights and identities of all

traditions in Northern Ireland are respected and safeguarded. The Police Service of Northern Ireland (PSNI, see below) takes primary responsibility for the prevention and investigation of all crime, including terrorism. The Armed Forces support the PSNI, but only when the security situation makes this necessary.

In *Responding to a Changing Security Situation: The Government's Approach*, updated in October 2003, the UK Government confirmed its aim to return to normal security arrangements in Northern Ireland as soon as possible, with the Armed Forces resuming a peacetime role. Troop levels in Northern Ireland have decreased year on year since 1992, with fewer than 13,000 remaining. Since the ceasefire in 1997, over half the military bases and installations have been closed, demolished or vacated and 102 cross-border roads have been reopened.

Reform of policing

A review of policing by an independent commission was set up under the chairmanship of Chris Patten. Its report was published in 1999 and its proposals are being implemented.

The *Police Service (Northern Ireland) Acts 2000* and *2003* contained measures to set up a new and more accountable police service and to redress the religious imbalance between Catholics and Protestants. The first group of recruits trained specifically for the new police service graduated in

The 2001 Census found that 167,490 people (10 per cent of the population) in Northern Ireland had some knowledge of the Irish language. Irish is one of the Celtic languages: others include Cornish and Welsh.

In April 2004 the Government set up a fund to support Irish language film and television production in Northern Ireland. The fund will provide £12 million over three years, to deliver at least 90 hours of Irish language broadcasting each year by 2007/08. It will also help at least 15 people to be trained in production and broadcasting skills each year.

2002. In June 2004, 14.9 per cent of regular officers in the police service were Catholic, compared with 7.6 per cent in March 2001. The Government aims to increase Catholic representation in the police service to 30 per cent by 2011.

In September 2003 the *Police (Northern Ireland) Act 1998* was amended to support fixed-term appointments of officers from the *Garda Siochana* (the Republic of Ireland's police force) to the PSNI.

A review of the Police and Criminal Evidence Order 1989, which provides the legislative framework for the operation of non-terrorist police powers in Northern Ireland, was announced in February 2004.

Human rights and equality

Human rights and equality were central to the Belfast (Good Friday) Agreement. The subsequent *Northern Ireland Act 1998* placed a statutory duty of equality on all public authorities and established the following bodies:

The Northern Ireland Human Rights Commission – to advise the Government on human rights issues. In 2003 the Commission published its second Strategic Plan covering the period 2003–06. The Plan identifies four goals: delivering a Bill of Rights for Northern Ireland; identifying and addressing human rights violations; promoting awareness and understanding of human rights; and increasing the effectiveness of the Commission.

The Equality Commission for Northern Ireland – to be responsible for fair employment, equal opportunities, racial equality, disability issues and enforcing the statutory duty of equality.

The Parades Commission – to help implement the *Public Processions (Northern Ireland) Act 1998*, which regulates public processions in Northern Ireland. The majority of parades are organised by the Protestant/Unionist community and take place from around Easter to the end of September.

The Victims Commission – to support victims of inter-community unrest in Northern Ireland.

Local government

Northern Ireland is divided into 26 local government districts (see map on page 36), each

---

Public administration review

A review of public administration, started by the Northern Ireland Assembly in 2002, published preliminary findings in May 2004. The main recommendations included:

- a significant reduction in the number of public bodies, including Health Service bodies;
- the number of local councils being reduced from 26 to 10, but having more powers; and
- aligning local council boundaries with those of other service providers in the locality.

Final proposals were expected to be published for consultation in autumn 2004.

The NIO has continued with the review while the Assembly has been suspended. It considers that the Executive should make the final decision, once devolution is resumed.

---

forming a single-tier (unitary) district council. They are mainly responsible for environmental health; refuse collection and disposal; leisure and recreation facilities; tourist amenities; building control and cemeteries. This is a narrower range of functions than local authorities elsewhere in the United Kingdom. However, the district councils nominate locally elected representatives to sit as members of the various statutory bodies dealing with other issues of local interest, for example, education, libraries and healthcare. They also have a consultative role in matters such as planning, roads and housing; and offer leadership and support in local economic development.

Local council elections are usually held every four years. All councils elect their members at the same time. The next elections will be held in 2005.

Finance

Unlike the other parts of the United Kingdom, local authorities in Northern Ireland are not financed through a council tax. Instead they raise revenue to help fund the services they provide by levying a domestic rate on homes and a business rate on commercial property. The district rate is fixed annually by each district council, and varies from district to district. Other public services are financed by the regional rate, which is set by the

Map 5.3 District councils, Northern Ireland

Moyle

Ballymoney

Derry

Limavady

Coleraine

Ballymena

Strabane

Magherafelt

Larne

Antrim

Nta

Cf

Omagh

Cookstown

ND

Belfast

Ards

Dungannon

Cr

Lisburn

Craigavon

Fermanagh

Armagh

Banbridge

Down

Newry
and Mourne

Republic of Ireland

Cf	Carrickfergus
Cr	Castlereagh
ND	North Down
Nta	Newtownabbey

Northern Ireland Assembly (or by the NIO when the Assembly is suspended). Additional finance comes from the general grant and reserves.

The rates system is being reviewed and in April 2004 the rating of vacant non-domestic property was introduced. A new domestic rating system is planned to come into effect from April 2007, which changes the basis of valuation from rental to assessed capital values. Regular revaluations will be carried out to ensure the new system reflects changes in the property market. The domestic sector was last revalued nearly 30 years ago.

In 2003/04 net revenue expenditure for local authorities in Northern Ireland was estimated at £338 million: £283 million financed from district rates, £50 million by general grant and £5 million from reserves.

Economy

The economy in Northern Ireland was traditionally based on shipbuilding, manufacturing and linen

production. In 2001 manufacturing accounted for 19 per cent of gross value added (GVA, see glossary and Table 22.12, page 357) in Northern Ireland while the service sector accounted for 68 per cent.

GVA at current prices was £20.5 billion in 2002, 2.3 per cent of the UK total. GVA increased by 5.6 per cent between 2001 and 2002, a bigger increase than in England, Scotland and Wales, and above overall UK growth of 5.1 per cent. However, GVA per head was £12,100, below the UK average of £15,300.

There were 750,000 people economically active in Northern Ireland in spring 2004, of whom 712,000 were in employment. Unemployment, at 5.0 per cent, was just above the UK rate of 4.8 per cent. Around 32 per cent of jobs are in the public sector, compared with 20 per cent of jobs in the United Kingdom overall.

Visitor numbers have increased since the Belfast (Good Friday) Agreement was signed in 1998, rising from 1.5 million to 1.9 million in 2003, and generating £291 million.

National day: 17 March, St Patrick's Day

National emblem: A number of emblems are used. The shamrock is associated with St Patrick and is used widely on St Patrick's Day. The Red Hand of Ulster is one of the few emblems used by both sides of the community in Northern Ireland, although it is more associated with the Unionist community.

National flag: The official flag is the Union flag, commonly called the Union Jack, the national flag of the United Kingdom. It is made up of the flag of St Patrick (a red diagonal cross on a white background) and the national flags of England and Scotland (see pages 12 and 29).

Agriculture and forestry account for almost 90 per cent of Northern Ireland's land area. There are 48 National Nature Reserves and 9 Areas of Outstanding Natural Beauty (AONBs).

In April 2002 Invest Northern Ireland (Invest NI) was established to promote economic development. It is funded by the Northern Ireland Executive through the Department of Enterprise, Trade and Investment. As a direct result of Invest NI activities, total commitments to invest £410 million were made in 2003/04. When added to commitments secured in the previous year, this brings Invest NI-supported investment in the Northern Ireland economy to some £1 billion. During 2003/04, over 2,750 new businesses were established with support from Invest NI.

The Economic Development Forum (EDF) provides a mechanism through which organisations can advise Northern Ireland ministers on issues relating to the development and future competitiveness of the economy. Membership includes representatives from central and local government, business organisations, trade unions, the education and agriculture sectors, and the voluntary and community sectors.

The EDF published *Working Together for a Stronger Economy* in 2002. It sets out seven strategic priorities to be addressed if the Northern Ireland economy is to be significantly strengthened by the year 2010. In March 2003 it published an *Action Plan* outlining 58 specific actions to improve the likelihood of achieving these priorities.

Northern Ireland receives around €1 billion from the EU Structural Funds allocation 2000–06 (see page 357). Discussions on further EU funding beyond 2006 are under way. However, there is acknowledgement that post-2006 support will focus on the accession members of the EU that joined in 2004 (see page 71).

Funding from the EU Programme for Peace and Reconciliation in Northern Ireland and the Border Region of the Republic of Ireland (PEACE II) provides a further €531 million (£375 million). This is supporting continued efforts to create a peaceful and stable society and to promote reconciliation. PEACE II has assisted more than 3,200 projects across all parts of Northern Ireland and the Border Region, covering one of the following priorities:

- economic renewal;

- social integration, inclusion and reconciliation;

- locally-based regeneration and development;

- cross-border co-operation; and

- technical assistance.

Although PEACE II was originally scheduled to run until 2004, the EU is developing proposals to extend it until 2006. The 2004 Spending Review provided £62 million for PEACE II in 2004/05 and £80 million in 2005/06.

International trade in goods

In 2003 exports of goods from Northern Ireland totalled £4.0 billion and imports of goods, £3.7 billion (Figure 5.4). The largest international trading partner was the EU, accounting for 58 per cent of both exports and imports. Machinery and transport accounted for 43 per cent of exports and 30 per cent of imports, while manufactured goods totalled 18 per cent of exports and 19 per cent of imports. Food and live animals accounted for 15 per cent of imports and 10 per cent of exports.

Figure 5.4 Distribution of international trade in goods, 2003, Northern Ireland

£ billion

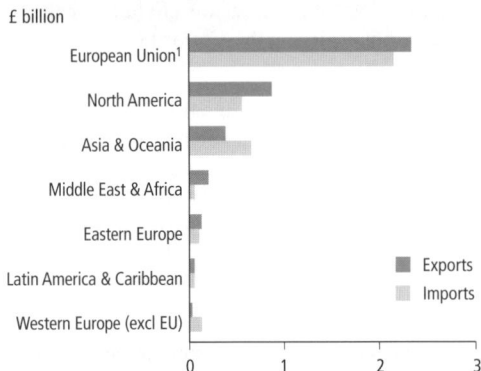

1 Excludes the ten countries that joined the EU in 2004.
Source: *UK Regional Trade in Goods Statistics*, HM Customs and Excise

Further reading

Northern Ireland Office Departmental Report 2004: The Government's Expenditure Plans 2004–05 to 2005–06. Cm 6229. The Stationery Office, 2004.

Websites

Northern Ireland Assembly
www.niassembly.gov.uk

Northern Ireland Executive
www.northernireland.gov.uk

Northern Ireland Office
www.nio.gov.uk

Department of Enterprise, Trade and Investment
www.detini.gov.uk

The Electoral Office for Northern Ireland
www.electoralofficeni.gov.uk

Northern Ireland Tourist Board
www.discovernorthernireland.com

Invest Northern Ireland
www.investni.com

WWW.

6 Government

The United Kingdom is a parliamentary democracy, based on universal suffrage. It is also a constitutional monarchy in which ministers of the Crown govern in the name of the Sovereign, who is Head of State and Head of the Government. There is no single document that forms the UK constitution; instead, the relationship between the State and the people relies on statute law, common law and conventions.[1]

The UK Parliament (the legislature) makes primary legislation, although it has devolved a range of issues to the Scottish Parliament, the National Assembly for Wales and, when it is sitting, the Northern Ireland Assembly (see chapters 3 to 5). Under the constitution, Parliament is supreme and has authority over government and law-making in the United Kingdom as a whole (see page 43). The executive comprises the Government (members of the Cabinet and other ministers responsible for policies); government departments and agencies; local authorities; public corporations; independent regulatory bodies; and certain other organisations subject to ministerial control. The Government derives its authority and membership from Parliament and can only stay in office if it is able to command a majority in the House of Commons. The judiciary (see chapter 14) determines common law and interprets legislation.

As Monarch, The Queen is head of the executive and plays an integral part in the legislature (see page 51). She heads the judiciary and is both the commander-in-chief of all the Armed Forces of

the Crown and 'supreme governor' of the established Church of England. In practice, the Monarch acts on the advice of her ministers.

In June 2003 the Government announced a series of constitutional changes designed to put the relationship between the executive, legislature and judiciary on a modern footing (see page 46).

Parliamentary electoral system

The United Kingdom is divided into 659 constituencies, each of which returns one Member of Parliament (MP) to the House of Commons. Constituencies vary in size and area; the average electorate is around 67,300. The largest electorate in December 2003 was the Isle of Wight (with 106,600 registered voters) and the smallest the sparsely populated Eilean Siar (21,300).

There are four Parliamentary Boundary Commissions – one each for England, Wales, Scotland and Northern Ireland – that review constituency size to ensure that constituencies have broadly similar numbers of electors. When the reviews for 2003 to 2007 have been completed, the four Commissions will become part of the Electoral Commission.

The Electoral Commission is an independent body set up under the *Political Parties, Elections and Referendums Act 2000* to oversee controls on donations to and campaign spending by political parties and others (see page 42). It also aims to ensure public confidence and participation in the democratic process in the United Kingdom, for example by recommending modernisation of the electoral process and promoting public awareness of electoral matters.

---

1 Conventions are rules and practices that are not legally enforceable but are regarded as indispensable to the working of government.

Table 6.1 State of the parties in the UK Parliament[1]

	MPs at 15 July 2004	MPs elected in 2001 General Election	% share of UK vote 2001 General Election
Labour	407	412	40.7
Conservative	163	166	31.7
Liberal Democrats	55	52	18.3
Scottish National	5	5	1.8
Plaid Cymru – The Party of Wales	4	4	0.7
Democratic Unionist	6	5	0.7
Ulster Unionist	5	6	0.8
Sinn Féin[2]	4	4	0.7
Social Democratic and Labour	3	3	0.6
KHHC[3]	1	1	0.1
Independent Conservative	1	.	.
Independent Labour	1	.	.
Other parties	0	0	3.8
Speaker and three deputies[4]	4	1	0.1

1 There have been a number of changes since the General Election. One Labour MP has changed parties and now sits as a Liberal Democrat. One Labour MP now sits as an Independent Labour MP and one Conservative MP sits as an Independent Conservative. One Ulster Unionist MP has left the party and now sits as a Democratic Unionist. The Liberal Democrats have gained two Labour-held seats in by-elections: Brent East in September 2003 and Leicester South in July 2004.
2 The Sinn Féin Members have not taken their seats.
3 The constituency of Wyre Forest was won by the independent Kidderminster Hospital and Health Concern candidate.
4 The Speaker and Deputy Speakers do not normally vote. At the 2001 General Election the Speaker stood for election in this capacity, while the Deputy Speakers were elected for their particular parties.
Source: House of Commons

Voters

UK citizens, and citizens of other Commonwealth countries and the Republic of Ireland resident in the United Kingdom, may vote in elections to the UK Parliament provided that they are aged 18 or over; included in the register of electors for the constituency; and not subject to any legal incapacity to vote.

Members of the Armed Forces, Crown servants and staff of the British Council employed overseas (together with their wives or husbands if accompanying them) may be registered as 'service voters' or at an address in the constituency where they would live if not serving abroad. British citizens living overseas are entitled to register at their last UK constituency and to vote for up to 15 years after moving abroad.

People not entitled to vote include members of the House of Lords, foreign nationals (other than qualifying Commonwealth citizens or citizens of the Republic of Ireland) resident in the United Kingdom, some patients detained under mental health legislation, convicted prisoners detained in

a penal institution, and people convicted within the previous five years of corrupt or illegal election practices.

Members of the House of Lords and EU citizens resident in the United Kingdom are eligible to vote in elections for local authorities, the National Assembly for Wales, the Scottish Parliament, the Northern Ireland Assembly, and the European Parliament.

Voting procedures

Voting is not compulsory in the United Kingdom and the simple majority system is used for Westminster elections. The Additional Member System and the d'Hondt system of proportional representation (see glossary) is used in the elections to the National Assembly for Wales, the Scottish Parliament and the Northern Ireland Assembly (see chapters 3 to 5) and to the European Parliament (see page 65). As in other EU countries, participation in voting at General Elections has declined, and the turnout in the 2001 General Election was 59 per cent, the lowest since the First World War.

At Westminster elections each elector may cast one vote and usually does so in person at a polling station. As part of its plans to modernise the electoral system, the Government has taken a number of measures designed to make voting more accessible for the electorate and allow people more flexibility in where and when they vote. These include the introduction in 2000 of postal voting on demand and the possibility of voting in a number of other ways in General Elections sometime after 2006.

In January 2004 the Government announced plans to improve electoral registers. The first phase will standardise local electronic electoral registers. The second phase will allow authorised users to access local registration data centrally and will support an e-enabled election in the future.

New voting methods have been tested at recent elections. In the May 2003 local elections, 59 pilot schemes took place in 61 local authorities in England, involving 6.4 million electors. There were 32 all-postal pilot schemes, while 17 multi-channel pilots included interactive digital television, touch-tone telephone, mobile phone text messaging and the Internet.

Local elections and elections to the European Parliament were held on the same day in June 2004. All-postal voting was piloted in four regions of England: North East, North West, Yorkshire and the Humber, and East Midlands. Turnout in the four pilot regions was 42.4 per cent, more than double that of the 1999 elections. Turnout was also higher in the local elections in the pilot regions than in the previous local elections.

In August 2004 the Electoral Commission published a report drawing on its evaluation of the all-postal voting pilot schemes in the 2004 elections. It recommended that postal voting should remain part of the UK electoral system, but noted that effectively swapping postal voting on demand with all-postal voting did not offer voters a choice of voting methods and recommended that all-postal pilot voting schemes should not continue.[2] Instead it recommended the development of a new foundation model of voting to enhance the degree of choice available to voters and to produce a more robust legal framework. It

plans to produce a report by 31 March 2005 on a new model for statutory elections and referendums, which will include provision for the introduction of additional voting channels, including the electronic channels that have been tested in the pilot schemes. The Government has welcomed the report and is considering the recommendations. It will look at how to strengthen and improve safeguards and at measures to prevent fraud.

Candidates

British citizens, and resident citizens of other Commonwealth countries and the Republic of Ireland, may be elected as MPs provided that they are aged 21 or over and are not disqualified. Disqualified people include members of the House of Lords; and holders of certain offices listed in the *House of Commons Disqualification Act 1975*.

Each candidate's nomination must be proposed and seconded by two electors registered in the constituency and signed by eight others. Candidates do not have to be backed by a political party. A candidate must deposit £500, which is returned if he or she receives 5 per cent or more of the votes cast.

Review of voting and candidacy age

In April 2004 the Electoral Commission published a review of voting and candidacy age, in response to growing concern about declining electoral participation among young people. Its main recommendations, which are being considered by the Government, were:

- the minimum voting age should remain at 18, in line with that in most other countries; and

- the age of candidacy should be reduced to 18, in line with the age of voting.

The maximum sum a candidate may spend on a General Election campaign is currently £5,483 plus 4.6 pence for each elector in a borough or district constituency, or 6.2 pence for each elector in a county constituency. A higher limit of £100,000 has been set for by-elections as they are often seen as tests of national opinion in the period between General Elections. All election expenses, apart from the candidate's personal expenses, are subject to these statutory rules. A candidate is also entitled

2 The Electoral Commission has recommended that the regional referendum in the North East in November 2004 should proceed as an all-postal ballot, as the process is already under way.

to send one election communication to each voter free of postal charges. The cost of free postage is met by central government.

The party political system

The party system, which has existed in one form or another since the 18th century, depends upon there being organised political groups, each of which presents its policies to the electorate for approval. In practice, most candidates in elections, and almost all winning candidates, belong to one of the main parties.

The origins of the Conservative Party go back to the 18th century, while the Labour Party emerged in the last decade of the 19th century. The Liberal Democrats were formed in 1988 when the Liberal Party, which also traced its origins to the 18th century, merged with the Social Democratic Party, formed in 1981. Other parties include two nationalist parties, Plaid Cymru – The Party of Wales (founded in 1925) and the Scottish National Party (founded in 1934). Northern Ireland has a number of parties. They include the Ulster Unionists, formed in the early part of the 20th century; the Democratic Unionists, founded in 1971 by a group that broke away from the Ulster Unionists; the Social Democratic and Labour Party, founded in 1970; and Sinn Féin, which is the political wing of the Irish Republican Army.

The party that wins most seats (although not necessarily the most votes) at a General Election, or that has the support of a majority of MPs in the Commons, usually becomes the Government. By tradition, the Sovereign invites the leader of that party to form a government. The largest minority party becomes the official Opposition, with its own leader and 'shadow cabinet'.

Since 1945 the traditional two-party system of government in the UK Parliament has been maintained, with power being held by either the Conservative Party or the Labour Party. Each has won eight General Elections in this period, the Labour Party being successful in the most recent General Election in 2001 (see Table 6.1 on page 40).

Financial controls over parties

The *Political Parties, Elections and Referendums Act 2000* contained provisions to make party funding more open and transparent, by restricting the sources of political donations, controlling spending on elections and regulating the finances of organisations campaigning at referendums.

Campaign expenditure

Campaign expenditure is regulated at elections to the UK and European Parliaments and to the Scottish Parliament, National Assembly for Wales and, when it is sitting, the Northern Ireland Assembly. During a General Election campaign a party is subject to limits which are calculated according to the number of seats it is contesting in England, Wales, Scotland and Northern Ireland; this excludes spending by candidates, for which there are separate limits (see page 41). Lower limits apply for elections to the other bodies. Third parties campaigning at elections (such as trade unions) are also subject to limits on expenditure incurred on election materials. There are separate rules governing expenditure on referendum campaigns.

Donations

Political parties in Great Britain are required to abide by regulations on accepting and reporting donations: these requirements have been disapplied to parties registered in Northern Ireland until February 2005. Parties may only accept donations of over £200 from 'permissible donors' – individuals on the UK electoral register and organisations (such as companies, trade unions and political parties) that are registered and do business in the United Kingdom. All donations of over £5,000 to a political party's central organisation must be reported to the Electoral Commission (see page 39) on a quarterly basis, and on a weekly basis during a General Election campaign. Parties must also report donations of over £1,000 made to party accounting units. Donations of more than £1,000 to holders of elective office and to members of registered parties must be reported by the individual, and 'members associations' (groups whose membership consists mainly or wholly of members of a particular registered party) must also report donations of over £5,000. Similar controls on donations apply to other organisations and individuals campaigning at elections and referendums.

Parliament

The UK Parliament is one of the oldest representative assemblies in the world, with its origins in the 13th century. During the 14th century two distinct Houses of Parliament began to emerge, with the 'Commons' sitting apart from the 'Upper House' from 1341. It was also accepted that there should be no taxation without parliamentary consent, which remains a fundamental principle.

Powers

There are three parts of Parliament – the elected House of Commons, the appointed House of Lords and the Sovereign. The agreement of all three is normally needed to pass laws, but that of the Sovereign is given as a matter of course.

Parliament at Westminster can legislate for the United Kingdom as a whole and has powers to legislate for any parts of it separately. However, by convention it will not normally legislate on devolved matters in Scotland or Northern Ireland without the agreement of the Scottish Parliament or, when it is sitting, the Northern Ireland Assembly. Under the Acts of Parliament that set up these administrations, the Westminster Parliament still has UK-wide responsibility in a number of areas (see appendix A, page 481).

As there are no legal restraints imposed by a written constitution, Parliament may legislate as it pleases, as long as the United Kingdom meets its obligations as a member of the European Union (see page 67). It can make or change law, and overturn established conventions or turn them into law. It can even legislate to prolong its own life beyond the normal period of five years without consulting the electorate.

In practice, Parliament does not assert itself in this way. Its members work within the common law and normally act according to precedent. The House of Commons is directly responsible to the electorate, and, during the 20th century, the House of Lords increasingly recognised the supremacy of the elected chamber.

Functions

The main functions of Parliament are:

- to pass laws;
- to provide (by voting for taxation) the means of carrying on the work of government;
- to scrutinise government policy and administration, including proposals for expenditure; and
- to debate the major issues of the day.

In performing these functions, Parliament helps to bring the relevant facts and issues to the attention of the electorate. By custom, Parliament is also informed before important international treaties and agreements are ratified. The making of treaties is, however, a royal prerogative carried out on the advice of the Government and does not need parliamentary approval.

Meetings

A Parliament has a maximum life of five years, but not all Parliaments serve their full term. The maximum life has been prolonged by legislation in rare circumstances, such as the two World Wars of the last century. The Sovereign dissolves Parliament and calls for a General Election on the advice of the Prime Minister.

The life of a Westminster Parliament is divided into sessions. Each usually lasts a year – normally beginning in November and ending in October or November – although a session may be longer if there has been a General Election. The two Houses do not normally sit at weekends, at Christmas, Easter and the late Spring Bank Holiday. There is also a recess in the summer from late July to October, but since 2003 both Houses return for about two weeks in September before a break that coincides with the political party conferences.

At the start of each session the Sovereign's speech to Parliament outlines the Government's policies and proposed legislative programme. Each session is ended by the Sovereign dismissing it – called 'prorogation'. Parliament then 'stands prorogued' for a few days until the new session begins. Prorogation brings to an end nearly all parliamentary business.

In the 2002/03 session the House of Commons sat on 162 days and the House of Lords on 174. New working hours were adopted in the House of Commons in January 2003 for an experimental period until the end of the current Parliament. They are designed to make it easier for MPs with families and those with provincial constituencies. The main changes involve earlier sitting days on Tuesdays, Wednesdays and Thursdays and fewer Friday sessions. The Select Committee on the Modernisation of the House of Commons is considering arrangements for the next Parliament.

The party system in Parliament

Leaders of the Government and Opposition, with members of the Cabinet and shadow Cabinet respectively, sit opposite one another on the front benches in the debating chamber of the House of Commons. Their supporters, 'the backbenchers', sit behind them. Benches to the right of the Speaker are used by the Government and its supporters; those to the left are occupied by the Opposition and members of the other parties. There are similar seating arrangements for the parties in the House of Lords, but many peers do not wish to be associated with a political party, and choose to sit on the 'crossbenches'.

The effectiveness of the party system in Parliament relies to a large extent on the relationship between the Government and the Opposition parties. Depending on the relative strengths of the parties in the House of Commons, the Opposition may try to overthrow the Government by defeating it on a 'matter of confidence' vote. In general, however, the Opposition contributes to the formulation of policy and legislation by constructive criticism; opposes government proposals with which it disagrees; tables amendments to Government Bills; and puts forward its own policies in order to improve its chances of winning the next General Election.

The Government Chief Whips in the Commons and the Lords, in consultation with their Opposition counterparts, arrange the scheduling of government business under the direction of the Prime Minister and the Leaders of the two Houses. The Chief Whips and their assistants, who are usually chosen by the party leaders, manage their parliamentary parties. Their duties include keeping members informed of forthcoming parliamentary business, maintaining the party's voting strength by ensuring members attend important debates, and passing on to the party leadership the opinions of backbench members.

The term 'whip' also applies to the weekly circular sent out by each Chief Whip to all their MPs or peers notifying them of parliamentary business. The degree of importance is indicated by the number of times that the debate or division is underlined. Items underlined once are routine and attendance is optional, while those underlined twice are more important and attendance is required unless – in the Commons – a 'pair' has been arranged with an Opposition MP who also intends to be absent. A 'three-line whip', when an item is underlined three times, indicates that attendance is required and pairing is not normally allowed. This is imposed on important occasions, such as second readings of major Bills and motions of no confidence.

House of Commons

The House of Commons consists of 659 elected MPs (see Table 6.1), of whom 529 represent constituencies in England, 40 in Wales, 72 in Scotland and 18 in Northern Ireland. In July 2004 there were 119 women MPs and 13 MPs who had declared that they were of minority ethnic origin.

After a Parliament has been dissolved, and a General Election has been held, the Sovereign summons a new Parliament. When an MP dies, resigns[3] or is made a member of the House of Lords, a by-election takes place.

MPs are paid an annual salary of £57,485 (from April 2004) and provided with between £66,458 and £77,534 for staff salaries and £19,325 for incidental expenses involved in running an office (excluding certain IT equipment which is provided centrally). For ministers' salaries see page 55. All MPs are entitled to travel allowances and to free stationery, inland telephone calls and postage from Parliament. There are various other allowances, such as a supplementary allowance payable to MPs for Inner London and certain other seats to reflect the higher cost of living in the capital.

Officers of the House of Commons

The chief officer of the House of Commons is the Speaker (see page 46), an MP elected by other MPs to preside over the House. Other officers include the Chairman of Ways and Means and two deputy chairmen, who are also MPs and may act as Deputy Speakers. They are elected by the House as nominees of the Government, but may come from the Opposition as well as the Government party. The House of Commons Commission, a statutory body chaired by the Speaker, is responsible for the administration of the House.

Permanent officers (who are not MPs) include the Clerk of the House of Commons – the principal

---

3 By tradition, an MP who wishes to resign from the House can do so only by applying for office as Crown Steward or Bailiff of the Chiltern Hundreds, or Steward of the Manor of Northstead. These positions disqualify the holder from membership of the House of Commons.

adviser to the Speaker on the House's privileges and procedures. The Clerk's other responsibilities relate to the conduct of the business of the House and its committees. The Clerk is also accounting officer for the House. The Serjeant at Arms, who waits upon the Speaker, carries out certain orders of the House. He is also the official housekeeper of the Commons' part of the Palace of Westminster and is responsible for security.

House of Lords

The House of Lords consists of:

- hereditary peers;
- life peers created to help carry out the judicial duties of the House (up to 12 Lords of Appeal in Ordinary or 'Law Lords' and a number of other Lords of Appeal);[4]
- all other life peers; and
- the Archbishops of Canterbury and York, the Bishops of London, Durham and Winchester, and the 21 next most senior bishops of the Church of England.

The number of peers eligible to sit is shown in Table 6.2, which also shows the representation of the main political parties. Crossbenchers, many of whom have specialist knowledge and expertise, do not vote with a political party. There were 125 women peers in July 2004.

Members of the House of Lords do not receive a salary for their parliamentary work, but they can claim for expenses incurred in attending the House and for certain travelling expenses.

The Government wants the House of Lords to be more representative of UK society. As a first step, under the *House of Lords Act 1999*, the number of hereditary peers entitled to sit in Parliament was reduced from over 750 to 92. The Government also set up a non-statutory independent House of Lords Appointments Commission to take over the Prime Minister's role in nominating non-political members of the House. In 2001 the Commission made its first appointments of 15 non-political life peers selected from a total of 3,166 public nominees. In September 2003 a consultation paper was issued containing the Government's proposals

Table 6.2 Composition of the House of Lords, July 2004

	Hereditary	Life peers	Bishops	Total
Conservative	47	159		206
Labour	4	187		191
Liberal Democrat	5	61		66
Crossbench[1]	33	146		179
Archbishops and bishops			26	26
Other[2]	2	33		35
Total members[3]	**91**	**586**	**26**	**703**

1 Includes Law Lords.
2 Comprises 1 Green, 1 Independent Labour, 1 Independent Socialist, 8 non-affiliated members and 24 newly created life peers who have not yet been introduced.
3 Excludes 11 peers on leave of absence.
Source: House of Lords

on the next stage of House of Lords reform, including proposals for removing the remaining hereditary peers. However, the Government has deferred a proposed Bill for the time being as it considers that it would be unable to secure the approval of the House of Lords for the Bill.

In June 2003 the Government announced a number of major constitutional changes, including the creation of the Department for Constitutional Affairs, which replaced the Lord Chancellor's Department (see page 46).

Officers of the House of Lords

The Speaker in the Lords, traditionally the Lord Chancellor, has limited powers compared with those of the Speaker of the House of Commons (see page 46). The Lords themselves control the proceedings with advice from the Leader of the House, who leads the governing party in the House and is a member of the Cabinet. Under the Government's proposed constitutional changes, the role of Speaker would no longer be fulfilled by the Lord Chancellor. In the light of this, the House of Lords set up a select committee to look at the Speakership of the House, and in November 2003 it recommended that the Speaker should be known as Lord Speaker.

As Clerk of the House of Lords, the Clerk of the Parliaments is responsible for the records of proceedings of the House of Lords and for the text of Acts of the UK Parliament. The Clerk is the accounting officer for the House, and is in charge of its administrative staff, known as the Parliament

---

4 The House of Lords is the final court of appeal for civil cases in the United Kingdom and for criminal cases in England, Wales and Northern Ireland. In June 2003 the Government announced its intention to create a new Supreme Court.

The Constitutional Reform Bill

The Constitutional Reform Bill, as introduced, provided for the abolition of the office of Lord Chancellor, who participates in all three branches of government: as head of the judiciary; as a Cabinet minister, with ministerial responsibility for much of the administration of justice; and as Speaker of the House of Lords. One of the aims of the Bill is to clarify the relationship between the judiciary and Parliament and the Government.

Under the Bill, statutory responsibilities relating to the judiciary would mostly be transferred to the Secretary of State for Constitutional Affairs or to the Lord Chief Justice, or shared between them. A new Supreme Court of the United Kingdom would replace the existing system of Law Lords operating as a Committee of the House of Lords.

The Bill received its second reading in the House of Lords in March 2004, where it was then considered by a special select committee. The Bill will be carried forward to the next parliamentary session if it does not complete all its stages in the current session.

Office. The Gentleman Usher of the Black Rod, known as 'Black Rod', is responsible for security, accommodation and services in the House of Lords' part of the Palace of Westminster.

Parliamentary privilege

To ensure that Parliament can carry out its duties without hindrance, certain rights and immunities apply collectively to each House and its staff, and individually to each member. These include:

- freedom of speech;

- first call on the attendance of Members, which means that members are free from arrest in civil actions and excused from serving on juries, or being forced to attend court as witnesses; and

- the right of access to the Crown, which is a collective privilege of the House.

Further privileges include the rights of the House:

- to control its own proceedings (so that it is able, for instance, to keep out 'strangers'[5] if it wishes);

- to decide upon legal disqualifications for membership and to declare a seat vacant on such grounds; and

- to punish for contempt.

Parliament has the right to punish anybody, inside or outside the House, who commits a breach of privilege – that is, offends against the rights of the House.

Parliamentary procedure

Parliamentary procedure is largely based on precedent and is set down by each House in a code of practice known as its 'Standing Orders'. The debating system is similar in both Houses. Every subject starts off as a proposal or 'motion' by a member. After debate, in which each member (except the person putting forward the motion) may speak only once, the motion may be withdrawn: if it is not, the Speaker or Chairman 'puts the question' whether to agree to the motion or not. The question may be decided without voting, or by a simple majority vote. The main difference between the two Houses is that in the House of Lords the Lord Chancellor, or the deputising Chairman, does not control procedure; instead such matters are decided by the general feeling of the House, which is sometimes interpreted by its Leader or a Government Whip.

In the Commons the Speaker has full authority to enforce the rules of the House and must uphold procedure and protect the rights of minorities in the House. The Speaker may or may not allow a motion to end discussion so that a matter may be put to the vote, and has powers to stop irrelevant and repetitious contributions in debate. In cases of serious disorder the Speaker can adjourn or suspend the sitting. The Speaker may order MPs who have broken the rules of behaviour of the House to leave the Chamber, or may suspend them for a number of days.

The Speaker supervises voting in the Commons and announces the final result. If there is a tie, the Speaker gives a casting vote (usually to keep the situation as it is), without expressing an opinion. Voting procedure in the House of Lords is broadly similar, except the Lord Chancellor can vote, but does not have a casting vote.

---

5 All those who are not members or officials of either House.

Public access to parliamentary proceedings

Proceedings of both Houses are normally public and are broadcast on television and radio, either live or, more usually, in recorded or edited form. Broadcasting on the Internet began on a pilot basis in 2002 and was made permanent in October 2003. Live coverage of both Houses and sittings in Westminster Hall is on *www.parliamentlive.tv*. The proceedings of both Houses, including speeches and parliamentary questions, are transcribed in the Official Report, *Hansard*, which is published the following morning, both in hard copy form and on *www.parliament.uk/hansard/hansard.cfm*.

Select committees

Select committees are appointed for a particular task, generally one of inquiry, investigation and scrutiny. They report to the House as a whole; in many cases they invite a response from the Government, which is also reported to the House. A select committee may be appointed for a Parliament, or for a session, or for as long as it takes to complete its task. Each committee is constituted on a basis that is in approximate proportion to party strength in the House, but the chairman is not necessarily drawn from the governing party. Members are normally backbenchers.

Select committees may question ministers, civil servants, interested bodies and individuals. Through hearings and published reports, they bring before Parliament and the public an extensive amount of fact and informed opinion, and build up considerable expertise in their subjects of inquiry.

The House of Commons has set up 15 committees to examine aspects of public policy, expenditure and administration across the main government departments and their associated public bodies. There are also regular Commons select committees, including the Public Accounts Committee and 'domestic' select committees covering the internal workings of Parliament. The chairmen of the select committees form the Liaison Committee.

Both Houses have a select committee to keep them informed of European Union (EU) developments, and to enable them to scrutinise and debate EU policies and proposals, while three Commons standing committees debate specific European legislative proposals.

In the House of Lords there are four major select committees on the European Communities; Science and Technology; Economic Affairs; and the Constitution. There are also select committees on aspects of public and private legislation, and on the internal workings of the House, while ad hoc committees are appointed to examine issues outside the remit of the main committees. The Lords' judicial work is conducted in the Appellate Committee.

Examination of government policy

The parliamentary system contains a number of checks to ensure that a government remains accountable. Through raising Parliamentary Questions, MPs seek information about the Government's intentions and can raise issues and grievances, including complaints brought to their notice by constituents. In the 2002–03 session nearly 59,600 questions were tabled: 4,100 oral questions and over 55,400 written questions. Oral statements are made by government ministers, when announcing a statement of government policy, such as the publication of a White Paper (see page 48), or in response to a significant event. The parliamentary convention is that Parliament should be first to hear a major announcement.

In addition to the scrutiny by select committees, both Houses offer opportunities for backbenchers to examine policy. In the House of Commons, these include:

- Question Time: for about an hour on Monday, Tuesday, Wednesday and Thursday when the House is sitting, ministers answer MPs' oral questions. Ministers are questioned on a rota agreed by the Government and Opposition parties. Prime Minister's Question Time takes place for 30 minutes every Wednesday.

- Adjournment debates: MPs use motions for the adjournment of the House to raise constituency cases or matters of public concern. There is a half-hour adjournment period at the end of the business of the day, and opportunities for private Members adjournment debates in Westminster Hall on Tuesdays and Wednesdays.

- Emergency debates: an MP wishing to discuss a 'specific and important matter that should have urgent consideration' may, at the end of Question Time, ask for an adjournment of the House. On the few occasions when this is successful, the matter is debated for three hours in what is known as an emergency debate, usually on the following day.

- Early day motions (EDMs): backbench MPs may express their views on particular issues in this way. A number of EDMs are tabled each sitting day; they are very rarely debated but can be useful in measuring the amount of support for the topic by the number of MPs who add their signatures to the EDM.

- Opposition days: on 20 days in each session opposition parties choose the business to be discussed. Of these days, 17 are allocated to the Leader of the Opposition and three to the second largest opposition party.

- Estimates days: the details of proposed government expenditure are debated on three days in each session.

- Procedural opportunities: criticism of the Government may also occur during the debate on the Queen's Speech at the beginning of each session, on motions of censure for which the Government provides time, and in debates on the Government's legislative and other proposals.

- Motions of no confidence: as a final act of parliamentary control, the House of Commons may force the Government to resign by passing a resolution of 'no confidence'. The Government must also resign if the House rejects a proposal which the Government considers so vital to its policy that it has declared it a 'matter of confidence' or if the House refuses to vote the money required for the public service. Motions of no confidence are relatively infrequent and the last successful one was in 1979.

Control of finances

The UK Parliament (and in particular the House of Commons) is responsible for overseeing revenue generation and public expenditure. No payment out of the central government's public funds can be made, and no taxation or loans authorised, except by Act of Parliament. However, limited interim payments can be made from the Contingencies Fund.

The Finance Act is the most important piece of annual legislation. It authorises the raising of revenue and is based on the Chancellor of the Exchequer's Budget statement (see page 371). Scrutiny of public expenditure is carried out by House of Commons select committees.

The law-making process in the UK Parliament

Statute law consists of Acts of Parliament (primary legislation) and delegated or secondary legislation (see page 51) made by ministers under powers given to them by an Act. While the interpretation of the law is refined constantly in the courts (see chapter 14), changes to statute law can only be made by Parliament. Since devolution, the Scottish Parliament and, when it is sitting, the Northern Ireland Assembly can also make primary or secondary legislation on devolved matters – see pages 33 and 494. Draft laws take the form of parliamentary Bills.

Public Bills

Bills that change the general law are called Public Bills and make up the major part of the parliamentary legislative process. They can be introduced into either House, by a government minister or any MP or peer. In the 2002–03 parliamentary session 138 Public Bills were introduced into Parliament and 46 became Acts of Parliament. Most Public Bills that become Acts of Parliament are introduced by a government minister and are known as 'Government Bills'. A Government Bill is generally accompanied by Explanatory Notes, which are designed to provide background information on the Bill and what it is seeking to achieve.

The main Bills forming the Government's legislative programme are announced in the Queen's Speech at the State Opening of Parliament. The Bills are introduced into one or other of the Houses over the following weeks.

Before a Government Bill is drafted, there may be consultation with professional bodies, voluntary organisations and others with an interest, including pressure groups (see page 51) looking to promote specific causes. The Government may publish a consultation paper, sometimes called a 'Green Paper', setting out proposals that are still taking shape and inviting comments from the public. 'White Papers', which are government statements of policy, often contain specific proposals for changes in the law. These may be debated in Parliament before a Bill is introduced.

As part of the process of modernising parliamentary procedures, more Bills are published in draft for pre-legislative scrutiny. The aim is to allow an input from backbenchers and other interested parties at an early stage, helping to save time and reducing the number of amendments made during the legislative process.

Other Bills

Bills introduced by other MPs or peers are known as 'Private Members' Bills. Early in each session backbench MPs ballot for the chance to introduce a Bill on one of the Fridays when such Bills have precedence over government business, and the first 20 MPs whose names are drawn win this privilege. There are also other opportunities for MPs to present a Bill, while peers may introduce Private Members' Bills in the House of Lords at any time. However, these Bills rarely become law – 13 were enacted in the 2002–03 session.

Private Bills are promoted by people or organisations outside Parliament (often local authorities) to give them special legal powers. They go through a similar process to Public Bills, but most of the work is done in committee, where procedures follow a semi-judicial pattern. Five Private Bills were enacted in the 2002–03 session.

Passage of Government Bills

Public Bills must normally be passed by both Houses. Government Bills likely to raise political controversy usually start in the House of Commons, while those of a technical nature but that are less likely to be politically controversial often start in the House of Lords. Government Bills involving new taxation or public expenditure are always introduced in the Commons. The process for a Commons Bill is shown in Figure 6.3.

Standing committees

House of Commons standing committees debate and consider Public Bills at the committee stage. The committee examines a Bill clause by clause and may amend it before reporting back to the House. Ordinary standing committees do not have names but are designated by letters, such as Standing Committee A. Each committee generally has around 18 members, with a party balance reflecting as far as possible that in the House as a whole. Committees for larger or more contentious Bills may have more members, up to a maximum of 50. In some cases a Committee of the Whole House may be established. This usually occurs for Bills of major constitutional importance, Bills that

need to be passed very quickly, and Bills that are considered uncontroversial.

In the House of Lords, Bills normally go through their committee stage in a Committee of the Whole House. However, other committees may be used, such as a Grand Committee (a Committee of the Whole House in which no votes are taken and that takes place away from the chamber of the House), which is regularly used for less contentious Bills.

Final stages

When a Bill has passed through all its parliamentary stages, it is sent to The Queen for Royal Assent, after which it becomes an Act of Parliament. The Royal Assent has not been refused since 1707.

Public Bills that have not been enacted by the end of the parliamentary session are usually lost. However, changes implemented in the 2002–03 parliamentary session allow for more Public Bills to be carried over to the next parliamentary session, particularly those that have undergone pre-legislative scrutiny in either House.

Limitations on the power of the Lords

The main legislative function of the House of Lords is to act as a revising chamber, complementing but not rivalling the elected House of Commons. As a result, there are some limitations on its powers. Under the *Parliament Acts 1911* and *1949*, the powers of the Lords in relation to 'money Bills' are very restricted. Bills authorising taxation or national expenditure are passed without amendment as a formality. A Bill dealing only with taxation or expenditure must become law within one month of being sent to the Lords, even if the Lords has not passed it.

The *Parliament Acts* also make it possible for a Bill to be passed by the Commons without the consent of the Lords in certain circumstances. This procedure has been used on only three occasions since 1949. The House of Lords does not usually prevent Bills from being enacted that the Commons is keen to pass, although the Lords will often amend and return them for further consideration. If no agreement is reached between the two Houses on a non-financial Commons Bill, the Lords can delay the Bill for a period that, in practice, is about a year. Following this, the Bill may be presented to The Queen for Royal Assent,

Figure 6.3 How legislation is made in the UK Parliament

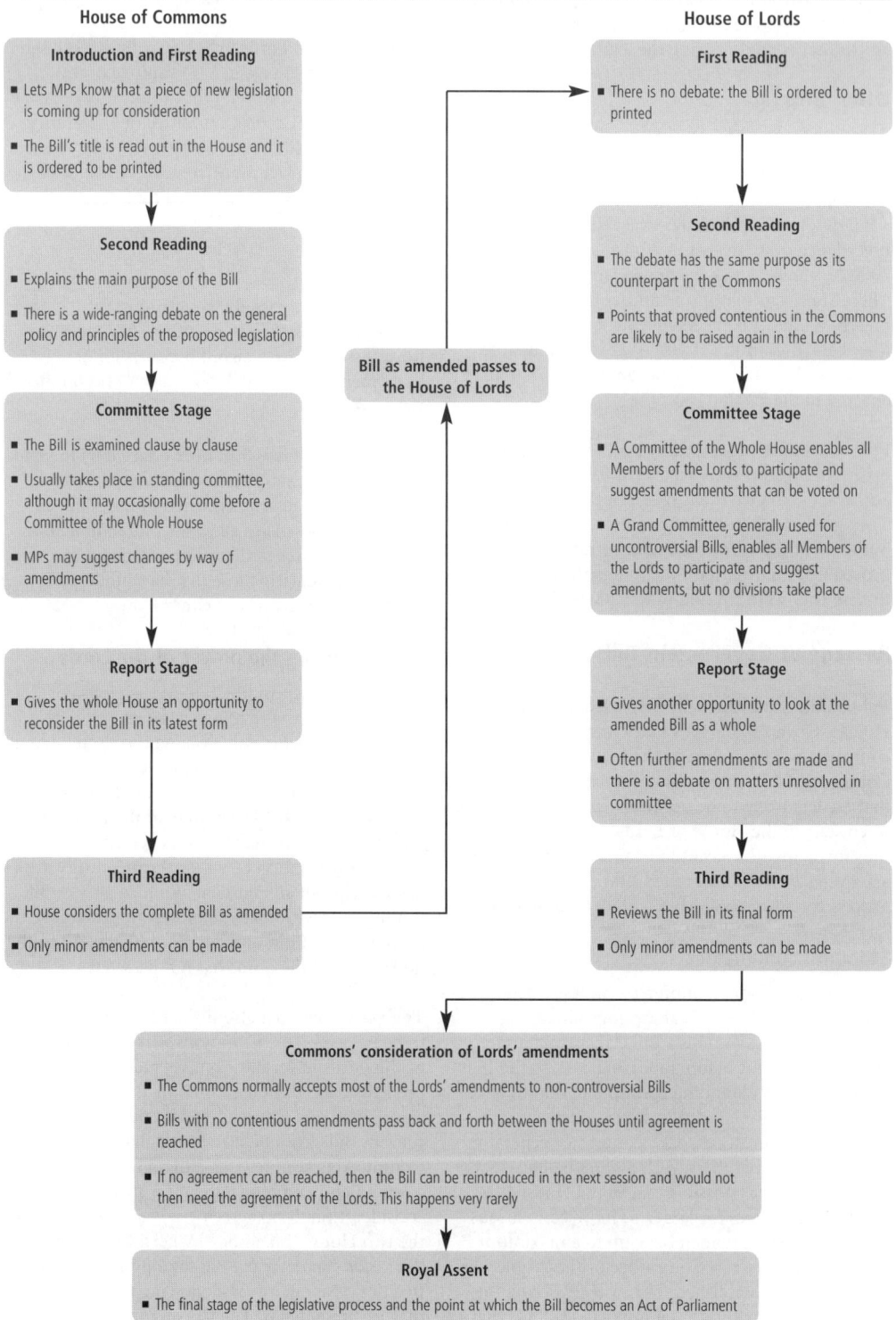

House of Commons

Introduction and First Reading

- Lets MPs know that a piece of new legislation is coming up for consideration
- The Bill's title is read out in the House and it is ordered to be printed

Second Reading

- Explains the main purpose of the Bill
- There is a wide-ranging debate on the general policy and principles of the proposed legislation

Committee Stage

- The Bill is examined clause by clause
- Usually takes place in standing committee, although it may occasionally come before a Committee of the Whole House
- MPs may suggest changes by way of amendments

Report Stage

- Gives the whole House an opportunity to reconsider the Bill in its latest form

Third Reading

- House considers the complete Bill as amended
- Only minor amendments can be made

House of Lords

First Reading

- There is no debate: the Bill is ordered to be printed

Second Reading

- The debate has the same purpose as its counterpart in the Commons
- Points that proved contentious in the Commons are likely to be raised again in the Lords

Committee Stage

- A Committee of the Whole House enables all Members of the Lords to participate and suggest amendments that can be voted on
- A Grand Committee, generally used for uncontroversial Bills, enables all Members of the Lords to participate and suggest amendments, but no divisions take place

Report Stage

- Gives another opportunity to look at the amended Bill as a whole
- Often further amendments are made and there is a debate on matters unresolved in committee

Third Reading

- Reviews the Bill in its final form
- Only minor amendments can be made

Bill as amended passes to the House of Lords

Commons' consideration of Lords' amendments

- The Commons normally accepts most of the Lords' amendments to non-controversial Bills
- Bills with no contentious amendments pass back and forth between the Houses until agreement is reached
- If no agreement can be reached, then the Bill can be reintroduced in the next session and would not then need the agreement of the Lords. This happens very rarely

Royal Assent

- The final stage of the legislative process and the point at which the Bill becomes an Act of Parliament provided the Commons has passed it in the current session and previous session. There is one important exception: any Bill to lengthen the life of a Parliament needs the full assent of both Houses.

Secondary legislation

To reduce unnecessary pressure on parliamentary time, primary legislation often gives ministers or other authorities the power to make detailed rules and regulations under an Act by means of secondary or 'delegated' legislation (usually in the form of 'statutory instruments' or 'SIs'). Such powers are normally delegated only to authorities directly accountable to Parliament or to the devolved legislatures, to minimise the risk of undermining the authority of the UK Parliament. The number of SIs has been increasing, and in 2003 was nearly 3,400.[6]

To save time on the floor of the House, the Commons uses standing committees to debate SIs, unless they are simply laid before the House or subject to negative resolution; actual decisions are taken by the House as a whole. In the Lords, debates on SIs take place on the floor of the House. In contrast to primary legislation, the Lords has the power of veto on non-financial SIs.

Joint committees

Joint committees, with a membership drawn from both Houses, are appointed in each session to deal with Consolidation Bills[7] and SIs. The two Houses may also agree to set up other joint committees. With the increase in pre-legislative scrutiny (see page 48), there has been a tendency for more draft Bills to be considered by a joint committee.

Pressure groups

Pressure groups are informal organisations that aim to influence Parliament and Government. They campaign on a wide range of issues, such as animal welfare, consumer and welfare rights, education, the environment, health and rural affairs. Some, like a number of trade unions, charities and professional associations, have large memberships. Others only have a few members. The Government consults with appropriate pressure groups on most major policy initiatives.

A common tactic of pressure groups is to ask members of the public to write to their MP about an issue, in order to raise awareness and, in the long term, to persuade the MP to support their cause, to raise the issue in the House of Commons and perhaps even effect a change in legislation. Many pressure groups employ full-time parliamentary workers or liaison officers, whose job is to develop contacts with MPs and peers sympathetic to their cause and to brief them on the issues. Occasionally pressure groups may organise a lobby of Parliament to express their concerns, with sometimes large numbers of people gathering outside or near Parliament.

The Monarchy

The Monarchy is the oldest institution of government. The Queen's full title is 'Elizabeth the Second, by the Grace of God, of the United Kingdom of Great Britain and Northern Ireland and of Her other Realms and Territories Queen, Head of the Commonwealth, Defender of the Faith'.

In addition to being the Sovereign of the United Kingdom, The Queen is Head of State of 15 other realms[8] and Head of the Commonwealth (see page 71). In each country where she is Head of State, Her Majesty is represented by a Governor-General, appointed by her on the advice of the ministers of the country concerned and independent of the UK Government. In the Isle of Man, Jersey and the Bailiwick of Guernsey Her Majesty is represented by a Lieutenant-Governor. In the Overseas Territories (see page 78) The Queen is usually represented by a Governor who is a member of the Diplomatic Service (see pages 59 and 80) responsible to the UK Government.

Succession

The title to the Crown derives partly from statute and partly from common law rules of descent. Despite interruptions in the direct line of succession, inheritance has always been how the Monarchy has passed down the generations, with sons of the Sovereign coming before daughters in succeeding to the throne. When a daughter does

---

6 In addition, over 600 SIs concerning Scotland were issued by the Scottish administration.
7 A Consolidation Bill brings together several existing Acts into one, with the aim of simplifying the statutes.

8 Antigua and Barbuda; Australia; the Bahamas; Barbados; Belize; Canada; Grenada; Jamaica; New Zealand; Papua New Guinea; St Kitts and Nevis; St Lucia; St Vincent and the Grenadines; Solomon Islands; and Tuvalu.

Figure 6.4 Principal members of the Royal Family from the reign of Queen Victoria to July 2004

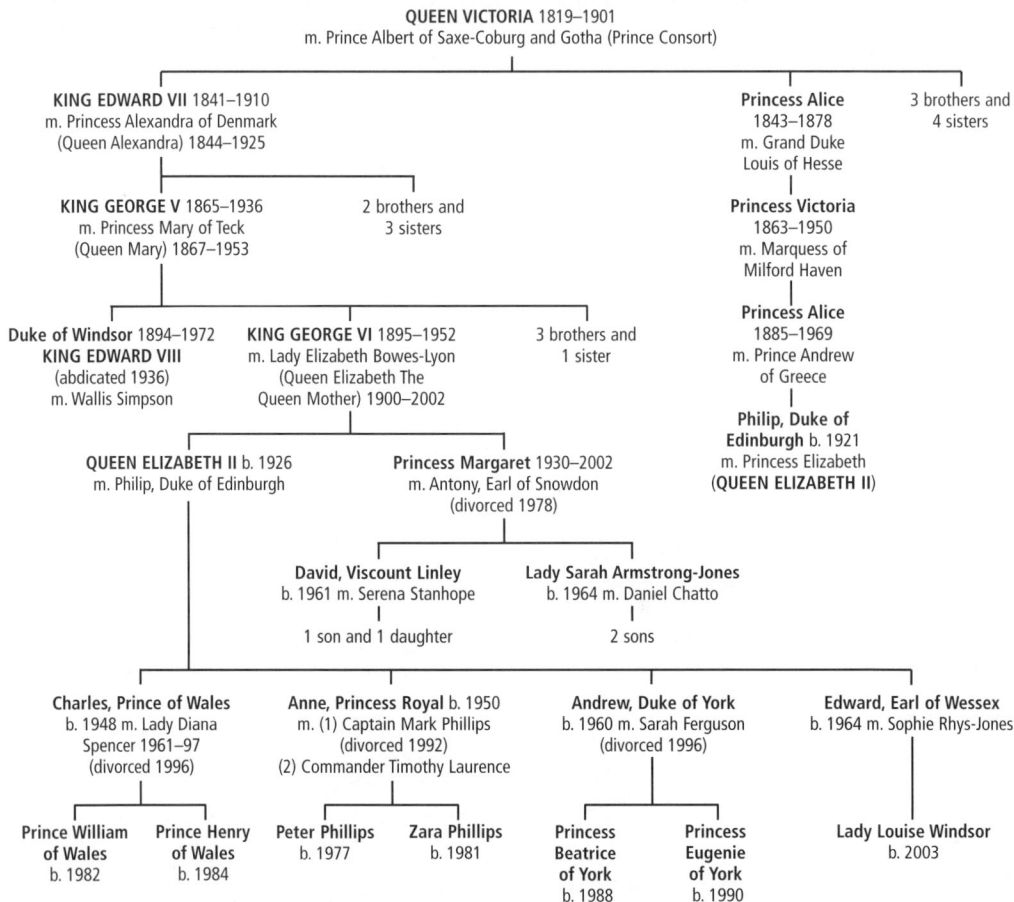

QUEEN VICTORIA 1819–1901
m. Prince Albert of Saxe-Coburg and Gotha (Prince Consort)

KING EDWARD VII 1841–1910
m. Princess Alexandra of Denmark
(Queen Alexandra) 1844–1925

Princess Alice 1843–1878
m. Grand Duke Louis of Hesse

3 brothers and 4 sisters

KING GEORGE V 1865–1936
m. Princess Mary of Teck
(Queen Mary) 1867–1953

2 brothers and 3 sisters

Princess Victoria 1863–1950
m. Marquess of Milford Haven

Princess Alice 1885–1969
m. Prince Andrew of Greece

Duke of Windsor 1894–1972 **KING EDWARD VIII** (abdicated 1936) m. Wallis Simpson

KING GEORGE VI 1895–1952 m. Lady Elizabeth Bowes-Lyon (Queen Elizabeth The Queen Mother) 1900–2002

3 brothers and 1 sister

Philip, Duke of Edinburgh b. 1921 m. Princess Elizabeth (**QUEEN ELIZABETH II**)

QUEEN ELIZABETH II b. 1926 m. Philip, Duke of Edinburgh

Princess Margaret 1930–2002 m. Antony, Earl of Snowdon (divorced 1978)

David, Viscount Linley b. 1961 m. Serena Stanhope — 1 son and 1 daughter

Lady Sarah Armstrong-Jones b. 1964 m. Daniel Chatto — 2 sons

Charles, Prince of Wales b. 1948 m. Lady Diana Spencer 1961–97 (divorced 1996)

Anne, Princess Royal b. 1950 m. (1) Captain Mark Phillips (divorced 1992) (2) Commander Timothy Laurence

Andrew, Duke of York b. 1960 m. Sarah Ferguson (divorced 1996)

Edward, Earl of Wessex b. 1964 m. Sophie Rhys-Jones

Prince William of Wales b. 1982 | Prince Henry of Wales b. 1984 | Peter Phillips b. 1977 | Zara Phillips b. 1981 | Princess Beatrice of York b. 1988 | Princess Eugenie of York b. 1990 | Lady Louise Windsor b. 2003

succeed, she becomes Queen Regnant, and has the same powers as a king. The 'consort' of a king takes her husband's rank and style, becoming Queen. No special rank or privileges are given to the husband of a Queen Regnant.

Under the Act of Settlement of 1701, only Protestant descendants of Princess Sophia, the Electress of Hanover (a granddaughter of James I of England and VI of Scotland), are eligible to succeed. The first seven members of the Royal Family in order of succession to the Throne are: The Prince of Wales, Prince William of Wales, Prince Henry of Wales, The Duke of York, Princess Beatrice of York, Princess Eugenie of York and The Earl of Wessex. Lady Louise Windsor, the daughter of The Earl and Countess of Wessex, became

eighth in line to the throne on her birth in November 2003.

The Sovereign succeeds to the throne as soon as his or her predecessor dies: there is no interval without a ruler. He or she is at once proclaimed at an Accession Council, to which all members of the Privy Council (see page 53) are called. Members of the House of Lords, the Lord Mayor, Aldermen and other leading citizens of the City of London are also invited.

Royal income, expenditure and business activity

Public funds (known as the 'Civil List') and government departments together meet the costs of The Queen's official duties. In 2000 a Royal Trustees' Report recommended that Civil List payments should remain at the 1991 level of £7.9 million a year for a further ten years from 2001. About 70 per cent of The Queen's Civil List provision is needed to meet the cost of staff. Under the Civil List, the Duke of Edinburgh receives an annual parliamentary allowance of £359,000 to enable him to carry out his public duties. Parliamentary annuities paid to other members of the Royal Family to carry out royal duties are reimbursed by The Queen. In return for the Civil List and other financial support, The Queen surrenders the income from the Crown Estate (£171 million in 2002/03) and other hereditary revenues to the nation. The Prince of Wales does not receive a parliamentary allowance since he is entitled to the annual net revenues of the Duchy of Cornwall.

According to the annual report of Civil List expenditure, issued in June 2004, The Queen's total expenditure as Head of State in 2003/04 was £36.8 million, of which £16.5 million was spent on the upkeep of the royal palaces and £4.7 million on royal travel (see box).

The Queen's private expenditure as Sovereign comes from the Privy Purse, which is financed mainly from the revenues of the Duchy of Lancaster;[9] her expenditure as a private individual is met from her own personal resources. Since 1993 The Queen has paid income tax on all personal and Privy Purse income. She also pays tax on realised capital gains on private investments and on assets in the Privy Purse. The Prince of Wales pays tax on the income from the Duchy of Cornwall that is used for private purposes.

The Monarch's role in government

Over time the Monarchy's power has been gradually reduced. The Queen's influence is mainly informal and, having expressed her views, she abides by the advice of her ministers. The Queen continues to perform a range of duties, such as summoning and dissolving Parliament, and giving Royal Assent to legislation passed by the UK or Scottish Parliament or, when it is sitting, by the Northern Ireland Assembly. She formally appoints

Royal travel

Members of the Royal Family carry out about 3,000 official engagements a year, both in the United Kingdom and overseas. Official engagements involve a significant amount of travel. The grant in aid for Royal travel was £5.7 million in 2003/04 and actual expenditure totalled £4.7 million.

In 2003/04 the Royal Train made 18 journeys, with an average distance of 1,184 kilometres per journey. Official flying for members of the Royal Family is provided by jet aircraft of The Royal Squadron, based at RAF Northolt, and a helicopter operated from Blackbushe in Hampshire. During 2003/04 the aircraft were used for Royal flying for 334 hours and the helicopter for 389 hours.

important office holders, including the Prime Minister and other government ministers (see page 54), the First Minister in Scotland, judges, officers in the Armed Forces, governors, diplomats, bishops and some other senior clergy of the Church of England. The Queen confers peerages, knighthoods and other honours.[10] In international affairs, as Head of State, she has the power to declare war and make peace, to recognise foreign states and conclude treaties.

The Queen holds Privy Council meetings, gives audiences to her ministers and officials in the United Kingdom and overseas, receives accounts of Cabinet decisions, reads dispatches and signs State papers. She is consulted on many aspects of national life, and must show complete impartiality.

The Privy Council

The Privy Council was once the chief source of executive power in the State, but as the system of Cabinet government developed in the 18th century, the Cabinet took on much of its role. The Privy Council remains the main way in which

---

9 The Duchy of Lancaster is a landed estate that has been held in trust for the Sovereign since 1399. It is kept quite apart from his or her other possessions and is separately administered by the Chancellor of the Duchy of Lancaster.

10 Although most honours are conferred by The Queen on the advice of the Prime Minister, a few – the Order of the Garter, the Order of the Thistle, the Order of Merit and the Royal Victorian Order – are granted by her personally.

A review of the honours system was set up under Sir Hayden Phillips. Its recommendations submitted in July 2004, included:

- setting up public networks to stimulate involvement so that nominations reflect the diversity of society and achievements of individuals;

- ensuring that the specialist committees that advise on honours are chaired by people independent of the Government and the civil service, and that non-civil service experts form a majority of the committee members; and

- reducing the number of public servants (members of the civil service, Diplomatic Service and the military) who receive awards from 27 per cent to 20 per cent within the next three to five years.

The Phillips Review recommendations will be considered alongside the Fifth Report to the House of Commons Public Administration Select Committee, which also proposes reforms to the honours system.

ministers advise The Queen on the approval of Orders in Council (such as those granting Royal Charters or enacting subordinate legislation) or on the issue of royal proclamations (such as the summoning or dissolving of Parliament).

The Privy Council consists of all members of the Cabinet, other senior politicians, senior judges and some individuals from the Commonwealth. Appointment is for life but only members of the Government participate in its policy work. The Prime Minister recommends membership of the Privy Council to the Sovereign. In August 2004 there were some 530 members.

Privy Council Office

The secretariat of the Privy Council is the Privy Council Office (PCO), the smallest autonomous government department. This is headed at ministerial level by the Lord President of the Council, a post that is usually combined with another senior post, currently that of Leader of the House of Lords. Much of the work of the PCO

is concerned with the affairs of about 400 institutions, charities and companies incorporated by Royal Charter, together with responsibilities in connection with higher education and with certain statutory regulatory bodies covering a number of the professions.

Committees of the Privy Council

Privy Council committees (of which the Cabinet is technically one) are normally made up of ministers with the relevant policy interest. The Judicial Committee, whose members have held high judicial office, is the final court of appeal from courts in UK Overseas Territories, those Commonwealth countries that have retained this method of appeal after independence, and in the Isle of Man, Jersey and the Bailiwick of Guernsey. The Committee also considers devolution issues concerning the powers and functions of the executive and legislative authorities in Scotland and Northern Ireland, and the competence and functions of the National Assembly for Wales.

Her Majesty's Government

The Government consists of ministers responsible for the conduct of national affairs. After a General Election, The Queen appoints the leader of the party that won the most seats in the House of Commons as Prime Minister. She appoints all other ministers on the Prime Minister's recommendation. About 100 members of the governing party receive ministerial appointments. Most ministers are MPs; the remainder sit in the Lords.

The composition of governments varies both in the number of ministers and in the titles of some offices. New ministerial offices may be created, others may be abolished, and functions may be transferred from one minister to another.

Prime Minister

The Prime Minister is head of the UK Government and is ultimately responsible for the policy and decisions of government. By tradition, the Prime Minister is also First Lord of the Treasury and Minister for the Civil Service. By modern convention, the Prime Minister always sits in the Commons.

The Prime Minister presides over the Cabinet and is responsible for allocating functions among ministers, has regular meetings with The Queen to inform her of the general business of the Government, and recommends a number of appointments to The Queen (including senior clergy). The Prime Minister represents the United Kingdom at major international events, such as the annual meeting of the Group of Eight leading industrialised countries (see page 72).

The Cabinet

The Cabinet is the supreme decision-making body in the UK Government. The Prime Minister chairs meetings of the Cabinet and appoints its members, normally about 20. In September 2004 there were 22 Cabinet ministers – 20 MPs and two peers – while a third peer, the Government Chief Whip in the House of Lords, also usually attends Cabinet meetings.

The Cabinet usually meets weekly, normally on a Thursday morning. It meets in private and its business is confidential, although after 30 years Cabinet papers usually become available for inspection in the National Archives.

Much of the work of the Cabinet is delegated to Cabinet committees. They provide a framework for collective consideration of, and decisions on, major policy issues and matters of significant public interest, and ensure that the views of all relevant ministers are considered. Some of the committees have subcommittees, which focus on a narrower range of issues. Cabinet committees include those dealing with defence and overseas policy; economic affairs, productivity and competitiveness; public services and public expenditure; the environment; and constitutional reform policy.

Ministerial responsibility

The Cabinet balances ministers' individual duties with their collective responsibility as members of the Government and takes the final decisions on all government policy. The convention of collective responsibility means that all ministers unanimously support government policy once it has been settled. The policy of departmental ministers must agree with the policy of the Government as a whole. Once the Government has decided its policy on a particular matter, each minister is expected to support it or resign. On rare occasions, ministers are allowed free votes in Parliament on important issues of principle or conscience. Ministers are individually accountable for the work of their departments and agencies, and have a duty to Parliament to answer for their policies, decisions and actions.

On taking up office ministers resign directorships in private and public companies, and must ensure that there is no conflict between their public duties and private interests. Detailed guidance on handling ministers' financial interests is set out in the Ministerial Code.

Cabinet and other ministers

The Deputy Prime Minister is First Secretary of State, deputising for the Prime Minister in the United Kingdom and abroad and chairing a number of Cabinet committees and subcommittees. The Office of the Deputy Prime Minister (ODPM) has responsibilities for regional policy; local government (including finance); and planning, housing and regeneration. The Chancellor of the Exchequer manages the business of HM Treasury and is responsible for presenting annually to Parliament the Budget and the Pre-Budget Report (see page 347).

Ministers in charge of the other main government departments are usually members of the Cabinet. Most have the title 'Secretary of State'.

Holders of various traditional offices, namely the Lord President of the Council, the Chancellor of the Duchy of Lancaster, the Lord Privy Seal, the Paymaster General and Ministers without Portfolio, may have few or no departmental duties. They are therefore available to carry out any duties the Prime Minister may wish to give them.

Ministers of state are middle-ranking ministers and are not usually in the Cabinet. They normally have specific responsibilities, usually reflected in their titles, for example, 'Minister for Lifelong Learning, Further and Higher Education'. The most junior ministers are parliamentary under-secretaries of state (or, where the senior minister is not a secretary of state, simply parliamentary secretaries).

Ministerial salaries

The salaries of ministers in the House of Commons (from April 2004) start at £86,173 a year for a parliamentary under-secretary, rising to £95,281 for a minister of state, £130,347 for a

Cabinet minister and £178,922 for the Prime Minister (inclusive of the parliamentary salary).

In the House of Lords the Lord Chancellor is entitled to a salary of £207,736 and the Attorney General £103,461. Other ministerial salaries in the Lords range from £67,255 for a parliamentary under-secretary to £77,220 for a minister of state and to £98,899 for a Cabinet minister.

Prime Minister's Office

The Prime Minister's Office, No 10 (so called after the Prime Minister's official residence at 10 Downing Street), supports him in his role as head of government. It works with the Cabinet Office to provide central direction for the development, implementation and presentation of government policy. No 10 is staffed by a mixture of civil servants and special advisers (see page 57) and is headed by a chief of staff.

A number of units within the Cabinet Office assist the Prime Minister including:

- the Prime Minister's Delivery Unit, which works in partnership with other departments to assess delivery and provide performance management for key priority areas;

- the Strategy Unit, which carries out long-term strategic reviews and policy analysis;

- the e-Government Unit (see page 63); and

- the Office of Public Services Reform, which is taking forward the Government's principles of public service reform.

The Cabinet Office

The Cabinet Office aims to make government more effective by providing a strong centre. It works to four objectives:

- supporting the Prime Minister in leading the Government;

- coordinating activity across government;

- improving delivery by building capacity in departments and the public services; and

- promoting standards that ensure good governance, including adherence to the Ministerial and Civil Service Codes.

Government Car and Despatch Agency

The Government Car and Despatch Agency (GCDA), an executive agency of the Cabinet Office. Its three main operations are the Government Car Service, which provides driver and car hire, a taxi booking service, protected security cars and specially trained drivers; the InterDespatch Service, which runs secure mail services within government and the wider public sector; and the Government Mail Service, which offers a range of mailroom, messenger and reprographic services, and secure mail screening. In 2004 the GCDA used 207 cars and 59 vans and other vehicles.

Government departments

The main role of government departments and their agencies is to implement government policy and advise ministers. They are staffed by politically impartial civil servants and generally receive their funding from money provided by Parliament. They often work alongside local authorities, non-departmental public bodies, and other government-sponsored organisations. The structure and functions of departments are sometimes reorganised if there are major changes in government policy or to improve efficiency. The Government has announced that the Inland Revenue and HM Customs and Excise will merge to form Her Majesty's Revenue and Customs (see page 371).

Most departments are headed by secretaries of state, supported by ministers. However, some are non-ministerial departments headed by a permanent office holder and secretaries of state with other duties are accountable for them to Parliament. Non-ministerial departments include the Food Standards Agency.

The functions and geographic remit of the main government departments and agencies are set out in appendix A, pages 481–95.

Non-departmental public bodies

A non-departmental public body (NDPB, sometimes known as a 'quango') is a national or regional public body, working independently of ministers to whom it is accountable. There are two main types of NDPB:

- Executive NDPBs have executive, administrative, commercial or regulatory functions. They work within a government framework and the degree of operational independence varies. Examples include the seven Research Councils.

- Advisory NDPBs provide independent and expert advice to ministers and their departments on particular matters. An examples is the Medicines Commission. Some Royal Commissions are also classified as advisory NDPBs.

Over 800 NDPBs are sponsored by UK government departments. The annual Cabinet Office directory *Public Bodies* is available electronically via the Cabinet Office website.

Parliament or Assembly, generally exercise executive powers. The duty of the individual civil servant is first and foremost to the minister in charge of the department or body in which he or she is serving, although a civil servant must remain politically impartial. A change of minister, for whatever reason, does not involve a change of staff.

With the exception of the Prime Minister, Cabinet ministers may each appoint up to two special advisers. The Prime Minister may also authorise the appointment of one or two special advisers by ministers who regularly attend Cabinet. The Prime Minister approves all appointments and they are paid for from public funds. In July 2004 there were 84 special advisers, including 28 in the Prime Minister's Office. Their appointments end when the Government's term of office finishes, or when the appointing minister leaves the Government or moves to another appointment.

The Civil Service

The constitutional and practical role of the Civil Service in Great Britain is to help the Government of the United Kingdom and the devolved administrations formulate their policies, carry out decisions and administer public services for which they are responsible. There is a separate Northern Ireland Civil Service (see page 59).

Civil servants are servants of the Crown; in effect this means the Government of the United Kingdom and the devolved administrations. Ministers, who are answerable to the appropriate

Civil servants

During the last ten years the number of civil servants in Great Britain declined up to 1999, but since then the number has risen (Table 6.5). In the year to October 2003 the number of permanent civil servants (on a full-time equivalent basis) rose by 3.5 per cent to 516,990. After taking account of the fall of 8.2 per cent in the number of casual staff, total staff rose by 3.2 per cent to 527,650. There has been a large increase in part-time working over the last ten years: in 2003, on a headcount basis, 16.4 per cent of permanent civil servants worked part time, compared with 9.2 per cent in 1993.

Table 6.5 Civil Service staff, Great Britain

	October 1993	October 2001	October 2002	October 2003	% change 1993–2003
Permanent staff					
Non-industrial	504,130	452,320	472,930	496,490	−1.5
Industrial	48,940	27,670	26,700	20,500	−58.1
Total permanent staff	553,080	479,990	499,630	516,990	−6.5
Casual staff	21,510	13,490	11,610	10,660	−50.4
Total staff (full-time equivalents)	**574,590**	**493,480**	**511,240**	**527,650**	**−8.2**
Total permanent staff (headcount):	572,900	504,440	526,900	546,670	−4.6
of whom: full-time	520,310	431,610	445,730	457,220	−12.1
part-time	52,590	72,830	81,170	89,460	70.1

Source: *Civil Service Statistics*, Cabinet Office

In April 2003 about half of all civil servants (full-time equivalent) provided services direct to the public. These included paying benefits and pensions, running employment services, staffing prisons, issuing driving licences, and providing services to industry and agriculture. The rest were divided between central administrative and policy duties; support services; and services that were largely financially self-supporting.

Equality and diversity

The Civil Service aims to create a culture in which the skills, experience and expertise that individuals bring are valued and used. In October 2003, on a headcount basis, some 52.4 per cent of civil servants were female; minority ethnic representation was 8.1 per cent; and about 4.3 per cent of staff employed were known to have a disability.

One of the Cabinet Office's targets is to ensure that the Civil Service becomes more open and diverse. In particular, there are targets that by 2004/05, 35 per cent of the Senior Civil Service (SCS) should be women, and 25 per cent of the top management posts should be filled by women. The figures in October 2003 were 27.5 per cent of SCS members and 23.9 per cent of those in the top management posts (including three at Permanent Secretary level). The 2004/05 target that 3.2 per cent of the SCS should be from declared minority ethnic backgrounds was met in October 2003, while the 1.7 per cent of the SCS with declared disabilities compared with a 2004/05 target of 3.0 per cent.

Civil Service Commissioners

The Civil Service Commissioners, who are independent of government, are responsible for ensuring that recruitment to the Civil Service is made on merit on the basis of fair and open competition. The Commissioners produce a recruitment code, monitor the recruitment policies and practices of departments and agencies, and participate in recruitment to the most senior posts. They also promote the Civil Service Code, which sets out the constitutional framework within which all civil servants work and the values they are expected to uphold.

Central management

As Minister for the Civil Service, the Prime Minister is responsible for the central coordination and management of the Civil Service. He is

Public sector efficiency and relocation

In the 2004 Budget the Government announced plans to cut its administration costs in real terms and to achieve efficiency gains across the public sector of 2.5 per cent a year over the three years of the 2004 Spending Review. The Spending Review (see page 368) included agreed departmental targets for achieving annual efficiencies of over £20 billion a year by 2007/08. It took account of an independent review of public sector efficiency by Sir Peter Gershon. Efficiency programmes include plans to achieve a gross reduction in Civil Service and military posts in administrative and support functions of 84,150 by 2007/08. Some 13,550 posts will be redeployed to support key front-line activities, leading to a net reduction in posts of 70,600.

The Government has accepted all the recommendations of an independent review of public sector relocation, the Lyons Review, which was published in March 2004. This found that the concentration of activity in and around London was inconsistent with government objectives for efficiency and regional development. Measures being taken include:

- relocation of staff – departments have confirmed 20,000 jobs for dispersal from London and the South East, which should be completed by 2010;
- slimming down of Whitehall headquarters, with departments reviewing the size and functions of their London offices; and
- a presumption against locating government functions in London and the South East, other than 'face-to-face' services.

supported by the Head of the Home Civil Service (whose function is combined with that of the Cabinet Secretary), who is responsible for leading the programme of Civil Service reform and for the most senior appointments in the Civil Service. The Cabinet Office oversees the central framework for management of the Civil Service. Responsibility for a range of terms and conditions has been delegated to departments and agencies, and to the devolved administrations in Scotland and Wales.

Executive agencies

Executive agencies were introduced to deliver government services more efficiently and effectively within available resources and to become more responsive to their customers. They are part of the Civil Service but have delegated authority to employ their own staff and organise service provision. Agencies are headed by chief executives who are personally responsible for day-to-day operations. They are normally directly accountable to the responsible minister, who in turn is accountable to Parliament.

The Diplomatic Service

The Diplomatic Service of some 6,000 people provides staff for the Foreign & Commonwealth Office (FCO, see page 80) in London and at UK diplomatic missions abroad. Terms and conditions of service are comparable with the rest of the Civil Service, but take into account the special demands of the Diplomatic Service, particularly the requirement to serve abroad. UK civil servants, members of the Armed Forces and individuals from the private sector may serve in the FCO and at overseas posts on loan or attachment.

Northern Ireland Civil Service

The Northern Ireland Civil Service (NICS) is modelled on its counterpart in Great Britain, and has its own Civil Service Commission. Its role is to support the Northern Ireland Executive in the administration of public services for which it has responsibility. During the suspension of devolution (see page 33), the NICS reports to the Secretary of State for Northern Ireland. There were about 27,000 permanent non-industrial civil servants in the NICS at 31 March 2004, on a full-time equivalent basis.

Local government

The structure of local government in each part of the United Kingdom is given in chapters 2 to 5. In July 2004 the Government announced a debate on what local government in England should look like in ten years' time (see chapter 2).

Elections

Local authorities in Great Britain consist of over 22,000 elected councillors. The procedure for local government voting is broadly similar to that for elections to the UK Parliament, except that proportional representation is used in Northern Ireland, and has been introduced in Scotland in time for the next local government elections in 2007. Eligibility rules for voters are also similar to those for UK parliamentary elections (see page 40), except that citizens of other EU Member States and Members of the House of Lords may vote. To stand for election, candidates must either be registered as an elector or have some other close connection within the electoral area of their candidature, such as their principal place of employment.

Powers

Local authorities work within the powers laid down under various Acts of Parliament. Their functions are far-reaching. Some are mandatory, which means that the authority must do what is required by law, while others are discretionary, allowing an authority to provide services if it wishes. In certain cases, ministers have powers to secure uniformity in standards to safeguard public health or to protect the rights of individual citizens. Where local authorities exceed their statutory powers, they are regarded as acting outside the law and can be challenged in court. Local councils' annual accounts must be audited by independent auditors appointed by the appropriate audit body.

The main link between local authorities and central government in England is the ODPM. However, the Departments for Education and Skills; Work and Pensions; Health; and Environment, Food and Rural Affairs; and the Home Office are also concerned with various local government functions.

As their work is largely in devolved areas, local authorities in Wales, Scotland and Northern Ireland now deal mainly with the devolved Parliament and Assemblies (see chapters 3 to 5).

Provision of local services

Many of the provisions of the *Local Government Act 2003*, which is designed to give greater freedom and flexibility to local authorities in England and Wales, took effect in November 2003. Local authorities have been given new powers intended to increase diversity and choice in public services. All local authorities can conduct advisory polls to help them engage with the wider community and business. Powers for the payment of government grants to authorities now have fewer restrictions on how the grants can be used.

In April 2004 a new regime for local government borrowing came into force under the Act. Local authorities no longer have to seek government permission for borrowing for capital investment, providing that they can afford to service the debt. Local authorities can also introduce Business Improvement Districts from October 2004 to enhance town centres and other areas.

Efficiency

The Government has introduced measures designed to improve the delivery and value for money of local services. The Comprehensive Performance Assessment (CPA) framework was introduced in 2002 and brings together assessments of individual local services and an assessment of the corporate capacity of each authority, to give an overall view of how each authority is performing and how well it is placed to deliver improvements. CPA has been introduced for all single-tier and county councils in England and is gradually being introduced for district councils. The Audit Commission is consulting on a revised CPA from 2005 onwards, which will provide a stronger focus on the importance of delivering value for money as well as looking at local government's community leadership role.

The duty of Best Value requires local authorities to deliver services by the most economic, efficient and effective means available to meet the requirements of their communities. Best Value Performance Indicators (BVPIs) were introduced in 2000/01.

The ODPM and the Local Government Association jointly launched the National Procurement Strategy for Local Government in October 2003. The three-year strategy includes a range of policies and programmes targeting improvements in procurement practices; local authorities spend around £40 billion a year. Nine new regional Centres of Procurement Excellence were announced in February 2004 to provide expertise to local authorities and to build on existing good practice.

Local Public Service Agreements (PSAs) are voluntary agreements negotiated between individual local authorities and the Government, under which an authority is rewarded by a grant if it achieves a demanding performance target. The Government has concluded agreements with 135 local authorities in England eligible for a local PSA. A second generation of local PSAs is being introduced, with the first agreements running from April 2004. The new PSAs focus on local priorities and building more effective local partnerships, both within and outside local government.

Employees

About 2.8 million people were employed by local authorities in the United Kingdom in June 2003. These include school teachers, the police, firefighters, and other non-manual and manual workers. Education is the largest service, with about 1.4 million jobs.

Internal organisation

Some districts have the ceremonial title of borough, or city, both granted by royal authority. Traditionally, their councillors choose a mayor (a provost in Scotland) to act as presiding officer and perform ceremonial duties. In certain large cities, he or she is known as the Lord Mayor. In Scotland the presiding officer of the council of the four longest

The Fire and Rescue Service

The *Fire and Rescue Services Act 2004* replaces the *Fire Services Act 1947* with a new framework designed to reflect a modern and efficient Fire and Rescue Service. Promoting fire safety has become a statutory duty for all fire and rescue authorities. The Act also places on a statutory footing the other activities now undertaken, including rescue from road traffic accidents and the Service's role in dealing with other emergencies, such as serious flooding and responding to the threat of terrorism.

The Act gives statutory effect to the Fire and Rescue National Framework, which sets out the strategic priorities of the Fire and Rescue Service. It also provides for the devolution of the remaining responsibilities for fire and rescue authorities in Wales to the National Assembly for Wales. Responsibility for the Service is already devolved in Scotland and Northern Ireland.

established cities – Aberdeen, Dundee, Edinburgh and Glasgow – is called the Lord Provost.

The *Local Government Act 2000* required local authorities in England and Wales to implement new decision-taking structures, including the option of a directly elected mayor. In most authorities the arrangements are based on one of three executive frameworks: a mayor and cabinet; a council leader and cabinet; or a mayor and council manager. Within these options local authorities have considerable flexibility to work under a constitution that reflects local circumstances. All local authorities have introduced new constitutions, with the majority opting for a style of executive where the leader of the cabinet is chosen by other councillors. By June 2004 there had been 30 referendums on mayors, leaders and cabinets, and 11 had voted in favour of a directly elected mayor.

Councillors are paid a basic allowance but may also be entitled to allowances and expenses for attending meetings or taking on special responsibilities.

Decision-making and scrutiny

All new decision-making structures are required to incorporate rigorous arrangements for review and scrutiny of councils' policies and the decisions they make. Some decisions, such as the acceptance of policies and the budget, are reserved for the full council, but most of those relating to the implementation of policy are for the executive. The executive is also responsible for preparing the policies and budget to propose to the council.

The public (including the press) is admitted to meetings of the executive when key decisions are being discussed. They also have access to agendas, reports and minutes of meetings and certain background papers. In addition, local authorities must publish a forward plan setting out the decisions that will be taken over the coming months. Local authorities may exclude the public from meetings and withhold papers only in limited circumstances. Provisions of the *Freedom of Information Act 2000* (see page 63) with regard to publication schemes apply to local authorities as public bodies, as will full implementation of the Act from January 2005.

Local authority finance

Local government expenditure accounts for about a quarter of public spending in the United

Kingdom. In 2003/04 expenditure by UK local authorities was an estimated £119.5 billion: £108.7 billion on current expenditure and £10.9 billion on net capital expenditure (Table 6.6).

Local authorities in Great Britain raise revenue through the council tax (see chapter 23); in England this meets about 25 per cent of their revenue expenditure. Their spending is, however, financed primarily by grants from central government or the devolved administrations and by the redistribution of revenue from national non-domestic rates, a property tax levied on businesses and other non-domestic properties. Capital expenditure is financed from several sources: central government capital grant; capital receipts from the disposal of land and buildings; and borrowing (including borrowing supported by the Government, and borrowing that is locally financed). The Government has powers to ensure that increases in local authority budgets and council tax are not excessive, and in April 2004 the Deputy Prime Minister announced that the 2004/05 budgets of 14 local authorities in England that set excessive increases for 2004/05 would be capped.

Following a review of local government funding in England, published in July 2004, the Government has agreed that council tax should be retained, but that there is a case for reform. It has therefore set

Table 6.6 Local authority current and capital expenditure, 2003/04,[1] UK

£ billion

	Current expenditure	Net capital expenditure	Total expenditure
Education and training	35.8	3.1	38.8
Social protection	29.3	0.2	29.5
Public order and safety	13.4	0.7	14.1
Transport	4.4	2.6	7.0
Environmental protection	4.6	0.6	5.2
General public services	4.1	0.4	4.5
Housing and community amenities	2.3	2.1	4.4
Recreation, culture and religion	2.6	0.9	3.5
Accounting adjustments	11.1	0.1	11.2
Miscellaneous other	1.1	0.2	1.3
Total local authority expenditure	**108.7**	**10.9**	**119.5**

1 Estimated expenditure based on local authority budget plans.
Source: *Public Expenditure Statistical Analyses 2004*, HM Treasury

up an independent inquiry to advise on how to take forward the review's findings. District councils in Northern Ireland continue to raise revenue through the levying of a domestic rate and a business rate (see page 35).

Standards and accountability

A number of safeguards are in place to ensure the probity of individuals in carrying out their public duties.

Committee on Standards in Public Life

The Committee on Standards in Public Life is an independent body reporting to the Prime Minister. It has responsibility for examining concerns about the standards of conduct of all holders of public office and making recommendations for changes to ensure the highest standards of propriety in public life.

Since its establishment in 1994 the Committee has produced nine reports. These have resulted in a number of changes, including a new regulatory regime for political party funding, overseen by the Electoral Commission (see page 39); and changes in the ethical framework for local government.

The Committee is conducting its tenth inquiry, and aims to report by the end of 2004. It is looking at the processes for maintaining high standards of conduct in public bodies, local government and the National Health Service.

Parliamentary standards

Arrangements governing parliamentary standards have been adopted following recommendations of the Committee on Standards in Public Life. These included:

- a new code of conduct for MPs;
- an improved Register of Members' Interests (MPs with a financial interest must declare it when speaking in the House or in Committee); and
- a new independent Parliamentary Commissioner for Standards, reporting to a strengthened House of Commons Select Committee on Standards and Privileges.

The Code of Conduct, revised in 2002, requires MPs, among other things, to uphold the law and the constitution, always act in the public interest, not bring the House of Commons into disrepute, observe the main principles of public life as set out by the Committee, and observe the House's rules such as on registering and declaring interests.

Responsibilities of the Parliamentary Commissioner for Standards include overseeing the maintenance of the Register, monitoring the operation of the Code of Conduct, and advising the Select Committee on Standards and Privileges on interpretation of the Code.

The House of Lords has its own register on similar lines to that for MPs, based on a separate Code of Conduct that came into force in 2002.

Commissioner for Public Appointments

The Commissioner for Public Appointments is independent of government and is responsible for regulating, monitoring and reporting on ministerial appointments to the boards of a range of public bodies – in 2002/03 ministers made nearly 3,500 appointments and reappointments to the boards of public bodies. The aim is to ensure that government departments have appointments systems that are visible, fair and open, and that all board appointments are made on merit. Departments are required to follow the Commissioner's Code of Practice; a new Code was issued in February 2004.

Complaints

Parliamentary Commissioner for Administration

The Parliamentary Commissioner for Administration – more usually known as the Parliamentary Ombudsman – investigates complaints from members of the public (that have been referred by MPs) alleging that they have been unfairly treated through maladministration. The Ombudsman is independent of government and reports to a select committee of the House of Commons. The Ombudsman's area of authority covers maladministration by government departments and certain other public bodies, but excludes complaints about government policy, the content of legislation and certain other matters.

When a complaint is upheld, the Ombudsman normally recommends that the department or other body makes some kind of redress (which might be financial in appropriate cases). There is no appeal against the Ombudsman's decision. The Ombudsman received 1,981 new complaints in 2003/04, an increase of 0.4 per cent on 2002/03.

Separate arrangements apply for complaints about the devolved administrations and devolved public bodies. In Wales complaints can be made directly to the Welsh Administration Ombudsman (from November 2004 the Welsh Public Services Ombudsman), in Scotland to the Scottish Public Services Ombudsman and in Northern Ireland to the Northern Ireland Ombudsman.

Local government

Complaints of maladministration by local authorities or by certain local bodies are investigated by independent Commissions for Local Administration, often known as 'the Local Ombudsman service'. There are Local Government Ombudsmen in England and Wales. In Scotland responsibility rests with the Scottish Public Services Ombudsman and in Northern Ireland there is a Commissioner for Complaints.

Modernising government

The Government has set out four principles of public service reform:

- high national standards designed to ensure that citizens have the right to high-quality services wherever they live;

- devolving decision-making, so that local leaders have responsibility and accountability for delivery;

- greater flexibility in the delivery of public services; and

- more choice for the customers of public services, including greater choice of service provider.

The Government has taken a number of measures to modernise and improve public services. PSAs set out each government department's plans to deliver results in return for the investment being made and include the department's aims, objectives and performance targets.

Electronic services in central and local government

The Government has set a target that all its services will be available electronically by the end of 2005. The Office of the e-Envoy (OeE), which had been helping to ensure that departments meet

Freedom of information

The *Freedom of Information Act 2000* will be brought fully into force on 1 January 2005. The Act will affect over 100,000 organisations, including central and local government, Parliament, the National Assembly for Wales, the Northern Ireland Assembly (when it is sitting), the Armed Forces, the police, hospitals, GPs and dentists, schools and publicly funded museums. The Act and associated environmental information regulations will apply in England, Wales and Northern Ireland. The Scottish Parliament has enacted separate legislation, which will also be fully operative from 1 January 2005.

The Act establishes a general statutory right of access so that a person who contacts a public authority seeking information will have the right to be told whether or not the authority has the information and, if so, to be sent it. There are exemptions specified under the Act, many of which are subject to a 'public interest' test: the authority will be required to disclose the information unless it can demonstrate that the public interest in withholding the information outweighs that in releasing it. Any decision not to disclose the information may be subject to appeal to the independent Information Commissioner.

this target, was reorganised in 2004 as the e-Government Unit. One of the key responsibilities of the new unit will be to help implement the efficiency decisions that were announced in the 2004 Spending Review (see page 368). By the end of March 2004, 74 per cent of central government services were available electronically.

There is a similar target for the electronic availability of local government services in England; in particular, local government is committed to making all its priority services electronically available by 2005.

In March 2004 the OeE launched 'Directgov' (*www.direct.gov.uk*), a new online service which is also available through digital TV. Directgov is designed to make it easier to find and access government services on the Internet. Over time it aims to become the first destination for people seeking information about public services. There are plans to offer information from up to 100 local authorities by the end of 2004.

The Government Gateway (*www.gateway.gov.uk*) acts as an 'intelligent hub' – verifying transactions from citizens and businesses, and routeing them to and from appropriate government departments. Examples of services that were on the Gateway by August 2004 included Export Licence Applications, electronic VAT returns and income tax self-assessment.

Government communications

Following an independent review published in January 2004, the Government has appointed a new Permanent Secretary for Government Communications, responsible for the strategy, coordination and effectiveness of government communications across Whitehall. He is taking forward, in consultation with departments, the review's recommendations concerning a redefinition of the overall role of government communications; the structures necessary to deliver this activity, some of which are run by the Government Information and Communications Service; and improved training and development of all communications specialists.

The UK in the European Union

As a Member State of the European Union (EU), the United Kingdom is bound by European Community (EC) legislation and agreements under EU law based on a series of treaties since the 1950s (see pages 67–69). Almost all UK government departments are involved in EU-wide business, and European legislation is an increasingly important element of government.

The EC enacts legislation that is binding in its entirety or its intention on the national governments of the Member States or, in certain circumstances, on individuals and companies within those states. UK government ministers take part in the discussions and decision-making, and all the Member States take the final decision collectively.

A constitutional treaty for the enlarged EU (see page 69) was finalised by the EU Heads of State and Government in June 2004.

The Office of the UK Permanent Representative to the European Union (UKREP), based in Brussels, participates in the negotiations on behalf of the UK Government, alongside Whitehall-based officials as necessary. Following UK devolution, the devolved administrations are consulted when the UK Government line on EU issues is developed.

Council of Ministers

This is the main decision-making body. Member States are represented by the ministers appropriate to the subject under discussion. When, for instance, health matters are being discussed, the UK Secretary of State for Health attends with his or her European counterparts. Ministers from the devolved administrations can also attend these meetings and, at the appropriate UK minister's request, devolved administration ministers can represent the United Kingdom. The Presidency of the Council changes at six-monthly intervals and rotates in turn among the Member States.

In some cases Council decisions must be unanimous; but in most cases they are taken by qualified majority voting where, until 31 October 2004, a proposal is adopted if it gets 88 or more of the total of 124 votes. Votes are weighted according to a country's population, and the United Kingdom has ten votes. The system will be adapted with effect from 1 November 2004 when the United Kingdom will have 29 out of 345 votes.

European Council

This usually meets four times a year, twice under each six-monthly Presidency, and comprises the Heads of State or Government (accompanied by their foreign ministers) and the President of the European Commission. The Council defines strategy and general political guidelines. At its meetings (referred to as European Summits), the Council will signal its commitment to particular courses of action.

European Commission

The European Commission is the EU's executive body and guardian of the treaties. It implements the decisions of the Council of Ministers as well as certain executive decisions under its own authority,

Table 6.7 European Parliament elections, June 2004

	Number of MEPs	% share of votes
Great Britain		
Conservative	27	26.7
Labour	19	22.6
UK Independence Party	12	16.2
Liberal Democrats	12	14.9
Green	2	6.3
Scottish National Party	2	1.4
Plaid Cymru – The Party of Wales	1	1.0
Other parties	0	11.0
Northern Ireland		
Democratic Unionist Party	1	32.0
Sinn Féin	1	26.3
Ulster Unionist Party	1	16.6
Other parties	0	25.1
Total	**78**	

Source: House of Commons

initiates legislation and ensures that Member States put it into effect. Each Commissioner is responsible for a specific policy area. The Commissioners are entirely independent of their countries, and serve the EU as a whole. From November 2004 the number of Commissioners will be set at 25, one for each Member State.

European Parliament

The number of directly elected Members of the European Parliament (MEPs) increased from 626 in 1999 to 732 in 2004, to take account of the increased membership of the EU (see page 71). The Parliament is consulted about major decisions and has shared power with the Council of Ministers over the EU budget (see page 69). In areas of legislation, its role varies between consultation, where it can influence but does not have the final say in the content of legislation; co-operation and assent procedures, where its influence is greater; and co-decision, where a proposal requires the agreement of both the Council and the European Parliament. The Parliament meets in full session in Strasbourg for about one week every month. Its committee work normally takes place in Brussels. Successive treaties have increased the Parliament's role in scrutinising the activities of the Commission and have extended its legislative and budgetary powers.

Elections to the European Parliament take place every five years. For the June 2004 election the number of MEPs in most existing Member States were reduced to accommodate representatives from the ten states that joined the EU in May 2004. The *European Parliament (Representation) Act 2003* made provision for the number of UK MEPs to be reduced from 87 to 78.

European legislation

Some European legislation is adopted jointly by the Council of Ministers and the European Parliament, some by the Council and some by the Commission under delegated powers. European laws can be split into four main types:

- regulations, which are directly applicable in all Member States, and have the force of law without the need for implementing further measures;

- directives, which are equally binding as to the result to be achieved but allow each Member State to choose the form and method of implementation;

European elections

As in the rest of the EU, the elections in the United Kingdom in June 2004 were conducted using a system of proportional representation: in Great Britain a vote for a 'closed' party list counted using the d'Hondt system (see glossary) and in Northern Ireland the single transferable vote system. The 78 seats were divided into 12 electoral regions: England, with 64 seats (split into nine regions, each returning between three and ten MEPs); Scotland (with seven seats); Wales (four seats) and Northern Ireland (three seats). The main features of the vote in the United Kingdom were a decline in the proportion of votes won by the Conservative Party and the Labour Party, both of which won fewer seats than in the 1999 election, and a rise in the proportion of votes gained by other parties. Both the UK Independence Party and the Liberal Democrats increased their number of seats, from 3 and 10 respectively in 1999, to 12 each in 2004. Turnout was significantly higher than in 1999, reaching 38.8 per cent.

- decisions, which, like regulations, do not normally need national implementing legislation and are binding on those to whom they are addressed; and

- recommendations and opinions, which are not legally binding.

Other EU institutions

The European Court of Justice, which comprises judges from the Member States, is the final authority on all aspects of Community law. It rules on questions relating to interpretation of the EU treaties, on secondary legislation in direct actions, and on cases referred to it by national courts. There is a Court of First Instance to deal with certain specified issues brought by individuals and companies. The United Kingdom is also represented on the European Court of Auditors, which is responsible for ensuring that the EU spends its money according to its budgetary rules and for the purposes for which it is intended.

The United Kingdom is represented on the Committee of the Regions by elected members from devolved administrations and local authorities. In addition, it is represented on the European Economic and Social Committee by appointees from employer and employee organisations, and producer and consumer groups.

Further reading

Cabinet Office Departmental Report 2004. Cm 6226. The Stationery Office, 2004.

Civil Service Statistics. Cabinet Office, annual.

Department for Constitutional Affairs Departmental Report 2003/04. Cm 6210. The Stationery Office, 2004.

The future of local government: developing a 10 year vision. ODPM, 2004.

Office of the Deputy Prime Minister Annual Report 2004. Cm 6206. The Stationery Office, 2004.

Websites

The UK Monarchy
www.royal.gov.uk

Cabinet Office
www.cabinet-office.gov.uk

Central government
www.direct.gov.uk

Department for Constitutional Affairs
www.dca.gov.uk

e-Government Unit
www.cabinet-office.gov.uk/e-government

Prime Minister's Office
www.pm.gov.uk

United Kingdom Parliament
www.parliament.uk

WWW.

7 International relations

The United Kingdom has global foreign policy interests. It belongs to more international organisations than any other country except France, and is a member of the European Union (EU), the North Atlantic Treaty Organisation (NATO, see page 91), the Group of Eight (G8, see page 72), the Commonwealth (see page 71) the Organisation for Security and Co-operation in Europe (OSCE, see page 72), as well as being a permanent member of the United Nations (UN) Security Council (see page 71).

In December 2003, the UK Government outlined priorities for UK foreign policy over the next five to ten years. They are:

- a world that is safer from global terrorism and weapons of mass destruction;

- the protection of the United Kingdom from illegal immigration, drug trafficking and other international crime;

- an international system based on the rule of law that is able to resolve disputes and prevent conflicts;

- an effective EU in a secure neighbourhood;

- the promotion of UK economic interests in an open and expanding global economy;

- sustainable development, underpinned by democracy, good governance and human rights;

- the security of UK and global energy supplies; and

- the security and good governance of the UK Overseas Territories.

The UK Government believes that no country can tackle these issues alone. The most important UK partnerships will remain within the EU and with the United States. The United Kingdom will also seek to develop stronger strategic relationships with states such as China, India, Japan and Russia, and will engage constructively with Islamic countries.

European Union

The United Kingdom joined the EU in 1973. The EU promotes coordinated social and economic progress and common foreign and security positions among its Member States, and has established a single market and an economic and monetary union. Principal EU institutions and its legislative processes are described on pages 64–66.

The Government published a White Paper, *Prospects for the EU*, in April 2004. This will form part of a regular series that sets out the forthcoming programmes of the Council of Ministers and the European Commission.

Treaties

A series of treaties created by Intergovernmental Conferences (IGCs) govern the structure and operation of the EU. Any amendments to the treaties must be agreed unanimously and must then be ratified by each Member State according to its own constitutional procedures. In the United Kingdom, Parliament must scrutinise and where necessary provide legislative powers to implement new EU treaties before they can be ratified.

Treaties of Rome

The 1957 Treaties of Rome established the European Community (EC) and the European Atomic Energy Agency (Euratom). The EC set out to create a common market encompassing the elimination of customs duties between Member States, free movement of goods, people, services and capital, and the removal of distortions in competition within this market. It also aimed to coordinate transport and establish common agricultural and economic policies. Euratom was set up to develop a common market in the peaceful uses of atomic energy. Under the Treaties of Rome, the Member States granted the European Commission a mandate to negotiate international trade agreements on their behalf.

The *1986 Single European Act*, which incorporated measures to complete the single market, reaffirmed these aims. It also provided, for the first time, a formal treaty basis for European political co-operation, the precursor to the common foreign and security policy (CFSP, see page 70); increased economic and social cohesion; and further developed the European monetary system.

Maastricht Treaty

The 1992 Maastricht Treaty, in force since 1993, established the European Union (EU), based on three 'pillars':

- pillar I – the EC;
- pillar II – new intergovernmental arrangements for a CFSP; and
- pillar III – increased co-operation on justice and home affairs (see page 71).

It amended the Treaties of Rome and encompassed moves towards economic and monetary union (see page 70) and a Cohesion Fund (see page 70). The Treaty also enshrined the principle of subsidiarity, under which action in areas where the EC and Member States share competence should be taken at European level only if objectives cannot be achieved by Member States acting alone, and can be better achieved by the EC. In addition, it introduced the concept of EU citizenship as a supplement to national citizenship. Qualified majority voting (see page 64) was extended and the Treaty introduced the co-decision procedure, which reinforced the role of the European Parliament in the legislative process.

Amsterdam Treaty

The 1997 Amsterdam Treaty, in force since 1999, further protected and extended citizens' rights by means of a new anti-discrimination clause. It

integrated the 'social chapter' (previously a separate protocol to the Maastricht Treaty) into the treaty framework following its adoption by the United Kingdom, and adopted new mechanisms to improve the operation of the CFSP. The immigration, asylum and civil judicial co-operation provisions of pillar III were brought in, while provisions for police and judicial co-operation in criminal matters were reinforced. The Treaty also introduced the possibility for groups representing a majority of Member States to co-operate and integrate more closely. Qualified majority voting was further extended, the number of areas subject to co-decision between the Council of Ministers and the European Parliament was increased, and the co-decision procedure was simplified.

Treaty of Nice

The Treaty of Nice was signed in 2001 and entered into force in 2003. It introduced changes to the EU institutional machinery in preparation for enlargement (see page 71). From 1 January 2005, the number of votes allocated to each Member State in the European Council changes to take account of prospective new members. The total rises from the 87 votes held by the 15 Member States until June 2004 to up to 345 votes held by a potential 27 Member States. France, Germany, Italy and the United Kingdom will each have 29 votes. Assuming 27 Member States, the total required for a qualified majority (see page 64) will increase from 62 to 255, and for a blocking minority from 26 to 91.

From 2005, the European Commission will comprise one member from each country, although when the EU reaches 27 members, the number of commissioners will be capped at a figure less than the total number of Member States. However, provisions in the Constitutional Treaty, if adopted, will supersede some of the Treaty of Nice provisions (see page 69).

Treaty of Accession

The Treaty of Accession, signed by 25 heads of state in Athens in April 2003, provided for the accession to the EU of ten members on 1 May 2004. Under the Treaty, nationals of the ten new Member States (see page 71) have the right to move freely within the EU from that date for all purposes except for work. The Treaty allows for the imposition of transitional work restrictions on nationals of the new Member States, except Cyprus and Malta, until 30 April 2011.

The United Kingdom has waived its right to impose these transitional work restrictions, subject to certain safeguards (see page 175).

EU Constitutional Treaty

In 2002, the Convention on the Future of Europe – under the presidency of former French President Valéry Giscard D'Estaing – began a fundamental review of EU institutions to consider how to make the expanded EU more democratic, effective and transparent.

In June 2003, the Convention's findings were presented in the form of a draft Constitutional Treaty at the Thessaloniki European Council.[1]

Under the Constitutional Treaty:

- Member States will confer competences on the EU;

- national parliaments will have a role in monitoring and enforcing subsidiarity (see page 68);

- a full-time president of the European Council will work alongside the existing presidents of the European Commission and the European Parliament;

- an EU foreign minister will bring together the roles of external relations commissioner and council high representative;

- a legally binding charter of rights will be introduced;

- the EU will become a single legal 'personality' (until the Treaty is ratified by all Members the EC and the EU have separate legal personalities);

- there will be greater co-operation on social security, justice and home affairs; and

- a simpler voting system will be introduced where decisions would pass if supported by at least 55 per cent of Member States, representing at least 65 per cent of the EU.

The UK Parliament will debate the Treaty in the autumn 2004. If it votes in favour of the proposed EU constitution, the UK Government will then hold a referendum.

Policies

The EC budget and broader EU policies are described below. Policies affecting specific UK sectors – for example, the Common Agricultural Policy – are covered in the appropriate chapters.

European Community budget

The EC's revenue consists of levies on agricultural imports from non-member countries, customs duties, a proportion of value added tax (VAT) receipts, and contributions from Member States based on gross national income (GNI). Increasingly, more revenue is being raised from contributions linked to GNI and less from VAT receipts and customs payments. The United Kingdom receives an annual budget rebate because of its disproportionately low share of receipts (notably agricultural funds) and higher than average contributions. The rebate has been in place since 1984 and is guaranteed until at least 2006.

Single market

The single European market, providing for the free movement of people, goods, services and capital within the EU, came into effect in 1993. Its benefits include the removal of customs barriers, the liberalisation of capital movements, the opening of public procurement markets and the mutual recognition of professional qualifications. Under the European Economic Area (EEA) Agreement that came into force in 1994, most of the EU single market measures also apply to Iceland, Liechtenstein and Norway.

Economic and monetary union

The Maastricht Treaty (see page 68) provided for the establishment of a European economic and monetary union in stages, culminating in the establishment on 1 January 1999 of a single currency, the euro, by the participating EU Member States.[2] Thirteen EU Member States are outside the euro area. These are Denmark, Sweden and the United Kingdom, and the ten new Member States that joined in May 2004: Cyprus, Czech Republic, Estonia, Hungary, Latvia, Lithuania, Malta, Poland, Slovakia and Slovenia. The UK Government has set out five economic tests that must be met before any decision to join can be made (see page 346).

---

1 The draft treaty was debated in an IGC of EU leaders between October 2003 and June 2004, and was agreed unanimously. It will be signed in autumn 2004. Before coming into force, it must be ratified by all 25 Member States.

2 The rate for Greece became fixed when it joined the euro on 1 January 2001.

Entente Cordiale

In April 2004, The Queen made a state visit to France to mark the centenary of the the the *Entente Cordiale*. The *Entente* was signed in London on 8 April 1904 to settle long-standing colonial disputes between France and the United Kingdom. It also ended hundreds of years of rivalry and paved the way for Franco–British diplomatic and military co-operation in the lead-up to the First World War (1914–18).

Conversion rates between the national currencies of the 12 participating Member States and the euro were fixed on 1 January 1999. The euro is the legal currency in the euro area and the European Central Bank has responsibility for formulating monetary policy for these countries.

Regional and infrastructure development

There are significant economic and social disparities between Member States. The EU implements a European regional policy financed by the European Funds – the Structural Funds and the Cohesion Fund.

The four Structural Funds are:

- the European Regional Development Fund, which finances infrastructure projects and schemes to promote development and diversification of industry;

- the European Social Fund, which supports human resource and equal opportunities schemes, and training measures for the unemployed and young people;

- the Guidance Section of the European Agricultural Guidance and Guarantee Fund, which supports agricultural restructuring and some rural development activities; and

- the Financial Instrument for Fisheries Guidance, which promotes the modernisation of the fishing industry.

The United Kingdom will receive €15.5 billion (over £10 billion) from the Structural Funds in 2000–06. In addition, a Cohesion Fund, set up under the Maastricht Treaty, provides direct finance for specific projects relating to environmental and transport infrastructure in Greece, Ireland, Portugal and Spain.

In the run up to enlargement (see page 71), the EU prepared financial programmes for the period 2000–06 to help the candidate countries prepare for membership. These include the Instrument for Structural Policies for Pre-accession (ISPA), which finances environment and transport projects with a budget of €7.28 billion (just under £5 billion), and the Special Accession Programme for Agriculture and Rural Development (Sapard), which supports agricultural development with a €3.64 billion (just under £2.5 billion) budget. They join the Phare programme (the main channel for EU financial and technical co-operation with Central and Eastern Europe), with a €10.92 billion (over £7 billion) budget, which aims to strengthen the administrative and institutional capacity of accession countries and to finance investment projects. The latter account for 30 per cent and 70 per cent of Phare's budget respectively.

After accession, the Structural Funds and the Cohesion Fund replace such assistance. The European Council meeting in Brussels in October 2002 set aside an additional €23 billion (over £15 billion) for structural spending in the new Member States for the period 2004–06.

Common foreign and security policy

The CFSP, introduced under the Maastricht Treaty (see page 68), provides for unanimous agreement among Member States on common policies and/or joint action on international issues, in the belief that Member States carry more weight when able to speak with one voice on international affairs than any single Member State alone. The Amsterdam Treaty (see page 68) preserves the principle of unanimity in all policy decisions but states that those decisions concerning common strategies, which are themselves unanimously agreed, will be by qualified majority voting. A Member State may prevent a vote being taken by qualified majority voting for 'important and stated reasons of national policy'. In addition, qualified majority voting does not apply to decisions having military or defence implications. A Member State may abstain and stand aside from an EU decision.

In 1998, the United Kingdom and France proposed the European security and defence policy (ESDP) with the aim of strengthening EU capacity to respond to crises, on the premise that the Union could play a coherent and effective political role only if this was backed up by a credible military capability. ESDP is designed to take on the Petersberg Tasks, established at the

Ministerial Council of the Western European Union in 1992. These were humanitarian and rescue tasks; peacekeeping tasks; and tasks of combat forces in crisis management, including peacemaking.

In 2003, the EU announced it was operational across the full range of these tasks, although it accepted that its capabilities were constrained by recognised shortfalls. During 2003, it successfully completed two military crisis management operations (in the Democratic Republic of Congo and the former Yugoslav Republic of Macedonia). Three civilian ESDP crisis management operations have also been launched – policing missions in Bosnia and the former Yugoslav Republic of Macedonia, and a rule of law mission in Georgia.

Justice and home affairs

The Maastricht Treaty established arrangements for increased co-operation among EU states on justice and home affairs issues. These include visa, asylum, immigration and other policies related to free movement of people; and police, customs and judicial co-operation in criminal matters (including co-operation through Europol).

This is a growing aspect of EU work and, since the Amsterdam Treaty came into force, includes both Community-based and intergovernmental areas of co-operation. A protocol annexed to the Amsterdam Treaty recognises the right of the United Kingdom to exercise its own frontier controls.

Enlargement

A key EU policy objective is to enlarge the Union to include those European nations that share its democratic values and aims, and that are functioning market economies, able to compete in the EU and to take on the obligations of membership. Ten new members – Cyprus, the Czech Republic, Estonia, Hungary, Latvia, Lithuania, Malta, Poland, Slovakia and Slovenia – joined the EU on 1 May 2004, in time to participate in the June elections to the European Parliament (see page 65).

The new Member States increased the population of the EU by around 75 million. Of the new members, Poland is the largest, accounting for around 8.5 per cent of both the population and the area of the enlarged EU. Malta has the smallest area, but is by far the most densely populated. At the European Council in December 2003, Bulgaria and Romania were given a target date of January

2007 for joining the EU. Accession negotiations with Turkey may be opened following the European Council meeting in December 2004, providing the Council decides that Turkey has fulfilled the Copenhagen political criteria relating to democracy, the rule of law, and respect for human rights and minorities.

Other international organisations

United Nations

The United Kingdom is a founder member of the UN and one of the five permanent members of the Security Council, along with China, France, Russia and the United States. It supports the purposes and principles of the UN Charter, including the maintenance of international peace and security, the development of friendly relations among nations, the achievement of international co-operation on economic, social, cultural and humanitarian issues, and the protection of human rights and fundamental freedoms.

The United Kingdom is the fourth largest contributor both to the UN regular budget – paying just over £48 million in 2003 – and to UN peacekeeping budgets, and is one of the largest voluntary contributors to UN funds, programmes and specialised agencies. In 2003, the total UK contribution to the UN exceeded £549 million. The UK Government advocates modernising the UN to enhance its effectiveness, including reforming the Security Council's composition. It is committed to reinforcing the UN's role in preventing and resolving conflicts around the world.

The Commonwealth

The Commonwealth has 53 members[3] including the United Kingdom (see map on page 73). It is a voluntary association of independent states, nearly all of which were once British territories. It promotes international peace and order, democracy, the rule of law, good governance, freedom of expression and human rights, as well as economic and social development. The Commonwealth Secretary-General has a role in conflict prevention and resolution, and the organisation provides election observer missions and democracy advisory services. The Commonwealth represents a combined population of 1.8 billion people.

---

3 Zimbabwe withdrew from the Commonwealth in December 2003.

The Queen is Head of the Commonwealth. The Commonwealth Secretariat, based in London, helps host governments to organise Commonwealth Heads of Government Meetings (CHOGMs – these take place in a different Commonwealth country every two years), ministerial meetings and other conferences. It administers assistance programmes agreed at these meetings, including the Commonwealth Fund for Technical Co-operation, which provides expertise, advisory services and training to developing countries in the Commonwealth. The next CHOGM is planned to be held in Valletta, Malta in November 2005, while Uganda will host the 2007 CHOGM.

North Atlantic Treaty Organisation

Membership of NATO is central to UK defence policy (see chapter 8). The main decision-making body is the North Atlantic Council. It meets at least twice a year at foreign minister level, and once a week at permanent representative level.

Group of Eight

The United Kingdom is one of the G8 leading industrialised countries. The other members are Canada, France, Germany, Italy, Japan, Russia (included as a full member from 1998, although the other countries continue to function as the G7 for some discussions) and the United States.

The G8 is an informal group with no secretariat. Its presidency rotates each year among the members, the key meeting being the annual summit of Heads of Government. Originally formed in 1975 (as the G7) to discuss economic issues, the G8 agenda now includes a wide range of foreign affairs and international issues.

The United States hosted the 2004 G8 summit in Georgia, in June. Topics discussed included famine and food security, peacekeeping, development, HIV/AIDS and corruption. The United Kingdom is to host the 2005 G8 summit.

Organisation for Security and Co-operation in Europe

The United Kingdom is a member of the OSCE, a regional security organisation of 55 states from Europe, Central Asia and North America. All decisions are taken by consensus. The OSCE is based in Vienna, where the United Kingdom has a permanent delegation. The main areas of work are:

- early warning and prevention of conflicts;
- observing elections and advising on human rights, democracy and law, and the media;
- post-conflict rehabilitation; and
- promoting security through arms control and military confidence-building.

The United Kingdom contributed around £21.3 million in 2003/04 to the OSCE.

Council of Europe

The United Kingdom is a founding member of the Council of Europe, which is open to any European state accepting parliamentary democracy, the rule of law and fundamental human rights. There are 45 full Member States. One of the Council's main achievements is the European Convention on Human Rights (see page 82). The United Kingdom is one of the major financial contributors to the Council of Europe, paying 12.4 per cent of the Council's budget, around £17.5 million in 2004/05.

Other international bodies

The United Kingdom is a member of many other international bodies. These include:

- the International Monetary Fund (IMF), which regulates the international financial system;
- the World Bank, which provides loans to developing countries;
- the Organisation for Economic Co-operation and Development (OECD), which promotes economic growth, support for less developed countries and trade expansion; and
- the World Trade Organisation (see page 383).

Other organisations to which the United Kingdom belongs or extends support include the Regional Development Banks for Africa, the Caribbean, Latin America and Asia, and the European Bank for Reconstruction and Development.

Map 7.1 The Commonwealth

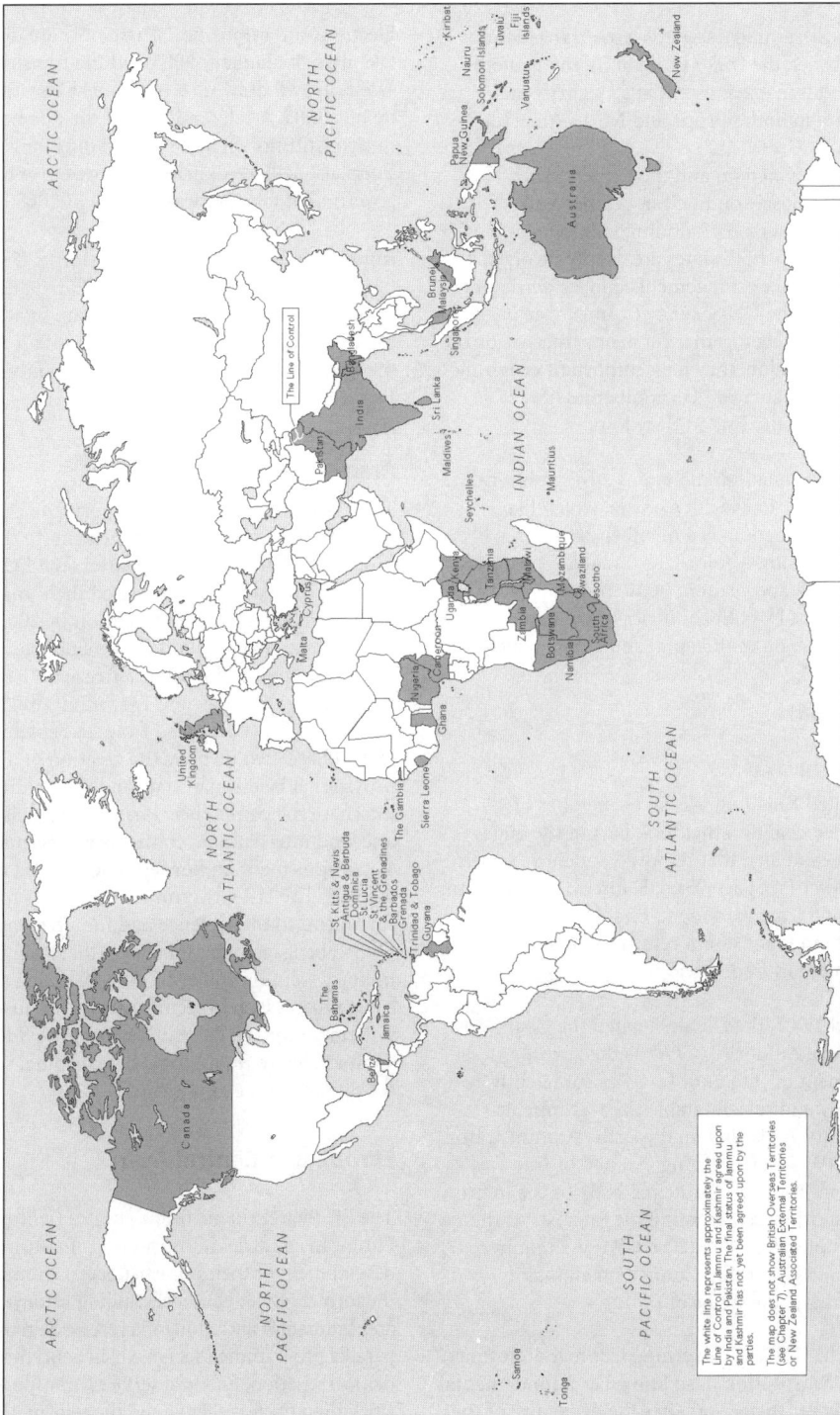

ARCTIC OCEAN

NORTH PACIFIC OCEAN

Kiribati

Tuvalu

Fiji Islands

New Zealand

Nauru

Solomon Islands

Vanuatu

Papua New Guinea

Australia

Brunei

Malaysia

Singapore

The Line of Control

Bangladesh

India

Sri Lanka

Pakistan

INDIAN OCEAN

Maldives

Seychelles

Mauritius

Malta

Cyprus

Uganda Kenya

Tanzania

Mozambique

Swaziland

Lesotho

Cameroon

Zambia

Malawi

Botswana

Namibia

South Africa

Nigeria

Ghana

The Gambia

Sierra Leone

United Kingdom

NORTH ATLANTIC OCEAN

SOUTH ATLANTIC OCEAN

St Kitts & Nevis
Antigua & Barbuda
Dominica
St Lucia
St Vincent
& the Grenadines
Barbados
Grenada
Trinidad & Tobago
Guyana

The Bahamas

Belize

Jamaica

Canada

ARCTIC OCEAN

NORTH PACIFIC OCEAN

SOUTH PACIFIC OCEAN

Samoa

Tonga

The white line represents approximately the
Line of Control in Jammu and Kashmir agreed upon
by India and Pakistan. The final status of Jammu
and Kashmir has not yet been agreed upon by the
parties.

The map does not show British Overseas Territories
(see Chapter 7), Australian External Territories
or New Zealand Associated Territories.

Regional relations

North America

The UK Government regards close transatlantic links between the United Kingdom, the United States and Canada as essential to security and prosperity in both Europe and North America.

The United Kingdom and the United States co-operate closely on nuclear, defence and intelligence issues. As founding members of NATO (see chapter 8), both states are deeply involved in Western defence arrangements and, as permanent members of the UN Security Council (see page 71), work closely together on major international issues. In addition, they have important economic links. More than 5,000 US companies have operations in the United Kingdom.

The United Kingdom maintains strong political and economic links with Canada, which like the United Kingdom is a member of the Commonwealth. A Joint UK–Canada Declaration in June 1997 and again in 2001 shows a commitment by both countries to greater co-operation on multilateral and global issues.

Middle East

Iraq

The United Kingdom was a key member of the US-led coalition that took part in the 2003 military campaign that removed Saddam Hussein from power (see page 95). UK forces, both civilian and military, are working to establish peace and lay the foundations for a return to democratic government in Iraq.

In March 2003, the UN designated the Coalition Provisional Authority (CPA) as the lawful government of Iraq until Iraq was sufficiently politically and socially stable to re-assume its sovereignty. A US diplomat was the Administrator of the CPA. The Governing Council of Iraq was formed in July as the principal body of the interim administration, representing the interests of the Iraqi people to the CPA. The CPA was required to consult the Governing Council on all major decisions and questions of policy.

In March 2004, the Governing Council drew up an interim constitution (also known as a fundamental law) to cover the period after the departure of the CPA and prior to the introduction of a permanent constitution. The CPA transferred power to an interim Iraqi government on 28 June 2004.

Elections for a transitional assembly are due to take place by January 2005 and the transitional assembly will draw up a permanent constitution by July 2005. A referendum will then be held on this constitution before full elections for a new internationally recognised representative Iraqi government take place at the end of 2005.

Improving security in Iraq is a priority. UK police trainers are involved in Basra, Baghdad and a training centre established in Jordan. In addition, the Coalition is developing the New Iraqi Army, the Civil Defence Corps, the border police and the Facilities Protection Service.

Arab–Israeli peace process

The UK Government fully supports the US initiative to give renewed momentum to the peace process. In April 2003 the Quartet (the EU, Russia, UN and United States) presented their 'roadmap' for a permanent two-state solution by 2005. Phase One stipulates an end to Palestinian violence, Palestinian political reform, a freeze on Israeli settlement expansion, and the withdrawal from Palestinian areas occupied from 28 September 2000. Phase Two involves the creation of a provisional Palestinian state and the holding of an international conference. Phase Three calls for a second international conference, a permanent status agreement on borders, and the end of conflict. The UK Government continues to press for an end to the violence and for a resumption of political engagement: it believes there can be no military solution to the conflict. A lasting solution must protect Israel's security, provide a just settlement for the Palestinians, and provide a comprehensive resolution of the dispute, including the Syrian and Lebanese tracks.

Europe and Central Asia

The EU Phare scheme primarily aids Central European countries in the process of reform and development of their infrastructure. Countries of the former Soviet Union (excluding Estonia, Latvia and Lithuania) and Mongolia receive help through a parallel programme (Tacis), which concentrates on democratisation, financial services, transport, energy (including nuclear safety) and the reform of public administration. The Community Assistance for Reconstruction, Development and Stabilisation (CARDS) programme focuses on countries in the Western Balkans.

The EU has strengthened relations with various countries in Eastern Europe through the conclusion of Europe (Association) Agreements. These agreements provide an institutional framework for supporting the process of integration ahead of the accession of these countries to the EU. There are Europe Agreements in force with Bulgaria and Romania. The EU also has an Association Agreement with Turkey. This agreement covers trade-related issues and other areas of co-operation.

EU Partnership and Co-operation Agreements are in force with Armenia, Azerbaijan, Georgia, Kazakhstan, Kyrgyzstan, Moldova, Russia, Ukraine and Uzbekistan. There are also Trade and Co-operation Agreements with Albania, the former Yugoslav Republic of Macedonia and Mongolia. The purpose of these agreements is to reduce trade barriers, promote wide-ranging co-operation and increase political dialogue.

Stabilisation and Association Agreements (SAA) also offer the prospect of ultimate EU membership and closer links to states in south-eastern Europe, provided that these countries meet EU conditions on democracy, electoral and media freedoms, economic reform, and respect for human rights and the rule of law. The EU signed its first SAA, with the former Yugoslav Republic of Macedonia, in April 2001. It concluded an SAA with Croatia in October 2001, and opened negotiations with Albania in January 2003, and with Bosnia and Herzegovina in November 2003.

Mediterranean

The United Kingdom and other EU Member States have developed closer links with 12 Mediterranean partners (Algeria, Cyprus, Egypt, Israel, Jordan, Lebanon, Malta, Morocco, the Palestinian Authority, Syria, Tunisia and Turkey) on the basis of the 1995 Barcelona Declaration, which promotes peace and prosperity in the region. The EU also has Euro-Mediterranean Association Agreements covering political dialogue, free trade and co-operation in a number of areas with Algeria, Egypt, Israel, Jordan, Lebanon, Morocco, the Palestinian Authority and Tunisia.

UK relations with Libya have improved following Libya's renunciation of Weapons of Mass Destruction in December 2003. The Prime Minister visited Libya in March 2004, the first UK Prime Minister to visit the country since 1943.

In February 2004, the United Kingdom welcomed the resumption of talks designed to reunify Cyprus (see page 84). In referendums held in April, Greek Cypriots overwhelmingly rejected the UN proposals, while Turkish Cypriots voted in favour. As a result, when Cyprus joined the EU in May, EU laws and benefits applied only to the Greek Cypriot community. The EU is seeking ways to end the economic isolation of the Turkish Cypriot state.

Africa

The UK Government has declared African development a policy priority. It supports efforts in the following areas:

- to prevent or end African conflicts;
- to promote trade, reduce debt and develop lasting prosperity; and
- to support African governments, organisations and individuals espousing the principles of democracy, accountability, the rule of law and human rights.

The UK Government supports the New Partnership for Africa's Development (NEPAD), an African-led strategy for sustainable growth and development, and plans to increase bilateral aid to Africa to £1 billion a year by 2005/06. The United Kingdom is working to reduce conflict in sub-Saharan Africa through the Africa Conflict Prevention Pool (see page 84).

With the EU and the Commonwealth, the UK Government has continued to protest at the violation of human rights in Zimbabwe, and has called for inter-party dialogue leading to free and fair elections. The United Kingdom has continued its programme of humanitarian assistance in response to the serious food shortage in Zimbabwe.

Since the abolition of apartheid and the election of the first African National Congress government in 1994, UK relations with South Africa have broadened into areas ranging from development assistance to military co-operation, and from sporting links to scientific partnerships. The EU and South Africa signed a trade, development and co-operation agreement in 1999, providing for the creation of a free trade area and for further substantial development assistance from the EU.

The UK Government welcomed South Africa's contribution to resolving conflicts in Burundi and the Democratic Republic of the Congo, and its efforts to deal with the problems of Zimbabwe. In 2004, the United Kingdom contributed £2 million to the African Union (AU) administered Trust Fund to help sustain the AU-led African Mission peacekeeping force in Burundi, which was successfully incorporated into the UN Mission in Burundi in June 2004. The United Kingdom also welcomed the August 2003 signing of a peace deal designed to end the civil war in Liberia. In February 2004, the UK Government announced it was contributing a further £9 million for reconstruction projects in Liberia. This commitment is in addition to £7.6 million contributions to support humanitarian agencies, £1 million to support West African peacekeepers, a £6 million contribution to EU efforts in Liberia, and £34.6 million to support the UN Mission in Liberia.

In July 2003, the United Kingdom contributed troops to a UN-mandated EU crisis management operation under the ESDP (see page 93) to stabilise Bunia in the Democratic Republic of the Congo, pending deployment of UN reinforcements. The mission was successful and ended in September when the UN peacekeeping force resumed its operations. In 2004, UK military personnel continued to participate in the UN peacekeeping missions in the Democratic Republic of the Congo and Sierra Leone.

Asia–Pacific region

The United Kingdom has well-established relations with Australia, China, Japan, the Republic of Korea, New Zealand and many South East Asian nations, and has defence links with most countries in the region. In 1997, the United Kingdom returned Hong Kong to Chinese sovereignty under the provisions of the 1984 Sino–British Joint Declaration. It continues to have responsibilities towards Hong Kong and the 3.6 million UK passport holders living there.

The United Kingdom is a member, with Australia, Malaysia, New Zealand and Singapore, of the Five Power Defence Arrangements, which was set up in 1971 and remains the only multinational defensive structure in the region. The United Kingdom is

also involved in English language teaching, co-operation in science and technology, and educational exchanges in the region.

The Asia–Europe Meeting (ASEM) process was inaugurated in 1996. ASEM's aim is to foster closer economic and political ties between EU countries and Brunei, China, Indonesia, Japan, the Republic of Korea, Malaysia, the Philippines, Singapore, Thailand and Vietnam. The fifth ASEM is planned to take place in Hanoi in October 2004.

The United Kingdom has long-standing and Commonwealth ties with the island countries of the Pacific. It is a dialogue partner of the Pacific Islands Forum, which works in support of member governments to enhance the social and economic well-being of the people of the South Pacific.

In October 2003, the UK Government pledged continued support for the Democratic Republic of Timor-Leste. The United Kingdom has pledged £12 million in the period 2002–05. It is one of six countries that are members of the 'core group' on East Timor at the UN.

Afghanistan

The United Kingdom made a major contribution to the military action leading to the defeat of the Taliban regime by a US-led coalition between October and December 2001. The Taliban had close links with the Al Qaida terrorist network, responsible for the attacks on the United States on 11 September 2001. An emergency *Loya Jirga* (Grand Council) met in Kabul in June 2002 to elect the President of the country, and approve a transitional administration.

In January 2004, the *Loya Jirga* agreed a new Constitution. The first post-Taliban presidential election is due to be held on 9 October, with elections for the legislative assembly to follow in spring 2005.

The UK Government is committed to the reconstruction of Afghanistan and has spent more than £300 million since September 2001 on humanitarian and reconstruction needs. The United Kingdom leads international assistance on counter-narcotics and has pledged £70 million (see page 87). It will also contribute 19 per cent of the European Commission's pledge of €1 billion (£0.67 billion) over five years.

In July 2003, the United Kingdom deployed a joint military–civilian Provincial Reconstruction Team (PRT) to Mazar-e-Sharif in northern Afghanistan. PRTs aim to help with the reform and reconstruction of security arrangements and to extend the authority of the central government, leading to improved security in the regions. In June 2004, the United Kingdom deployed a second PRT in northern Afghanistan and a Forward Supporting Base coordinating support for other PRTs in the north. The UK PRTs are now part of the NATO-led International Security Assistance Force (ISAF), to which the United Kingdom also contributed troops in Kabul.

Latin America and the Caribbean

Links with Latin America date from the early 19th century. The rise of democracy and increasingly free market economies have enabled the United Kingdom to strengthen its ties with the region, and it is one of the largest investors after the United States.

Links with the countries of the Caribbean go back centuries, and there are about 570,000 British citizens of Caribbean origin resident in the United Kingdom. The first UK/Caribbean Forum, held in 1998 in the Bahamas, marked a new longer-term process of co-operation between the United Kingdom and the region. The Forum is a biennial event, hosted alternately by the United Kingdom and a Caribbean country. The fourth meeting took place in the United Kingdom in May 2004.

The EU plays an increasingly important role in the UK's relationship with Latin America and the Caribbean (LAC). The first summit of EU, Latin American and Caribbean Heads of State and Government took place in 1999. A second meeting was held in May 2002, when the EU and Chile concluded negotiations on a trade association agreement. The EU has a similar agreement with Mexico, and is negotiating one with the Mercosur bloc, which comprises Argentina, Brazil, Paraguay and Uruguay. In May 2004, the third EU–LAC summit took place in Mexico.

Overseas Territories

UK Overseas Territories (OTs) have a combined population of about 198,000 (see page 78). Governors are appointed by The Queen and are responsible for external affairs, internal security,

defence and, in some OTs, international financial services. Most domestic matters are delegated to locally elected governments and legislatures. The British Indian Ocean Territory, the British Antarctic Territory, and South Georgia and the South Sandwich Islands have non-resident Commissioners, rather than Governors. None of the Territories has expressed a desire for independence.

The United Kingdom aims to provide the OTs with security and political stability, to ensure efficient and honest government, and to support their economic and social advancement. The Foreign & Commonwealth Office (FCO) and Department for International Development (DFID) support OTs that qualify to access finance from European Development Fund (EDF) and other benefits under the 2001 EU/Overseas Countries and Territories Overseas Association Decision. EDF funding is used to improve local transport infrastructure, and to promote trade development and diversification, inward investment and regional co-operation.

The FCO Overseas Territories Economic Diversification Programme Budget was established in 2001 to help the OTs develop a sustainable economic future by diversifying their economies. In 2003/04, £500,000 was available. The FCO Good Government Fund for the OTs allocated over £3 million in 2003/04 to activities promoting good governance, law enforcement and human rights. Offshore financial service industries are important in several of the OTs. The UK Government's policy is to ensure that these meet international standards of regulation and that effective steps are taken to combat financial crime and regulatory abuse.

Under the *British Overseas Territories Act 2002* all existing OT citizens (with the exception of those deriving their citizenship solely from a connection with the UK Sovereign Base Areas of Cyprus) are automatically British citizens, with the right of abode in the United Kingdom. By the end of 2003, some 18,000 British OT citizens had applied for British Citizens passports. A constitutional review, designed to bring the Territory constitutions up to date to reflect a more modern relationship between the UK and OT Governments, is being carried out. An OT Consultative Council, which brings together UK Ministers and the Chief Ministers or their equivalents from each territory, meets in London annually.

The Overseas Territories at a glance

Anguilla (capital: The Valley)
Area: 90 square kilometres
Population: 11,600 (2001 estimate)
Economy: tourism, financial services, fishing
History: British territory since 1650.

Bermuda (capital: Hamilton)
Area: 53 square kilometres
Population: 62,000 (2000 census)
Economy: reinsurance, tourism
History: first British settlers in 1609–12. Government passed to the Crown in 1684.
UN World Heritage Site: town of St George and related fortifications.

British Antarctic Territory
Area: 1.7 million square kilometres
Population: no indigenous population. The United Kingdom has two permanent British Antarctic Survey stations, staffed by 40 people in winter and 200 in summer. Other Antarctic Treaty nations also have bases in the Territory
History: the British claim dates back to 1908. By October 2002, 45 states, including the United Kingdom, had become Members of the Antarctic Treaty System, which provides a framework for the peaceful use of the Antarctic.

British Indian Ocean Territory (capital: Diego Garcia)
Area: 54,400 square kilometres of ocean, including the Chagos Archipelago land area
Population: military. No indigenous inhabitants
Economy: territory used for defence purposes by the United Kingdom and United States
History: ceded to Britain by France under the 1814 Treaty of Paris.

British Virgin Islands (capital: Road Town)
Area: 153 square kilometres
Population: 21,000 (2002 estimate)
Economy: tourism, financial services
History: annexed by Britain in 1672.

Cayman Islands (capital: George Town)
Area: 260 square kilometres
Population: 42,000 (2003 estimate)
Economy: tourism, offshore finance
History: the 1670 Treaty of Madrid recognised Britain's claim to the islands.

Falkland Islands (capital: Stanley)
Area: 12,173 square kilometres
Population: 2,400, plus military garrison. (2001 census)
Economy: fisheries, tourism, agriculture
History: first known landing in 1690 by British naval captain, John Strong. Under British administration since 1833, except for brief Argentine occupation in 1982.

Gibraltar (capital: Gibraltar)
Area: 6.5 square kilometres

Population: 28,200 (2001 census)
Economy: tourism, banking and finance
History: ceded to Britain in 1713 under the Treaty of Utrecht.

Montserrat (capital: Plymouth)
Plymouth was destroyed by volcanic activity which has rendered the south of the island an exclusion zone.
Area: 102 square kilometres
Population: 4,500
Economy: construction, tourism
History: colonised by English and Irish settlers in 1632.

Pitcairn, Ducie, Henderson and Oeno (capital: Adamstown)
Area: 4.5 square kilometres
Population: 47
Economy: fishing, agriculture and postage stamp sales
History: occupied by mutineers from the British ship *Bounty* in 1790; annexed as a British colony in 1838
UN World Heritage Site: Henderson Island.

St Helena (capital: Jamestown)
Area: 122 square kilometres
Population: 5,000 (1998 census)
Economy: fishing, agriculture and tourism
History: taken over in 1658 by the British East India Co.

Ascension Island (Dependency of St Helena)
Area: 90 square kilometres
Population: 950 (2001 census)
Economy: communications and military base
History: the British garrison dates from Napoleon's exile on St Helena after 1815.

Tristan da Cunha (Dependency of St Helena)
Area: 98 square kilometres
Population: 278 (2001 census)
Economy: fishing
History: occupied by a British garrison in 1816
UN World Heritage Site: Gough Island Wildlife Reserve.

South Georgia and the South Sandwich Islands
Area: Some 170 kilometres long, varying in width from 2 to 40 kilometres
Population: no indigenous population. British Antarctic Survey stations at King Edward Point and Bird Island
History: first landing by Captain Cook in 1775.

Turks and Caicos Islands (capital: Cockburn Town)
Area: 430 square kilometres
Population: 20,200 (2001 census)
Economy: tourism, property development, real estate, international finance and fishing
History: Europeans from Bermuda first occupied the islands around 1678, then planters from southern states of America settled after the American War of Independence in the late 18th century.

New laboratory in Antarctica

A £3 million laboratory opened at the British Antarctic Survey's Rothera Research Station, Adelaide Island, in January 2004. The Bonner Laboratory replaces a research facility destroyed by fire in 2001 and is made of fire-retardant materials. It is equipped with laboratories, offices, an aquarium and a dive facility complete with recompression chamber. Rothera is a centre for biology, geoscience and atmospheric science programmes. Its work includes long-term biological monitoring that contributes to understanding global climate change.

Falkland Islands

The Falkland Islands are the subject of a territorial claim by Argentina. The UK Government does not accept the Argentine claim and is committed to defending the Islanders' right to live under a government of their own choosing. This right of self-determination is enshrined in the UN Charter and is embodied in the 1985 Falkland Islands Constitution.

The United Kingdom and Argentina seek to co-operate on issues of common interest affecting the South Atlantic, such as conservation of fish stocks and surveying the continental shelf. However, difficulties remain. In 2003 Argentina imposed restrictions on charter flights through its airspace, threatening tourism in the Falklands. Efforts to resolve the matter were continuing in 2004.

Gibraltar

British and Dutch forces captured Gibraltar in 1704 and Spain ceded the island to Britain in perpetuity under the 1713 Treaty of Utrecht. However, Spain has long sought its return. In July 2002, the UK Government indicated that although a number of issues remained to be resolved, the United Kingdom and Spain had reached a broad measure of agreement on the principles that should underpin a lasting settlement:

- that the United Kingdom and Spain should share sovereignty over Gibraltar;
- that there should be more internal self-government;

- the retention of UK traditions, customs and way of life;
- the retention of the right to UK nationality for Gibraltarians, who should also gain the right to Spanish nationality;
- the retention of Gibraltar's own institutions; and
- that Gibraltar could, if it chose, participate fully in the EU single market and other EU arrangements.

The Government of Gibraltar organised a referendum on the question of joint sovereignty with Spain in November 2002 and of those participating, almost 99 per cent voted against the principle. The UK Government stressed that the principle of Gibraltarian consent, as set out in Gibraltar's 1969 Constitution, remained central to its approach. The UK Government continues to believe that dialogue with both Spain and Gibraltar is the best way to secure a permanent settlement to the dispute.

Gibraltar has an elected House of Assembly. Responsibility for 'defined domestic matters' is devolved to elected local ministers. The Territory is within the EU, as part of the United Kingdom Member State, although it is outside the common customs system and does not participate in the Common Agricultural or Fisheries Policies or the EU VAT arrangements. The people of Gibraltar have been declared UK nationals for EU purposes.

The *European Parliament (Representation) Act 2003* allows the people of Gibraltar to vote in elections to the European Parliament. Gibraltar forms part of the English South West electoral region, which returns seven Members of the European Parliament (MEPs). In the European parliamentary elections in June 2004, 57.5 per cent of the electorate in Gibraltar voted.

Overseas Territories Environment Programme

In December 2003, the United Kingdom launched the Overseas Territories Environment Programme (OTEP), a joint initiative between the FCO and DFID, which doubles the amount of money available to the OTs for sustainable environment work. The £3 million fund is designed to save precious eco-systems from destruction.

A review of the Financial Services Commission, which regulates Gibraltar's financial services, took place in 2004. The review evaluated the extent to which the regulation of financial services in Gibraltar matches relevant UK and EU standards. Its report should be published in autumn 2004.

300th anniversary celebrations

The Gibraltar Government arranged a number of events in 2004 to celebrate the 300th anniversary of the capture of the Rock of Gibraltar by British and Dutch forces. It invited 500 UK war veterans to visit Gibraltar to commemorate all UK servicemen who have given their lives in defence of Gibraltar during the last 300 years, and to mark the special relationship that exists between Gibraltar and the UK Armed Forces.

Administration of foreign policy

Foreign & Commonwealth Office

The FCO is headed by the Secretary of State for Foreign and Commonwealth Affairs, a cabinet minister (see page 55) who is also responsible for the Diplomatic Service (see page 59). The FCO maintains diplomatic, consular and commercial relations with about 190 countries, and the United Kingdom has 233 diplomatic posts worldwide. As well as about 2,000 diplomats from the United Kingdom, the diplomatic missions overseas employ 9,860 locally engaged staff. Staff in the diplomatic missions deal with political, commercial and economic work, entry clearance to the United Kingdom, and consular work, aid administration, information and other activities.

The Global Opportunities Fund was set up to fund projects around the world relating to UK foreign policy priorities (see page 67). The projects are coordinated through six themes: counter-terrorism; climate change and energy; engaging with the Islamic world; re-uniting Europe; strengthening relations with emerging markets; and human rights, democracy and good governance.

Under the 2004 Spending Review announced in July 2004, the FCO budget will increase from

£1.5 billion in 2004/05 to £1.7 billion in 2007/08. The extra funds will help to improve the security of diplomatic posts, following the bomb attacks on the British Consulate and the HSBC bank headquarters in Istanbul in November 2003 in which several people were killed, and help the FCO to continue to meet its international priorities. The Global Opportunities Fund was allocated £60 million a year for the period 2005/06 to 2007/08.

Consular services

In 2003, UK residents made 61.5 million trips abroad, a figure that has tripled over the past 20 years. Most enjoy a trouble-free trip, although FCO consular staff helped well over 85,000 UK nationals in 2003/04. Consular staff typically offer help and advice to: those who have been the victims of crime; those who find themselves injured or sick overseas; and the friends and families of UK citizens who die while overseas.

They also replace lost or stolen passports, assist in emergencies, natural disasters and major incidents, and act as a point of contact between UK citizens who have been imprisoned overseas and their families in the United Kingdom.

The Public Diplomacy Strategy Board was established in 2002 to improve government efforts to promote the image of the United Kingdom overseas. The Board meets three times a year, and includes senior personnel from other government departments (including the devolved administrations, see chapters 3 to 5), non-governmental organisations, the British Council, BBC World Service (see page 261), VisitBritain (see page 478) and the private sector. A £2 million Public Diplomacy Campaign Fund supports up to two major campaigns each year.

The FCO Public Diplomacy Challenge Fund (PDCF) was launched in early 2003 with an annual budget of about £2.5 million. It supports public diplomacy projects generated by Embassies and High Commissions.

The main elements of FCO-funded public diplomacy work are:

- the FCO website and the *www.i-uk.com* portal site, launched in 2002, which provides information on the United Kingdom;
- scholarship schemes for overseas students (see page 141) and programmes for influential foreign visitors;
- the BBC World Service;
- the British Council;
- British Satellite News, used extensively by overseas radio and television broadcasters to supplement their news coverage. BSN has a bilingual website; and
- the London Press Service, a UK-based online news and information service supplying material for publication overseas.

The FCO executive agency, Wilton Park in Steyning, West Sussex, organises conferences in the United Kingdom that are attended by politicians, business people, academics and other professionals from all over the world. It aims to organise a minimum of 40 conferences a year and contributes to the analysis and discussion of key international policy challenges and issues.

British Council

The British Council is the principal UK agency for educational and cultural relations overseas. Operating in 110 countries, its work includes teaching English, promoting UK education and training, running information centres, supporting good governance and human rights, and encouraging appreciation of UK science, arts, literature and design.

In 2003–04, the British Council employed 1,700 teachers in 126 teaching centres overseas and administered over 1 million professional and academic examinations. Other activities during the period included:

- collaborating in 1,950 arts events around the world;
- issuing 7.5 million books and videos to 300,000 British Council library members;
- dealing with 2.3 million enquiries; and
- helping over 15,000 UK people aged between 15 and 25 to meet and work with overseas partners in more than 600 projects.

The Council is financed partly by a grant from the FCO and partly by income from revenue-earning

activities such as English language teaching and the administration of examinations. Some of the programmes organised by the Council as part of the UK aid programme receive funding from DFID (see page 82). Under the 2004 Spending Review, its budget is set to rise from £173 million in 2004/05 to £197 million in 2007/08.

Educational exchanges

The British Council recruits teachers for work overseas, organises short overseas visits by UK experts, encourages cultural exchange visits, and organises academic interchange between UK universities and colleges and those in other countries. In 2003–04 the Council arranged nearly 2,500 work placements and more than 200 study visits in 31 countries across Europe.

Human rights

The UK Government has stated its commitment to work for improvements in human rights standards around the world. In September 2004, it published the seventh *Annual Report on Human Rights*.

International conventions

United Nations

Universal respect for human rights is an obligation under the UN Charter. Expressions of concern about human rights do not, therefore, constitute interference in the internal affairs of another state.

The UK Government supports the Universal Declaration of Human Rights, which the UN General Assembly adopted in 1948. Since this is not a legally binding document, the General Assembly in 1966 adopted two international covenants on human rights, imposing legal obligations on those states ratifying or acceding to them. The United Kingdom ratified both in 1976. One deals with economic, social and cultural rights and the other with civil and political rights. Other international instruments that the United Kingdom accedes to include those on:

- the elimination of racial discrimination;
- the elimination of all forms of discrimination against women;
- the rights of the child;
- the elimination of torture and other cruel, inhuman or degrading treatment or punishment;

- the prevention of genocide;
- the abolition of slavery; and
- the status of refugees.

Council of Europe

The United Kingdom is also bound by the Council of Europe's Convention for the Protection of Human Rights and Fundamental Freedoms (ECHR), which covers areas such as:

- the right to life, liberty and a fair trial;
- the right to marry and have a family;
- freedom of thought, conscience and religion;
- freedom of expression;
- freedom of peaceful assembly and association;
- the right to have a sentence reviewed by a higher tribunal; and
- the prohibition of torture and inhuman or degrading treatment.

The rights and obligations of the ECHR are enshrined in UK law by the *Human Rights Act 1998*. In October 2003, the United Kingdom ratified Protocol 13 to the ECHR banning the death penalty in all circumstances.

International Criminal Court

The United Kingdom supported the establishment of an International Criminal Court to try cases of genocide, crimes against humanity and war crimes. Ratification took place in 2001. Over 90 other states have ratified the Statute (although not the United States, which does not recognise its jurisdiction) and the Court came into existence in July 2002. The Court is based in The Hague in The Netherlands and its powers are not retrospective.

Development co-operation

UK development aid policy is linked to internationally agreed development targets, the Millennium Development Goals. The UK Government is shifting its assistance from individual projects to direct support to governments that are implementing agreed poverty reduction strategies and better financial management. The *International Development Act 2002* outlaws the use of UK aid for any other purpose than poverty reduction. DFID plans to spend 90 per cent of its bilateral aid budget in the poorest countries by 2005/06.

Official development assistance (ODA) is set to rise from 0.26 per cent of gross national income (GNI) in 1997 to 0.47 per cent by 2007/08. At this rate of progress, the Government anticipates that it will meet the UN target of 0.7 per cent of GNI by 2013. Most of the ODA is channelled through DFID.

In 2003/04, DFID's expenditure was £3.9 billion (Figures 7.2 and 7.3). Almost £2 billion was spent bilaterally, of which 48 per cent went to Asia, and 43 per cent to Africa, and £1.8 billion went to multilateral agencies.

Under the 2004 Spending Review DFID's budget is planned to rise to £4.5 billion in 2005/06, £5.0 billion in 2006/07, and £5.3 billion in 2007/08. From these resources, UK bilateral aid to Africa will increase to at least £1.25 billion a year by 2008.

Millennium Development Goals

All members of the UN made a commitment in 2000 to meet the Millennium Development Goals by 2015:

- reduce extreme poverty and hunger by halving the proportion of people whose income is less than $1 a day and the proportion of people who suffer from hunger;
- achieve universal primary education;

Figure 7.2 DFID bilateral aid programme, by aid type, 2003/04

Total: £2.0 billion

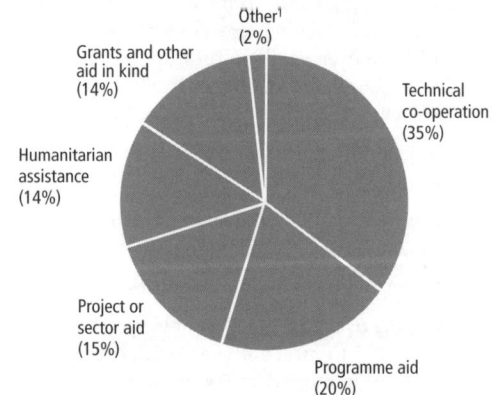

Other[1] (2%)
Grants and other aid in kind (14%)
Technical co-operation (35%)
Humanitarian assistance (14%)
Project or sector aid (15%)
Programme aid (20%)

1 Debt relief (1%), and aid and trade provision (1%).
Source: Department for International Development

Figure 7.3 DFID multilateral aid programme, by recipient agency, 2003/04

Total: £1.8 billion

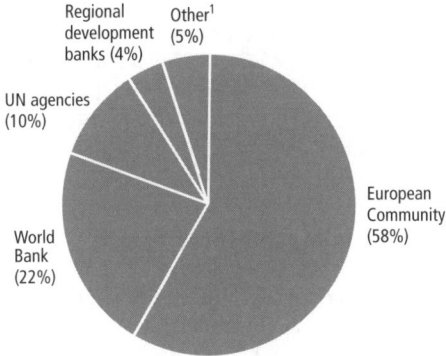

Regional development banks (4%)

Other[1] (5%)

UN agencies (10%)

World Bank (22%)

European Community (58%)

1 Includes Global Environmental Assistance (2%), International Monetary Fund (1%) and other agencies.
Source: Department for International Development

- promote gender equality and empower women by eliminating gender inequality in primary and secondary education;

- reduce under-five-year-old child mortality by two-thirds;

- improve maternal health by reducing maternal mortality by three-quarters;

- combat HIV/AIDS, malaria, and other diseases;

- ensure environmental sustainability, including reducing by half the number of people without access to clean drinking water; and

- develop a global partnership for development.

In 2003, the UK Government announced a proposal for an International Finance Facility (IFF) to help meet these goals by 2015. Its founding principle is long-term but conditional funding guaranteed to the poorest countries by the richest. The IFF would be a temporary financing mechanism that would 'frontload' donor commitments made at the UN International Conference on Financing in Monterrey in 2002 – resources promised in the long-term would be invested in tackling the causes rather than the symptoms of poverty in the short term. It would gain additional money from the international capital markets by issuing bonds, and aims to double levels of international aid for the world's

poorest countries, from just over $50 billion a year in 2003 to $100 billion a year in the years to 2015. The IMF and the World Bank have carried out an in-depth study of the IFF proposal and a report will be published in autumn 2004.

Debt relief

The UK Government is pressing for continued progress on implementation of the revised 1999 Heavily Indebted Poor Countries (HIPC) debt initiative, which is designed to deliver broader and faster relief to countries committed to poverty reduction. The United Kingdom is the second largest bilateral contributor to the HIPC Trust Fund. It has cancelled the aid debts for all the poorest countries, not just HIPC countries, affecting debt of around £1.2 billion.

Health

Three of the eight Millennium Development Goals involve health. The United Kingdom was an advocate for the Global Fund for AIDS, TB and Malaria (GFATM) to increase access to effective treatments against these diseases. Launched in January 2002, the Fund has attracted $5 billion in pledges over eight years from 43 countries as well as major foundations and private donors. At least £1.5 billion of UK aid is planned for HIV/AIDs related work between 2005/06 and 2007/08.

Good governance and human rights

The UK Government believes the quality of governance has a major impact on economic growth and the effectiveness of services. It focuses on issues such as:

- democratic accountability (bringing poor people into the democratic process);

- fundamental freedoms (including rights to education, health and an adequate livelihood);

- combating child labour;

- tackling corruption and money laundering;

- better revenue and public finance management;

- access to basic services; and

- personal safety and security in the community, with access to justice.

Conflict and natural disasters

Many of the 40 poorest countries are either engaged in armed conflict or have only recently emerged from such conflict. UK objectives are to reduce the tensions that lead to conflict, limit the means of waging warfare, and provide timely and effective humanitarian assistance and support needed for long-term reconstruction.

The United Kingdom seeks to improve the quality and speed of response to a disaster; promote early transition from emergency assistance to rehabilitation and reconstruction; and help countries to reduce their vulnerability to natural, environmental and industrial disasters. It is also committed to strengthening the response of multilateral institutions to humanitarian relief and crisis management.

In 2001, two conflict prevention pools were set up to bring together FCO, MoD and DFID skills and resources in conflict prevention activity. The Global Conflict Prevention Pool has carried out conflict prevention and peacebuilding activities in, among other areas, the Balkans, India, the Middle East, Nepal, Pakistan, the former Soviet Union and Sri Lanka. The budget for the Global Conflict Prevention Pool will be maintained at £74 million a year between 2005 and 2008. The United Kingdom worked through the Africa Conflict Prevention Pool to underpin African (and subsequently UN) peace support operations in Burundi, Côte d'Ivoire and Liberia in 2003/04. It also played a role in the peace processes in the Democratic Republic of the Congo, Somalia, Sudan and Uganda, as well as continuing its peace-building programmes in Angola, Rwanda and Sierra Leone. The budget for the Africa Conflict Prevention Pool is £60 million in 2004/05.

By early June 2004, the United Kingdom had earmarked £18 million in response to the humanitarian crisis in Darfur in western Sudan. The United Kingdom has committed £544 million to humanitarian and reconstruction assistance in Iraq for the period April 2003 to March 2006.

In June 2003, the 18 leading humanitarian donor governments agreed in Stockholm to pursue a series of measures, known as the Good Humanitarian Donorship initiative, to improve the effectiveness and efficiency of international humanitarian action. The UK Government is a strong supporter of this initiative, which seeks to promote more equitable resource allocation, more robust needs assessment and stronger coordination and strategic prioritisation.

In November 2003, the National Audit Office published a report *Department for International Development: Responding to Humanitarian Emergencies* that concluded that DFID responded quickly and flexibly to humanitarian emergencies, particularly when dealing with sudden disasters, and that it had contributed to the saving of lives.

Peacekeeping and security

The UN is the principal body responsible for the maintenance of international peace and security. In April 2004, it was maintaining 14 peacekeeping operations around the world involving about 53,000 military personnel and civilian police from 96 countries. The United Kingdom contributes military personnel to UN operations around the world (see also page 94).

The United Kingdom has a contingent of 410 troops in the UN Force in Cyprus, established in 1964 to help prevent the recurrence of fighting between Greek and Turkish Cypriots. Since the hostilities of 1974, when Turkish forces occupied the northern part of the island, the Force has been responsible for monitoring the ceasefire and for control of a buffer zone between the two communities.

The United Kingdom helps to fund the International Criminal Tribunal in The Hague, established to bring to trial those indicted for war crimes in the former Yugoslavia, and provides staff, information and forensic science expertise. UK forces have been at the forefront of SFOR's efforts to detain war crimes suspects.

The United Kingdom provides about 110 civilian police, along with specialist officers, local government administrators and judicial experts to the UN interim civilian administration, which is helping to establish self-government in the province. The United Kingdom maintains its commitment to the Kosovo Force, contributing around 220 personnel.

Arms control

The United Kingdom has a national interest in preventing proliferation of weapons of mass destruction and promoting international control, given the global reach of modern weapons. The terrorist attacks in the United States of 11 September 2001 highlighted the need to prevent terrorists from obtaining such weapons.

Weapons of mass destruction

Proliferation Security Initiative

The Proliferation Security Initiative (PSI) was launched by the United States in May 2003. Under PSI, nations are trying to establish a coordinated and effective basis to prevent states and others from trafficking in weapons of mass destruction

and delivery systems. The United Kingdom has taken a leading role in the development of PSI.

Nuclear weapons

The UK Government remains committed to the Treaty on the Non-Proliferation of Nuclear Weapons (NPT), which entered into force in 1970. The United Kingdom is recognised as a nuclear weapons state under the NPT (see also page 94).

The United Kingdom has ratified the Comprehensive Test Ban Treaty (CTBT). The CTBT, with its permanent verification system, will come into force upon ratification by the remaining

Butler Inquiry into Weapons of Mass Destruction

In February 2004, the Government established a committee of inquiry to review the intelligence on weapons of mass destruction (WMD), chaired by Lord Butler of Brockwell. The committee's terms of reference were:

- to investigate the intelligence coverage available in respect of WMD;

- to investigate the accuracy of the intelligence on Iraqi WMD up to March 2003; and

- to make recommendations on gathering, evaluation and use of intelligence on WMD.

The Butler Inquiry reported its findings in July 2004. Its conclusions included the following:

- The importance of co-operation with international agencies such as the UN Special Commission and the International Atomic Energy Agency, supported by the contribution of intelligence from national agencies.

- Further steps are needed to integrate the relevant work of the Defence Intelligence Staff (DIS) with the rest of the intelligence community.

- The Security and Intelligence Coordinator should review the size and resources of the Assessments Staff (who make objective assessments of the intelligence reports).

- The 'informality' of government procedures in the context of policy-making towards Iraq risks reducing the scope for informed collective political judgement.

- Part of the reason for doubt over a high proportion of human intelligence sources arose from weaknesses in the effective application by Secret Intelligence Service (SIS) of its validation procedures and in their proper resourcing.

- In general the intelligence material was correctly reported and the intelligence community made good use of the technical expertise available to the Government. The Committee found no evidence of deliberate distortion or judgements being altered to meet the policy concerns of senior officials.

- The claim that Iraq could use weapons of mass destruction within 45 minutes should not have been made in the Government's weapons dossier without explaining what the claim referred to.

- There is a strong case for the chairperson of the Joint Intelligence Committee to be someone with experience of dealing with Ministers in a senior role and who is demonstrably beyond influence.

- It would be helpful to bring together more closely counter-proliferation expertise by creation of a 'virtual' network across government.

These and other conclusions and recommendations have implications for the way in which intelligence business will be conducted in the future. This is being taken forward by the Cabinet Office in consultation with Departments and the Intelligence Agencies.

12 of 44 named states (in Annex 2 of the Treaty) that participated in the 1996 Conference on Disarmament and that possessed nuclear power or research reactors at that time. The UK Government has also participated in efforts to start negotiations on a treaty banning the future production of fissile material for use in nuclear weapons.

The United Kingdom welcomed the Treaty of Moscow (Strategic Offensive Reductions Treaty) between Russia and the United States. This came into force in 2003 and aims to reduce the strategic nuclear warheads that are deployed by these two countries by two-thirds by 2012.

Biological weapons

The 1972 Biological and Toxic Weapons Convention (BTWC) provides for a worldwide ban on such weapons, but there are no effective compliance mechanisms. The United Kingdom continues to look for ways of strengthening the Convention.

The BTWC Fifth Review Conference in 2002 unanimously agreed a programme for 2002–05 that includes national implementation of the Convention; capabilities for investigating cases of alleged use of biological or toxin weapons or suspicious outbreaks of disease; sharing best practice on disease surveillance; and developing a code of conduct for scientists. The UK Government strongly supports and continues to participate in this programme of follow-up work.

Chemical weapons

The 1993 Chemical Weapons Convention, which came into force in 1997, provides for a worldwide ban on these weapons. The Organisation for the Prohibition of Chemical Weapons (OPCW), which is responsible for verification, held its first Review Conference in May 2003.

The United Kingdom is committed to providing assistance to Russia for the destruction of its huge chemical weapons stockpile. UK assistance is focused on Shchuch'ye in the Urals, Russia's main chemical weapon destruction facility. Following completion of a first project in 2003 (construction of the water supply), the United Kingdom is procuring equipment for the electricity substation that directly supports the destruction facility. The United Kingdom is contributing some £4.5 million and the Czech Republic, the EU and Norway are also contributing through the UK programme.

The United Kingdom plans to continue working closely with other donors, including Canada, in implementing further projects at Shchuch'ye.

Conventional Armed Forces

The UK Government continues to work with its NATO and OSCE partners to develop and improve agreements on enhancing stability in the Atlantic–Eurasia region. The main agreements reached are:

- the Conventional Armed Forces in Europe (CFE) Treaty (entered into force in 1992 and adopted in 1999), is widely regarded as a linchpin of European security;

- the Vienna Document, developed under the auspices of the OSCE, is a politically binding agreement concerning the promotion of stability by building transparency, confidence and trust across the OSCE area; and

- the 1992 Open Skies Treaty permits overflight and photographing of the entire territory of the 30 participating states to monitor their military capabilities and activities. The Treaty entered into force on 1 January 2002.

The UN Register of Conventional Arms, which came into effect in 1992, is intended to allow greater transparency in international transfers of conventional arms and to help identify excessive arms build-up in any one country or region. Countries are requested on a voluntary basis to report imports and exports of seven categories of major conventional weapons that have been assessed as having the greatest potential to be destabilising. Participation in the Register has grown since its inception; by the end of July 2003, 165 Member States had participated at least once, while almost all the major producers, exporters and importers of conventional arms were reporting regularly to the Register.

Landmines

The United Kingdom signed the Ottawa Convention banning the use, production, trade, transfer and stockpiling of anti-personnel landmines in 1997, and destroyed its stockpile after the Convention entered into force in 1999.

The United Kingdom has a programme to support humanitarian demining activities. This aims to help affected countries develop the capacity to clear landmines and to improve the coordination of international demining resources.

Export controls

The United Kingdom is committed to maintaining one of the most rigorous and transparent arms export control systems in the world. It is a founding member of all the international regimes that control the export of conventional arms, and of dual-use technologies with both civilian and military applications, particularly those that might also contribute to the development of weapons of mass destruction, and missiles capable of delivering such weapons.

In 1997, the UK Government issued new criteria for assessing licence applications for arms exports that, among other things, prohibit the granting of licences where there is a clear risk that these exports might be used for internal repression or international aggression. At the same time, it banned the export of certain items for use in torture. It is committed to preventing UK companies from manufacturing, selling or procuring such equipment, and is seeking a global ban.

In 1998, EU Member States agreed on a Code of Conduct on Arms Exports, setting common standards to which all EU members would adhere. In 2003 the United Kingdom also supported an EU common position on trafficking and brokering.

Export Control Act

Under the *Export Control Act 2002*, which came into force in May 2004, a licence is required for all trafficking and brokering activities in military equipment that take place wholly or partly in the United Kingdom. Extraterritorial controls have been introduced on trafficking and brokering of military equipment to embargoed destinations, and the export of torture equipment or long-range missiles to any destination by UK persons anywhere in the world. The Act has also introduced new controls on the transfer abroad of military technology by electronic means.

International terrorism

The UK Government regards acts of terrorism as unacceptable in all circumstances and opposes concessions to any terrorist demands. It wishes to eliminate terrorism as a force in international affairs.Working bilaterally with other like-minded

governments, and multilaterally through the UN, EU, G8 and other international and regional organisations, it aims to promote effective and sustained action against terrorist groups and to foster closer international coordination of the fight against terrorism. The United Kingdom has been at the forefront of international efforts to increase controls on the transfer of man-portable air defence systems (MANPADS), which pose a significant threat to civilian aircraft. This work includes co-operative action to collect, secure and, wherever possible, destroy MANPADS.

The UK Government has stepped up assistance to countries that lack the means to tackle terrorism, and is committed to challenging the political, social and economic conditions that terrorists exploit. It has allocated £60 million a year for the period 2005/06 to 2007/08 to the FCO Global Opportunities Fund (see page 80), which includes a counter-terrorism programme. The United Kingdom has ratified all 12 UN terrorism conventions.

International crime

The UK Government strongly supports international efforts to combat illegal drugs, working with producer and transit countries.

Working with international partners, the UK Government helps Latin American, Caribbean and Central Asian states to stem the transit of drugs from and across their territories. The United Kingdom is one of the biggest contributors to the UN Office on Drugs and Crime. The United Kingdom plays a role in coordinating international anti-narcotics assistance to support Afghanistan's fight against drugs under the Afghanistan National Drug Control Strategy, which came into effect in May 2003. To support implementation of the Strategy, the United Kingdom has committed £70 million.

With its EU partners, the United Kingdom is confronting serious and organised international crime through Europol, which supports investigations and operations conducted by national law enforcement agencies. EU Member States also belong to the International Criminal Police Organisation (Interpol). The National Criminal Intelligence Service UK (see page 205) provides liaison with Interpol. Over 100 law enforcement liaison officers are stationed in UK missions in key countries, in co-operation with the host governments.

The United Kingdom supports international efforts to counter financial crime, through its membership of the Financial Action Task Force against money laundering, and by backing regional anti-money laundering groups.

Further reading

Foreign & Commonwealth Office UK International Priorities – A strategy for the FCO. Cm 6052. The Stationery Office, 2003.

Foreign & Commonwealth Office Departmental Report 2004. Cm 6213. The Stationery Office, 2004.

Department for International Development Departmental Report 2004: The Government's Expenditure Plans 2002–03 to 2006–07. Cm 6214. The Stationery Office, 2004.

Human Rights Annual Report 2004. Foreign & Commonwealth Office, 2004.

Review of Intelligence on Weapons of Mass Destruction (the Butler Review). The Stationery Office, 2004.

Websites

Foreign & Commonwealth Office
www.fco.gov.uk

Department for International Development
www.DfID.gov.uk

Ministry of Defence
www.mod.uk

British Council
www.britcoun.org

Commonwealth Secretariat
www.thecommonwealth.org

Council of Europe
www.coe.int

European Union (Europa)
www.europa.eu.int

Organisation for Security and Co-operation in Europe
www.osce.org

United Nations
www.un.org

WWW.

8   Defence

Defence policy

The United Kingdom contributes to international peace and security through membership of a variety of international organisations (see chapter 7) and is a permanent member of the United Nations (UN) Security Council. It is a leading military contributor to the North Atlantic Treaty Organisation (NATO) alliance (see page 91) and operations involving the European Union (EU, see page 93). The security and stability of Europe and the maintenance of the transatlantic relationship with the United States are fundamental to UK security and defence policy.

The Ministry of Defence (MoD) is responsible for implementing defence policy and is also the headquarters of UK military services. Its primary objective is to deliver security for the people of the United Kingdom and its Overseas Territories (OTs, see page 77) by defending them, including against terrorism, and to act as a force for good by strengthening international peace and stability.

In December 2003 the MoD published a White Paper, *Delivering Security in a Changing World*. It gives an assessment of the security environment, and is a policy baseline for the MoD to make decisions to provide the Armed Forces with the structures and capabilities they need to carry out the operations they can expect to undertake in the future. The main conclusions of the White Paper were:

- There are no major conventional military threats to the United Kingdom or to other members of NATO. The three challenges to peace and security are those posed by international terrorism; the threat associated with weapons of mass destruction; and the consequences of failed and failing states.

- The United Kingdom will remain engaged in potential areas of instability in and around Europe, the Near East, North Africa and the Gulf. But it must improve its ability to carry out military activities further afield than envisaged in the 1998 Strategic Defence Review (SDR), to encompass sub-Saharan Africa and South Asia, and to meet the wider threat from international terrorism.

- There is a need to strike the right balance of capabilities to meet the demands of the eight strategic military effects – prevent, stabilise, contain, deter, coerce, disrupt, defeat and destroy.

- The structure of the Armed Forces needs to be optimised to be able to support three concurrent small and medium scale operations, where at least one is an enduring peace support operation, including the ability to act as lead or framework nation for coalition operations.

- The United Kingdom will retain the ability to prepare at longer notice for the less frequent, but more demanding, large scale operations, while concurrently conducting a small scale operation. The full spectrum of military capabilities is not required at large scale, as the most demanding operations could only conceivably be undertaken alongside the United States, either as part of NATO or leading a coalition. The United Kingdom would choose what capabilities to contribute.

- Modernising the UK Armed Forces will continue, concentrating on speed, precision, agility, deployability, reach and sustainability. Key to this will be the ability to exploit the benefits of advancing technology.

- The MoD will support the Home Office and other civil authorities charged with the safety and security of the United Kingdom, through routine military activities and being prepared to provide support in a crisis.

UK security

The Armed Forces are responsible for safeguarding UK territory, airspace and territorial waters. They also operate around the world to protect UK interests and are responsible for the defence of the UK OTs. In addition, they assist the civil authorities in both the United Kingdom and the OTs.

Maritime defence

The Royal Navy is responsible for the delivery of the UK Strategic Nuclear Deterrent (see page 94). Ships of the Navy and Royal Fleet Auxiliary patrol, police and defend UK territorial waters and protect UK rights and interests (including offshore oil and gas reserves) in the surrounding seas and around the world. The maintenance of a 24-hour, year-round presence in the waters around the British Isles, in conjunction with the RAF's maritime patrol aircraft, upholds the security of the seas and reassures merchant and other types of shipping. Threats to UK-flagged ships overseas, particularly in view of the continuing global terrorist threat, also remain a national responsibility. The United Kingdom maintains a worldwide expeditionary capability based around aircraft carriers that operate RAF Joint Force Harriers.

Land defence

The Army aims to have the capability to defend the United Kingdom and its OTs. It is also committed to such tasks as offering military aid to peacekeeping and humanitarian operations, responding to regional conflicts outside the NATO area, and contributing forces to counter a strategic attack on NATO. It works closely with the other Services and is geared towards rapid reaction and mobility, pre-empting a crisis if possible. It usually acts with its allies but can act alone.

Air defence

A system of layered defences maintains the air defence of the United Kingdom and the surrounding seas. The Air Surveillance and Control System (ASACS), supplemented by the NATO Airborne Early Warning Force to which the RAF contributes six aircraft, provides continuous radar cover. The RAF contributes four squadrons of Tornado F3 air defence aircraft, supported by tanker aircraft, and in wartime, an additional F3 squadron. Royal Navy air defence destroyers may also be linked to the ASACS, providing radar and electronic warfare coverage, and surface-to-air missiles. Ground-launched Rapier missiles defend the main RAF bases. Naval aircraft also contribute to UK air defence.

Northern Ireland

The Armed Forces support the police in Northern Ireland in maintaining law and order and countering terrorism (see page 34). The number of units deployed depends on the prevailing security situation. In May 2004 there were 12,000 military personnel deployed in Northern Ireland.

Overseas garrisons

The United Kingdom maintains garrisons or detachments in Ascension Island, Belize, Brunei, the Sovereign Base Areas of Cyprus, Diego Garcia, the Falkland Islands and Gibraltar. Gibraltar contains support, logistics, communications and training facilities in the western Mediterranean, while Cyprus provides base facilities in the eastern Mediterranean. The garrison on the Falkland Islands reflects the Government's commitment to uphold the islanders' right to determine their own future (see page 79). The garrison in Brunei is maintained at the request of the Brunei Government and the unit in Belize is for jungle warfare-training.

UK intelligence and security services

The United Kingdom has three intelligence and security services:

- the Secret Intelligence Service (SIS), also known as MI6, is responsible for obtaining information and conducting operations in support of UK foreign policy objectives, and seeks to counter threats to UK interests worldwide;

- the Security Service (also known as MI5) is responsible for protection against threats to national security, primarily from terrorism and espionage. In February 2004, the Government announced plans to expand MI5 from about 2,100 employees to 3,000 by 2008;

- the Government Communications Headquarters (GCHQ) carries out signals intelligence supporting national security, military operations and law enforcement, and also helps to secure government communications and key systems supporting UK infrastructure.

The SIS and GCHQ are responsible to the Foreign and Commonwealth Secretary, while the Security Service is responsible to the Home Secretary. The planned budget for these agencies in 2004/05 is £1.2 billion. The MoD has its own defence intelligence staff, which provides intelligence analyses, assessments, advice and strategic warnings.

Other tasks

Other activities include the provision of military aid to the civil authorities, such as:

- emergency cover during the firemen's strike of 2003;

- assisting the police in response to terrorist threats and helping in the fight against drugs;

- assistance in dealing with terrorist devices and bombs left over from both world wars;

- fishery protection duties;

- military search and rescue; and

- other support to the civil community, for example during floods.

In January 2004 the Government published the Civil Contingencies Bill, aimed at modernising and improving the way the United Kingdom deals with potential threats from terrorist incidents or other civil emergencies. The Bill would allow the Government to restrict public access to 'sensitive sites', evacuate affected areas, deploy the Armed Forces, requisition property, ban public gatherings and set up a special court to deal with a disaster.

International security

North Atlantic Treaty Organisation

The defence of the United Kingdom and its economic and wider interests is linked to the security of the Euro-Atlantic area. NATO is the primary means of guaranteeing that security and embodies a unique defence and security partnership between North America and Europe. Membership of NATO is a cornerstone of UK defence policy. The United Kingdom is a founder member and most of its forces are assigned to the organisation.

NATO formally admitted seven new members in March 2004: Bulgaria, Estonia, Latvia, Lithuania, Romania, Slovakia and Slovenia. The expansion was the biggest in the history of NATO and brings NATO's membership to 26. Further rounds of

enlargement may take place in the future with Albania, Croatia and the former Yugoslav Republic of Macedonia.

NATO was created in 1949 in response to the ideological, political and military threat from communism and the former USSR. It has adapted to changes in the security environment in Europe, which have involved a fundamental transformation in the alliance's relationship with Russia after the terrorist attacks in the United States in 2001. In 2002 the NATO–Russia Council (NRC) replaced the NATO Russia Permanent Joint Council. The NRC provides NATO allies and Russia with a mechanism for consultation, consensus-building, co-operation and joint action on security issues of common interest, including terrorism, crisis management and non-proliferation. Work has been progressing well, with NATO and Russia working as equal partners.

NATO's security tasks are:

- to provide a firm basis for stability and security in the European and Atlantic areas;

- to serve as a transatlantic forum for any issues that affect Allied interests;

- to deter and defend against any threat of aggression directed towards any NATO Member State wherever that threat may arise – an attack on one member is treated as an attack on all;

- to contribute to effective conflict prevention and crisis management; and

- to promote partnership, co-operation and dialogue with other countries in the Euro-Atlantic area, including Russia.

NATO reassessed its defence policy after 11 September 2001. NATO foreign ministers agreed in 2002 that alliance forces could be used wherever they were needed to counter the new threats of terrorism and weapons of mass destruction. Subsequent decisions were that NATO should take the lead role on the International Security Assistance Force (ISAF) in Afghanistan, and offer assistance to Poland in its operation in Iraq.

Heads of State and Government of NATO members also adopted measures in 2002 aimed at strengthening the alliance's preparedness and ability to manage the full spectrum of security challenges, including terrorism and the spread of weapons of mass destruction. The transformation of NATO will involve:

- a new command structure and headquarters to meet the new security climate;
- a NATO Response Force (NRF);
- the development of new capabilities to fill critical combat shortfalls; and
- reform of NATOs administration.

In August 2003, NATO's international staff was re-organised into six main divisions. The NRF was inaugurated in October 2003. It is expected to achieve initial operational capability within one year and to reach full operational capability by the end of 2006.

NATO's multinational Chemical, Biological, Radiological and Nuclear Defence Battalion achieved initial operational capability in December 2003. It is designed to provide a response and defence against the use of weapons of mass destruction both inside and beyond NATO's area of responsibility.

At the 2004 NATO Summit held in Istanbul, one of the key themes was strengthening NATO's partnerships. NATO was looking in particular to increase co-operation with the Caucasus and Central Asia, and to reinforce links in the Mediterranean. NATO also remains committed to developing its relationship with Ukraine, through the NATO–Ukraine Commission. In 2002, NATO and Ukraine launched an action plan to develop closer political and practical co-operation.

Anniversary of the Crimean War

The year 2004 marked the 150th anniversary of UK involvement in the Crimean War. On 20 September 1854 a joint invasion force of more than 60,000 British, French and Turkish troops went into battle against Russia in the Crimea.

Florence Nightingale is famous for the help she gave to the sick and wounded during the Crimean War. That she was described as a 'passionate statistician' is less well known. She compiled quantities of statistics in her drive for hospital reform and standardised the reporting of deaths using *Miss Nightingale's scheme for Uniform Hospital Statistics*.

The UK in NATO

Maritime forces

Most Royal Navy ships are available to NATO, with a continued commitment declared to two of its standing naval forces, the provision of a High Readiness Force Maritime Headquarters and contributions to the NATO Response Forces. The United Kingdom also contributes to NATO's maritime augmentation forces, which are held at the lowest state of readiness and, in peacetime, comprise ships mainly in routine refit or maintenance.

The main components of the UK fleet available to NATO are:

- Invincible class aircraft carriers operating Joint Force Harrier aircraft and Sea King or Merlin anti-submarine helicopters;
- destroyers and frigates and mine counter-measure vessels;
- nuclear-powered attack submarines for long-range, stealth operations and precision land attack with Tomahawk missiles;
- amphibious forces, including a commando brigade of the Royal Marines, and specialist amphibious shipping providing a self-contained expeditionary capability; and
- survey vessels and a collection of logistic support ships.

Land forces

The key land component of NATO's Rapid Reaction Forces is the multinational HQ of the Allied Command Europe Rapid Reaction Corps (ARRC) and its supporting forces. The HQ ARRC is capable of deploying at short notice up to four NATO divisions, and is commanded by a UK General. The United Kingdom provides two of the ten divisions available to the Corps. Up to 55,000 UK troops may be assigned to HQ ARRC for operations. An air-mobile brigade, assigned to one of the Corps' multinational divisions, is also based in the United Kingdom.

Air forces

The RAF contributes its full range of air capability to NATO's Graduated Readiness Forces, allocating around 120 aircraft and 40 helicopters. The RAF maintains an airlift capability, both strategic and tactical, that can contribute to supply and troop airlift facilities for deployed forces, including the ARRC. It also provides Nimrod maritime patrol aircraft and search and rescue helicopters. In addition, it is the main European provider of air-to-air refuelling, and normally contributes 25 per cent of the NATO airborne early warning and control component.

The RAF has offered air force elements, including the UK Joint Force Air Component Command Headquarters, for the initial rotations of the NATO Response Force (NRF), a joint force held at high readiness for a variety of missions. The RAF also provides elements to the Joint Nuclear, Biological and Chemical (NBC) Regiment (in co-operation with the Army) that provides a range of specialist capabilities. Both the NRF and the NBC are to be operational by the end of 2006.

European security and defence policy

NATO remains the cornerstone of European territorial defence for its members and the natural choice for an operation involving European and American Allies. However, in 1998, it was agreed that the European countries needed to improve their ability to implement their common foreign and security policy objectives in circumstances where NATO is not involved. The EU needed the ability to use military and police forces in addition to the other economic, humanitarian and judicial responses available.

In 1999 the EU launched its European security and defence policy (ESDP), with the aims of strengthening European military capabilities (to benefit NATO, the EU and Member States) and of enabling the EU to undertake crisis management operations where NATO was not involved militarily. Later that year the EU set itself the goal of being able to deploy 60,000 troops capable of conducting crisis management tasks within 60 days and to sustain them for a year.

By May 2003 more than 100,000 troops had been pledged and the goal achieved, although it was limited by recognised shortfalls in certain capabilities. The UK contribution to forces available to the EU involves around 12,500 ground troops, 18 warships and 72 combat aircraft. However, as with NATO and UN operations, national forces are offered to EU operations on a case-by-case basis, dependent on national decisions, and working to national rules of engagement.

The UK Government has ensured ESDP develops alongside NATO. The EU has a strategic

partnership with NATO in crisis management, and in December 2002 the two organisations signed a joint agreement ensuring that the EU could have access to NATO planning in order to run its own military operations. The EU's first military peace support operation drawing on NATO capabilities started in March 2003, to help build peace and security in the former Yugoslav Republic of Macedonia. This concluded successfully in December 2003. In June 2003, the EU began its first operation without recourse to NATO, rapidly deploying over 2,000 troops to stabilise the security environment in the Democratic Republic of the Congo. The EU also has two police missions in Bosnia and the former Yugoslav Republic of Macedonia.

The EU is planning its third military operation, in close consultation with NATO, to deploy some 7,000 troops in a stabilisation mission to Bosnia, following on from the conclusion of NATO's SFOR operation in December 2004. This will be the largest ESDP operation yet, and the first since the EU enlarged to 25 countries in May 2004 (see page 71). The EU will be leading the military operation for the first year.

A new civil/military unit is planned that will improve EU coordination of civil and military responses. This will have the capacity to set up an operations centre to run a joint civil/military operation in certain circumstances.

European military capability will continue to be strengthened. Member States have agreed to make available to the EU by 2007 'battlegroups' of around 1,500 troops capable of rapid deployment within 15 days and of being sustained for an initial period of 30 days. These groups would be provided either by one nation or multinationally, and would be deployed primarily in support of the UN. In June 2004 a new goal was agreed for the year 2010 that focuses on the speed of response and quality of European capability, such as improving inter-operability and how well forces can be deployed and sustained.

In June 2004 the EU agreed to set up a European Defence Agency by the end of 2004. This will:

- promote and facilitate the development of new European capabilities;

- evaluate the capabilities offered by EU Member States;

- foster defence research and development; and
- work with the Commission to develop a more open and internationally competitive defence market in Europe.

Wider security interests

UK forces working within NATO, assisting the UN, operating in coalition with allies, or acting alone may undertake military tasks to promote wider UK security interests. Since the attacks in the United States on 11 September 2001, UK Armed Forces have taken a prominent role in the fight against terrorism. The United Kingdom, for example, contributed considerable forces in the Iraq conflict in the early part of 2003 (see page 95), and maintained a large force in Iraq in 2004.

United Nations

As a permanent member of the Security Council the United Kingdom has particular responsibility to ensure the success of the UN. It supports the UN by offering forces for selective operations and providing officers to key posts in UN missions.

The United Kingdom is actively training peacekeeping troops from third party countries, particularly in Africa. This will give the UN a pool of quality manpower to call upon, and will enable African states to do more of their own peacekeeping. The United Kingdom is also working with EU partners on the 'battlegroup' concept (see page 93) to offer rapid deployment capacity for temporary and focused support of UN operations. A large proportion of the newly formed Joint Rapid Reaction Forces could be made available for future UN peacekeeping operations, although the decision to deploy these forces rests with the United Kingdom.

The United Kingdom contributes some 7.4 per cent of the costs of UN peacekeeping and in 2004 had 22 military observers and 434 troops deployed on UN operations worldwide, including in the Democratic Republic of the Congo, Cyprus, Ethiopia-Eritrea, Georgia, Liberia and Sierra Leone. Over 2,500 troops are deployed with NATO on UN-mandated operations in Bosnia-Herzegovina and Kosovo, including experienced specialist personnel in the UN humanitarian mine action programme. In March 2004, following violent clashes in Kosovo, a further 750 UK personnel were temporarily deployed in Kosovo.

Other activities

UK forces are involved in operations against traffickers in illicit drugs. In the Caribbean, for example, a Royal Navy destroyer or frigate works closely with the United States, the OTs in the area, and the regional authorities to combat such trafficking.

UK forces have also participated in international evacuation or humanitarian relief operations in Angola, the Caribbean and Central America, the Democratic Republic of the Congo, East Timor, Eritrea, Mozambique, Rwanda, Sierra Leone and Somalia.

In recognition of the changed post-Cold War strategic environment, a new defence mission, 'defence diplomacy', was created to give greater priority, impetus and coherence to various activities designed to prevent conflicts and promote peacetime diplomacy.

Three military tasks contribute to the defence diplomacy mission:

- arms control, non-proliferation, and confidence and security building measures;
- outreach activities designed to contribute to security and stability in Central and Eastern Europe, particularly in Russia but also extending to the Trans-Caucasus and Central Asia, through bilateral assistance and co-operation programmes; and
- military assistance programmes with overseas forces and defence communities not covered by outreach.

Nuclear forces

The United Kingdom, along with other members of NATO, has radically reduced its reliance on nuclear weapons, although it retains four Trident submarines as the ultimate guarantee of national security.

The United Kingdom maintains one Trident submarine on patrol throughout the year. It carries a load of 48 warheads. The submarine's missiles are not targeted and it is normally on several days' 'notice to fire'. Trident submarines on patrol also carry out a variety of secondary tasks without compromising their security. These include hydrographic data collection, equipment trials and exercises with other vessels.

The Trident Strategic Weapon System has three component parts:

- four Vanguard-class ballistic missile submarines – HMS *Vanguard*, *Vigilant*, *Victorious* and *Vengeance*. The four submarines enable the United Kingdom to maintain a continuous deterrent patrol at sea over the life of the Trident force;
- 58 Trident D-5 long-range ballistic missiles carried and launched by the Vanguard-class submarines; and
- fewer than 200 operationally available UK-designed and built nuclear warheads with which to equip the D-5 missiles.

The United Kingdom is the only nuclear power that has reduced its nuclear capability to a single system. It continues to support mutual, balanced and verifiable reductions in the number of nuclear weapons worldwide (see page 85). The Government will include UK nuclear weapons in any multilateral negotiations when it is satisfied that sufficient progress has been made to do so without endangering UK security interests.

The Defence White Paper published in December 2003 (see page 89) confirmed that the Government's nuclear policy set out in the 1998 SDR remained unchanged. Decisions on whether to replace Trident are likely to be needed within the next few years.

Defence equipment

Modern equipment is an essential part of the UK restructuring programme to increase the flexibility and mobility of the Armed Forces. A range of equipment and systems will enter service with the Armed Forces over the next few years.

Improvements in the Royal Navy equipment programme include the introduction of:

- the Astute-class attack submarines;
- two new aircraft carriers, which will deploy the new jointly operated RN/RAF F35 Joint Combat Aircraft;
- the Type 45 destroyer, which will deploy an anti-air missile system developed with France and Italy;
- two new landing platform dock ships, *Albion* and *Bulwark*. These operate with high-speed landing craft, enabling the swift insertion or

Iraq

UK forces played a pivotal role in the US-led coalition assault on Iraq, which began on 20 March 2003 and ended the following month on 14 April. On 22 May 2003 the UN Security Council approved Resolution 1483 lifting economic sanctions against Iraq and recognising the status of the United States and the United Kingdom as occupying powers. The United Kingdom continued to command multinational divisions in the south of the country during 2003 and 2004. UK forces will remain in Iraq with the consent of the Iraqi government for as long as they are needed, with the scale of UK commitment dependent on the security situation and progress in handing over responsibility to Iraqi security forces.

In December 2003, the MoD published a report, *Operations in Iraq: Lessons for the Future*. The key points in the report included:

- the rapid deployment of a balanced joint force of 46,000 personnel was an exceptional achievement and the operation demonstrated the extent to which the UK Armed Forces can deliver the expeditionary capabilities envisaged in the 1998 Strategic Defence Review (SDR) and the 2002 SDR New Chapter;
- the operation confirmed the need for highly versatile UK forces that are able to mount small and medium-sized operations on a routine basis, while also being capable of meeting less frequent but larger and more demanding commitments.

withdrawal of vehicles, troops, refugees or evacuees. They will be supported by the new Royal Fleet Auxiliary Bay Class amphibious shipping component;

- updates to the Swiftsure and Trafalgar submarines to provide enhanced capabilities, including the ability to launch Tomahawk Land Attack Missiles; and
- six new roll-on/roll-off ferries, providing significant strategic lift capability.

The Army needs a balanced structure of light, medium and heavy forces. A new light brigade will be established and the number of armoured brigades will be reduced from three to two. The Army front line is being strengthened through the introduction of:

- the Bowman communications system;
- Apache attack helicopters equipped with new anti-tank missiles;
- improved Rapier and new Starstreak air defence missiles; and
- the Mobile Artillery Monitoring Battlefield Radar (MAMBA), which can accurately detect enemy artillery positions and can be deployed almost anywhere.

Improvements within the RAF include the introduction of:

- the Eurofighter Typhoon combat aircraft and new Nimrod maritime patrol and attack aircraft;
- EH101 and Chinook support helicopters;
- the C-17, C-130J, A400M transport aircraft and new air-to-air refuelling aircraft to replace VC10 and TriStar aircraft; and
- significant new weapons systems including the Storm Shadow Stand-Off Missile, the ASRAAM and Meteor air-to-air missiles and a new precision guided bomb.

In addition, the Joint Force Harrier force will be replaced with the F35 Joint Combat Aircraft operating from aircraft carriers and from land.

The Armed Forces

The Service Personnel Plan of April 2004 set out a strategy for recruiting, training and retaining Armed Forces personnel and for responding to social and demographic trends. Table 8.1 shows the rank structure of the UK Armed Forces.

Commissioned ranks

Commissions are granted either by promotion from the ranks or by direct entry based on educational and other qualifications. All three Services have school, college and university sponsorship schemes.

Commissioned ranks receive initial training, dependent on their Service, at the Britannia Royal Naval College, Dartmouth; the Commando

Training Centre, Lympstone, Devon; the Royal Military Academy, Sandhurst; or the Royal Air Force College, Cranwell. Specialist training follows and may include degree courses at Service establishments or universities. The Joint Services Command and Staff College at Shrivenham (Wiltshire) provides courses of higher training for officers, designed to emphasise the joint approach to tactical and operational levels of conflict.

Non-commissioned ranks

Engagements for non-commissioned ranks vary widely in length and terms of service. Subject to a minimum period, entrants may leave at any time if they give 18 months' notice (12 months' for certain engagements). Discharge may also be granted on compassionate or medical grounds.

After basic training, non-commissioned personnel receive supplementary specialist training throughout their careers. Study for educational qualifications is encouraged. The MoD, with Department for Education and Skills assistance, has started screening new entrants to identify those with literacy or numeracy needs. A network of tutors, teaching assistants and computer hardware and software will be used to support the development of these basic skills. Beyond this, Service trade and technical training is wherever possible accredited to nationally recognised qualifications ranging from National Vocational Qualifications to postgraduate degrees. For young people wishing to join the Armed Forces the Army Foundation College offers a 42-week course combining military training and the opportunity to acquire national qualifications. The course aims to attract high-quality recruits who will go on to fill senior posts in front-line roles.

Work is under way to rationalise specialist training across the three Services and an increasing emphasis is placed on technology in training delivery. The MoD has recently introduced the Defence e-learning Delivery and Management Capability, designed to allow training to be provided to the student at the point of need, be that in the front line or a headquarters environment.

Defence Medical Services

The Defence Medical Services (DMS) provides primary care for all three Services, involving the provision of an occupational, environmental and

6–8 October 2003 UK Nobel Prize winners announced.

Above: **6 October** Professor Sir Peter Mansfield receives the Nobel Prize for Medicine for pioneering work in the development of magnetic resonance imaging (MRI) technology. Sir Peter, pictured in front of a whole body scanner at the University of Nottingham, shares the award with American Paul C Lauterbur. MRI scans allow doctors to see detailed images of the internal organs without the use of X-rays.

7 October Professor Anthony Leggett (*below*), who has joint UK/US citizenship, gets the Nobel Prize for Physics, along with Russian-American Alexei Abrikosov and Russian Vitaly Ginzburg, for their work on superconductors and superfluids.

8 October Professor Clive Granger gets the Nobel Prize for Economics with American Professor Robert Engle, for work on macroeconomic modelling. He developed methods of analysing economic time series with common trends (cointegration), helping to reduce the effect of statistical fluctuations. Pictured (*below left*) receiving the award in December.

9 October 2003–18 January 2004 Gothic art exhibition at the Victoria & Albert Museum.

Above: Margaret of York's crown made of silver gilt, enamel, precious *stones* and pearls (c.1461–74). Margaret was the sister of Edward IV and was married to Charles, Duke of Burgundy.

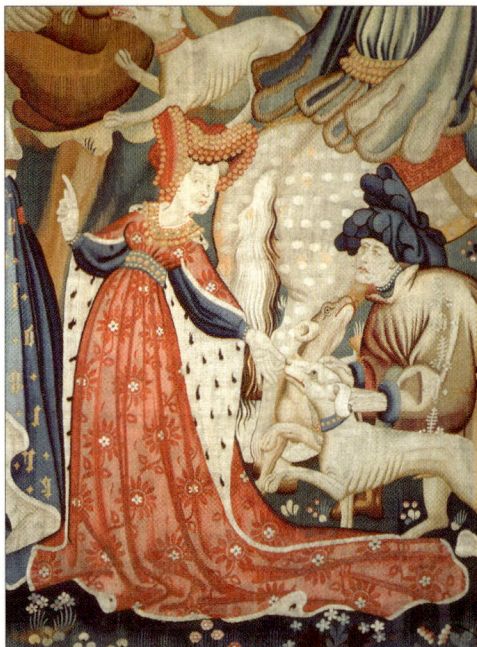

Above: Boar and bear hunt detail from Devonshire hunting tapestry (1425–30) in warp and weft wool.

Left: The Weoley Cup, colourless glass, blown, tooled enamelled and gilt. The glass came from Venice c.1500, and the mount was made in London in 1547.

Below: Gilt bronze effigy (1449–50) of Richard Beauchamp, 13th Earl of Warwick. Beauchamp was a leading political figure, serving under kings Henry IV, V and VI.

Table 8.1 Rank structure of the Armed Forces

Royal Navy[1]	Royal Marines[1]	Army	Royal Air Force
Commissioned officers	*Commissioned officers*	*Commissioned officers*	*Commissioned officers*
Admiral of the Fleet	–	Field Marshal	Marshal of the RAF
Admiral	General	General	Air Chief Marshal
Vice Admiral	Lieutenant General	Lieutenant General	Air Marshal
Rear Admiral	Major General	Major General	Air Vice Marshal
Commodore	Brigadier	Brigadier	Air Commodore
Captain	Colonel	Colonel	Group Captain
Commander	Lieutenant Colonel	Lieutenant Colonel	Wing Commander
Lieutenant Commander	Major	Major	Squadron Leader
Lieutenant	Captain	Captain	Flight Lieutenant
Sub-Lieutenant	Lieutenant/2nd Lieutenant	Lieutenant/2nd Lieutenant	Flying Officer/Pilot Officer
Midshipman	–	Officer Designate	Officer Designate
Non-commissioned ranks	*Non-commissioned ranks*	*Non-commissioned ranks*	*Non-commissioned ranks*
Warrant Officer Class 1	Warrant Officer Class 1	Warrant Officer Class 1	Warrant Officer
Warrant Officer Class 2	Warrant Officer Class 2	Warrant Officer Class 2	–
Chief Petty Officer	Colour Sergeant	Staff Sergeant	Flight Sergeant/Chief Techn
Petty Officer	Sergeant	Sergeant	Sergeant
Leading Rate	Corporal	Corporal	Corporal
–	–	Lance Corporal	–
Able Rate	Marine	Private (Classes 1 to 3)	Junior Technician/ Leading Aircraftman/ Senior Aircraftman
–	–	Private (Class 4)/Junior	Aircraftman

1 The Royal Navy and the Royal Marines make up the Naval Service.
Source: Defence Analytical Services Agency

public health medical service as well as the traditional general practice. Secondary health care is principally provided through the NHS with six Military Hospital Units based in NHS Trusts across the United Kingdom. The DMS also has hospitals in Cyprus and Gibraltar. In January 2003 there were nearly 350 more fully trained medical personnel than in January 1999 and over 500 more are being trained.

Reserve forces

The United Kingdom relies heavily on the reserve forces that support UK regular forces by serving both at home and overseas. The reserves also play a crucial role in responding to natural disasters within the United Kingdom, such as flooding.

Over 6,000 reservists were called up for the conflict in Iraq, and reserves are also serving in peacekeeping and humanitarian operations in Bosnia, Kosovo and Sierra Leone. There are two types of reserves:

- regular reserves, who are former members of the regular Armed Forces liable for service in an emergency; and

- volunteer reserves, who are recruited directly from the civilian community. They may join the Royal Naval Reserve, the Royal Marines Reserve, the Territorial Army or the Reserve Air Forces (which comprise the Royal Auxiliary Air Force and the Royal Air Force Reserve).

Table 8.2 Strength of Service[1] and civilian personnel, April 2004

Naval Service[2]	40,880
Army	112,750
RAF	53,390
Regular reserves	210,000
Volunteer reserves	45,380
Civilians[3]	109,050

1 Figures are for UK Regular Forces and exclude Gurkhas, full-time reserve service personnel, the Home Service Battalions of the Royal Irish Regiment, and mobilised reserves.
2 Figures include data for Royal Marines.
3 93,620 are UK-based; 15,430 are locally employed.
Source: Defence Analytical Services Agency

PDSA Dickin Medal 60th anniversary

In December 2003 Buster, a Royal Army Veterinary Corps search dog, was awarded a PDSA Dickin Medal for outstanding devotion to duty during the conflict in Iraq. Buster discovered an arsenal of weapons and explosives hidden in a house in Safwan.

Maria Dickin founded The People's Dispensary for Sick Animals, better known as PDSA, in 1917. She instigated the PDSA Dickin Medal in 1943. It is known as 'the animals' Victoria Cross'. One of the early recipients was Gustav, the pigeon that flew from Normandy to Thorney Island in 1944 bringing first news of how the D-Day landings were progressing.

The reserves – both individuals and formed units – need to be fully integrated with regular formations. They need to be readily available for service, where necessary through selective compulsory call-out, in situations short of a direct threat to the United Kingdom. Reserves are also liable for service in peace support operations. Training for this role takes place at the Reserve Training Mobilisation Centre at Chilwell. Royal Navy and RAF volunteer reserve numbers have increased and, while the Territorial Army has fallen to about 41,000, it is more closely integrated with the regular Army, with an emphasis on combat support.

Administration

Defence management

The Secretary of State for Defence is the cabinet minister charged with making defence policy and providing the means by which it is conducted. The Secretary of State is supported by three Ministers and is also the Chairman of the Defence Council and of the three Service Boards: the Admiralty Board, the Army Board and the Air Force Board.

The Permanent Secretary at the MoD is the Government's principal civilian adviser on defence and has primary responsibility for policy, finance and administration of the Department. The Chief of the Defence Staff (CDS) is the professional head of the Armed Forces and the principal military adviser to the Secretary of State and the Government.

The defence budget

The defence budget for 2004/05 is expected to be £29.7 billion. Under the 2004 Spending Review, the budget will increase from £30.9 billion in 2005/06 to £32.1 billion in 2006/07. This growth aims to provide the necessary investment in the Armed Forces' capabilities and structures to deal with extra priorities outlined in the 2003 Defence White Paper (see page 89).

Defence procurement

The largest element of the defence budget is expenditure on equipment and spares. The Defence Procurement Agency buys weaponry and equipment for the Armed Forces. The Defence Logistics Organisation purchases spares and stores to support equipment in service.

The 1998 SDR aimed to provide better, cheaper equipment more quickly resulting in 'Smart Acquisition'. Smart Acquisition applies to the procurement of new equipment and to its support in service, as well as stores and supplies. It is being extended to non-equipment areas, such as infrastructure and services of the defence estate.

A National Audit Office report on major MoD projects published in January 2004 found that in-year costs rose by over £3 billion in 2003 and were 6.1 per cent above the approved level. Nearly 90 per cent of the cost overrun was caused by four delayed major projects that pre-dated the introduction of Smart Acquisition: the Eurofighter Typhoon warplane; Nimrod reconnaissance planes; Astute submarines; and Brimstone air-launched anti-tank missiles.

International defence equipment co-operation

The United Kingdom is a founder member of OCCAR, an armament co-operation organisation formed with France, Germany, Italy and now Belgium, for managing joint procurement activities. It also participates in NATO's Conference of National Armaments Directors, has significant co-operative efforts with the United States, and is a member of the six (European) nation Letter of Intent Framework Agreement, aimed, among other things, at reducing

D-Day anniversary

The year 2004 marked the 60th anniversary of the D-Day landings in France in June 1944 – the beginning of the Allied campaign to liberate Europe during the Second World War. Events on 6 June in France included American, Canadian and UK ceremonies on the Normandy beaches, memorial services, an event at Arromanches attended by 17 Heads of State and Government, a naval review, a flypast and a parachute drop by American, Canadian and UK troops.

restrictions towards an open and competitive defence equipment market. The UK Government expects that the new European Defence Agency (see page 93) will contribute significantly towards improving the coordination of armaments procurement within the EU. Significant co-operative programmes in which the United Kingdom participates include:

- production of the Eurofighter Typhoon (with Germany, Italy and Spain);
- the Principal Anti-Air Missile System (with France and Italy) for use by the Type 45 destroyer;
- a 'Beyond Visual' Anti-Air Missile System (with France, Germany, Italy, Spain and Sweden) to arm Typhoon, Rafale and Gripen;
- the EH101 helicopter (with Italy);
- the Airbus A400M military transport aircraft (with Belgium, France, Germany, Spain and Turkey);
- a guided missile for use with the Army's Multiple Launch Rocket System; and

- a replacement aircraft, the Joint Strike Fighter, to replace the Harrier and Sea Harrier.

Further reading

Ministry of Defence: The Government Expenditure Plan 2003–2004 to 2005–2006. Cm 5912. Ministry of Defence. The Stationery Office, May 2003.

Delivering Security in a Changing World. Cm 6041. Ministry of Defence. The Stationery Office, December 2003.

Delivering Security in a Changing World: Future Capabilities. Cm 6269. Ministry of Defence. The Stationery Office, July 2004.

Websites

Ministry of Defence
www.mod.uk

NATO
www.nato.int

UK Army
www.army.mod.uk

Royal Air Force
www.raf.mod.uk

Royal Navy
www.royalnavy.mod.uk

Defence Statistics
www.dasa.mod.uk

WWW.

9 The social framework

The population of the United Kingdom has grown and changed significantly over the last half century. Increased life expectancy and lower fertility rates have led to an ageing population, while immigration has led to ethnic diversity. Living arrangements and relationship patterns have changed; more people are living alone, cohabitation before marriage is increasingly common and there has been a rise in births outside marriage. Many more women now participate in the labour market, although they still earn less than men and are under-represented in senior management. The standard of living has risen, but some people and communities are still affected by poverty and social exclusion.

Population

The UK population was estimated to be 59.6 million in mid-2003, an increase of 0.2 million on the previous year. Projections based on the 2002 mid-year estimates suggest that the population will continue to increase and peak at around 65 million in 2050 before beginning a gradual decline.

Age and gender

The United Kingdom has an ageing population. Between 1971 and 2003 there was an 18 per cent decrease in the number of children aged under 16. In contrast there was a 28 per cent increase in the number of people aged 65 and over, and a 128 per cent increase in those aged 85 and over.

Projections suggest that this ageing trend will continue and that the number of people aged 65 and over will exceed those aged under 16 by 2013 (Figure 9.1). Even allowing for the increase in state pension age for women from 60 to 65 between

2010 and 2020, there could be fewer than 2.2 people of working age for every person of pensionable age in the 2050s, compared with 3.35 in 2002. The mean age of the population is projected to rise from 39.3 years in 2002 to 43.6 years in 2031. Longer-term projections suggest it will reach 45 years by about 2050, but will only rise slightly thereafter.

Figure 9.1 Under 16s and people aged 65 and over, UK

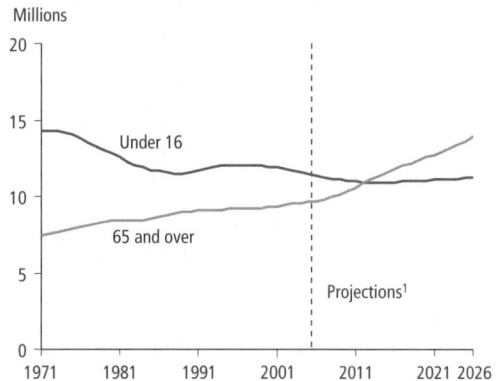

1 2002-based projections.
Source: Office for National Statistics; Government Actuary's Department; General Register Office for Scotland; Northern Ireland Statistics and Research Agency

Lower fertility rates (see page 103) and lower mortality rates have both contributed to the ageing trend. Latest estimates of life expectancy at birth (2000–02) in the United Kingdom were 75.7 years for males and 80.4 years for females. This represents an increase over the last 30 years of around 7 years for men and 5 years for women.

More boys than girls are born each year, but there are more females than males in the overall population – 30.4 million females compared with 29.1 million males in 2003, with women beginning to outnumber men from the age of 22. Among those aged 90 and over, women outnumber men by more than three to one.

Births and deaths

There were 695,600 live births in the United Kingdom in 2003, a live birth rate of 11.7 per 1,000 population. Projections suggest that the number will remain relatively constant at around 680,000 over the next 40 years.

Some 611,800 deaths were registered in the United Kingdom in 2003, a crude rate of 10.3 per 1,000 population. The number of deaths each year has remained relatively constant over the last century,

Modernisation of registration services

The registration service for England and Wales was established in 1837 and provides a national system for the registration of births, deaths and marriages. There have been relatively few changes over the years and the law still requires that every birth and death must be registered in person in the area where it occurred. The registrar uses pen and ink to enter the information onto a paper register, and issues a certificate.

In July 2004 a draft Order was presented to Parliament which would enable members of the public to register births and deaths on-line, by telephone, or in person at any register office. New records of births and deaths would be kept in a central database, to which existing records could be added over time. This should make it easier for people to apply for a passport or driving licence or to deal with a relative's estate using information held electronically, without having to provide a paper certificate.

The Order is expected to take about a year to complete its passage through Parliament. The Government is also considering proposals to modernise the procedures governing how people give notice to marry.

in spite of population growth. They are projected to decrease slightly over the next decade. However, as the ageing of the population continues, deaths are then projected to increase, and are expected to exceed births from 2031.

A rising standard of living, and developments in medical technology and practice, have contributed to large declines in mortality rates over the last hundred years. Death rates are higher for males than females in almost all age groups, but the gap between the sexes has narrowed in recent decades.

Households and families

There were 24.1 million private households in Great Britain in spring 2004, an increase of 30 per cent since 1971. Household growth has outpaced the population (which only grew by 6 per cent to 2003) because of the trend towards smaller households. By spring 2004, 29 per cent of households in Great Britain consisted of one person (Figure 9.2), compared with 18 per cent in 1971.

Figure 9.2 Households, by type, spring 2004, Great Britain

Total: 24.1 million

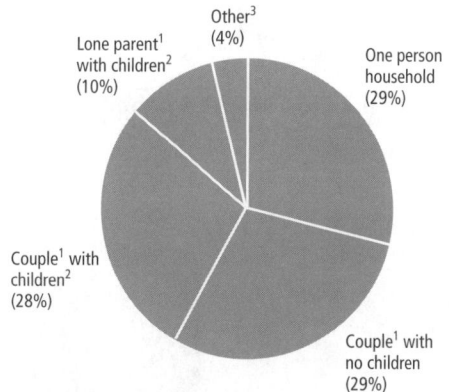

Lone parent[1] with children[2] (10%)

Other[3] (4%)

One person household (29%)

Couple[1] with children[2] (28%)

Couple[1] with no children (29%)

1 Other individuals who were not family members may also be included.
2 Includes dependent and non-dependent children.
3 Households consisting of two or more unrelated adults, and households with more than one family.
Source: Labour Force Survey, Office for National Statistics

Marriage, cohabitation and divorce

The majority of men and women marry at some stage of their lives, but the proportion of the population who are married has decreased. In

1971, 71 per cent of men and 65 per cent of women aged 16 and over in England and Wales were married; in 2002 this was 54 per cent of men and 50 per cent of women. Over the same period, the proportion of the population who were single or divorced increased, while the proportion who were widowed remained fairly constant. First marriages accounted for 83 per cent of all marriages in 1970 but for only 59 per cent in 2002 (Figure 9.3).

Results from the General Household Survey suggest that 12 per cent of 16- to 59-year-olds in Great Britain were cohabiting in 2002/03. For the non-married population in this age group the figure was one in four (Figure 9.4).

About 160,700 divorces were granted in the United Kingdom in 2002, 2.5 per cent more than 2001 (Figure 9.3). The median length of marriage for couples divorcing in England and Wales in 2002 was 11.1 years. There has been little change in this duration since data first became available in 1963, when it was 11.5 years. Divorce rates are affected by religious, social, cultural and legal differences, resulting in wide variation between EU Member States. The UK divorce rate was 2.7 per 1,000 population in 2002, higher than the EU-25 (see glossary) average of 2.0.

Figure 9.3 Marriages and divorces, UK

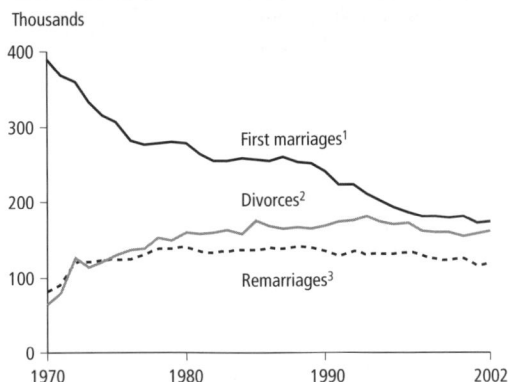

Thousands

1 For both partners.
2 Includes annulments.
3 For one or both partners.
Source: Office for National Statistics; General Register Office for Scotland; Northern Ireland Statistics and Research Agency

Family formation

More than three quarters of conceptions in 2001 led to a maternity (a live or stillbirth). This proportion has fallen steadily from 91 per cent in 1970. Conceptions to teenage women are more likely to lead to an abortion – 40 per cent of such conceptions were terminated by a legal abortion in

Figure 9.4 Non-married people[1] cohabiting, by age and sex, 2002/03, Great Britain

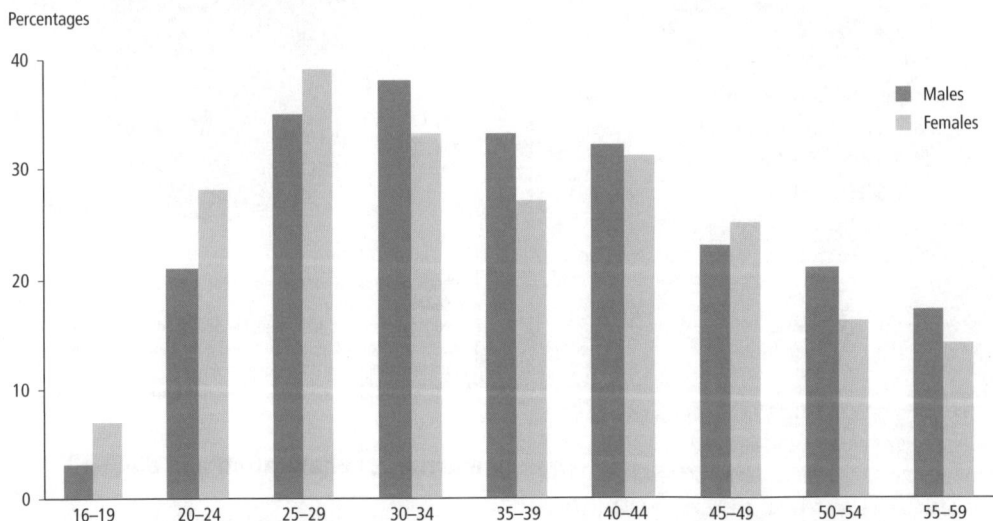

Percentages

1 Includes those respondents describing themselves as separated.
Source: General Household Survey, Office for National Statistics

Parenting after separation

The majority of children with separated parents are in touch with both parents, although the nature and frequency of this contact varies widely. Approximately 10 per cent of parents whose relationships end in separation make applications to the courts for orders concerning the future contact and residence arrangements for their children. Whether or not they obtain a court order, some parents lose touch with their children and are unhappy with this outcome.

The Government published a consultation document in July 2004 with proposals for improving the outcome for children when their parents separate. *Parental Separation: Children's Needs and Parents' Responsibilities* (which applies to England and Wales) emphasises the provision of better information and advice, the avoidance, where possible, of contested court hearings, and new measures to ensure that agreements and court orders are followed. It rejects any automatic 50:50 division of the child's time between the two parents on the grounds that a 'one size fits all' formula would not be in the best interests of most children.

2001, compared with 15 per cent of conceptions to women aged 30 to 34. Since the 1970s fertility rates in the United Kingdom have been below the level needed for the long-term natural replacement of the population. This reflects a trend towards later childbearing, smaller families and a rise in childlessness. Fertility rates for women under 30 years are far lower than 30 years ago, while in the last two decades fertility rates at 30 years and over have risen (Table 9.5). However, the data for 2003 indicate that fertility in each age group except the under 20s was higher than in 2001.

In England and Wales, the mean age[1] of women at the birth of their first child was 26.7 years in 2002 – six years older than in 1971. Fifteen per cent of women born in 1955 were still childless at the age of 45, compared with 9 per cent of those born in 1945.

---

1 This figure has been standardised to allow for changes in the age structure of the population.

Most children are born to married couples, but an increasing proportion of births occur outside marriage – 41 per cent in England and Wales in 2003, compared with 8 per cent in 1971. Most of this growth is accounted for by the increase in births to cohabiting couples. Of all births outside marriage in 2003 in England and Wales, 64 per cent were jointly registered births by parents living at the same address.

The EU-25 (see glossary) average for births outside marriage in 2002 was 29 per cent, ranging from 3.5 per cent in Cyprus to 56 per cent in Estonia and Sweden.

Migration

Population movements occur both within the United Kingdom and internationally. During the second half of the 20th century there was an internal movement of people from the coal, shipbuilding and steel industry areas in the north of England, Wales and Scotland to the south of England and the Midlands. Over the same period there was immigration from Commonwealth countries, followed more recently by an increase in the number of people seeking asylum in the United Kingdom.

Internal migration

In 2002, it is estimated that Wales gained 14,300 people from migration within the United Kingdom, Scotland gained 4,300 people, and Northern Ireland lost around 300 people. England experienced a net loss of 18,400 people. At a regional level, the greatest net loss due to internal migration occurred in London, where 107,800 more people moved from the capital to other regions of the country than moved into London.

International migration

Although the United Kingdom experienced a net loss of people due to migration during the 1970s and early 1980s, the position has reversed and since the late 1990s net migration into the United Kingdom has increasingly been a factor in population growth. A migrant is defined as someone who changes his or her country of usual residence for at least a year, so that the country of destination becomes the country of usual residence. It is estimated that 153,400 more people migrated to, rather than from, the United Kingdom in 2002,

Table 9.5 Fertility rates: by age of mother at childbirth, UK

Live births per 1,000 women

	1971	1981	1991	2001	2003
Under 20[1]	50.0	28.3	32.9	27.9	26.8
20–24	154.4	106.8	88.9	68.2	70.3
25–29	154.6	130.4	119.9	91.7	95.4
30–34	79.4	69.5	86.5	88.2	94.6
35–39	34.3	22.4	32.0	41.4	46.1
40 and over[2]	9.2	5.0	5.3	8.2	9.6
All ages GFR[3]	84.3	62.1	63.6	54.5	56.3
All ages TFR[4]	n/a	1.82	1.82	1.63	1.71
Total births (thousands)	901.6	730.7	792.3	669.1	695.6

1 Live births to women aged under 20 per 1,000 women aged 15 to 19.
2 Live births to women aged 40 and over per 1,000 women aged 40 to 44.
3 Gross fertility rate (GFR) total live births per 1,000 women aged 15 to 44.
4 Total fertility rate (TFR) is the number of children that would be born to a woman if current patterns of fertility persisted throughout her childbearing life.
Source: Office for National Statistics

a decrease of 11 per cent on the 2001 level. The number of in-migrants to the United Kingdom increased from 479,600 in 2001 to 512,800 in 2002. There were 359,400 out-migrants in 2002, 51,700 more than in 2001.

Immigration law

Immigration into the United Kingdom is largely governed by the *Immigration Act 1971*. Rules made under this Act set out the requirements to be met by those who are subject to immigration control and seek entry to, or leave to remain in, the United Kingdom. The 1971 Act has been amended by subsequent legislation, including the *Immigration and Asylum Act 1999*, the *Nationality, Immigration and Asylum Act 2002* and the *Asylum and Immigration (Treatment of Claimants, etc.) Act 2004*.

Nationals of the European Economic Area (EEA) – EU Member States and Iceland, Liechtenstein and Norway – are not subject to substantive immigration control. They may work in the United Kingdom without restriction and, provided they are working or able to support themselves financially, have the right to reside in the United Kingdom. Slightly different arrangements have been introduced for most of the countries that joined the EU in 2004 (see pages 71 and 175).

Visas

Under the Immigration Rules, nationals of certain countries must obtain a visa before they can visit

the United Kingdom. Nationals from other countries subject to immigration control must obtain entry clearance when coming to work or settle. Visas and other entry clearances are normally obtained from the nearest UK diplomatic post in a person's home country. In 2002 there were around 2 million applications for visas or other entry clearance, with around 1.7 million being successful.

Settlement in the United Kingdom

In 2003, 143,000 people were granted permanent settlement in the United Kingdom, 21 per cent more than in 2002 (Table 9.6). Of these grants, 38 per cent were to Asian nationals, and a further 31 per cent to African nationals.

Managed migration

The Government believes that managed migration can help overcome recruitment difficulties, bring innovation and capital into the country and counteract the effects of the ageing population. It has taken a number of steps to encourage people with skills and expertise to come and work in the United Kingdom, by overhauling the work permit[2] system and by introducing special schemes for certain categories of migrant, including entrepreneurs, temporary workers in hotels and catering, and overseas nurses, doctors and dentists who graduate in this country and wish to switch

2 Employers must apply for a work permit for a specific vacancy and demonstrate they cannot fill the post with a domestic worker.

Table 9.6 Grants of settlement by region, UK

Thousands

	Asia	Africa	Americas	Europe[1]	Oceania	Other[2]	All regions[1]
1981	30.0	4.1	6.3	6.6	4.5	7.5	59.1
1991	24.9	9.6	7.2	5.5	2.4	4.2	53.9
1996	27.9	13.0	8.5	7.5	3.5	1.4	61.7
2001	44.2	31.9	12.0	14.0	5.5	0.9	108.4
2002	46.6	39.2	11.7	14.0	6.2	0.5	118.3
2003	54.9	44.6	16.6	18.8	7.2	1.1	143.2

1 Includes European Economic Area (EEA) countries except for 2001 when these data were not available. EEA nationals are not obliged to seek settlement and the figures relate only to those who choose to do so.
2 From 1996 these are mainly British overseas citizens and those whose nationality was unknown.
Source: Home Office

to work permit employment. Around 136,000 work permits were granted in 2002.

Under the Highly Skilled Migrant Programme, skilled individuals who are not EEA nationals (see page 104) can apply to come to the United Kingdom to seek work or self-employment opportunities. They do not need to find a specific job before applying. Applications are assessed on a points-based system in the following areas:

- educational qualifications;
- work experience;
- past earnings;
- achievement in a chosen field; and
- achievements of spouse or partner.

There is also a special category for overseas doctors wishing to become self-employed GPs.

Successful applicants are granted leave to enter the United Kingdom for one year, following which further leave may be granted depending on the individual's employment status.

Asylum

The United Kingdom has a tradition of giving asylum to those in need of protection, and is a signatory to the 1951 United Nations Convention and its 1967 Protocol relating to the Status of Refugees. These provide that lawful residents, who have been granted refugee status, should enjoy treatment at least as favourable as that accorded to the indigenous population.

In the late 1980s applications to the United Kingdom for asylum started to rise sharply, from

around 4,000 a year in the period from 1985 to 1988, to a record 84,130 in 2002.[3] In 2003 the number of applications fell to 49,405, a decrease of 41 per cent on the previous year. In the first six months of 2004 applications for asylum averaged 2,810 a month. This was 37 per cent lower than in the same period a year earlier. Reforms to the asylum system and measures to secure the Channel Tunnel and move UK border controls to France are thought to have contributed to this overall decline.

The main nationalities applying for asylum in the United Kingdom in 2003 were: Somali (5,090 applicants); Iraqi (4,015 applicants); Chinese (3,450 applicants); Zimbabwean (3,295 applicants); and Iranian (2,875 applicants).

Around 64,940 initial asylum decisions were made in 2003. Of these decisions, 6 per cent were grants of asylum, compared with 10 per cent in 2002. A further 11 per cent of decisions in 2003 were grants of exceptional leave to remain,[4] humanitarian protection or discretionary leave and 83 per cent were refusals. Many failed asylum seekers appeal against refusal: of the 81,725 appeals determined by adjudicators in 2003, 16,070 (20 per cent) were successful. The backlog of cases awaiting an initial decision was 23,900 at the end of 2003, compared with 41,300 a year earlier.

The 41 per cent fall in applications to the United Kingdom during 2003 compared with a 19 per cent drop across the EU-25 as a whole. When the

3 Figures for asylum applications and decisions are based on the principal applicant and exclude dependants.
4 Humanitarian protection and discretionary leave replaced exceptional leave to remain on 1 April 2003.

relative size of each country is taken into account, applications to the United Kingdom equalled the EU average (1.0 applicants – including dependants – per 1,000 population). Austria had the highest rate at 4.0 per 1,000 population, while Portugal had the lowest (fewer than 0.01 per 1,000 population).

Support for asylum seekers

The National Asylum Support Service (NASS) provides support to qualifying asylum seekers until a decision is made on their claim. The support is in the form of cash benefits: a single adult aged 25 or over receives approximately £39 a week. NASS also provides short-term emergency accommodation and longer-term accommodation, on a 'no choice' basis, placing applicants at a number of dispersal areas across the United Kingdom. Children of compulsory school age in families seeking asylum must attend school, and asylum seekers and their dependants are eligible to receive free healthcare. Support for living costs and help with housing is no longer available to those who do not claim asylum when they arrive at a port, or as soon as possible thereafter, and who cannot give a satisfactory explanation. Once people are granted refugee status or humanitarian protection they are entitled to claim public funds.

Assistance with legal costs is available in some cases, through the Legal Services Commission in England and Wales, the Scottish Legal Aid Board and the Law Society of Northern Ireland. Unless exempted by the *Immigration and Asylum Act 1999*, immigration advisers who do not belong to designated professional bodies must register with the Office of the Immigration Services Commissioner, who is responsible for ensuring that they meet good practice requirements.

Recent reforms to asylum and immigration law

The *Asylum and Immigration (Treatment of Claimants, etc.) Act 2004* unifies the immigration and asylum appeals system into a single tier of appeal with limited onward review or appeal. The Act includes measures to:

- make it an offence to arrive in the United Kingdom without a valid immigration document when the person cannot show they have a reasonable excuse;

- deal with situations where it is deemed that a country other than the United Kingdom is best placed to consider someone's asylum or human rights claim substantively;

- withdraw family support after appeal from those who are in a position to leave the United Kingdom;

- make community work an obligation for failed asylum seekers who receive support because they cannot return home;

- require non-EEA foreign nationals to demonstrate they have entered the United Kingdom lawfully before giving notice of an intended marriage at a designated registry office; and

- enhance the powers of the Office of the Immigration Services Commissioner.

Citizenship

Under the *British Nationality Act 1981,* there are several forms of British nationality:

- British citizenship generally applies to those with a close connection with the United Kingdom, the Channel Islands or the Isle of Man;

- British Overseas Territories citizenship applies to people with a close connection with one of the Overseas Territories (see page 77);

- British National (Overseas) Status, for people who, before July 1997, were connected with Hong Kong; and

- for those connected with a former British colony, Ireland (before 1949), or former British India, or a territory that was formerly under British protection, there are categories such as British Overseas citizenship, British subject, and British protected person.

British citizens have the right to live permanently in the United Kingdom and are free to leave and re-enter the country at any time. British citizenship is acquired automatically at birth by a child born in the United Kingdom or a 'qualifying territory' (if born on or after 21 May 2002) if his or her mother (or father, if the child is legitimate) is:

- a British citizen; or

- settled in the United Kingdom; or

- settled in that 'qualifying territory' (if appropriate).

British citizenship may also be acquired by registration or naturalisation, and in some circumstances by children who have been adopted. Among those entitled to apply for registration are British nationals, children born in the United Kingdom who did not automatically acquire British citizenship at birth, and stateless people. Naturalisation is at the Home Secretary's discretion and there are a number of residential and other requirements.

In 2003, 124,315 people (Figure 9.7) were granted British Citizenship in the United Kingdom (3 per cent more than in 2002) and 10,680 were refused or withdrew their application. Residence in the United Kingdom continued to be the most frequent basis on which people were granted British citizenship, amounting to 44 per cent of grants in 2003, while marriage to a British citizen accounted for nearly 30 per cent.

Figure 9.7 Grants of British citizenship in the UK, by previous nationality, 2003

Total: 124,315

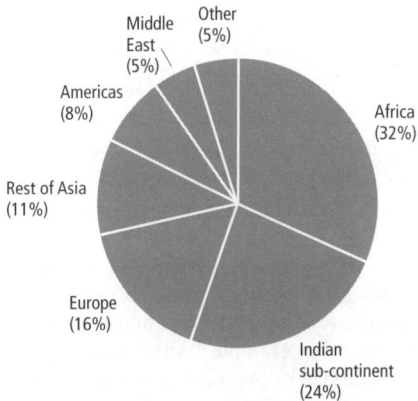

Source: Home Office

The *Nationality, Immigration and Asylum Act 2002* introduced a citizenship ceremony, including a citizenship oath and pledge (see box), and a requirement that naturalisation applicants demonstrate knowledge about life in the United Kingdom. The Prince of Wales and the Home Secretary attended the first ceremony in the London Borough of Brent in February 2004.

Ceremony of naturalisation

Oath of allegiance:

I, (name), (swear by almighty God/do solemnly and truly declare and affirm) that, on becoming a British citizen, I will be faithful and bear true allegiance to Her Majesty Queen Elizabeth II, Her Heirs and Successors according to law.

Pledge

I will give my loyalty to the United Kingdom and respect its rights and freedoms. I will uphold its democratic values. I will observe its laws faithfully and fulfil my duties and obligations as a British citizen.

Identity cards

The United Kingdom (along with Denmark, the Republic of Ireland, and Latvia) is one of four countries in the EU where people do not carry identity cards, either compulsorily or voluntarily. In April 2004 the Home Office consulted on a draft Identity Cards Bill that would establish a legislative framework for the gradual introduction of a national scheme.

The Government hopes that the introduction of identity cards will help to prevent identity fraud, counter the threat of global terrorism and ensure that free public services are only accessed by those entitled to them. It intends in the first instance to build on documents such as passports and driving licences. Although eventually it may be compulsory to register and hold an identity card, the Government is not proposing to make it compulsory to carry such a card or to produce it without good reason. However, in time it may be necessary to produce a card in order to access public services.

The draft Bill covers everyone aged 16 or over who is legally resident in the United Kingdom for three or more months.

Ethnicity and identity

For centuries people from overseas have settled in the United Kingdom, either to escape political or religious persecution or in search of better economic opportunities. Irish people have a long history of migration to the United

Kingdom, and many Jewish refugees arrived towards the end of the 19th century and in the 1930s. Substantial immigration from the Caribbean and the Indian subcontinent dates principally from the 1950s and 1960s, when the Government encouraged immigration from these areas to tackle labour shortages. Many people of south Asian descent also entered the United Kingdom from Kenya, Malawi and Uganda in the 1960s and 1970s. Recent trends in asylum applications have also added to the cultural and religious diversity of the UK population (see page 105).

In the 2001 Census, 4.6 million people (8 per cent of the UK population) described themselves as belonging to a minority ethnic[5] group. These groups have a younger age profile than the White

Table 9.8 Population by ethnic group,[1] April 2001, UK

	Total population		Minority ethnic population
	Thousands	%	%
White	54,154	92.1	.
Mixed	677	1.2	14.6
Asian or Asian British			
Indian	1,053	1.8	22.7
Pakistani	747	1.3	16.1
Bangladeshi	283	0.5	6.1
Other Asian	248	0.4	5.3
Black or Black British			
Black Caribbean	566	1.0	12.2
Black African	485	0.8	10.5
Black Other	98	0.2	2.1
Chinese	247	0.4	5.3
Other	231	0.4	5.0
All minority ethnic population	4,635	7.9	100
All population	58,789	100	.

1 Different versions of the ethnic group question were asked in England and Wales, and in Scotland and Northern Ireland, to reflect local differences in the requirement for information. However, results are comparable across the UK.
Source: Census, Office for National Statistics

5 In this section the term 'minority ethnic' does not include people from White minorities, such as White Irish and 'Other White'.

population, reflecting past immigration and fertility patterns. In Great Britain, 691,000 people identified themselves as White Irish and 1.4 million people as 'Other White'.

People from minority ethnic groups were more likely to live in England than in the rest of the United Kingdom. They made up 9 per cent of the population of England in 2001 compared with 2 per cent of the population of both Wales and Scotland and 1 per cent of the population of Northern Ireland. Nearly half (45 per cent) of the total minority ethnic population lived in London, where they comprised 29 per cent of all residents. However, the extent to which individual ethnic groups were concentrated in London varied considerably; for example, 78 per cent of Black Africans lived in London compared with just 19 per cent of Pakistanis.

Equal opportunities

Race equality

People from certain ethnic groups are more likely to experience poverty and social exclusion. The Households Below Average Income Series published by the Department of Work and Pensions (DWP) shows that the percentage of people living in low-income households in 2002/03 was higher when the household reference person (HRP – see glossary) belonged to a minority ethnic group, particularly when the HRP was of Pakistani/Bangladeshi descent.

In areas such as education, health, housing and the labour market, there are considerable variations between minority ethnic groups and within the White group. For example, Indian, White Irish, Chinese and Black African, were more likely to be working in a professional occupation in Great Britain in 2001/02 than people who described themselves as White British.

Race relations policy and legislation

The Home Office has overall responsibility for policy and legislation on racial equality. The equality unit in the Scottish Executive is also responsible for work in this area. In Great Britain, the *Race Relations Act 1976* makes it unlawful to discriminate on grounds of race, colour, nationality (including citizenship), or ethnic or national origins (referred to as 'racial grounds').

The Act applies to employment, training, education and the provision of goods and services. Legislation along similar lines was introduced in Northern Ireland in 1977.

Amendments introduced under the *Race Relations Act 1976 (Amendment) Regulations 2003* also ensure that Great Britain meets the standards of protection from racial discrimination and harassment required by the EC Article 13 Race Discrimination Directive of 2000.

The *Race Relations (Amendment) Act 2000* extended the scope of the 1976 Act to cover the way most public authorities carry out their public functions. Public authorities listed under the Act have a statutory general duty to work to eliminate unlawful racial discrimination and promote equal opportunities and good relations between people from different racial groups. Certain listed public bodies also have specific duties to fulfil. These include producing and publishing a race equality scheme to explain how they will meet these general duties, and monitoring the ethnic origin of staff and applicants for jobs, promotion and training. The Commission for Racial Equality (CRE, see below) has published a statutory code of practice to provide guidance to public bodies on how to meet these duties. In May 2004 the CRE also released a draft employment code to update and replace the statutory code issued in 1984.

The *Crime and Disorder Act 1998* created racially aggravated versions of a number of existing offences in England and Wales, including assault, criminal damage and harassment. These racially aggravated offences carry a higher maximum penalty. Scottish criminal law provides for the statutory aggravation of any offence on the grounds of racial (or religious) prejudice and the specific offence of racially aggravated harassment or behaviour.

In May 2004 the Government announced a period of consultation on community cohesion and race equality, prior to the launch of a new strategy in autumn 2004. The consultation paper, *Strength in Diversity*, covers issues such as citizenship and identity, eradicating racism and extremism, and tackling inequality.

Commission for Racial Equality

The CRE was set up under the *Race Relations Act 1976*, to tackle racial discrimination and promote equal opportunities and good race relations in Great Britain. The CRE has the power to investigate companies and organisations if it has sufficient evidence that unlawful racial discrimination has taken place, and it can issue non-discrimination notices, requiring them to change their policies and practice. The CRE also provides legal advice to people who think they have been discriminated against; in 2003 around 900 people made formal applications for assistance.

In 2003 the CRE supported the work of 93 organisations in Great Britain. Most of these were racial equality councils – voluntary bodies jointly funded by the CRE and local authorities whose job it is to promote good race relations locally.

In Northern Ireland equivalent responsibilities rest with the Equality Commission for Northern Ireland, whose remit also covers other types of unlawful discrimination.

Gender

The economic and domestic lives of women have changed considerably over time, and women have taken an increasingly important role in the labour market. In 1971, 55 per cent of women of working age in the United Kingdom were in employment, compared with 91 per cent of men. By spring 2004, in Great Britain, the rate for women was 70 per cent while the rate for men was 79 per cent. The likelihood of women being in employment, however, varies considerably according to whether or not they have dependent children. Employment rates are lowest for those women with a child under the age of five (53 per cent in spring 2004).

The pay gap between men and women who work full-time narrowed between 2002 and 2003, to the lowest since records began. The average gross weekly earnings of women working full-time in April 2003 were 75.4 per cent of those for men (£396 compared with £525).

Causes of the gender pay gap include the fact that men and women tend to work in different occupations and the impact of family responsibilities, as well as the possibility of pay discrimination. A much higher proportion of women than men work in administrative and secretarial jobs, for example, while a higher proportion of men work in skilled trades (see Table 11.3 on page 147).

Equal opportunities policy and legislation

Under the *Equal Pay Act 1970,* women and men in Great Britain are entitled to equal pay when doing work that is the same or broadly similar, work that is rated as equivalent, or work that is of equal value. The *Sex Discrimination Act 1975* (as amended) makes it unlawful in Great Britain to discriminate between men and women in employment and vocational training, education, and the provision and sale of goods, facilities, services and premises. The Act also outlaws discrimination in employment and training on the grounds of gender reassignment and being married. Similar legislation on sex discrimination and equal pay applies in Northern Ireland.

There are two Ministers for Women, supported by the Women and Equality Unit based in the Department of Trade and Industry. They are responsible for a range of gender equality issues in Government and are sponsors of the Equal Opportunities Commission (EOC). The Equality Unit in the Scottish Executive and the Gender Policy Unit in the Northern Ireland Executive are also responsible for work in this area.

The Civil Partnership Bill, introduced into Parliament in March 2004, would give same sex couples in England and Wales the option of gaining formal legal recognition for their relationship. A range of rights and responsibilities would apply to those who choose to register as civil partners. These include:

- a duty to provide reasonable maintenance for the civil partner and for children of the family;
- civil partners to be assessed in the same way as spouses for child support;
- equitable treatment for the purposes of life assurance;
- employment and pension benefits;
- recognition under intestacy rules;
- access to fatal accidents compensation;
- protection from domestic violence; and
- recognition for immigration and nationality purposes.

A number of other EU Member States have already introduced a form of civil partnership registration – the first to do so was Denmark in 1989.

The *Gender Recognition Act 2004* gives transsexual people the right to seek legal recognition in their acquired gender. If recognition is granted, they will be regarded for almost all purposes as being of their acquired gender. This means that a legally recognised transsexual person will be able to marry in their acquired gender, obtain a new birth certificate, and receive State benefits and pensions. The Act includes a few exemptions, for example in respect of sports governing bodies, who may in some circumstances restrict participation in competitive events of someone seeking to compete in their acquired gender. The Act follows two judgments in the European Court of Human Rights in 2002, when the United Kingdom was found to have breached the Convention rights of transsexual people.

Equal Opportunities Commission

The EOC was established under the *Sex Discrimination Act 1975*. It is an independent statutory body, which has the powers to:

- work towards the elimination of discrimination on the grounds of sex or marital status;
- promote equality of opportunity between women and men;
- review, and propose amendments to, the *Sex Discrimination Act* and the *Equal Pay Act*; and
- provide legal advice and assistance to individuals who have been discriminated against.

Northern Ireland has its own Equality Commission responsible for tackling discrimination and promoting gender equality. It is an independent public body established under the *Northern Ireland Act (1998)*. The Commission also promotes equality of opportunity between persons of different religious beliefs, political opinions, ethnic groups, age, marital status and sexual orientation, between those with and without a disability, and between those with and without dependants.

Disability

According to the DWP, there were around 10 million disabled adults and 700,000 disabled children in the United Kingdom in 2002/03, using the definition of disability in the *Disability Discrimination Act 1995* (see below). Despite significant progress in recent years, disabled people still do not have the same opportunities to participate in society. In spring 2004, for example, 50 per cent of the 7 million disabled people of working age in the United Kingdom were in employment, compared with 80 per cent of non-disabled people. People with learning difficulties and mental health problems were the least likely to be in employment.

The unemployment rate for disabled people was higher than for non-disabled people (7.8 per cent and 4.6 per cent respectively). The likelihood of being long-term unemployed was also higher, at 33 per cent of unemployed disabled people compared with 18 per cent of non-disabled people.

Disability rights policy and legislation

The *Disability Discrimination Act 1995* protects disabled people in the United Kingdom against discrimination in the areas of employment, access to goods, facilities and services, buying or renting land or property and education. The Act allows the Government to set minimum standards so that disabled people can use public transport more easily. The definition of disabled under the Act requires a mental or physical impairment that has an adverse effect on someone's ability to carry out normal day-to-day activities over a period of at least twelve months. The adverse effect must be substantial and long-term.

The rights of access afforded to disabled people under the Act place a duty on businesses to adjust the way they provide services to the public, changing their policies, practices and procedures where reasonable. From October 2004 service providers will have to take steps to remove, alter or provide means of avoiding physical features that make it impossible or unreasonably difficult for disabled people to use their services. The Government also intends to introduce a statutory duty on public bodies to promote equality for disabled people.

There is a Minister for Disabled People, supported by the Disability Unit in the DWP. The Unit provides advice and policy information relating to disability in the United Kingdom. The Equality Unit in the Scottish Executive is also responsible for work in this area.

A draft Disability Discrimination Bill was published in December 2003. It proposes measures to extend the scope of existing legislation to cover most public sector activities and to place a new duty on public bodies to promote equal opportunities for disabled people.

Disability Rights Commission

The DRC, established under the *Disability Rights Commission Act 1999*, is an independent body, funded by the Government, that works towards eliminating discrimination and promoting equal opportunities for disabled people in Great Britain. It also promotes good practice with employers and service providers and advises the Government on the working of the disability discrimination legislation. In 2003/04 the DRC received over 120,000 calls to its helpline. It has provided legal representation and support in 215 legal cases since 2000.

Proposed Commission for Equality and Human Rights (CEHR)

A White Paper published in May 2004 (*Fairness For All: A New Commission for Equality and Human Rights*) contains plans for a new body to bring together the work of the CRE, EOC and DRC and to promote human rights. The proposed CEHR would also take responsibility for new legislation outlawing workplace discrimination on grounds of religion or belief and sexual orientation and, in time, age. Primary legislation will be required to establish the CEHR. The Government has also confirmed that it will take steps to introduce a statutory duty on public bodies to promote gender equality.

Low-income households

Although there have been substantial long-term improvements in the standard of living, there remain concerns about the relative deprivation of some people and communities. The distribution of income and wealth is uneven. For example:

- the average original income[6] of the top 20 per cent of UK households in 2002/03 (£60,300) was around 15 times greater than for those in the bottom 20 per cent (£4,000). Benefits and, to a lesser extent, taxes reduce this inequality so that the ratio for final income is four to one;

---

6 Original income is income before any state intervention in the form of taxes and benefits.

- in 2002/03, 17 per cent of the population of Great Britain lived in households with a low income (see glossary), before housing costs are taken into account, although this has fallen since the peak of 21 per cent in 1992. Lone parent families, pensioners and children are more likely to live in a low-income household than people of working age who do not have children; and
- the wealthiest 10 per cent of the UK population owned 56 per cent of marketable wealth in 2001, or 72 per cent of marketable wealth excluding the value of dwellings.

In all, 17 per cent of the UK population was at risk of poverty (that is living in a low income household) in 2001, compared with 15 per cent for the EU-25 (see glossary) as a whole. The variation between Member States was quite wide, ranging from 8 per cent in the Czech Republic to 21 per cent in the Republic of Ireland and Slovakia.

Social exclusion

The term 'social exclusion' describes individuals or areas suffering from a combination of linked problems, such as unemployment, poor skills, low incomes, unfair discrimination, poor housing, high crime, bad health and family breakdown.

The Social Exclusion Unit (SEU), based in the Office of the Deputy Prime Minister, was set up in 1997 to reduce social exclusion in England. The Unit liaises with the Welsh, Scottish and Northern Ireland administrations, which have their own strategies for tackling social exclusion. Previously published reports have led to new policies to tackle, for example, truancy, rough sleeping,

Action on debt

The SEU published *Action on Debt*, a report and fact pack, in April 2004 following an announcement in the Budget that the Government would work with both the financial services sector and voluntary and community bodies to improve the availability of free debt advice for those in need of it. The report is aimed at managers and decision makers in several sectors including health, employment, justice and neighbourhood renewal, and sets out how they can work together and individually to help alleviate debt among those with the lowest incomes.

Joseph Rowntree Foundation

The Joseph Rowntree Foundation celebrated its centenary in 2004. It was originally set up by Joseph Rowntree, a Quaker and businessman, and is one of the largest social policy research and development charities in the United Kingdom. Its budget for 2004 is £8.6 million. Of this, about £5.5 million is used to fund research and development work that focuses on the causes of social disadvantage and ways of overcoming them through improved policy and practice. The Foundation does not carry out research in-house, but supports projects carried out by academic and other institutions. It also engages in practical housing and care work through the Joseph Rowntree Housing Trust.

teenage pregnancy and neighbourhood renewal. The Unit published *A Better Education for Children in Care* in 2003, *Mental Health and Social Exclusion* in 2004 and (also in 2004) *Tackling Social Exclusion: Taking stock and looking to the future – Emerging Findings.*

Neighbourhood Renewal

In 2001, *A New Commitment to Neighbourhood Renewal: A National Strategy Action Plan* set out the Government's plans for delivering economic prosperity, safe communities, high-quality education, decent housing and better health to the poorest parts of the country (see page 320). The plan is implemented by the Neighbourhood Renewal Unit.

Social participation

Many voluntary and community organisations are involved in activities that improve the quality of life in the local community, working in areas as diverse as social welfare, education, sport, heritage, the environment and the arts. The National Council for Voluntary Organisations is the umbrella body for the voluntary sector in England. It has a growing membership of over 3,500 in 2004, ranging from large national charities to small local community groups.

The 2003 Home Office Citizenship Survey found that in the 12 months prior to interview, 28 per cent of the population aged 16 and over in England had been involved at least once a month in formal volunteering – defined as giving unpaid help through groups, clubs or organisations in order to benefit other people or the environment. Thirty seven per cent of the population had been involved in informal volunteering at least once a month, by giving unpaid help to someone who was not a family member.

The Government encourages links between the statutory, voluntary and community sectors. The Active Community Unit at the Home Office aims to promote and develop the voluntary and community sector and encourage people to become actively involved in their communities. The Government has set a target to increase voluntary and community sector participation by 5 per cent by 2006.

The Youth Service is a partnership between local government and voluntary organisations concerned with the informal personal and social education of young people aged 11 to 25 (5 to 25 in Northern Ireland). Local authorities manage their own youth centres and clubs and provide most of the public support for local and regional organisations. In England there is also a nationwide support service for 13- to 19-year-olds (Connexions – see page 127).

Charities

The Charity Commission is established by law as the regulator and registrar for charities in England and Wales. To become a registered charity an organisation must have purposes that are exclusively philanthropic, such as:

- the relief of financial hardship;
- the advancement of education;
- the advancement of religion; or
- other charitable purposes for the benefit of the community, such as urban and rural regeneration or the relief of unemployment.

In 2003/04 around 8,300 applications were received for registration from organisations, of which more than 6,200 were accepted and placed on the Public Register of Charities. Around 5,200 charities were removed from the register. There were approximately 165,000 registered charities in England and Wales at the end of March 2004.

An organisation based in England and Wales must register with the Charity Commission if it fulfils both the requirements for charitable status and the minimum requirements for registration. Some charities, called exempt charities, cannot register, and are not subject to the Commission's supervisory powers. These include, among others, some educational institutions, including most universities and national museums. Charities elsewhere in the United Kingdom are not required to register with a government organisation, but do need to seek recognition of their charitable status with the Inland Revenue for tax purposes.

The Charity Commission aims to provide effective regulation of charities in England and Wales in order to increase their efficiency and effectiveness and to promote public confidence and trust. The Commission has powers to investigate abuse and mismanagement and, where necessary, will intervene to protect charities from crime and remedy problems. Over 400 investigations were carried out in 2003/04.

The Charities Aid Foundation (CAF) is a registered charity that works to increase resources for the voluntary sector in the United Kingdom and overseas. It provides services that are both charitable and financial and undertakes a comprehensive programme of research and is a leading source of information on the voluntary sector.

Funding

At the end of March 2004, the total annual income of all registered charities in England and Wales was estimated at over £32 billion. Approximately 7 per cent of registered charities receive nearly 90 per cent of the total annual income recorded, while around two-thirds have an income of £10,000 or less a year and account for under 1 per cent of the annual total.

Voluntary organisations may receive income from several sources, including:

- central and local government grants;
- contributions from individuals, businesses and trusts;
- earnings from commercial activities and investments; and
- fees from central and local government for services provided on a contractual basis.

Busy year for RNLI

The Royal National Lifeboat Institution (RNLI) had its busiest year in 2003. Lifeboats were launched a record 8,901 times and 7,987 people were rescued.

The number of lifeboats launched has more than doubled since 1986. This increase is partly a result of changing patterns of sea use by the public and improved search and rescue techniques. The rapid increase in the use of mobile phones (see page 252) is another factor and, for 2003, a long hot summer.

The RNLI is a registered charity providing a 24-hour service to cover search and rescue requirements up to 50 miles out from the coast. It depends on voluntary contributions and legacies. There are more than 4,600 crew members, most of whom are volunteers.

Figure 9.9 Gross amounts donated from payroll giving schemes, UK

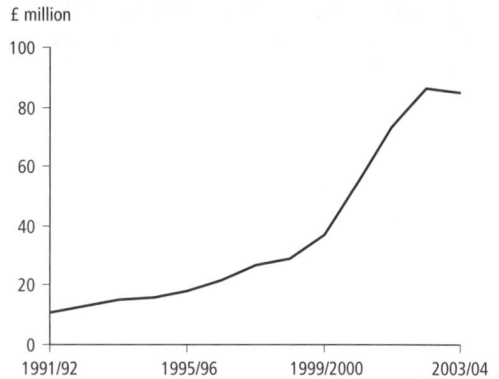

£ million

Source: Inland Revenue

Since its introduction in 1994, the National Lottery (see page 275) has given charities and voluntary organisations substantial funding for projects across a range of activities. Another valuable source of revenue for charities is through tax relief and tax exemptions. When an individual makes a donation under the Gift Aid scheme the charity can claim back the basic rate of tax, increasing the value of the donation by 28 per cent based on current tax rates. In addition, gifts of land and property, and gifts of quoted stocks and shares can be offset against income. All gifts and bequests to charities are exempt from inheritance tax.

Under the Payroll Giving scheme, available since 1987, employees can make a tax-deductible gift to charity on a regular basis from their payroll. It is open to all employed (and some retired) taxpayers, provided their employer is registered with a payroll giving agent. Around 2 per cent of those on PAYE who have access to such a scheme participate by making donations through their payroll. The average donation is around £5 per month, and in 2002/03, over 500,000 PAYE employees gave in this manner. Payroll giving has more than doubled between 1999/2000 and 2003/04, from £37 million to £85 million (Figure 9.9).

Sustainable development

A widely used definition of sustainable development is 'development that meets the needs of the present without compromising the ability of future generations to meet their own needs'. The Government has set out four key objectives that need to be met simultaneously to achieve this:

- social progress that recognises the needs of everyone;

- effective protection of the environment;

- prudent use of natural resources; and

- maintenance of high and stable levels of economic growth and employment.

The Government's sustainable development strategy, A Better Quality of Life, identifies a core set of around 150 indicators of sustainable development with a subset of 15 headline indicators to provide an overview of progress. The indicators relate, as far as possible, to the United Kingdom as a whole and cover economic and social, as well as environmental concerns. The nine English regions have their own versions of the 15 headline indicators.

The strategy also sets out a number of guiding principles – for example the need to take a long-term perspective; to support economic growth in all countries; to combat poverty and social exclusion; and not to allow a lack of full scientific knowledge to be used as a reason for postponing cost-effective measures to prevent environmental degradation when there are threats of serious or irreversible damage (the precautionary principle).

The Government reports annually on progress towards sustainable development. *Achieving a Better Quality of Life: Review of progress towards sustainable development,* covering 2003 as well as reviewing progress since 1999, was published in March 2004 along with *Quality of Life Counts,* an update of the indicators. This is the last progress report in this format. The Government plans to have a new scheme in place early in 2005, and in April 2004 announced a joint consultation with the devolved administrations on developing a new strategy.

The Department for Environment, Food and Rural Affairs (Defra) funds the Sustainable Development Research Network, which was set up to contribute to sustainable development in the United Kingdom by facilitating the better use of evidence and research in policymaking. The Sustainable Development Commission, an advisory non-departmental public body reporting to the Prime Minister and leaders of the devolved administrations, acts as an advocate and independent adviser to government on the actions needed.

The National Assembly for Wales has a legal duty to promote sustainable development in its functions. It has adopted a sustainable development scheme for Wales, *Learning to Live Differently,* to provide a framework for this duty. Its list of headline indicators reflects Welsh concerns and priorities such as the percentage of Welsh speakers, the amount of electricity produced by renewable sources and Wales' global ecological footprint. The latest data on the 12 headline indicators for Wales were published in March 2004.

The Scottish Executive has identified resource use, energy and travel as priority areas and adopted a number of sustainable development targets. Progress is measured via indicators such as the proportion of household waste recycled and the total number of households living in fuel poverty.[7] The Scottish Executive published its latest progress report in February 2004.

---

7 The need for a household to spend more than 10 per cent of its income on fuel to maintain a satisfactory heating regime.

The Department of the Environment (DoE) is developing a sustainable development strategy for Northern Ireland, together with a set of indicators. This strategy is linked to the DoE's efforts to introduce environmental legislation on air quality and waste management. It will complement:

- the *Regional Development Strategy for Northern Ireland 2025,* which seeks to provide a development framework that will work towards balanced and sustainable development. The first annual monitoring report was published in October 2003;

- the *Growing for a Green Economy Strategy,* which seeks to achieve sustainable economic development through more efficient business practices; and

- the *Northern Ireland Biodiversity Strategy.*

International development and co-operation

The UK Government has identified four key areas when considering sustainable development in an international context:

- working with others to eliminate global poverty and raise living standards in developing countries;

- working with others to tackle the global pressures on the environment and resources;

- promoting a fair and open trade system that respects the environment; and

- strengthening the place of sustainable development in the work of international organisations.

Overseas aid and trade

In the 2004 Spending Review, the Government made a commitment to increase its overseas aid budget (see page 82) to 0.47 per cent of gross national income (GNI) by 2006/07.

In 2003, the Export Credits Guarantee Department (see page 386) announced it would make available at least £50 million of guarantees each year to help the UK renewable energy sector assist developing countries to limit greenhouse gas emissions. It aims to encourage UK companies to export renewable energy goods and services, by offering them insurance against the risks of non-payment, and to help developing countries meet their power generation requirements in a sustainable way.

Fairtrade

Fairtrade is a trading partnership that aims to achieve greater equity in international trade. It offers better trading conditions to, and secures the rights of, marginalised farmers and workers in the developing world, helping to reduce poverty and improve living standards. The Fairtrade Foundation, which certifies and promotes Fairtrade, was set up by a number of agencies including the charities Cafod, Christian Aid, Oxfam, Traidcraft Exchange, and the World Development Movement.

The year 2004 is the tenth year of the Fairtrade mark and, in March 2004, announced that sales of Fairtrade products in the United Kingdom in 2003 totalled an estimated retail value of over £92 million – 46 per cent higher than in 2002. By the end of 2003, UK shoppers were spending over £2 million a week on products with the Fairtrade Mark compared with £2.7 million spent in the whole of 1994.

Further reading

A Better Quality of Life: A Strategy for Sustainable Development for the UK. The Stationery Office.

Asylum Statistics, United Kingdom. Home Office.

Birth Statistics. Office for National Statistics. (Available only on the ONS website)

Control of Immigration: Statistics, United Kingdom. Home Office.

Facts about Men and Women. Equal Opportunities Commission. (Available on the EOC website)

Family Spending. Office for National Statistics. The Stationery Office.

Focus on Ethnicity and Identity (January 2004) and other reports in the *Focus on…* Series. Office for National Statistics. (Available only on the ONS website)

Health Statistics Quarterly. Office for National Statistics. The Stationery Office.

Households Below Average Income Series. Department for Work and Pensions.

Individual Incomes of Men and Women. (Available only on the Women and Equality Unit website)

International Migration. Office for National Statistics. The Stationery Office.

Key Population and Vital Statistics. Office for National Statistics. The Stationery Office.

Living in Britain: Results from the General Household Survey. Office for National Statistics. The Stationery Office.

Marriage, Divorce and Adoption Statistics. Office for National Statistics. (Available only on the ONS website)

Parental Separation: Children's Needs and Parents' Responsibilities. Cm 6273. The Stationery Office, 2004.

Patterns and Trends in International Migration in Western Europe. Eurostat.

Persons Granted British Citizenship, United Kingdom. Home Office.

Population Trends. Office for National Statistics. The Stationery Office.

Social Trends. Office for National Statistics. The Stationery Office.

United Kingdom National Accounts – the Blue Book 2004. Office for National Statistics. The Stationery Office.

Websites

Charities Aid Foundation
www.cafonline.org

Charity Commission
www.charitycommission.gov.uk

Commission for Racial Equality
www.cre.gov.uk

Department for Constitutional Affairs
www.dca.gov.uk

Department for Work and Pensions
www.dwp.gov.uk

Disability Rights Commission
www.drc.org.uk

Equal Opportunities Commission
www.eoc.org.uk

Equality Commission for Northern Ireland
www.equalityni.org

Equality Research and Information (Northern Ireland)
www.equality.nisra.gov.uk

Eurostat
http://europa.eu.int/comm/eurostat

Government Actuary's Department
www.gad.gov.uk

Home Office
www.homeoffice.gov.uk

Home Office Immigration and Nationality Directorate
www.ind.homeoffice.gov.uk

National Youth Agency
www.nya.org.uk

Neighbourhood Renewal Unit
www.neighbourhood.gov.uk

Neighbourhood Statistics
www.neighbourhood.statistics.gov.uk

Office for National Statistics
www.statistics.gov.uk

Scottish Executive
www.scotland.gov.uk

Social Exclusion Unit
www.socialexclusionunit.gov.uk

Sustainable Development Commission
www.sd-commission.gov.uk

Sustainable Development, UK Government
www.sustainable-development.gov.uk

Sustainable Development, Scottish Executive
www.sustainable.scotland.gov.uk

Sustainable Development, Welsh Assembly Government
www.wales.gov.uk/themessustainabledev

Women and Equality Unit
www.womenandequalityunit.gov.uk

WWW.

10 Education and training

Parents are required by law to ensure that their children receive full-time education between the ages of 5 and 16 in Great Britain and between 4 and 16 in Northern Ireland. In 2004, almost three-quarters of 16-year-olds in the United Kingdom remained in full-time education after this age, either in school or further education colleges. Around 44 per cent of young people in England entered universities or other institutions of higher education. However, increasing emphasis is also placed on lifelong learning as a way of creating skills and improving employment prospects in a changing labour market.

Pre-school children

Early or pre-school education is expanding to ensure that all children begin their compulsory education with key skills such as listening, concentration and learning to work with others, and that they have a basic foundation in literacy and numeracy.

The proportion of three- and four-year-olds enrolled in schools in the United Kingdom rose from 29 per cent in 1973/74 to 65 per cent in 2003/04 (see Figure 10.1). In 2003/04, 35 per cent of children in this age group were enrolled in other settings offering early education such as playgroups in the private and voluntary sectors, either instead of, or in addition to, their school place.

In England, every three- and four-year-old is entitled to a free, part-time early education place if their parents want one. Places can be in the state, private or voluntary sector, as long as the provider agrees to work to curricular goals.

In Wales free, part-time early years places must be provided for four-year-olds and a pilot scheme to implement a foundation phase of education for three- to seven-year-olds began in September 2004. In Scotland local authorities have a duty to secure a free pre-school education place for all three- and four-year-old children whose parents want one. Children in Northern Ireland are entitled to one year's free pre-school education in the year immediately before they start compulsory primary education.

Childcare

Affordable and accessible childcare (for pre-school children or during out-of-school hours when children are older) helps support parents who want to work or train, as well as providing development

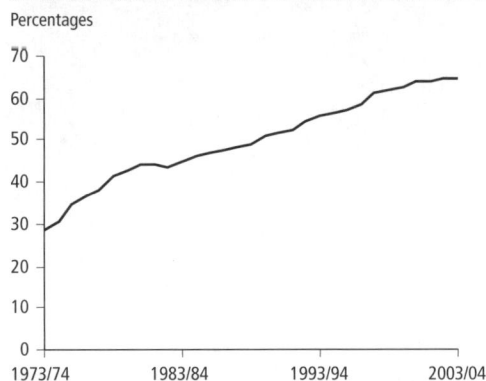

Figure 10.1 Children under five[1] in schools as a percentage of all children aged three and four, UK

Percentages

1 Pupils aged three and four at 31 December each year.
Source: Department for Education and Skills; National Assembly for Wales; Scottish Executive; Northern Ireland Department of Education

and social opportunities for children. Provision is expanding, with places in day nurseries, with childminders, and in holiday schemes and out-of-school clubs. Childcare is often privately run and paid for by parents, but low and middle income families can receive help with the costs of childcare through the tax credit system.

Throughout the United Kingdom the Sure Start programme (see page 167) brings together a range of initiatives (including early education and childcare) to improve the health and well-being of families and children. In England, for example, there will be up to 2,500 children's centres by March 2008. These will offer childcare and early education, and a range of family and health services, in the most disadvantaged communities. In addition, there will be childcare provision in at least 1,000 primary schools.

Schools

About 94 per cent of pupils in the United Kingdom receive free education paid for from public funds, while 6 per cent attend independent fee-paying schools (see page 121).

State schools

In England and Wales state schools are classified into three broad categories. Community schools are mainly schools that were traditionally owned

and funded by Local Education Authorities (LEAs). Foundation schools include many of the former grant-maintained schools. Voluntary schools are divided into controlled and aided, of which many are connected to a particular religious faith. LEAs are responsible for employing staff and for admission arrangements in community and voluntary controlled schools. The school governing body performs this role in foundation and voluntary aided schools.

All state schools in Scotland are directly managed by local authorities. However, there are also eight grant-aided schools, seven of which are special educational needs schools. In Northern Ireland, although all state schools are open to all religions, most Protestant children attend one of the 633 controlled schools, managed by education and library boards, while most Catholic children attend one of the 545 voluntary-maintained schools. There are, in addition, 54 voluntary grammar schools, which tend to be either Catholic or non-denominational in character. Integrated schools aim to educate Catholic and Protestant children together; these schools may be either controlled or grant-maintained. The Government has a statutory duty to encourage integrated education as a way of breaking down sectarian barriers. Publicly financed schools can apply to become integrated, following a majority vote by parents. In 2004, 6 per cent of children in Northern Ireland attended an integrated school.

Table 10.2 Number of schools, 2003/04,[1] UK

Type of school	England	Wales	Scotland	Northern Ireland	United Kingdom
State nursery	463	37	2,836	100	3,436
State primary	17,758	1,602	2,248	911	22,519
State secondary	3,395	227	386	233	4,241
of which specialist schools	1,446	.	.	.	1,446
Non-maintained schools	2,165	59	117	17	2,358
of which CTCs[2] or academies	21	.	.	.	21
Special schools[3]	1,131	43	225	47	1,446
Pupil referral units	357	29	.	.	386
All schools	**25,269**	**1,997**	**5,812**	**1,308**	**34,386**

1 Provisional. Includes 2002/03 data for Wales and Scotland.
2 City Technology Colleges.
3 Catering for children with special educational needs (see page 121). Most special schools are publicly maintained.
Source: Department for Education and Skills; National Assembly for Wales; Scottish Executive; Northern Ireland Department of Education

Table 10.3 Number of pupils by school type, 2003/04,[1] UK

Type of school	Thousands
State nursery[2]	150
State primary	5,113
State secondary	3,997
Non-maintained schools	629
Special schools[3]	109
Pupil referral units	12
All schools	**10,009**

1 Figures based on head counts.
2 Nursery classes within primary schools are included in primary schools except for Scotland, where they are included in nursery schools.
3 Includes maintained and non-maintained sectors.
Source: Department for Education and Skills; National Assembly for Wales; Scottish Executive; Northern Ireland Department of Education

Some education milestones in England and Wales

Pre 1870 Education for the poor is provided in a variety of settings – for example through charities, voluntary societies, workhouses, dame schools, and the Ragged School Union. Much of it is rudimentary.

1870 School Boards are set up to build and maintain schools out of local rates where existing provision is insufficient.

1880 Attendance at school is made compulsory for children up to the age of ten years.

1902 School Boards are abolished and their duties handed over to local borough or county councils, who set up new secondary and technical schools.

1906 Local authorities are allowed to provide school meals.

1918 The school leaving age is raised to 14.

1944 Education Act provides universal free education and brings in the 11-plus examination.

1951 Introduction of General Certificate of Education (GCE) Ordinary levels (O-levels) and Advanced levels (A-levels).

1964 Government announces plans to replace grammar and secondary modern schools with mixed ability comprehensives.

1988 GCSEs replace O-levels and the National Curriculum is introduced (see page 123)

Primary schools

In England and Wales, all children must attend school no later than the start of the term after their fifth birthday. Primary schools consist mainly of infant schools for children aged 5 to 7, junior schools for those aged 7 to 11, or combined junior and infant schools for both age groups. However, first schools in some parts of England cater for ages 5 to 9 or 10 as the first stage of a three-tier system: first, middle and upper. Middle schools cover various age ranges between 8 and 14 and usually lead on to comprehensive upper schools.

In Scotland, where children start school at the same age, public primary schools normally lead to the transfer to secondary school at the age of 12.

In Northern Ireland, primary schools cater for children aged 4 to 11. Some children are educated in the fee-charging preparatory departments of grammar schools.

Secondary schools

In January 2004, 88 per cent of secondary pupils in the maintained sector in England and all such pupils in Wales attended comprehensive schools. These generally take pupils without reference to ability or aptitude, providing a wide range of secondary education for all or most of the children in a district. All Scottish state pupils also attended non-selective schools.

Secondary education in Northern Ireland is currently organised largely on selective lines, with grammar schools admitting pupils on the basis of '11-plus' transfer tests in English, mathematics and science. In 2003/04, 41 per cent of secondary pupils attended grammar schools. In January 2004 the Minister with responsibility for education announced new arrangements for post-primary education, including the ending of transfer tests in autumn 2008.

Travel to school

The way children travel to school has changed greatly over the years, with fewer walking to school and more travelling in cars. In 1989–91, 27 per cent of trips to school taken by 5- to 10-year-olds in Great Britain were by car or van; by 1999–2001 this had risen to 39 per cent. The average length of the school journey has also increased over the same period – from 2.0 to 2.6 kilometres for children aged 5 to 10 and from 4.5 to 4.8 kilometres for those aged 11 to 16.

Special educational needs

A child has special educational needs (SEN) if he or she has significantly greater difficulty in learning than other children of the same age, or a disability which makes it difficult to use normal educational facilities. Approximately 1.5 million pupils with SEN were identified in the United Kingdom in 2003/04. Each one has the right to receive a broad and balanced education and state schools must publish information for parents about their SEN policy.

In England, an SEN code of practice came into force in 2002. It includes rights and duties introduced by the *Special Educational Needs and Disability Act 2001* and associated regulations. A new strategy, *Removing Barriers to Achievement*, which aims to improve opportunities for children with SEN, was published in February 2004. It envisages that more children with SEN will attend mainstream schools, but there will also be a clear and continuing role for special schools for those with the most severe and complex needs.

An SEN code of practice for Wales came into effect in April 2002 and in Scotland the provisions of the *Education Additional Support for Learning (Scotland) Act 2004* are expected to commence in autumn 2005. In Northern Ireland legislation similar to the 2001 Act will come into force from September 2005.

Independent schools

Independent schools are not funded by the state and obtain most of their finances from fees paid by parents. An independent school is defined as any school that provides full-time education for five or more pupils of compulsory school age or one or more pupils with a statement of special needs or who is in public care. Independent schools are required to register with the appropriate government department and are subject to inspection.

The Independent Schools Council (ISC) represents the seven independent schools' associations in the United Kingdom and has overall responsibility for the Independent Schools Inspectorate (ISI). In England the ISI inspects schools in the ISC every six years, using criteria approved by Ofsted (see page 140) and the Department for Education and Skills (DfES). In Wales all schools are inspected by the Office of HM Chief Inspector in Wales (Estyn, see page 141). Independent schools have to pass an inspection to qualify for membership of an association within ISC. All other independent schools are inspected by the relevant national inspectorates.

In England, the Independent/State School Partnership Scheme, set up in 1997, aims to encourage the sharing of experience and good practice between the two school sectors. In 2004/05, 46 partnerships received funding of £1.4 million for one- and two-year projects. In 2005/06, £2 million will be available for new partnerships.

Raising standards

Achievement and attainment tables

Performance tables were introduced for English schools in 1993, and renamed School and College Achievement and Attainment Tables in July 2004, following a number of changes to their contents. The primary school tables show how much value each school has added, based on progress made by individual pupils between the first two Key Stages (see page 123), together with test results in English, mathematics and science, and rates of pupil absence. Secondary school tables provide similar information, but also include the examination achievements of pupils reaching school leaving age. School and college (post-16) tables show the achievements of students in a range of intermediate and advanced qualifications.

In Wales and Northern Ireland results are published by individual schools. Scotland includes attainment as one of a range of measures used to monitor progress towards the five national priorities in education (see page 124).

Specialist schools

The Government intends that 95 per cent of all secondary schools in England will become specialist schools or academies by 2008. Specialist schools receive extra funding to establish curriculum centres of excellence that support improvement throughout the school and specialist work in partner schools and the wider community. Although they focus on one or two chosen specialisms, these schools must still meet the full national curriculum requirements (see page 125). Any maintained secondary school in England can apply to be designated as a specialist school in the following subject areas: arts, business and enterprise, engineering, humanities, languages, mathematics and computing, music, science, sports or technology. There were 1,955 schools in the specialist schools programme in March 2004, of which 1,446 were operational. High performing schools will be able to take on other roles and responsibilities, such as becoming training schools or taking on a second specialism.

Academies

Academies are state-funded independent schools in England. They may be set up:

- to replace existing schools that have been facing challenging circumstances;
- as part of a wider school reorganisation; or
- where there is an unmet demand for school places.

Sponsors from the private and voluntary sectors, church and other faith groups help to set up and run these schools. They provide free education to secondary age pupils of all abilities, including provision for children with SEN. Academies aim to offer a broad and balanced curriculum, including a specialism. The first three opened in 2002, with another nine in 2003.

Under its Five Year Strategy (see page 123) the Government intends that 200 academies will be open or under development by 2010.

Other initiatives

The Excellence in Cities programme, which was developed for disavantaged areas of England, is delivered locally by schools working in partnership with their local authorities. The programme provides additional resources and guidance for schools in the most disadvantaged communities. There were 57 whole authority partnerships involved in the programme in July 2004, and 51 'excellence clusters', which focus on smaller pockets of disadvantage.

In July 2003 the Leading Edge Partnership programme was established with 103 partnerships involving two or more secondary schools in England. Each partnership receives funding of £60,000 a year for three years for an agreed programme of activities designed to raise the performance of schools that are struggling to improve standards, and to address under-achievement among pupils from poorer socio-economic backgrounds and certain minority ethnic groups. The second round of the programme commenced in September 2004.

The Scottish Executive published a consultation paper and draft bill, *Ensuring Improvement in Our Schools*, in 2003. This included a proposal that Scottish Ministers, acting on the advice of Her Majesty's Inspectorate of Education (HMIE) (see page 141), should be able to require an education authority to secure improvement in its schools. Similar powers would apply in respect of the eight grant-aided schools. The consultation ended in January 2004.

Truancy

Unauthorised absences in English primary and secondary schools accounted for 0.7 per cent of half-days in 2002/03, the equivalent of 7.5 million sessions missed in a year. During the fourth round of nationally coordinated truancy sweeps, which took place in March 2004, police and educational welfare officers across England found 5,000 young people who did not have a valid reason to be out of school. Of these, one-third were accompanied by an adult.

In Wales, unauthorised absences accounted for 0.6 per cent of half-days in primary schools and 1.6 per cent of half-days in secondary schools in 2002/03. In Scotland, on average, 5,600 pupils (0.8 per cent) in local authority schools were absent without authorisation each school day in 2002/03.

The Attendance Strategy, part of the Improving Behaviour and Attendance Programme, started in April 2003 in 60 LEAs in England with particularly high rates of absence. Eight specialist attendance consultants worked closely with LEA Education Welfare Services to promote best practice and

Five Year Strategy for Children and Learners

The *Five Year Strategy for Children and Learners* was published by the DfES in July 2004, building on the *Education Act 2002* and backed by an increase in resources in the July 2004 Spending Review (see page 139). The Strategy covers education and learning for all age groups, including adults, as well as childcare.

For parents with children under five, key points include:

- the establishment of children's centres providing childcare, education, health, employment and parenting support;

- support for parents to stay at home with children from birth until age two, if they want to; and

- the development of dawn-to-dusk schools with breakfast, childcare and after-school clubs, to help working parents.

For primary school children, the strategy includes:

- more tailored learning in reading, writing and mathematics;

- giving every child the opportunity to learn a foreign language, play music (see box on page 125) and take part in sport; and

- a closer relationship between parents and schools to encourage family learning.

Key points at secondary school level include:

- guaranteed three-year budgets for every school from 2006;

- 95 per cent of secondary schools in England to become specialist schools by 2008;

- helping popular schools to expand so that there are more places available where parents want them;

- providing 200 academies by 2010;

- continuing the renewal and refurbishment programme of all secondary schools over the next 15 years;

- making it easier for schools to obtain foundation status and take control of their own land, buildings and other assets; and

- setting up 'foundation partnerships' in which schools group together to raise standards and to provide places for those with SEN or those pupils who are hard to place.

Post-secondary school provisions include:

- free tuition for people learning basic skills;

- Adult Learning Grants for adults studying for Level 2 qualifications (the equivalent of five good GCSEs); and

- access to university for anyone with the potential to benefit, grants for students that need them, and an end to up-front fees.

---

monitor progress through half-termly absence data collection.

Curriculum

All state schools in the United Kingdom must provide religious education, but parents have the right to withdraw their children from these classes. In Northern Ireland the main Christian churches have approved a core syllabus for religious education, which must be taught in all grant-aided schools.

Sex and relationship education, including education about HIV/AIDS and other sexually transmitted diseases, is compulsory in UK secondary schools and voluntary in primary schools.

England, Wales and Northern Ireland

Children follow the National Curriculum in England, the National Curriculum for Wales in Wales and the Northern Ireland Curriculum in Northern Ireland. The curricula contain programmes of study for age groups split into Key Stages (Table 10.4). These stages outline what pupils are entitled to be taught and set out expected standards of performance. The programmes of study represent a statutory minimum – schools have flexibility to add other elements, to choose how they teach the content of the curriculum, and to focus more or less time on particular aspects. Following the *Education Act 2002*, the early education curriculum for three- and four-year-olds in the pre-compulsory

Better education for children in care

Fewer than one in ten children in care in England in 2001 achieved five GCSEs grades A*-C, compared with half of all young people; and just 1 per cent went on to university. In Scotland in 2003, four out of ten care leavers achieved some qualifications compared to 95 per cent for Scotland as a whole, and 6 per cent of care leavers went to university. The UK Government and the devolved administrations aim to narrow the gap between the educational attainment of children in care and that of their peers by 2006.

In September 2003, to coincide with the publication of the Green Paper *Every Child Matters*, the Social Exclusion Unit published *A Better Education for Children in Care*. Measures to help children in care fulfil their potential include more books and computers to improve learning at home, more encouragement to stay on at school after age 16, and more joint training for teachers, social workers and carers.

phase is now part of the National Curriculum in England. There are four Key Stages covering the ages of compulsory schooling. Key Stages 1 and 2 are studied in primary schools, and Stages 3 and 4 in secondary school. The National Curriculum requires all pupils in Wales to study Welsh up to the age of 16. A major review of the Northern Ireland Curriculum has taken place and proposals for a revised curriculum agreed. Legislation will be in place by September 2006. There will be greater flexibility to enable schools to provide a curriculum appropriate to the needs of individual pupils and greater emphasis on the development of skills and attributes.

Scotland

There is no statutory national curriculum in Scotland. There are five national priorities in education set out under the following headings:

- achievement and attainment;
- framework for learning;
- inclusion and equality;
- values and citizenship; and
- learning for life.

Table 10.4 Organisation of compulsory school years

	Pupil ages	Year group	Attainment expected in final year of the group[1]
England and Wales			
Key Stage 1	5–7	1–2	Level 2
Key Stage 2	7–11	3–6	Level 4
Key Stage 3	11–14	7–9	Level 5/6
Key Stage 4	14–16	10–11	GCSE
Northern Ireland			
Key Stage 1	4/5–8	1–4	Level 2
Key Stage 2	8–11	5–7	Level 3/4
Key Stage 3	11–14	8–10	Level 5/6
Key Stage 4	14–16	11–12	GCSE
Scotland			
(Curriculum	5–7	P1–P3	Level A
following	7–8	P3–P4	Level B
national	8–10	P4–P6	Level C
guidelines from	10–11	P6–P7	Level D
ages 5 to 14)	11–13	P7–S2	Level E
NQ[2]	14–15	S3–S4	Standard Grade

1 For more details see pages 125–126.
2 Standard Grades are now part of the National Qualifications (NQ) framework in Scotland. They are broadly equivalent to GCSEs.
Source: Department for Education and Skills; National Assembly for Wales; Scottish Executive; Northern Ireland Department of Education

Music manifesto

Prominent figures from the music industry, education and music organisations came together in July 2004 to promote music education and launch the music manifesto which aims to put music at the heart of every school.

The manifesto commits its signatories to five key priorities to drive improvement:

- to give every young person access to a range of music experiences;

- to provide opportunities for young people to develop their musical interests and skills;

- to identify and nurture young musicians with talent;

- to develop teachers of music education; and

- to improve the support provided for music-making.

The content and management of the curriculum are the responsibility of educational authorities and individual head teachers. National guidelines for pupils aged 5 to 14 set out the ground to be covered and the way pupils' learning should be assessed and reported.

There are curriculum guidelines for languages, mathematics, information and communication technology (ICT), environmental studies, expressive arts, religious and moral education, health education, and personal and social development. Pupils can study a modern European language during the last two years of primary education.

There are 58 units in primary schools where education takes place through the Gaelic language. In some other schools Gaelic can be learned as a second language.

Attainment

In England, the attainment of pupils in test and teacher assessment for core subjects at ages 7 and 11 has remained broadly unchanged since 2002. At age 14 results in the core subjects of English, maths, science and ICT have risen every year since

Table 10.5 Compulsory subjects at Key Stages

	England	Wales[1]	Northern Ireland[2]
All Key Stages			
English	•	•	•
Welsh/Irish		•	•
Mathematics	•	•	•
Science	•	•	•
Physical education	•	•	•
Design and technology	•		•
ICT[3]	•		
Cross-curricula themes			•
Key Stages 1 to 3			
History	•	•	•
Geography	•	•	•
Art and design	•	•	•
Music	•	•	•
Technology		•	
Key Stages 3 and 4			
Citizenship	•		
Modern foreign language	•	•	•
Cross-curricula themes[4]			•
Humanities			•

1 In Wales, art and design is art; technology includes design and ICT. A language is optional at Key Stage 4.
2 Irish is taken in Irish-speaking schools. Science includes technology at Key Stages 1 and 2. Design and technology is taken at Key Stages 3 and 4 only.
3 Information and communications technology.
4 Cross-curricula themes include cultural heritage, education for mutual understanding, health education and ICT at Key Stages 1 to 4, and economic awareness and careers education at Key Stages 3 and 4. At Key Stage 4 pupils must choose a humanities subject.
Source: Department for Education and Skills; National Assembly for Wales; Scottish Executive; Northern Ireland Department of Education

2000. Girls consistently out-perform boys at Key Stage 1, the greatest difference being for writing. At Key Stage 3 girls continued to out-perform boys in all core subjects, although the gap narrowed to three percentage points in 2003. Table 10.6 shows the results of teacher assessments in England – unlike tests, these are carried out in all three subjects at each stage.

In Scotland, the upward trend in literacy and numeracy levels since 1997 continued in 2003. Attainment levels for pupils aged 5–14 increased in reading and writing at all stages and at almost every stage in maths. Girls out-performed boys at all stages and in all subjects.

Climbing the languages ladder

A new voluntary recognition assessment scheme that will allow people of all ages, from seven-year-olds to adults, to gain credit for their language skills, was piloted in 2004 in French, German and Spanish. The National Recognition Scheme, also known as the Language Ladder, is being developed by the University of Cambridge Local Examinations Syndicate with funding from the DfES.

People at all stages of education are assessed in listening, speaking, reading and writing in their chosen language. The scheme will be rolled out across England from September 2005 in eight languages: French, German, Spanish, Italian, Japanese, Chinese, Urdu and Punjabi.

The Language Ladder is part of the Government's National Languages Strategy for England that also aims to ensure that by the end of the decade every pupil from age 7 to 11 will have the opportunity to study foreign languages and develop their interest in the cultures of other nations. Language Pathfinder projects are being funded in 19 LEAs until July 2005 to support the introduction of languages in primary schools.

Table 10.6 Pupils reaching expected standards according to teacher assessments, 2003, England

Percentages

	English	Mathematics	Science
Key Stage 1[1]			
Boys	80	87	87
Girls	88	89	89
Key Stage 2[2]			
Boys	65	71	78
Girls	76	73	80
Key Stage 3[3]			
Boys	56	65	60
Girls	73	68	63

1 Percentage of pupils achieving level 2 or above.
2 Percentage of pupils achieving level 4 or above.
3 Percentage of pupils achieving level 5 or above.
Source: Department for Education and Skills

Table 10.7 Pupils attaining target levels in each subject, 2002/03, Scotland

Percentages

	P3	P6	S2
Mathematics	95	79	54
Reading	87	85	61
Writing	86	75	51

Source: Scottish Executive

Qualifications

Examinations in England, Wales and Northern Ireland are typically taken at the following ages:

- 16 – General Certificate of Secondary Education (GCSE, graded A* – the highest grade – to G);
- 17 – General Certificate of Education Advanced Subsidiary (AS level, graded A to E) which is equivalent to 50 per cent of an A level; and
- 18 – General Certificate of Education Advanced (A level, graded A to E).

In Scotland, the National Qualifications (NQ) Framework covers Standard Grade (usually taken at age 16 and graded 1 to 7, with grade 1 the highest); and Access, Intermediate 1 and 2, Higher and Advanced Higher qualifications (usually taken at ages 17 and 18 and graded A to C – except for Access qualifications, which have no external assessment component).

Specifications and assessment procedures must comply with national guidelines and be accredited by the Qualifications and Curriculum Authority in England, by its Welsh counterpart, Qualifications, Curriculum and Assessment Authority for Wales/Awdurdod Cymwysterau, Cwricwlwm ac Asesu Cymru, or the Northern Ireland Council for Curriculum, Examinations and Assessment. These independent government agencies are responsible for ensuring that the curriculum and qualifications are of high quality, coherent and flexible. NQs in Scotland are managed by the Scottish Qualifications Authority.

In 2002/03, 53 per cent of pupils in the United Kingdom gained five or more GCSE grades A* to C or equivalent, compared with 45 per cent in 1995/96 (Figure 10.8).

How pupils in the United Kingdom are assessed

England and Wales
Pupils are assessed formally at the ages of 7, 11 and 14 by their teachers and/or by national tests in the core subjects of English, mathematics and science and additionally in ICT at age 14. At age 14, pupils are also assessed in other subjects. In Wales there is no statutory national testing at age 7, and the Welsh Minister for Education has published proposals for alternatives to formal testing at 11 and 14.

Northern Ireland
Pupils are formally assessed at the age of 14 in English, mathematics and science. The requirements are broadly similar to those in England and Wales. Assessment takes the form of teacher assessment and tasks or tests.

Scotland
Progression is measured by attainment of six levels, based on the expectation of the performance of the majority of pupils at certain ages between 5 and 14 (see Table 10.4). Pupils are assessed by their teachers and by tests in reading, writing and mathematics which are selected and administered from a national catalogue. Tests can take place at any time during the school year and at any age.

Figure 10.8 Pupils obtaining GCSE or equivalent qualifications,[1] 2002/03, UK

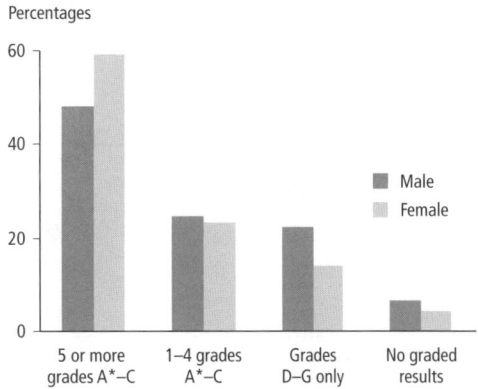

Percentages

1 Percentage of pupils aged 15 at the start of the academic year, or in year S4 in Scotland, who obtained the grade shown. See text for explanation of Scottish qualifications.
Source: Department for Education and Skills; National Assembly for Wales; Scottish Executive; Northern Ireland Department of Education

In 2002/03, an estimated 39 per cent of young people in schools and further education in the United Kingdom achieved two or more GCE A levels or equivalent (Figure 10.9). The performance gap between the sexes widened from two percentage points in 1992/93 to nine in 2002/03.

Careers

All young people in full-time education in the United Kingdom are entitled to career information, advice and guidance.

In England, GCSEs in vocational subjects were introduced in 2002, replacing the General National Vocational Qualification Part One. Northern Ireland also introduced vocational GCSEs at this time. They are available in eight subjects: applied art and design; applied business; engineering; health and social care; applied ICT; leisure and tourism; manufacturing; and applied science. In Scotland the General Scottish Vocational Qualification is the equivalent.

In Wales, a six-year pilot of a new Baccalaureate qualification began in 2003. This has a common core curriculum of key skills, Wales, Europe and the world (including a language module), work-related education and personal and social education. Twenty-four schools and colleges were involved by September 2004.

In England, Connexions is the Government's support service for all young people aged 13–19. It provides integrated information, advice and guidance, and access to personal development opportunities. These aim to help to remove barriers to learning and progression and ensure that young people make a smooth transition to adulthood and working life. It offers confidential support on any issue the young person chooses, including educational and career options. The service is delivered through 47 local Connexions Partnerships and a network of personal advisers based in a variety of settings, including schools, colleges and community centres. There is also a confidential telephone helpline and an interactive online advice service.

Figure 10.9 Achievement at GCE A level or equivalent,[1] UK

Percentages

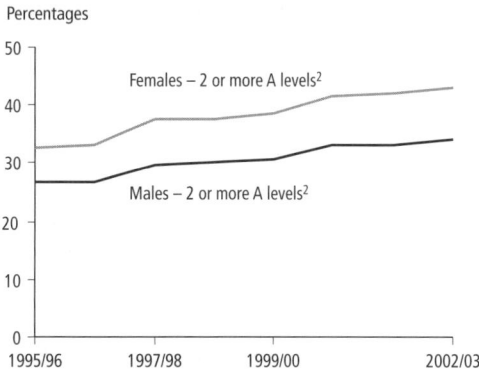

Females – 2 or more A levels[2]

Males – 2 or more A levels[2]

1995/96   1997/98   1999/00   2002/03

1 As a percentage of those aged 17 (16 in Scotland) at the start of the academic year. Two AS levels count as one A level pass. Includes pupils from schools and further education colleges.
2 Three or more Highers in Scotland.
Source: Department for Education and Skills; National Assembly for Wales; Scottish Executive; Northern Ireland Department of Education

Careers Wales works with schools and colleges to deliver information, advice and guidance to all age groups. It also facilitates work experience placements for students in schools and further education colleges and provides additional help to those most at risk of failing to realise their potential. Careers Scotland offers a careers advisory service to all ages and, like Careers Wales, provides support to vulnerable young people.

The Scottish Executive's strategy for Enterprise in Education, *Determined to Succeed*, started in 2003. It focuses on the following key themes:

- enterprise and entrepreneurial education;

- work-based vocational learning with a relevant qualification for those over 14; and

- appropriately focused careers education.

Under the strategy, Careers Scotland provides a range of career education for all pupils in Scotland's schools.

In Northern Ireland careers guidance is delivered by the Department for Employment and Learning's Careers Service. The Careers Service is provided to young people in education and training and to unemployed young people and adults, with a priority focus on 14- to 19-year-olds

Reforms for 14- to 19-year-olds

The Working Group for 14–19 Reform (*www.14-19reforms.gov.uk*) published its interim report in February 2004. The Working Group was particularly concerned with low post-16 participation and achievement, and with simplifying the curriculum, the assessment system, and the framework of vocational qualifications.

The report proposed a diploma framework for 14–19 education in England organised around four levels – entry, foundation, intermediate and advanced. The diploma would provide a way into apprenticeships (see page 134), employment, or further learning. At each level the diploma would include a common core content covering mathematical skills, communication and ICT, and include an extended project or personal challenge. Young people would be able to choose from a range of specialised diplomas, suitable for specific employment sectors or areas of further learning, and open diplomas, in which they could pursue a more mixed pattern of subjects.

The interim report was followed by a period of consultation, with final recommendations presented to the Government in autumn 2004.

who are vulnerable to social exclusion. It works closely with the Department for Education and the Department for Enterprise, Trade and Investment to develop a coherent strategy for business–education liaison in Northern Ireland.

Young people and adults

Further education

After compulsory education is finished, young people can choose to stay on at school, attend college or take part in work-based learning. Three-quarters of 16- to 18-year-olds in the United Kingdom continue in further education and training either in school sixth forms, sixth form colleges or further education colleges, or with work-based learning providers. The further education and training sector delivers a broad range of learning, including:

16 October 2003 200th anniversary of the birth of civil engineer Robert Stephenson, 1803–59 *(right)*. Robert worked closely with his father, locomotive engineer, George Stephenson, and the *Rocket* steam locomotive was built under Robert's direction.

© PRIVATE COLLECTION

Below: Illustrations of *(top)* the *Lancashire Witch* and *(second from top)* the prototype of the *Rocket,* both built by George and Robert Stephenson. The *Rocket's* main challengers at the Rainhill trials were *Novelty (third from top)* and *Sans Pareil (bottom).*

Below: One of Robert Stephenson's designs was the Conwy tubular bridge, built across the River Conwy, Gwynedd, in 1849 as part of the Chester to Holyhead Railway. The main span of the bridge is 125 metres. Just behind is Telford's suspension bridge, and on the left is Conwy Castle.

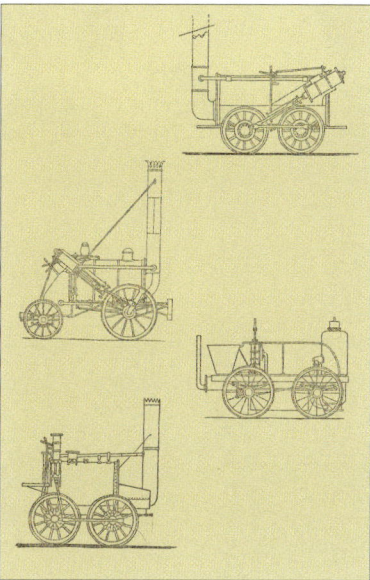

© PRIVATE COLLECTION

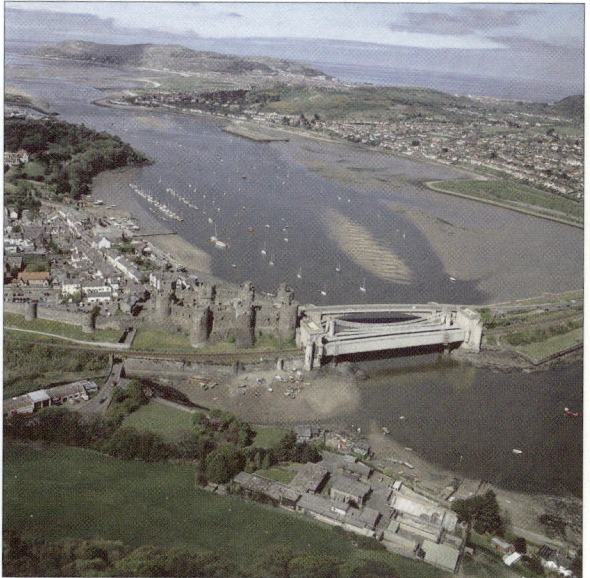

© JASON HAWKES/CORBIS

18 October 2003–18 April 2004 Wildlife Photographer of the Year exhibition at the Natural History Museum. The exhibition also toured around the United Kingdom.

Above: Wildlife Photographer of the Year Winner – Gorilla and boy by Gerhard Schulz (Germany).
Below left: Animal Behaviour: Birds Category Winner – Barn owl, a vole's-eye view by Nick Oliver (UK).
Below right: Animal Portraits Category Winner – Dalmation pelican by Helmut Moik (Austria).

24 October 2003 *Left:* The last passenger flight of Concorde takes off from New York bound for London Heathrow.

Below: Concorde travels by barge past the Houses of Parliament in London on its way to the Museum of Flight in Edinburgh.

8 November 2003 Maggi Hambling's *Scallop (front and back)* is unveiled on a beach at Aldeburgh in Suffolk. The 3.65-metre sculpture celebrates composer Benjamin Britten; its solid steel structure has been pierced with the words *I hear those voices that will not be drowned*, taken from Britten's opera *Peter Grimes*.

22 November 2003 *Right:* Jonny Wilkinson kicks the winning drop goal in the last seconds of the Rugby Union World Cup final between Australia and England at Telstra Stadium in Sydney, and *(below)* the England Rugby Squad celebrates its victory.

© PA PHOTOS

© MANUEL BLONDEAU/PHOTO & CO/CORBIS

- academic and vocational learning for
  16- to 19-year-olds;

- vocational education and training for adults
  seeking employment;

- workforce development for employers;

- second chance general education for adults;
  and

- learning for leisure and personal
  development.

The National Council for Education and Training
for Wales (ELWa, see page 135) has developed a
bilingual learning strategy. One of the aims is to
encourage increased bilingual and Welsh medium
provision in further education institutions to
complement that in schools. Students can
continue their studies through the medium of
Welsh or bilingually in a number of sixth forms
and further education institutions. ELWa is also
developing a strategy for developing Welsh
medium vocational training, while Welsh for
Adults is a popular programme that allows adult
learners to acquire or improve their Welsh
language skills.

Centres of Vocational Excellence (CoVEs)

CoVEs aim to meet the skill requirements of
employers by providing vocational skills training
across a wide range of occupations, such as
catering, computing and construction. The
Learning and Skills Council (LSC, see page 135)
aims to develop a network of at least 400 CoVEs
across England by the end of March 2006. CoVEs
are mainly based in further education colleges, but
the programme has been extended to develop
centres with work-based learning providers. By
August 2004 there were over 260 CoVEs, 225 of
which were based within colleges.

Networks of Excellence

A Networks of Excellence pilot programme
operates in Wales. It aims to establish networks in
six key economic sectors. Their purpose is to
create and support links between colleges and
industry by involving employers in the design and
delivery of courses, and to ensure that the needs of
business sectors are met.

Student support

Young people aged 16–19 in further education in
England are entitled to free learning and do not

Table 10.10 Students[1] in further and higher education, by type of course and sex, 2002/03, UK

Thousands

	Males	Females
Further education[2]		
Full-time	509	517
Part-time	1,424	2,278
All further education	1,933	2,795
Higher education[3]		
Undergraduate		
Full-time	535	645
Part-time	262	428
Postgraduate		
Full-time	105	102
Part-time	134	158
All higher education	1,038	1,336

1 Home and overseas students.
2 Excludes adult education centres.
3 Includes Open University.
**Source: Department for Education and Skills, National
Assembly for Wales, Scottish Executive and Northern Ireland
Department of Education**

have to pay tuition or other fees. Further
Education Learner Support Funds (£69 million in
2004/05) are available to help students aged 16 to
19 in particular financial difficulty. This funding is
available for course-related costs, including
transport, childcare, residential and other day-to-
day costs, where the Education Maintenance
Allowance (see page 130) is insufficient.

Care to Learn, a new universal childcare scheme,
supports young parents under the age of 19 in
England who want to continue in or enter into
education or training by paying their childcare
and associated travel costs. Since the scheme was
introduced in August 2003, it has supported
almost 2,400 young parents who can claim the cost
of childcare up to £5,125 per child per annum.

Adults on government-funded courses are
expected to make a financial contribution towards
the cost of their tuition fees unless they are on a
low income or studying basic skills. Learner
Support Funds for those aged 19 and over in
2004/05 include Hardship Funds, which can help
towards the cost of books, equipment, transport
and tuition fees (£54 million), Childcare Support
Funds (£40 million) and Residential Bursaries
(£3 million).

Educational Maintenance Allowances

Educational Maintenance Allowances (EMAs) were introduced across England in September 2004, for young people who continue in further education at school or college. EMA aims to reduce the drop-out rate from education at age 16. All young people aged 16 from households with incomes of £30,000 or less are eligible for means-tested EMA payments of between £10 and £30 a week in return for strong attendance and commitment at school or college. Young people aged 17 and over who live in the 56 EMA pilot areas can also apply. Payments are made direct to students. Young people can also receive up to three annual bonuses of £100 if they remain on their course and make good progress.

The DfES estimates that the EMA should be helping an additional 72,000 young people to stay on in further education by 2006–07. Similar schemes have also been introduced in Scotland, Wales and Northern Ireland.

The Government is piloting the Adult Learning Grant in England for people aged 19 and over studying for their first qualification equivalent to NVQ level 2 or level 3. The maximum payment is £30 per week for all adults studying at level 2, but only for those aged 19 to 30 studying for a level 3 qualification.

ELWa and the Scottish Further Education Funding Council provide similar help for eligible students in further education. In 2002/03 the Welsh Assembly Government introduced Assembly Learning Grants: eligibility depends upon age, income and course of study. By the end of February 2004, over 22,000 students in Wales had applied for the grants, 90 per cent of whom were successful.

In Northern Ireland funding and support is provided through the Further Education Funding Formula. Funding is also provided to colleges and students through a number of special budgets, which are designed to widen access, increase participation, address skills shortages and enhance the role of the sector in supporting economic development.

The Connexions Card

All 16- to 19-year-olds in England qualify for a free Connexions Card, a smartcard which enables young people to collect reward points for learning at school, college, work-based training or voluntary activities. Points can be exchanged for various free or discounted goods and services from businesses taking part in the scheme.

Higher education

Around 40 per cent of young people in Great Britain take degree and other advanced courses in universities and other colleges, compared with around 20 per cent at the beginning of the 1990s.

Universities and higher education colleges

There are 89 university institutions in the United Kingdom, including the Open University. This figure does not include the constituent colleges of the universities of London and Wales, both of which have a federal structure. UK universities enjoy academic freedom, appoint their own staff, admit students and award their own degrees. The universities of Oxford and Cambridge date from the 13th century and the Scottish universities of St Andrews, Glasgow and Aberdeen from the 15th century. The University of Edinburgh was established in the 16th century.

In addition, there are 60 higher education colleges. Some are very specialised, such as art and design, teacher education and agriculture colleges, while others are multi-disciplinary. Some award their own degrees and qualifications, while in others these are validated by a university or national body. Applications for full-time first degrees and Higher National Diploma courses are usually made through the Universities and Colleges Admission Service (UCAS). Over 374,000 applicants were accepted into higher education through UCAS in 2003. Around 29,000 students were accepted as deferred entrants for places after the following academic year – accounting for nearly 8 per cent of accepted applications.

Students at university in England, Wales and Northern Ireland usually spend three years of study, leading to a bachelor's degree, such as a Bachelor of Arts or Bachelor of Science. There are some four-year courses, especially for those studying languages, while medical and veterinary courses normally require five or six years. A full-time first degree in Scotland (where students usually start a year earlier) generally takes four years for Honours and three years for the broad-based Ordinary degree.

In 2003 some 273,000 students gained a first degree in the United Kingdom compared with around 159,000 students in 1992 and 102,000 in 1982. Fifty-six per cent of first degree graduates were women, and 11 per cent gained their award through part-time study.

Postgraduate studies in the United Kingdom usually lead to a taught or research masters degree, such as a Master of Arts or Master of Science, or to a research doctorate (PhD). A masters degree usually lasts one year full-time or two years part-time. A PhD usually lasts three years full-time or six years part-time. Applications for postgraduate study are processed separately by each institution and are made directly to the university.

A 'New Route PhD' was introduced in 2001 as a response to the changes in knowledge and skills demanded of PhD graduates in a rapidly expanding worldwide market. It lasts four years and combines the traditional PhD research project with a programme of broader coursework and professional skills development.

The Open University

Founded in 1969 and copied the world over, the Open University (OU) is a non-residential university offering over 420 undergraduate, postgraduate and other courses for students wishing to study in their own time. The OU has an 'open entry' policy: students do not need any formal academic qualifications to register for most courses. There are short residential schools for some courses and teaching is through a variety of media, including specially-produced textbooks, interactive CD-ROMs and audio-visual material. Many OU learning resources are delivered online; some 160,000 of the 200,000 students study in this way. Students can use computer conferencing, the local tutorial centre network, phone or email to contact their tutors and fellow students.

Other distance learning

With the growth of the Internet, more UK universities and colleges now offer study through distance learning. Courses are available at many levels, including degree and postgraduate qualifications. The DfES offers advice on which institutions are recognised as having degree awarding powers and recommends that a check is made before applying for an online course.

Widening access

The Government's aim is, by 2010, to increase participation in higher education towards 50 per cent of those aged 18 to 30, and also to make significant progress year-on-year towards fair access and reduce non-completion rates. In Scotland the Age Participation Index, which is used to measure participation of those aged under 21, shows that just over 50 per cent of young Scots go into higher education.

Programmes being introduced to widen participation include 'AimHigher' (in England, Scotland and Northern Ireland) and 'Reaching Wider' partnerships in Wales.

Finance

In 2002/03 central government spent £6.3 billion on higher education in the United Kingdom. Government finance is distributed to higher education institutions by Higher Education Funding Councils in England, Wales and Scotland, and by the Department for Employment and Learning in Northern Ireland. The private University of Buckingham is the only independent university in the United Kingdom and does not receive public funds.

In addition to charging tuition fees, institutions provide paid training, research or consultancy for commercial firms, and many establishments have endowments or receive grants from foundations and benefactors.

Student finance in England and Wales

Eligible full-time students in England and Wales receive help towards their tuition fees and loans and grants towards living costs.

Most students do not pay the full fee. How much help a student gets depends on their own and their family's income. Students from low-income backgrounds do not pay anything. In 2004/05 the maximum contribution was £1,150 per year.

Low interest student loans provide help with living costs. The maximum loan available in

2004/05 for eligible full-time students living away from home is £4,095 (£5,050 for those in London). All eligible students are entitled to 75 per cent of this amount, with the remaining 25 per cent being income based. Loans are only repaid once the student has left their course, and when they are earning over £10,000 a year (increasing to £15,000 in April 2005). In 2004/05 non-repayable Higher Education Grants of up to £1,000 became available to students from low-income backgrounds.

Additional non-repayable help is targeted at certain students, particularly those with disabilities, and those with children or adult dependants. The Access to Learning Fund, available through universities and colleges, helps students on low incomes who may need extra financial support for their course and to stay in higher education.

Help is also available for eligible part-time students. Those on low incomes can obtain a grant towards tuition fees of up to £575 a year and a grant of £250 per year to help with course costs.

Scotland

Student loans and supplementary grants are also the main source of help with living costs in Scotland. Young students from low-income families are entitled to have up to £2,150 of their annual loan entitlement replaced by a non-repayable bursary. Since 2000/01 tuition fees have not been payable by eligible full-time Scottish-domiciled students or European Union (EU) students studying in Scotland. Some graduates who have started courses since 2001/02 are required to make a one-off Graduate Endowment payment when they complete their course and start earning over £10,000 a year (mature students, lone parents and disabled students are exempt). Graduates liable for this payment can add the amount to their student loan account. The payment for students starting their courses in 2003/04 is £2,092.

Northern Ireland

In Northern Ireland support for higher education students generally operates on a similar basis to England and Wales. However, in September 2003 means-tested bursaries of up to £2,000 became available to low-income families.

Postgraduate support

Most postgraduates have to pay a significant contribution towards tuition fees. In 2004/05 the assumed fee for a one-year masters programme in England is in the region of £3,000, although this varies with the programme of study and the institution. Some postgraduates receive an award from a public body, some support themselves through a mixture of public and private finance, and others receive funding through scholarships and bursaries. Most public funding is provided by Research Councils (see chapter 25) that operate throughout the United Kingdom, the Students Awards Agency for Scotland and the Department for Employment and Learning in Northern Ireland. Employers may offer support by paying for all or part of the tuition fees and/or other costs such as examination fees and books, and by allowing paid leave for study.

Adult education

Adult education courses are designed to meet a range of social and community needs. Subjects that can be studied include languages, administration, ICT, sport and fitness, and craft skills. Education for adults provided by LEAs is carried out in a wide range of locations, including LEAs' own premises, local community centres, libraries, museums, schools and adult and further education colleges.

Overall, about half of LEAs provide adult and community learning through direct delivery; the other half are through contracts with other providers, predominately voluntary sector organisations, community learning centres and colleges. The duty to secure such education rests with the LSC in England (see page 135).

Adult education in Scotland is a statutory duty of education authorities and is generally known as community learning and development. In Northern Ireland it is provided by the further education sector, supplemented by the work of a range of non-statutory providers.

The Workers' Educational Association (WEA) is the largest UK voluntary provider of adult education. Founded in 1903, it runs over 10,000 courses each year through local and regional centres, providing learning for more than 110,000 adults. The WEA is a national charity and is supported by the Government through funding from the LSC in England, ELWa in Wales, and by the Scottish Executive and local authorities in Scotland.

Higher education reforms

The Higher Education Act 2004 aims to widen access to universities and help them remain competitive in the world economy. It takes forward the proposals set out in the White Paper, *The Future of Higher Education.* The new legislation covers higher education in England and Wales but some provisions will also affect higher education in other parts of the United Kingdom.

Measures in the Act and associated secondary legislation include:

- introducing variable tuition fees: from 2006 until at least 2010, provided that they have agreed access plans in place, institutions in England will be able to charge any amount between zero and £3,000, payment of which can be deferred until the graduate's income reaches £15,000 a year. The National Assembly for Wales has decided that variable fees will not be introduced in Wales before 2007, if at all;

- creating an Office for Fair Access in England, charged with agreeing the access plans of any

institution wishing to increase fees above the standard fee of around £1,200;

- re-introducing maintenance grants of up to £2,700 a year to help students from lower income households. Institutions charging the maximum £3,000 fee will be required to provide at least an additional £300 a year for students who qualify for the full £2,700 grant;

- creating a new UK-wide Arts and Humanities Research Council that will take over the funding of arts and humanities research;

- designating an independent body to review student complaints that are not related to matters of academic judgement;

- measures to prevent student debt being written off on discharge of bankruptcy;

- powers to help reduce bureaucracy by allowing data sharing with higher education institutions and other public bodies; and

- measures enabling the transfer of the majority of student support functions to Wales.

Literacy and numeracy

Skills for Life, the national strategy for improving adult literacy and numeracy in England, covers the literacy, language (English for speakers of other languages) and numeracy needs of all post-16 learners, including those with learning difficulties or disabilities, from pre-entry level up to and including level 2 (equivalent to GCSE grades A*–C – see page 124). All basic skills provision is free to the learner no matter where or how it is delivered.

The first definitive national profile of adult literacy and numeracy skills in England was published by the DfES in October 2003. It revealed that 5 million adults aged 16 to 65 had literacy skills that mean they would be unable to pass a GCSE in English; 15 million people had numeracy skills below this level.

The National Basic Skills Strategy for Wales began in 2001 and seeks to tackle basic skills deficiencies in all age groups. It is being implemented by the Basic Skills Agency.

The Scottish Adult Literacy and Numeracy strategy was also launched in 2001 with the publication of the *Adult Literacy and Numeracy in Scotland* report, which made 21 recommendations for developing a world-class service. Since then a national research and development unit, Learning Connections, has been established within Communities Scotland to support the strategy. In Northern Ireland the Essential Skills for Living strategy started in October 2002. A common curriculum has since been established and a series of essential skills qualifications developed, ranging from entry level to level 2. Over 240 tutors have enrolled on level 4 qualifications, increasing tutor capacity within the sector. Existing tutors have also benefited from enhanced in-service training.

Work-related training

The Government has several initiatives to help people train for work and achieve occupationally specific qualifications such as National Vocational

Qualifications (NVQs, see below). These include the New Deal (see page 151), Apprenticeships (see below) and work-based learning for adults – open to those aged 25 and over who have been unemployed for six months or longer.

Vocational qualifications

NVQs and the equivalent Scottish Vocational Qualifications (SVQs) are occupationally specific qualifications, based on competencies, which are assessed in the workplace. They cover sectors such as engineering, construction and health and social care. They also cover all-sector areas such as administration, management and customer services.

The qualifications are derived from national standards developed by employer-led bodies and approved across the United Kingdom by the Qualifications and Curriculum Authority or the Scottish Qualifications Authority. NVQs or SVQs are awarded at five levels.

There are also a range of awarding body 'own brand' vocational qualifications accredited into the National Qualifications Framework (NQF) which include Business and Technology Council (BTEC) and City and Guilds Craft awards. NQs in Scotland also include a range of vocational subjects.

Vocational GCSEs and Vocational A levels are an alternative to GCSEs and GCE A levels in England, Wales and Northern Ireland (see page 126) and are offered at levels 2 and 3 respectively of the NQF. A revised NQF was introduced in September 2004.

The Scottish Credit and Qualifications Framework brings all mainstream academic and vocational Scottish qualifications into a single unified framework, enabling learners, employers and the public in general to understand better how different Scottish qualifications relate to each other.

Apprenticeships

Apprenticeships provide structured learning programmes for young people that combine work-based training with off-the-job learning. Apprenticeships offer training to NVQ level 2 and Advanced Apprenticeships to level 3. More than 80 sectors of business and industry offer Apprenticeships, ranging from accountancy to

Vocational and academic comparability

Vocational and academic qualifications are broadly comparable at the following levels:

- an NVQ or SVQ level 5 is comparable to a higher degree;
- an NVQ or SVQ level 4 is comparable to a first degree, BTEC Higher National qualifications, an RSA Higher Diploma, a nursing qualification or other higher education;
- an NVQ or SVQ level 3 is comparable to two GCE A levels, and to vocationally related qualifications awarded by NQF accredited bodies. Examples are an RSA Advanced Diploma, City and Guilds Level 3 Progression Awards and BTEC National Diplomas; and
- an NVQ or SVQ level 2 is comparable to five GCSEs at grades A* to C, an RSA diploma, a City and Guilds Level 2 or a BTEC First Diploma.

sport. Each has its own guidance on entry requirements. The Government's aim is that more than a quarter of all young people in England will start an Apprenticeship before they are 22 years old. Apprenticeships are also being opened up to adults so that learners over 25 can capitalise on their prior learning and experience by achieving an Apprenticeship qualification. In Scotland, Modern Apprenticeships are available at level 3 and are broadly equivalent to Advanced Apprenticeships in England. They combine work-based training with study for an SVQ at level 3 or above. They are available in around 80 occupational sectors and are designed by the Sector Skills Council to ensure that they meet employers' needs. People of all ages can benefit from the programme.

Young Apprenticeships were introduced for 14- to 16-year-olds in England in September 2004, involving about 1,000 students. They provide a route for well motivated pupils at Key Stage 4 to undertake industry specific vocational qualifications with employers and training providers. All young people entering the initial programme must meet minimum achievement criteria at Key Stages 2 and 3.

England

Entry to Employment (E2E) is an entry to level 1 work-based learning programme for young people aged 16–18 who are not yet ready to enter an Apprenticeship, employment or structured learning at level 2. Each E2E programme is flexible but all students undertake learning in three core areas: basic and key skills; vocational development; and personal and social development.

Programme Led Pathways (PLPs), a route into Apprenticeships and Advanced Apprenticeships, were introduced in England in August 2004. PLPs are for young people aged 16 and over not in employment or waiting to start employment. The young person has access to the technical certificate and key skills part of the Apprenticeship and is expected to transfer to an employer to complete the remaining part of the qualification in the workplace.

Foundation Degrees, a vocational higher education qualification, were introduced in England in 2001. They are also available in Wales and Northern Ireland. They address a skills gap, identified by employers, at associate professional and higher technician level. Over 24,000 students were studying for Foundation Degrees in 2003/04 – an increase of 100 per cent over the previous year.

Wales

The Welsh Assembly Government, in collaboration with ELWa (see opposite), has integrated work-based learning programmes for adults and young people into a single All Age programme. The All Age programme is targeted at those people who have difficulties finding employment and aims to develop social skills, literacy, numeracy, ICT and other skills. The Modern and Foundation Modern Apprenticeship routes are now open to all and the Modern Skills Diploma for Adults, which was introduced in 2001, provides high-level (level 3 and above) skills training. All the programmes are open to those in employment.

Other initiatives in Wales include the development of the Credit and Qualifications Framework, the introduction of Individual Learning Accounts (ILA Wales), and the Learning Worker Project pilot for those in employment without a level 3 qualification.

Scotland

In Scotland all young people aged between 16 and 18 are entitled to training under the government-funded Skillseekers scheme. The emphasis is on training leading to a recognised qualification, up to SVQ level 3, and provided through an individual training plan with employer involvement.

Northern Ireland

In Northern Ireland the Jobskills Programme is available to all 16- to 17-year-olds. It provides training to NVQ level 2 with progression routes to NVQ level 3 through Modern Apprenticeship arrangements. Jobskills also provides Access training with pre-vocational and vocational strands for those young people entering training with physical or learning disabilities or with motivational problems and who are not immediately capable of undertaking a level 2 programme.

Learning providers

England

In England, the LSC is the planning and funding body for all post-16 education and training other than higher education. With a budget of around £8.7 billion for 2004/05 its objectives include maximising the achievement and participation of young people in education and training, increasing demand for learning by adults, improving the level of basic skills in the workplace, increasing employer engagement and improving the quality of provision.

Wales

ELWa has a similar remit to the LSC. It is responsible for post-16 education and training, with the exception of higher education. From April 2006, ELWa is being merged into the Welsh Assembly Government.

There are 21 local voluntary partnerships (Community Consortia for Education and Training) linking LEAs, schools, colleges, voluntary organisations, private training providers, employers and trade unions. Higher education remains the responsibility of the Higher Education Funding Council for Wales.

Scotland

A network of Local Enterprise Companies is responsible for the delivery of the Scottish Executive's national training programmes. They run under contract to two non-departmental public bodies: Scottish Enterprise and Highlands and Islands Enterprise.

Northern Ireland

The Department for Employment and Learning of the Northern Ireland Executive is responsible for higher and further education, employment, skill development and lifelong learning.

Sector Skills Councils

The Sector Skills Development Agency funds and supports a new UK-wide network of Sector Skills Councils (SSC). These have replaced National Training Organisations. SSCs are independent organisations developed by groups of employers in industry and business sectors. They bring together employers, trade unions and professional bodies, working with the Government to develop the skills needed by UK businesses.

New Technology Institutes

New Technology Institutes (NTIs) are formed through partnerships between higher education institutions, further education colleges, and private sector partners; 18 have been set up in England. NTIs advise and support small and medium sized enterprises (SMEs) on the effective adoption of new technology and business practices. They collaborate with local employers and regional and national organisations, such as the Small Business Service (see page 355) and Regional Development Agencies (see page 357), to identify skills gaps and to tailor NTI activity to local needs.

Learndirect

Learndirect is a network of online learning and information services provided by Ufi Ltd. Learndirect's services are being developed to meet the skills needs of businesses, and to widen the participation in learning of adults who are poorly qualified or who may have had negative experiences of learning in more formal environments. In October 2003 there were more than 2,000 learndirect centres across England, Wales and Northern Ireland, including more than 50 learndirect premier business centres providing services for SMEs. There is also a network of 460 learndirect scotland learning centres. Following a review of learndirect in Wales, a distinct Ufi Cymru organisation was set up in 2004.

Financial support

Career development loans are designed to help people pay for vocational education or learning in Great Britain. Loans of between £300 and £8,000 are provided through three major banks. Interest payments during training and for one month after are funded by the Government. The loans help to pay for courses lasting up to two years and, if relevant, for up to one year's practical work experience where it forms part of the course. Around 17,300 loans were taken out in 2003/04, totalling nearly £74 million. Over 200,000 loans have been taken out since the scheme began in 1988.

Teaching and other staff

Since 1997/98 the decline in the overall number of teachers in the United Kingdom has reversed (Figure 10.11). However, the number of male teachers has continued to fall. In 2001/02 women made up 68 per cent of full-time teachers in UK schools.

England and Wales

New teachers in state primary and secondary schools must be graduates and hold Qualified Teacher Status (QTS). In independent schools it is strongly recommended that new teachers obtain QTS. It can be achieved in a number of ways, including a one-year Post Graduate Certificate in Education (PGCE) course or a three- or four-year Bachelor of Education degree (BEd).

Graduate and Registered Teacher Programmes offer the opportunity for trainees to earn a salary while following a teacher training programme in a school. These schemes are particularly suitable for mature career changers, school support staff, people who have had previous teaching experience and overseas-trained teachers who do not hold QTS (who can make use of the Overseas Trained Teacher Programme – available in England only).

All teachers working in state schools must be registered with the General Teaching Council for England or for Wales. These are teachers' professional bodies which, among other things, have the power to strike a teacher from the register on grounds of professional misconduct or incompetence. As a result of a National Agreement on Raising Standards and Tackling Workloads signed in 2003, teachers in England and Wales are

Figure 10.11 Full-time teachers,[1] UK

Thousands

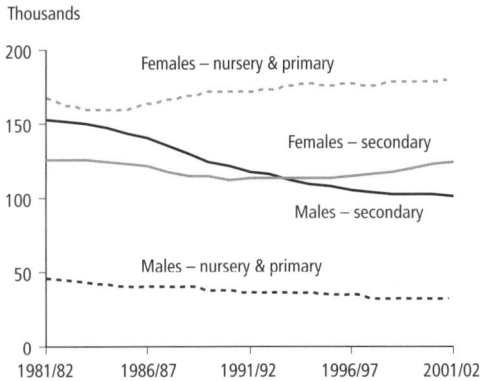

1 Qualified teachers only. As at 31 March of each year.
Source: Department for Education and Skills; National Assembly for Wales; Scottish Executive; Northern Ireland Department of Education

no longer required to undertake administrative and clerical tasks on a routine basis and the number of hours that a teacher can be required to cover for absent colleagues is limited to 38 hours a year. From September 2005 all teachers will be given guaranteed time within the school day – equal to at least 10 per cent of their timetabled teaching time – for planning, preparation and assessment.

Scotland

All teachers in education authority schools must be registered with the General Teaching Council for Scotland. The Council gives advice to the Scottish Executive on teacher supply and the professional suitability of teacher training courses. It is also responsible for disciplinary procedures under which a teacher guilty of professional misconduct may be removed temporarily or permanently from the register.

Teacher qualification procedures are similar to those in England and Wales, including the BEd degree and the PGCE. There is also a combined degree, sometimes known as a concurrent degree. All pre-service courses are validated by a higher education institution accredited by the Council and approved by the Scottish Executive. The Education Inspectorate has powers to inspect teacher education and training.

Northern Ireland

All entrants to teaching in grant-aided schools are graduates and hold an approved teaching qualification. Initial teacher training is integrated with induction and early in-service training, the latter covering a period of three years. The General Teaching Council in Northern Ireland has similar duties to those in England and Wales. As with the rest of the United Kingdom, the main teacher training courses are the BEd degree and the PGCE. The education and library boards have a statutory duty to provide curricular support services and in-service training.

Teaching assistants

The term teaching assistant refers to a person whose primary role is either to assist the teacher in the classroom, or to provide support for individual pupils. There are no obligatory qualifications for this role, although some local authorities have their own requirements. However, National Occupational Standards for teaching assistants and NVQs (levels 2 and 3) based on these standards are available. The role of teaching assistants is expanding with new higher level teaching assistants.

Teachers' TV

In 2003 the DfES proposed a new, editorially independent, digital television channel dedicated to teachers and all those who work in schools. The channel launch is planned for early 2005 and will deliver three types of programming:

- classroom resources (ideas, lesson plans, reviews and teaching tips);

- training and development materials (for improving the skills of the schools workforce); and

- management information, news and developments that affect the education sector as whole.

Teachers' TV will broadcast for 18 hours a day via digital terrestrial, cable and satellite channels.

Headteachers

In England the National College for School Leadership provides a range of programmes for the development of school leaders at all levels. The three national headship training programmes are: the National Professional Qualification for

Headship (NPQH) for aspiring headteachers; the Headship Induction Programme – formerly the Leadership and Management Programme for New Headteachers; and the Leadership Programme for Serving Headteachers. Since April 2004 it has been mandatory for all first-time heads in local education authority maintained schools or non-maintained special schools to hold the NPQH or to be working towards it.

Wales and Northern Ireland have their own versions of the NPQH, adapted to suit their respective school systems. In Wales the NPQH will become mandatory in 2005; the Welsh Professional Headship Induction Programme (PHIP) and the Leadership Programme for Serving Heads mirror their counterparts in England. In Scotland the Scottish Standard for Headship, gained through the Scottish Qualification for Headship, will become mandatory from August 2005.

Allied professions

Some of the other professions involved in education and training are described below.

Childcare

There are a range of relevant qualifications for those working in childcare. For example, in nursery work, trainees under supervision work towards a level 2 qualification on the NQF (see page 134) in Early Years Education, Childcare and Playwork. On-the-job progression can then be made to a managerial or supervisory position by working towards a level 3 qualification.

Careers advisers

In England and Wales fully qualified advisers are required to hold a relevant qualification at NVQ or SVQ level 4 or equivalent. In England career guidance is delivered by Connexions (see page 127) personal advisers, who must also have successfully completed Connexions specific training.

Further and higher education

There were around 57,000 full-time further education and 78,000 full-time higher education academic staff in the United Kingdom in 2002/03.

All those entering further education teaching in England must have, or gain within given timescales, an appropriate teaching qualification. A framework

of professional standards for teaching is being developed by the Higher Education Academy for 2005/06. In Wales the Further Education Teachers' Qualifications Regulations 2002 require new further education teachers to hold or work towards a stage 3 further education teaching qualification. The Welsh Assembly Government will be making regulations under the provisions of the *Education Act 2002* to ensure that new principals of further education institutions in Wales gain or hold a principalship qualification.

In Scotland lecturers on full-time permanent contracts are encouraged to obtain a qualification, and the Scottish Further Education Funding Council provides funding to cover the cost of training.

In Northern Ireland a Postgraduate Certificate in Further and Higher Education is required if an approved teaching qualification is not already held.

Administration and management

State schools in England and Wales are maintained by LEAs (see page 119). With a few exceptions, this is also the position in Scotland. In Northern Ireland all schools are funded by the five education and library boards. Further education colleges in the United Kingdom are legally independent institutions with independent governing bodies that include nominations from the local community and businesses. Universities and higher education colleges are legally independent corporate institutions with individual governing bodies.

A number of government departments are responsible for education policy:

- the DfES in England;

- the Welsh Assembly Government Department for Training and Education;

- the Scottish Executive Education Department (primary and secondary education) and the Scottish Executive Enterprise, Transport and Lifelong Learning Department; and

- the Department of Education and the Department for Employment and Learning in Northern Ireland.

LEAs are responsible for pre-16 provision in Great Britain and they fund schools largely on the basis of pupil numbers. The DfES funds post-16 education institutions directly. Specific central government grants are made to LEAs in Great Britain to improve school performance in literacy, numeracy and ICT. The Government also allocates some resources directly to schools in England for them to use as they wish. The costs of the education and library boards are met directly by the Northern Ireland Executive.

School management

England and Wales

All state schools work in partnership with LEAs. They receive their recurrent funding, through the LEAs' school funding formulae, as budget shares. A school is free to spend its budget share as it sees fit provided it does so 'for the purposes of the school'. Schools are run by headteachers and governing bodies, comprising parents, headteacher, school staff, LEA and local community representation.

The *Education Act 2002* established a 'Power to Innovate' which enabled the Government to exempt the governing bodies of schools and LEAs in England and Wales from educational legislation for a limited period. The power lifts regulatory requirements so an applicant can carry out a specific innovative project, initially for a period of up to three years, that has the potential to raise standards of education.

From September 2005, LEAs will be responsible for coordinating admissions to all schools in their area through a locally agreed scheme which ensures that parents receive a single offer of a school place and that all receive that offer on the same day. LEAs for community and voluntary controlled schools and governing bodies for foundation and voluntary aided schools (the admission authorities) are responsible for determining and applying admission arrangements for individual schools. Before doing so, they must take part in discussions with local schools, churches and others, to coordinate admission arrangements, taking account of statutory codes of practice. Any disagreements on school organisation or admissions in England are referred to an independent adjudicator; those regarding religious or denominational admission criteria are referred to the Secretary of State for Education and Skills. In Wales the National Assembly determines school organisation proposals and deals with objections to admissions arrangements.

Admission authorities are not allowed to introduce selection by ability, unless it is for sixth form admission or is designed to ensure that pupils of all abilities are admitted and that no one level of ability is over- or under-represented. Where existing partial selection by ability is challenged, the adjudicator (in Wales the National Assembly Government) decides whether it should continue.

In England there are 164 designated grammar schools which select all pupils on ability. Local parents are allowed to petition for a ballot and (if sufficient numbers locally wish it) to vote on whether to keep these selective admission arrangements.

Scotland

Nearly all Scottish schools are education authority schools financed by the authorities and central government. The headteacher is responsible for decision-making on at least 80 per cent of school-level expenditure.

In May 2002, 84 per cent of eligible education authority schools had a school board consisting of elected parents and teachers and members co-opted from the local community. In addition to promoting contact between parents, school and community, they are involved in procedures to appoint senior staff and to determine the community use of school premises. They may also take on further executive functions by delegation from their education authority.

The eight grant-aided schools are all run by boards of managers that receive government grants.

Northern Ireland

Boards of governors are responsible for the management of individual schools and include elected parents and teachers among their members. Virtually all schools have delegated budgets under which school governors determine spending priorities.

Rights of parents

England and Wales

Parents have a statutory right to information about schools and to express a preference for a school for their child. There is an appeal system if their choice is not met. Parents must be given a copy of the annual report from the school governors, which includes summaries of the school's results in National Curriculum assessment tests, public examinations, vocational qualifications (if applicable) and rates of pupil absence. This will be replaced by a school profile in September 2005.

Parents must be given a written annual report on their child's achievements in all subjects, including results of tests and examinations. Arrangements must also be made for the discussion of reports with teachers.

Parents are also entitled to see or be provided with a copy of their child's pupil record within 15 school days of making a written request. Unless there is a court order preventing it, all parents have a right to participate in decisions about their child's education.

Home/school agreements set out the responsibilities of schools, pupils and parents and are a statutory requirement for all maintained schools.

Scotland

Parents have a statutory right to request their choice of school and the education authority must meet this request except in certain circumstances set out in law. There is an appeal system if their choice is not met. Information is published on budgeted school running costs, examination results, pupil attendance and absence, 5–14 attainment targets and results, and the destinations of school leavers. Schools are required to provide parents with information about their children's attainment in each subject, pupil attainment targets, teachers' comments on their progress, and to provide access to their child's educational records.

Northern Ireland

The system of reporting to parents is broadly similar to that in England and Wales, except that no annual performance tables on a school-by-school basis are published.

Educational standards

England and Wales

The Office for Standards in Education (Ofsted) in England and the Office of Her Majesty's Chief Inspector in Wales (Estyn) aim to improve the quality and standards of education through independent inspection, regulation and advice.

Schools are inspected at least once in six years, and more often where weaknesses have been identified in an earlier inspection. All schools must produce an action plan to address the key issues raised in the inspection report. A school failing to provide an acceptable standard of education is deemed to need special measures and is subject to regular monitoring visits by inspectors.

LEAs are expected to monitor, challenge and support schools causing concern and must produce a statement of action when schools are placed in special measures. They may use their intervention powers to add additional governors, take back a school's delegated budget or replace the governing body with an interim executive board.

Ofsted inspects all 16–19 education and training in sixth form and further education colleges (that are conducted with the Adult Learning Inspectorate), teacher education and LEAs. Ofsted is also responsible for the regulation of all early years childcare providers.

The Adult Learning Inspectorate performs the same function as Ofsted for post-19 provision in colleges and for work-based learning, adult and community learning and learndirect. In Wales, Estyn has responsibility for all these areas as well as for the provision of careers guidance.

Scotland

In Scotland, HM Inspectorate of Education operates as an executive agency of the Scottish Executive. It inspects, reviews and reports on state and independent schools, further education colleges and the education functions of local authorities. Reports are published and are usually followed up within two years.

Northern Ireland

The Education and Training Inspectorate monitors, inspects and reports on standards of education and training provided by schools, colleges and other grant-aided organisations, and provides information and policy advice to the Department of Education, the Department of Culture, Arts and Leisure, and the Department for Employment and Learning.

International links

Large numbers of people from other countries come to the United Kingdom to study, and many UK people work and train overseas. The British Council (see chapter 7) encourages links between educational institutions in the United Kingdom and developing countries.

The Commonwealth Education Fund

The Commonwealth Education Fund was set up in 2002 to highlight the need for universal primary

education in the Commonwealth and to raise children's awareness of development issues. Actionaid, Oxfam and Save the Children administer the fund. The Government provided a grant of £10 million to the fund until December 2005, and matches contributions by businesses and others. There are estimated to be 70 million children in the Commonwealth who do not go to school.

European Union

The Socrates education programme supports partnerships between schools, colleges and universities, by promoting the European dimension in education through language learning, mobility opportunities for educational staff, pupils and students and a range of multinational projects.

The Leonardo da Vinci vocational training programme supports co-operation in vocational training across Europe through multinational pilot projects, work placements and trainer exchanges, and research projects.

Overseas students and teachers in the UK

In 2001/02 there were 97,900 overseas students in further education in the United Kingdom, and 247,400 overseas students in higher education. Most pay fees covering the full costs of their courses. Nationals of other EU states generally pay the lower level of fees applicable to UK home students.

In order to teach in maintained schools in England and Wales, it is generally necessary to hold QTS (see page 136). Regulations do not allow for the automatic recognition of teaching qualifications gained abroad unless the teacher is a national of the European Economic Area (see page 69) or Switzerland. Other nationals can be appointed under certain circumstances as temporary unqualified teachers for up to four years. These may gain QTS through a school-based training programme, or, in England only, through the Overseas Trained Teachers programme.

Government scholarship schemes

The Government makes provision for foreign students to study in the United Kingdom through its Chevening Programme and other scholarship schemes. In 2002/03 about 3,400 overseas scholarships were awarded under scholarship schemes funded by the Foreign & Commonwealth Office (FCO), and other government departments. In addition to the Chevening Programme, these are the Commonwealth Scholarships and Fellowship Plan, Department for International Development Shared Scholarships, Marshall Scholarships, and North Atlantic Fellowships.

Other schemes

The Overseas Research Students Award Scheme, funded by the higher education funding councils, provides help for overseas full-time postgraduate students with outstanding research potential. In addition, most UK universities and colleges offer bursaries and scholarships for which graduates of any nationality are eligible. Other public and private scholarships are available to students from overseas and to UK students who want to study in other countries.

The Teachers' International Professional Development Programme aims to provide teachers with opportunities for international study visits or exchanges which will enable them to benefit from good practice, develop international educational links with other schools, carry out research and share information with a network of other participants.

Further reading

Department for Education and Skills Departmental Report. Cm 6202. Department for Education and Skills, 2004.

Education and Training Statistics for the United Kingdom. Department for Education and Skills. Annual.

Education for the 21st Century – Post Primary Review. Department of Education, Northern Ireland, 2001.

Excellence and Enjoyment – a strategy for primary schools. Department for Education and Skills, 2003.

Five Year Strategy for Children and Learners, Cm 6272. Department for Education and Skills, 2004.

The Future of Higher Education. White Paper. Cm 5735. Department for Education and Skills, 2003.

The Learning Country – A Comprehensive Education and Lifelong Learning Programme to 2010 in Wales. National Assembly for Wales, 2001.

Websites

Department for Education and Skills
www.dfes.gov.uk

Scottish Executive
www.scotland.gov.uk

Welsh Assembly Government
www.learning.wales.gov.uk

Department of Education (Northern Ireland)
www.deni.gov.uk

Department for Employment and Learning (Northern Ireland)
www.delni.gov.uk

WWW.

11 The labour market

Both full-time and part-time employment in the United Kingdom have risen over the last decade. The increase has been predominantly in the service sector, in which over three-quarters of employees now work. At the same time unemployment has fallen considerably since the last peak at the end of 1992 and in spring 2004 reached its lowest rate since the introduction of the International Labour Organisation (ILO) measure of unemployment in 1984.

Patterns of employment

The Labour Force Survey (LFS)[1] carried out by the Office for National Statistics shows that, on a seasonally adjusted basis, 29.7 million people aged 16 and over were economically active in the United Kingdom in spring 2004, comprising 28.3 million in employment[2] and 1.4 million unemployed (Table 11.1). The number in employment represented an increase of 206,000 on the previous year. The employment rate among those of working age (men aged 16 to 64 and women aged 16 to 59) was 74.7 per cent, unchanged from spring 2003. The economic activity rate for people in this age group was 78.6 per cent. Some 7.8 million people of working age were economically inactive.

One of the main long-term trends in the labour market is the increased participation of women in employment. In spring 2004, 70 per cent of working-age women were in employment,

1 The LFS data in this chapter do not take account of October 2004 revisions (see page vii).

2 There are two main measures of employment: the number of people in employment and the number of jobs; they differ because one person can have more than one job.

Definitions

Economic activity
The labour market can be divided into two groups: the economically active and inactive. The economically active are defined as those who are either in employment (employee, self-employed, unpaid family worker or on a government-supported training programme) or unemployed and actively seeking work. The economically inactive are people who do not meet either of these criteria: for example those in retirement and those not actively seeking work.

Unemployment
The unemployment figure is based on LFS estimates of the number of people without a job who are seeking work. It refers to the number available to start work within two weeks who have either looked for work in the previous four weeks or are waiting to start a job they have already obtained. It is based on ILO guidelines and is the official measure of UK unemployment.

Employment and unemployment rates
The employment rate is the percentage of people in a given age group who are in employment. The unemployment rate is the percentage of the economically active who are unemployed.

Redundancy rate
The ratio of the number of redundancies in one quarter to the number of employees in the previous quarter, measured as redundancies per 1,000 employees.

Table 11.1 Employment, spring 2004, UK

Thousands, seasonally adjusted

	Males	Females	Total
All aged 16 and over	22,813	24,371	47,184
Total economically active	16,109	13,624	29,733
of whom:			
In employment	15,285	13,016	28,301
Unemployed	824	608	1,432
Economic activity rate (%)[1]	83.6	73.2	78.6
Employment rate (%)[1]	79.3	69.8	74.7
Unemployment rate (%)	5.1	4.5	4.8

1 For men aged 16 to 64 and women aged 16 to 59.
Source: Labour Force Survey, Office for National Statistics

compared with 58 per cent in 1984. Among many reasons for their greater involvement is that more women delay having children until their thirties and are then more likely to return to work afterwards, making use of a range of childcare options. Other reasons include the increasing levels of educational attainment among women and changing social attitudes to women working. The difference in employment rates between men and women has narrowed from 19 percentage points in 1984 to 10 percentage points in 2004.

Differences in employment rates within the regions of the United Kingdom are generally greater than differences between regions. The Annual Local Area LFS shows that in 2002/03 the greatest contrast in rates was found between local authorities in London. The capital includes Tower Hamlets, with the lowest employment rate in Great Britain (53 per cent), and Richmond upon Thames, with a rate of 82 per cent. The local authorities with the highest employment rate in Great Britain are Forest Heath (in the East), and Tandridge (in the South East), both with rates of 88 per cent.

Young people

The economic activity of young people is closely linked to their participation in full-time education (FTE). Of those 16- to 17-year-olds not in FTE in spring 2004, 77 per cent were economically active, and of these 27 per cent were unemployed. For those in FTE, 44 per cent were economically active. Youth unemployment decreased slightly between spring 2003 and 2004 with 389,000 people aged 18 to 24 unemployed at the latter

date. The number of young people unemployed for more than two years decreased by 5,000 to 18,000 over the same period (a fall of 21 per cent).

Older workers

There were 6.3 million people aged between 50 and state pension age[3] in employment in spring 2004, representing 22 per cent of all people in employment in the United Kingdom. Their employment rate was unchanged on the previous year at 70 per cent. The economic inactivity rate among men aged 50 to 64 increased from 23 per cent in 1984 to peak at 29 per cent in 1995 and was 26 per cent in spring 2004. The rate for women aged 50 to 59 declined from 41 per cent to 31 per cent between 1984 and 2004. Over 90 per cent of people above state pension age were economically inactive (see page 143) in spring 2004, but 995,000 were in employment, of whom 660,000 were women.

In spring 2004, 15 per cent of the unemployed were aged 50 and over, of whom 33 per cent had been unemployed for more than 12 months. The Government will be bringing forward legislation to outlaw age discrimination in employment and training by 2006 (see page 154). Its Age Positive website promotes the Code of Practice on Age Diversity in Employment.

Disabled people

The LFS uses the definition of disability in the *Disability Discrimination Act*, which includes both work limiting and non-work limiting disabled people. In spring 2004 there were about 7 million people of working age with long-term disabilities in the United Kingdom, of whom just under half were in employment. The unemployment rate among long-term disabled people in spring 2004 was 8 per cent, a fall of around 3 percentage points since spring 1998.

Households with no one in work

The number of workless households (among households where at least one adult was of working age) was 3.0 million in spring 2004, some 150,000 fewer than in 1999. This represented a rate of worklessness of 16.1 per cent in spring 2004, compared with 17.3 per cent in 1999.

3 60 for women and 65 for men.

Lone parents

In spring 2004 the rate of worklessness for lone parent households with dependent children was 42.1 per cent, down 1.2 percentage points from the previous year and down 6.0 percentage points from spring 1999. The number of such households in spring 2004 was 751,000, some 40,000 fewer than five years earlier.

Working patterns

For the past decade, about three-quarters of those in employment have been full-time workers, with the remainder working part time. A significant number of people have alternative employment patterns, such as second and temporary jobs. There is also a growing number of people who have a flexible work pattern.

Part-time work

There were nearly 7.4 million people in part-time work in the United Kingdom in spring 2004 (Table 11.2), of whom 78 per cent were women. Over the past decade the number of people working part time has increased by over 1 million, but as a proportion of all those in employment it has remained at around 25 per cent. People work part time for a variety of reasons. In spring 2004, 74 per cent did not want a full-time job while 8 per cent were working part time because they could not find full-time work.

Table 11.2 Employment status of the workforce,[1] UK

Thousands

	2000	2003	2004
Employees	23,904	24,394	24,458
Self-employed	3,258	3,521	3,616
Unpaid family workers	111	88	104
Government-supported training and employment programmes	141	92	123
Total in employment	**27,413**	**28,095**	**28,301**
of whom:			
Full-time workers	20,503	20,816	20,930
Part-time workers	6,910	7,279	7,371
Temporary employees	1,695	1,501	1,488
Workers with a second job	1,171	1,128	1,073

1 Spring figures, seasonally adjusted.
Source: Labour Force Survey, Office for National Statistics

Secondary and temporary work

Just over 1 million people had a second job in spring 2004 and about 1.5 million people (6 per cent of employees) were engaged in temporary jobs (Table 11.2). Around a quarter worked in a temporary job because they could not find a permanent one. The *Employment Act 2002* gives fixed-term employees the right to equal treatment on pay, pensions, holidays, sick pay and training. Temporary employment is lower in the United Kingdom than in most other European Union countries.

Flexible working patterns

Government policy has stressed the importance of maintaining a healthy work-life balance. Flexible working arrangements can make a contribution to this. A fifth of employees working full time in the United Kingdom and a quarter of those working part time had some type of flexible working arrangement in spring 2004. Flexible working hours was the most common form of arrangement for full-time employees from both sexes. It was also the most common arrangement for men who worked part time, whereas term-time working was the most common for women who worked part time (see also page 146).

The *Second Work-Life Balance Study*, published by the Department for Trade and Industry (DTI) in October 2003, found strong support for extending flexible working practices from both employers and employees. The survey of employers found that 84 per cent agreed with the statement 'employers should make special effort to accommodate the particular difficulties facing parents of young and disabled children in balancing their work and family life', and 94 per cent of employers agreed with the statement 'people work best when they can balance their work and other aspects of their lives'.

Hours of work

The most common hours worked by those in employment in the United Kingdom were between 31 and 45 hours in spring 2004. A slightly higher proportion of men (57 per cent) than women (46 per cent) worked these hours. The next most common length for men was over 45 hours (32 per cent) whereas for women it was between 16 and 30 hours (30 per cent). A higher

Flexible arrangements for parents

Regulations introduced across the United Kingdom in April 2003 give parents of children under 6 or parents of disabled children under 18 the right to request a flexible work pattern: either a change to the hours they work; a change to the times when they are required to work; or the opportunity to work from home. Employers have a statutory duty to consider such applications and may only refuse on business grounds.

In April 2004 the DTI published results of its first flexible working employee survey. The survey questioned employees in September, October and November 2003, and February 2004. It found that 52 per cent of all employees in Great Britain were aware of the right of working parents to request flexible working and that the large majority (86 per cent) of flexible working requests made since April 2003 were either fully or partly accepted by employers.

proportion of women (44 per cent) than men (11 per cent) worked 30 hours or less a week.

Hours worked tend to be longest in agriculture and construction, and shortest in public administration, education and health, and other services. These differences between industries reflect the mix of part-time and full-time workers, as well as any difference in the standard working week.

Regulations implementing an EC Directive on working time are in force in the United Kingdom. They apply to full-time, part-time and temporary workers and provide for:

- a maximum working week of 48 hours (on average), although individual workers can choose to work longer;
- a minimum of four weeks' annual paid leave;
- minimum daily, weekly and in-work rest periods;
- a limit for night workers of an average eight hours' work in a 24-hour period; and
- a right for night workers to receive free health assessments.

From August 2004 these regulations were extended to the working time of junior doctors, with the

Travelling to work

According to the 2001 Census, 62 per cent of people aged 16 to 74 who were in employment in England and Wales travelled to work in a car or van. Far smaller proportions (14 per cent) used public transport and 13 per cent went on foot or on a bicycle. Fifty eight per cent of workers travelled less than 10 kilometres to their workplace and only 5 per cent travelled 40 kilometres or more. The majority (80 per cent) of those who walked to work travelled less than 2 kilometres to their workplace. Of those who used the train, just under a quarter (23 per cent) travelled 40 kilometres or more.

implementation of the maximum 48-hour working week to be phased in by 1 August 2009. There are specific provisions for 16- and 17-year-olds in respect of entitlement to rest and health assessments and specific working time and night work limits.

Self-employment

In spring 2004, 3.6 million people (nearly three-quarters of whom were men) were self-employed in the United Kingdom (Table 11.2). This represented 13 per cent of those in employment, a small increase since spring 2003. Those who were self-employed were most likely to work in construction or banking, finance and insurance, and less likely to work in manufacturing, transport and communication.

Occupations and industries

There has been a long-term growth in managerial and professional occupations and a decline in skilled trades, elementary occupations[4] and process, plant and machine operatives.

The patterns of occupations followed by men and women in the United Kingdom are quite different (Table 11.3). More than a fifth of women in

---

4 Occupations involving mainly routine tasks which do not require formal qualifications, but usually have a period of formal on-the-job training.

Table 11.3 Employment by sex[1] and occupation, spring 2004,[2] UK

Percentages

	Males	Females
Managers and senior officials	18	11
Professional occupations	13	12
Associate professional and technical	13	14
Administrative and secretarial	5	22
Skilled trades	20	2
Personal service	2	14
Sales and customer service	5	12
Process, plant and machine operatives	12	2
Elementary occupations	12	12
All employees[3] (million)	**15.2**	**13.0**

1 Aged 16 and over.
2 Not seasonally adjusted.
3 Includes a few people who did not state their occupation.
  Percentages are based on totals that exclude this group.
Source: Labour Force Survey, Office for National Statistics

Table 11.4 Workforce jobs by industry, March 2004,[1] UK

	Jobs (thousands)	Jobs (per cent)	Percentage change 1984–2004
Agriculture and fishing	420	1.4	−36.5
Energy and water	203	0.7	−64.3
Manufacturing	3,654	12.1	−32.4
Construction	2,111	7.0	15.5
Services	23,936	78.9	37.6
of which:			
Distribution, hotels & restaurants	7,040	23.2	25.3
Transport & communication	1,813	6.0	13.5
Finance & business services	5,828	19.2	80.0
Public administration, education & health	7,362	24.3	28.3
Other services	1,893	6.2	57.3
All jobs	**30,325**	**100**	**17.3**

1 Seasonally adjusted.
Source: Office for National Statistics

employment were in administrative and secretarial work in spring 2004, while men were most likely to be employed in skilled trades or as managers and senior officials. These occupations were less likely to be followed by women. Conversely women were more likely than men to be employed in the personal services and in sales and customer services. Only the professional and associated occupations, and elementary occupations, were followed by similar proportions of men and women.

Employment by sector

One of the major long-term trends in employment in the United Kingdom has been the large increase in employment in service industries (Table 11.4). Between March 1984 and March 2004 the number of workforce jobs in service industries increased from 17.4 million to 23.9 million, a rise of 38 per cent, compared with a rise in the total number of jobs of 17 per cent. Growth in finance and business services was particularly strong, up by 80 per cent over this period.

In recent years most other sectors have experienced falling levels of employment. The biggest long-term decline has been in energy and water, with a reduction of 64 per cent between 1984 and 2004, reflecting, among other things, a large fall in jobs in the coal industry.

Pay and conditions

Earnings

According to the New Earnings Survey (NES), average gross weekly earnings for full-time adult employees whose pay was not affected by absence were £476 in Great Britain in April 2003 (an increase of 2.4 per cent since April 2002), and £405 in Northern Ireland (Table 11.5). London had by far the highest average earnings within the United Kingdom (£637 a week) and the North East had the lowest (£402 a week). Across all regions in the United Kingdom, men earned more than women. However, female employees in London earned more on average than male employees from many of the other regions.

In Great Britain average hourly pay, excluding overtime, for full-time male adult employees whose pay was not affected by absence was £12.88 in April 2003, compared with £10.56 for female employees. Expressed in percentage terms, women were paid 82.0 per cent of the male rate – the narrowest gender pay gap since the NES began in 1970. For full-time employees in Northern Ireland the hourly rate for men was £10.64, compared with £9.51 for women.

Directors and chief executives of major organisations were the highest paid occupation,

Table 11.5 Average gross weekly pay,[1] April 2003, UK

£

	Males	Females	All
England	533.5	400.9	483.4
North East	437.8	347.3	402.1
North West	483.1	367.9	437.6
Yorkshire and the Humber	463.8	360.4	425.5
East Midlands	467.3	357.4	428.7
West Midlands	477.1	363.7	435.8
East	528.5	382.7	475.9
London	716.5	516.5	636.9
South East	560.9	415.7	505.6
South West	485.1	364.7	440.6
Wales	448.3	357.3	414.5
Scotland	483.7	372.4	436.8
Great Britain	525.0	396.0	475.8
Northern Ireland	437.7	355.2	404.5

1 Full-time employees on adult rates, whose pay was unaffected by absence.
Source: New Earnings Survey 2003, Office for National Statistics; Department of Enterprise, Trade and Investment, Northern Ireland

receiving over ten times the average gross weekly pay of those working as retail cashiers and check-out operators (Table 11.6).

Table 11.6 Highest and lowest paid occupations,[1] April 2003, Great Britain

Average gross weekly pay (£)

Highest paid
Directors and chief executives of major organisations	2,301
Medical practitioners	1,186
Financial managers and chartered secretaries	1,124
Solicitors and lawyers, judges and coroners	926
Marketing and sales managers	889

Lowest paid
Kitchen and catering assistants	228
Waiters and waitresses	218
Bar staff	218
Launderers, dry cleaners and pressers	218
Retail cashiers and check-out operators	208

1 Full-time employees on adult rates, whose pay was unaffected by absence. Certain occupations have been excluded due to the small size of the sample.
Source: New Earnings Survey 2003, Office for National Statistics

National minimum wage

The statutory national minimum wage (NMW) was introduced in 1999. In October 2004, largely based on the recommendations of the Low Pay Commission, the Government introduced a new NMW for people who are under 18 and above school leaving age. Minimum wage rates, from 1 October 2004, are:

- £4.85 an hour for those aged 22 or above;
- £4.10 an hour for workers aged 18 to 21, and for those aged 22 or over receiving accredited training in the first six months of a new job with a new employer; and
- £3.00 an hour for those who are under 18 and above school leaving age.

Almost all workers who are 16 or over are covered by the NMW, including casual workers, agency workers, part-time workers, overseas workers and workers in small businesses. Workers not covered include the majority of the self-employed and members of the Armed Forces.

The NMW is enforced through a combination of measures. For example:

- employers are required by law to keep records to prove they are paying the NMW;
- Inland Revenue Compliance Officers investigate all complaints about non-payment of the NMW; they visit employers thought to be likely to pay below the minimum wage and take enforcement action where necessary; and
- individuals can take action through an employment tribunal or civil court.

The DTI and Inland Revenue publicise employer obligations and employee rights, mainly through direct advertising, the DTI employment rights website and the NMW helpline.

Fringe benefits

Fringe benefits offered by some employers include schemes to encourage financial participation by employees in their companies, pension schemes, medical insurance, subsidised meals, company cars and childcare schemes.

Many companies have adopted employee share schemes, where employees acquire shares or options to buy shares from their employer. An all-employee share ownership plan, called Share

Incentive Plan was introduced in 2000, allowing employees to buy shares from their pre-tax and National Insurance contribution (see page 161) salary and to receive free shares, with tax incentives for longer-term shareholding.

Workforce skills

The demand for different types of skills varies across the United Kingdom and this is reflected in the organisations responsible for managing skills, described in chapter 10.

The Government published a Skills Strategy and Delivery Plan for England in 2003, which sets out how it aims to close the productivity gap with competitors through a highly skilled, productive workforce. The Strategy identified particular gaps in basic skills such as literacy, numeracy and use of IT. It also identified skills gaps at intermediate and higher levels – for example there is a need for more people with technician, higher craft and associate professional qualifications, and a need to develop high quality leadership and management skills, particularly at middle management level in companies, and in small and medium-sized enterprises.

The New Deal for Skills forms part of the Skills Strategy and was announced in the 2004 Budget. It is a joint project between the Department for Work and Pensions (DWP) and the Department for Education and Skills with involvement from the Learning and Skills Council (see page 135), Jobcentre Plus (see page 153), the DTI and the Treasury. It aims to improve the support to the low-skilled by creating a new skills guidance service, co-located with Jobcentre Plus where possible, and improving mechanisms of financial support for those for whom training provides a route back to work.

The New Deal for Skills takes forward the recommendations set out in the February 2004 report of the National Employment Panel, *Welfare to Workforce Development*. The Panel is an employer-led body that provides independent advice to Ministers.

The National Employers Skills Survey 2003 found that about 2.4 million workers in England were described by their employers as not proficient in their jobs. One in five job vacancies remained unfilled because of a lack of skilled applicants and 44 per cent of the employers experiencing skills shortages said they were losing business as a result.

The Scottish Executive's strategy for lifelong learning, *Life Through Learning; Learning Through Life*, was published in 2003. It sets out five goals to achieve the best possible match between the learning opportunities open to people and the skills necessary to strengthen Scotland's economy.

Futureskills Scotland (part of Scottish Enterprise and Highlands and Islands Enterprise carried out the Skills in Scotland 2003 survey. It found that skills shortages were uncommon, and were concentrated in skilled trades and personal service occupations, and among the other services, health and social work, and agriculture industries.

The Department for Employment and Learning in Northern Ireland is developing a Skills Strategy in conjunction with other Northern Ireland departments and agencies and has established a Skills Task Force.

Skills Monitoring Surveys were carried out in Northern Ireland in 2000 and 2002 and the next is scheduled for early 2005. In addition, a series of skills forecasting studies on specific industry sectors have been completed.

Investors in People

Investors in People (IiP) is the National Standard that sets a level of good practice for improving an organisation's performance through its people. It links the training and development of employees to the organisation's business objectives. Reported benefits include increased productivity, higher profits, lower rates of absenteeism and improved morale. Investors in People UK is responsible for the promotion, quality assurance and development of the Standard. In March 2004 over 7 million employees worked in IiP recognised organisations.

Unemployment

There has been a steadily downward trend in the number of unemployed people since 1993, apart from a slight increase between spring 2001 and spring 2002 (Figure 11.7). The unemployment rate in spring 2004 was down 0.2 percentage points on spring 2003 and, at 4.8 per cent, was at its lowest level since the introduction of the ILO measure of unemployment in 1984. This represents about

Figure 11.7 Unemployment¹ in the UK

Millions

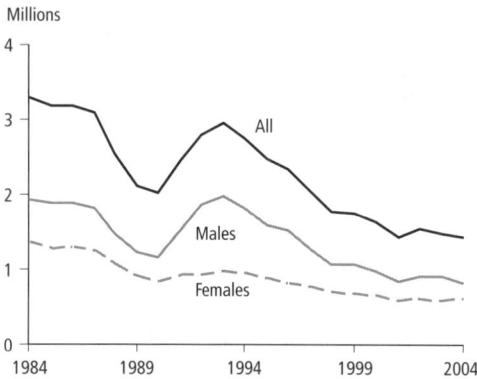

1 At spring each year, seasonally adjusted.
Source: Labour Force Survey, Office for National Statistics

1.4 million unemployed people (see Table 11.1) and compares with the EU-15 average in 2003 of 8.1 per cent and a rate of 6.0 per cent in the United States.

Within the United Kingdom, unemployment rates in spring 2004 were highest in Scotland (6.1 per cent), followed by Northern Ireland (5.0 per cent), England (4.7 per cent) and Wales (4.6 per cent). In addition, there were significant variations in unemployment rates within regions.

In recent years there has been a substantial fall in long-term unemployment. In spring 2004 some 290,000 people aged 16 and over had been unemployed for over a year, of whom 135,000 had been out of work for over two years. These figures represent falls of 9 per cent and 13 per cent respectively since spring 2003.

In June 2004, 851,000 people were claiming unemployment-related benefits, representing 2.7 per cent of the total UK workforce. Around two-thirds of claimants had been claiming benefits for less than six months.

Redundancies

Redundancy levels in the United Kingdom have remained roughly constant since the statistical series began in 1995. In spring 2004 the redundancy rate was 5.9 per 1,000 employees, compared with 6.4 per 1,000 in spring 2003. The highest redundancy rate was in manufacturing at 12.1 per 1,000. The redundancy rate in the services sector was 4.3 per 1,000 employees.

Economic inactivity

In spring 2004, 7.8 million people of working age in the United Kingdom were economically inactive, of whom 61 per cent were women. When including those over state pension age (65 for men and 60 for women) there were 17.5 million economically inactive people.

Figure 11.8 shows that inactivity rates were highest for people over the state pension age although around 10 per cent of men and women of this age were still economically active. Given many 16- to 17-year-olds continue in full-time or part-time education after they complete their compulsory education, the inactivity rate for this group is also fairly high. Inactivity rates among men were lowest for those aged 25 to 34 and 35 to 49, at around 8 per cent, and for women the rate was lowest for 35- to 49-year-olds at 22 per cent.

Sickness and disability were the major reasons for economic inactivity among working-age men in spring 2004. Looking after the family or home was the most common reason for inactivity among working-age women – 45 per cent said this was the main reason for not seeking work. Government

Figure 11.8 Economic inactivity rates,¹ by sex and age, spring 2004, UK

Percentages

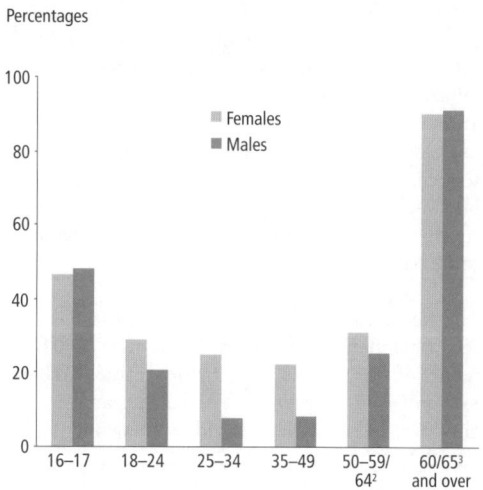

1 The number of people who are not in work, but who do not satisfy all the criteria for unemployment (see page 143) as a percentage of the population in each age group. Data are seasonally adjusted.
2 Females aged 50–59, males aged 50–64.
3 Females aged 60 and over, males aged 65 and over.
Source: Labour Force Survey, Office for National Statistics

policy is aimed at helping those who are currently inactive to make the transition towards activity, primarily through the New Deal programmes (see page 152) and Jobcentre Plus (see page 153).

Labour market policy

The Government's strategy for ensuring employment opportunity for all was set out in its Green Paper, *Towards Full Employment in a Modern Society*, published in 2001. It is based on:

- helping people to move from welfare to work, through extending the series of New Deal programmes (see page 152);

- easing the transition to work by removing barriers to working and ensuring that people are financially secure when moving from welfare to work;

- making paid work more attractive, through promoting incentives to work and reforming the tax and benefits system (see chapters 23 and 12); and

- securing progression in work through lifelong learning, to ensure that people are well trained and able to adapt to changing economic circumstances.

Although the UK employment rate has increased over the last ten years the Government wants to increase the employment opportunities for certain sections of society who may experience disadvantage such as lone parents, people on sickness and disability benefits, and those who have been on benefits for a long time – particularly in areas where there are high concentrations of economic inactivity. In December 2003 it published *Full employment in every region*, which outlines its strategy of:

- making the benefit system encourage those people who are economically inactive but capable of, and often interested in, work;

- improving the financial incentives for people on sickness and disability benefits, and for people living in areas where housing rents are high, so that they gain more by returning to work; and

- providing more flexible opportunities for training and childcare and reducing other barriers to work.

Welfare to work

The DWP operates a number of programmes aimed at helping people into work, including:

- Employment Zones – working in 13 areas of Great Britain where there are high concentrations of unemployment;

- Action Teams for Jobs – operating in 63 areas in Great Britain, these aim to remove the barriers to employment faced by jobless people and, by working with employers, to move them into suitable vacancies;

- StepUP – a programme aimed at providing guaranteed jobs for up to 50 weeks in areas of high unemployment, for those who have not been successful on the New Deal;

- Progress2work – a £40 million programme helping recovering drug misusers find employment. Progress2work-LinkUP, which began in October 2002, is piloting the same approach with a wider group, including ex-offenders, alcohol misusers and the homeless;

- Adviser Discretion Fund – which gives Jobcentre Districts flexibility to address the specific barriers to work affecting their communities; and

- Ambition Programmes – industry-specific training and recruitment programmes in sectors such as IT, retailing, energy, construction and the public sector.

The Government's welfare to work policy is also delivered throughout the United Kingdom through a number of 'New Deal' programmes, targeted at specific groups (see Table 11.9). In 2004/05 the provision for expenditure on New Deals includes £330 million for young people, £256 million for the 25 plus programme, £95 million for lone parents and £42 million for disabled people.

Recruitment and job finding

There are many ways in which people look for work in the United Kingdom. According to the LFS, in spring 2002, more than half of all employees obtained their current job either by hearing about it from someone who worked there or by replying to an advertisement. In spring 2004 there were an estimated 631,000 vacancies in the United Kingdom, 48,300 more than in spring 2003.

Table 11.9 New Deal programmes

Young people

Target group	18- to 24-year-olds who have been unemployed and claiming Jobseeker's Allowance (JSA) for six months.
Main features	Begins with a period of advice and guidance, called 'the gateway'. This is followed by an intensive programme of activity, involving subsidised employment, self-employment, training or placement with a voluntary organisation (options include an element of education and training). A period of follow-through for 4 to 6 months comprises regular interviews with personal advisers.

25 plus

Target group	Compulsory for people aged 25 and over who have been claiming JSA for 18 months or more (or 18 months out of the previous 21 months).
Main features	A gateway period of up to 4 months, with weekly interviews and jobsearch support from a personal adviser. An intensive period of 13 weeks, for those aged 25 to 49, with a mix of subsidised activities based on needs, including employment, work-focused training, work placements and self-employment support. A follow-through period of 6 weeks that can be extended to a maximum 13 weeks.

50 plus

Target group	A voluntary programme for those aged over 50 who have been claiming work-related benefits for 6 months or more.
Main features	Offers personal advice, jobsearch help and financial support through the Working Tax Credit. An in-work training grant of up to £1,500 over 2 years. Advice on starting up a business.

Lone parents

Target group	Compulsory meeting with a personal adviser to discuss work issues and give advice on in-work benefits – further participation is voluntary. From October 2005, lone parents whose youngest child is aged 14 or 15 will be required to attend extra interviews to access support.
Main features	Participation in a work trial (if appropriate). Help with the costs of approved training or education courses. Help with costs incurred while training, such as travel expenses and registered childcare costs. Outreach service for those living in isolated communities, and those who do not generally come into contact with government agencies.

Disabled people

Main features	Delivered by a range of organisations called Job Brokers, whose job is to help disabled people locate and move into work. Job Brokers advise about jobsearch and training, and offer support when the jobseeker starts work. Disabled people are eligible for inclusion in all New Deal activities without a qualifying period.

Partners

Target group	Partners of people claiming a range of work- and sickness-related benefits, with the aim of reducing the number of workless households.
Main features	Offers help with jobsearch activities, training opportunities, and a short course to refresh or boost skills before starting a job, or help and support with setting up a new business.

Jobcentre Plus

In Great Britain the Jobcentre Plus network provides help in finding jobs and pays benefits to people of working age. It has responsibility for running local offices formerly managed by the Employment Service and the Benefits Agency, including Jobcentres and social security offices. By the end of March 2004 around 400 Jobcentre Plus offices had been opened. The DWP expects the network of offices will be completed by 2006. Until this time, services in some areas will continue to be provided in social security offices and Jobcentres. A similar programme to combine Jobcentre and social security offices is under way in Northern Ireland. The new offices are known as 'Jobs and Benefits'.

All Jobcentre Plus vacancies are now available on the Internet, on one of the largest job banks in the world. Vacancies are also available through electronic touch-screen kiosks, known as 'Jobpoints', which are replacing traditional vacancy display boards in Jobcentres. The DWP is planning to install Jobpoints in locations such as libraries, supermarkets, prisons, and community centres.

Employers with a vacancy can use the Employer Direct service, which provides a single national telephone number for employers to have their vacancies advertised on the Internet and on all Jobpoints. From summer 2004 a new service – Employer Direct Online – enabled employers to notify their vacancies over the Internet.

Advisory services

Most people who make a claim for a working-age benefit have to take part in a meeting with a personal adviser, for example to discuss help to find work or support such as training or childcare. If the individual is claiming benefits other than JSA (see page 172), it is his or her decision whether or not to look for work.

Jobcentre Plus advisers assess eligibility for JSA and provide advice about jobs, training and self-employment opportunities. To receive the allowance, each unemployed person has to complete a Jobseeker's Agreement, which sets out his or her availability for work, the types of job that are being looked for, and the steps that, if taken, offer the best chance of securing work.

Employment agencies

There are many private employment agencies, including several large firms with significant branch networks. The law governing the conduct of employment agencies is less restrictive in the United Kingdom than in many EU countries, but agencies must comply with legislation that establishes minimum standards designed to protect agency users, both workers and employers.

The Recruitment and Employment Confederation is the association representing the private

recruitment and staffing industry in the United Kingdom. It has a membership of over 6,000 recruitment agencies and over 8,000 recruitment consultants. All members must abide by a code of good recruitment practice.

New website for foreign workers

In December 2003 the Government launched a website (*www.workingintheuk.gov.uk*) that provides information about the rules for foreign nationals who want to work legally in the United Kingdom, including information on applying for a work permit. The site also provides advice for employers on preventing illegal working and includes other information on immigration policy.

Industrial relations

Individual employment rights

Employment protection legislation provides a number of safeguards for employees. For example, most employees have a right to a written statement setting out details of the main conditions, including pay, hours of work and holidays.

Employees with at least two years of continuous employment with their employer are entitled to lump sum redundancy payments if their jobs cease to exist and their employers cannot offer suitable alternative work.[5]

Minimum periods of notice are laid down for both employers and employees. Most employees who believe they have been unfairly dismissed have the right to complain to an employment tribunal (see page 154), subject to the general qualifying period of one year's continuous service. If the complaint is upheld, the tribunal may make an order for re-employment or award compensation.

Legislation prohibits discrimination in employment, training and related matters, on grounds of sex or marital status, or gender reassignment, disability, race, nationality (including citizenship) or ethnic or national origin

---

5 The statutory redundancy payment is calculated according to a formula based on a person's age, the number of years of continuous service up to a maximum of 20 years and his or her weekly pay up to the current maximum of £250 per week. However, many employers pay more than the statutory amount.

(see page 108). In December 2003 new employment regulations came into force in Great Britain. The Employment Equality (Sexual Orientation) and the Employment Equality (Religion or Belief) Regulations 2003, implemented parts of the EC Employment Directive, and extended protection against discrimination in employment and training to cover sexual orientation and religion or belief. Northern Ireland has separate legislation implementing the Directive and discrimination in employment, training and related matters on grounds of political opinion is also unlawful.

Between July and October 2003, the Government conducted a consultation exercise outlining proposals that would implement the part of the EC Employment Directive relating to age discrimination. It is planned that legislation outlawing age discrimination in employment and vocational training will come into force in October 2006.

The purpose of the *Equal Pay Act 1970* is to eliminate pay discrimination between women and men, when doing work that is the same or broadly similar, work that is rated as equivalent, or work that is of equal value. Regulations under the Act that came into force in 2003 lengthened the time limit for bringing cases, and the time limit for which arrears payments can be made. An Equal Pay Questionnaire was introduced in April 2003, designed to help employees who believe they may not have received equal pay to request relevant information from their employers.

The Disability Rights Commission, the Equal Opportunities Commission and the Commission for Racial Equality have powers to investigate cases of discrimination at work in Great Britain. The Equality Commission in Northern Ireland has similar powers.

Legislation that was due to come into force in October 2004 provides more protection for disabled people against discrimination in the workplace. The employment and vocational training provisions of the *Disability Discrimination Act 1995* were extended to employers with fewer than 15 employees and to most previously excluded occupations, such as police officers, firefighters and partners in businesses.

All pregnant employees have the right to statutory maternity leave with their non-wage contractual

benefits maintained, and to protection against detriment and dismissal because of pregnancy. Statutory maternity, paternity and adoption pay are described in chapter 12. The *Employment Act 2002* included provisions for paternity, maternity, adoption, and flexible working for parents of young or disabled children.

Employment tribunals

Employment tribunals in Great Britain have jurisdiction over complaints covering a range of employment rights, including unfair dismissal, redundancy pay, equal pay, and discrimination. New tribunal regulations, including provisions to deter cases with weak claims and defences, took effect in 2001 and reforms brought about by the *Employment Act 2002* were due to come into force in October 2004. These included:

- provision for cost recovery for management time in vexatious cases;

- requirements on employers to provide statutory grievance procedures at the workplace to help resolve disputes; and

- requirements on employees, in most cases, to begin these procedures before taking a complaint to a tribunal.

A similar tribunal system operates in Northern Ireland, and similar reforms are being introduced.

Between March and June 2004, the Government carried out a consultation on new rules of tribunal procedure for dealing with complex equal value cases. These involve workers claiming equal pay on the basis that they are doing work of equal value to that of someone of the opposite sex, rather than the same or a similar job. The Government plans to introduce these new regulations by the end of 2004.

In March 2003 the Government announced plans to bring the top ten non-devolved tribunals (including employment tribunals) into a new, unified Tribunals Service. Full proposals were published in a White Paper – *Transforming Public Services: Complaints, Redress and Tribunals* – by the Department for Constitutional Affairs in July 2004.

Labour disputes

The largest annual number of working days lost through stoppages in the United Kingdom was in 1926, the year of the General Strike, when just over

160 million working days were lost. The coal industry accounted for 146 million of these days. Since 1970 there have been peaks in 1972, 1979 and 1984 (Figure 11.10). In 1972, a miners' strike accounted for 45 per cent of the 24 million days lost. A strike by the engineering workers in 1979 resulted in just over half of the 29 million days lost. Another miners' strike in 1984 was responsible for over 80 per cent of the 27 million days lost.

In 2003 there were 133 stoppages of work arising from labour disputes in the United Kingdom, and 0.5 million working days were lost as a result, down from 1.3 million in 2002. In 2003, 28 per cent of the working days lost were in the public administration and defence sector, with the next highest sector being education, at 26 per cent. Stoppages over wage rates and earnings accounted for 56 per cent of days lost.

Figure 11.10 Working days lost as a result of labour disputes, UK

Millions

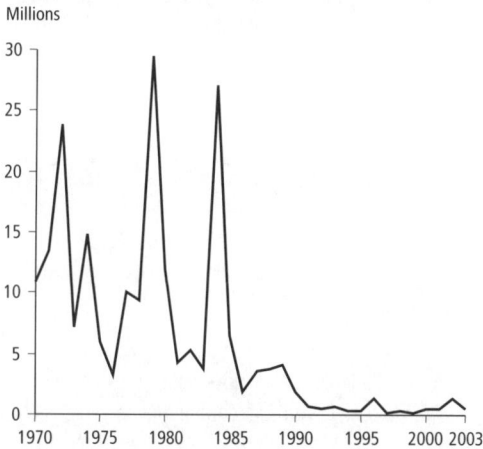

Source: Office for National Statistics

Trade unions and employers' organisations

Trade unions

Trade unions have members in nearly all occupations. As well as negotiating pay and other terms and conditions of employment with employers, they provide benefits and services, such as educational facilities, financial services, legal advice and aid in work-related cases. In autumn 2003 there were around 7.4 million trade union

members in the United Kingdom according to the LFS.[6] The proportion of employees who were union members was 29 per cent in 2003 (compared with 32 per cent in 1995), and the proportion among all those in employment was 27 per cent (29 per cent in 1995). By occupation, employee membership is highest among professionals, nearly half of whom were trade union members in 2003. Membership was lowest for sales and customer service employees of whom around one in ten were members.

The largest union in the United Kingdom is the public service union UNISON, which has around 1.3 million members. Other unions with membership over 500,000 are:

- Amicus – formed by the merger in 2002 of the Amalgamated Engineering and Electrical Union and the Manufacturing, Science and Finance union;

- the Transport and General Workers Union; and

- the GMB – a general union with members in a wide range of industries.

At the end of March 2004 there were 195 trade unions on the list maintained by the Certification Officer, who, among other duties, is responsible for certifying the independence of trade unions. Entry on the list is voluntary but to be eligible a trade union must show that it consists wholly or mainly of workers and that its principal purposes include the regulation of relations between workers and employers or between workers and employers' associations. A further 20 unions were known to the Certification Officer.

Trades Union Congress

The national body of the trade union movement in England and Wales is the Trades Union Congress (TUC), founded in 1868. In January 2004 its affiliated membership was 69 trade unions, which together represented some 6.4 million people.

There are six TUC regional councils for England and a Wales Trades Union Council. The TUC annual congress meets in September and a General Council represents the TUC between annual meetings.

6 There are two main sources of information on trade union membership: the ONS Labour Force Survey and data provided by trade unions to the Certification Office. Differences in coverage can result in different estimates – in 2002/03 there were 7.7 million trade union members in the United Kingdom according to the Certification Office.

In Scotland there is a separate national body, the Scottish Trades Union Congress, to which UK unions usually affiliate their Scottish branches. Nearly all trade unions in Northern Ireland are represented by the Northern Ireland Committee of the Irish Congress of Trade Unions (ICTU). Most trade unionists in Northern Ireland are members of unions affiliated to the ICTU, while the majority also belong to unions based in Great Britain, which are affiliated to the TUC.

The TUC participates in international trade union activity, through its affiliation to the International Confederation of Free Trade Unions and the European Trade Union Confederation. It also nominates the British workers' delegation to the annual ILO Conference.

Trade union and industrial relations law

Legal requirements governing trade unions include the following:

- All individuals have the right not to be dismissed or refused employment (or the services of an employment agency) because of membership or non-membership of a trade union.
- Where a union is recognised by an employer for collective bargaining purposes, union

officials are entitled to paid time off for certain trade union duties and training.

- A trade union must elect every member of its governing body, its general secretary and its president. Elections must be held at least every five years and be carried out by a secret postal ballot under independent scrutiny. Measures in the *Employment Relations Act 2004* (see box) will change the requirements on unions to hold a postal ballot for presidents.

- If a trade union wishes to set up a political fund, its members must first agree in a secret ballot a resolution adopting those political objectives as an aim of the union. The union must also ballot its members every ten years to maintain the fund. Individual members have a statutory right to opt out of contributing to the fund.

- For a union to have the benefit of statutory immunity when organising industrial action, the action must be wholly or mainly due to a trade dispute between workers and their own employer. Industrial action must not involve workers who have no dispute with their own employer (so-called secondary action) or involve unlawful forms of picketing. Before

---

Employment Relations Act 2004

The *Employment Relations Act 2004* is mainly concerned with collective labour law and trade union rights. The Act includes measures to:

- improve the process whereby a trade union gains recognition by an employer, through statutory means;

- tackle intimidation by unions or employers during statutory union recognition ballots. The measures will outlaw practices such as dismissing union activists or threatening workers in an attempt to influence a ballot;

- simplify the law on industrial action ballots and ballot notices;

- provide the Secretary of State with the power to make funds available to independent trade unions and federations of trade unions to modernise their operations;

- define more closely the actions that employers and unions should undertake when taking steps to resolve industrial disputes;

- widen the ability of the unions to lawfully expel or exclude individuals whose political behaviour is incompatible with trade union membership;

- ensure that union members have clear rights to use their union's services;

- improve trade union regulation;

- allow the Secretary of State to include non-postal methods of balloting in statutory union elections and ballots; and

- remove the requirements for union presidents (or their equivalents) to be elected by a secret postal ballot of the entire membership, provided they are already elected members of the union executive.

calling for industrial action, a trade union must obtain the support of its members in a secret postal ballot.

Employers' organisations

Many employers in the United Kingdom are members of employers' organisations, some of which are wholly concerned with labour matters, while others are also trade associations concerned with commercial matters in general. Employers' organisations are usually established on an industry basis rather than a product basis, for example, the Engineering Employers' Federation. At the end of March 2004, there were 85 employers' associations on the list maintained by the Certification Officer and a further 80 were known to the Certification Officer. Most national organisations belong to the Confederation of British Industry (see page 363).

ACAS

The Advisory, Conciliation and Arbitration Service (ACAS) is an independent statutory body with a general duty of promoting the improvement of industrial relations. ACAS aims to operate through the voluntary co-operation of employers, employees and, where appropriate, their representatives. Its main functions are collective conciliation; provision of arbitration and mediation; advisory mediation services for preventing disputes and improving industrial relations through the joint involvement of employers and employees; and the provision of a public enquiry service. ACAS also conciliates in disputes on individual employment rights, and runs a voluntary arbitration system for resolving unfair dismissal claims. In April 2004 the arbitration service provided by ACAS in England and Wales to resolve complaints concerning unfair dismissal was extended to Scotland. The scheme is optional and both employer and employee must choose arbitration rather than a tribunal hearing.

In Northern Ireland the Labour Relations Agency, an independent statutory body, provides similar services to those provided by ACAS.

Health and safety at work

There has been a long-term decline in injuries to employees in the United Kingdom, partly reflecting a change in industrial structure away from the traditional heavy industries, which tend to have higher risks. In Great Britain in 2003/04 there were 235 deaths of employees and the self-employed from injuries at work, which represented a fatal injury rate of almost one per 100,000 workers. Falls from a height, being struck by a moving vehicle and being struck by a moving/flying object continue to be the three most common kinds of accident, accounting for 29 per cent, 29 per cent and 12 per cent of fatal injuries respectively. In Northern Ireland in 2002/03 there were 21 fatal accidents in the workplace.

The main legislation in this area in Great Britain is the *Health and Safety at Work, etc. Act 1974.* It imposes general duties on everyone concerned with work activities, including employers, the self-employed, employees, and manufacturers and suppliers of materials for use at work. Associated Acts and regulations deal with particular hazards and types of work. Employers with five or more staff must prepare written statements of their health and safety policy and their assessment of significant risks and bring them to the attention of their staff. The regulatory regime for health and safety at work in Northern Ireland broadly mirrors that of England, Scotland and Wales. The principal legislation is contained in the Health and Safety at Work (Northern Ireland) Order 1978 as amended by the Health and Safety at Work (Amendment) (Northern Ireland) Order 1998.

The DWP has lead responsibility for the sponsorship of the Health and Safety Commission (HSC) and the Health and Safety Executive (HSE). Other government departments have specific health and safety responsibilities, for example, the DTI for civil nuclear matters and the Department for Transport for rail passenger safety. The Health and Safety Executive for Northern Ireland has responsibility for enforcing legislation there.

Health and Safety Commission

The HSC has responsibility for developing policy on health and safety at work in Great Britain, including proposals for new or revised regulations and approved codes of practice. In February 2004 the HSC published *A strategy for workplace health and safety in Great Britain to 2010 and beyond.* The strategy aims to:

- work with others, especially on workplace health, and form closer working relations between HSE and local authorities;

- promote effective health and safety management, the case for health and safety, and worker involvement;
- focus on key ways to reduce workplace injury and ill health; and
- develop more effective ways of communicating HSC and HSE aims.

The HSC has advisory committees covering subjects such as toxic substances, genetic modification and occupational health. There are also several industry advisory committees, each covering a specific sector of industry.

Health and Safety Executive

The HSE is the primary means of carrying out the HSC's policies. It provides technical advice and enforces health and safety law through its inspectorates. In premises such as offices, shops, warehouses, restaurants and hotels, legislation is enforced by inspectors appointed by local authorities, working as agents of the HSC under guidance from the HSE.

The Health and Safety Laboratory, an agency of the HSE, supports investigations of incidents and workplace situations. It also carries out longer-term research on occupational health and safety problems.

Further reading

A strategy for workplace health and safety in Great Britain to 2010 and beyond. Health and Safety Commission. 2004.

Full employment in every region. HM Treasury and the Department for Work and Pensions. The Stationery Office. 2003.

Labour Market Bulletin. Northern Ireland Department for Employment and Learning. Annual.

Labour Market Trends. Office for National Statistics. Monthly.

Towards Full Employment in a Modern Society. Department for Education and Employment, HM Treasury and the Department of Social Security. Cm 5084. The Stationery Office. 2001.

Transforming Public Services: Complaints, Redress and Tribunals. Department for Constitutional Affairs, 2004.

Welfare to Workforce Development. National Employment Panel Skills Advisory Board. 2004.

Websites
Department for Education and Skills
www.dfes.gov.uk

Department for Employment and Learning (Northern Ireland)
www.delni.gov.uk

Department of Trade and Industry
www.dti.gov.uk

Department for Work and Pensions
www.dwp.gov.uk

Health and Safety Executive
www.hse.gov.uk

Learning and Skills Council
www.lsc.gov.uk

Office for National Statistics
www.statistics.gov.uk

Trades Union Congress
www.tuc.org.uk

WWW.

12   Social protection

Social protection refers to the support that is provided by central government, local authorities, private bodies, voluntary organisations and individuals to those who are in need or at risk. Recipients of such help include children and families; older people and survivors (such as widows); those who are sick, physically disabled or sensorily impaired; people with learning disabilities or mental health problems; and low earners and the unemployed. The Government provides social protection principally through the social security system and health and personal social services. Services relating specifically to health are included in chapter 13.

The social security system is designed to secure a basic standard of living for people in financial need. It provides income during periods of inability to earn (including periods of sickness and unemployment), pensions for retired people, financial help for low-income families and assistance with costs arising from disablement. The provision of these benefits is administered by the Department for Work and Pensions (DWP) in Great Britain (mainly through the Jobcentre Plus network and The Pension Service) and the Social Security Agency of the Department for Social Development in Northern Ireland. The Inland Revenue administers tax credits (see page 161).

Personal social services refers to the assessment for, and provision of, practical help and support for older people, disabled people, vulnerable children and young people, those with mental health problems or learning disabilities, and their families and carers. These services may be residential, day care, short-break or 'domiciliary' (provided for people needing support to live in

their own homes). In certain circumstances, direct cash payments may be made to enable individuals to obtain relevant services for themselves.

In Great Britain the social services departments of local authorities are responsible for ensuring the direct provision or commissioning of services and for ensuring that people receive a high-quality service, regardless of the provider. In Northern Ireland services are provided by Health and Social Services (HSS) Trusts.

Central government is responsible for establishing national policies, securing resources, issuing guidance and overseeing standards. An independent body is responsible for inspecting and regulating social care services in each part of the United Kingdom (see page 162).

Various voluntary, charitable and not-for-profit organisations also offer care, assistance and support to vulnerable members of society. Examples include the Anchor Trust, which works with older people; Barnardo's, which helps children and young people (and their families); and Mencap, which supports people with learning disabilities, their parents and carers. Citizens Advice (see page 479) offer free and impartial advice on a wide range of issues including benefits, housing, debt, legal matters, employment, and immigration.

Expenditure

Average UK social protection expenditure per head was £3,842 in 2001, similar to the EU average (Figure 12.1). These figures include central and local government expenditure on social security and personal social services, sick pay paid by

Figure 12.1 Expenditure[1] on social protection in the EU, 2001

£ thousand per head

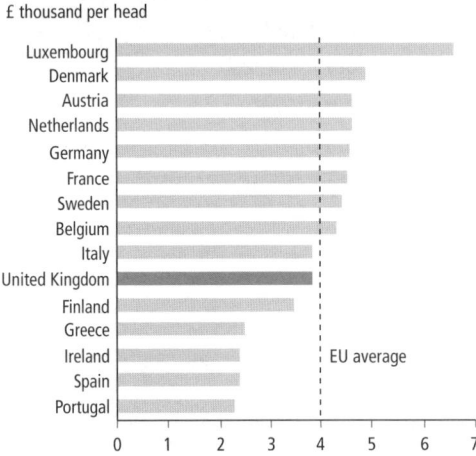

1 Before deduction of tax, where applicable. Tax credits are generally excluded. Figures are Purchasing Power Parities per inhabitant.
Source: Social Protection in Europe, Eurostat

Figure 12.2 Local authority personal social services expenditure,[1] 2002/03, England

Total: £15.2 billion

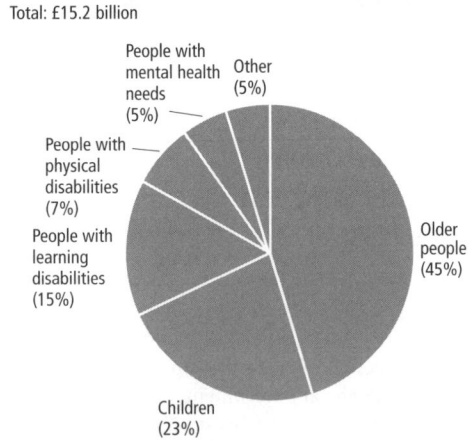

1 All figures include overhead costs.
Source: Department of Health

employers, payments made from occupational and personal pension schemes, and administration costs, but they exclude most tax credits. In order to allow direct comparisons they are expressed in Purchasing Power Parities (which take account of the general level of prices within each country). As well as different levels of expenditure in the EU countries, the figures reflect differences in demographic structures, unemployment rates and other social, institutional and economic factors.

Social security is the largest single area of UK government spending, amounting to an estimated £131 billion in 2003/04 – 28.5 per cent of total managed expenditure. Over half of government expenditure on social security benefits (excluding tax credits) goes on pensioners.

In 2002/03 gross expenditure on personal social services by local authorities was £15.2 billion in England. Expenditure on older people accounted for 45 per cent of the total and on children for 23 per cent (Figure 12.2). In Wales, spending on personal social services was £1.0 billion, while spending on social work amounted to £2.2 billion in Scotland and £600 million in Northern Ireland.

The social security system

Benefits

Social security benefits can be grouped into four types:

- contributory, paid to people who have made the required contributions to the National Insurance Fund (see page 161);

- means-tested, available to people whose income and savings are below certain levels;

- benefits which are neither contributory nor means-tested, mainly paid to offset extra costs of, for example, disability, or paid universally (for example Child Benefit); and

- payments made by employers to employees who are sick, expecting a baby or adopting a child (these payments are based on earnings and the terms and conditions of employment).

Most benefits are increased annually in line with percentage increases in retail prices. The main benefits (payable weekly) are described on pages 161 and 171.

From April 2003 the Government began paying benefits, state pensions and war pensions directly into bank, building society or Post Office accounts. This method of payment, called Direct Payment, is being phased in over two years. By October 2003, almost half of those receiving benefits or pensions had switched to direct payments.

Tax credits

Administered by the Inland Revenue, tax credits have been introduced with the aim of improving the way the Government supports families with children and working people on low incomes, including disabled workers. The main tax credits are the Working Tax Credit and Child Tax Credit.

National Insurance contributions (NICs)

With the exception of a small National Health Service (NHS) allocation, all NICs are paid into the National Insurance Fund. All contributory benefits and their administrative costs are paid out of the Fund.

Entitlement to many benefits, for example Retirement Pension, Incapacity Benefit and contributory Jobseeker's Allowance, is dependent upon the payment of NICs or the award of credits.

Employees and the self-employed aged under 65, and employers, are all liable to pay contributions once an individual's earnings exceed a certain amount. Where an employer operates a final salary pension scheme (see page 164), the employee and his or her employer pay a reduced rate of contribution to offset the cost of the contribution to the pension. The current NIC rates are set out on the Inland Revenue website. Self-employed people pay lower NICs than employees but receive fewer benefits; in particular they are not eligible for the State Second Pension (see page 164).

Social care providers

Providers of care range from families, friends and volunteers to large statutory, voluntary and private

---

Table 12.3 Selected key benefits and tax credits (from April 2004)

State Retirement Pension

A taxable benefit payable, if the contribution conditions have been met, to women from the age of 60 and men from the age of 65 (from 2020, the state pension age for both men and women will be 65). The full basic pension is £79.60 a week for a single person and £127.25 for a married couple – lower rates apply for those who have not paid full contributions. It is not possible for people in work to choose to contract out of the basic scheme. There is an additional state pension scheme (see page 164), although many people contract out of this and belong instead to occupational schemes (run by employers), or personal pension plans.

Child Benefit

A tax-free, universal, non-contributory payment of £16.50 a week for the eldest qualifying child and £11.05 for each other child. It is not affected by income or savings and is payable for children up to the age of 16, and for those under 19 who continue in full-time, non-advanced education.

Income Support

Payable to certain people aged between 16 and 59 who are not required to be available for work, and whose savings are below £8,000 (£16,000 for people in residential care or a nursing home). Those eligible include lone parents, carers, and long-term sick and disabled people. Income Support is based on circumstances, including age and whether the claimant is single, a lone parent or has a partner. The rates are £33.50 for a person aged 16–17, £44.05 for someone aged 18–24 and £55.65 a week for people aged 25 or over. Couples aged 18 or

over receive £87.30. There are additional allowances for dependent children and premium payments for those with extra expenses, for example people with disabled children.

Pension Credit

Guarantees everyone aged 60 or over a weekly income of at least £105.45 a week for a single person or £160.95 for a couple. For pensioners aged 65 or over some existing income and savings are not taken into account, in order to avoid penalising people who have saved in the past.

Working Tax Credit (WTC)

For people on low incomes who usually work at least 16 hours a week and are:

- aged 16 or over and responsible for at least one child; or
- aged 16 or over and disabled; or
- aged 25 or over and usually work at least 30 hours a week.

In addition to the basic credit, there are additional elements for single parents and couples, disabled people, childcare costs, and people aged 50 or over who are returning to work after a period on benefit. WTC is administered by the Inland Revenue.

Child Tax Credit (CTC)

A payment to support families with children. It is for people who are aged 16 or over and responsible for at least one child or young person who lives with them. As with WTC, it is administered by the Inland Revenue. The amount of CTC paid depends on income and the number of children. There are additional amounts for children aged under one and for those with disabilities.

sector organisations. In April 2004 a single comprehensive inspectorate for social care in England was formed, bringing together the work previously undertaken by the Social Services Inspectorate (SSI); the SSI/Audit Commission joint review team; and the social care functions of the National Care Standards Commission.

The Commission for Social Care Inspection (CSCI) is responsible for:

- inspecting all public, private, and voluntary social care organisations, including local social services authorities;

- registering services that meet national minimum standards;

- publishing an annual report to Parliament on national progress on social care and an analysis of where resources have been spent;

- validating all published performance assessment statistics on social care; and

- publishing star ratings for social services authorities.

In Wales and Scotland, the independent agencies responsible for inspecting and regulating social care services have a remit that also includes private hospitals and clinics. They are the Care Standards Inspectorate for Wales (CSIW) and the Scottish Commission for the Regulation of Care (the Care Commission). Social services authorities, however, are inspected by separate bodies, the Social Services Inspectorate for Wales and, in Scotland, the Social Work Services Inspectorate.

In Northern Ireland, a new Health and Personal Social Services Regulation and Improvement Authority will become responsible for monitoring and regulating the quality of health and care services. It was set up in April 2004 and will become fully operational in April 2005.

Informal carers

Much of the care given to people with long-term physical or mental ill-health, a disability, or problems relating to old age is provided by family members, friends, and neighbours. The 2001 Census found that one in ten people in the United Kingdom (5.9 million people) were providing unpaid care (looking after, giving help or support) to family members, friends, neighbours or others. The majority of these carers (68 per cent) were providing unpaid care for up to 19 hours a week, but around 21 per cent (1.3 million people) did so for 50 or more hours a week.

Carers can receive financial help from the Government. The Carer's Allowance is paid to full-time carers who are aged 16 or over and who are spending at least 35 hours a week looking after someone who is getting Attendance Allowance, Disability Living Allowance (at the middle or highest rate for personal care) or Constant Attendance Allowance. The rate of Carer's Allowance in April 2004 was £44.35 a week. For every complete tax year it is received, this is counted as a contribution to the State Second Pension.

Carer's Allowance is not paid to full-time students or if the carer is earning over £79 a week (after allowable expenses). Carers entitled to the Allowance and on low income may be able to qualify for the carer premium, paid with income-related benefits such as Pension Credit or Income Support. The carer premium from April 2004 is £25.55 a week.

The *Carers and Disabled Children Act 2000* provides carers in England and Wales with the right to have their need for services assessed by the local authority, and for the local authority to provide services direct to carers. The Act also extended the power of local authorities to offer direct payments to carers. Local authorities can help young carers using powers in the *Children Act 1989*, which allow them to provide services to other family members – such as helping a disabled parent fulfil his or her parenting role – where that is the best way to help the child.

The *Carers (Equal Opportunities) Act 2004* will be implemented from April 2005. It applies to England and Wales. The Act aims to:

- ensure that all carers know they are entitled to an assessment of their needs;

- place a duty on councils to consider a carer's outside interests (work, study or leisure) when carrying out an assessment; and

- promote better joint working between councils and the health service to ensure support for carers is delivered in a coherent way.

Under the *Community Care and Health (Scotland) Act 2002,* the ability of carers to provide care is assessed independently of the needs of the person receiving care. The Act also requires local authorities to take account of a carer's contribution and views before deciding what services to provide for the cared-for person.

Local authorities

Local authority social services departments provide support and services to children and their families, older people and those with learning disabilities, physical disabilities or mental health needs. These include the assessment of needs, the provision of help, such as meals on wheels and home help, and the running of day centres and residential homes. Efforts are made in the provision of services to promote independence and choice, and to help disabled people live as independently as possible. A new framework for delivering housing support services, the Supporting People programme, began in 2003 (see page 306).

The General Social Care Council in England, the Care Council for Wales and the Scottish Social Services Council are responsible for promoting high standards of conduct and training for social care workers by agreeing and issuing statutory codes of practice, setting up a register of social care workers, dealing with matters of conduct, and regulating and supporting social work education and training. All three bodies began registering social care workers on a phased basis from April 2003, starting with qualified social workers.

Residential and nursing homes

Care homes provide a range of facilities for people who cannot manage at home, and some are registered to provide nursing care. Most care homes are run by the independent sector. The cost of care and accommodation is funded in a number of ways: by the NHS where the person's primary need is for healthcare, by local authority social services, or by the individual following a means test. The details of such funding vary in each part of the United Kingdom (see page 166).

Under the *Care Standards Act 2000*, national minimum standards for care homes for people aged 18–65 and for care homes for older people came into force in England in 2002 and were slightly amended in June 2003. The standards cover such areas as choice of home, health and personal care, daily life and social activities, complaints and protection, environment, staffing, management and administration. Broadly similar standards apply in Wales and Scotland.

Table 12.4 Places available in residential care homes[1] at 25 May 2004, England

	Number of places (thousands)
Public sector[2]	
Older people	32.0
People with physical or sensory or learning disabilities	8.0
People with mental health problems	1.8
All places in the public sector	**35.8**
Independent sector[3]	
Older people	143.0
People with physical or sensory or learning disabilities	38.6
People with mental health problems	30.5
All places in the independent sector	**176.5**

1 Some categories are dual registered so totals are less than the sum of their constituent parts.
2 Places in staffed residential care homes.
3 Residential places in private, voluntary and small homes (less than four places) and dual registered places.
Source: Commission for Social Care Inspection

Older people

Pensions

In 2001/02 the State Retirement Pension was received by around 11 million people (including those living overseas) and accounted for £42 billion of social security benefit expenditure. In 2002/03, according to the Family Resources Survey, 59 per cent of employees of working age and 44 per cent of self-employed people of working age were contributing to either an occupational or a personal pension scheme or both (see page 164).

State pensions

The basic State Retirement Pension (see page 161) is based on NICs and is payable when people reach state pension age, unless they choose to defer. Under proposals in the Pensions Bill (see page 165), those choosing to defer taking their pension by at least a year will be able to take the deferred pension as a lump sum instead of higher weekly payments.

It is possible to build up an additional state pension based on NICs and earnings. The State Second Pension replaced the State Earnings-Related Pension Scheme (SERPS) from 2002.

The State Second Pension provides an additional pension for low and moderate earners, and for certain carers and people with a long-term illness or disability who have not been able to make contributions. Any SERPS entitlement that has already been built up is protected, both for those who have already retired and for those who have not yet reached pensionable age.

Occupational pensions

An occupational pension scheme is an arrangement that employers make to provide pensions for their employees when they retire. These schemes may also provide a tax-free lump sum on retirement, and benefits for the dependants of an employee if he or she dies. It is common for both employer and employee to contribute, based on a percentage of the employee's earnings. All employers with five or more employees are required to provide their employees with access to a stakeholder pension scheme if they do not provide access to an occupational scheme or to a personal pension with an employer contribution of at least 3 per cent.

There are two main types of occupational pension scheme:

- final salary (sometimes known as defined benefit) schemes, which offer a predetermined level of pension benefit, expressed as a fixed proportion of the employee's final salary for every complete year as a scheme member. The scheme may give members the option to convert part of the pension to a tax-free lump sum or it may specifically provide a separate tax-free lump sum; and
- money purchase schemes, in which the contributions of the employer and the employee are invested. The size of the fund depends on the amount of these contributions and the performance of the investment. When an employee retires or leaves the scheme, he or she can receive a proportion of the fund as a tax-free lump sum, while the remainder must be used to purchase an annuity (an arrangement by which a life assurance company pays a regular income, usually for life, in return for a lump-sum premium).

Personal and stakeholder pensions

Personal pensions are provided through financial services companies, such as insurance companies, banks, investment companies and building societies. Employers may make contributions in addition to those of employees. The money in the fund is invested to provide a pension when the owner retires.

Stakeholder pensions are a form of personal pension introduced by the Government to provide a pension option for people who do not have access to a good occupational or personal pension. Regulations provide that transfers can be made without charge from one stakeholder pension to another arrangement (including a different stakeholder) and for people to vary the amount they contribute to the scheme.

Regulation

The Occupational Pensions Regulatory Authority (Opra) is the regulator of pension arrangements offered by employers in the United Kingdom and seeks to ensure that pension schemes comply with the legislation.

Opra's Pension Schemes Registry maintains a register of UK tax-approved occupational and personal pension schemes. It also offers a service, which will be taken over by the DWP in April 2005, for tracing pension schemes when people have lost touch.

The Government has announced that Opra will be replaced by a new Pensions Regulator in April 2005 (see page 165).

The Office of the Pensions Advisory Service gives help and advice to people who have problems with state, company, personal or stakeholder pensions and has a telephone helpline. The Pensions Ombudsman deals with complaints of maladministration against occupational and personal pension schemes and adjudicates on disputes.

Pension reform

As people are living longer, the pensions industry is required to support a greater number of pensioners for longer periods. This increased pressure on pension funds has been exacerbated in recent years by falling share prices – pension funds generally rely on financial stock market returns to pay policyholders. As a result, many employers have closed their final salary schemes to new employees, increased employee contributions or, in a few cases, wound up existing schemes. There have also been some instances where employees have lost pension rights when their employer went out of business.

In June 2003, following an independent review and a Green Paper, the Government published *Simplicity, security and choice: Working and saving for retirement: Action on Occupational Pensions*. This was followed in February 2004 by the introduction of the Pensions Bill, which is designed to protect members of pension schemes through a number of measures, including:

- a Pension Protection Fund for defined benefit pension schemes in the United Kingdom which will protect the pension rights of members of underfunded pension schemes whose employers have become insolvent; and

- a new Pensions Regulator from April 2005, with a legal framework that will enable it to tackle the areas of greatest risk to members' benefits and powers to educate and advise those who administer or advise on pensions.

In an amendment to the Bill in May 2004 the Government proposed a £400 million fund to help workers who have already lost their pensions. It will pay the money over a 20-year period to assist people who lost their pension when their employer went out of business. Stakeholders will be consulted on how the fund will operate.

Simplicity, security and choice: Informed choices for working and saving, published in February 2004, contains proposals that would help people to make informed choices about saving and could equip them to plan better for financial security in retirement.

Other financial support

In addition to the State Retirement Pension, people aged 60 or over are eligible for other benefits. For those on low incomes, the Pension Credit (see page 161) replaced the Minimum Income Guarantee in October 2003.

Most people aged 60 or over are entitled to a Winter Fuel Payment of up to £200 for each eligible household. A further payment of up to £100 is paid to households that include someone aged 80 or over. From 2004/05, a new Age-Related

Payment is being paid with the Winter Fuel Payment to people aged 70 or over, to help with council tax bills and other expenses.

Free NHS prescriptions and eye tests are provided to those aged 60 or over. People receiving Pension Credit can also get free NHS dental treatment, wigs and fabric supports, vouchers towards the cost of glasses or contact lenses, and refunds of necessary travel costs to hospitals for NHS treatment (including check-ups). Pensioners aged 75 or over can claim a free television licence. Across the United Kingdom older people are entitled to free travel or concessionary fares on public transport (see page 330).

Care services for older people

Some £6.9 billion was spent by English local authorities on older people in 2002/03, 45 per cent of their total spending on personal social services (Figure 12.2).

Domiciliary care

Wherever possible, services are designed to help older people live at home. These services may include domestic help, the provision of meals in the home, sitters-in, night attendants and laundry services, as well as direct payments, day centres, lunch clubs and recreational facilities.

In England 661,000 older people (8.4 per cent of all people aged 65 or over) were being helped to live at home by local authorities at the end of March 2003. Gross expenditure on day and home care provision for older people amounted to almost £2 billion in 2002/03.

In Northern Ireland, around 22,000 older people (9.6 per cent of people aged 65 or over) were receiving home care services at 31 March 2003. During 2002/03, over £92 million was spent on day and home care for older people, and just over 11 million hours of home help and home care were provided.

Residential care

According to the 2001 Census nearly 324,000 people over retirement age were living in residential care or nursing homes in Great Britain, and around 19,000 were living in medical and care establishments in Northern Ireland. Residents who need regular and frequent care from a registered nurse are cared for in homes that are registered to

Table 12.5 Pensioners[1] in receipt of selected social security benefits, 2002/03, UK

Percentages

	Working Families' Tax Credit or Income Support/MIG[2]	Housing Benefit	Council Tax Benefit	State Retirement Pension	Incapacity or Disablement Benefits[3]	Child Benefit	Any benefit or tax credit
Pensioner couple	7	10	17	98	26	1	99
Single pensioner							
Male	14	25	33	98	20	0	99
Female	24	27	38	97	20	0	99

1 Single person or couple living as married and any dependent children, where the head of household is over state pension age (60 for females and 65 for males).
2 Working Families' Tax Credit and Disabled Person's Tax Credit ceased to exist from April 2003. They have been replaced by Working Tax Credit (and Child Tax Credit). Minimum Income Guarantee was replaced by Pension Credit in October 2003.
3 Incapacity Benefit, Disability Living Allowance (Care and Mobility components), Severe Disablement Allowance, Industrial Injuries Disability Benefit, War Disablement Pension, Attendance Allowance and Disabled Person's Tax Credit.
Source: Family Resources Survey 2002–2003, Department for Work and Pensions

provide nursing care. In England, residents' care and accommodation is funded by the NHS (where the person's primary need is for healthcare), by social services or by the individual following a means test.

The Welsh Assembly Government has implemented a policy to ensure that the services of a registered nurse are free of charge in all care settings. Funding has been set at £100 a week for each self-funder who is assessed as needing nursing care. Similar arrangements, with funding up to £100 apply in Northern Ireland.

In Scotland, the *Community Care and Health (Scotland) Act 2002* provides for free personal care, and for free nursing care in care homes that provide nursing. The Act allows people to make top-up payments if they wish to enter more expensive accommodation than the local authority would normally pay for (they may also defer these payments until their home is sold after death).

Families and children

Financial support

CTC and WTC (see page 161) provide financial support for children and their families. The level of CTC was increased by 13 per cent in April 2004 in order to try to reduce child poverty.

All pregnant employees have a right to 26 weeks' ordinary maternity leave and most can take a

further 26 weeks' additional maternity leave. Statutory Maternity Pay is paid directly from the employer for a maximum of 26 weeks to women who have been working for the same employer for 26 weeks and who earn on average at least £79 a week. It is paid at a rate equal to 90 per cent of their average weekly earnings for the first 6 weeks and a standard rate of £102.80 a week for the remaining 20 weeks, or at the 90 per cent rate if average earnings are less than £102.80.

Women who are not eligible for Statutory Maternity Pay because, for example, they are self-employed or have recently changed jobs or left their job, may qualify for a weekly Maternity Allowance, which is paid for up to 26 weeks at a standard rate of £102.80, or at a rate equal to 90 per cent of their average weekly earnings if this is less than £102.80.

Fathers who have 26 weeks' service with their employer have a right to two weeks' paternity leave within eight weeks of the child's birth. Those whose average weekly earnings are at least £79 per week qualify for Statutory Paternity Pay, which is paid at the same standard rate as Statutory Maternity Pay – £102.80 per week (or 90 per cent of average weekly earnings if this is less than £102.80).

Employees who adopt a child have a right to take 52 weeks' adoption leave and receive Statutory Adoption Pay for 26 weeks, paid at the same rate as Statutory Maternity Pay. To qualify, they must have worked for their employer for 26 weeks. Where a couple adopt jointly, they can choose which one of them will take adoption leave and pay. The other may take paternity leave and may qualify for Statutory Paternity Pay if their average weekly earnings are at least £79.

Subject to certain qualifying requirements, both mothers and fathers are entitled to 13 weeks' unpaid parental leave before the child's 5th birthday. Parents of disabled children can take 18 weeks before the child's 18th birthday. Parents of children aged under 6 and parents of disabled children aged under 18 have the right to request flexible working patterns. Employers have a duty to consider these requests and may only refuse on business grounds (see also page 146).

A Child Trust Fund will be set up in April 2005. The fund will provide every child born after September 2002 with an initial endowment at birth of £250 (or £500 for the poorest families). Parents, family members and friends will be able to make additional contributions, up to an annual limit of £1,200. Children will be able to access their accounts when they reach the age of 18.

Child Support Agency

The function of the Child Support Agency (CSA) is to ensure that parents who live apart meet their financial responsibilities to their children. The Northern Ireland Child Support Agency has a similar role. Both agencies:

- assess claims for child support maintenance;

- trace and contact non-resident parents;

- help conclude paternity disputes when a man denies he is a child's father;

- calculate child maintenance; and

- arrange, collect and pass on maintenance payments to the parent who is caring for the child, taking action to make the non-resident parent pay if necessary.

In March 2003 the way that child support payments are calculated was changed for new applicants and for people whose case is linked to a new application. The new scheme provides a simpler system that is designed to get money to more children more quickly. It enables non-resident parents to calculate their liability even before the CSA has completed an assessment.

Other support for families and children

Local authorities in England, Wales and Scotland, and HSS Trusts in Northern Ireland, are required to safeguard and promote the welfare of any children in need and, so far as is consistent with that, to promote the upbringing of children by their parents. The services provided to those with assessed needs include advice, guidance, counselling, help in the home and family centres. Help can be given to the immediate family of the child or to any other member of the family, if it is done with a view to safeguarding and promoting the child's welfare. Local authorities can provide these services directly or arrange them through another agency such as a voluntary organisation. They are required to publicise the help available to families in need.

Local authorities also help people fleeing domestic violence, often working with specialist voluntary organisations that provide refuges where women and children receive short-term accommodation and support, pending a more permanent solution.

In 2003 a Minister for Children, Young People and Families was appointed, with responsibilities for a broad range of policies and programmes to meet the needs of children and young people in England. The Children Bill (see page 168) contains plans to create a Children's Commissioner in England. Wales already has a Children's Commissioner: Scotland and Northern Ireland have Commissioners for Children and Young People.

Sure Start

In England, the Sure Start Unit brings together a number of programmes for children and families – from pregnant mothers to children up to age 14 (or 16 for those with special needs). They include universal, free part-time early education for three- and four-year-olds, and childcare services such as day nurseries, childminders, after-school clubs and holiday schemes. Early education and childcare are provided by the state, private and voluntary sectors, often through local Sure Start programmes and children's centres in the most disadvantaged communities.

In the 2004 Budget, the Government announced increased funding for Sure Start programmes in England, including early education and childcare, in order to continue expanding services for young children and families. Spending will rise by £669 million between 2004/05 and 2007/08.

In Wales, Cymorth – the Children and Youth Support Fund – provides support with the aim of improving the life chances of children and young people from disadvantaged families. Through Sure Start Scotland, all 32 local authorities are funded to work in partnership with health services and voluntary organisations to identify need and deliver services to vulnerable families with very young children. The Scottish Executive is also working towards an Integrated Strategy for the Early Years covering from pre-birth to six-year-olds and their families. In Northern Ireland, some 19,000 under-fours and their families have access to Sure Start programmes.

Day care

Day care facilities are provided for children by day nurseries, childminders, playgroups, and out of school clubs, run privately or by voluntary organisations or, in some cases, by local authorities.

Children Bill

Following its Green Paper, *Every Child Matters*, which was published in September 2003, the Government introduced the Children Bill in March 2004. It contains measures that are intended to protect children from harm, promote their well-being and support all children to develop their full potential. The proposals include:

- a duty on agencies to co-operate to improve the well-being of children and young people;

- a duty on key agencies to safeguard children through Local Safeguarding Children Boards;

- a database with basic information about every child;

- a Director of Children's Services in every local authority to ensure clear accountability;

- enabling pooled budgets between health, education and social care professionals;

- an integrated inspection framework; and

- an independent Children's Commissioner to champion the views of children and young people.

Many of the proposals will apply in Wales as well as England.

The Office for Standards in Education (Ofsted) (see page 140) is responsible for the regulation of childminding and day care for children under eight years of age in England. Its Early Years Directorate registers and inspects childcare provision and assesses its suitability on the basis of National Standards which set minimum levels of quality for day care.

In Wales, CSIW (see page 162) is responsible for ensuring that childminders and providers of day care for young people are suitable and that they comply with regulations and national minimum standards. The Care Commission is responsible for regulating day care providers in Scotland. National care standards for early education and childcare aged up to 16 have been published, and HM Inspectorate of Education and the Care Commission operate an integrated inspection regime in conjunction with these standards and other key documents.

In Northern Ireland, the new Regulation and Improvement Authority will take over the regulation of day care providers and other services, covering provision for children aged up to 12, from local HSS Trusts. The Authority should be fully operational by April 2005.

Child protection

Child protection is the joint concern of a number of different agencies and professions. Local authority-led area child protection committees determine how the different agencies should co-operate to help protect children in their area from abuse and neglect. The Children Bill (see box) proposes that the committees will be superseded by statutory Local Safeguarding Children Boards.

Local authority social services departments help children who are in need, including those considered to be at risk of significant harm, and each department holds a register of children considered to be at risk. There were around 32,700 children on child protection registers in the United Kingdom at 31 March 2003.

In England and Wales a child may be brought before a family proceedings court if he or she is suffering, or is likely to suffer, significant harm. The court can commit children to the care of the local authority under a care order or a supervision order. However, an order is made only if the court is also satisfied that this will positively contribute to the child's well-being and be in his or her best interests. All courts have to treat the welfare of children as the paramount consideration when reaching any decision about their upbringing. There is a general principle that, wherever possible, children should remain at home with their families.

In Scotland, children who have committed offences or are in need of care and protection may be referred to the Children's Reporter. If compulsory intervention is needed, the child will be brought before a Children's Hearing, which can impose a supervision requirement on a child. In some cases, this requirement will be conditional on the child living away from home – for example where the Hearing believes the child will receive the right help or supervision from foster parents, in a children's home or at a special residence. Supervision requirements are reviewed at least once a year until ended by a Children's Hearing. The Scottish Executive carried out a review of the Children's Hearings system during 2004/05.

In September 2003 the Government published a report, *Keeping children safe*. This was a response to a review of arrangements for safeguarding children and an inquiry into the death of an eight-year-old girl at the hands of those caring for her. The conclusions of the report have been taken into account in the proposed changes to the child protection regime in the Children Bill (see page 168).

In Scotland, a Child Protection Review, similarly prompted by the death of a child, produced a report, *It's Everyone's Job to Make Sure I'm Alright*, in 2002. In response, the Scottish Executive announced a number of measures including a three-year reform programme for child protection services, and a Framework for Standards in Child Protection and a Children's Charter, which were launched in March 2004.

Fostering and children's homes

Local authorities and HSS Trusts in Northern Ireland must provide accommodation for children who have no parent or guardian, who have been abandoned, or whose parents are unable to provide for them. They have a duty to ensure that the welfare of children being looked after away from home is properly safeguarded. This includes protecting their health, providing for their education and ensuring contact with their

families. As far as possible they work in partnership with the parents of children who are in their care.

When a child in local authority care is the subject of a care order imposed by the court, the local authority shares legal responsibility for that child with their parents. Although it consults with the child's parents about where the child should live, the local authority will usually be responsible for deciding this, taking account of the child's circumstances, wishes and feelings. Children can also enter care as a result of a voluntary agreement between their parents and the local authority. Children looked after under voluntary agreement are referred to as 'accommodated'.

Table 12.6 Children looked after by local authorities,[1] March 2003, England

	Thousands
Foster placements	41.1
Children's homes and hostels[2]	6.7
With parents	6.4
Placed for adoption	3.4
Living independently or in residential employment	1.2
Residential schools	1.1
Other	1.0
Total	**60.8**

1 Excludes children looked after under an agreed series of short-term placements.
2 Includes local authority, voluntary sector and private children's homes and secure units.
Source: *Children Looked After by Local Authorities*, Department for Education and Skills

Younger children are placed wherever possible with foster carers, sometimes as a short-term measure (for example when parents are temporarily unable to look after their child because of family illness) or, if necessary, for longer periods. Children's homes can be run by local authorities, or by private or voluntary organisations.

In the year ending 31 March 2003 there were some 41,100 children in foster care and 6,700 in children's homes in England (Table 12.6). In Wales there were just over 4,500 children being looked after by local authorities, the majority of whom were in foster homes. In Scotland, just under 11,400 children were being looked after, of whom 14 per cent were in residential accommodation and the remainder were living at home with their parents or elsewhere in the community. In Northern Ireland, 2,400 children were being looked after – 64 per cent in foster care and 12 per cent in children's homes.

Local authorities in England and Wales have a duty to assess and meet the needs of young people leaving care. Each care leaver should have a written plan (called a Pathway Plan) and the support of a personal adviser. Local authorities must keep in touch with care leavers and ensure they have access to suitable accommodation.

All children's homes and fostering services are required to register with the CSCI (see page 162) or its equivalent bodies in Scotland and Wales. The CSCI is responsible for inspecting all children's homes to assess the quality of care provided.

Adoption

There were 5,459 adoption orders in England and Wales in 2002. An adoption order gives parental responsibility for a child to the adopting parent(s) and must be obtained by relatives and step-parents seeking to adopt, as well as by non-relatives who have been approved by an adoption agency. Adoption orders can be granted to applicants by the High Court, county courts and magistrates' courts. People who adopt a child may be eligible for time off work and Statutory Adoption Pay (see page 166).

The *Adoption and Children Act 2002* will modernise the legal framework for domestic and inter-country adoption in England and Wales. The child's welfare will be the paramount consideration in all decisions to do with adoption. Unmarried couples will be legally allowed to adopt children together, as well as single people and married couples. The Act also introduces new restrictions on bringing a child into the United Kingdom for adoption, on arranging adoptions and on advertising children for adoption. The restriction on advertising also applies in Scotland and Northern Ireland. The Act is being implemented gradually and should come fully into force in September 2005.

The National Adoption Standards for England are intended to ensure that children, prospective adopters, adoptive parents and birth families receive a consistent and high-quality adoption

service no matter where they live. The CSCI (see page 162) is responsible for the registration and inspection of voluntary adoption agencies and the inspection of local authority adoption services in England. The CSIW has similar responsibilities in Wales, as has the Care Commission in Scotland. Adoption standards are in place in Wales and Scotland and standards for Northern Ireland will be issued at a later date.

The Adoption Register for England and Wales holds information on children waiting to be adopted and approved adoptive families waiting to adopt, and can suggest matches between children and approved adopters. The aim is to tackle delays in finding suitable adoptive families where a local family cannot be found or the child needs to move away from the area.

People with a sickness or disability

According to the 2001 Census 10.9 million people, or 18.5 per cent of the UK population, reported a long-term illness, health problem or disability that limited their daily activities or work.

The Disability Rights Commission aims to eliminate discrimination against disabled people, promote equal opportunities, encourage good practice and advise the Government on the operation of the *Disability Discrimination Act 1995* (see page 111). The Equality Commission (see page 110) has a similar role in Northern Ireland.

The Department of Health publication *A Practical Guide for Disabled People or Carers* provides information about services from government departments and agencies, the NHS and local government and voluntary organisations. The Disability Unit in the DWP runs a website to help disabled people learn more about their rights and the relevant legislation for disabled people in the United Kingdom. The Department for Social Development in Northern Ireland has produced a guide to public services for people with disabilities and people over pensionable age.

An initiative to help people with an illness or disability to find work, Pathways to Work, is being piloted in seven areas of England, Wales and

Scotland with a budget of £1 billion over two and a half years from 2002/03 to 2005/06. The initiative provides:

- early support from personal advisers, including work-focused interviews and action plans;
- specialist programmes, including new condition management (rehabilitation) services provided jointly by Jobcentre Plus and the NHS; and
- greater financial incentives to work, including a Return To Work Credit of £40 a week for 52 weeks for those finding a job that pays less than £15,000 a year.

Disabled people benefit from a range of concessions on public transport (see page 330). They may also be eligible for WTC (which replaced Disabled Person's Tax Credit in April 2003) (see page 161) and cold weather payments. People injured as part of activity in the Armed

Forces may be entitled to War Disablement Pension (see page 174).

Care services for people with physical disabilities

Local authority social services departments and HSS Trusts in Northern Ireland help with social rehabilitation and adjustment to disability. They are required to identify the number of disabled people in their area and to provide and publicise services. These may include advice on personal and social problems arising from disability, as well as occupational, educational, social and recreational facilities, either at day centres or elsewhere.

Other services may include minor adaptations to homes such as ramps for wheelchairs, or bath rails, the delivery of cooked meals, support with personal care at home and direct payments with which disabled people can purchase support to meet their assessed need. Local housing authorities

Table 12.7 Main benefits available to sick and disabled people from April 2004

Statutory Sick Pay
Employers are responsible for paying this up to a maximum of 28 weeks. There is a single rate of £66.15 a week for all qualifying employees, provided their average gross weekly earnings are at least £79.

Incapacity Benefit
Paid to people of working age who become sick or disabled and stop working or looking for work as a result. Entitlement begins when entitlement to Statutory Sick Pay ends or, for those who do not qualify for Statutory Sick Pay, from the fourth day of sickness. Payments, which depend on age and the length of illness, range from £55.90 to £74.15 a week.

Severe Disablement Allowance
A tax-free benefit for people who have not been able to work for at least 28 weeks because of illness or disability but who cannot get Incapacity Benefit because they have paid insufficient NICs. The benefit is £44.80 a week, plus additions of up to £15.55 depending on the person's age when he or she became incapable of work. Additions for adult dependants and for children may also be paid. In April 2001 this Allowance was abolished for new claims. From that date, people aged 16 to 20, or 16 to 25 if they were in education or training at least three months immediately before age 20, can instead claim Incapacity Benefit without having to satisfy the contribution conditions.

Disability Living Allowance
A non-contributory tax-free benefit to help severely disabled people aged under 65 with extra costs incurred as a result of disability. Entitlement is measured in terms of personal care and/or mobility needs. There are two components: a care component which has three weekly rates – £58.80, £39.35 and £15.55 – and a mobility component with two weekly rates, of £41.05 and £15.55. It is payable to those aged three or over who have severe difficulty walking, or aged five or over who need help getting around.

Attendance Allowance (AA)
Paid to people who need help to look after themselves. It is paid if a person becomes ill or disabled on or after his or her 65th birthday and needs help for at least six months. There are different rates depending on whether the claimant needs care during the day, during the night, or both, and on the extent of the disability. AA ranges from £39.35 to £58.80 a week depending on circumstances and is not normally affected by savings or income.

Industrial Injuries Disablement Benefit
For people who have been disabled by an accident at work or through a prescribed disease caused by a particular type of employment. The rate is between £14.71 and £120.10 a week depending on the level of disablement and age.

provide assistance with major adaptations such as stairlifts and ground-floor toilets. Alternatively, local authorities and voluntary organisations may provide severely disabled people with residential accommodation, either on a permanent basis or temporarily in order to relieve their existing carers. Special housing may be available for those able to look after themselves.

Services for people with learning disabilities

In England, the Government's policies for improving services for people with learning disabilities, their families and carers were set out in *Valuing People: A New Strategy for Learning Disability for the 21st Century,* published in 2001. Learning Disability Partnership Boards have been set up in local council areas to take forward the Valuing People programme at local level. Until 2006 there will be a team of regionally based workers providing support to Partnership Boards and sharing good practice.

In Scotland, the Scottish Executive is working with local agencies through Partnerships in Practice agreements to improve the lives of people with learning disabilities in line with its review, *The same as you?*, published in 2000.

Social services departments and HSS Trusts in Northern Ireland can provide or arrange short-term care, support for families in their own homes, residential accommodation and support for various types of activity outside the home.

People with learning disabilities may also be able to receive direct payments from local authorities to let them buy for themselves the support that will meet their assessed needs. The aim is to ensure that, as far as possible, people with learning disabilities can lead full lives in the community. The NHS provides specialist services when the ordinary primary care services cannot meet healthcare needs.

People with a mental health problem

Under the Care Programme Approach in England, each service user should receive an assessment leading to an agreed care plan. A care coordinator is appointed to keep in contact with the service user, and review the plan regularly in the light of the individual's changing needs. The separate Welsh Mental Health Strategy employs many of the same principles in delivering services in Wales.

In Scotland, each NHS board works with its local authority care partners, with users of mental health services and with their carers in order to develop joint strategies and provide local and comprehensive mental health services. These plans are expected to conform to the Framework for Mental Health Services and to comply with standards set by Quality Improvement Scotland. The *Mental Health (Care and Treatment) (Scotland) Act 2003* aims to provide more appropriate services and rights for people with mental health problems who receive compulsory treatment. The Act will be implemented before 2005. Meanwhile, the Scottish Executive is working on a Code of Practice and other guidance. Northern Ireland has an integrated health and social services structure allowing a multi-disciplinary approach to care management.

Arrangements made by social services authorities for providing care in the community include direct payments, home help, day centres, social centres and residential care. Social workers are increasingly being integrated with mental health staff in community mental health teams under single management. Help may be provided to find housing, secure an adequate income, and sustain basic daily living – shopping, cooking, and washing. In certain circumstances social workers can apply for a person with a mental disorder to be compulsorily admitted to and detained in hospital. There are safeguards for patients to ensure that the law is used appropriately.

Unemployed people

Claimants for Jobseeker's Allowance (JSA) must be capable of, available for, and actively seeking work. They must normally be aged at least 18 and under pension age. JSA can be either contribution-based or income-based:

- Contribution-based JSA is available to those who have paid sufficient NICs. They are entitled to a personal JSA for up to six months (£53.95 a week from April 2004 for a person aged 25 or over), regardless of any savings or partner's income.

- Income-based JSA: those on a low income are entitled to an income-based JSA, payable for as long as the jobseeker requires support and continues to satisfy the qualifying conditions.

Help with travel arrangements

Local authorities have a duty to provide transport to and from social services facilities, such as day centres. An Audit Commission report in 2001 estimated that local authorities in England and Wales were spending over £150 million a year on such transport. Some 63,000 adults in England had help with transport as part of their community care service during 2002/03. Arrangements vary, and include the use of dedicated coaches, buses, minibuses, taxis and hired cars.

Non-emergency patient transport services are available to take people to and from outpatient appointments and clinics and for non-urgent transfers between hospitals. They are free of charge where there is a medical need. There are about 14 million non-emergency patient journeys in ambulances each year. According to the government report on Transport and Social Exclusion, *Making the*

Connections, over 1.4 million people miss their appointments or do not use healthcare services because of transport problems. The report called for an expansion of the criteria for patient transport services, to include medical, mobility, transport and financial grounds.

People on low incomes can get help with travel to hospital for treatment through the Hospital Travel Grants Scheme. Community Care Grants are available from the Social Fund (see page 174) to help people with travel costs to visit a relative in hospital.

The Scottish Executive is funding four pilot schemes for demand-responsive transport in urban areas. One of them, operating in four areas of Glasgow, will help people who have travel difficulties and those on low incomes to attend health appointments and visit patients in hospital.

The amount a claimant receives comprises an age-related personal allowance (£55.65 a week from April 2004 for a single person aged 25 or over), plus other allowances. Some allowances are determined by circumstances on a basis similar to Income Support (see page 161).

Recipients of JSA and people aged under 60 who receive Income Support can benefit from a *Back to Work Bonus*. The aim of this scheme is to encourage people to keep in touch with the labour market by undertaking small amounts of work while claiming benefit. It allows people to accrue a tax-free lump sum of between £5 and £1,000 if working part-time while in receipt of Income Support or JSA. There are a number of other financial benefits for unemployed people to help them back into employment, including various New Deals (see chapter 11).

People on low incomes

People on low incomes can claim Income Support or, for those over 60, Pension Credit (see box on page 161). In 2002/03 there were around 4.1 million people receiving Income Support in the United Kingdom. Other benefits for which

unemployed people and those on low incomes may be eligible include exemption from NHS charges, vouchers towards the cost of spectacles, publicly funded legal help and free school meals for their children. People on low incomes, pensioners, widows, widowers and long-term sick people on Incapacity Benefit may be eligible for extra help to meet the cost of value added tax (VAT) on their fuel bills.

Housing Benefit is an income-related, tax-free benefit which helps people on low incomes meet the cost of rented accommodation. The amount paid depends on personal circumstances, income, savings, rent and whether other people are sharing the home. It also normally depends on the general level of rents for properties with the same number of rooms in the locality. Most single people aged under 25 who are not lone parents and who are renting privately have their Housing Benefit limited to the average cost of a single non-self-contained room (that is, with shared use of kitchen and toilet facilities) in the locality.

Council Tax Benefit helps people to meet their council tax payments (the tax set by local councils to help pay for services – see page 376). The scheme offers help to those claiming Income Support and income-based JSA and others with low incomes. In Northern Ireland, where council tax was not introduced, Housing Benefit helps with the cost of rent and/or rates.

The Social Fund provides payments in the form of loans or grants to help with expenses which are difficult to meet on a low income. These payments can be:

- budgeting loans for intermittent expenses;
- community care grants to help, for example, people resettle into the community from care, or to remain in the community, to ease exceptional pressure on families, to set up home as part of a planned resettlement programme or to meet certain travel expenses; and
- crisis loans to help people in an emergency or as a result of a disaster where there is serious risk to health or safety.

Budgeting loans and community care grants are available only to people who are receiving social security benefits and some tax credits.

Asylum seekers receive limited cash benefits and may qualify for other services (see page 106).

Widows and widowers

Bereavement Payment is a one-off payment to widows aged under 60, and widowers aged under 65 – or those aged 60/65 or over whose spouses were not entitled to a basic State Retirement Pension when they died. It is payable provided the spouse paid a minimum number of NICs.

Widowed Parent's Allowance is a regular payment for widows or widowers bringing up children. It is based on the late spouse's NICs and continues while the children are still dependent.

Bereavement Allowance is a regular payment, also based on the late spouse's NICs, which is payable for 52 weeks to widows and widowers aged 45 or over who are not bringing up children.

A number of charities and voluntary organisations advise and support people who have been bereaved. A consortium of some of the leading bodies has published a set of national standards for bereavement care.

War pensioners

The Veterans Agency is part of the Ministry of Defence (MoD). It provides advice and help with new and ongoing claims for war disablement pensions and war widows' and widowers' pensions. In addition, the Agency is the single point of contact within the MoD for providing information and advice on issues of concern to veterans and their families.

The War Pensioners' Welfare Service, through working closely with ex-Service organisations and other statutory and voluntary organisations, provides a comprehensive advice and support service for all war pensioners and war widows and widowers living in the United Kingdom and the Republic of Ireland.

In Great Britain there were approximately 260,000 beneficiaries of War Disablement and War Widow's/Widower's Pensions in 2003. The majority are Second World War veterans, but there are also small numbers of First World War veterans, ex-National Servicemen and those disabled in more recent conflicts. War Disablement Pension is payable to ex-members of the Armed Forces as a result of disability due to Service. It also can be claimed by, among others, civilians, merchant seamen and members of the Polish forces under British command, although special conditions apply in these cases. War Widow's/Widower's Pension is payable to widows and widowers of ex-members of the Armed Forces where death is due to or hastened by Service.

There are proposals for a new Armed Forces Pension Scheme and a new compensation scheme for those killed or injured in service, to replace the current schemes with effect from 2005/06.

Arrangements with other countries

As part of the European Union's efforts to promote the free movement of labour, regulations provide for equality of treatment and the protection of benefit rights for people who move between Member States. The regulations also cover retired pensioners and other beneficiaries who have been employed, or self-employed, as well as dependants. Benefits covered include Child Benefit and those for sickness, maternity, unemployment, retirement, invalidity, accidents at work and occupational diseases. The Government introduced special measures for nationals of most of the ten countries that joined the European Union in May 2004. Workers from these countries (excluding Malta and Cyprus) are able to take up employment in the United Kingdom provided that they are registered under a new workers' registration scheme. If they enter the United Kingdom in the hope of finding employment they are not entitled to income-related benefits.

The United Kingdom has reciprocal social security agreements with a number of other countries that also provide cover for some national insurance benefits and family benefits.

Further reading

Department for Work and Pensions Departmental Report: The Government's Expenditure Plans 2003–04 to 2005–06. Cm 6221. The Stationery Office, 2004.

Department of Health Departmental Report. The Government's Expenditure Plans 2003/2004 to 2004/2005. Cm 6204. The Stationery Office, 2004.

Simplicity, security and choice: Informed choices for working and saving. Cm 6111. The Stationery Office, 2004.

Every child matters, Cm 5860. The Stationery Office, 2003

It's everyone's job to make sure I'm alright: Report of the Child Protection Audit and Review. Scottish Executive, 2002.

Keeping children safe. Cm 5861. The Stationery Office, 2003.

Websites

Citizens Advice
www.adviceguide.org.uk

Department for Social Development, Northern Ireland
www.dsdni.gov.uk

Department for Work and Pensions
www.dwp.gov.uk

DWP disability website
www.disability.gov.uk

Department of Health
www.dh.gov.uk

Department of Health, Social Services and Public Safety, Northern Ireland
www.dhsspsni.gov.uk

Inland Revenue
www.inlandrevenue.gov.uk

National Assembly for Wales
www.wales.gov.uk

Northern Ireland Social Security Agency
www.ssani.gov.uk

Pension Guide
www.pensionguide.gov.uk

The Pension Service
www.thepensionservice.gov.uk

Scottish Executive
www.scotland.gov.uk

www.

13   Health

The state of public health

Over the past century major social and economic trends such as improvements in nutrition and housing, advances in medicine and technology, and the development of health services that are freely available to all have led to significant improvements in the nation's health. In 1901, males born in the United Kingdom could expect to live to around 45 years of age and females to around 49. By 2002 life expectancy at birth had increased to 76 and 81 years respectively.

Declines in infant mortality have contributed to the increases in life expectancy over the past century. In 1921, 84.0 children per 1,000 live births in the United Kingdom died before the age of one; by 2002 the rate was 5.2 per 1,000 (Figure 13.1).

Cancer

About a third of people in the United Kingdom will be diagnosed with cancer during their lifetime and about a quarter will die from the disease. As average life expectancy has risen, the population at risk of cancer has grown, with two-thirds of cases occurring in those aged over 65. There are over 200 different types of cancer but the four major types – lung, colorectal, breast and prostate – account for over half of all cases diagnosed.

Since the mid-1970s there has been a steep decline in the death rate for lung cancer among males (Figure 13.2). This can be closely linked to the proportion of the population who smoke (see Figure 13.5). In contrast, the lung cancer death rate among females continued to rise until 1988, since when there has been little change. The death rate for females is still only half that for men, but

Figure 13.1 Infant mortality,[1] UK

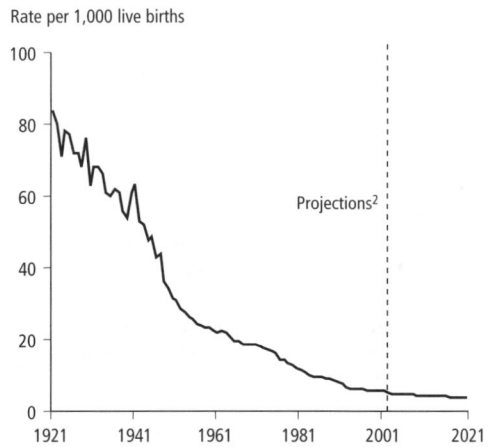

Rate per 1,000 live births

Projections[2]

1 Deaths within one year of birth.
2 2002-based projections for 2003 onwards.
Source: Office for National Statistics; General Register Office for Scotland; Northern Ireland Statistics and Research Agency; Government Actuary's Department

the difference between the sexes has narrowed considerably.

Breast cancer is the most common cause of cancer death among women. Death rates peaked in the late 1980s but have since fallen steadily and now only just exceed the rate for lung cancer. The improvement can be linked to advances in treatment and to the introduction of a national screening programme (see page 192). For prostate cancer, which only affects men, the death rate peaked in 1992 but has since declined. Since the mid-1990s, prostate cancer has been the second most common cause of cancer death among men.

Colorectal cancer is the third most common cause of cancer death among both males and females.

Figure 13.2 Death rates from selected cancers,[1] UK

Rates per 100,000 population

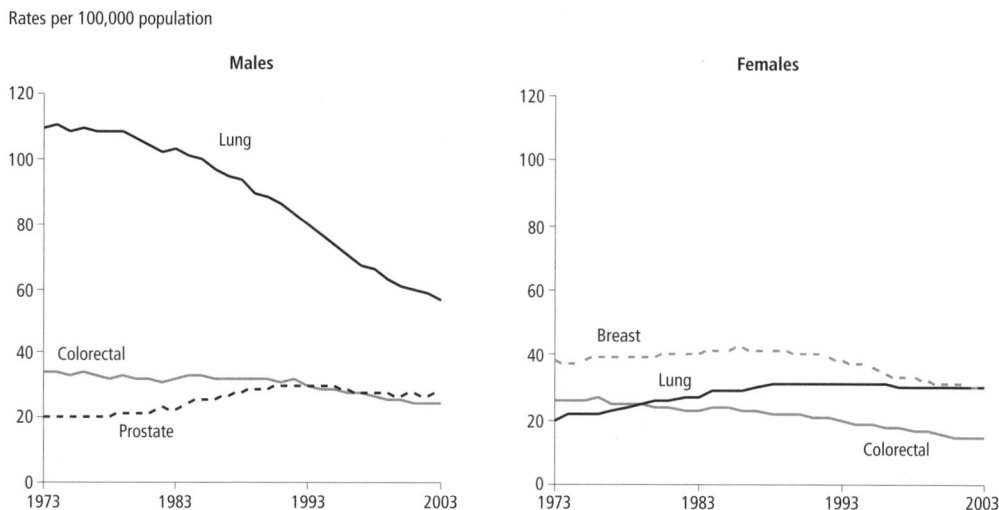

1 Data have been age standardised using the European standard population. Age standardised death rates enable comparisons to be made over time (and between males and females), which are independent of changes in the age structure of the population.
Source: Office for National Statistics

Death rates have gradually declined since 1976, by 28 per cent among males and 44 per cent among females, widening an existing gap between the sexes in death rates for this form of cancer.

Survival rates from lung cancer are low compared with the other most common cancers. For those diagnosed with lung cancer in England and Wales between 1996–99, the five-year survival rate (adjusted for overall levels of mortality from other causes in the general population) for both men and women was around 6 per cent. Cancers with the highest five-year survival rates included: melanoma, at 77 per cent for men and 87 per cent for women, female breast cancer at 78 per cent, prostate cancer at 65 per cent and cervical cancer at 61 per cent.

Circulatory disease

The United Kingdom has one of the highest premature death rates from circulatory disease (which includes heart disease and strokes) in Europe. A number of risk factors have been identified, including smoking, obesity, drinking alcohol and lack of regular exercise. Over the past 30 years, while circulatory diseases have remained the most common cause of death among males and females of all ages in the United Kingdom, they have also shown by far the greatest decline. In 1973, age-standardised death rates from circulatory

diseases were 7,000 per million males and 4,300 per million females. By 2003 the death rates had fallen by over half for both sexes, to 3,100 and 1,900 respectively.

Chronic diseases

In the United Kingdom, there are some 17.5 million people living with chronic conditions like diabetes and asthma. People with chronic diseases account for up to 80 per cent of GP consultations in England, around 180 million visits a year. In March 2004 the Department of Health (DH) announced that a specialist team would be set up at a demonstration site within each of the 28 Strategic Health Authority (SHA) areas.

Infectious diseases

Although diseases such as measles, tuberculosis (TB) and whooping cough became far less common during the last century, they can still give cause for concern. Between 1993 and 1994 for example, measles registrations nearly doubled, from 12,000 to 23,500, before the underlying downward trend resumed. In 2002 the number of cases of measles notified in the United Kingdom was 3,700. In contrast notifications of TB have increased quite steadily since 1987 and the disease is now more common than either measles or whooping cough. In 2002 there were around 7,200 cases, compared with 6,100 in 1991. The rise has been particularly noticeable in London, with a TB notification rate of 39 per 100,000 population in 2002, compared with 15 per 100,000 in the West Midlands (which had the next highest rate), and just 4 per 100,000 in Northern Ireland.

Immunisation

Government targets are for 95 per cent of children to be immunised by the age of two against diphtheria, tetanus, polio, whooping cough, Haemophilus influenzae b (Hib), meningitis C and measles, mumps and rubella (MMR). In recent years, publicity questioning the safety of the MMR combined vaccine has led to a fall in the proportion of children immunised. In 2002/03, 82 per cent of children in the United Kingdom had received the vaccine, compared with 91 per cent in 1991/92. Although regional variations were generally small, the figure in London was 72 per cent.

Vaccination against influenza is intended primarily for people in high risk groups, which include those with chronic heart disease, lung disease, renal disease or diabetes. Older people are vulnerable to influenza, and a free National Health Service (NHS) vaccination is available to everyone aged 65 and over. The extension of free vaccination and a national advertising campaign have been major factors in the increased uptake among this group. In 2002/03 nearly 70 per cent of over-65s in England were vaccinated.

MRSA

Methicillin-resistant *Staphylococcus aureus* (MRSA) is a hospital-acquired infection which is resistant to treatment by penicillin and methicillin antibiotics. There is currently no known vaccine, although a new drug is currently under trial in the United Kingdom. MRSA was first identified in 1961, the same year that methicillin came into use. Reports of MRSA bloodstream infections have increased significantly since the mid-1990s and a recent study has shown that between 1993 and 2002 the number of deaths involving MRSA in England and Wales rose from 51 to 800. This was matched by an increase in laboratory reports of MRSA bacteraemia, from 210 in 1993 to 5,310 in 2002. Steps to tackle MRSA and other 'superbugs' are described on page 184.

Sexually transmitted infections

Diagnoses of sexually transmitted infections made in genito-urinary medicine clinics in England, Wales and Northern Ireland have been increasing, especially among young people. In 2003, genital chlamydia was the most common sexually transmitted infection diagnosed, with just over 89,800 cases. This was 9 per cent more than in 2002 and more than double the 34,100 cases in 1996.

Since 1996 the number of Human Immunodeficiency Virus (HIV) diagnoses in the United Kingdom has risen each year. The Communicable Disease Surveillance Centre reported that by the end of 2002 the estimated number of people living with HIV in the United Kingdom was 49,500, an increase of 20 per cent compared with 2001. In 2003, 6,600 new HIV cases were diagnosed (Figure 13.3). By contrast, the numbers of AIDS diagnoses and deaths in HIV-infected individuals declined after the introduction of effective therapies in the mid-1990s, and in more recent years have remained relatively constant, with 766 reports of AIDS and 475 deaths reported for 2003.

Figure 13.3 HIV and AIDS diagnoses,[1] and deaths in HIV-infected individuals, UK

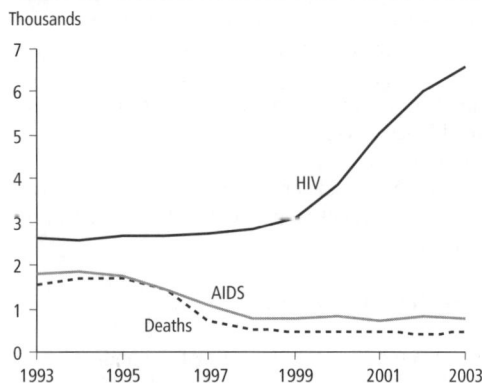

Thousands

1 Numbers of diagnoses recorded, particularly for recent years, will rise as further reports are received.
Source: Health Protection Agency

Substance misuse

Alcohol

The consumption of alcohol in excessive amounts can lead to an increased likelihood of problems such as high blood pressure, cancer and cirrhosis of the liver. DH advice is that consumption of three or four units[1] a day for men and two or three units a day for women should not lead to significant health risks. Consistently drinking more than this is not advised. In 2002/03, 38 per cent of men and 23 per cent of women in Great Britain exceeded the recommended amount of alcohol on at least one day in the week before being interviewed (Table 13.4).

Table 13.4 Adults exceeding daily benchmarks[1] of alcohol, 2002/03, Great Britain

		Percentages
	Males	Females
16–24	49	42
25–44	46	31
45–64	38	19
65 and over	16	5
All aged 16 and over	38	23

1 On heaviest drinking day in last week. See footnote on this page for benchmarks.
Source: General Household Survey, Office for National Statistics

Alcohol-related deaths in England and Wales have been rising for years. Between 1979 and 2000 the number more than doubled, from 2,506 to 5,543. Of the deaths in 2000, 85 per cent were due to chronic liver disease and cirrhosis. In 2000 the age-standardised rate for alcohol-related deaths among men was 13 per 100,000 population, almost twice the rate among women (7 per 100,000). Services to combat alcohol misuse are described on page 196.

Smoking

More cancer deaths in the United Kingdom can be attributed to smoking tobacco than to any other single risk factor. Over the past 30 years, the reduction in lung cancer deaths can be closely linked to the fall in the proportion of the population who smoke.

1 A unit of alcohol is 8 grams by weight or 10 millilitres (ml) by volume of pure alcohol. This is the amount contained in half a pint of ordinary strength beer or lager, a single measure of pub spirits (25 ml), one glass of ordinary wine or a small pub measure of sherry or other fortified wine.

In 1974, 51 per cent of men and 41 per cent of women in Great Britain reported that they were regular cigarette smokers. By 2002/03 this had fallen to 27 per cent of men and 25 per cent of women (Figure 13.5). The figures for Northern Ireland were 35 per cent of men and 32 per cent of women in 1986, falling to 27 per cent and 26 per cent respectively by 2002. Measures to encourage a further reduction are described on page 196.

In Great Britain in 2002/03, 20 per cent of men and 18 per cent of women in the managerial and professional group smoked, compared with 32 per cent and 31 per cent respectively among the routine and manual group. The differences in Northern Ireland were even more marked. In 2002, men in semi-skilled manual occupations were twice as likely to smoke as professional men (33 per cent compared with 17 per cent). Women in semi-skilled manual occupations were three times as likely to smoke as professional women (35 per cent compared with 11 per cent).

Figure 13.5 Prevalence of adult[1] cigarette smoking, Great Britain

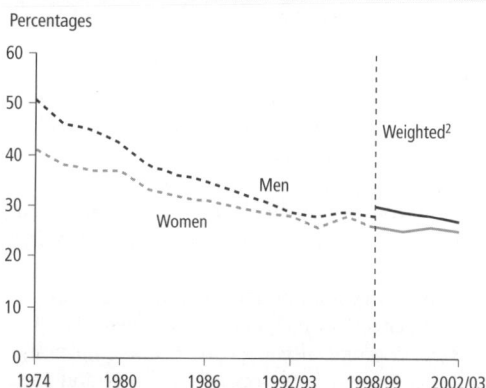

Percentages

1 People aged 16 and over. From 1988 data are for financial years. Between 1974 and 2000/01 the surveys were run every two years.
2 From 2000/01 data are weighted to compensate for non-response and to match known population distributions. Weighted and unweighted data for 1998/99 are shown for comparison.
Source: General Household Survey, Office for National Statistics

Drugs

Results from the 2002/03 British Crime Survey (see page 204) indicate that 16 per cent of men and 9 per cent of women aged 16 to 59 in England and Wales had taken an illicit drug in the previous year. Young people are more likely than older people to use drugs. The most commonly used drug in 2002/03 among those aged 16 to 24 years was cannabis. Cocaine and ecstasy were the most commonly used Class A drugs (see glossary) among those aged 16 to 59. Since 1996 there has been an increase in the use of cocaine among young people, especially among young men. In contrast, the use of amphetamines has declined.

In 2002 there were almost 2,700 deaths due to drug-related poisoning in England and Wales, a 7 per cent fall compared with 2001. Almost 70 per cent of these deaths were among males. Heroin and/or morphine were involved in 790 deaths; more than any other drug, but the lowest figure since 1999. In contrast, the number of deaths involving methadone remained relatively stable at just over 200, while deaths involving cocaine rose to their highest recorded level of almost 140. Continuing recent trends, deaths involving paracetamol fell to their lowest recorded level of around 460. Measures to prevent the misuse of drugs are described on page 196.

Diet and nutrition

The DH recommends that a healthy diet should include at least five portions of a variety of fruit and vegetables (excluding potatoes) a day. The 2000–01 National Diet and Nutrition Survey showed that only 13 per cent of men and 15 per cent of women aged 19 to 64 in Great Britain were consuming this amount on an average daily basis. The proportion of men and women eating the recommended amount increased with age. Less than 5 per cent of men and women aged 19 to 24 were consuming an average five or more portions a day, compared with 24 per cent of men and 22 per cent of women aged 50 to 64.

Obesity is linked to heart disease, diabetes and premature death. The body mass index (BMI) is a measure for assessing an individual's weight relative to their height, and a BMI score of over 30 is taken as the definition of obesity for adults aged 16 and over. In recent years the proportion of the population who are obese or overweight has been rising. In 2002, 22 per cent of men and 23 per cent of women aged 16 and over in England were classified as obese. A further 43 per cent of men and 34 per cent of women were overweight (Figure 13.6).

Figure 13.6 Overweight and obese[1] adults, England

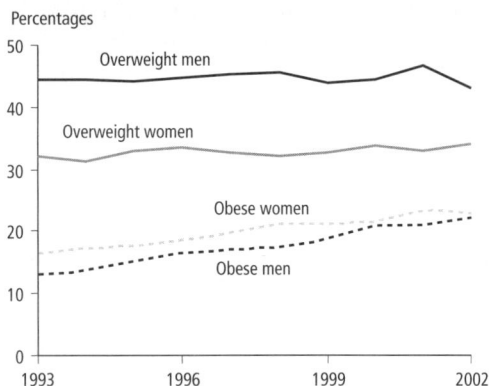

1 Using the body mass index (BMI) for people aged 16 and over. BMI score is calculated as weight (kg)/height (m)². Overweight is defined as a BMI score of over 25 to 30, and obese as over 30.
Source: Health Survey for England, Department of Health

The National Health Service

The NHS was created in 1948 to provide healthcare for the UK resident population, based on need, not the ability to pay. It is made up of a range of health professionals, support workers and organisations. The NHS is funded by taxation and is accountable to Parliament. All taxpayers, employers and employees contribute to the cost, so that members of the community who do not require healthcare help to pay for those who do. Most forms of treatment are provided free, but others, such as prescription drugs and eye tests, may incur a charge.

In England the NHS is overseen by the DH, which is responsible for developing and implementing policies and for the overall regulation and inspection of health services. The devolved administrations have similar responsibilities in other parts of the United Kingdom. The DH represents UK health interests at an international level, principally through the European Union (EU) and the World Health Organisation.

NHS Direct

NHS Direct, a nurse-led telephone helpline, was launched in England in 1998. It aims to provide fast and convenient access to health information and advice, helping people to care for themselves and their families, when it is appropriate to do so, and directing them to the most appropriate level of care when they need professional help. NHS Direct Online (*www.nhsdirect.nhs.uk*), an Internet extension of the telephone-based services, features an electronic version of the NHS Direct self-help guide, an encyclopedia of over 400 health topics and an interactive enquiry service for health information. By mid 2004, the telephone service and the website were each receiving over 500,000 calls or visits every month.

Wales has a similar telephone and Internet service, NHS Direct Wales *(www.nhsdirect.wales.nhs.uk)* which offers advice in both English and Welsh. The service in Scotland is known as NHS 24 *(www.nhs24.com)*.

In April 2004 comprehensive health information from the *British Medical Journal* (BMJ) was launched on NHS Direct Online. 'BMJ Best Treatments' provides information on the most common health conditions including explanations of elective surgery procedures, details of other treatments available, and advice on pre- and post-operative care. It also offers information on the choice of possible treatments for 60 chronic conditions, ranking them according to effectiveness and highlighting the risks and benefits of each.

Electronic initiatives

The NHS is making increasing use of new technology in patient care and has a major information technology (IT) development programme. This is focusing on improving the IT infrastructure and developing electronic national services for prescriptions, patient records and appointments.

NHSnet is a range of voice and data services used by the NHS, covering radio, telephone and computer-based communications. In February 2004 a £530 million, seven-year contract providing broadband Internet access linking all NHS organisations in England was awarded to BT. The New National Network, also known as N3, will enable transmission of voice and video information as well as data such as emails, medical information, test results and GP payment information. The network will ensure secure transmission of all confidential medical information. An equivalent scheme, HPSSnet, has been set up by Northern Ireland Health and Personal Social Services (HPSS).

In the longer term, it is intended that NHSnet will support electronic booking systems and replace paper-based health records with electronic versions. By 2010 the Government intends that every patient in England will have an individual electronic care record, containing a summary of key personal and health data. The NHS Care Records Service will connect more than 30,000 GPs and 270 acute, community and mental health NHS Trusts (see page 183) in a single, secure national system. It will be of particular use to accident and emergency (A&E) staff who will be able to access information about emergency patients and help diagnose them more quickly. The information on the NHS Care Records will grow over time and eventually people will have access to their own records, enabling them to be more involved in making decisions about their care and treatment.

The NHS in England

The *Health and Social Care (Community Health and Standards) Act 2003* legislated for the next stage in the Government's programme of NHS reform and investment. Key provisions include:

- the establishment of NHS Foundation Trusts (see page 183), which enjoy new freedoms and are locally accountable;
- the establishment of two independent regulators – the Commission for Healthcare Audit and Inspection (CHAI – see page 198) and the Commission for Social Care Inspection (CSCI – see chapter 12, page 162);
- recovery by the NHS of hospital treatment and/or ambulance costs where patients have received compensation for injuries;
- a new duty on Primary Care Trusts (PCTs) (see page 183) to provide or secure the provision of primary dental services; and
- the replacement of the Welfare Food Scheme (see page 192).

Reducing health inequalities and avoidable ill health are key aims in the Government's health strategy. The 2002 report, *Securing Our Future Health: Taking a Long-Term View*, assessed the resources required to provide high-quality health services in the future. The report illustrated the considerable difference in expected cost depending on the extent to which people engaged in living healthier lifestyles. In February 2004 a follow-up report, *Securing Good Health for the Whole*

Population, recommended that the Government develops a more coherent strategy to reduce preventable illness caused by unhealthy behaviour, such as smoking and physical inactivity. Other recommendations include:

- HM Treasury should produce a framework for the use of economic instruments in relation to public health, such as tax credits or a tax on unhealthy ingredients in food;

- the Government should set consistent national objectives to improve the nation's health; PCTs and other agencies should devise local targets, based on national objectives but taking account of local needs;

- the cost-effectiveness of public health strategies and treatments should be evaluated;

- measures of productivity in the NHS should move away from narrow definitions of output, to overall measures of health outcomes, and compare the effectiveness of prevention and cure; and

- an annual report on the state of the nation's health should be produced.

The Government welcomed the report and said it proposed to build on it through a formal public consultation exercise and a White Paper to be published later in the year. The consultation document, *Choosing Health?* set out a number of issues for debate, including smoking in public places; encouraging walking; access to fruit and vegetables; food labelling; preventing and treating sexually transmitted infections; and healthy workplaces. Members of the public were able to take part in the consultation through media polls and through the DH website.

The Government also aims to increase the choice patients have over when, where and how they are treated. In December 2003 it published *Building on the Best*. Plans include:

- giving patients a choice of provider for planned surgery;

- making it possible for patients to get repeat prescriptions from their pharmacist without having to go back to their GP;

- expanding the range of medicines available over the counter without prescription;

- developing new ways for people to receive primary care, such as at nurse-led clinics; and

- making it easier for patients to receive treatment that best suits their lifestyle – for

example, allowing commuters to register with a GP near their workplace.

In line with the policy of devolving more power and responsibility to front-line organisations and staff there will be fewer national performance targets over the three-year period from 2004, allowing flexibility for local targets to meet local needs. In July 2004 the DH published *National standards, local action: health and social care standards and planning framework 2005/06 – 2007/08*. The document sets out 24 core healthcare standards that all providers of care to NHS patients have to meet, covering the seven key areas: safety; clinical and cost-effectiveness; governance; patient focus; accessible and responsive care; care environment and amenities; and public health. There are also ten developmental standards setting out what providers should be seeking to achieve over the coming years. The CHAI (see page 198) will assess the performance of providers against these standards.

Strategic Health Authorities

The health administration structure in England came into effect in 2002. The *NHS Reform and Health Care Professions Act 2002* provided for 28 SHAs, with typical populations of between 1.5 and 2.4 million. They are responsible for creating a framework for local health services, and for

NHS National Tariff

A National Tariff for clinical procedures was introduced in April 2004 and will be phased in throughout England by 2008. It means that hospital trusts will be paid a fixed fee for each type of operation, whether they treat the patient themselves or purchase treatment from the private sector. The tariff sets a fixed price (for elective treatment) for 48 different procedures, including:

- cataract operation – £786;

- heart valve surgery – £10,199;

- heart bypass – £8,080;

- hip replacement – £5,568;

- hernia surgery – £956; and

- knee replacement – £6,182.

building capacity, supporting performance improvement and managing the performance of PCTs and of NHS Trusts (though not NHS Foundation Trusts – see below) in their areas.

Primary Care Trusts

Responsibility for deciding which health services the local population needs and for ensuring the provision of these services lies with the 303 local PCTs across England. They are responsible for providing all services, including hospitals, dentists, mental health services, Walk-in Centres, NHS Direct (see page 180), patient transport (including A&E), population screening, pharmacies and opticians, and for developing health improvement programmes and seeing that local NHS organisations work effectively with local authorities and social services. In 2004/05, 81 per cent of the total NHS budget will be controlled by PCTs.

Care Trusts

Care Trusts are NHS bodies that work in both health and social care and can be established where NHS organisations and local authorities agree to work together. A Care Trust is usually set up where it is felt that closer integration between health and social care is needed or would be beneficial at a local level. Seven Care Trusts had been established by August 2003.

NHS Trusts

NHS Trusts are the organisations responsible for running most NHS hospitals. Although the statutory functions of the Trusts were not changed following NHS reorganisation, they are now overseen by the SHAs.

NHS Foundation Trusts

The *Health and Social Care (Community Health and Standards) Act 2003* (see page 181) included provision for the creation of NHS Foundation Trusts. These are independent legal entities, owned by their members (who include patients, staff and local people). They are outside the DH's accountability and performance management systems. Foundation Trusts are granted a licence to operate by an independent regulator and are controlled by a Board of Governors elected annually by the members. Foundation Trusts have greater powers and flexibility than traditional NHS hospitals. In particular they may:

- borrow from the private sector;

- retain their surpluses and money from the sale of land and assets; and

- exercise a greater degree of flexibility in setting pay and benefits packages.

Although Foundation Trusts will be able to raise income by charging for the treatment of private patients, their private work is limited by a cap on the proportion of their income that can come from private treatment. The licence given to each Trust specifies which services it is required to provide as a condition of its authorisation. This list will initially mirror the clinical services provided by the Trust at the time of its establishment. In addition, service agreements with PCTs will specify that the services provided must comply with national quality and safety standards. Foundation Trusts will be assessed against national clinical and quality standards by the CHAI (see page 198).

The first ten Foundation Trusts were established in April 2004, with a further ten in July 2004. Only NHS Trusts attaining three stars under the Government's star rating system are eligible to apply for Foundation Trust status. However, the Government hopes that over the next four to five years all NHS Trusts will become Foundation Trusts.

Walk-in Centres

NHS Walk-in Centres are a network of nurse-led centres where no appointment is necessary. They offer quick access to a range of services, including healthcare advice and information, and treatment for minor ailments and injuries. They are intended to complement GP surgeries and reduce pressure on GPs. Thirteen new centres were due to open in 2004/05, bringing the total number in England to 65. They are funded from a three-year £40 million investment package announced in July 2003.

Health education

Established in 2000, the Health Development Agency (HDA) works to improve the health of people and communities in England, and to reduce health inequalities. In partnership with others, it gathers evidence of what works, advises on standards and develops the skills of all those working to improve health. Following a review of the DH's arm's length bodies (see box, page 184) it was announced in July 2004 that the functions of the HDA would be taken on by the National Institute for Clinical Excellence (see page 197).

Hospital 'superbug' action plan

In July 2004 the Government published plans to improve cleanliness and reduce the level of hospital-acquired infections such as MRSA (see page 178). The measures include:

- publishing hospitals' infection rates;
- a new target for hospitals to reduce MRSA rates year on year;
- a national review of infection control and cleanliness by the CHAI (see page 198);
- cleanliness inspections by the patients' forum in each Trust, four times a year;
- putting matrons in charge of cleaning staff; and
- sharing national and international best practice.

Review of 'arm's length bodies'

The DH's arm's length bodies (ALBs) carry out a wide range of regulatory, standard-setting and public welfare functions, as well as providing central services to the NHS. In October 2003 the Secretary of State for Health announced a review of these bodies. In July 2004 the report *Reconfiguring the Department of Health's Arm's Length Bodies* was published. This sets out the Government's conclusions based on the review and the input of the ALBs. Over time the number of ALBs will be reduced from 38 to 20. By 2007/08 the Government anticipates savings in expenditure of around £500 million and a reduction in posts of around 25 per cent.

NHS and Independent Treatment Centres

NHS Treatment Centres provide pre-booked surgery and diagnostic tests. They are a way of increasing the number of routine operations the NHS can perform in some of the specialities where waiting times are longest.

By July 2004, 27 NHS-run Treatment Centres were open, and a further 19 were in development. Two independent Treatment Centres were also open. There will be an estimated 80 Treatment Centres by the end of 2005, treating an additional 250,000 patients a year.

The NHS in Wales

In Wales, the operation of the NHS is the responsibility of the Welsh Assembly Government, which has the power to make changes to the structure of the NHS in Wales through secondary or 'delegated' legislation (see page 51). There are 22 Local Health Boards (LHBs) in Wales, which replaced the five Health Authorities in April 2003. The LHBs report to three regional offices within the NHS Wales Department of the National Assembly.

A Health and Well-being Partnership Council, chaired by the Health and Social Services Minister, brings together key personnel from the NHS, local government, the voluntary and independent sectors, staff and professional groups, and patients'

representatives, to ensure the direction and leadership of the agenda for health and well-being. The Council is supported by a network of similar partnerships at a local level.

The *Health (Wales) Act 2003* contains measures aimed at giving patients more say in the running of the NHS and providing information to protect and improve public health in Wales. These include:

- reform of the Community Health Councils and powers for the establishment of an Association of Welsh Community Health Councils;
- establishment of a Wales Centre for Health (WCH); and
- establishment of Health Professions Wales (HPW).

WCH will bring together information and evidence on public health issues, and provide advice to policy makers. It will also lead the development of multi-professional education and training for public health, coordinate professional surveillance of health trends and undertake risk assessments of threats to health and well-being.

HPW was established in April 2004 to support education and training for a range of healthcare professions, including laboratory staff, nurses, midwives, health visitors, physiotherapists and radiographers.

Since devolution, the Welsh Assembly Government has determined its own spending priorities for the budget for the NHS in Wales. The planned health budget for 2004/05 is £4.3 billion, an increase of £1.7 billion on 1999/2000. Much of this additional investment is being directed towards tackling the priorities outlined in *Improving Health in Wales* (published in 2001): coronary heart disease, cancer services, mental health services, intensive care, primary and community care, children's services and local priorities set out in Health Improvement Programmes. Other measures will address waiting lists and waiting times, pressures on admissions, and human resource development for the NHS workforce.

An Inequalities in Health Fund was established in 2001 to stimulate and support new local action to tackle factors that cause health inequalities, including inequities in access to health services. The Fund, which has concentrated on coronary heart disease as its first priority, is supporting more than 60 projects in disadvantaged communities across Wales.

In 2003 Health Commission Wales was established as an independent agency under the Welsh Assembly Government. It has responsibility for planning and commissioning specialised health services, including cancer and cardiac services and the Welsh Blood Service (see page 194). Funding allocated to Health Commission Wales in 2004/05 was £403 million.

The NHS in Scotland

The Scottish Executive's Health Department is responsible for the leadership of NHSScotland and for the development and implementation of health and community care policy.

Scotland has 15 NHS Boards, each of which is responsible for all NHS services in its area. The Boards and 32 local authorities work together to strengthen the local focus of health provision, and every local authority has a seat on its principal NHS Board. Other NHS bodies, such as the Scottish Ambulance Service, NHS Health Scotland and NHS Quality Improvement Scotland (see page 197), provide services on a national basis.

In 2003 the Scottish Executive's Health Department published *Improving Health in Scotland – The Challenge*. This outlined a

framework for the delivery of a more rapid rate of health improvement in the four priority areas of:

- early years – stressing the importance of infant and child health to later life;

- teenager transition – encouraging young people to make healthy lifestyle choices, with all schools involved in a health promotion programme by 2007;

- the workplace – engaging employers in improving health at work; and

- communities – active health improvement programmes introduced through Community Planning Partnerships, which will bring together the NHS, local authorities and the voluntary sector at a local level.

Action in the priority areas will include work to tackle key health risk factors including diet, physical activity, alcohol, tobacco and mental health.

To achieve these aims, the Executive's core spending on health is planned to rise from £7.2 billion in 2003/04 to £8.0 billion in 2004/05 – this represents approximately a third of the devolved Scottish budget. The distribution of NHS funds across Scotland reflects relative healthcare needs, including those caused by deprivation and by geographical remoteness.

For 2004/05, the Scottish Executive allocated a capital budget for the NHS in Scotland of £350 million, a 13 per cent increase on 2003/04. Almost £240 million will be distributed to Health Boards to improve healthcare facilities and services, with a further £108 million to support a number of centrally funded initiatives, including:

- £39 million for the West of Scotland cancer centre; work commenced in July 2004;

- £14 million for the development of GP premises to improve access for patients;

- £2 million for the roll-out of colorectal cancer screening across Scotland;

- £13 million for the purchase of linear accelerators for cancer treatment; and

- £5 million for the provision of Positron Emitting Tomography scanners across Scotland.

The White Paper *Partnership for Care*, published in 2003, set out a package of proposed reforms that included:

- establishment of unified NHS Boards and the abolition of NHS Trusts, with requirements to devolve authority to front-line staff;

- establishment of community health partnerships to provide greater accountability and integration with social services;

- guaranteed waiting times for treatment, initially for certain heart surgery, but to be extended to other services;

- establishment of a new Scottish Health Council to ensure that the NHS Boards fulfil their new duties; and

- increased involvement of, and accountability to, patients through the introduction of an integrated care record, a new statement of patient's rights and responsibilities, and a new complaints procedure.

After smoking, poor diet is the most significant contributor to poor health in Scotland, being linked to high levels of cancer and heart disease.

By 2005 the Executive has set targets to:

- double the average intake of fruit and vegetables to more than 400 grams a day;

- reduce the average intake of food energy from total fat from 41 per cent in 1995 to no more than 35 per cent; and

Health and well-being constituency profiles for Scotland

In March 2004, NHS Health Scotland published health and well-being profiles which compare each Scottish parliamentary constituency with the national average. The profiles, which include 80 indicators, also show the changes in the ten years to 2001. The profiles showed that for Scotland as a whole over the decade:

- life expectancy for males increased by 3 per cent or 2.1 years, and for females by 2.4 per cent or 1.8 years;

- infant mortality decreased by 32.4 per cent;

- the rate of heart disease fell by 35.4 per cent; and

- hospital admissions attributable to alcohol increased by 52 per cent overall and by 22 per cent for teenagers.

- reduce the average intake of food energy from saturated fatty acids from 17 per cent in 1995 to no more than 11 per cent.

In 2003 the Scottish Executive published its first national physical activity strategy *Let's Make Scotland More Active*. This aims to increase physical activity levels in people of all ages. It sets targets that by 2022, 50 per cent of adults will be taking at least 30 minutes of moderate activity every day, and 80 per cent of children will be taking at least 60 minutes of moderate activity a day.

NHS 24 was launched in Scotland in 2002. This is a nurse-led telephone advice service similar to NHS Direct in England (see page 180). The first call centre covered the Grampian region. The service will be fully operational across Scotland by the end of 2004. There are also plans to introduce a NHS 24 online service.

The NHS in Northern Ireland

The Department of Health, Social Services and Public Safety (DHSSPS) is responsible for the development and implementation of health, community care and public safety policy in Northern Ireland.

There are four Health and Social Services Boards (Eastern, Northern, Southern and Western) which are agents of the DHSSPS. The Boards are responsible for planning, commissioning and purchasing health services for residents in their areas.

Unlike other parts of the United Kingdom, health and personal social services are provided as an integrated service by 19 Health and Social Services Trusts. The HSS Trusts manage front-line health staff and services and control their own budgets.

Since 2000, the Government has produced a written contract with the people of Northern Ireland setting out, within the limits of the financial resources available, the plans and priorities for tackling problems and improving public services. The latest document, *Priorities and Budget 2004–06*, identifies the following priorities for health and social services in Northern Ireland:

- reduction in preventable deaths, diseases and injuries;

- more responsive hospital services;

- accessible and effective primary care;

- improvements in the quality of health and social care provided;

- better support for those who need care in the community;

- better life chances for children; and

- safeguarding the rights and interests of children.

In response to *Priorities and Budget,* DHSSPS published *Priorities for Action 2004/05* which details how the Department, Boards and Trusts will achieve these targets and how resources are deployed for the benefit of the local community.

DHSSPS has implemented a number of initiatives to modernise service delivery and ensure that high quality services are provided for all the people of Northern Ireland. One example is *Investing for Health* (2002). This is a framework of action to improve health and well-being and reduce health inequalities and is based on partnership working among departments, public bodies, local communities, voluntary bodies and district councils. *Investing for Health* has resulted in a Five Year Tobacco Action Plan; a Teenage Pregnancy and Parenthood Strategy and Action Plan; Promoting Mental Health Strategy and Action Plan; Home Accident Prevention Strategy and Action Plan; Sexual Health Strategy; Physical Activity Strategy; Food and Nutrition Strategy; and a Health Promoting Schools Initiative.

In February 2004 the Strategic Investment Programme was announced. This included over £300 million of capital investment in the HPSS. Some £72 million of this money will be used over the next three years for a programme of hospital developments as set out in *Developing Better Services – Modernising Hospitals and Reforming Structures.* This document details the way forward for acute service provision in Northern Ireland and sets out proposals for new organisational structures to manage health and social services. In addition, capital monies will provide for:

- increased hospital capacity, additional renal capacity and expansion of magnetic resonance imaging to all main hospitals;

- new secure accommodation for the mentally ill, and a new Acquired Brain Injury service; and

- a new cancer centre at the Belfast City Hospital.

Finance

In 2003/04 an estimated 74 per cent of the NHS was financed through general taxation, with 21 per cent from National Insurance contributions (see chapter 12) and 5 per cent from charges and other receipts.

The April 2002 Budget announced increases in National Insurance contributions from April 2003 to provide extra funding for the NHS. As a result, public spending on health will increase from £66.3 billion in 2002/03 to £107.2 billion in 2007/08. This will result in the proportion of UK GDP spent on health services increasing from 7.6 per cent to 9.2 per cent over this five-year period. Government plans for public expenditure on health for the three financial years from 2004/05 are set out in Table 13.7.

Table 13.7 Government expenditure plans for the NHS,[1] UK

		£ billion
	Total public expenditure	*of which* capital investment
2004/05	81.1	3.7
2005/06	88.6	4.7
2006/07	97.4	5.6

1 The public health spending figures are based on the UN Classification of the Functions of Government (COFOG), as used in the Public Expenditure Statistical Analysis 2004.
Source: HM Treasury

Some NHS funding is raised from other, non-government, sources. For example, some hospitals increase revenue by taking private patients, who pay the full cost of their accommodation and treatment. Hospitals can also use private finance for NHS capital projects, under the Private Finance Initiative, which aims to promote commercial partnership between the public and private sectors (see page 370). This involves new NHS facilities being designed, built, maintained and owned by the private sector, which then leases them back to the NHS. The NHS retains control of key planning and clinical decisions.

Charges

Around 650 million prescription items, worth around £7.5 billion, were dispensed in the community in England in 2003. The proportion of items provided in the community free of charge was 86 per cent. The following groups are exempt from prescription charges:

- people aged 60 and over;

- children under 16 and full-time students under 19;

- women who are pregnant or have given birth in the previous 12 months;

- people with certain medical conditions;

- NHS in-patients; and

- people who receive (or whose partners receive) certain social security benefits (see chapter 12), or who qualify on low income grounds.

There are charges for most types of NHS dental treatment, including examinations. However, the following people are entitled to free treatment: women who begin a course of treatment while pregnant or within 12 months of having a baby; children under 18; full-time students under 19; NHS in-patients (where treatment is carried out by a hospital dentist); NHS hospital dental service out-patients; community dental service patients; and adults on low incomes or receiving the same benefits or tax credits as for free prescriptions.

Free NHS sight tests are available for people aged 60 and over, children up to the age of 16, full-time students under the age of 19, adults on low incomes or receiving the same benefits or tax credits as for free prescriptions, patients whose sight test is carried out in a hospital eye department as part of their treatment; and people who have, or are at particular risk of, eye disease. Around 10.5 million sight tests were paid for by PCTs and Local Health Boards in England and Wales in the year ending 31 March 2004.

Fraud prevention

The NHS Counter Fraud Service was established in 1998 and incorporated into the NHS Counter Fraud and Security Management Service (CFSMS) in April 2003. The CFSMS estimates that since 1999 counter-fraud work has benefited the NHS by £320 million, compared with costs of £20 million.

NHS workforce

The NHS is one of the largest employers in the world. In 2003 there were the equivalent of over 1 million full-time direct care employees in NHS hospital and community health services in Great Britain (Table 13.8).

Table 13.8 NHS hospital and community health service staff,[1] 2003, Great Britain

	Thousands
Direct care staff	640
of which	
Medical and dental	81
Nursing, midwifery and health visitors	377
Other non-medical	182
Management and support staff	336
General medical practitioners	39
General dental practitioners	22
All staff	**1,037**

1 Figures on a full-time equivalent basis.
Source: Department of Health; National Assembly for Wales; NHSScotland

Doctors and dentists

Only people on the medical or dentists' registers may practise as doctors or dentists in the NHS. University medical and dental schools are responsible for undergraduate teaching, and the NHS provides hospital and community facilities for training.

Full registration as a doctor requires five or six years' training in a medical school, in a hospital and in the community, with a further year's hospital experience. The regulating body for the medical profession in the United Kingdom is the General Medical Council and the main professional association is the British Medical Association.

For a dentist, five years' training at a dental school and satisfactory completion of one year's mandatory vocational training are required before becoming eligible to work as a principal or associate in the General Dental Services of the NHS. All NHS general dental practitioners are paid by a combination of capitation fees for children registered with the practice, continuing care payments for adults registered, and a prescribed scale of fees for individual treatments. The regulating body for the dental profession in the United Kingdom is the General Dental Council, and the main professional association is the British Dental Association.

Regulation of controlled drugs

The fourth report of the Shipman Inquiry, the *Regulation of Controlled Drugs in the Community*, was published in July 2004. The inquiry was set up following the conviction in January 2000 of a Manchester GP who had murdered patients by administering controlled drugs. The report makes three groups of recommendations:

- setting up an integrated and multidisciplinary inspectorate to monitor and audit the prescription, storage, distribution and disposal of controlled drugs;

- restrictions that would discourage or prevent health professionals from prescribing in circumstances in which it could be considered unsafe or unwise for them to do so; and

- measures to tighten up the handling and safekeeping of controlled drugs along each part of the supply chain, from the supplier to the patient's home, and to provide a complete audit trail, both in the NHS and in the private sector.

The final report of the inquiry, on the monitoring of medical practitioners, is expected later in 2004.

The *Health and Social Care (Community Health and Standards) Act 2003* gave PCTs the responsibility for ensuring the delivery of high quality dental services to meet all reasonable requirements within their area. Financial resources for commissioning local dental services will be devolved to PCTs from October 2005, at which time a new dental contract will also come into force. In July 2004 the Government announced plans to recruit an extra 1,000 dentists by October 2005, accompanied by extra investment of £368 million in NHS dentistry.

Nurses, midwives and health visitors

The majority of nursing students undertake the pre-registration Diploma in Higher Education programme, which emphasises health promotion as well as care of the sick and enables students upon qualification to work either in hospitals or in the community. The programme lasts three years (full-time) and consists of periods of university study combined with practical experience in a hospital and in the community. Midwifery education programmes for registered general/adult nurses take 18 months, while the direct entry programme lasts three years (full-time). Health visitors and district nurses are registered adult nurses who have a further specialist qualification and care for clients in the community.

The Nursing and Midwifery Council is responsible for regulating and registering nurses and midwives throughout the United Kingdom.

Nurse consultants

In 2000 the first nurse consultant posts were introduced. The NHS Plan committed the Government to establishing 1,000 such posts by 2004, and by June 2004 over 870 posts had been filled. The positions combine specialist practice with leadership, consultancy, education and research responsibilities.

Modern matrons

In 2001 the first 'modern matron' posts were created in England. Each matron is in overall charge of a group of hospital wards, helping to ensure high standards of care. They set and monitor standards for cleaning and catering, and can take action where these are not met. Over 3,000 appointments had been made by April 2004.

Pharmacists

Only people on the register of pharmaceutical chemists may practise as pharmacists. Registration requires four years' training in a school of pharmacy, followed by one year's practical experience in a community or hospital pharmacy approved for training by one of the regulatory bodies for the profession – the Royal Pharmaceutical Society of Great Britain and the Pharmaceutical Society of Northern Ireland.

Community pharmacists are paid professional fees for dispensing NHS prescriptions. From 2003, supplementary prescribing was introduced with the aim of speeding access to medicines for patients with conditions such as asthma, diabetes, coronary heart disease and high blood pressure. This allows suitably trained pharmacists and nurses to issue repeat prescriptions to patients, avoiding the need for them to revisit their doctors.

Opticians

The General Optical Council regulates the professions of optometrists (ophthalmic opticians) and dispensing opticians in the United Kingdom. Only registered optometrists may test sight. In general, optometric training takes four years (five years in Scotland), including a year of practical experience under supervision. Dispensing opticians usually take a two-year full-time course with a year's practical experience, or a three-year part-time day-release or distance-learning course while employed with a registered optician.

Other health professions

The Health Professions Council is a UK-wide regulatory body responsible for setting and monitoring the standards of professional training, performance and conduct of 12 healthcare professions: arts therapists, chiropodists, clinical scientists, dieticians, biomedical scientists, occupational therapists, orthoptists, paramedics, physiotherapists, prosthetists and orthotists, radiographers, and speech and language therapists.

Council for the Regulation of Health Care Professionals

The Council for the Regulation of Health Care Professionals was established in 2003 to oversee the individual regulators of healthcare professions in the United Kingdom. The Council is responsible for ensuring consistency in the work of the regulators, and helps Parliament to hold them to account. The creation of the Council met a commitment set out in the 2000 NHS Plan and was also one of the recommendations made in the 2001 report of the public inquiry into children's heart surgery at the Bristol Royal Infirmary.

Recruitment

Delivering the NHS Plan, published in 2002, set new targets for 15,000 extra consultants and GPs, 35,000 nurses, midwives and health visitors, and 30,000 therapists and scientists by 2008.

Several initiatives have been put in place to recruit new staff and encourage former NHS healthcare professionals to return to the service. The 'Return to Practice' initiative, which seeks to attract former staff back to the NHS, has been running since February 1999. Under this scheme, nearly 17,500 nurses, midwives and health visitors had returned to work in the NHS by December 2003.

The GP returners scheme offers incentives to doctors returning to work in the NHS. The scheme includes a package of financial and working measures designed to adapt work to individual GPs' needs. Benefits include:

- salaried refresher training tailored to individual needs;

- a 'golden hello' payment up to £12,000;

- flexible working options enabling full- or part-time hours; and

- support and advice on childcare.

In February 2004 the Government announced the launch of a recruitment and retention strategy to increase the number of radiographers working in the NHS in England. The strategy will receive £3.4 million funding over two years and will focus on increasing the workforce, encouraging qualified radiographers to return to the NHS and developing career paths for all radiography staff.

NHS online recruitment service

In December 2003 the Government launched an online recruitment service for the NHS, which allows candidates to view job advertisements and apply for positions on one website (*www.jobs.nhs.uk*). Forty-six NHS organisations were selected to pilot the service, which was rolled out across the NHS in England in April 2004. The service will complement the NHS careers service, which provides information to people wishing to start or return to a career in the NHS. A daily total of around 1,500 jobs is displayed.

The NHS is also recruiting from abroad, and in 2000 set a target of recruiting 1,000 doctors and 2,000 nurses by March 2005, focusing on countries where there are surpluses of suitably qualified staff. To increase capacity and reduce waiting times, the Government has also introduced an overseas clinical teams initiative whereby surgeons and their existing teams of suitably qualified medical specialists are being employed by the NHS. The Government's top priority area for overseas teams is for them to work in new NHS Treatment Centres (see page 184).

Services for children, women, men and older people

Children

Activities promoting the health of children include: prevention of childhood accidents; immunisation and vaccination (see page 178); screening and health surveillance; and health education on diet and exercise.

Babies and pre-school children

A comprehensive programme of health surveillance for pre-school children is run by community health services and GPs. They receive an annual payment for every child registered on the programme (in Scotland this is carried out by the Community Paediatric Service, which may be based in a primary care or acute services trust).

Health visitors have a central role in health promotion and in identifying the healthcare needs of under-fives and helping to ensure access to services. They visit new-born babies at home between 10 and 14 days after birth. Later checks usually take place at:

- six to eight weeks (with a physical examination by a health visitor, GP or clinic doctor);
- six to nine months (including hearing and sight assessments);
- 18 months to two years; and
- pre-school, at three to four-and-a-half years.

School health services

Children attending state schools have access to the school health service. School nurses check hearing, sight, speech and weight, administer vaccinations and are involved in health education, counselling and sex education. The service also assists teachers with pupils who have medical needs.

Child guidance and child psychiatric services provide help and advice to families and children with psychological or emotional problems. In recent years, efforts have been made to improve co-operation between community-based child health services and local authority education and social services for children. This is particularly important in the prevention of child abuse and for the health and welfare of children in care.

The Food in Schools programme is a joint venture between the DH and the Department for Education and Skills. A range of nutrition-related activities and projects has been developed as part of the programme, to complement existing healthier-food initiatives in schools.

Pilot projects run in over 300 schools during the 2003/04 academic year included healthier breakfast clubs, tuck shops, vending machines, lunch boxes and cookery clubs. Schools are also being encouraged to carry out an 'audit' during the school day and develop food policies for the whole school. The results of the pilot projects will be brought together and made available to schools across England from the beginning of 2005.

The National School Fruit Scheme ensures that all children aged four to six receive free fruit on each school day. Each year from 2004, about 440 million pieces of fruit will be distributed to over 2 million children in some 18,000 schools in England.

In Wales, a Food and Fitness Task Group for children and young people helps to plan and coordinate food and fitness initiatives. Schools in the Welsh Network of Healthy School Schemes are being encouraged to audit their activity related to food and nutrition. Over 350 schools have developed fruit tuck shops and a healthy vending pilot project is under way in secondary schools. The primary school breakfast scheme, which provides a free healthy breakfast at school, was introduced in September 2004 and will be available to all schools wishing to participate by January 2007.

In Scotland, nutritional standards for school meals were set out with the publication of *Hungry for Success* in February 2003. The Scottish Executive committed funding of £64 million over three years to develop nutritional standards for school meals and provide free fruit three times a week to all primary 1 and 2 children. The Executive also provided funding of £24 million over three years to develop the Active School Co-ordinators Programme, which aims to encourage children to be more physically active.

Children's National Service Framework

The Children's National Service Framework (NSF), published in 2004, set new national standards for children in England, across both the NHS and social services. It has a broad remit covering eight areas: hospital services; the ill child; child and adolescent mental health services;

disabled children; children in special circumstances; healthy children and young people; maternity; and medicines. The first module, on hospital services, was published in 2003.

Women

Women have particular health needs related to certain forms of cancer and to pregnancy.

Screening

Under the UK breast cancer screening programme, every woman aged between 50 and 64 is invited for a breast X-ray every three years by computerised call-up and recall systems. In England the upper age limit was raised to 70 in 2004, and the same change is being made on a phased basis in Wales and Scotland. In 2002/03, 1.3 million women of all ages were screened in England, and 9,849 cases were diagnosed.

National policy for cervical screening is that women should be screened every three to five years (three-and-a-half to five-and-a-half years in Scotland) so as to detect indications of the long developmental stage that may proceed to invasive cancer. The programme invites women aged 20 to 64 (20 to 60 in Scotland) for screening. However, since many women are not invited immediately when they reach their 20th birthday, the age group 25 to 64 is used to give a more accurate estimate of coverage of the target population. By the end of March 2003, 81 per cent of women aged 25 to 64 had been screened at least once in the previous five years in England, 86 per cent in Scotland, 81 per cent in Wales and 73 per cent in Northern Ireland.

Maternity

A woman is entitled to care throughout pregnancy, birth and the postnatal period. Care may be provided by a midwife, a community-based GP, a hospital-based obstetrician, or a combination of these. Special preventive services are provided under the NHS to safeguard the health of pregnant women and mothers with young children. Services include free dental treatment; health education; and vaccination and immunisation of children against certain infectious diseases (see page 178).

The Welfare Food Scheme supports mothers on low incomes. The scheme was originally created in 1940 as a wartime measure to protect the health of young children during times of rationing. The scheme provides tokens for free liquid milk and infant formula milk to those who qualify on the grounds of low income or receipt of tax credits.

In February 2004 the Government announced reforms to the scheme to be phased in across England from early 2005. Under the new scheme called Healthy Start, milk tokens will be replaced with weekly vouchers that can be used to buy fresh produce as well as milk. The scheme will be expanded to cover all pregnant women under the age of 18, regardless of family income. The vouchers will be worth at least £5.60 a week to families with children under one, and at least £2.80 a week to those with children over one.

In England and Wales, two guides are given to first-time mothers free of charge. *The Pregnancy Book* is a complete guide to a healthy pregnancy, labour and giving birth as well as life with a new baby. *Birth to Five* is a guide to the early stages of development, nutrition, weaning and common childhood ailments. The Scottish equivalent is *Ready, Steady, Baby!* produced by NHS Health Scotland. New mothers also receive a Personal Child Health Record to record immunisations, tests, birth details and health checks.

Teenage pregnancy

The Social Exclusion Unit's report on teenage pregnancy in England, published in 1999, set out a national strategy to halve the rate of under-18 conceptions by 2010, with an interim reduction of 15 per cent by 2004. It also aims to increase the participation of teenage parents in education and work, to reduce their risk of social exclusion. To aid delivery of these aims, every top-tier local authority has a ten-year teenage pregnancy strategy and a detailed three-year action plan. Between 1999 and 2001 the conception rate for women aged under 18 in England and Wales fell from 45.9 to 42.3 per 1,000 women aged 15 to 17 years, but there was a slight increase (to 42.8) in 2002.

Abortion

Under the *Abortion Act 1967*, as amended, a time limit of 24 weeks applies to the largest category of abortion – risk to the physical or mental health of the pregnant woman – and also to abortion because of a similar risk to any existing children of her family. There are three categories to which no time limit applies:

7 December 2003 Winner of the Turner Prize, potter Grayson Perry, dressed as his alter ego Claire, with two of his vases at Tate Britain in London.

9 December 2003 Buster, a five-year-old springer spaniel, pictured with his handler Sgt Danny Morgan, is awarded the People's Dispensary for Sick Animals (PDSA) Dickin Medal, 'the animals' Victoria Cross', for sniffing out a cache of arms, explosives and bomb making equipment in Iraq.

9 December 2003 The M6 Toll Road *(below right)*, the first private motorway in the United Kingdom, opens in the West Midlands to help ease motorway congestion in the area *(below left)*. The 43-kilometre motorway cuts journey times around the city of Birmingham by an estimated 45 minutes.

© RAF HENDON

© RAF HENDON

© RAF HENDON

17 December 2003 The Royal Air Force Museum at Hendon unveils *Milestones of Flight*, an exhibition that traces the history of the first century of powered flight.

Top: Hawker Tempest V, which came into service towards the end of WW II.

Centre: BAe Harrier GR3, famous for its vertical take-off and landing capabilities, which came into service in 1969.

Bottom: Eurofighter Typhoon, which came into service in 2003. It operates as a fighter but, as the design evolves, will also operate as a bomber and ground attack aircraft.

- prevention of grave permanent injury to the physical or mental health of the woman;
- where there is a substantial risk of serious foetal handicap; or
- where continuing the pregnancy would involve a risk to the life of the pregnant woman greater than if the pregnancy were terminated.

The Act does not apply in Northern Ireland.

In 2003 the number of legal abortions performed on women resident in England and Wales rose by 3.2 per cent to 181,600. The age-standardised rate rose from 17.0 to 17.5 abortions per 1,000 women aged between 15 and 44. In Scotland in 2002 the number fell by 2.9 per cent to 11,800 with the overall age-standardised rate falling from 11.3 to 10.4 per 1,000 women aged between 15 and 44.

Men

The lower life expectancy of men (see page 176) is the most significant indication of the health inequalities that exist between the sexes. Two possible reasons are that men tend to have less healthy lifestyles in terms of diet, smoking and higher alcohol and drug intake, and that they are involved in more accidents. They also risk later diagnosis and treatment because, according to some experts, they do not consult a doctor as quickly as women do when a problem arises.

In recent years, Government and other health campaigns have aimed to raise awareness and improve treatments for male-specific cancers. In both England and Scotland the respective Cancer Plans set out the Government's and Scottish Executive's intention to introduce prostate cancer screening as soon as techniques are sufficiently developed. In the meantime, a prostate cancer risk management programme has been launched in both England and Scotland. One element of this is a project for prostate specific antigen (PSA) testing. Extra Government funding for research has also been allocated. In 2003/04, funding for the NHS Prostate Cancer Programme was £4.2 million, a twentyfold increase since 1999.

Older people

The NSF for Older People sets out national standards for care across health and social services in England. These standards apply whether an

older person is being cared for at home, in a residential setting or in a hospital. The NSF focuses on conditions that are particularly significant for older people and that have not been covered in other NSFs (see page 197). Two of the aims for 2004 were that:

- every general hospital that provides care for stroke victims should have a specialised stroke service; and
- every general practice should be using protocols agreed with local specialist health and social care services to diagnose, treat and care for patients with depression and dementia.

The Diabetes NSF includes a target that by 2006 at least 80 per cent of people with diabetes will be offered screening for the early detection of diabetic retinopathy (a cause of blindness in older people).

Mobile centres for treatment of cataract patients

From February 2004 cataract patients in areas of England with the longest waiting times were able to get treatment at mobile centres. The two new mobile treatment centres move around England, performing an extra 44,000 cataract operations over the next five years.

Hospital and specialist services

District general hospitals offer a broad spectrum of clinical specialities, supported by a range of other services, such as anaesthetics, pathology and radiology. Almost all have facilities for the admission of emergency patients, either through A&E departments or as direct referrals from GPs. Treatments are provided for in-patients, day cases, out-patients and patients who attend wards for treatment such as dialysis.

Some hospitals provide specialist services covering more than one region or district, for example for heart and liver transplants and rare eye and bone cancers. There are also specialist hospitals, such as the Great Ormond Street Hospital for Children, Moorfields Eye Hospital, and the National Hospital for Neurology and Neurosurgery, all in London. These hospitals combine specialist treatment facilities with training and international research.

Organ transplants

United Kingdom Transplant (a special health authority of the NHS) provides a 24-hour support service to all transplant units in the United Kingdom and the Republic of Ireland for the matching and allocation of organs for transplant. In some cases transplants are multi-organ. United Kingdom Transplant is also responsible for maintaining the NHS Organ Donor Register. In July 2004 the Government announced that, as part of the implementation of its arm's length bodies Review (see page 184), UK transplant would merge with the National Blood Authority to create a new National Blood and Transplant Authority.

The number of organ transplants carried out in the United Kingdom during 2003/04 was 2,863, the highest on record. This figure included 1,787 kidney transplants, for which there was a waiting list of 4,989 patients at the end of that year, and 679 liver transplants.

At the end of 2003 there were five designated adult cardio-thoracic transplant centres and one paediatric transplant centre in England, and one adult centre in Scotland. There are six designated adult and three paediatric liver transplant units in England and one adult unit in Scotland.

People who are willing to donate their organs after death may carry a donor card. The NHS Organ Donor Register contained around 11 million names at December 2003. The Government aims to have 16 million people registered by 2010.

Blood services

Blood services are run by the National Blood Service in England and north Wales, the Welsh Blood Service, the Scottish National Blood Transfusion Service, and the Northern Ireland Blood Transfusion Service.

Over 3 million donations are made each year by voluntary unpaid donors in the United Kingdom.

These are turned into many life-saving components and products for patients. Red cells, platelets and other components with a limited 'life' are prepared at blood centres, while the production of plasma products is undertaken at the Bio Products Laboratory in Elstree (Hertfordshire) and the Protein Fractionation Centre in Edinburgh.

Use of human tissue

In December 2003 the Government published the *Human Tissue Bill.* This arose from events at the Bristol Royal Infirmary and the Royal Liverpool Children's Hospital (Alder Hey), when organs and tissue from children who had died were removed, stored and used without proper consent. This practice had been fairly widespread and the law in this area was not clear and consistent.

Most of the provisions in the Bill will apply in England, Wales and Northern Ireland. It seeks to establish a new body – the Human Tissue Authority – which would oversee the use of human tissue for a wide range of purposes, including anatomical examination, education and training, research and transplantation. The consent of the donor or family members would form the basis for keeping or using tissues and cells. The Bill would also make it an offence, throughout the United Kingdom, to analyse DNA without consent (as envisaged in the genetics White Paper – see page 200). In time the Human Tissue Authority will be merged with the Human Fertilisation and Embryology Authority (see page 200) to form the Regulatory Authority for Fertility and Tissue.

Each of the four blood services coordinates programmes for donor recruitment, retention and education, and donor sessions are organised regionally, in towns and workplaces. Donors are aged between 17 and 70. Blood centres are responsible for blood collection, screening, processing and supplying hospital blood banks. They also provide laboratory, clinical, research and specialist advisory services and facilities. They are subject to nationally coordinated quality audit programmes, through the Medicines and Healthcare products Regulatory Agency (MHRA, see page 199).

Ambulance and patient transport services

NHS ambulances are available free to the public through the 999 telephone system for medical emergencies and accidents, as well as for doctors' urgent calls. Non-emergency patient transport services are free to NHS patients considered by their doctor, dentist or midwife to be medically unfit to travel by other means.

In many areas volunteer drivers provide a hospital car service for non-urgent patients. Patients on low incomes may be eligible for reimbursement of costs of travelling to hospital.

Emergency response

In 2003/04 the number of emergency calls to the NHS in England rose by 8 per cent to 5.3 million; the number of incidents attended by 7 per cent to 4.3 million; and the number of emergency patient journeys by 6 per cent to 3.4 million. Paramedics using cars or motorcycles and 'approved first responders' (such as a doctor) helped to ensure that the ambulance services met their target of responding to 75 per cent of Category A calls (those which are immediately life threatening) within eight minutes. There were 16 dedicated air ambulance services in England and Wales in April 2004, all operating as independent charitable trusts. Scotland has two helicopters and four fixed-wing aircraft funded by the Scottish Executive.

Hospices

Hospice (or palliative) care is a special type of care for people whose illness may no longer be curable. It focuses on controlling pain and other distressing symptoms, and on providing psychological support to patients, their families and friends, both during the illness and into bereavement. Palliative care services mostly help people with cancer, although patients with other life-threatening illnesses are also cared for.

The first hospices in the United Kingdom were opened in 1967 and were provided on a voluntary basis. Most care continues to be provided by the voluntary sector, but is also increasingly provided within NHS palliative care units, and by hospitals and community palliative care teams. The care may be provided in a variety of settings: at home (with support from specially trained staff), in a hospice or palliative care unit, in hospital or at a hospice day centre. There were 216 hospice or palliative care units in the United Kingdom in January 2003, providing around 3,000 beds.

In June 2003 there were 28 children's hospices in England, providing respite care from birth to 16 years of age. Palliative care networks for children are being established across England to coordinate how and where services are provided. In Scotland there are two children's hospices, the second of which became operational in April 2004.

The National Council for Hospices and Specialist Palliative Care Services brings together voluntary and health service providers in England, Wales and Northern Ireland, to provide a coordinated view of the service. Its Scottish counterpart is the Scottish Partnership for Palliative Care.

Sexual health

The Government's public health strategy includes the provision of sexual health services. Free contraceptive advice and treatment are available from GPs and family planning clinics, which also offer tailored services for young people. Clinics provide condoms and other contraceptives free of charge and emergency or 'morning after' pills are available from pharmacists without a prescription.

The DH has developed a national sexual health and HIV strategy to bring together initiatives in these areas, including work on chlamydia (see page 178). The first phase of a national screening programme for chlamydia was launched in 2002 at ten sites across England. In January 2004 the Government announced the introduction of a further 16 programmes covering 50 PCTs across England. The programmes primarily target women aged 16 to 24, as this group is at greatest risk of infection.

In Wales, recent sexual health promotions have included condom distribution schemes and sexually transmitted infection and HIV prevention campaigns. Following the Welsh Assembly Government's *Strategic Framework for Promoting Sexual Health*, a Review of HIV and Sexual Health Services has been commissioned. The Scottish Executive is also developing plans for a sexual health strategy.

Alcohol

In March 2004 the Government published the *Alcohol Harm Reduction Strategy for England*. This identifies a need for greater awareness of alcohol misuse issues among health service staff, and an improvement in their ability to deal with them. It proposes pilot schemes to find out whether earlier identification and treatment of those with alcohol problems can improve health and lead to longer-term savings. It also proposes measures aimed at achieving a long-term change in attitudes to irresponsible drinking and behaviour, including:

- making the 'sensible drinking' message easier to understand and apply;
- targeting information campaigns at those most at risk, in particular binge drinkers and chronic drinkers;
- ensuring better information for consumers on products and at point of sale;
- creating alcohol education programmes for schools that can change attitudes and behaviour, as well as raise awareness; and
- moves to ensure television advertising does not target young drinkers or glamorise irresponsible behaviour.

In 2002 the Scottish Executive published a *Plan for Action on Alcohol Misuse*. This aims to reduce alcohol-related harm in Scotland and prioritises action to reduce binge drinking and harmful drinking by children and young people.

In Northern Ireland, the *Strategy for Reducing Alcohol Related Harm* was published in 2000 and is being implemented with the drug strategy. A review has commenced to determine the overall effectiveness of the Northern Ireland drugs and alcohol strategies and the structures and activities developed to take them forward.

There is also close co-operation between statutory and voluntary organisations. In England, Alcohol Concern and other voluntary organisations play a prominent role in improving services for problem drinkers and their families, increasing public awareness of alcohol misuse, and improving training for professional and voluntary workers. In Scotland local action is coordinated through a network of 22 local action teams, while Alcohol Focus Scotland promotes responsible drinking and offers a range of training and counselling services.

Tobacco

Cigarette advertising on UK television has been banned since 1965. During 2003/04 a number of wider restrictions came into effect under the *Tobacco Advertising and Promotions Act 2002*. This will lead to a ban on most forms of tobacco advertising, promotion and sponsorship in the United Kingdom, including magazines, newspapers, billboards, the Internet, and sponsorship of cultural and sporting events.

NHS smoking cessation services offer information, counselling and motivational help to smokers who want to stop. In England, the Government target for 2002/03 was for 100,000 smokers to have quit by the four-week follow-up stage. Results show that of the 234,900 smokers who set a quit date in 2002/03, 124,100 reported that they had successfully quit at the four-week stage. A target of 800,000 successful quitters at the four-week stage has been set for the three years 2003/04 to 2005/06 combined. In July 2004 the Government announced a new target to reduce adult smoking rates to 21 per cent or less by 2010 (from 26 per cent in 2002), with a reduction among routine and manual groups to 26 per cent or less (from 31 per cent).

Drugs

The misuse of drugs, such as heroin, cocaine and amphetamines, is a serious social and health problem (see page 179). The Government launched its ten-year anti-drugs strategy *Tackling Drugs to Build a Better Britain* in 1998. In 2002 an updated version of the strategy was published, building on the progress and lessons learned. This focused on the most dangerous drugs and the communities and individuals most affected by them. It aims to discourage young people from using drugs in the first place and to provide support to parents and family members who are concerned about drugs.

The DH has a target to double the participation of problem drug users in drug treatment programmes in England by 2008, and to increase year on year the proportion of users successfully sustaining or completing treatment programmes.

Within the UK strategy, there are separate strategies for Wales, Scotland and Northern Ireland. Programmes are delivered at a local level by Drug Action Teams or similar teams composed of all those involved in drugs issues (for example PCTs, the social and probation services, and the police). They agree a strategy that applies the national policy to the particular conditions in their area.

Medical standards

Standards of care

NHS Charters

Your Guide to the NHS, which in 2001 replaced the earlier Patient's Charter, provides information on how to get treatment and sets out minimum standards of service, targets for the NHS and improvements in the NHS Plan. It also details what patients have a right to expect from the NHS and what is expected from patients. A new guide for Scotland *The NHS and You* was published in 2004.

National Service Frameworks

The aim of NSFs is to set national standards and reduce variations in service within the NHS. Since 1999 in England, NSFs for mental health, coronary heart disease, cancer, diabetes and older people (see page 193) have been published. In addition an NSF for renal services is being developed in a modular format. *Part One: Dialysis and Transplantation* was published in January 2004 with *Part Two: Prevention and End of Life Care* to follow. The first part of the Children's NSF, which included the standard for hospital services, was published in 2003 and the remainder in 2004. An NSF for long-term conditions (with a particular focus on neurological conditions) is also in preparation.

National Institute for Clinical Excellence

NICE was established in 1999 to develop national standards for best practice in clinical care within the NHS in England and Wales. NICE publishes three types of guidance:

- technology appraisals on the use of new and existing medicines and treatments: by July 2004, 80 had been published;

- clinical guidelines on the appropriate treatment and care of people with specific diseases and conditions: by July 2004, 29 had been published; and

- interventional procedures on whether techniques used for diagnosis or treatment are safe and work well enough for routine use: by July 2004, 79 had been published. (This category of guidance applies to Scotland as well as England and Wales.)

The Institute's membership is drawn from the health professions, the NHS, academics, health economists and patients.

In October 2003, new treatments referred to NICE for appraisal in its next work programme included those for people with chemotherapy induced anaemia, and heart failure. New clinical guidelines will include topics such as breast and prostate cancers, puerperal/perinatal mental health, and the management of chronic fatigue syndrome.

NHS Quality Improvement Scotland is responsible for developing and running a national system of quality assurance in healthcare for the NHS in Scotland. This involves setting clinical standards, reviewing and monitoring performance and providing a single source of national advice on effective practice. It also takes the lead on patient safety and is responsible for investigating any cases of serious service failure.

Treatment centres for ME sufferers

In January 2004 the Government announced the creation of 12 new centres in England to support people with chronic fatigue syndrome, also known as ME, backed by extra investment of £8.5 million. The centres will provide access to specialist assessment, diagnosis and advice; develop education and training resources for health professionals; and support clinical research into the causes and treatment of the condition.

Complaints

There are three levels to the NHS complaints procedure: the first involves resolution of a complaint locally, following a direct approach to the Patients Advice and Liaison Service at the relevant NHS service provider; the second involves an independent review procedure if the complaint is not resolved locally; and as a final resort, patients may approach the Health Service Commissioner (in Northern Ireland, the Commissioner for Complaints) if they are still dissatisfied. The majority of complaints do not proceed beyond the local level.

Since 30 July 2004 the CHAI (see page 198) has been responsible for the independent review of complaints. The Government is planning to issue amended regulations setting out the reformed local resolution process during 2005 after considering relevant recommendations made by the Shipman Inquiry report (see page 189) and other inquiries.

The Independent Complaints Advocacy Service provides assistance to people who wish to complain about the NHS in England.

In 2002/03, 63 per cent of complaints about hospital and community health services in England were resolved within the performance target of 20 working days. The top four subjects of these complaints were clinical treatment (34 per cent); the attitude of staff (13 per cent); delays and cancellations to outpatient appointments (12 per cent); and communication/ information to patients (9 per cent). These have consistently been the top complaints since 1996/97, when such figures were first collected.

In Wales, a revised NHS complaints procedure was introduced in April 2003. Key changes include:

- strengthened local resolution (first stage) with the offer of independent complaints facilitation/mediation;
- independent review (second stage) by a pool of trained lay reviewers appointed by, and accountable to, the Welsh Assembly Government; and
- support to complainants by independent advocates based at Community Health Councils.

Health Service Commissioners

England and Wales each have Health Service Commissioners who are responsible for investigating complaints about health service bodies that have not been dealt with to the satisfaction of the member of the public concerned. The English and Welsh posts are held by one person who is also Parliamentary Commissioner for Administration (the Ombudsman, see page 62). The Health Service Commissioner reports annually to Parliament and to the Welsh Assembly Government.

In Scotland, complaints about the health service can be directed to the Scottish Public Services Ombudsman, who is also the Parliamentary and Housing Commissioner and who reports to the Scottish Parliament. In Northern Ireland complaints about health and social services bodies are investigated by the Commissioner for Complaints.

Health Service Commissioners can investigate complaints that a person has suffered hardship or

injustice as a result of a failure in a service provided by a health service body (including action by health professionals arising from the exercise of clinical judgement); complaints of a failure to provide a service to which the patient was entitled; or maladministration.

Inspection and regulation

The *NHS Reform and Health Care Professions Act 2002* introduced changes to the way in which health and social services are regulated. Further legislation included in the *Health and Social Care (Community Health and Standards) Act 2003* (see page 181) introduced two new independent inspectorates: the CHAI and the CSCI (see page 162). The Act also provided new healthcare inspection powers for the National Assembly for Wales through the establishment of Healthcare Inspectorate Wales. Separate arrangements will continue in Scotland.

Commission for Healthcare Audit and Inspection

The CHAI became fully operational from April 2004. Known as the Healthcare Commission, it is responsible for investigating the performance of all NHS organisations and private hospitals in England. It has also assumed responsibility for the financial monitoring work of the Audit Commission (see page 369) within the NHS in England, the work of the Commission for Health Improvement and the private healthcare role of the National Care Standards Commission. Following assessments, the Healthcare Commission publishes star ratings for all NHS organisations in England and recommends special measures where there are persistent problems. It also publishes an annual report to Parliament on national progress on healthcare in England and Wales and how resources have been used. In Wales, HIW, which became operational in April 2004, has the same responsibilities for undertaking reviews and investigations into the provision of healthcare by NHS bodies in Wales. The voluntary and private healthcare sector in Wales is regulated by the Care Standards Inspectorate for Wales.

Safety

Health Protection Agency

The Health Protection Agency (HPA) was established in April 2003 with a remit covering biological, chemical and radiological hazards, infectious disease control and health emergency planning. The *Health Protection Agency Act 2004* established the HPA as a UK-wide non-departmental public body. In addition to the above health functions, the UK Government and the devolved administrations will look to the HPA to provide all the functions currently carried out by the National Radiological Protection Board (NRPB), which is being wound up. The extent to which the Agency undertakes health functions will vary in different parts of the United Kingdom, to take account of the different needs and wishes of the DH and the devolved administrations.

Medicines and medical equipment

The Medicines and Healthcare products Regulatory Agency (MHRA) was established in 2003. It is responsible for the regulation of both medicines and healthcare products in the United Kingdom and for safeguarding the interests of patients and users by ensuring that medicines, equipment and other products meet appropriate standards of safety, quality and performance, and that they comply with relevant EC Directives.

Only medicines that have been granted a marketing authorisation issued by the MHRA or the European Medicines Agency may be supplied to the public. Marketing authorisations are issued following scientific assessment on the basis of safety, quality and effectiveness.

In January 2004 the Chief Pharmaceutical Officer published *Building a safer NHS for patients – improving medication safety*. The report examined the causes and frequency of medication errors, highlighted drugs and clinical settings that carry particular risk, and identified models of good practice for health professionals and NHS organisations to follow when prescribing drugs.

Food safety

Under the *Food Safety Act 1990*, it is illegal to sell or supply food that is unfit for human consumption or falsely or misleadingly labelled. The Act covers a range of commercial activities related to food production, the sources from which food is derived, such as crops and animals, and articles that come into contact with food. There are also more detailed regulations, which apply to all types of food and drink and their ingredients. Local authorities are responsible for enforcing food law in two main areas: trading

standards officers deal with the labelling of food, its composition and most cases of chemical contamination; and environmental health officers deal with hygiene, cases of microbiological contamination of foods, and food that is found to be unfit for human consumption.

The Food Standards Agency (FSA) is responsible for food safety and standards in the United Kingdom and represents the Government on these issues in the European Union. The FSA has offices in Scotland, Wales and Northern Ireland. Its key aims are to:

- reduce foodborne illness by 20 per cent between 2001 and 2006 by improving food safety throughout the food chain;
- help people to eat more healthily;
- promote honest and informative labelling to help consumers;
- promote best practice within the food industry; and
- improve the enforcement of food law.

Research

The Medical Research Council (MRC, see also page 395) supports medical research in the United Kingdom by providing funding for research programmes and infrastructure, and by investing in training and employment, both in universities and its own research centres. The MRC receives an annual grant from the Office of Science and Technology (part of the Department of Trade and Industry). In 2003/04 the MRC received £410 million and realised a further £68 million from external sources, such as joint-funding initiatives and commercial activities.

The MRC advises the Government on matters relating to medical research, and co-operates with Health Departments throughout the United Kingdom, the NHS and other government departments concerned with biomedical and health service research. It also works closely with other research councils, medical research charities, industry and consumers, to identify and respond to current and future health needs.

Human fertilisation and embryology

The world's first 'test-tube baby' was born in the United Kingdom in 1978, a result of the technique of in-vitro fertilisation. The social, ethical and

Increase in research funding

In the March 2004 Budget, the Government announced an extra £100 million for the NHS for medical research and development. As a result, the combined government budget for medical research will rise from £1.0 billion in 2004 to £1.2 billion a year by 2008. The additional funding will be used to research the treatment and cure of Alzheimer's, stroke, diabetes and mental health, and to develop new medicines for children. The creation of the UK Clinical Research Collaboration will bring together the NHS, the MRC, medical charities, industry and patients, to speed up the development and availability of new medicines and treatments.

legal implications were examined by a committee of inquiry and led eventually to the passage of the *Human Fertilisation and Embryology Act 1990*. The Human Fertilisation and Embryology Authority (HFEA) licenses and inspects centres providing certain infertility treatments, undertaking human embryo research or storing gametes or embryos. It also maintains a code of practice giving guidance to licensed centres and reports annually to Parliament. As part of the implementation of the review of the DH's arm's length bodies (see page 184), the HFEA will, subject to legislation, be merged with the Human Tissue Authority (see page 194), to form the Regulatory Authority for Fertility and Tissue.

Genetic profiling and other advances in genetics have the potential to improve health and healthcare through more precise diagnosis, better targeted and more effective use of existing drugs, and new gene-based drugs and therapies. The 2003 genetics White Paper, *Our inheritance, our future – realising the potential of genetics in the NHS*, set out a plan for the NHS, including the investment of £50 million over three years from 2004, to help realise the benefits of genetics in healthcare. New initiatives include:

■ a substantial investment in upgrading genetics laboratories, and more genetics counsellors, consultants and laboratory scientists;

■ more than £7 million on initiatives to introduce genetics-based healthcare into mainstream NHS services;

■ a Genetics Education and Development Centre to take the lead in education and training in genetics for all healthcare staff; and

■ research in pharmacogenetics, gene therapy and health services research.

The White Paper also set out the safeguards against, and controls on, inappropriate or unsafe use of developments in genetics. In addition to existing controls on gene therapy and use of genetic test results by insurance companies, the Government will introduce new legislation to ban DNA theft, meaning it will become an offence to test someone's DNA without their consent except for medical or police purposes. This is being taken forward in the Human Tissue Bill (see page 194).

Health arrangements with other countries

The member states of the European Economic Area (EEA – see page 104) have special health arrangements under which EEA nationals resident in a member state are entitled to receive emergency treatment, either free or at a reduced cost, during visits to other EEA countries. These arrangements also apply in Switzerland. Treatment is provided, in most cases, on production of a valid Form E111. There are also arrangements for people who go to another EEA country specifically for medical care, or who require continuing treatment for a pre-existing condition. From the end of 2005 the Form E111 will be replaced by the European Health Insurance Card.

Unless falling into an exempted category (for instance people engaging in employment, taking up permanent residence or seeking asylum in the United Kingdom), visitors to the United Kingdom are generally expected to pay for all non-emergency treatment. The United Kingdom also has a number of bilateral agreements with some other countries, such as Australia and New Zealand.

In December 2003 the Government announced changes to the legislation that allows the NHS to charge overseas visitors for treatment. The new regulations, which came into effect in April 2004, prevent the following people (among others) from receiving free treatment:

- failed asylum seekers and others with no legal right to be in the country, for conditions arising after their legal status has been finally determined;

- the dependants and spouse of someone who is permanently resident in the United Kingdom visiting the country briefly just to obtain free treatment. They will only be entitled to free treatment if they permanently reside in the country; and

- business travellers to the United Kingdom and their dependants who fall ill or are injured on a trip to the UK.

There were also changes made to the rules covering UK pensioners who spend part of the year living in another EEA country. The new rules make it easier for them to receive free NHS treatment, by allowing them to spend up to six months out of the country every year and still be eligible. Overseas students studying full time in the United Kingdom became fully exempt from charges.

Health provision outside the NHS

Private healthcare

As an alternative to the NHS, people are entitled to pay for their own health and social care, for example by joining a private healthcare organisation or simply paying for private treatment when the need arises. In addition, there is the option of private medical insurance, which, depending on the premium paid, will cover people's healthcare in times of need. In 2002, 6.7 million people in the United Kingdom were covered by private medical insurance, more than three times the number in 1971 (2.1 million).

The UK market for private dentistry has expanded rapidly in recent years, growing by almost 50 per cent in real terms between 1997 and 2001, to a value of over £1 billion. Around 7 million people in the United Kingdom regularly receive private dental treatment.

Partnerships

In 2000 the DH signed an agreement with the independent healthcare sector (which comprises the private and voluntary sectors), covering care, and workforce and service planning. It involves the NHS using the independent sector's spare capacity; transfer of patients between the two sectors; exchange of information; and joint working on preventive and rehabilitation services.

The publication of *Growing Capacity: independent sector diagnosis and treatment centres* in 2002 marked the launch of a procurement process for a series of independent sector diagnosis and treatment centre projects, with expressions of interest being invited from both UK and overseas independent healthcare providers (see page 184). When fully operational there are expected to be 34 independent sector treatment centres in England providing services for NHS patients. These will complement 46 NHS-run centres that will treat an additional 144,000 patients a year when fully operational by the end of 2005.

In April 2004 the Government announced two supplementary contracts to be run by Nuffield Hospitals and Capio Healthcare UK, to perform almost 25,000 hip, knee and other operations for the NHS in 2004/05. The combined contract value is about £75 million and will make use of existing spare capacity in independent hospitals.

Complementary and alternative medicine

There has been an increasing interest in, and use of, complementary and alternative medicine (CAM) in recent years. An ONS survey published in 2001 found that one in ten people in the United Kingdom had used a complementary therapy in the last year.

Two CAM professions (osteopaths and chiropractors) are regulated by law. In March 2004 the Government published proposals to regulate herbal medicine and acupuncture practitioners. The proposals would mean that those who meet the required standards of competence will be included on a register of practitioners who are entitled to practise. Sanctions, including removal from the register, will be applied to those whose fitness to practise is impaired.

In November 2003 NICE (see page 197) published clinical guidance giving cautious endorsement of some complementary medicines in easing the symptoms of multiple sclerosis. The guidelines recognised the role of therapies such as fish oils, reflexology and t'ai chi.

Further reading

The NHS Improvement Plan: Putting People at the Heart of Public Services. Cm 6268. The Stationery Office, 2004.

National Standards, Local Action: Health and Social Care Standards and Planning Framework. Department of Health, 2004.

Reconfiguring the Department of Health's Arm's Length Bodies. Department of Health, 2004.

Building on the Best: Choice, Responsiveness and Equity in the NHS. Cm 6079. The Stationery Office, 2003.

Department of Health Departmental Report 2004. The Government's Expenditure Plans. Cm 6204. The Stationery Office, 2004.

Improving Health in Wales – A Plan for the NHS with its Partners. Welsh Assembly Government, 2001.

Improving Health in Scotland – The Challenge. Scottish Executive Health Department, 2003.

Priorities for Action 2004/05. Department of Health, Social Services and Public Safety, Northern Ireland, 2004.

Health Statistics Quarterly. Office for National Statistics. The Stationery Office.

Scottish Health Statistics. Information and Statistics Division, NHSScotland.

Health Statistics Wales. National Assembly for Wales.

Health and Social Care in Northern Ireland: A Statistical Profile (2002). Department of Health, Social Services and Public Safety.

Equality and Inequalities in Health and Social Care in Northern Ireland: A Statistical Overview (2004). Department of Health, Social Services and Public Safety.

Websites

Department of Health
www.dh.gov.uk

Welsh Assembly Government
www.wales.gov.uk

Scottish Executive Health Department
www.scotland.gov.uk

NHSScotland, Information and Statistics Division
www.show.scot.nhs.uk/isd

Department of Health, Social Services and Public Safety, Northern Ireland
www.dhsspsni.gov.uk

Commission for Healthcare Audit and Inspection
www.chai.org.uk

Health Protection Agency
www.hpa.org.uk

NHS Direct
www.nhsdirect.nhs.uk

NHS Gateway
www.nhs.uk

WWW.

14   Crime and justice

The legal framework

The United Kingdom has three legal systems (operating in England and Wales, Scotland and Northern Ireland) and three systems of criminal justice. In each system there is emphasis on the independence of both prosecuting authorities and the judiciary, but unlike many countries, there is no single criminal or penal code that sets out the principles on which the justice system operates.

The criminal law presumes that a person is innocent until proven guilty. The standard of proof required is that the evidence should establish guilt 'beyond reasonable doubt'. In civil law – which is primarily concerned with regulating disputes between individuals or organisations – a case only has to be proved on the 'balance of probabilities'. In both criminal and civil cases, the courts make their decisions on an adversarial rather than an inquisitorial basis.

In all three legal systems many areas of law have developed over the centuries through the decisions of the courts. Consistency is achieved because the decisions of higher courts are binding on those lower down. The House of Lords is currently the ultimate appeal court in the United Kingdom, except for Scottish criminal cases. However, in June 2003, the Government announced its intention to create a new independent Supreme Court, separate from the House of Lords, which would take over its judicial functions. These plans would also bring to an end the post of Lord Chancellor (see page 213) and establish an independent Judicial Appointments Commission. A Constitutional Reform Bill (see page 46) to enact these changes was published in February 2004.

Statutes passed by the Westminster or Scottish Parliaments are the ultimate source of law. As the United Kingdom is a member of the European Union (EU, see page 67) there is also a legal duty to comply with European Community (EC) law. Courts in the United Kingdom are obliged to apply the latter in cases where the two conflict. A statute may confer power on a minister, local authority or other executive body to make delegated legislation (see page 51).

EC law is derived from the EC treaties, from the Community legislation adopted under them, and from the decisions of the European Court of Justice. Under the Treaties of Rome, that court has

International co-operation against crime

Measures in the *Crime (International Co-operation) Act 2003* are intended to improve international co-operation against terrorism, money laundering, people trafficking and financial crime. They include:

- paving the way for the United Kingdom to have access to the Schengen information database of missing and wanted persons and items, covering the whole of the EU;

- improved arrangements for police surveillance between EU countries;

- mutual recognition between EU countries of orders to freeze evidence, so that the authorities in one country will act swiftly on the court order of another;

- modernising UK counterfeiting laws to cover payment methods such as direct debit;

- making terrorist offences committed outside the United Kingdom by UK citizens offences under UK law; and

- recognition of driving disqualifications across EU Member States.

the highest authority to decide points of EC law. Where a point arises before a UK court, it may refer the point of law to the Court of Justice for it to decide. Sometimes a court is obliged to make a reference to the European Court.

The European Convention on Human Rights was incorporated into UK law under the *Human Rights Act 1998*. It guarantees the right to a fair trial, to freedom of thought and expression, and to respect for family and private life. All public authorities, including the courts, must act compatibly with these rights. The rights in the Convention do not take precedence over an Act of Parliament. Where they conflict, the higher courts may make a declaration of incompatibility and Parliament then decides what action to take.

Crime in the United Kingdom

There are two main measures of the extent of crime in the United Kingdom: surveys of the public and the recording of crimes by the police.

The British Crime Survey (BCS – covering England and Wales) and similar surveys of the public in Scotland and Northern Ireland give a more complete measure of many types of crime because they include offences that are not reported to the police. They also give a more reliable picture of trends, as they are not affected by the extent to which the public report crime to the police or by variations in police recording practice. Recorded crime statistics are affected by reporting and recording practices. In England and Wales there have been major changes to the recording of crimes since 1997/98.

The BCS[1] estimated that 11.7 million crimes were committed against adults living in private households in England and Wales in the 12 months before interview in 2003/04, a 5 per cent decrease on the previous year (Figure 14.1). The risk of being a victim of crime during this period was estimated at around 26 per cent, one-third lower than the risk in 1995 (40 per cent).

The most recent surveys in Scotland (covering crime in 1999) and Northern Ireland (covering crime in 2000–01) both estimated that the risk of

1 The BCS sample does not include children or people living in institutions; and murder, fraud, sexual offences and victimless crimes such as illegal drug use are not covered.

Figure 14.1 British Crime Survey offences,[1] England and Wales

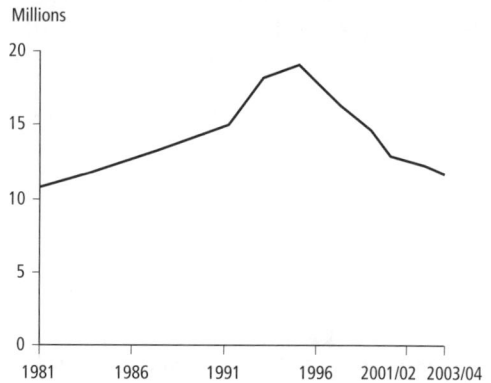

Millions

1 Data refer to survey years, 1981, 1983, 1987, 1991, 1993, 1995, 1997, 1999, 2000, 2001/02, 2002/03 & 2003/04. Until 2000, respondents were asked to recall their experience of crime in the previous calendar year. From 2001/02, when the BCS became a continuous survey, the recall period was changed to the 12 months prior to interview.
Source: British Crime Survey, Home Office

being a victim of crime was 20 per cent. In both cases, crime had fallen since the previous survey.

In England and Wales the term 'recorded crime' is used for crime and attempted crime recorded by the police and notified to the Home Office (so called 'notifiable offences'). All indictable and triable-either-way offences (see page 214) have to be notified, but few of the 'summary' offences (such as motoring offences) that are dealt with by magistrates. Similar terminology is used in Northern Ireland, but in Scotland the term 'crimes' is reserved for the more serious offences (roughly equivalent to indictable and triable-either-way) while less serious crimes are called 'offences'.

Differences in legal systems and recording practices mean that recorded crime statistics from the different parts of the United Kingdom are not exactly comparable. However, Table 14.2 suggests that the crime rate is higher in England and Wales, and that a higher proportion of crime is detected (see glossary) in Scotland.

In 2003/04 in England and Wales, 52 per cent of offences recorded by the police involved forms of theft or burglary, while 19 per cent involved violence (Figure 14.3).

Table 14.2 Recorded crime, 2003/04

	England & Wales	Scotland[1]	Northern Ireland
Notifiable offences	5,935	407	128
Detection rate[2] (percentages)	23	47	27
Offences per 1,000 population	113	80	75

1 Figures for Scotland refer to 2003.
2 Detections are referred to as clear ups in Scotland.
Source: Home Office, Scottish Executive, Police Service of Northern Ireland

Offenders

In 2002, 481,000 people were cautioned for, or found guilty of an indictable offence in England and Wales – about 3 per cent more than in 2001. Young people aged between 16 and 24 were by far the most likely to be cautioned or convicted and in every age group the rate for males was much higher than that for females (Table 14.4).

Some 125,000 people were convicted in Scottish courts in 2002, 4 per cent more than in 2001. There were increases in convictions for crimes such as serious assault, shoplifting, drugs and drink-driving, partly offset by decreases for crimes such as robbery, other theft and speeding.

National crime agencies

National agencies operating solely in England and Wales, Scotland or Northern Ireland are covered

Table 14.4 Offenders found guilty of, or cautioned for, indictable offences, 2002, England and Wales

Rates per 10,000 population

	Males	Females
10–15	196	74
16–24	606	119
25–34	292	61
35 and over	53	12
All aged 10 and over	177	37

Source: Home Office

later in the chapter. However, a number of agencies have a wider remit.

The British Transport Police (BTP) aims to ensure a safe railway environment that is free from disruption and the fear of crime. BTP's remit covers rail operators, staff and passengers throughout Great Britain and also includes the London Underground, the Docklands Light Railway and two tram systems – the Midland Metro and Croydon Tramlink. The force dealt with 83,000 crimes and 50,000 minor offences in 2003/04. A Police Authority for the BTP was set up in 2004.

The National Criminal Intelligence Service (NCIS) works on behalf of all UK law enforcement agencies. It provides strategic and tactical intelligence on serious and organised crime, both nationally and internationally. It is the gateway for UK law enforcement enquiries overseas via the International Criminal Police Organisation (Interpol), the European Police Office (Europol) and the overseas liaison officers networks. It also coordinates on behalf of police forces with the Security Service, in accordance with the Security Service Act 1996. Subject to legislation, NCIS will become part of a new Serious Organised Crime Agency in 2006 (see below).

The Serious Fraud Office (SFO) investigates and prosecutes serious and complex fraud in England, Wales and Northern Ireland. It employs multi-disciplined teams of lawyers, accountants, police officers and other specialists and has wide powers that go beyond those normally available to the police and prosecuting authorities. Under the Criminal Justice Act 1987, staff authorised by the Director of the SFO have powers to require a person to answer questions, provide information or produce documents for an investigation.

Figure 14.3 Recorded crime in 2003/04, England and Wales

Total: 5.9 million

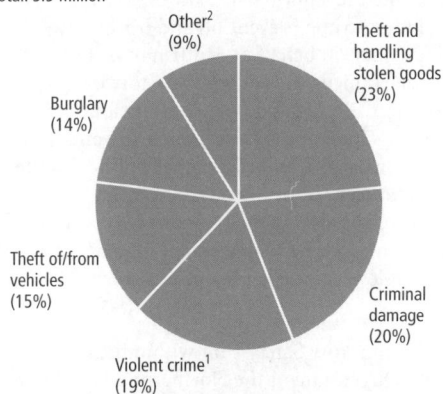

Other[2] (9%)
Theft and handling stolen goods (23%)
Burglary (14%)
Theft of/from vehicles (15%)
Violent crime[1] (19%)
Criminal damage (20%)

1 Robbery, violence against the person and sex offences.
2 Including fraud and forgery, and drug offences.
Source: Home Office

Vehicle crime

The risk of a vehicle-owning household in England and Wales having its car stolen is about once every 77 years. The Home Office Car Theft Index for 2003 showed that older cars (aged 11–15 years) are more likely to be stolen than new cars (three years old or less). Cars that were 13 years old (registered in 1989) were most at risk, with a theft rate of 30 cars per 1,000 registered, compared with just 5 per 1,000 for cars registered in each year between 1996 and 2001. The more sophisticated security measures now fitted as standard to new cars are thought to be the main reason for the difference.

Measures to reduce crime

Various agencies and departments are involved in a range of crime reduction measures with the aim of reducing the social and economic costs that crime can have on individuals and on society as a whole.

Organised crime

A new strategy for tackling organised crime was set out in a White Paper in March 2004 (*One Step Ahead: a 21st Century Strategy to Defeat Organised Crime*). The proposed measures include:

- new powers to disrupt criminal activity and convict those responsible;
- better use of existing powers such as tax, immigration and planning laws;
- the creation of a new Serious Organised Crime Agency; and
- closer co-operation between the Immigration Service, Special Branch and Customs.

It is proposed that the Serious Organised Crime Agency will come into existence in April 2006, bringing together the responsibilities of the National Crime Squad (see page 212), the NCIS, the investigative and intelligence work of HM Customs and Excise, and the Home Office's responsibilities for immigration crime. The agency will employ experts with technological, financial, criminal intelligence and investigative skills. People smuggling and drug trafficking are two of the areas that will be targeted.

Community safety

The *Crime and Disorder Act 1998*, as amended by the *Police Reform Act 2002*, places a statutory requirement on responsible authorities to work with other local agencies and organisations to develop and implement strategies to tackle crime and disorder and misuse of drugs in their area. These statutory partnerships are known as Crime and Disorder Reduction Partnerships (CDRPs), or Community Safety Partnerships (CSPs) in other parts of the United Kingdom. The responsible authorities are the police, local authorities, fire and police authorities and Primary Care Trusts (health authorities in Wales). There are 376 partnerships in England and Wales, supported and monitored by ten Home Office regional teams in the Government Offices (see page 12) and the National Assembly for Wales (see page 18).

The Building Safer Communities Fund is a three-year programme for CDRPs, running from 2003/04. The aim is to encourage problem-solving approaches based on a knowledge of 'what works'. Examples include:

- tackling drug-related crime and strengthening communities against drugs;
- tackling repeat victimisation through anti-burglary projects;
- measures to reduce anti-social behaviour through pub watch schemes; and
- work with young people at risk of truancy and offending.

Within the Scottish Executive Justice Department, the Crime Prevention Unit has responsibility for developing crime prevention and community safety policy on behalf of Scottish ministers. All 32 local councils in Scotland have formed non-statutory CSPs bringing together the four key agencies – local authorities, police, fire and health boards or trusts – as well as other public, private and voluntary sector organisations. The Scottish Executive has also formed a Scottish Forum on Community Safety, which brings together at a national level all the key agencies involved.

The Community Safety Unit within the Criminal Justice Directorate of the Northern Ireland Office is helping to establish 26 local CSPs. These partnerships are developing local action plans, based on an audit of crime and disorder issues.

Anti-social behaviour

Anti-social behaviour covers a wide range of unacceptable behaviour and disorder, including harassment, intimidation, graffiti, vandalism, drunk and disorderly behaviour, begging and litter. The *Anti-Social Behaviour Act 2003* included measures to help tackle such behaviour in England and Wales, for example:

- widening the use of fixed penalty notices against problems such as noise nuisance, truancy and graffiti;

- encouraging parents to prevent and tackle anti-social behaviour by their children;

- enabling the swift closure of premises used in connection with the production, use or supply of class A drugs (see glossary);

- allowing for the dispersal of groups in order to counter ongoing or likely harassment, intimidation, alarm or distress to members of the public; and

- changes to improve the operation of anti-social behaviour orders (ASBOs).

ASBOs, first introduced in 1999, are effective for a minimum of two years. They are civil orders that can be used to prohibit an offender (aged ten or over) from committing specific anti-social acts or from entering defined areas. The Home Office published its national action plan and launched the TOGETHER campaign against anti-social behaviour in October 2003.

The *Antisocial Behaviour etc. (Scotland) Act 2003* provided for the extension of ASBOs to 12- to 15-year-olds; the extension of electronic tagging to

---

Mobile phone use while driving

It has been illegal to use a mobile phone while driving in Great Britain since December 2003, and since March 2004 in Northern Ireland. The maximum penalty, if the matter goes to court, is £1,000 for drivers of cars and £2,500 for drivers of buses, coaches, vans and lorries. The law does permit 999 calls made in a genuine emergency and the use of hands-free equipment, if drivers have proper control of their vehicle.

---

under 16s; and parenting orders to make parents act in the best interests of their children. The Scottish Executive is providing £95 million over 2004 to 2006 to fund the implementation of the provisions of the Act.

Domestic violence

Domestic violence accounts for nearly a fifth of all violent crime in England and Wales. In 2002, 36,000 incidents of domestic abuse were reported to Scottish police and 13 women were killed by their partner or former partner. The Domestic Violence, Crime and Victims Bill, introduced into Parliament at the end of 2003, proposed the biggest overhaul of domestic violence legislation in England and Wales for 30 years. It includes a range of measures that would provide additional protection and support for victims and help to bring perpetrators to justice. Many of the elements in this Bill are already in place in Scots law.

The Government's strategy on domestic violence, of which the Bill is a part, was outlined in the consultation paper *Safety and Justice,* published in June 2003. It focuses on the prevention of domestic violence; protection and justice; and support for victims.

Drugs misuse

According to the Home Office, about 4 million people in England and Wales use at least one illicit drug each year and drug misuse results in £10 billion to £18 billion a year in social and economic costs. There are strong links between illegal drug use and crime.

The UK-wide drugs strategy *Tackling Drugs to Build a Better Britain* was introduced in 1998 and updated in 2002 following a review. It focuses on:

- helping young people resist drug misuse;

- protecting communities from drug-related anti-social and criminal behaviour;

- enabling people to overcome drug problems through treatment; and

- reducing the supply of illegal drugs on the streets.

In England, 147 local Drug Action Teams (DATs) bring together representatives of relevant agencies including health and education authorities, social services and the voluntary sector. DATs work with CDRPs (see page 206) to help the police and communities tackle drug problems and associated crime, and contribute to the delivery of the National Drug Strategy. Similar arrangements apply in Scotland, Wales and Northern Ireland.

The Criminal Justice Interventions Programme (CJIP), which began in April 2003, is a three-year programme to develop and integrate measures for directing drug misusing offenders out of crime and into treatment. It involves criminal justice and treatment agencies working together with other services to provide a tailored solution for those individuals who commit crime in order to fund their use of Class A drugs (see glossary).

Interventions under the CJIP include drug testing those who have committed certain types of offence; enhanced arrest referral (designed to encourage drug users to take up appropriate treatment after arrest); community sentencing; throughcare and aftercare (treatment and support that begins after sentencing and continues during and after release from prison); legislative changes to introduce bail restrictions for those testing positive for the use of cocaine, heroin or crack; and additional support for young people.

The programme initially concentrated on areas with high levels of acquisitive crime, but a year after it was launched, the Government announced that it would be expanded to another 36 police Basic Command Unit (BCU) areas, bringing the total to 66. The throughcare and aftercare parts of the programme and enhanced arrest referral are being phased in across England and Wales.

Cannabis reclassification

In January 2004 cannabis was reclassified from a Class B to a Class C drug (see glossary) across the United Kingdom. This means that the maximum penalty for possession has been reduced from five years' imprisonment to two years', although police guidance in England and Wales recommends that, in the absence of aggravating factors, adults should usually be given a warning and have the drug confiscated. The maximum penalty for supply, dealing, production and trafficking remains at 14 years' imprisonment, as the maximum penalty for Class C substances was raised when cannabis was reclassified.

Scotland, Wales and Northern Ireland have their own drug strategies within the UK framework. The Scottish Executive has provided funding for pilot arrest referral schemes. Although not directly linked to the criminal justice process, they provide another route into treatment for drug misusing offenders. Drug treatment and testing orders (DTTOs) have been made available to courts in Scotland on a phased basis since 1999. At present courts covering 70 per cent of the population in Scotland can make a DTTO and all will have access to the order by mid-2005. Scotland has retained the sentencing option of probation with a condition of treatment, which is intended for lower tariff offenders than those subject to the DTTO.

Terrorism

Permanent measures to counter terrorism on a UK-wide basis were contained in the *Terrorism Act 2000* and the *Anti-Terrorism, Crime and Security Act 2001*. Provisions in these Acts – which extended the definition of terrorism to cover ideological and religious motivation – include:

- an offence of inciting terrorist acts abroad from within the United Kingdom;
- powers to seize suspected terrorist cash at borders;
- a judicial authority to consider applications for extensions of detention of terrorist suspects;
- specific offences relating to training for terrorist activities;
- offences relating to weapons of mass destruction;
- better security at airports and nuclear sites; and
- an extension of police powers to detain and question those suspected of terrorist offences.

The 2001 Act also gave the Home Secretary the power to certify and detain foreign nationals who are believed to be international terrorists and a threat to national security. The provision applies to people whose removal from the country is temporarily or indefinitely prevented by a point of law relating to an international agreement such as the European Convention on Human Rights, or by a practical consideration.

At the end of February 2004 the Home Office began a six-month consultation process to review the existing counter-terrorist provisions and consider how to take legislation forward.

An emergency EU Justice and Home Affairs council meeting was held in Brussels in March 2004, following terrorist bombings in Madrid. The UK Government secured agreement on various proposals aimed at combating terrorism across the EU. These included an agreement to establish new common standards for the retention of communications data and an agreement to implement proposals to improve the exchange of data between countries (for example in respect of lost or stolen passports).

In the same month the Government announced £15 million additional funding to help Special Branch police disrupt and prevent attacks against the United Kingdom.

Justice in England and Wales

The criminal justice system in England and Wales consists of several agencies and departments, which are together responsible for maintaining law and order and for the administration of justice (see Figure 14.5 overleaf). The government departments involved are:

- The Home Office deals with matters relating to criminal law, the police, prisons and probation. The Home Secretary also has general responsibility for internal security.

- The Department for Constitutional Affairs (DCA) deals with matters relating to the judiciary and (through the Court Service, see page 212) administers the courts. Under proposals in the Constitutional Reform Bill (see page 46) the Lord Chief Justice would become the professional head of the judiciary in England and Wales, assuming the new title of President of the Courts of England and Wales.

- The Law Officers' Departments comprise the Crown Prosecution Service (CPS), the SFO (see page 205) and the Customs and Excise Prosecution Office. The CPS is responsible for the independent prosecution of nearly all criminal cases instituted by the police.

Criminal justice agencies

The police service

There are 43 police forces organised on a local basis in England and Wales. The Metropolitan

Police Service and the City of London force are responsible for policing London.

Police forces are maintained in England and Wales by local police authorities. In the 41 police areas outside London they normally have 17 members – nine locally elected councillors, three magistrates and five independent members. The authorities set local policing objectives in consultation with the chief constables and local community, while the Government sets ministerial priorities for the police as a whole. All police forces are subject to inspection by HM Inspectorate of Constabulary (HMIC), which reports to the Home Secretary.

Table 14.6 Police officer strength,[1] at 31 March 2004, England and Wales

	Numbers
ACPO ranks[2]	224
Chief Superintendents	540
Superintendents	947
Chief Inspector	1,885
Inspector	6,600
Sergeant	19,382
Constable	110,986
All ranks	140,563

1 Full-time equivalent staff, including staff on career breaks or maternity/paternity leave.
2 Chief constable and deputy or assistant chief constable.
Source: Home Office

Each police force also has a Special Constabulary – a volunteer force with full constabulary powers. The main role of special constables is to carry out local intelligence-based patrols and crime reduction initiatives, targeted at specific crime problems. They give up a few hours a week, typically evenings or weekends, supporting regular officers and local communities. There were 11,000 special constables in post at the end of March 2003.

Police powers

Police powers and procedures are defined by legislation and accompanying codes of practice. Evidence obtained in breach of the codes may be ruled inadmissible in court. The codes must be available in all police stations.

Police officers can stop and search people and vehicles if they reasonably suspect that they will find stolen goods, offensive weapons or

Figure 14.5 Structure of the criminal justice system, England and Wales

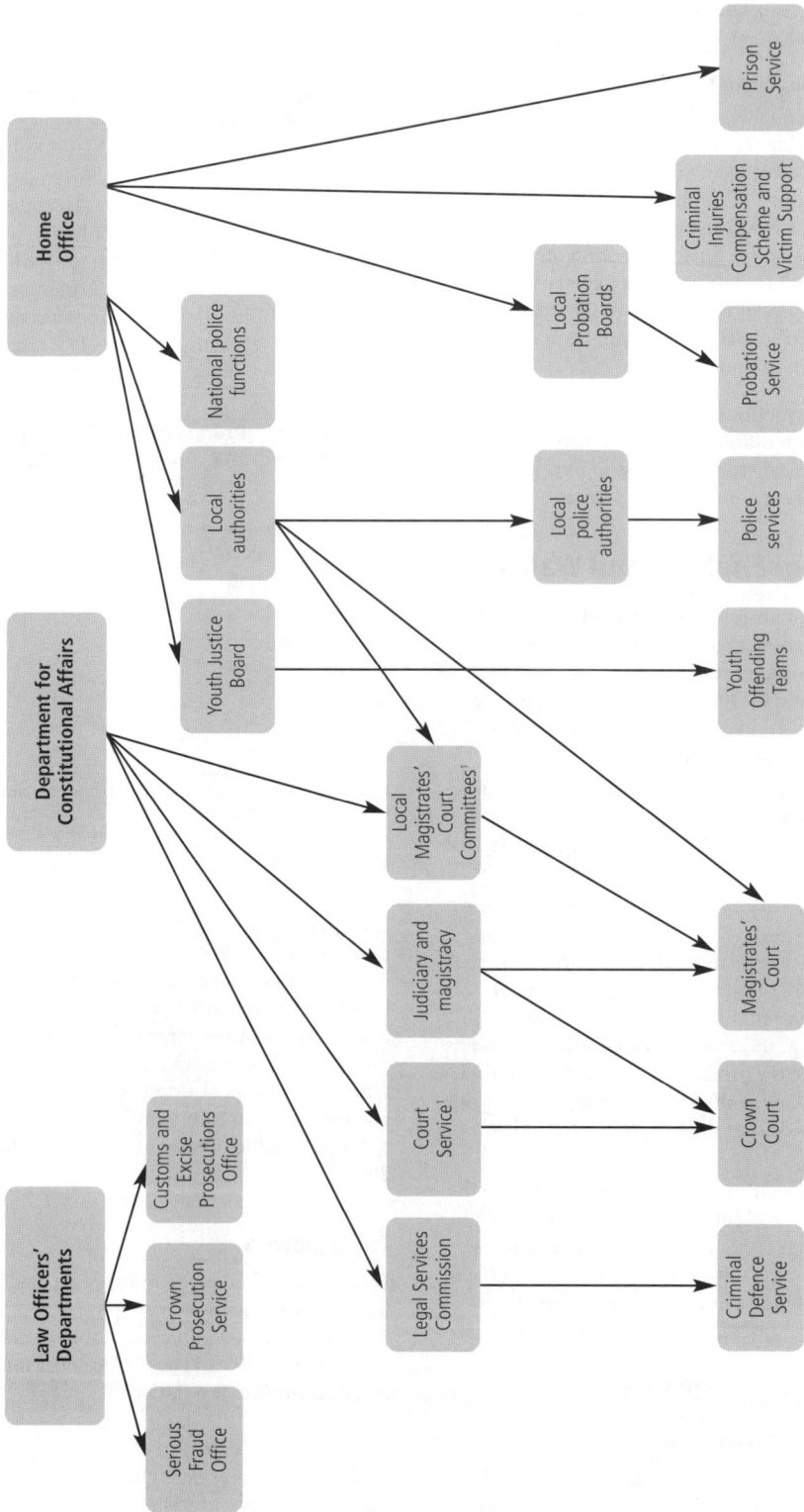

1 The functions of the Court Service and Magistrates' Court Committees will be combined in HM Courts Service in April 2005.
Source: Based on *A Guide to the Criminal Justice System in England and Wales*, Home Office, 2000

implements that could be used for burglary and other offences. The officer must record the grounds for the search and the person searched is entitled to a copy of the officer's report. The police stopped and searched 868,900 people and 26,400 vehicles in England and Wales in 2002/03. The total of 895,300 stops and searches was 21 per cent more than in 2001/02. The same proportion (13 per cent) led to an arrest as in the previous two years.

The police may arrest a suspect on a warrant issued by a court, but can also do so without a warrant for arrestable offences (those for which the sentence is fixed by law or for which the term of imprisonment is five years or more).

Suspects must be cautioned before the police can ask any questions about an offence. As a result of the *Criminal Justice Act 2003,* a suspect for an arrestable offence can be detained in police custody without charge for up to 36 hours. Someone suspected of a serious arrestable offence can be held for up to 96 hours, but not beyond 36 hours unless a warrant is obtained from a magistrates' court. The Act also allows the police to take fingerprints and DNA samples from people who have been arrested and detained at police stations. This was only previously possible once the person had been charged.

As another result of the 2003 Act, the CPS is responsible for determining the charge in all but minor and routine offences. In certain cases a caution (reprimand or formal warning for youth offenders) may be more appropriate than a prosecution. A caution is not the same as a conviction, and will only be given if the person admits the offence. Young offenders (those aged 10–17) are given a reprimand for most first offences, and a final warning for a second offence, at which point they are referred to the local Youth Offending Team (see page 218). However, each case is looked at individually and all factors, including the seriousness of the offence and the impact on the victim, are considered before deciding on the best course of action.

Once a person is charged, he or she may be released on bail to attend a magistrates' court. If not granted police bail, the defendant must be brought before a court as soon as possible. There is a general right to bail, but magistrates may withhold it. In certain circumstances, the prosecution may appeal to a Crown Court judge against the granting of bail by magistrates.

Complaints against the police

Members of the public can make complaints against the police if they feel they have been treated unfairly or improperly, if they feel the police have not given them sufficient information, or if they are not happy with the outcome of an investigation by the police. Under the *Police Reform Act 2002*, a new system has been set up, and the Independent Police Complaints Commission (IPCC) replaced the Police Complaints Authority in April 2004. The IPCC has the power to supervise or manage a police investigation or to conduct its own investigation. It is also responsible for monitoring the way complaints are handled by local police forces.

Community relations

A number of measures have been taken in recent years to improve relations between the police and the community. These include stricter regulation of stop and search powers, ten-year minority ethnic employment targets for recruitment, regression and retention in the police service; a complete overhaul in the way racist incidents are handled; and community and race relations training for over 130,000 police personnel. Racial discrimination by the police was made unlawful by the *Race Relations (Amendment) Act 2000*, which also gave them a duty to promote race equality.

The *Police Reform Act 2002* included powers for the Home Secretary to make statutory codes of practice and regulations governing policing practices and procedures.

Community Support Officers (CSOs) play a complementary role to police officers in tackling disorder and anti-social behaviour. They carry out routine patrols to increase visible policing in the community, and provide reassurance to the public. CSOs help free up the time of police officers, enabling them to tackle more serious crimes. The *Police Reform Act* allows chief officers to give CSOs limited powers to deal with anti-social behaviour and disorder, including a power of detention for 30 minutes (currently being piloted in six forces); issuing penalty notices for minor offences; and dealing with abandoned vehicles.

Neighbourhood wardens are employed by local authorities and housing associations to provide a highly visible, uniformed and semi-official presence in residential and public areas, town centres and high-crime areas. Their overall purpose is to improve quality of life and contribute to the regeneration of their areas.

Specialist crime bodies

The National Crime Squad (NCS) is concerned with serious and organised crime that transcends national and international boundaries – for example, money laundering, counterfeiting, and the illegal trafficking of arms or drugs. The NCS will form part of the new Serious Organised Crime Agency in 2006 (see page 206).

The Forensic Science Service (FSS) is an executive agency of the Home Office that provides forensic science services to police forces through its seven regional laboratories. As well as being a source of training, consultancy and scientific support, it operates the national DNA database in England and Wales, which is used to match DNA profiles taken from suspects to profiles from samples left at scenes of crime.

The Police Scientific Development Branch of the Home Office provides technical, operational and policy support for the UK law enforcement community, including police forces. It evaluates, develops, and advises on science and technology, equipment and techniques.

Prosecution authorities

The CPS is a single independent authority for England and Wales which, in common with other agencies of the criminal justice system, is organised in 42 local areas, each with its own Chief Crown Prosecutor. The head of the CPS is the Director of Public Prosecutions (DPP), who is superintended by the Attorney General. The responsibilities of the CPS include:

- giving pre-charge and early advice to the police, in accordance with statutory guidance issued by the DPP;

- deciding on the appropriate charge or other disposal (for example a caution or reprimand);

- continuously reviewing each case throughout its lifetime;

- dealing with disclosure issues;

- conducting the prosecution of cases in the magistrates' and Crown courts;

- preparing and conducting cases, including instructing counsel for hearings and/or applications in all higher courts; and

- keeping victims informed of the progress of cases, including informing and if necessary meeting with them when charges are altered or dropped.

HM Crown Prosecution Service Inspectorate is the independent Inspectorate for the CPS. Its purpose is to promote improvement in the efficiency, effectiveness and fairness of the prosecution service through a process of inspection, evaluation and identification of good practice.

Other prosecuting authorities include the SFO (see page 205), which also answers to the Attorney General, and bodies such as the Inland Revenue, HM Customs and Excise commissioners, local authorities and trading standards departments, all of which prosecute cases in their own discrete areas of work. Individual citizens may bring private prosecutions for most crimes, but some need the consent of the Attorney General and these cases may be taken over by the DPP.

Criminal courts

The Court Service, an executive agency of the DCA, is responsible for the administration of the Crown Court, High Court and Court of Appeal. Magistrates' courts are administered locally by Magistrates' Courts Committees, working within a national framework set by the DCA. However, the *Courts Act 2003* provided for a new unified courts administration to be created by April 2005, combining the functions of the Court Service and the Magistrates' Courts Committees. This will be called HM Courts Service, and will operate as an agency of the DCA.

About 96 per cent of criminal cases are dealt with at a magistrates' court. Cases may be tried by lay magistrates (usually three sitting together) or by a District Judge (Magistrates' Court) who usually sits alone. District Judges are legally qualified and salaried, while magistrates (also known as Justices of the Peace) are unpaid, and advised on the law and procedure by a qualified clerk.

Magistrates cannot normally pass sentences of imprisonment that exceed six months or fines exceeding £5,000. From December 2005 magistrates will be able to give consecutive sentences of up to 12 months, as a result of the *Criminal Justice Act 2003*. In triable-either-way cases the magistrates may commit the offender to the Crown Court if a more severe sentence is thought necessary.

The Crown Court tries more serious criminal cases, as well as hearing appeals from the magistrates' courts. It sits in 78 main Crown Court Centres, divided into six regions known as circuits. Trial of cases is by a jury[2] of 12 people (see page 216) selected at random from the Electoral Register and directed on matters of law by a judge. Only a High Court Judge can try the more serious offences.

A Coroner (usually a senior lawyer or doctor) must hold an inquest if a person died a violent or unnatural death, or died while in prison or in other specified circumstances. He or she may also need to hold an inquest if the cause of death remains unknown following a post-mortem examination.

The Coroner's Court establishes how, when and where the death occurred. A Coroner may sit alone or, in certain circumstances, with a jury. Following a consultation process in 2003 a programme of reform of the coroner service in England and Wales is under way, and is expected to be completed by around 2008.

The judiciary

Judges are appointed from the ranks of practising barristers and solicitors. They have independence of office and can be removed only in rare and limited circumstances involving misconduct or incapacity. They are not subject to ministerial control or direction.

Most judicial appointments are filled through advertised open competition. Applicants are considered by a panel consisting of a judge, a lay member and a senior civil servant who acts as chairman, with input from members of the judicial community through a consultation process. Chosen candidates are then recommended to the Lord Chancellor.

Appointments to the High Court are also advertised, although not confined to those who apply. Candidates are considered by a wide consultation process, and discussed with the senior judiciary, following which the Lord Chancellor makes his recommendations to The Queen.

---

2 Under provisions in the *Criminal Justice Act 2003* a judge may sit alone in a limited number of cases involving threats and intimidation of juries. The Act also paved the way for judge-alone trial in a small number of exceptionally long, complex fraud cases.

The Constitutional Reform Bill (see page 46), which would abolish the post of Lord Chancellor, also seeks to replace the current arrangements for appointing judges with an independent Judicial Appointments Commission (JAC). The Secretary of State for Constitutional Affairs would only be able to appoint candidates recommended by the JAC and would have limited powers to reject its recommendations.

The Lord Chancellor has traditionally been regarded as the head of the judiciary: under proposals in the Bill the Lord Chief Justice would become the professional head of the judiciary in England and Wales, assuming the new title of President of the Courts of England and Wales.

The legal profession

Although people are free to conduct their own cases if they so wish, barristers and solicitors, or other authorised litigators, generally represent the interests of parties to a dispute. Barristers practise as individuals, but may join a group of other barristers in Chambers. Solicitors usually operate in partnership with other solicitors, but some are self-employed. Large firms employ not only qualified solicitors, but also legal executives and support staff. The Bar Council is the regulatory and representative body for barristers, and the Law Society performs a similar function for solicitors.

The Legal Services Ombudsman oversees the way in which the relevant professional bodies handle complaints about barristers, solicitors and other legal practitioners.

The prison service

Since the end of June 2004, the National Offender Management Service (NOMS – see page 214) has had overall responsibility for HM Prison Service (HMPS). There are 139 prisons in England and Wales, including ten that are privately run. Accommodation includes high security prisons, open prisons, young offender institutions and remand centres.

Adult male sentenced prisoners are classified into different groups for security purposes, ranging from Category A (whose escape would seriously endanger the public or the security of the state) to Category D (prisoners who can reasonably be trusted in open conditions). Women are held in separate prisons or in separate accommodation in mixed prisons. Remand prisoners (those currently awaiting trial) enjoy wider rights and privileges than convicted prisoners.

Every prison establishment in England and Wales has an Independent Monitoring Board comprising volunteers drawn from the local community and appointed by the Home Secretary. They perform a 'watchdog' role on behalf of ministers and the general public by providing day-to-day independent oversight of prisons to ensure that prisoners are being cared for decently and with humanity.

National Offender Management Service

Following an independent review of correctional services, the Home Secretary announced in January 2004 that the prison and probation services would work more closely as a single service. The National Offender Management Service (NOMS) will focus on reducing reoffending by ensuring that offenders are managed throughout their sentence, both in custody and in the community. Over time, it is anticipated that the private and voluntary sectors will have an increased opportunity to provide services to NOMS. The process of establishing NOMS began in June 2004.

HM Inspectorate of Prisons is an independent body that inspects prisons and reports on the treatment of prisoners and prison conditions. It submits annual reports to the Home Secretary. Each prison establishment is visited about once every three years.

Probation service

The National Probation Service (NPS) is based in 42 areas, with the same boundaries as the police and CPS. The NPS supervises offenders in the community under direct court orders and on release on licence from custody. The caseload on any given day is in excess of 200,000. Each year the NPS assists magistrates and judges in their sentencing decisions through the provision of about 253,000 pre-sentence reports, and 10,000 bail information reports.

HM Inspectorate of Probation reports independently to ministers on the performance of the NPS. The Prisons and Probation Ombudsman

investigates complaints from prisoners and those subject to probation supervision, or those upon whom reports have been written. The Ombudsman is appointed by the Home Secretary and is independent of both the Prison Service and the NPS.

The prosecution process

When deciding whether or not to charge, the CPS must first consider whether there is enough evidence to provide a realistic prospect of conviction, and then consider whether it would be in the public interest to prosecute. This two-stage test is set out in the Code for Crown Prosecutors. If there is insufficient evidence or prosecution would not be in the public interest, the CPS has the authority to discontinue or otherwise terminate the proceedings. It has a continuing duty to review cases and can determine whether to continue with a charge or deal with the matter by way of a caution, reprimand or final warning.

The flow of cases through the criminal justice system is shown in Figure 14.7.

Court procedures

Summary offences are the least serious and may be tried only in the magistrates' court. Indictable-only offences, such as murder, manslaughter or robbery, must be tried by a judge and jury in the Crown Court on 'indictment'.[3] Triable-either-way offences are dealt with as summary offences unless the magistrates decide the case is more suitable for the Crown Court, or the defendant elects to be tried in the Crown Court.

Trial

The law presumes an accused person is innocent until proved guilty beyond reasonable doubt by the prosecution. Accused people have a right at all stages to stay silent; however, when questioned, failure to mention facts that they later rely upon in their defence may not be helpful to their case. If the defendant pleads guilty, the judge will decide upon the appropriate sentence.

Criminal trials normally take place in open court (that is, members of the public and press are allowed to hear the proceedings) unless there are specific reasons why this would not be

---

3 An indictment is a written accusation against a person, charging him or her with serious crime triable by jury.

Figure 14.7 The prosecution process, England and Wales

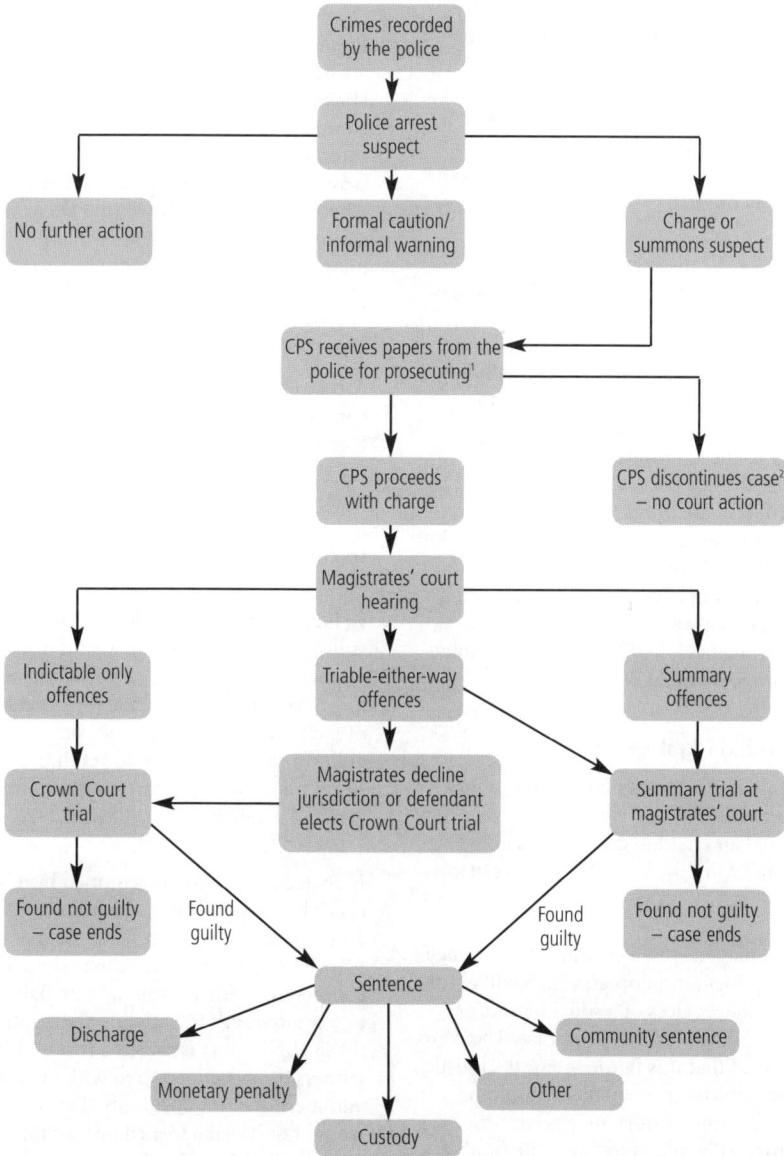

1 Although the majority of prosecutions are handled by the Crown Prosecution Service, other organisations can also bring prosecutions.
2 A case will be under continued review, and may be discontinued at any stage before the hearing at the magistrates' court or the prosecution may offer no evidence. In addition, the charge may be altered up to the final decision of the court.
Source: Based on *A Guide to the Criminal Justice System in England and Wales*, Home Office, 2000

appropriate. If a 'not guilty' plea is entered, the prosecution and defence form opposing sides in an adversarial system. They call and examine witnesses and present opposing versions of the case. Strict rules of evidence govern how this may be done. Written statements by witnesses are allowed with the consent of the other party or in limited circumstances at the discretion of the court. Otherwise evidence is taken from witnesses testifying orally on oath.

The *Courts Act 2003* includes provisions for a Criminal Procedure Rule Committee. Working to a programme agreed by the criminal justice ministers, the Committee will make rules for all criminal courts in England and Wales, including magistrates' courts, the Crown Court and the Court of Appeal (Criminal Division). The membership of the Committee has been devised to ensure that the key parties involved in a criminal trial have the opportunity to help in modernising and streamlining the criminal trial process. The aim will be to make rules that are both simple and simply expressed. It is expected that the Committee will be established later in 2004 and that the first Criminal Procedure Rules will come into force in 2005.

Publicly funded legal service

Advice and assistance are available without reference to an individual's means to anyone who is arrested and held in custody at a police station, or other premises, or who appears before a court.

A defendant charged with a criminal offence may apply for a representation order, which will entitle him or her to the services of a solicitor and/or barrister, depending on the type of case. The court must be satisfied that it is in the interests of justice that publicly funded representation should be granted. In the Crown Court, judges have the power to order a defendant to pay some or all of the defence costs.

In criminal proceedings, the Legal Services Commission, through the Criminal Defence Service, makes arrangements for duty solicitors to assist unrepresented defendants in the magistrates' courts. Advocacy assistance is also available in some other specified circumstances. During 2002/03 over 1.5 million acts of assistance were granted by the Criminal Defence Service at a total net cost of around £526 million. Criminal legal aid

work in the Crown Court and higher courts amounted to a further £569 million.

Public Defender Offices are being piloted in eight areas. In these areas the Public Defender Service (PDS) directly employs solicitors and offers a complete service to clients from the police station, through the magistrates' court and on to the Crown Court as appropriate. Clients may choose whether to be represented by PDS or duty solicitors. An independent evaluation of these pilots is due to report in 2005.

The jury

Around 500,000 jurors are selected at random by computer every year. They are chosen from the Electoral Register for the surrounding area near the Crown Court and must be aged over 18 and under 70. They are expected to attend the court for around two weeks or for the duration of any trial for which they are selected.

In jury trials, the judge decides questions of law, sums up the case to the jury, and discharges or sentences the accused. A jury is independent of the judiciary, and is responsible for deciding questions of fact. The jury's verdict may be 'guilty' or 'not guilty' and the latter would result in an acquittal. Juries may, subject to certain conditions, reach a verdict by a majority of at least 10–2.

If an accused person is acquitted by a jury, there is no right of appeal from the prosecution and the accused cannot be tried again for that same offence, except in serious cases where new and compelling evidence has come to light. However, an acquittal may be set aside and a retrial ordered if the High Court is satisfied that a juror or a witness has been interfered with or intimidated, and there is a real possibility that the acquittal would not have happened but for the interference or intimidation. Any attempt to interfere with jurors or witnesses is a criminal offence.

Sentencing and appeals

The court sentences the offender after considering all the relevant information, which may include pre-sentence or any other specialist reports, and a mitigating plea by the defence. A range of sentences are available, depending on the type of court and the seriousness of the offence:

Table 14.8 Offenders sentenced for indictable offences, 2002, England and Wales

							Percentages
	Discharge	Fine	Community sentence	Fully suspended sentence	Immediate custody	Other	All sentenced (thousands)
Theft and handling stolen goods	20	19	37	0	22	2	126.7
Drug offences	19	44	18	0	17	1	49.0
Violence against the person	10	11	44	1	31	3	37.8
Burglary	3	2	42	0	51	1	26.4
Fraud and forgery	16	15	45	2	21	2	18.1
Criminal damage	21	16	45	0	11	7	10.8
Motoring	5	40	27	1	26	0	8.5
Robbery	0	0	22	0	76	1	7.7
Sexual offences	5	6	28	1	59	2	4.4
Other offences	10	43	19	1	17	11	47.4
All indictable offences	15	23	33	1	25	3	336.7

Source: Home Office

- discharge (which can be absolute, or conditional on not committing another offence);
- monetary (for example fines, compensation orders and confiscation orders);
- custody (which can be immediate or suspended in whole or in part); and
- community sentence.

In 2002, 336,700 offenders were sentenced for indictable offences in England and Wales. Table 14.8 shows how the form of sentence varied according to the type of offence committed. A majority of those convicted of drug offences were fined or discharged, while a majority of those convicted of robbery, sexual offences or burglary were given immediate custodial sentences. Overall, one in three offenders were given community sentences.

Community sentences

A community punishment order (formerly community service) means that the offender has to do a certain number of hours of unpaid work for the community. If the offender is in employment, he or she will be expected to do it during his or her own time. The work is organised by the NPS. A community rehabilitation order (formerly probation order) means that, for the duration of the order, the offender will be under the supervision of a probation officer. Offenders who

fail to comply with the terms of an order may be taken back to court where they can be re-sentenced for the offence. Other types of community sentence include attendance centre orders, and drug treatment and testing orders. In order to provide more flexible options for sentencers, the *Criminal Justice Act 2003* has created a single community sentence under which the various types of community order are available.

Custodial sentences

Imprisonment is the most severe penalty available to the courts, and is generally only available for the more serious offences, each of which has a maximum prison term usually specified by an Act of Parliament. Life imprisonment is the mandatory sentence for murder, and is also available for certain other serious offences. There are mandatory minimum sentences for serious repeat offenders. Any time spent in custody before the trial usually counts towards the prison sentence.

One in four of those convicted of an indictable offence in 2002 in England and Wales were given a custodial sentence (Table 14.8). The prison population has increased in recent years. In December 2003 there were over 74,000 prisoners, an increase of 2 per cent over the previous year.

Appeals

A person convicted by a magistrates' court may appeal to the Crown Court against the conviction and/or the sentence imposed, or on a point of law, by judicial review or case stated, to the High Court. Appeals from the Crown Court go to the Court of Appeal (Criminal Division). This normally sits in London at the Royal Courts of Justice and is presided over by the Lord Chief Justice, who is the most senior judge in England and Wales.

A further appeal can be made to the House of Lords on points of law of public importance, if permission is given. Under proposals in the Constitutional Reform Bill (see page 46), the judicial functions of the House of Lords would be undertaken by an independent Supreme Court.

The Criminal Cases Review Commission, which is independent of both government and the courts, reviews alleged miscarriages of justice that have been through the appeal process. It can refer the case back to the Court of Appeal if it considers there is a real possibility that a conviction or sentence would not be upheld. This only occurs in a very small number of cases. Referral of a case to the Commission depends on some new argument or evidence coming to light that was not raised at the trial or on appeal.

Youth justice

The youth justice system comprises Youth Offending Teams (Yots), the police, youth courts and the institutions in which young people are held in custody. The Youth Justice Board (YJB) for England and Wales is a non-departmental public body that maintains and oversees the operation of the youth justice system as a whole.

Every local authority in England and Wales is served by a Yot, made up of representatives from the police, NPS, social services, health, and education. Yots also have access to services concerned with drug and alcohol misuse, and in some cases housing staff. The Yot uses a national assessment system to identify the specific problems that make the young person offend and to measure the risk he or she poses to others. This enables the Yot to identify suitable programmes to address the needs of the young person with the intention of preventing further offending.

Youth courts

When someone under the age of 18 is charged with an offence, his or her case is heard by either a youth court or the Crown Court depending on the severity of the offence and whether he or she is co-accused with an adult. The youth court is a magistrates' court especially established to deal with young people. It is served by Youth Panel Magistrates and District Judges. They have the power to give detention and training orders of up to 24 months, as well as a range of community sentences. Youth courts are less formal than adult courts and hearings are not held in public. However, the victim of the crime can ask to attend the hearing, and victims often have the opportunity to make an input to the sentencing process through the Yot.

Sentencing

Young people who plead guilty to a first offence in court must receive a referral order, unless they are given an absolute discharge or fine, or the offence is so serious that a custodial sentence is required. The young person is required to attend a Youth Offender Panel, which is made up of a Yot officer and two volunteers from the local community. The Panel agrees a contract lasting between 3 and 12 months with the young person, his or her parents or carers, and the victim (where appropriate). The contract can include attending programmes to address offending behaviour, repairing the harm done by their offence or one of a variety of other actions.

Reparation orders require the young person to address the harm caused by the offence. Reparation can be made to the victim or to the community. Examples include cleaning up graffiti or undertaking appropriate community work. The order is overseen by the Yot. Other non-custodial sentences can include fines, action plan orders, attendance centre orders, and supervision orders.

Custodial sentences

The main custodial sentence for offenders aged 12 to 17 is the detention and training order. Half of the order is spent in custody and the other half under supervision in the community, although early release from custody is available in certain circumstances.

There are three types of secure accommodation in which a young person can be placed: secure training centres, local authority secure children's homes and young offender institutions. The Youth Justice Board is responsible for purchasing bedspaces, placing young people in appropriate secure accommodation and setting the standards for these facilities.

Civil justice

Jurisdiction in civil matters in England and Wales is administered mainly by the county courts and the High Court, the latter handling the more substantial and complex cases. County courts also handle family proceedings, such as divorce, domestic violence and matters affecting children. Magistrates' courts have civil jurisdiction in family matters (when they sit as a Family Proceedings Court) and in miscellaneous civil orders, but do not deal with divorce cases.

Most civil disputes are dealt with through statutory or voluntary complaint mechanisms, or through mediation and negotiation. Arbitration is common in commercial and building disputes. Ombudsmen have the power to determine complaints in the public sector and, on a voluntary basis, in some private sector activities (for example, banking, insurance and pensions). Many cases where a claim is issued do not go to trial because the parties settle out of court. Other cases are determined without trial because the case has no merit (summary judgment), or the defendant does not respond to the claim (judgment in default), or the defendant offers to pay by instalments.

Successful actions taken in the civil courts can result in damages being awarded to the individual pursuing the claim. The amount awarded in each case varies according to the circumstances.

The number of claims issued in the civil courts has declined following a peak in the late 1980s and early 1990s (Figure 14.9). In 2003, 1.57 million claims were entered, a decrease of over 3 per cent since 2002. Money claims represented 86 per cent of the total. Most of the remainder were actions for the recovery of residential premises.

The Court Service (see also page 212) is responsible for the administration of the Court of Appeal, High Court, county courts, probate service and a number of tribunals.

Tribunals

There are some 80 tribunals in England and Wales which together deal with over 1 million disputes a year. Most are concerned with cases that involve the rights of private citizens against decisions of the State in areas such as social security, income tax and mental health. Some tribunals deal with other disputes, such as employment.

Figure 14.9 Writs and summonses issued in England and Wales

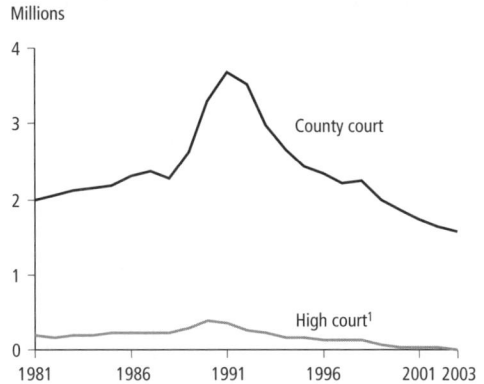

Millions

1 Queen's Bench Division.
Source: Court Service

A new unified tribunals service was announced in 2003. The new service has at its core the top ten non-devolved tribunals, covering areas such as employment, immigration, tax and pensions. A White Paper, *Transforming Public Services: Complaints, Redress and Tribunals*, was published in July 2004. This set out more detailed plans for unifying the tribunals into a new dispute resolution service, which is planned to start in 2006.

Courts

The High Court is divided into three Divisions:

- The Queen's Bench Division deals with disputes relating to contracts, general commercial matters and breaches of duty – known as 'liability in tort' – covering claims of negligence, nuisance or defamation.

- The Chancery Division deals with disputes relating to land, wills, companies and insolvency.

- The Family Division deals with matrimonial matters, including divorce, and the welfare of children.

Appeals in most civil cases were reformed by the *Access to Justice Act 1999*. In most cases a person must obtain permission before he or she can appeal. The general principle is that appeal 'lies' to the next level of judge in the court hierarchy. A county court appeal lies from a District Judge to a Circuit Judge and from a Circuit Judge to a High

Court Judge. In the High Court appeal lies from a master or District Judge of the High Court to a High Court Judge and from a High Court Judge to the Court of Appeal.

As in criminal cases, appeals from magistrates' courts in civil matters go to the High Court, on matters of law, or to the Crown Court, if the case is to be re-heard. A further appeal on points of law of public importance would go to the House of Lords.

Proceeding with a claim

Where a claim is not settled, or is subject to summary or default judgment, there is a system of three tracks to which disputed claims are assigned by a judge. These are the:

- small claims track, for most cases worth less than £5,000, at an informal hearing by a District Judge;
- fast track, for most cases from £5,000 to £15,000, with a fixed timetable from allocation to trial; and
- multi-track, for cases worth over £15,000 or of unusual complexity or significance, which are supervised by a judge and given timetables tailored to each case.

Publicly funded legal services

The Legal Services Commission administers the Community Legal Service (CLS). The CLS Fund provides legal help and representation to qualifying applicants, depending on their personal financial circumstances and the merits of their case. It supports eligible people in cases of divorce and other family issues, and also in non-family cases including welfare benefits, debt, housing and property, immigration and nationality, clinical negligence, and actions against the police.

Recipients may be asked to make a contribution, depending on their personal financial circumstances and the outcome of the case. During 2003/04 there were 925,000 acts of assistance under the CLS and the total net expenditure was £898 million. In recent years, there has been a switch in emphasis to encourage early resolution of disputes without recourse to protracted and expensive legal action.

In addition to providing legal help and representation in civil matters, CLS activities extend to providing access to legal advice for the wider community, in particular via its website (www.justask.org.uk). CLS Partnerships bring together organisations offering legal and advice services into local networks in England and Wales. These include solicitors, Citizens Advice (see page 479), law centres, local authority services and other independent advice centres.

Justice in Scotland

The Scottish Parliament makes laws on matters devolved to it (see chapter 4 and appendix A).

The Advocate General for Scotland is one of the three UK law officers, along with the Attorney General and Solicitor General for England and Wales, and is the UK Government's principal legal adviser on Scots law. The Lord Advocate and the Solicitor General for Scotland are the Scottish law officers, as well as being the only non-elected members of the Scottish Cabinet. They provide the Scottish Executive with advice on legal matters and represent its interests in the courts.

The Scottish Executive Justice Department, under the Minister for Justice, is responsible for the police service in Scotland, for civil and criminal justice, criminal justice social work services, prisons, courts administration, legal aid, and liaison with the legal profession. The Department is also responsible for the operation of Scots law as it relates to international law and relations with other legal systems, including those of other parts of the United Kingdom.

Advocates (broadly speaking the Scottish equivalent of barristers) and Solicitor-Advocates (who are accredited specifically for civil or criminal business) have audience in the Supreme Courts. Solicitors in Scotland (numbering 9,120 in October 2003) have audience in the Sheriff and District Courts (see page 222) and in the other courts and tribunals. They practise largely in partnerships and incorporated practices.

The professional body for advocates is the Faculty of Advocates. For solicitors the regulator is the Law Society of Scotland, which also regulates conveyancing and executry practitioners. The Scottish Legal Services Ombudsman oversees the way in which these bodies handle complaints against practitioners.

Scots law

The legal principles, rules and concepts of Scots law can be traced from diverse sources, including Roman law, canon law and the influences of other European systems. The main sources are judge-made law, certain legal treatises having 'institutional' authority, legislation, and EC law. The first two sources are sometimes referred to as the common law of Scotland. Legislation, as in the rest of the United Kingdom, consists of statutes (Acts of the UK or Scottish Parliament) or subordinate legislation authorised by the Scottish or UK Parliament. Many statutory offences are shared with England and Wales through UK-wide legislation (for example road traffic law) and laws relating to issues such as environmental pollution.

Criminal justice agencies

The police

Scotland has eight 'territorial' police forces. Other police forces or UK law enforcement agencies that operate in Scotland include the British Transport Police (see page 205), the NCIS (see page 205) and HM Customs and Excise.

Legal responsibility for policing is shared by police authorities or joint boards (both made up of local authority councillors); chief constables; and Scottish ministers. Police authorities or joint boards determine the budgets and the resources available to each force. They also appoint senior police officers (with the agreement of Scottish ministers) and determine the number of police officers and support staff for their areas. Once appointed, such staff come under the control of the Chief Constable for the area. The Chief Constable also has sole responsibility for operational decisions about police deployment and law enforcement in the area.

Scottish ministers make regulations concerning the terms and conditions of police officers. They are advised by the Police Negotiating Board (on pay and conditions) and the Police Advisory Board for Scotland (on other matters).

Police numbers in Scotland reached a record whole-time equivalent of 15,645 at the end of March 2004, an increase of 835 since March 1999.

Police powers

The police have a general duty to uphold and enforce the law and to maintain the peace in Scotland. They are provided with powers through both common law and statutory law to carry out this duty, including powers of arrest and detention.

The police in Scotland can arrest someone without a warrant, under wide common law powers, if suspects are seen or reported as committing a crime or are a danger to themselves or others. Someone suspected of a serious offence may be held for police questioning without being arrested, but for no more than six hours without being charged. If arrested, suspects must be charged and cautioned. The case is then referred to the Procurator Fiscal (see page 222).

As in England and Wales, the police have responsibility for a number of other tasks including criminal investigation, traffic management and community liaison. They also rely on a number of specialist support services such as forensic science laboratories, air support and underwater search teams. In addition, there are several centrally provided police services, known as 'common police services' maintained or funded by the Scottish Ministers. These include the Scottish Criminal Record Office, the Scottish Police College and the Scottish Drug Enforcement Agency (Operational and Intelligence Groups).

Scotland has community wardens similar to the neighbourhood wardens in England and Wales (see page 211). Community wardens can perform a variety of tasks depending on the needs and priorities of the community, but do not have police powers. Following pilot schemes, community warden schemes were extended to every local authority area in Scotland in April 2004. Most schemes are run by the local authorities.

HM Inspectorate of Constabulary (HMIC) is independent of police forces, police authorities and the Scottish Executive. HMIC has a statutory duty to submit an annual report to Scottish ministers on the state and efficiency of Scotland's police forces. As HMIC is not a regulatory body it has no powers to direct the police. It makes recommendations based on professional judgement.

Complaints against the police

A complaint alleging criminal conduct against a police officer is investigated on behalf of the Lord

Advocate by the Area Procurator Fiscal for the force area in which the officer serves. The decision on whether to prosecute is made by the Solicitor General for Scotland. Complaints alleging misconduct on the part of a police officer are investigated by the officer's force, either at local level or by the Deputy Chief Constable, and, if upheld, can result in penalties ranging from a warning, to dismissal from the service. In cases of serious criminal behaviour or misconduct it is open to the regional Procurator Fiscal or the police force to request the appointment of investigating officers from another force. Police authorities have responsibility for dealing with complaints against chief officers.

HMIC has a statutory authority to respond to referrals from dissatisfied complainants by considering the manner in which their complaints have been dealt with by chief constables.

Prosecution authorities

The Crown Office and Procurator Fiscal Service provides Scotland's independent public prosecution service. It is a department of the Scottish Executive and headed by the two Scottish Law Officers (see page 220). They are assisted by Advocate Deputes and are known collectively as Crown Counsel. Advocate Deputes are usually experienced, practising advocates who are appointed for a period of about three years.

The Department is the sole public prosecution authority in Scotland. It is responsible for making decisions about and bringing prosecutions for almost all criminal offences – statutory (devolved and reserved) and non-statutory (common law). Unlike in England, there is no general right of prosecution. The prosecution is undertaken by the Lord Advocate in the interests of the public as a whole, rather than on behalf of the police and other agencies such as HM Customs and Excise or individual citizens.

Scotland does not have a coroner's office. The Department has the duty to investigate sudden, suspicious or unexplained deaths. It decides if criminal proceedings or a fatal accident inquiry should be held and conducts such proceedings and inquiries.

Criminal courts

There are two types of criminal procedure in Scotland – solemn and summary. Solemn

procedure covers the most serious cases involving trial on indictment before a judge or sheriff sitting with a jury. A Scottish jury is made up of 15 people and a simple majority (8–7) is sufficient to establish guilt or innocence. Three verdicts are available: 'guilty', 'not guilty', or 'not proven'. A not proven verdict is the equivalent of not guilty in that it is an acquittal. Summary procedure covers less serious offences involving a trial by sheriff sitting alone or a magistrate who may sit alone or in a bench of three.

Scotland has a three-tier criminal court system. These are, in order of precedence, the High Court of Justiciary (the High Court), the Sheriff Courts and the District Courts. In addition there are separate drug courts, youth courts and children's hearings, and a pilot domestic abuse court is planned by the end of 2004.

The High Court of Justiciary, established in 1672, is the supreme criminal court. It handles the most serious crimes such as murder and rape. It is peripatetic, sitting in cities and larger towns as required. As an appeal court it sits only in Edinburgh. It comprises the Lord Justice General, the Lord Justice Clerk, and another 30 judges known formally as Lords Commissioners of Justiciary.

The 49 Sheriff Courts deal mainly with less serious offences. They can sit under either summary or solemn procedure. The maximum sentence a Sheriff Court can impose under summary procedure is three months or, for a second or subsequent offence of dishonesty or personal violence, six months (unless a lower or higher statutory maximum is specified for a particular offence). The maximum fine is £5,000. Under solemn procedure, the maximum sentence is five years' imprisonment or an unlimited fine. If the court considers its sentencing powers to be insufficient it can remit a case to the High Court.

District Courts sit under summary procedure only and are managed by local authorities. Each court comprises one or more Justices of the Peace (lay magistrates) who sit alone or in threes with a qualified legal assessor as convener or clerk of court. They handle cases of breach of the peace, drunkenness, minor assaults, petty theft, and offences under the *Civic Government (Scotland) Act 1982*. As the lowest level of criminal court, the district court has limited sentencing powers. Lay justices can impose sentences of imprisonment or detention up to a maximum of 60 days, and can impose fines of up to £2,500 (unless a lower or higher statutory maximum is specified for a particular offence). However, in the Glasgow District Court there are professional stipendiary magistrates who have the same sentencing powers as a sheriff sitting in a summary court.

The Scottish Court Service, an executive agency of the Scottish Executive Justice Department, is responsible for the administration, organisation and staffing of the Supreme Courts (the High Court and, in relation to civil matters, the Court of Session) and the Sheriff Courts.

Around 143,000 people were proceeded against in Scottish criminal courts in 2002; of whom 125,000 had a charge proved. Of the latter, 4 per cent were dealt with under solemn procedure, 63 per cent in sheriff summary courts, and 33 per cent in district and stipendiary magistrates' courts.

Reform of summary justice

The McInnes report was published in March 2004 after a two-year review of the way that the justice system in Scotland deals with less serious offences. It recommended:

- the creation of a single unified summary court managed by the Scottish Court Service;
- an all professional judiciary – consisting of sheriffs and new 'summary sheriffs' – both with identical sentencing powers in summary cases; and
- enhanced sentencing powers to allow summary courts to impose sentences of one year's imprisonment and a maximum £20,000 fine.

The Scottish Executive is consulting on these recommendations.

Prison service

The Scottish Prison Service (SPS) is an executive agency. In 2002/03 there were 16 prison establishments (15 public and one private), and an average daily prison population of 6,475, of whom fewer than 280 were women.

The main statutory duty of HM Inspectorate of Prisons for Scotland is the regular inspection of individual establishments. Matters that are inspected and reported on include physical conditions, quality of prisoner regimes, morale of staff and prisoners, facilities available to staff and prisoners, questions of safety and decency, and the establishment's contribution to preventing re-offending.

Complaints from prisoners that have not been resolved through the internal grievance system of the SPS are investigated by the Scottish Prisons Complaints Commission.

There are statutory arrangements governing the early release of prisoners. Offenders serving terms of less than four years may be automatically released at specific points in their sentences. Those detained for longer require Parole Board approval. Ministers are statutorily obliged to give effect to the Parole Board's directions.

Criminal justice social work

There is no separate probation service as in England and Wales. Instead, the Scottish Executive funds local authorities to provide criminal justice social work. This includes supervising offenders subject to community disposals, providing reports to court to assist sentencing and providing supervision to certain categories of offenders following release from custody.

Local authorities have a statutory responsibility for prisoners sentenced to over four years in prison on their release, and for those sentenced to supervised release orders and extended sentences. Throughcare is provided to prisoners and their families from the point of sentence or remand, during the period of imprisonment, and following release into the community. Local authorities also provide voluntary aftercare, which consists of supervision, support and assistance to people who request such a service within 12 months of their release from custody. This service might be in the form of advice on access to benefits, accommodation, education and training or alcohol or drugs rehabilitation.

Legal aid

The Scottish Legal Aid Board manages legal aid in Scotland. Its main tasks are to grant (or refuse) applications for legal aid; to pay solicitors or advocates; and to advise Scottish ministers on legal aid matters. Where legal aid is granted to the accused in criminal proceedings, he or she is not required to contribute towards expenses.

Sentencing and appeals

Of the 125,000 convictions in Scottish courts in 2002, 13 per cent resulted in a custodial sentence and 12 per cent in a community sentence. Sixty-three per cent of all convictions resulted in a fine or compensation order as the main penalty, compared with 73 per cent in 1993.

Non-custodial disposals

Non-custodial disposals available to Scottish courts include fines, community service orders, probation orders, restriction of liberty orders, and drug treatment and testing orders. Community reparation orders (see page 218) will be introduced as a result of the *Antisocial Behaviour etc. (Scotland) Act 2004.*

An offender given a community service order is required to carry out unpaid work of benefit to the community for between 80 and 240 hours in summary proceedings, and 300 hours in solemn proceedings.

Offenders can be placed on probation for a period of between six months and three years. The order has an action plan in which the offender agrees to address his or her offending behaviour and its underlying causes. Additional conditions can be attached in respect of unpaid work, place of residence, curfew conditions, financial recompense to the victim, and attendance at a programme for alcohol or drug treatment.

Restriction of liberty orders require an offender to be restricted to a specific place for a maximum of 12 hours a day up to a maximum of 12 months, and/or from a specified place or places for 24 hours a day up to 12 months. The legislation also provides for the use of electronic monitoring equipment to monitor the offender's compliance with the order. Electronic monitoring may also be used as a condition of a probation order or a drug treatment and testing order, or as a condition of licence for those under supervision in the community.

In 2002 15,200 convictions resulted in a community sentence, 12 per cent more than in 2001. These mainly comprised probation and community service orders, with the average length of a community service order being 153 hours.

Custodial sentences

In Scotland a court must obtain a social enquiry report before imposing a custodial sentence if the accused is aged under 21 or has not previously served a custodial sentence. The number of custodial sentences imposed in 2002 was 16,800, of which 82 per cent were for six months or less.

Appeals

The High Court of Justiciary also sits with at least three judges as the Scottish Court of Criminal Appeal. In both solemn and summary procedure a convicted person may appeal against conviction, or sentence, or both. The Court may dispose of an appeal in a number of ways, including authorising a retrial if it sets aside a conviction. There is no appeal from this court to the House of Lords. Just under 2,500 appeals were concluded in 2002, equivalent to 2 per cent of total convictions in that year. Of these, 3 per cent resulted in a conviction being quashed and 15 per cent in a reduced sentence.

The Scottish Criminal Cases Review Commission considers alleged miscarriages of justice and refers cases meeting the relevant criteria to the Court of Appeal for review. It will usually do this only if the normal appeal procedure has been exhausted.

Youth justice

Criminal proceedings may be brought against any child aged eight or over, but the instructions of the Lord Advocate are necessary before anyone under 16 is prosecuted. Many of the children under 16 who have committed an offence or are considered to be in need of care and protection may be referred to the Children's Reporter, who decides whether the child should be brought before a children's hearing. The hearing consists of three lay people who are not lawyers. The hearing members decide whether compulsory supervision is required and, if so, in what form.

In 2002 the Scottish Executive launched a ten-point action plan for dealing with problem young offenders. Two points in particular sought to tackle this issue. Firstly a fast-track Children's Hearing to deal with persistent offenders in the under-16 age group was introduced in January 2003 as a pilot scheme in 43 areas. Secondly, a two-year pilot youth court was launched in June 2003 to deal with 16- and 17-year-olds (who would otherwise be prosecuted under the standard summary sheriff court procedure). The court has designated sheriffs, a range of specially tailored community programmes at its disposal, and a

14 January 2004 Ray Harvey, winner of the Concept Boat 2003 award at the Schroders London Boat Show, with HRH The Princess Royal. Ray's boat, Sport Submarine (53), is a fast sport boat that also functions as an open submarine for two suitably equipped aqualung divers. It was the 50th anniversary of the Boat Show, and the first at its new venue at ExCeL in London's Docklands.

25 January 2004 Members of the cast of *The Office* at the Golden Globes awards in Beverly Hills, USA. It is the first time a UK television programme has been nominated, and it won two Globes. *(Back row from left)* Ricky Gervais holding his Best Actor in a TV Comedy award, with Martin Freeman, Lucy Davis, and *(front row)* Ash Atalla, and Stephen Merchant holding the Best TV Comedy award.

14 January 2004 The first UK fuel cell bus begins service in London. The bus runs on hydrogen stored in pressurised cylinders. The only emission is water vapour.

6 February 2004 200th anniversary of the death of Joseph Priestley, the scientist who is sometimes credited with the discovery of oxygen (the Swedish scientist Karl Scheele had independently discovered the gas two years earlier). His scientific research into the nature and properties of gases led him to a technique for dissolving carbon dioxide in water to produce a pleasant, fizzy drink – soda water – although it was 100 years later that the soft drinks industry began.

Top right: An illustration of Priestley's electrical machine. As a result of his work on electricity, he was elected a Fellow of the Royal Society in 1766.

16 February 2004 A permanent Prisons of War exhibition opens at Edinburgh Castle covering the late 18th century, when Edinburgh was the main 'prison of war' in the north. The vaults were filled with hundreds of captured sailors from France, Holland, Spain and the new state of America, as well as Irish and British inmates.

16–20 February 2004 London Fashion Week is held in the King's Road, Chelsea. There were 170 exhibiters and nearly 40 shows during the five-day event, attracting about 5,000 visitors. *(Left)* Danish designer Jens Laugesen featured monochrome fluid designs, while *(right)* Glaswegian Jonathan Saunders used bold prints.

© CHRIS MOORE PHOTOGRAPHIC LTD

© TIM GRIFFITHS

© PA PHOTOS

17 February 2004 Justin Hawkins, lead singer of rock group The Darkness, on stage during the annual Brit Awards 2004 at Earls Court. The Darkness won three Brit Awards – Best British Group, Best British Rock Act and Best Album.

21 February 2004 A display of items from the 1,400-year-old tomb of an Anglo-Saxon king, discovered at Prittlewell in the suburbs of Southend, opens at Southend Museum.

Top: Seventh century gold foil crosses that were probably laid on the body or sewn on a shroud, a gold buckle that could also be used to hold a reliquary, and a sample of coins found *(above)*.
Left: Archaeologists carefully excavate the tomb.
Below: A pair of coloured glass vessels and a pair of glass jars.

Below: A Roman coin from the four-day reign of Emperor Domitianus in 271 AD was found buried in a field in Oxfordshire in a pot of coins *(right)* dating from 250 to 275 AD and spanning the reigns of five emperors. The coin went on display at the British Museum in February 2004.

Front view

Rear view

fast-track process that ensures all offenders make their first appearance in the court within ten days of being charged. A second pilot youth court was set up in June 2004 and will run for two years.

All the community sentences available to the courts in Scotland can be used to deal with young offenders.

Civil justice

Most civil business in Scotland is conducted in one of 49 Sheriff Courts (see page 222). The matters dealt with include debt, claims for compensation, contract disputes, divorce, eviction, anti-social behaviour, and various applications under statutes concerned with matters such as licensing and bankruptcy. An appeal is possible from the Sheriff to the Sheriff Principal and then to the Court of Session. Appeal to the House of Lords from the Court of Session is available.

The Court of Session, which sits in Edinburgh, is the supreme civil court in Scotland. It is both a court of first instance for the initial consideration of cases and the court of appeal for most civil matters, although Sheriffs Principal can also hear appeals at local level. The jurisdiction of the Court of Session as a court of first instance is broadly the same as the jurisdiction of the Sheriff Court. However, some matters can only be raised in the Court of Session, such as the judicial review of decisions by administrative authorities.

Tribunals in Scotland deal with a range of matters including employment, education, children's hearings, immigration, social security and tax. Most tribunals are supervised by the Scottish Committee of the Council on Tribunals, which has a statutory role to review the constitution and working of tribunals in Scotland.

Justice in Northern Ireland

Northern Ireland's legal system is broadly similar to that in England and Wales. The Lord Chancellor is responsible for court administration through the Northern Ireland Court Service, while the Northern Ireland Office (NIO, see page 31), under the Secretary of State, deals with policy and legislation concerning criminal law, the police and the penal system. The Lord Chancellor has general responsibility for legal aid, advice and assistance.

A major review of the criminal justice system was set up under the 1998 Belfast (Good Friday) Agreement (see page 32) and reported in 2000. Key recommendations included:

- a focus on promoting human rights within the criminal justice system;
- a new Public Prosecution Service building on the work of the existing Director of Public Prosecutions Office;
- an independent Judicial Appointments Commission;
- an Independent Criminal Justice Inspectorate;
- an Independent Northern Ireland Law Commission;
- improvements to youth justice arrangements – including the creation of a Youth Justice Agency; and
- the development of North/South co-operation on criminal justice matters.

The review received broad support from most political parties and from practitioners in the criminal justice system. As a result, the majority of the recommendations have been, or are in the process of being, implemented. Those recommendations that required legislation were enacted in the *Justice (Northern Ireland) Act 2002.*

Criminal justice agencies

The police

In 2001 the Royal Ulster Constabulary became the Police Service of Northern Ireland (PSNI) in line with recommendations made by the Independent Commission on Policing. The Commission's report followed the Belfast (Good Friday) Agreement of 1998, which said there should be 'a new beginning to policing in Northern Ireland, with a police service capable of attacting and sustaining support from the community as a whole'. Under the process of change an Oversight Commissioner was appointed, as well as an independent Policing Board with Unionist and Nationalist participation and broad powers to hold the police to account. The Board works with district policing partnerships in the 26 district council areas. Complaints against the police are investigated by an independent Police Ombudsman.

PSNI strength at the end of March 2004, including student officers in training, was 7,489. This was complemented by 1,572 full-time and 864 part-time reserve officers. The first batch of recruits appointed under the system of 50:50 recruitment of Catholics and non-Catholics graduated in 2002.

Prosecution authorities

Following the review of the criminal justice system in Northern Ireland an independent prosecution service is being set up and will be responsible for undertaking all criminal prosecutions. The Public Prosecution Service for Northern Ireland will be headed by the Director of Public Prosecutions and will replace the existing Department of the Director of Public Prosecutions for Northern Ireland. It is anticipated that this service will be fully implemented by December 2006.

The courts

The Northern Ireland Court Service is accountable to the UK Parliament through the Parliamentary Secretary at the DCA and the Lord Chancellor. It is responsible for the administration of the Supreme Court, county courts, magistrates' courts, coroners' courts and for certain tribunals.

The Supreme Court of Judicature comprises the Court of Appeal, the High Court and the Crown Court. All matters relating to these courts are under the jurisdiction of the UK Parliament. The Court of Appeal consists of the Lord Chief Justice (as President) and two Lords Justices of Appeal. The High Court is made up of the Lord Chief Justice and five other judges. The practice and procedure of the Court of Appeal and the High Court are virtually the same as in the corresponding courts in England and Wales. Both courts sit in the Royal Courts of Justice in Belfast.

The Court of Appeal has power to review the civil law decisions of the High Court and the criminal law decisions of the Crown Court, and may in certain cases review the decisions of county courts and magistrates' courts. Subject to certain restrictions, an appeal from a judgment of the Court of Appeal can go to the House of Lords. As in the rest of the United Kingdom, a Criminal Cases Review Commission, which is independent of both government and the courts, reviews alleged miscarriages of justice.

The High Court is divided into a Queen's Bench Division, Chancery Division, and a Family Division, along similar lines to the courts in England and Wales (see page 219). The Crown Court deals with all serious criminal cases.

County courts and magistrates' courts differ in a number of ways from those in England and Wales. County courts are presided over by one of 14 county court judges, two of whom – in Belfast and Londonderry – have the title of Recorder. Appeals from the county courts go to the High Court. Although primarily civil law courts, the county courts also handle appeals from the magistrates' courts in both criminal and civil matters. In civil matters, the county courts decide most actions in which the amount or the value of specific articles claimed is below a certain level. They also deal with actions involving title to, or the recovery of, land; equity matters such as trusts and estates; mortgages; and the sale of land and partnerships.

The day-to-day work of dealing summarily with minor local criminal cases is carried out in magistrates' courts presided over by a full-time, legally qualified resident magistrate. The magistrates' courts also exercise jurisdiction in certain family law cases and have a very limited jurisdiction in other civil cases.

Prison service

The Northern Ireland Prison Service, established in April 1995, is an executive agency of the NIO. It operates under the direction and control of the Secretary of State for Northern Ireland, within a statutory framework based on the *Prison Act (Northern Ireland) 1953* and the Prison and Young Offenders Centre Rules (Northern Ireland) 1995.

The Prison Service has three operational establishments: Maghaberry Prison, a high-security prison housing male prisoners, as well as accommodating male immigration detainees at its facility in Belfast; Magilligan Prison, a medium-security prison housing adult male prisoners that also has low-security accommodation for selected prisoners nearing the end of their sentence; and Hydebank Wood, a medium- to low-security young offenders centre and prison that accommodates all young male offenders aged between 17 and 21, and all female prisoners including young offenders and immigration detainees. The overall annual prison population in Northern Ireland increased by 12 per cent from an average of 1,026 in 2002 to an average of 1,152 in 2003.

Each prison has a Board of Visitors or Visiting Committee comprising volunteers appointed by the Secretary of State for Northern Ireland.

Probation Board

The Probation Board for Northern Ireland is a non-departmental public body established under the Probation Board (Northern Ireland) Order 1982. It is primarily charged with carrying out risk assessments and providing pre-sentence reports for the courts, the statutory supervision of offenders in the community, and the performance of social welfare duties in prisons and young offender centres.

During 2003/04 the Board received 8,267 requests for reports from the courts, 5 per cent more than in the previous year. Its caseload of clients subject to court orders at 31 March 2004 was 3,251, an increase of nearly 7 per cent on the previous year.

Youth Justice Agency

The Youth Justice Agency is an executive agency within the NIO, replacing the former Juvenile Justice Board in April 2003. It provides community-based services, youth conferencing and secure custody and works in partnership with others to divert young people from crime and assist their integration into the community. Youth justice policy is the responsibility of the Criminal Justice Directorate of the NIO.

Further reading

Department for Constitutional Affairs: Departmental Report 2003/04. Cm 6210. The Stationery Office, 2004.

Home Office Annual Report 2003–2004. Cm 6208. The Stationery Office, 2004.

Crime in England and Wales, 2003/2004. Home Office. 2004.

Criminal Statistics, England and Wales. The Stationery Office (annual publication).

Websites

Community Legal Service
http://www.clsdirect.org.uk

Crime Statistics for England and Wales
www.crimestatistics.org.uk

Criminal Justice System
www.cjsonline.org

Department for Constitutional Affairs
www.dca.gov.uk

HM Prison Service (England and Wales)
www.hmprisonservice.gov.uk

Home Office
www.homeoffice.gov.uk

Legal Services Commission
www.legalservices.gov.uk

Northern Ireland Office
www.nio.gov.uk

Police services of the United Kingdom
www.police.uk

Scottish Executive
www.scotland.gov.uk

Youth Justice Board
www.youth-justice-board.gov.uk

WWW.

15   Religion

Everyone in the United Kingdom has a legal right to freedom of thought, conscience and religion. Religious organisations and groups may conduct their rites and ceremonies, promote their beliefs within the limits of the law, own property, and run schools and a range of other charitable activities. Although the United Kingdom is predominantly Christian, most world religions are represented. In particular there are large Muslim, Hindu, Sikh and Jewish communities.

Religious affiliations in the UK

The 2001 Census was the first to include a religion question in England, Wales and Scotland (although a census was taken of places of worship in 1851). Censuses in Northern Ireland have included a question on religion since 1926.

The Census question in England and Wales was voluntary and designed to measure religious identification in the broad sense. It asked 'What is your religion?'. Different questions were used in Scotland and Northern Ireland, to reflect local differences in the requirement for information.

Over three-quarters (77 per cent) of the population of Great Britain said that they identified with a religion in the 2001 Census. Fifteen per cent said they had no religion, and the remainder (8 per cent) did not answer the question. Of those who identified with a religion, 93 per cent (41 million people) said they were Christian.

Of the 3 million people who belonged to a religion other than Christianity, just over half identified themselves as Muslims, with smaller numbers of Hindus, Sikhs, Jews and Buddhists. London had a higher proportion of all these religions among its population than other regions.

Some 8.6 million people in Great Britain stated that they had no religion. Organisations such as the British Humanist Association and the National Secular Society represent the views of some of those who do not identify with a religion.

The faith communities

Christians

The Christian community in the United Kingdom consists of many denominations. Of these, the Anglican and Catholic Churches and the Church of Scotland have some of the largest memberships. Several other Christian denominations are known collectively as the 'Free Churches', including Methodists, Baptists, Presbyterians and the United Reformed Church.

Anglicans

The four Anglican churches in the United Kingdom are the Church of England, the Church in Wales, the Scottish Episcopal Church, and the

A new i-church

In March 2004 the Church of England announced the creation of its first Internet parish (www.i-church.org), providing a spiritual ministry for people who are unable, or do not wish, to join a local congregation. Applications for the post of 'web pastor' were invited by the Diocese of Oxford, whose pioneering initiative is being funded by the Church Commissioners. Alyson Leslie was subsequently appointed to the post, and the i-church was dedicated at a service in Oxford on 30 July 2004.

Church of Ireland (Northern Ireland). They form part of a worldwide communion of 38 Anglican churches.

The Church of England is divided into two geographical provinces, each headed by an archbishop, and numerous dioceses (regions under the care of a bishop). The province of Canterbury has 30 dioceses, including the Diocese in Europe; and the province of York has 14 dioceses. The dioceses are divided into archdeaconries and deaneries, which are in turn divided into 13,000 parishes, although in practice many parishes are grouped together.

The Archbishop of Canterbury is Diocesan Bishop of Canterbury, Primate of All England and leader of the Anglican Communion. He takes the lead in respect of Anglican relationships with other Christian churches in the United Kingdom and abroad, and he also leads in respect of Anglican relationships with other faiths.

The Archbishops' Council is the centre of an administrative system dealing with inter-Church relations, inter-faith relations, social questions, recruitment and training for the ministry, and missionary work. The General Synod, elected from the laity and clergy of each diocese and numbering 581 members, normally meets twice a year. It has the power to prepare legislation – called Measures – about any matter to do with the Church of England. Parliament may accept or reject such Measures, but cannot amend them. If accepted, they become part of the law of the land.

The Archbishops of Canterbury and York, the Bishops of Durham, London and Winchester, and the 21 senior diocesan bishops from other dioceses of the Church of England have seats in the House of Lords (see page 45).

Archbishops, bishops and the deans of some Church of England cathedrals are appointed by The Queen on the advice of the Prime Minister. The Crown Appointments Commission, which includes lay and clergy representatives, plays a key role in the selection of archbishops and diocesan bishops.

The 33 Church Commissioners, accountable to the General Synod and to Parliament, are responsible for the management of a large part of the Church of England's invested assets. The Crown appoints a

A changing priesthood

The year 2004 was the tenth anniversary of the ordination of the first women priests in the Church of England. The number of full-time stipendiary women clergy in 2002 was 1,262, compared with 7,920 male clergy. The ordination of women remains a controversial issue for some sections of the Anglican congregation and women cannot be appointed as bishops. There has also been debate about the appointment of openly gay clergy. In July 2003, for example, Canon Jeffrey John withdrew from his appointment as suffragan Bishop of Reading (assistant to the diocesan Bishop) following opposition from the evangelical wing of the Church and from Anglicans abroad.

Member of Parliament from the governing party to the unpaid post of Second Church Estates Commissioner, to represent the Commissioners in Parliament. The Church Commissioners currently meet some 20 per cent of the Church of England's total running costs, providing support for parish, bishops and cathedral ministry and the pensions of the clergy. Parishes and dioceses meet the remaining costs.

Catholics

There are eight provinces of the Catholic Church in the United Kingdom – four in England, two in Scotland, one in Wales and one that includes Northern Ireland. The Roman Catholic Archbishops for England, Wales and Scotland have their seats in the Archdioceses of Westminster, Cardiff and Glasgow. Northern Ireland is covered by the Archdiocese of Armagh. The Bishops' Conference is a permanent institution of the Catholic Church whereby the bishops of a country together exercise pastoral, legislative and teaching offices as defined by the law of the Church. There is a Bishops' Conference of England and Wales, and another for Scotland. The Irish Episcopal Conference covers all of Ireland.

There are 22 territorial Catholic dioceses in England and Wales and eight in Scotland. Northern Ireland is covered by seven dioceses, some of which extend into the Republic of Ireland. Each diocesan bishop is appointed by the Pope and governs according to Canon Law and through reference to a Council of Priests, a College of

Consultors, a Finance Committee and a Pastoral Council.

Church of Scotland

The Church of Scotland is the largest Protestant church in Scotland and has a Presbyterian form of government – that is, government by church courts, composed of ministers, elders and deacons. There are over 1,500 congregations, governed locally by courts known as Kirk Sessions. The courts above these are the 'Presbyteries', responsible for a geographical area made up of a number of parishes. The General Assembly, or Supreme Court, meets annually under the convenership of an elected moderator, who serves for one year.

Other Christians

The rise of the Puritan movement in the 16th and 17th centuries led to a proliferation of nonconformist churches. The term 'Free Churches' is often used to describe these Protestant churches which, unlike the Church of England and the Church of Scotland, are not 'established' Churches (see page 234). Free Churches include Methodist, Baptist, The United Reformed, Presbyterian, Salvation Army and a variety of Pentecostal churches.

The British Methodist Church (which covers only Great Britain, there being a separate Irish Methodist Church), is the largest of the Free Churches in the United Kingdom. Originating in the 18th century following the evangelical revival under John Wesley, it has around 6,400 places of worship. The present Church is based on the 1932 union of most of the separate Methodist Churches.

The Baptists, dating from the 17th century, are mainly organised in associations of churches, most of which belong to the Baptist Union of Great Britain. The union covers England, a significant proportion of the English-speaking Baptist churches in Wales, and two Baptist Churches in Scotland (both of which also belong to the Baptist Union of Scotland). There is also a Baptist Union in Wales and an Association of Baptist Churches in Ireland (which covers both Northern Ireland and the Republic).

The United Reformed Church was formed in 1972 from the union of the Congregational Church in

England and Wales with the Presbyterian Church in England. In 1982 and 2000 there were further unions with the Reformed Churches of Christ and the Congregational Union of Scotland.

Among the other Free Churches are the Presbyterian Church in Ireland, the Presbyterian (or Calvinistic Methodist) Church of Wales, the Union of Welsh Independents, and a number of independent Scottish Presbyterian churches which are particularly active in the Highlands and Islands.

The Salvation Army was founded in the East End of London in 1865 by William Booth. It runs over 900 local church and community centres.

The Religious Society of Friends (Quakers) was founded in the middle of the 17th century under the leadership of George Fox. Unitarians and Free Christians, whose origins go back to the Reformation, belong to a similar tradition. The Christian Brethren, founded in the 19th century, comprises the Open Brethren, the Reunited Brethren and the Plymouth Brethren No. 4.

People of different cultures coming to settle in the United Kingdom since the Middle Ages have contributed to the diversity of Christian denominations. Christian communities founded by migrants include those of the Orthodox, Lutheran and Reformed Churches of various European countries, the Coptic Orthodox Church, Armenian Church and a number of Churches originating in Africa, such as the Cherubim and Seraphim Churches. These tend to be concentrated in the larger cities of the United Kingdom, particularly London, and use a variety of languages. The largest is the Greek Orthodox Church, many of whose members are of Cypriot origin.

Other developments within the Christian tradition have included the rise of Pentecostalism and the charismatic movement (which emphasises personal religious experience and divinely inspired powers). A number of Pentecostal bodies were formed in the United Kingdom at the turn of the 20th century. The two main organisations in the United Kingdom tracing their origins back to this period are the Assemblies of God, and the Elim Pentecostal Church. They have since been joined by other Pentecostal groupings with roots in the Black community. Immigration from the Caribbean and Africa since the Second World War has led to a significant number of Black Majority Churches, many of which are Pentecostal.

The Christian 'house church' movement (or 'new churches') began in the 1970s when some of the charismatics began to establish their own congregations.

Muslims

By the early 19th century Muslim seamen, mainly from Yemen and the Indian subcontinent, had settled in several areas of the United Kingdom, including the dockland areas of Cardiff, South Shields and London. There was further settlement after the First World War, and again in the 1950s and 1960s as people arrived to meet the shortage of labour following the Second World War.

The 1960s and 1970s saw the arrival of significant numbers of Muslims of Asian origin from Kenya and Uganda, as well as those arriving directly from the Indian subcontinent. There are well-established Turkish Cypriot, Nigerian and Arab Muslim communities, and more recently Muslims from Somalia, Iraq, Bosnia and Kosovo have sought refuge in the United Kingdom. In addition, there are smaller numbers of White and Black Caribbean Muslims. The principal Sunni and Shi'a traditions are both represented among the UK Muslim community. The Muslim Council of Britain, founded in 1997, represents 400 national and regional Muslim bodies as well as local mosques, professional associations and other organisations. The Council aims to promote co-operation, consensus and unity on Muslim affairs in the United Kingdom and serves as an advocacy and representative body for British Muslims.

The London Muslim Centre

A large number of residents and visitors attended the opening of a new Muslim community centre in Whitechapel, East London in June 2004. Built next to the East London Mosque, facilities at the centre include a gym, library, crèche, exhibition centre and classrooms. Members of the public contributed to the construction costs, and further funding was provided by the European Regional Development Fund and by central and local government. The centre was opened by Shaykh Abdur-Rahman al-Sudays, Imam of the Ka'bah in Makka (Mecca). One of the centre's aims is to improve dialogue between Islam and other faiths.

Hindus

Most Hindus in the United Kingdom are of Gujarati or Punjabi origin with smaller numbers from Uttar Pradesh, West Bengal and the southern states of India and Sri Lanka. Others settled from countries to which earlier generations of Indians had migrated such as Kenya, Malawi, Tanzania, Uganda and Zambia.

The main umbrella bodies for Hindus are the National Council of Hindu Temples (UK), the Hindu Council UK and more recently the Hindu Forum of Britain (formed in March 2004). Other national bodies serving the Hindu community include Vishwa Hindu Parishad (UK).

Sikhs

Most of the Sikh community in the United Kingdom originates from the Indian part of the Punjab, although a minority came via East Africa and other former British colonies to which members of their families had previously migrated. The community in the United Kingdom is believed to be the largest outside the Indian subcontinent.

The Network of Sikh Organisations represents over 100 Sikh organisations in the United Kingdom. It promotes understanding of the Sikh way of life, organises events and celebrations for the major Sikh festivals, and provides advice and information.

Jews

Jews settled in England after the Norman Conquest in 1066. They were banished by royal decree in 1290, but re-admitted following the English Civil War (1642–51). Sephardic Jews, who originally came from Spain and Portugal, have been present since that time. The majority of Jews in the United Kingdom today are Ashkenazi, descended from people who emigrated or fled persecution in the Russian Empire between 1881 and 1914, or Nazi persecution in Germany and other European countries from 1933 onwards. Sixty per cent of those Ashkenazi households who are affiliated to synagogues acknowledge the authority of the Chief Rabbi. The Reform Syna-gogues of Great Britain, the Masorti Synagogues, the Union of Liberal and Progressive Synagogues and the Union of Orthodox Hebrew Congregations together account for most of the remaining synagogue-affiliated community membership.

The Board of Deputies of British Jews is the officially recognised representative body for the Jewish community. Founded in 1760, the Board's representation is through deputies elected by synagogues and deputies elected by community organisations. It serves as the voice of the community to both government and the wider non-Jewish community and calls on the Chief Rabbi and the Communal Rabbi of the Spanish and Portuguese Jews' Congregation for religious advice and guidance when needed.

Buddhists

The Buddhist community in the United Kingdom includes people of White, Chinese and other ethnic groups. Various traditions are represented. The Network of Buddhist Organisations, founded in 1993, links various educational, cultural, charitable and teaching organisations. The Buddhist Society promotes the principles, but does not adhere to any particular school of Buddhism.

Other traditions

Jainism was brought to the United Kingdom mainly by immigrants from the Gujarat and Rajasthan areas of India. The Zoroastrian religion is mainly represented by the Parsi community from India; the founders of the UK community originally settled here in the 19th century. The Bahá'í movement originated in Persia in the 19th century. Rastafarianism, with its roots in the return-to-Africa movement, emerged in the West Indies early in the 20th century and arrived in the United Kingdom with immigration from Jamaica in the 1950s.

Other religious groups in the United Kingdom were originally founded in the United States in the 19th century, including a number deriving from the Christian tradition. Examples include a growing number of Mormons (the Church of Jesus Christ of Latter-day Saints), and Jehovah's Witnesses, Christadelphians, Christian Scientists, and Seventh-day Adventists.

A number of newer religious movements, established since the Second World War and often with overseas origins, are now active in the United Kingdom. Examples include the Church of Scientology, the Transcendental Meditation movement, the Unification Church and various New Age groups.

Places of worship

There are around 16,000 Anglican churches, and 42 Anglican cathedrals which serve as focal points of the dioceses. The Catholic Church has nearly 4,590 churches and the Church of Scotland over 1,500. The Church in Wales also has about 1,500 places of worship.

Liverpool Cathedral

After marking the 25th anniversary in October 2003 of the completion of its construction, Liverpool's Anglican cathedral celebrated its centenary with a special service at 4.00 pm on 19 July 2004 – exactly 100 years since King Edward VII laid the foundation stone. The Cathedral is the largest in Britain, with an area of 9,987 square metres and its bells are said to have the highest and heaviest peal in the world. The architect was Sir Giles Gilbert Scott.

English Heritage (see page 290) provides funds for repairs to Anglican and Catholic cathedrals through its Cathedral Repairs Grant Scheme. It provided almost £40 million through the scheme between 1991 and 2004. In January 2004 it announced a new £2 million funding package for 20 cathedrals in England, including £200,000 each for Lincoln, Salisbury, Leicester and Truro cathedrals and St George's Chapel, Windsor.

In his 2004 Budget, the Chancellor of the Exchequer announced that the Listed Places of Worship Grant Scheme, launched in 2001, will be expanded to allow a full VAT refund for eligible repair and maintenance work. Under current plans, the scheme will remain in place until March 2006. It applies to listed places of worship of all religions throughout the United Kingdom. The Repair Grants for Places of Worship in England Scheme, which runs from 2002 to 2005, is funded jointly by English Heritage and the Heritage Lottery Fund. All faith groups and denominations, Christian and non-Christian, are eligible to apply if they are formally constituted religious organisations. In 2003/04, £30 million was made available for urgent repairs.

Since 1969 over 1,600 churches in England have become redundant and around £33 million has been raised from their disposal. Redundant churches are increasingly being used for residential property or as civic, cultural or community centres. The Churches Conservation Trust, funded jointly by the Government and the Church of England, preserves Anglican churches of particular cultural and historical importance that are no longer used as regular places of worship. In 2004, 332 churches were maintained in this way. A number of outstanding buildings from other denominations and faiths are cared for by the Historic Chapels Trust.

There are over 1,000 mosques and numerous community Muslim centres throughout the United Kingdom. Mosques are not only places of worship but also offer instruction in the Muslim way of life, and facilities for education and welfare. They range from converted buildings in many towns and suburbs to the Central Mosque in Regent's Park, London, with its associated Islamic Cultural Centre. The main conurbations in London, the Midlands, the North West and North East of England, and Scotland, Wales and Northern Ireland also have their own central mosques with a range of community facilities.

The first Hindu temple, or mandir, was opened in London in the 1950s and there are now 143 in the United Kingdom; many are affiliated to the National Council of Hindu Temples (UK). The Swaminarayan Hindu Temple in Neasden, north-west London, is the largest and was the first purpose-built Hindu temple in Europe. There are also a number of meeting places in addition to the official places of worship. There are over 200 Sikh temples, or gurdwaras, in the United Kingdom, the vast majority located in England and Wales. They cater for the religious, educational, welfare and cultural needs of their community. In March 2003 the largest gurdwara outside India was opened in Southall, west London.

There are about 300 Jewish synagogues in the United Kingdom, but there are many additional congregations that do not have their own purpose-built synagogue buildings. There are over 400 Buddhist centres in the United Kingdom at which meditation or spiritual practice can take place, although it is not considered essential to go to a temple and practice can take place at home. Examples include the Wat Buddhapadipa Temple in London, the Amaravati Monastery in Hertfordshire and the Kagyu Samye Ling Tibetan Centre in Dumfriesshire and Galloway.

Religious ceremonies and festivals

Although there are secular alternatives, religious traditions play a major role in commemorating births, marriages, deaths and other important life events.

In 2002 around 38 per cent of UK marriages were solemnised with a religious ceremony, compared with approximately 60 per cent in 1971. There are, however, wide variations within the United Kingdom. Seventy-two per cent of marriages in Northern Ireland in 2002 involved a religious ceremony, compared with 62 per cent in Scotland and 34 per cent in England and Wales.

Of the 85,870 religious ceremonies in England and Wales in 2002, 68 per cent were solemnised in the Church of England or the Church of Wales; 12 per cent in nonconformist churches; another 12 per cent in the Catholic Church; 5 per cent in other Christian bodies and 3 per cent in other faith traditions.

The two most important periods in the Christian calendar are Easter and Christmas, which are major public holidays in the United Kingdom. Festivals and events observed by other religions – such as Eid ul-Fitr and Eid ul-Adha (Muslim), Diwali and Janmashtami (Hindu), Vaisakhi (Sikh), the High Holy Days and Passover (Jewish), and the Birthday of the Buddha – are adding to the visible diversity of life in the United Kingdom today.

Religious education

In England and Wales all maintained schools must provide religious education and a daily act of collective worship, although parents can withdraw their children from either or both of these activities. In maintained schools without a religious designation, each local education authority is responsible for producing a locally agreed syllabus, which must reflect Christianity as the main religious tradition of the country, while taking account of the teachings and practices of the other principal religions represented in the United Kingdom. There are no nationally prescribed attainment targets, nor assessment levels or programmes of study for religious education, but the subject must be provided up to but not including sixth form level.

State supported schools that are designated as having a religious character are often called faith schools. In these schools collective worship is in the tenets of the faith of the school. In 2004 there were about 6,230 primary and almost 600 secondary state supported faith schools in England. All but around 40 of these were associated with Christian denominations.

State supported faith schools can be either foundation or voluntary controlled (both of which are entirely funded by the local education authority) or voluntary aided (where school and parent organisations make a contribution to capital expenses). Voluntary aided schools (61 per cent of the total) are responsible for setting their own admission policies, and the religious education they provide is in accordance with the tenets of their own faith. Voluntary controlled schools teach the locally agreed religious education syllabus and the local authority sets admissions policies.

Since December 2003 independent schools, including academies (see page 122), have been able to apply to be designated as schools with a religious character. This allows them to employ teaching staff with the same religious beliefs as the school. Independent schools are not funded by the state. They draw their funding from fees paid by parents, donations and appeals. Of the 2,300 registered independent schools, which include academies, about 1,000 describe themselves as having a religious character and, by mid-2004, 478 had successfully applied for designation.

In April 2004 the Qualifications and Curriculum Authority published a consultation document for a non-statutory national framework for religious education in England. The proposed framework acknowledged the fact that many people have no formal beliefs.

Citizenship became a statutory national curriculum subject in secondary schools in England in 2002. Pupils are taught about the diversity of national, regional, religious and ethnic identities in the United Kingdom, and the need for mutual respect, tolerance and understanding.

In Scotland, education authorities must ensure that schools provide religious education and regular opportunities for religious observance. The law does not specify the form of religious education, but it is recommended that pupils should be provided with a broad-based curriculum, through which they can develop a knowledge and understanding of Christianity and other world religions, and develop their own beliefs, attitudes, moral values and practices. Roman Catholic schools account for nearly all of the 440 state supported faith schools in Scotland.

In Northern Ireland the main Churches have approved a core syllabus for religious education and this must be taught in all grant-aided schools, though parents may withdraw their children from attendance at religious education or collective worship. Integrated education (where Protestant and Catholic pupils are taught together) is encouraged and all schools must be open to pupils of all religions, although in practice most Catholic pupils attend Catholic maintained schools or Catholic voluntary grammar schools, and most Protestant children are enrolled at controlled schools or non-denominational voluntary grammar schools. However, the number of inter-denominational schools is gradually increasing and in 2003/04, 16,494 primary and secondary pupils enrolled at integrated schools compared with 11,382 pupils in 1998/99.

Religion and society

The influence of Christianity and other religions in the United Kingdom has always extended far beyond the comparatively narrow spheres of organised and private worship. Religious organisations are actively involved in voluntary work and other services to the community, and many faith groups maintain active links with government.

Church and state

Two Churches have special status with regard to the State. In England, since the rejection by Henry VIII of the supremacy of the Pope in 1534, the Anglican Church of England has been legally recognised as the official, or 'established', Church. The Monarch is the 'Supreme Governor' of the Church of England and must always be a member of the Church, and promise to uphold it. A similar position was occupied by the Presbyterian Church of Scotland until the early 20th century. This continues to be recognised as the national Church in Scotland, but the Monarch holds no constitutional role in its government, although she is represented at the General Assembly (see page 230) through the office of the Lord High Commissioner. Neither of the established Churches are funded by the State. There are no established Churches in Wales or Northern Ireland.

Charitable work

In 2004 there were nearly 11,400 charities in England and Wales with a religious objective (excluding those registered as a place of worship). Christian Aid, CAFOD (Catholic Agency for Overseas Development), Muslim Aid and Islamic Relief (the two largest Muslim charities), Khalsa Aid (a Sikh charity) and UK Jewish Aid are among the many UK-based charities that organise appeals and deliver relief aid globally.

Within the United Kingdom the Salvation Army is an important provider of accommodation for homeless people, and offers other services including work with alcoholics, prison chaplaincy and a family-tracing service. The Quakers have a long tradition of social concern and peacemaking. Trusts with a Quaker history, such as the Cadbury and Rowntree Trusts (see also page 112), support many social initiatives, particularly funding for housing.

British and Foreign Bible Society (BFBS)

The BFBS celebrated its bicentenary on 8 March 2004 with a special service at St Paul's Cathedral. Founded in London in 1804, the Society's original aim was to increase the availability of Christian Scriptures in England and Wales. By 2003, however, there was a worldwide fellowship of 136 national Bible Societies, working in more than 200 countries and territories. Each Society is a non-denominational organisation whose purpose is to translate, produce and distribute the Bible 'without note or comment' in a range of languages and at prices they can afford. By the end of 2002 the Societies had helped to ensure that the Bible, or some part of it, had been translated into over 2,000 languages.

The Church Urban Fund, established by the Church of England, is an independent charity, which raises money to enable those living in the most disadvantaged urban areas to set up local projects to alleviate the effects of poverty. Although rooted in the Christian faith, the fund does not restrict its grants on the basis of religious belief.

The General Assembly of the Church of Scotland, through its Board of Social Responsibility, is the largest voluntary social work agency in Scotland.

Links with government

In October 2003 the Foreign & Commonwealth Office (FCO) held its first 'Multi Faith Week': a

Pilgrimage

Pilgrimage to sacred sites is an integral aspect of worship for some faiths. Each year about 20,000 British Muslims travel to Makka to perform the Hajj, where they join around two million other pilgrims. The Hajj is an important expression of faith and a journey involving significant emotional and physical demands. Since 2000 a British Hajj Delegation has travelled to Makka to provide consular, pastoral and medical assistance to British pilgrims. The Delegation is a team of volunteers from the British Muslim community and is accompanied by Muslim staff from the Foreign & Commonwealth Office.

Walsingham in Norfolk first became a place of pilgrimage in medieval times. There are two shrines – one Anglican and one Catholic. In 2003, listeners to BBC Radio voted Walsingham 'the nation's favourite spiritual place', beating other nominations such as Iona and Durham Cathedral. During 2004 the image of Our Lady of Walsingham (from the Anglican shrine) was taken on her own pilgrimage to a series of secular locations, including Pentonville Prison in London, Oxford University, a comprehensive school in Wales, Wolverhampton General Hospital, Aldershot Barracks and Gatwick Airport. Prayers and other events were held at each location.

series of seminars, open days and receptions to help build relationships with faith communities. The FCO also provides support to the British Hajj Delegation (see box).

In 2003 the Home Office set up a Faith Communities Unit, which is responsible for engaging with faith communities and promoting inter-faith dialogue. *Working Together: Co-operation between Government and Faith Communities,* published in 2004, provides guidance on national, regional and local consultations, and advice for faith communities on getting the most out of their dealings with government. The report also recommends that consideration be given to the involvement of organisations representing those with non-religious beliefs, such as humanists and secularists.

In England the Inner Cities Religious Council, based in the Office of the Deputy Prime Minister, provides a forum in which the Government and faith communities work together on neighbourhood renewal and social inclusion. Chaired by a government minister, the Council's members are from the Christian, Muslim, Hindu, Sikh and Jewish faiths.

The ecumenical Churches Regional Network coordinates church involvement in English Regional Development Agencies and church input to regional initiatives. Inter-faith forums and councils have been established in many of the English regions.

Churches in Scotland have created a Scottish Churches Parliamentary Office for formal representation of their interests in the Scottish Parliament. The Scottish Inter Faith Council works with the Scottish Executive and other national and local agencies to help ensure they are aware of the interests of faith communities. In Wales, the Churches have worked together to appoint a Churches National Assembly Liaison Officer to relate to the National Assembly for Wales.

Legal rights and responsibilities

The European Convention on Human Rights, which was incorporated into the *Human Rights Act 1998,* guarantees everybody in the United Kingdom the right to religious freedom, conscience and religion, subject to the law. In Great Britain religious discrimination is unlawful in the areas of employment and training under an

EC Directive that came into effect in December 2003. Its provisions do not apply in Northern Ireland, where separate legislation prohibits discrimination on a number of grounds, including religious belief in employment, training and the provision of goods, facilities and services. In addition, a public authority, in carrying out its functions relating to Northern Ireland, is obliged to have regard to the need to promote equality of opportunity between persons of different religious beliefs and to have due regard to the desirability of promoting good relations between such people.

In England and Wales certain offences motivated by religious hatred are subject to a higher maximum penalty. In addition, the Attorney General's power to challenge unduly lenient court sentences was extended from October 2003. Certain offences can be referred to the Court of Appeal for review where it is felt that a tougher sentence is merited. The *Criminal Justice (Scotland) Act 2003* also makes specific provision for offences aggravated by religious prejudice. Where a person commits such an offence, Scottish courts must take the religious prejudice into account when sentencing the offender, and state any extra element of the sentence because of this.

In July 2004 the Home Secretary announced the Government's intention to introduce legislation making incitement to religious hatred a criminal offence in England and Wales.

Relations between religious traditions

Ecumenical movements

Churches Together in Britain and Ireland (CTBI) is the main coordinating body for the Christian Churches in the United Kingdom and promotes discussion of Christian faith and doctrinal issues in the Christian community. It also coordinates the work of its 33 member Churches or groupings of Churches in the areas of social responsibility, international affairs, church life, world mission, racial justice, care of international students and inter-faith relations. Its international aid agencies – Christian Aid, CAFOD and SCIAF (Scottish Catholic International Aid Fund) – are major charities. Member Churches are also grouped in separate ecumenical bodies, according to country: Churches Together in England, Action of Churches

Together in Scotland, Churches Together in Wales (Cytûn), and the Irish Council of Churches.

The respective leaders of the Anglican and Methodist Churches signed a national covenant in November 2003, marking a commitment to unity which envisages a movement towards shared services, clergy and resources.

The Scottish Churches' Initiative for Union began in 1996, incorporating the Church of Scotland, Methodist Church, Scottish Episcopal Church and United Reformed Church. The Church of Scotland voted to withdraw in May 2003. The Scottish Episcopal Church reaffirmed its commitment to the goal of unity in June 2004.

Co-operation between faiths

The Inter Faith Network for the UK links nearly 100 organisations with an interest in inter-faith relations, including the representative bodies of the Bahá'í, Buddhist, Christian, Hindu, Jain, Jewish, Muslim, Sikh and Zoroastrian communities. The Network promotes good relations between faiths in the United Kingdom, and runs a public advice and information service on inter-faith issues. In October 2003 it published *Local Inter Faith Activity in the UK: A Survey* – the results of a research project into inter-faith initiatives across the United Kingdom. The project found nearly 140 inter-faith and multi-faith local bodies, 43 per cent of which had come into existence since the beginning of 2000. The Scottish Inter Faith Council also aims to promote good relations between the different faith communities in Scotland.

The Council of Christians and Jews works for better understanding among members of these two religions, and deals with educational and social issues. The Three Faiths Forum and the Calamus Foundation have as their focus relationships between the Christian, Jewish and Muslim traditions.

Some individual faith communities also have units or programmes dedicated to inter-faith relations. For example, CTBI has a Churches' Commission on Inter Faith Relations, which aims to enable the churches to engage effectively in dialogue with other faith communities in Britain and Ireland and to facilitate a network of information and experience among Christians about inter-faith relations. The Inter-faith Unit of the Islamic Foundation was set up with the specific aim of developing better relations between the Muslim and Christian traditions.

Further reading

UK Christian Handbook – Religious Trends 2003/2004, No. 4, Christian Research.

Religions in the UK Directory, 2001–03, Religious Resource and Research Centre at the University of Derby and The Inter Faith Network for the UK, 2001.

Religion in England and Wales: findings from the 2001 Home Office Citizenship Survey, Home Office Research Study 274, 2004.

Websites

Churches Together in Britain and Ireland
www.ctbi.org.uk

Inter Faith Network for the UK
www.interfaith.org.uk

ODPM/Inner Cities Religious Council
www.neighbourhood.gov.uk/faith_communities.asp

Office for National Statistics
www.statistics.gov.uk

WWW.

16 Culture

The United Kingdom has a strong tradition in literature, theatre, popular and orchestral music and the performing arts. These, together with collections in UK museums and galleries, act as a magnet for overseas visitors and make a substantial contribution to the economy. According to economic estimates made by the Department for Culture, Media and Sport (DCMS), the creative industries accounted for 8 per cent of UK Gross Value Added in 2002 (see glossary and page 357), and creative employment provided 1.9 million jobs in Great Britain in 2003.

Participation

With the exception of the cinema, the percentage of the population who attend various types of cultural event has remained fairly stable since the early 1990s (Table 16.1). Admissions to UK cinemas, however, fell to 167.3 million in 2003 from a record 176 million in 2002.

Table 16.1 Attendance[1] at cultural events, Great Britain

Percentages

	1993/94	1998/99	2003/04
Cinema	50	57	61
Plays	24	22	25
Art galleries/exhibitions	22	21	24
Classical music	12	11	13
Ballet	7	6	8
Opera	7	6	8
Contemporary dance	3	4	6

1 Percentage of resident population aged 15 and over attending 'these days'.
Source: Target Group Index, BMRB International

Attendance at some of the major museums and galleries in England also rose between 2001/02 and 2002/03, with the National Museums Liverpool, Natural History Museum, and the Victoria and Albert Museum recording the biggest increases.

Churches and cathedrals are also an important part of the nation's cultural heritage, attracting many visitors. York Minster and Canterbury Cathedral receive over 1 million visitors each a year. Kew Gardens in London, the National Botanic Gardens in Carmarthenshire, Royal Botanics in Edinburgh and the Botanic Gardens in Belfast and are also popular destinations for people with an interest in gardening and horticulture. Windsor Castle, the Tower of London and the Roman Baths in Bath are among the top heritage attractions.

Highlights of 2003–04

Among the many cultural highlights from mid-2003 to mid-2004 were:

- the London Symphony Orchestra (LSO) marked its 100th birthday in June 2004 with a huge musical celebration. Many of the world's greatest artists and conductors, including Mstislav Rostropovitch and Michael Tilson Thomas, joined the LSO on stage at London's Barbican Centre (see also page 242);

- gardens, museums and galleries throughout the United Kingdom ran a series of Treasure Trails to celebrate the 250th anniversary of the Royal Society of Arts. All the exhibits on display were designed, built or inspired by the RSA, an RSA Fellow or medallist. Among the industrial designers featured at London's

Transport Museum (see also page 245) was Eric Ottaway who designed the famous red Routemaster Bus;

- Ricky Gervais, star of *The Office*, became the first UK actor to win a TV comedy-acting award at the Golden Globes. *The Office* also won the award for the best comedy;
- a record 70 buildings received awards from the Royal Institute of British Architects (RIBA);
- East London schools joined the University of East London and Newham Sixth Form College to stage *Cascade 2004*, an exhibition of young people's artwork supporting London's bid to stage the Olympic Games in 2012. A colourful wire and papier-mâché sculpture of Olympic figures in action formed the centrepiece of the exhibition;
- Jonathan Ive, designer of Apple's iMac and iPOD, was named by a panel of culture experts as the most influential person in British culture on BBC TV's *Cultural Movers and Shakers* programme.

Awards

A selection of major award winners is given in Table 16.2 on page 240.

Live performance

Festivals

Hundreds of professional arts festivals take place in the United Kingdom each year. Some, like the

Fifty years of Lord of the Rings

The year 2004 marked the 50th anniversary of the publication of the first two parts of JRR Tolkien's epic *Lord of the Rings* trilogy. *The Fellowship of the Ring* and *The Two Towers* were both published in 1954. A special set of ten stamps, designed by HGV, was issued by the Royal Mail in February. The stamps, illustrating places and characters from the novels, were taken from Tolkien's original drawings apart from one by his son, Christopher, featuring a map of Middle Earth. Tolkien's celebrated fantasy came first in The Big Read, a BBC poll to find the best-loved UK novel.

Edinburgh International Festival

Edinburgh International Festival is one of the world's greatest celebrations of the arts. The 2004 event featured performances of music, theatre, opera and dance, as well as lectures and discussions. Highlights included three productions from Hanover State Opera and an 11-hour theatrical performance of Claudel's *Le Soulier de Satin*. The Edinburgh Festival Fringe, with a wide variety of programmes (including street events), takes place alongside the main events. In recent years it has proved a fertile training ground for comedians and actors, who have progressed to successful careers elsewhere. Other annual Edinburgh events include the International Film Festival, the Jazz Festival and the Edinburgh Mela Festival. The Edinburgh International Book Festival, which celebrated its 21st birthday in 2004, is the largest literary festival in Europe, welcoming over 200,000 visitors.

Cardiff and Brighton Festivals, last for a month and offer a wide variety of programmes.

The Aldeburgh Festival, founded by Benjamin Britten, focuses on classical music. The Hay Festival, held in Hay-on-Wye, originally focused on literature – the town is renowned for its second-hand bookshops – but has broadened its range in recent years and its programme now includes musical events and contributions from guest speakers. Film festivals include the annual London Film Festival, the Leeds Children's and Young People's Film Festivals and the Brief Encounters short film festival in Bristol.

Glastonbury, one of the world's biggest outdoor festivals, features many forms of culture: pop and dance music, fringe theatre, painting, sculpture and textile art. About 150,000 people attended the 2004 festival. There were over 2,000 performances at over 30 different venues from artists from all over the world. The WOMAD (World of Music, Arts and Dance) festival celebrates many forms of music, arts and dance from countries and cultures all over the world. WOMAD was originally inspired by UK musician Peter Gabriel. Since the first festival in 1982, WOMAD has presented more than 140 events in various different countries. UK

Table 16.2 Selected major award winners, 2004,[1] UK

Award	Category	Title of Work	Winner
Art			
Turner Prize (2003)		ceramic pots	Grayson Perry, also known as Claire
Literature			
Whitbread Prizes (2003)	Novel and Overall	*The Curious Incident of the Dog in the Night-Time*	Mark Haddon
	Children's	*The Fire-Eaters*	David Almond
	Poetry	*Landing Light*	Don Paterson
	First Novel	*Vernon God Little*	DBC Pierre
	Biography	*Orwell: The Life*	DJ Taylor
Man Booker Prize (2003)		*Vernon God Little*	DBC Pierre
Orange Prize for Fiction		*Small Island*	Andrea Levy
Popular music			
Brit Awards	Best Male Artist		Daniel Bedingfield
	Best Female Artist		Dido
	Best Group		The Darkness
	Best Newcomer		Busted
	Outstanding Contribution		Duran Duran
The Ivors	Best Song Musically & Lyrically	*Leave Right Now*	Francis Eg White (writer)
	Songwriters of the Year		The Darkness
Film			
BAFTA Awards	Best Film	*The Lord of the Rings: the Return of the King*	Peter Jackson
	Best British Film	*Touching the Void*	Kevin Macdonald
	Best Actor	*Lost in Translation*	Bill Murray
	Best Actress	*Lost in Translation*	Scarlett Johansson
	Best Supporting Actor	*Love Actually*	Bill Nighy
TV and video			
BAFTA Awards	Best Drama Series	*Buried*	World Productions/ Channel 4
	Best Soap	*Coronation Street*	Granada/ITV1
	Best Sport	*Rugby World Cup Final*	ITV1
	Best Drama Serial	*Charles II: The Power and the Passion*	BBC One and A&E
	Best Actor	*State of Play*	Bill Nighy
	Best Actress	*The Wife of Bath – Canterbury Tales*	Julie Walters
Theatre			
Olivier Awards	Best Actor	*Of Mice and Men*	Matthew Kelly
	Best Actress	*Honour*	Eileen Atkins
	Best New Play	*The Pillowman*	Martin McDonagh
	Best Director	*Caligula*	Michael Grandage
Architecture			
Stirling Prize (2003)		*Laban Dance Centre*	Herzog & de Meuron

1 Unless otherwise indicated.

events in 2004 included the WOMAD Festival at Rivermead, Reading.

Festivals in Wales include Brecon Jazz and the Llangollen International Eisteddfod, which attracted performers from over 40 countries in 2004. The Belfast Festival is the largest of its kind in Ireland, attracting over 50,000 visitors. Featuring both Irish and international artists and performers, the two-week arts extravaganza includes theatre, dance, literature, jazz, classical, popular and folk music, visual arts, and comedy. Journeys and migrations were the themes for the 2004 festival.

Royal National Mod

The 100th Royal National Mod took place in Oban on the west coast of Scotland in October 2003. The festival celebrates Gaelic language and culture through competitions in music, drama, dance, arts and literature. Visitors came from Australia, Canada, Ireland, the United Kingdom and the United States to take part in the competition. The first Mod was held in Oban in 1892.

Drama

Musicals, thrillers, and comedies provide most of the material for London's West End theatre productions. *The Mousetrap* by thriller-writer Agatha Christie opened in 1952 and is the longest-running play, with over 20,000 performances by the end of 2002. *Les Misérables*, based on Victor Hugo's novel, and Andrew Lloyd Webber's *The Phantom of the Opera*, are among the most popular and longest-running musicals.

Clwyd Theatr Cymru in Mold is the national English-speaking theatre company for Wales. The Welsh language theatre company, *Theatr Genedlaethol Cymru*, was established in Llanelli in autumn 2003 and toured theatres throughout Wales in 2004. There is also a national network of production companies for theatre for young people.

In Scotland, the Royal Lyceum Theatre and the King's and Festival Theatres in Edinburgh, and the Citizen's Theatre Glasgow, have full programmes

covering a wide range of productions. The Traverse Theatre in Edinburgh is Scotland's main centre for new writing. The creation of a National Theatre of Scotland (NToS) was announced in September 2003 with start-up funding from the Scottish Executive of £7.5 million over two years. The NToS will commission productions to tour a range of venues across Scotland.

Northern Ireland has six major theatres, including the Opera House and Waterfront Hall in Belfast and the new Millennium Forum in the city of Londonderry. It also has several independent theatre companies specialising in productions of new work.

Music

Classical music

A range of professional orchestras perform regularly throughout the United Kingdom, offering a varied repertoire of classical works from the great composers to more experimental pieces. Four major symphony orchestras are based in London: the London Symphony Orchestra, the Philharmonia, the London Philharmonic, and the Royal Philharmonic.

In the English regions the Bournemouth Symphony, City of Birmingham Symphony, the Hallé (based in Manchester) and the Royal Liverpool Philharmonic orchestras are all well known and highly rated. In Wales the BBC National Orchestra of Wales offers a year-round programme of orchestral and choral music – the latter featuring the BBC National Chorus of Wales. The Royal Scottish National orchestra is based in Glasgow and the Scottish Chamber Orchestra performs throughout Scotland and overseas. The Ulster Orchestra is Northern Ireland's only fully professional orchestra.

Three well-established events in the classical musical calendar are the Leeds International Piano Competition for young pianists, held every three years and won by Antti Siirala of Finland in 2003; the biennial BBC Singer of the World in Cardiff Competition, won by Tommi Hakala from Finland in 2003; and the biennial BBC Young Musicians contest, won in 2004 by 16-year-old violinist Nicola Benedetti.

The Henry Wood Promenade Concerts (the BBC Proms), held in the Royal Albert Hall in London,

LSO celebrates centenary

The London Symphony Orchestra (LSO), the first independent, self-governing orchestra in the United Kingdom, was founded in 1904. Many distinguished conductors and composers have been associated with the orchestra over the last 100 years, including Hans Richter, Sir Thomas Beecham, Sir Edward Elgar and Sir Colin Davies. The LSO was the first UK orchestra to travel overseas, visiting Paris in 1906, and the first to visit the United States, in 1912. Today the LSO tours the world and is the only UK orchestra to hold an annual residency at the Lincoln Center in New York.

During 2004/05 the LSO is performing over 100 concerts, featuring many great international artists, at its home in London's Barbican Centre. As part of the centenary, the LSO's education and community Discovery programme will launch a new programme of work to involve people of all ages and abilities in making music alongside the players.

are the world's largest music festival. The themes of the 2004 series were 'Back to Bohemia', 'East/West' and 'England at the Crossroads: 1934'. In September 2004 the BBC presented the eighth season of 'Proms in the Park' in Belfast, Manchester, Swansea and Hyde Park, London. All four concerts featured top classical and pop artists live on stage and linked up to the Royal Albert Hall for the finale of the traditional Last Night of the Proms concert.

English and Welsh choral societies have done much to foster the oratorio tradition at the leading music festivals. English ecclesiastical choral singing is a speciality of the choirs of cathedrals and Oxford and Cambridge colleges.

Opera

London's Royal Opera House (ROH) at Covent Garden attracts performers with international reputations. Glyndebourne Opera (East Sussex), which relies on private patrons for its summer season, is another prestigious venue. The English National Opera returned to play at the newly restored London Coliseum in February 2004. The

restoration has provided more public space, returned the auditorium to its original rich colour scheme, and installed a new glass roof with views of the Coliseum's famous tower.

Welsh National Opera will move to a permanent home at the Wales Millennium Centre in Cardiff when it opens in November 2004. Consisting of the 1,900-seat lyric theatre, a studio theatre and a dance theatre, with an additional concourse space for live performances, the centre will host an international showcase of opera, musicals, ballet and dance.

Scottish Opera for All toured Scotland's schools in 2004 with its innovative production of the *Minotaur*. Schoolchildren had a backstage view of opera production, and workshops with musicians and singers allowed them to perform their own version of the *Minotaur*.

Popular music

Turnover in the music industry was estimated at over £2 billion in 2003, employing about 125,000 people. In 2003, over 236 million albums and 36 million singles were sold in the UK domestic market. In Scotland, Edinburgh hosted the MTV Europe Awards in November 2003, generating an estimated £9 million for the economy.

Top fives

Top five singles in 2003
1 Black Eyed Peas *Where is the Love*
2 Gareth Gates featuring The Kumars *Spirit in the Sky*
3 R Kelly *Ignition (remix)*
4 Michael Andrews featuring Gary Jules *Mad World*
5 Will Young *Leave Right Now*

Top five artist albums in 2003
1 Dido *Life for Rent*
2 Justin Timberlake *Justified*
3 Christina Aguilera *Stripped*
4 Daniel Bedingfield *Gotta Get Thru This*
5 Norah Jones *Come Away with Me*

UK and US artists continue to dominate the pop charts. Coldplay's *Clocks* won a Grammy Award for Record of the Year in 2003. Rock band The Darkness shot to fame during 2003. By February 2004 they had sold 1.2 million copies of their debut album, *Permission to Land*, in the United Kingdom and almost 1 million copies elsewhere in the world. The Darkness won Best Group at the 2004 Brit Awards, while the award for Best British Female went to Dido (see Table 16.2).

Folk music is popular in all parts of the United Kingdom. In Northern Ireland, for example, traditional musicians perform in pubs and clubs, playing fiddles and other Celtic instruments. Scottish and Welsh festivals uphold Gaelic and Celtic traditions in music and song.

Dance

Two major dance companies based in London are the English National Ballet and the Royal Ballet. Other important ballet companies include the Birmingham Royal Ballet and the Northern Ballet Theatre. Scottish Ballet is Scotland's National Dance Company and the fourth largest in the United Kingdom. Its Associate Programme offers children and young people the opportunity to take courses taught by professional dancers.

Independent Ballet Wales is renowned for presenting classical ballet in an unpretentious and original way. Each year the company of eight dancers and two technicians tours around 90 venues throughout the United Kingdom, including schools, arts centres and universities. Its productions are re-choreographed to suit each venue. It also runs workshops and classes.

The Laban Centre in south-east London, which opened in 2003, is the new home for one of Europe's leading institutions for contemporary dance training and is the largest contemporary dance space in the world. Contemporary dance companies with established reputations are Diversions, Spring Loaded and the Richard Alston Dance Company. The Ballet Boyz, Michael Nunn and William Trevitt, were commissioned by television's Channel 4 to write and present *The Rough Guide to Choreography*, which aims to demystify and widen audiences for contemporary dance. In March and April 2004 Scotland's national dance centre, Dance Base in Edinburgh, produced the entertaining *Off Kilter*, a witty look at Scottish culture with choreography performed to both traditional and world music.

The Critics' Circle

The Critics' Circle is an association of UK critics, founded in 1913. It has nearly 300 members, most of whom write for national and regional newspapers and magazines.

The Critics' Circle has four sections representing dance, drama, film and music. The first three sections hold award ceremonies each year, with critics voting for the winners.

In 2003, the English National Ballet won two dance awards: the Company Prize for Outstanding Repertoire (Classical) and Michael Corder for Best Choreography (Classical). In the drama awards, Eve Best was voted Best Actress for *Mourning Becomes Electra* and Michael Sheen Best Actor for *Caligula*. The Attenborough Award for the best British film was won by Peter Mullan's *The Magdalene Sisters*.

Film and broadcasting

Film

In 2003, cinemas took £742 million at the box office in the United Kingdom, compared with £755 million in 2002. An estimated 57,000 people were employed in the film and video production and distribution and film exhibition sectors. In 2002, film exports were worth £656 million.

There were record levels of film production in the United Kingdom in 2003. Thirty major feature films attracted inward investment of £729 million, compared with £266 million in 2002. These included *Harry Potter and the Prisoner of Azkaban*, *King Arthur* and *Troy*. There were 44 UK-produced films such as *Thunderbirds* and *Bride and Prejudice* (the Bollywood version of *Pride and Prejudice*). In addition, there were 99 UK co-productions, compared with 66 in 2002, indicating the growth and importance of international partnerships to the UK film industry.

Figure 16.3 Cinema admissions, UK

Millions

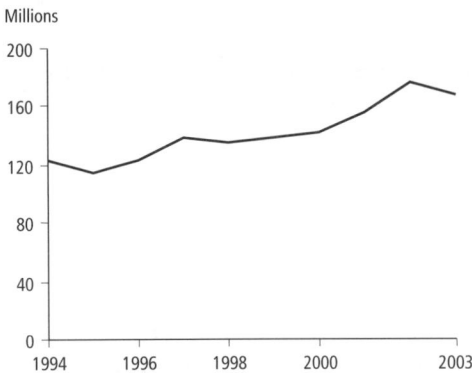

Source: CAA/Gallup/Nielsen EDI

Lord of the Rings: The Return of the King was the most popular film with UK cinema-goers in 2003, followed by *Finding Nemo*. The United Kingdom was involved in the production of three of the top ten most popular films, *Love Actually*, *Calendar Girls* and *Johnny English*.

The Government provides tax relief to encourage film production in the United Kingdom. Companies shooting films wholly or partly in the United Kingdom can write off 100 per cent of production expenditure against their liabilities for tax. There are plans to extend tax credits to film distribution in a bid to widen audiences for new UK films.

Television

Around 95 per cent of UK households own a television set, and, on average, people watched 26 hours of television a week in 2003.

The kinds of programmes produced in the United Kingdom vary enormously. Soaps (long-running series with multiple characters and plots) such as *EastEnders* and *Coronation Street* regularly top the ratings. Sporting events, such as the Euro 2004 football championships, and shows such as *Pop Idol* and *Who Wants to be a Millionaire?*, were also popular in 2004. Individual programmes receiving BAFTA awards in 2004 in recognition of particular merit included *The Office Christmas Special* (comedy) and *The Deal* (drama).

Radio

The BBC broadcasts a wide spectrum of classical music, jazz and world music (both live and recorded) on Radio 3. BBC Radio 1 broadcasts rock and pop, and much of the output of BBC Radio 2 is popular and light music.

Among the independent stations, Classic FM offers mainly classical music and Virgin Radio plays rock and pop. Much of the output of UK local radio stations consists of popular and light music, phone-ins and news.

BBC Radio 4's output is mainly talk-based and includes current affairs and documentaries, discussions and full-length plays. It is estimated that over 90 per cent of the adult population aged 15 and over tune into radio, with BBC local and national stations having just over half of the audience share.

More details on the pattern of radio listening, and the range of new digital stations available to listeners, can be found in chapter 17.

Visual arts

Museums and galleries

There are around 1,860 registered museums and galleries in the United Kingdom. These include the major national museums, about 1,000 independent museums, and others supported by local authorities, universities, the Armed Services, the National Trust and English Heritage.

In December 2001 free admission was reintroduced to all national museums and galleries. Over the next two years the number of visitors to these museums and galleries increased by 72 per cent with over 5 million more visitors in each of 2002 and 2003.

There were 33.5 million visitors to all DCMS-sponsored museums and galleries in 2002/03, increasing to 34.7 million visitors in 2003/04. Over 1.2 million visits were made to national museums and galleries in Wales in 2003/04. In 2003 a record number of visits (over 0.75 million) were made to the National Museums and Galleries of Northern Ireland, 7 per cent more than in 2002.

The Designation Scheme was launched in 1997 to recognise and protect collections of national and international importance held in England's non-national museums. Designated collections are held in 62 museums or museum services across England. The scheme is administered by The Museums, Libraries and Archives Council (MLA), on behalf of the DCMS.

Renaissance in the Regions is a major new initiative from the MLA to revitalise England's regional museums. Regional museum 'Hubs' or centres of excellence have been established in each English region with funding of £70 million over four years from 2003/04. Visits by schoolchildren to museums in Phase One of the initiative increased by 28 per cent in 2003/04.

London's Transport Museum

London's Transport Museum tells the story of London's transport history since the early 1800s. Displays and special exhibitions explore the impact of public transport on the growth of London and the lives of Londoners. The collection was started in the 1920s with two Victorian horse buses and an early motor bus. Since then it has grown to over 350,000 items ranging from horse-drawn trams, red double-decker buses and tube trains to posters, uniforms and early versions of the innovative London Underground map, designed by HC Beck.

The website *www.24hourmuseum.org.uk* provides a gazetteer of all UK museums and galleries, a magazine, search facilities and educational resources. The site provides live information on over 2,800 institutions.

SCRAN (*www.scran.ac.uk*), the Scottish Cultural Resources Access Network, is a history and culture site providing access to images, films, sounds and virtual reality records from museums, galleries, archives and media.

The Arts Council of Wales supports a network of galleries throughout Wales including Oriel Davies Gallery in Newtown and Ffotogallery, which is dedicated to the promotion of photographic art in Wales.

Architecture and design

The Royal Institute of British Architects (RIBA), with about 30,000 members, has been promoting and advancing architecture since receiving its Royal Charter in 1837. Architecture Week, held in June and organised by Arts Council England in partnership with RIBA, is a national celebration of contemporary architecture with events around the country.

In England, the Commission for Architecture and the Built Environment (CABE) is responsible for promoting high standards in the design of buildings and spaces between them. Its urban unit, CABE Space, was launched in May 2003 and is responsible for encouraging good quality parks and green spaces. In Scotland, a new body, Architecture and Design Scotland (ADS), will promote architecture from 2005, taking over and developing the work of the Royal Fine Art Commission for Scotland.

30 St Mary Axe

30 St Mary Axe, built on the site of the former Baltic Exchange, is the newest addition to London's skyline. At 180 metres, the 40-storey tower, affectionately called 'the Gherkin' because of its unusual curvilinear shape, is the second tallest in the City of London. It was designed by Norman Foster and partners, for Swiss Re. The building incorporates a range of innovative features, including use of natural ventilation and daylight to reduce energy consumption. It also boasts London's highest restaurant with a 360-degree panorama over the city and beyond.

Better use of design by business, the public sector and educational bodies, is supported and encouraged in the United Kingdom by the Design Council. The Council is funded by a grant from the Department of Trade and Industry.

Crafts

'Crafts' in the United Kingdom is an umbrella term covering a huge range of activities, from the making of ceramics and textiles to handmade toys and other personal and household products.

The Crafts Council is the national development agency for contemporary craft. It supports and showcases the best in craft practice across the United Kingdom, aiming to raise the profile of crafts to an international audience. It runs an international exhibition programme at its London gallery, organises the annual Chelsea Crafts Fair and in 2004 launched COLLECT, the art fair for contemporary objects, at the Victoria and Albert Museum. Craft Forum Wales supports craft business groups in Wales. In Scotland, the Scottish Arts Council has a Crafts department that promotes crafts and helps craftworkers. The Arts Council of Northern Ireland has played a leading role in establishing an inter-agency Craft Development Unit for Northern Ireland.

The Government's £13 million Culture Online programme uses new technologies to reach people who do not normally participate in arts and culture. Projects in the programme include World War Two Remembered, with Age Concern and the BBC, which enables older people to use computers and the Internet to record their memories; and SoundWorlds, which helps people to discover and create music.

The written word

In 2002 UK publishers issued over 125,000 separate titles (including new and revised editions). The UK book industry exported books worth £1.3 billion in 2003 (see Table 27.11 on page 427).

Among the leading trade organisations are the Publishers Association (PA), which has 200

Poems on the Underground
Since 1986 the journeys of millions of London commuters have been brightened by Poems on the Underground, displays of poetry on advertising posters in tube trains. *The Lake of Innisfree*, by WB Yeats, John Clare's *Emmonsails Heath in Winter* and AC Jacobs's *Spring* were some of the poems to feature in 2004. Other transport systems that have also introduced poem posters include those in New York, Barcelona, Moscow and Shanghai.

members; and the Booksellers Association, with 3,000 members. The PA, through its international division, promotes the export of British books. The Welsh Books Council promotes the book trade in Wales in both Welsh and English and the Gaelic Books Council supports the publication of books in Gaelic. Other trade organisations include the Scottish Publishers Association and the Independent Publishers Guild. Booktrust encourages reading and the promotion of books through an information service and a children's library.

Book awards

Gold and Platinum Book Awards were launched in September 2001. By March 2004 Platinum Awards (granted to those with sales of 1 million or over) had been awarded to:

Louis de Bernières *Captain Corelli's Mandolin*

Helen Fielding *Bridget Jones's Diary: A Novel*

Helen Fielding *Bridget Jones: Edge of Reason*

Frank McCourt *Angela's Ashes: A Memoir of a Childhood*

Tony Parsons *Man and Boy*

Dave Pelzer *A Child Called 'It'*

JK Rowling *Harry Potter and the Philosopher's Stone*

JK Rowling *Harry Potter and the Chamber of Secrets*

JK Rowling *Harry Potter and the Prisoner of Azkaban*

JK Rowling *Harry Potter and the Goblet of Fire*

JK Rowling *Harry Potter and the Order of the Phoenix*

Pamela Stephenson *Billy*

World Book Day is celebrated annually in the United Kingdom. The second World Book Day Online Festival was held in 2004, with virtual events on the Internet.

Libraries and archives

Local authorities in Great Britain and education and library boards in Northern Ireland have a duty to provide a free lending and reference library service. There are almost 5,000 public libraries in the United Kingdom. In Great Britain more than 34 million people (60 per cent of the population) were registered members of their local library in 2001/02, and 10 million people make a visit to a public library at least once every two weeks. Those who are not registered members can also use many of the local library facilities.

Many libraries have collections of CDs, records, audio- and video-cassettes, DVDs and musical scores for loan to the public, while a number also lend from collections of works of art, which may be originals or reproductions. Most libraries hold documents on local history, and all provide services for children.

About 361 million books and 42 million audio-visual items were borrowed from UK public libraries in 2002/03. Children's author Jacqueline Wilson, whose works include *The Story of Tracy Beaker*, became the most borrowed author in 2003, ending Catherine Cookson's 17-year reign. Of the 20 most-borrowed books at libraries, 16 were written by Jacqueline Wilson. Other authors popular with borrowers include Danielle Steel, Jack Higgins and crime novelist Agatha Christie.

Nearly all libraries have personal computers with Internet connections for public use. The People's Network is a £120 million programme funded through the National Lottery (see page 251) to set up information communications technology (ICT) learning centres in all UK public libraries. A further £50 million is enabling library material to be stored and accessed in digitised form.

Mobile libraries

Many people living in isolated rural communities rely on mobile libraries to borrow books and access information services. There are over 660 mobile libraries in the United Kingdom providing a whole range of services, including Internet access. Each mobile library serves hundreds of local communities on a weekly, fortnightly or monthly basis. It will carry about 3,500 items including books, talking books and videos.

The British Library

The British Library, the national library of the United Kingdom, is custodian of one of the most

important research collections in the world (150 million items spanning 3,000 years). The reading rooms, including the Business and Intellectual Property Centre, are open to those who need to see material (manuscripts, newspapers, journals, stamps, maps and CD-ROMs as well as books) that is not readily available elsewhere and to those whose work or studies require the facilities of the national library. The library's Internet catalogue has details of more than 10 million documents from the past 500 years, including books, journals and reports.

UK publishers are legally obliged to deposit a copy of each new publication in the British Library. The National Libraries of Scotland and of Wales, the Bodleian at Oxford and the Cambridge University Library (and the Library of Trinity College, Dublin) can also claim copies of all new British publications.

Archives

In 2003 the Public Record Office and the Historical Manuscripts Commission combined to form a new organisation, The National Archives. Its building in Kew houses the records of the superior courts of law of England and Wales and those of most government departments, as well as manuscripts of historical documents, such as the *Domesday Book* (1086) and autograph letters and documents of the sovereigns of England. The *Freedom of Information Act (FOI) 2000*, which comes into force in January 2005, gives people a general right of access to information held by public authorities. This means the 30-year period after which most public records were available for inspection will no longer apply. The National Archives has set up an FOI implementation team and is developing procedures for responding to requests for information when the Act is implemented.

The National Archives also provides information and advice about historical papers outside the public records, and advises private owners, grant-awarding bodies, record offices, local authorities and the Government on the acquisition and maintenance of manuscripts. It maintains the National Register of Archives (the central collecting point for information about British historical manuscripts) and the Manorial Documents Register, both of which are available to researchers.

The National Archives of Scotland in Edinburgh and the Public Record Office of Northern Ireland in Belfast serve a similar purpose.

Cultural opportunities

The National Curriculum in England and Wales specifies that all children at school should receive training in the arts, music and literature (see page 125). In Scotland, expressive arts are a key component of the pre-school and 5 to 14 curricular guidelines. In Northern Ireland, creative and expressive studies are part of the curriculum in all publicly-financed schools, while cultural heritage is one of six cross-curricular themes.

In England, Artsmark is a national award scheme run by Arts Council England and supported by the DCMS, the Department for Education and Skills (DfES), and other relevant agencies. An Artsmark is awarded to schools that show a demonstrable commitment to the full range of the arts – music, dance, drama, and art and design.

Other initiatives to encourage cultural excellence in schools include:

- a national grants scheme commencing in September 2004 to complement the Music and Dance (Aided Pupil) scheme to help exceptionally talented young musicians and dancers to benefit from the best specialist training locally;
- Youth Music, established in 1999 to provide music-making opportunities for children and young people up to the age of 18, concentrating on those who live in areas of social and economic need;
- the Scottish Executive's Youth Music Initiative, which provides access to free music tuition for all schoolchildren across Scotland;
- Creative Partnerships, a nationwide initiative managed by Arts Council England and sponsored by the DCMS with additional support from the DfES, which aims to give schoolchildren aged 5 to 18 and their teachers the opportunity to explore their creativity by working with professionals;
- The music manifesto, a unique coalition of prominent people from the music industry, the education world and leading music organisations, which was launched in July 2004 to promote music education; (see page 125); and
- Scotland's Schools Cultural Coordinators programme for heritage, arts and culture, which identifies ways of maximising the potential contribution of culture to young people's education.

In Northern Ireland, Creative Youth Partnership, a three-year scheme that aims to create and support arts programmes, activities and initiatives for children and young people aged from 3 to 25 years, was launched in 2004. Funding of £1.6 million has been provided by the Department of Culture, Arts and Leisure, the Arts Council of Northern Ireland and the Department of Education.

For those wishing to pursue a career in the arts, training available at post-16 tends to concentrate on particular specialisms. The DfES allocates £14 million a year in grants for drama and dance students for tuition and maintenance in England and Wales. Over 800 students a year cover their tuition fees in this way, on the same basis as other higher and further education pupils. All training must be at accredited institutions and towards recognised qualifications, with annual evaluation by the DfES to ensure that standards are maintained.

The Royal National Theatre's Education Programme encourages access to drama through youth theatre projects, touring productions, workshops, rehearsed readings, work in schools and a nationwide membership scheme.

Professional training in music is given at universities and conservatoires. Professional training for dancers and choreographers is provided mainly by specialist schools, while all government-funded dance companies provide dance workshops and education activities.

The National Film and Television School is financed jointly by the Government and the film, video and television industries. It offers postgraduate and short-course training for directors, editors, camera operators, animators and other specialists.

Most practical education in art and design is provided in the art colleges and fine and applied art departments of universities and in further education colleges and private art schools. Some of these institutions award degrees at postgraduate level. The Royal College of Art in London is the only wholly postgraduate school of art and design in the world. Art is also taught to degree level at the four Scottish art schools.

The Scottish Dewar Arts Awards support exceptionally talented young people who have limited financial resources. The awards aim to foster excellence in the arts and offer young people from less privileged backgrounds an opportunity to develop their talent to the highest level.

A new Creative & Cultural Industries Sector Skills Council is being established to coordinate UK training and professional development in this sector.

Administration

Many artists and performers engaged in cultural activity rely on subsidies and funding from the Government and other patrons of the arts. The Government also has a role in protecting the rights of authors through copyright legislation (see page 250); providing a regulatory framework for cultural activities in areas such as film classification; and encouraging greater public participation in the arts.

Public sector involvement in the arts is expressed in a number of ways:

- through the work of the four administrations directly responsible for culture in England, Wales, Scotland and Northern Ireland;

- through local government support for local initiatives; or

- through intermediate groups such as the arts councils, which act independently from the Government but are publicly funded and take on the role of patrons of the arts.

The policy responsibilities of the DCMS include the arts, public libraries and archives, museums and galleries and the built heritage in England, and UK-wide responsibilities for broadcasting, creative industries, and the National Lottery (see page 251).

DCMS objectives for the arts include:

- creating an efficient and competitive market by removing obstacles to growth and unnecessary regulation;

- broadening access to cultural events and to the built environment;

- raising the standards of cultural education and training; and

- ensuring that everyone has the opportunity to achieve excellence in areas of culture and to develop talent, innovation and good design.

Table 16.4 DCMS expenditure on selected areas of cultural life

			£ million
	1991/92	1996/97	2003/04[1]
Museums, galleries and libraries[2]	333	336	868
Historic buildings (England)	.	162	347
The arts (England)	212	195	334
Tourism (UK)	44	46	58

1 Data are estimated outturn.
2 Includes museums and galleries (England), libraries (UK) and museums' library archives (UK).
Source: Department for Culture, Media and Sport

Table 16.4 shows how DCMS expenditure is allocated.

The National Assembly for Wales has responsibility for the arts in Wales and has published a culture strategy, *Creative Future.* The Scottish Executive's National Cultural Strategy provides the basis for the administration of the arts in Scotland and a Cultural Commission has been set up to review the delivery and governance of culture. In Northern Ireland responsibility for the arts rests with the Department of Culture, Arts and Leisure.

Local authorities

Although policy is formulated by the UK Government (for England) and the devolved administrations, many initiatives and services are provided at a local level. Local authorities maintain many museums and art galleries, and the network of public libraries. They also provide grant aid for professional and amateur orchestras, theatres, and opera and dance companies.

Arts councils

Arts Council England, the Arts Council of Wales, the Scottish Arts Council and Arts Council of Northern Ireland are independent development bodies that distribute government grants and Lottery funding to a wide range of artists and arts organisations. This can be through open application schemes or by regular funding over a long term. The arts councils also commission research into the impact of the arts on society and develop forward strategies.

Arts Council England funds major national arts organisations in England, including the Royal Opera, the Royal Ballet, the Birmingham Royal Ballet, English National Opera, the Royal Shakespeare Company, the Royal National Theatre, the South Bank Centre and the main touring companies, such as Opera North and English National Ballet. Arts Council England also funds a wide range of community, experimental and culturally diverse work by individual artists and large and small companies. In 2003/04 it made 3,647 grants for the arts, ranging in value from £500 to £100,000.

The Arts Council of Wales supports major companies such as the *Theatr Genedlaethol Cymru* (Welsh Language National Theatre of Wales), Welsh National Opera and over 130 other organisations. The Scottish Arts Council supports more than 100 artistic organisations, as well as investing in individual artists. It supports festivals from Edinburgh to Orkney and the national companies: Scottish Ballet, the Royal Scottish National Opera, Scottish Opera and the Scottish Chamber Orchestra. During 2004, the Scottish Arts Council invested over £60 million in the arts. The Arts Council of Northern Ireland allocated more than £7.3 million to 129 arts organisations in 2004/05.

The Museums, Libraries and Archives Council

The MLA is the strategic agency working with, and on behalf of, museums, archives and libraries across the United Kingdom, and advising the Government on policy issues. It has regional agencies in each of the nine English regions and provides funding through these agencies. It has responsibility for a number of initiatives, including:

- the portable antiquities scheme, set up to record archaeological objects. Information from the scheme is now available online. Over 30,000 records offer an important research tool for both academics and the public;

- schemes for museum registration and designation of collections (see page 245); and

- the Acceptance in Lieu Scheme, whereby pre-eminent works of art may be accepted by the Government in settlement of tax and allocated to public galleries.

UK Film Council and *bfi*

The UK Film Council oversees the majority of public funding for film in the United Kingdom. It aims to stimulate a competitive, successful and vibrant film industry and to promote the widest possible enjoyment and understanding of cinema throughout the nations and regions of the United Kingdom. It aims to ensure that the economic, cultural and educational aspects of film are represented effectively at home and abroad. It also supports UK Film Council US (the former British Film Office in Los Angeles), which acts as its information and marketing satellite in the United States.

The UK Film Council supports new and innovative film-makers as well as the production of mainstream films, and training schemes to develop the UK film industry workforce of the future. It is the principal funder of the British Film Institute (*bfi*), which promotes audience appreciation of film through cultural and educational initiatives across the United Kingdom. The Council works with Sgrîn Cymru, Scottish Screen and the Northern Ireland Film and Television Commission to develop film across the United Kingdom. It also provides funding (£7.5 million a year) to the nine English regional screen agencies.

Cinema licensing and film classification

Local licensing conditions differ from area to area, but local authorities have a duty to prohibit children from viewing unsuitable films. In assessing films, authorities normally rely on the judgement of an independent non-statutory body, the British Board of Film Classification (BBFC), to which all items are submitted. The BBFC is also legally responsible for classifying videos. Responsibility for the policy on film and video classification lies with the DCMS.

Authors' copyright and performers' protection

Original literary, dramatic, musical or artistic works (including computer programs and databases), films, sound recordings, broadcasts and the typographical arrangement of published editions are automatically protected by copyright in the United Kingdom if they meet certain legal requirements. The copyright owner has rights against unauthorised reproduction, distribution, public performance, rental, broadcasting and adaptation of his or her work (including putting material on the Internet without permission). In most cases the author is the first owner of the copyright, and the term of copyright in literary, dramatic, musical and artistic works is for the life of the author and for 70 years thereafter. There are similar rules governing copyright on films. Sound recordings and broadcasts are protected for a period of 50 years.

National Lottery

The introduction of the National Lottery in 1994 significantly altered the funding of arts projects in the United Kingdom. During the early years of the Lottery, the focus of arts funding was on major capital projects. Some shift in emphasis occurred from 1998 onwards, with the allocation of funds to smaller, local projects. By June 2004 the Arts Councils across the United Kingdom had awarded over 32,000 grants worth a total of over £2.3 billion. The UK Film Council had awarded over 1,600 Lottery grants worth over £107 million.

In addition, the DCMS has established the National Endowment for Science, Technology and the Arts (NESTA), which uses the income generated by £250 million of Lottery funds to support projects and inventions in the arts and sciences.

Sponsorship

Total UK business investment in the arts in 2002/03 was £120 million, compared with £111 million in 2001/02. Arts & Business promotes and encourages partnerships between business and the arts. It has 400 business members and manages the Arts & Business New Partners Programme on behalf of Arts Council England and the DCMS.

Many arts organisations also benefit from the fund-raising activities and financial support of friends, groups and private individuals. For

example, theatre companies have traditionally relied on the support of 'angels', individual sponsors investing often quite small amounts of money to meet the costs of putting on a show, in the prospect of subsequently recouping their investment from box office proceeds.

Further reading

Department for Culture, Media and Sport: Annual Report 2004. Cm 6220. The Stationery Office, 2004.

Websites

Department for Culture, Media and Sport
www.culture.gov.uk

Arts Council England
www.artscouncil.org.uk

Arts Council of Wales
www.artswales.org.uk

Scottish Arts Council
www.scottisharts.org.uk

Arts Council of Northern Ireland
www.artscouncil-ni.org

The National Archives
www.nationalarchives.gov.uk

Department of Culture, Arts and Leisure (Northern Ireland):
www.dcalni.gov.uk

Museums and Galleries of Northern Ireland
www.magni.org.uk

WWW.

17 Communications and the media

Communications are moving into the digital age. Technology is changing the way people in the United Kingdom work, spend their leisure time, access information and communicate with each other. The number of UK households using new forms of communication has increased rapidly in recent years (Figure 17.1). Ownership of mobile phones has grown from 17 per cent of households in 1996/97 to 85 per cent in February 2004.

With the advent of digital television and radio, alongside the continuing expansion of cable and satellite television, there has been a proliferation of new public service and independent channels. Since December 2003 the Office of Communications, Ofcom, has been responsible for regulating TV and radio (apart from the BBC) as well as telecommunications and wireless communications (see page 262), but the press remains self-regulated. Both broadcast and non-broadcast media (including the press) are major vehicles for advertising (see page 265).

Telecommunications

Turnover of the telecommunications services sector in Great Britain grew by 6 per cent in 2003 to £50.8 billion.

Telephone services

A total of 396 billion minutes of telephone calls were made from fixed and mobile links in 2003 (Table 17.2). Calls from fixed phones increased by 2 per cent and accounted for 85 per cent of all calls in 2003, down from 86 per cent in 2002. Calls from mobile phones grew by 13 per cent to 59 billion minutes in 2003.

The telephone is one of the most common consumer durable goods in the home. At the end of 2003, there were just under 35 million fixed lines in the United Kingdom, although this figure has been falling over the past few years with the increased popularity of mobile phones.

British Telecommunications (BT) is the biggest fixed-line UK operator with over 71 per cent of revenue market share although competitors have increased their share of the market, especially the business market. BT runs one of the world's largest public telecommunications networks, with around 29 million exchange lines. BT's group turnover in the year to March 2004 was £18.5 billion. The two main cable operators are ntl and Telewest, with 2.5 million and 2.1 million telephony lines respectively.

A variety of new telecommunications services have emerged. For example, many companies offer their

Figure 17.1 Households with selected durable goods, UK

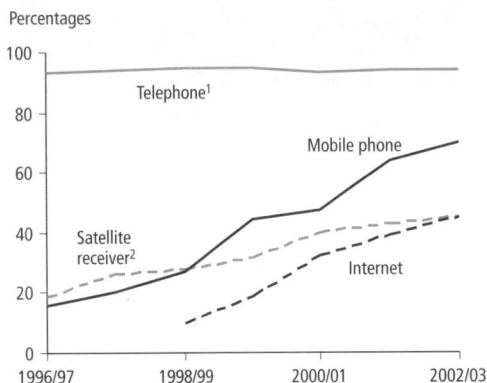

Percentages

1 Includes both fixed-line and mobile phones.
2 Includes digital and cable receivers.
Source: Family Expenditure Survey and Expenditure and Food Survey, Office for National Statistics

Table 17.2 Telephone call minutes, 2003, UK

	Call minutes (billion)	Percentage of all calls
Fixed link		
Local calls	74.2	18.8
National calls	46.4	11.7
International calls	6.2	1.6
Calls to mobile phones	15.6	3.9
Other calls[1]	194.1	49.1
All calls[2]	336.6	85.1
Cellular services		
UK calls	56.9	14.4
Outgoing international calls	0.8	0.2
Calls while abroad	1.3	0.3
All calls	59.0	14.9
Total	**395.6**	**100**

1 Other calls include number translation services, premium rate calls, directory enquiries, operator calls, the speaking clock, public payphones and calls to Internet Service Providers (ISPs).
2 Figures may include a small amount of double counting, as in some instances calls supplied by an operator to a reseller may be counted by both operator and reseller.
Source: Ofcom

customers information services using 0845 and 0800 telephone numbers.

Mobile telephones

At the end of March 2004 there were 54.7 million active mobile phone customers in the United Kingdom, compared with just under 50 million a year earlier. The five network suppliers are Orange (part of France Telecom), O$_2$, Vodafone, T-Mobile (a subsidiary of Deutsche Telekom) and 3, which launched its services in 2003. There are also around 50 independent service providers. In 2003, Vodafone had the largest market share in terms of total retail revenue at 32 per cent.

Messaging services such as text messaging (SMS) and picture messaging (MMS) are growing in popularity. The networks handled 21.3 billion messages in 2003, a 23 per cent increase on 2002. Text and picture messaging accounted for between 14 and 19 per cent of each network's retail revenue.

BT and Cable and Wireless have been working with Ofcom to develop new technology that can trace the location of people making emergency calls on mobile phones. In February 2004, the

London Ambulance Service became the first UK organisation to adopt the new technology. The Service receives about 750 calls from mobile phones each day, around 25 per cent of total calls.

Regulation

Ofcom (see page 262) is responsible for promoting competition and choice, and protecting the interests of consumers.

The *Communications Act 2003* represents a substantial move towards complete deregulation of the telecommunications industry, by replacing the previous licence-based system in the United Kingdom with a 'general conditions of entitlement' regime. The Act also provides for the implementation of a series of EU directives that together make up the new regulatory framework for European electronic communications. The directives emphasise, among other things, lighter regulation and greater consistency across Europe.

In September 2003, Ofcom's predecessor Oftel issued a Good Practice Guide for Service Delivery for Disabled and Elderly Customers in the United Kingdom. The guide aims to ensure that mobile product and service providers are meeting the needs of these customers, for example by producing handsets that are compatible with hearing aids or that are large enough to be gripped easily.

The Internet

By April 2004, 53 per cent of UK households had Internet access at home, compared with 10 per cent in 1998/99.

A growing number of homes and businesses are using high-speed broadband connections. According to Ofcom, there were nearly 4.5 million such connections in the United Kingdom by the end of June 2004, compared with around 2.2 million at the end of June 2003. Over 40,000 new connections were being made each week by the end of December 2003.

The National Statistics Omnibus Survey found that 58 per cent of adults in Great Britain had used the Internet in a three month period prior to being interviewed between April 2003 and February 2004. Table 17.3 shows the most common reasons given by those who used the Internet – these include email and finding information about goods or services. Among those

Table 17.3 Adults who have accessed the Internet,[1] April 2003 to February 2004, Great Britain

Percentages

Communication	
Using email	84
Telephoning over the Internet/video conferencing	6
Using chat rooms or sites	21
Information search and online services	
Finding information about goods or services	81
Finding information about travel and accommodation	69
Activities for school, college or university	28
Other educational activities	25
Reading or downloading online news	34
Playing or downloading music	25
Downloading other software	23
Listening to web radio	15
Playing or downloading games	13
Purchasing goods, services and banking	
Buying or ordering goods, tickets or services	50
Internet banking	36
Other financial services	8
Others	
General browsing or surfing	68
Activities for current or future job	35
Selling goods or services	7

1 Data are for adults who had accessed the Internet in the three
　months before being interviewed.
Source: Omnibus Survey, Office for National Statistics

using the Internet for buying or ordering goods, tickets and services for personal or private use in the 12 months prior to interview, the most popular purchases were for travel, accommodation or holidays (52 per cent), tickets for events (39 per cent), music or CDs (38 per cent), and books, magazines, e-learning or training material (37 per cent).

Computers continue to be the preferred method for accessing the Internet in Great Britain (99 per cent). However, between April 2003 and February 2004, 11 per cent of adults who had used the Internet in the three months prior to interview had done so via a mobile phone.

Postal services

The Post Office was founded in 1635. It pioneered mail services and was the first service in the world to introduce adhesive postage stamps as proof of advance payment for mail. Under the provisions of the *Postal Services Act 2000*, the Post Office ceased to be a statutory corporation and its property, rights and liabilities now belong to Royal Mail Holdings plc, a company wholly owned by the Crown. It has an operating subsidiary, Royal Mail Group plc. Royal Mail Group serves its UK customers through two main operations – Royal Mail and Parcelforce Worldwide – and a subsidiary company, Post Office Ltd, and employs around 200,000 people.

Competition and regulation

The Postal Services Commission, known as Postcomm, is responsible for licensing postal operators throughout the United Kingdom, including Royal Mail. Every company that delivers letters weighing up to 100 grams needs a licence from Postcomm. It also regulates the price and quality of services provided by Royal Mail.

In January 2003 Postcomm opened the market for some business mail services. The first category opened to competition – bulk mail above 4,000 items per mailing from a single user at a single site in a similar format – was worth about £1.7 billion in its first year, representing about 30 per cent of the UK letter market by value. Postcomm is reviewing options for the next stage of competition.

By 1 April 2004 Postcomm had awarded long-term licences (valid for a minimum of seven years) to six postal operators in addition to Royal Mail. Four other companies held interim licences, valid for a minimum of 12 months.

Since January 2004 domestic customers have been entitled to compensation when mail is delayed for three days or more. There is a separate scheme for bulk business users.

Royal Mail operations

Royal Mail delivers to all 27 million UK addresses. It missed its quality of service targets for 2003/04, delivering 90.1 per cent of first-class mail by the next working day against a target of 92.5 per cent. Deliveries were seriously affected by industrial action in autumn 2003 and a fire at one of its major mail centres.

The volume of mail has continued to grow despite competition from other forms of communication, increasing by 5 per cent between 2000/01 and 2003/04. Mail is collected from over 113,000 post boxes across the United Kingdom, and from Post Office branches and large postal users. The UK postcode system allows mechanised sorting down to part of a street on a delivery round and, in some cases, to individual addresses.

Parcelforce Worldwide provides a range of delivery services throughout the United Kingdom, handling 40 million items in 2003/04. As well as delivering to all UK addresses, it offers a range of services to 239 countries and territories worldwide.

At July 2004, there were around 16,000 Post Office branches in the United Kingdom, of which some 560 were directly run by Post Office Ltd. The rest are owned by the people who run them, including franchisees and subpostmasters and subpostmistresses. Post Office branches handle a wide range of transactions, with a total turnover of £977 million in 2003/04. They act as agents for Royal Mail and Parcelforce Worldwide, government departments and local authorities, and also provide banking services. Post Office branches offer access to current accounts for seven UK banks, and to basic bank accounts for a further 17, as well as providing access to National Savings and Investments (see page 463). Post Office Ltd is developing its own provision of personal banking services. The first product, an unsecured personal loan, was introduced in March 2004. Post Office Ltd also provides the largest foreign exchange services in the United Kingdom.

About 29 million customers visit a Post Office branch each week. The number of people using the Post Office to collect benefit payments is falling, due to the Government's programme to pay benefits directly into bank, building society or Post Office accounts. People can still receive their benefits at the Post Office by opening a Post Office card account.

In October 2002, parliamentary approval was given for Government funding to assist the Post Office in a programme involving the closure of up to 3,000 urban Post Office branches across the United Kingdom. The aim of the programme is to create a more streamlined network of viable branches, while ensuring that over 95 per cent of the urban population still lives within one mile of a Post Office branch. By July 2004, 1,273 branches had been closed. Postwatch, the postal industry's independent watchdog, ensures that there is full public consultation on every proposed closure, and actively opposes closures where it feels they will restrict access to postal services or affect people in deprived areas. In addition, the Government is providing £450 million over three years to support the rural Post Office network.

The Travelling Post Office makes its final journey

On 9 January 2004, the Travelling Post Office (TPO) completed its final journey. These overnight mail trains – where the post was sorted en route – had been running since 1838. However, modern automated equipment can sort 30,000 letters an hour, compared with 3,000 an hour on the TPO. Mail is now transported by air and road only, although Royal Mail has not ruled out using trains again. The new arrangements are expected to save Royal Mail an estimated £9 million a year.

Television

Terrestrial television

There are five public service broadcasters in the United Kingdom: the BBC (British Broadcasting Corporation), ITV1, Channel 4, Five, and S4C (*Sianel Pedwar Cymru*), which broadcasts Welsh-language programmes. They each have a statutory public service remit that governs the minimum level of different types of programming they should provide. The broadcasting regulator Ofcom is conducting a review to find out how far the public service broadcasters are fulfilling their remit. The first phase of the review, published in April 2004, states that the broadcasters are only partly fulfilling the requirements of the *Communications Act 2003*. Ofcom's findings suggest that there is too much reliance on programmes with obvious popular appeal, and that the audience share for public service broadcasters is falling. Ofcom has invited further consultation with groups including viewers. The results will be fed into the BBC's Charter review process (see page 256).

Local television services began in 1998. There are 18 local service licences, which make use of spare frequencies as and when they are available.

The BBC

The BBC was formed in October 1922 by a group of leading wireless manufacturers. By 1925, it was broadcasting radio programmes to most of the United Kingdom. In its early days, the BBC's output concentrated on plays, concerts, talks and variety programmes. News could only be broadcast after 7.00 pm, to avoid affecting newspaper sales. In 1936, the BBC launched the world's first regular high-definition television service from Alexandra Palace in north London.

The BBC now broadcasts nearly 55,000 hours of television each year to national and regional audiences on its analogue and digital channels. It provides two national networks financed mainly by a TV licence fee – in 2004, a colour licence cost £121.00 and a black and white licence £40.50. BBC One is a mainstream channel, broadcasting popular programmes across a range of genres including documentaries and current affairs, features, drama and light entertainment, sport, religion and children's programmes. BBC Two

The Hutton report

In May 2003 a news item was aired on BBC Radio 4's *Today* programme about the evidence relating to Iraq's alleged weapons of mass destruction. In July 2003, Dr David Kelly, a government weapons inspector – and the alleged source of the *Today* story – committed suicide. Lord Hutton conducted an inquiry into the circumstances leading to Dr Kelly's death. His report, published in January 2004, criticised the reporting of the BBC journalist who made the allegations against the Government, saying that they were 'unfounded'. The report also criticised BBC managers for failing to check the details of the story as soon as the Government objected to the allegations. This led to the resignation of the BBC's Chairman and its Director-General. In a statement, the BBC said that it believed it must re-state its core editorial values, look hard at issues of accountability and transparency, and work to sustain editorial quality across the full range of its programmes. A new Chairman was appointed in April and new Director-General in May 2004.

40 years of BBC Two

BBC Two celebrated its 40th birthday on 20 April 2004. It was originally launched at least partly to encourage people to buy new television sets in order to receive its 625-line transmission – a technological advance which paved the way for colour television. A special programme broadcast on the anniversary featured clips from classic BBC Two shows including *Monty Python's Flying Circus* from the late 1960s, David Attenborough's natural history programme *Life on Earth* from 1979 and award-winning comedy *The Office* from 2001 (see also chapter 16).

aims for more innovation and originality in its programming, often catering for specialist audience interests. For details of BBC digital television channels, see page 258.

Network programmes are made at, or acquired through, Television Centre in London and six bases throughout the United Kingdom (Belfast, Birmingham, Bristol, Cardiff, Glasgow, and Manchester). Programmes are also commissioned from independent producers, and the BBC must ensure that at least 25 per cent of its original programming comes from the independent sector. In 2003/04, the BBC achieved this target with 29 per cent of qualifying programmes being independent productions.

Education is a central component of the BBC's public service commitment. A range of programmes is broadcast for primary and secondary schools, further education colleges and the Open University (see page 131). There are also educational programmes for people learning from home, or doing evening classes. Books, pamphlets, computer software, and audio and video material supplement the programmes.

The BBC operates under a Royal Charter. The Charter and Agreement were granted in 1996 and will expire in 2006. Before the Charter is renewed, the Department for Culture, Media and Sport (DCMS) is carrying out a detailed review of the BBC and its work, including its digital and on-line services, and plans to publish a Green Paper in late 2004 which will be sent out for consultation. This will be followed by a White Paper setting out the Department's recommendations on the BBC's future.

24 February 2004 The first exhibition of UK art since the Islamic revolution of 1979 opens at the Tehran Museum of Contemporary Art in Iran. The exhibition includes works by Damien Hirst, Anish Kapoor and Gilbert and George. *(Above)* A selection of bronze works by Barbara Hepworth and Henry Moore with Barbara Hepworth's *Spring* in the foreground.

Above: Red on Green by Scottish-born artist Anya Gallaccio. This ephemeral piece was made on site, from 1,000 red roses grown in Delfuz on the Iran-Iraq border. The work was created to change through the course of the exhibition and here it is seen on day three. By the end of the exhibition all the roses had decayed and turned brown.

26 February 2004 HRH The Prince of Wales at Brent Town Hall attending the first citizenship ceremony in the United Kingdom, when 16 adults and 3 children acquired British citizenship. At the ceremonies new citizens take the traditional oath of allegiance to The Queen and pledge to uphold UK democratic values.

3 March 2004 *Below:* Work starts on dismantling Isambard Brunel's *(left)* first iron bridge over the Grand Union Canal at Paddington. The bridge, which locked together like a jigsaw without needing bolts, was found inside a brick bridge that was being demolished. It will be reconstructed, possibly over the canal near its original site.

8 March 2004 Official opening of the Graduate Centre, designed by Daniel Libeskind, at the London Metropolitan University in Holloway Road. The building was inspired by the Orion constellation and is entirely clad with stainless steel panels with large geometrical cuts as windows.

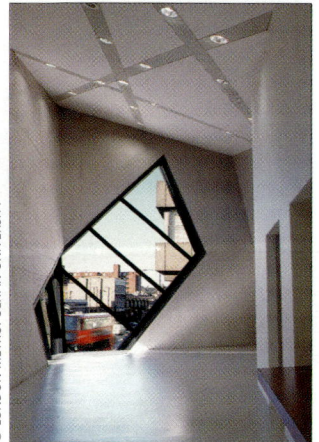

10 March 2004 200th anniversary of the Royal Horticultural Society, the leading gardening charity in the United Kingdom, founded to promote excellence in the art, science and practice of horticulture.

Above: RHS Garden at Hyde Hall, Essex, one of the driest areas of the United Kingdom.

Left: Springtime in the Jubilee Arboretum at Wisley, Surrey, the main base of the RHS. To complement the spring-flowering trees, substantial collections of *Narcissus* have been planted.

Below left: RHS Garden at Rosemoor, Devon, which includes a formal garden, extensive herbaceous borders, herb and cottage gardens, and extensive stream and lakeside plantings.

Below right: Walkway between different parts of the garden at Wisley.

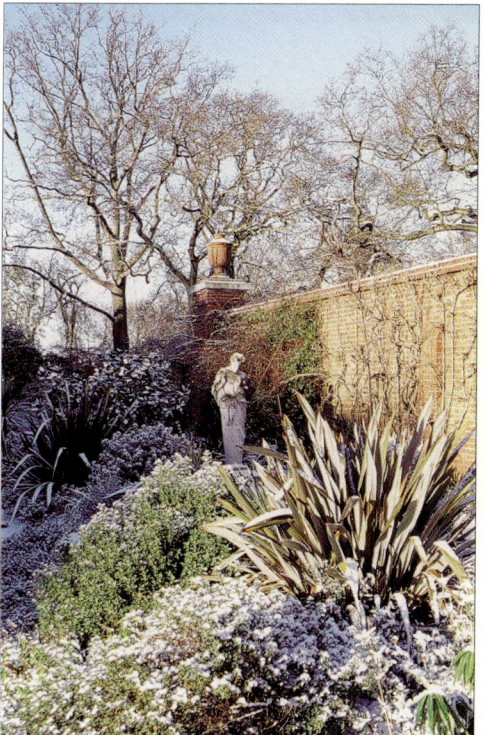

18–28 March 2004 Wrexham Science Festival, with more than 150 events and displays, aims to make science exciting and relevant to people of all ages.

Left: Professor John Brown, Astronomer Royal for Scotland, holds an evening of 'magiscience' entitled *Black Holes and White Rabbits*.

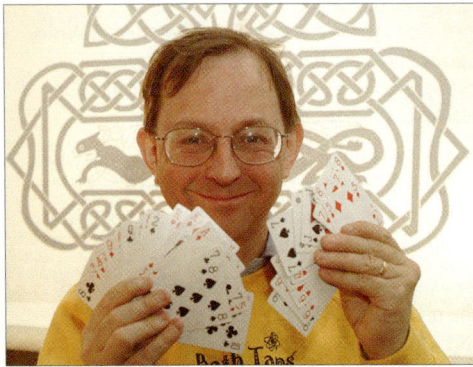

Centre: Maths for the Terrified – Professor Chris Budd from the Royal Institution demonstrates that maths need not be scary and can be fun.

22 March 2004 250th anniversary of the Royal Society of Arts, founded by painter and social activist William Shipley *(above)*. The RSA was set up *'to embolden enterprise, enlarge science, refine arts, improve manufactures and extend commerce'*.

The first meeting of the RSA was held in Rawthmell's coffee house in Covent Garden. The RSA moved to its current premises in the Adelphi, London *(above)* in 1774. The building was specially designed for the Society by Robert Adam.

The ITV network

ITV began broadcasting in the United Kingdom in September 1955. Today, the ITV network's analogue services are broadcast on Channel 3 as ITV1. This is a federation of regionally based commercial TV companies, which are licensed to supply programmes in the 14 independent geographical television regions. In February 2004 Carlton Communications and Granada plc – two of the major regional licence-holders – merged to form ITV plc, which now owns most of the regional ITV licences. There are three other ITV broadcasting companies: SMG, which runs Scottish TV and Grampian; Ulster TV; and Channel TV. Until October 2003, there were two licences for London, one for weekdays and the other for the weekend. The ITV merger means that a single company is now responsible for delivering all regional services in the capital for the first time in ITV's history. A separate company, GMTV, provides a national breakfast-time service, transmitted on the ITV network.

All Channel 3 licences were renewed for a further ten-year period from 1999, 2000 and 2001. Under the *Communications Act 2003*, Channel 3 licensees, Channel 4 and Channel 5 will also be offered new digital licences. These will be valid until the end of December 2014 or 18 months after the switchover from analogue to digital (see page 259), whichever is later. The licences will be issued before the end of 2004, following consultation.

ITV1 is a mainstream channel that aims to attract the widest possible audience. Programmes are broadcast 24 hours a day throughout the country. Independent Television News (ITN) provides a shared national and international news service for the ITV network. From February 2004, ITV's national, international and regional news services came together as a single division to enable a more effective use of resources.

ITV1 companies are obliged to operate a national programme network. The ITV network centre, which is owned by the companies, independently commissions and schedules programmes. ITV1 also provides 27 dedicated regional and sub-regional services for the 14 independent regions.

Operating on a commercial basis, licensees derive most of their income from selling advertising time. Their financial resources and programme production vary considerably, depending largely on the population of the areas in which they operate.

Newspaper groups can acquire a controlling interest in ITV companies, although measures are in force to deter any undue concentrations of media ownership (see page 264).

Channel 4 and S4C

Channel 4 provides a national 24-hour television service. It is a statutory corporation, licensed and regulated by Ofcom, and funded by selling its own advertising time. Its remit is to provide programming that demonstrates innovation, experiment and creativity in form and content; appeals to the tastes and interests of a culturally diverse society; includes a significant number of educational programmes; and exhibits a distinctive character. Channel 4 does not make programmes but commissions them from independent producers or acquires them from other programme providers, including a number from overseas. The Channel 4 Group also runs a number of commercial businesses, including digital channels E4 and FilmFour, which are managed via a wholly owned subsidiary, 4Ventures.

In Wales the fourth analogue channel is allocated to S4C, which is regulated by the Welsh Fourth Channel Authority and funded by an annual grant from the Treasury and advertising revenue. Members of the Welsh Authority are appointed by the UK Government. S4C must ensure that a significant proportion of programming – the majority aired between 6.00 pm and 10.00 pm – is in Welsh. At other times it transmits Channel 4 programmes.

An independent review of S4C, requested by the Authority, was published in July 2004. The document recommends that S4C:

- reviews its programme distribution operations;
- agrees a formula with the BBC for the supply of programmes and other services; and
- plays a more integral role in the developing national cultural and economic agendas in Wales.

Other recommendations cover S4C's digital services.

Five

The newest UK analogue terrestrial channel went on air in 1997, its ten-year licence having been awarded by competitive tender to Channel 5 Broadcasting Ltd. Five reaches over 80 per cent of the population and is financed by advertising revenue. It broadcasts a range of programmes, including current affairs, children's programmes, films, drama, and sport. It also produces 17 per cent of UK regional TV programmes.

Text services

Teletext is a text-based data service, broadcast on Channels 1 to 5 using the spare signal capacity in analogue terrestrial television services. Most domestic television sets can decode teletext signals, which are displayed as text and simple graphics. Teletext services include regularly updated information on a variety of subjects, including news, sport, travel, weather and entertainment. Between January and September 2003, teletext services attracted 18 million viewers a week. Teletext is now also available on digital TV, the Internet and mobile phones.

The BBC broadcasts its 'Ceefax' teletext service within the BBC One and Two signals. For ITV1, Channel 4 and Five, the teletext service is provided under ten-year broadcasting licences, granted by

Reality TV

The past few years have seen an increase in the number of 'reality' TV programmes shown in the United Kingdom. These include 'fly-on-the-wall' documentaries, capturing real-life events as they unfold, and 'constructed documentaries' where non-actors are filmed interacting with each other in artificial environments. Viewing figures for 'factual entertainment' programmes rose by 20 per cent between 1998 and 2002.

In 2003, the most successful reality TV shows were *I'm a Celebrity – Get Me Out of Here!* and *Pop Idol.* The final of the third series of *I'm a Celebrity* … attracted an average of 14.1 million viewers – an audience share of 54.5 per cent. The final of *Pop Idol* was watched by 11.1 million people. Other popular shows include *Fame Academy,* where young people are filmed while being coached to become singers and musicians. Around 4.5 million people voted in the 2003 *Fame Academy* final.

Ofcom (see page 262). All terrestrial channels provide subtitles via teletext for people with hearing difficulties on most of their programmes.

Digital television

By the end of March 2004 nearly 13.1 million, or 53 per cent, of UK households were accessing digital television via either terrestrial or satellite transmitters.

Digital technology provides a more efficient way of delivering television. Computer technology is used to convert sound and pictures into a digital format and to compress them. This means that several television channels can be carried in the same amount of space as analogue signals use to carry one channel. Digital signals can be received by standard aerials, satellite dishes or through cable networks, but have to be decoded and turned back into sound and pictures using a separate set-top box or a decoder built into the television.

A single frequency carrying the signals of several digital services is called a multiplex. There are six terrestrial multiplexes capable of supporting services in the United Kingdom. One is reserved for and operated by the BBC, and the other five are licensed by Ofcom. One of these is reserved for Channel 3, Channel 4 and public teletext services, and another for Five and S4C. The other three multiplexes are licensed to the BBC and Crown Castle International.

Most UK digital terrestrial television (DTT) services are free-to-view but there are also a few pay services, operated by Top Up TV. Freeview, marketed by DTV Services Ltd and run by its three shareholders – the BBC, Crown Castle International and British Sky Broadcasting (BSkyB), was launched in October 2002 as an umbrella brand for UK DTT services, and offers about 30 TV channels and 21 radio channels, along with interactive services. By the end of March 2004, 3.5 million households were receiving Freeview.

All services from the public service broadcasters that are available on analogue terrestrial are also available on DTT. Other services available on DTT include four news channels; BBC Parliament (coverage of proceedings in the House of Commons, House of Lords, the Parliament in Scotland and the Assemblies in Wales and Northern Ireland); BBC Three (new entertainment, comedy, contemporary drama and music); BBC Four (in-depth coverage of culture, the arts, science, history, business and current affairs); two daytime children's channels from the BBC; ITV2 (an additional service from the ITV network); and S4C2 (an additional service from S4C, which provides over 80 hours of programmes in Welsh each week). There are also several shopping and entertainment channels.

The Government is looking at ways to exploit the potential of digital TV. In December 2003, the Cabinet Office published a policy framework aimed at encouraging government departments to consider the benefits of delivering public services via digital television. The Learning and Skills Development Agency has published a report that sets out to raise awareness and stimulate debate on interactive digital TV as a learning medium.

Switching to digital

The Government intends eventually to stop the transmission of analogue terrestrial television. It believes that the switchover to digital television could start as early as 2007, and be completed by 2012. The Digital Television Project is a partnership between the Government,

Interactive digital TV

Digital TV offers three types of interactive service: stand-alone information; transactional services (like shopping, banking and email); and enhanced programming, where viewers can access additional audio and video features. These services can be delivered either through TV channels or as video on demand, where viewers have complete freedom to decide what is transmitted to them and when. For video on demand, viewers need a dedicated broadband digital connection to their TV.

BBCi, the BBC's interactive TV service, offers continuous news updates and enhanced programming features such as quizzes, polls, and additional audio and video features. For example, viewers watching the BBC's coverage of the FA Cup Final in May 2004 could switch between the live football match, earlier highlights, statistics, player profiles and news.

broadcasters, industry, consumer and other groups. The Project's action plan aims to enable ministers to decide how and when to implement digital switchover and help prepare a subsequent implementation project. The Project aims to complete its work by the end of 2004.

Non-terrestrial television

There are two main non-terrestrial television delivery systems (platforms) in the United Kingdom – cable and digital satellite television. These are funded mainly by subscription income. Both platforms offer packages of subscription-only television services, including some premium services such as film and sports channels and pay-per-view events. Both cable and satellite are required to carry the public service channels at no additional cost to the viewer.

On both platforms, the selection of channels available via subscription is broadly similar, but there are some services that are unique to each platform. Available services include Eurosport, the Cartoon Network, UKTV channels (programmes from TV archives), E4 (additional services from Channel 4) and the Discovery Channel (science and nature documentaries).

Foreign language services are also provided. Some are designed for minority ethnic groups within the United Kingdom, while others aimed primarily at audiences in other countries. Viewers in the United Kingdom can similarly receive a variety of television services from other European countries.

Cable television

Cable television services are delivered to consumers via underground networks of cables. The signals are decoded using a converter box, which is rented from the cable provider. Cable customers can also access telephone services and, in the case of digital cable, broadband Internet services.

By June 2004 the cable network passed around 12.5 million UK homes, mostly in urban and suburban areas. The two main cable providers are ntl and Telewest, and both networks are in the process of converting from analogue to digital. By June 2004, there were 3.4 million cable television subscribers, with digital cable accounting for 2.5 million of these.

Analogue cable television systems can carry around 65 television services, as well as a range of telecommunications services. Digital cable television can carry around 200 services (TV and radio), plus interactive services.

Digital satellite

Referred to as 'direct to home', satellite television signals are received through a specially designed antenna (or 'dish') mounted on the outside of a building, and are decoded using either a set-top box or an integrated digital television.

Most satellite television in the United Kingdom is provided by BSkyB, which had just over 7 million subscribers at the end of June 2004. Sky Television was launched in 1989 as an analogue-only service, and began simultaneous digital broadcasting in 1998. In October 2001 the analogue signal was switched off and the service renamed Sky Digital, the first digital-only TV platform in the United Kingdom. It has been fully interactive since 1999.

In June 2004, Sky Digital offered over 420 TV and radio services. Most of the more popular channels are accessible only by subscription to BSkyB, but there is also a wide variety of free-to-view channels. By the end of 2004, BSkyB will be introducing a package of free-to-view television services which viewers will be able to receive without a subscription.

Radio

Radio is popular in the United Kingdom, with 90 per cent of the adult population listening each week in the quarter to June 2004. News, talk and music are the main output of radio stations.

The BBC has five national radio networks, which together transmit all types of music, news, current affairs, drama, education, sport, comedy and a range of features programmes. There are also 40 BBC local radio services covering England and the Channel Islands, and national radio services in Wales, Scotland, and Northern Ireland, including Welsh and Gaelic language stations. At the end of June 2004, BBC radio had a 53 per cent share of the total UK radio audience (Table 17.4).

There were 274 independent local radio (ILR) services by the end of July 2004, providing music, local news and information, sport, education and

Table 17.4 Share of radio listening by station, spring 2004, UK

Percentage of listening hours

BBC	
BBC Radio 1	8.3
BBC Radio 2	16.2
BBC Radio 3	1.1
BBC Radio 4	11.0
BBC Radio Five Live	4.5
BBC World Service	0.6
BBC local/regional	10.9
All BBC	53.1
Commercial	
Classic FM	4.5
talkSPORT (Talk radio)	1.8
Virgin radio (AM only)	1.6
All national commercial	10.1
All local commercial	34.9
All commercial	45.0
Other listening[1]	1.9

1 Other listening includes any UK station that does not subscribe to RAJAR as well as non-UK and private radio stations.
Source: Radio Authority Joint Audience Research/RSL

consumer advice. The first (and only) national commercial digital radio multiplex started in 1999 (see page 261).

BBC network radio

BBC network radio, broadcasting to the whole of the United Kingdom, transmits nearly 44,000 hours of programmes each year on its five networks:

- Radio 1, a contemporary music station that also provides news and information, serving a young target audience;

- Radio 2, offering a wide range of popular and specialist music, news, information and entertainment for a mainstream audience;

- Radio 3, covering classical music and jazz, drama, documentaries and discussion;

- Radio 4, offering news and current affairs coverage, complemented by drama, science, the arts, religion, natural history, medicine, finance, comedy and gardening features; it also carries parliamentary coverage and cricket on its longwave frequency, and broadcasts BBC World Service programmes overnight; and

- Five Live, broadcasting news, current affairs and extensive sports coverage.

BBC World Service

The BBC World Service has been broadcasting for over 70 years. It broadcasts in 43 languages (including English) and had an estimated global weekly audience of 146 million listeners in June 2004. As well as news, programmes cover the arts, drama, business, documentaries, religion, science and technology and sport.

While maintaining shortwave broadcasts for mass audiences, the BBC World Service is making programmes widely available on FM frequencies and delivering services in major languages through digital broadcasting and on the Internet.

BBC Monitoring, the international media monitoring arm of the BBC World Service, monitors and translates news, information and comment from more than 3,000 radio, TV, press, Internet and news agency sources around the world. Users of the service include government departments, journalists, academics and businesses.

Independent national radio

There were three independent national radio services operating in 2004, licensed and monitored by Ofcom (see page 262):

- Classic FM, which broadcasts mainly classical music, together with news and information;
- Virgin 1215, which plays rock and pop music (and is supplemented by a separate Virgin station that operates under a local London licence and broadcasts on an FM frequency); and
- talkSPORT, a speech-based service.

Independent local radio

Independent local radio (ILR) stations broadcast a wide range of programmes and news of local interest, as well as music and entertainment, traffic reports and advertising. There are also stations serving minority ethnic communities. Ofcom awards independent local radio licences in an open competition. The success of local licence applications is determined by the extent to which applicants would broaden the range of radio

services available in the area, cater for the tastes and interests of people in the area, and demonstrate evidence of local demand or support, and have the necessary resources to maintain the service for the 12-year licence period.

Digital radio

Around 44 million people in the United Kingdom live in areas where national digital radio services are available. Ofcom has awarded one national commercial multiplex licence carrying eight programme services. It has also awarded licences for 44 local digital multiplexes, which carry about 300 commercial radio services between them.

As with digital TV, digital radio allows more stations to be broadcast within a similar amount of radio spectrum. Listeners to digital radio can hear analogue stations, plus a wide range of 'digital only' services including more stations and additional text information.

40 years of pirate radio

The year 2004 marks the 40th anniversary of pirate radio stations – stations that broadcast without a licence. Radio Caroline, which began transmitting from a boat off the coast of Essex in spring 1964, was the first UK offshore station. Caroline built up an audience of 8 million listeners, and launched the careers of broadcasters such as John Peel and Tony Blackburn. Radio Caroline still exists as a digital and satellite station.

Pirate stations can interfere with legal broadcasts and disrupt vital safety communications. Penalties under the *Wireless Telegraphy Act 1949* include fines, seizure of all equipment and even imprisonment. In 2003, the Radiocommunications Agency prosecuted 71 pirate broadcasters.

At the end of June 2004, 1.7 million listeners in the United Kingdom were tuning into the BBC's digital radio stations. The stations are:

- 1Xtra, broadcasting contemporary black music for a young audience;
- Radios 1–4, Five Live and the BBC World Service;

- 6 Music, broadcasting contemporary and classic pop and rock music;

- Five Live Sports Extra;

- BBC Asian Network, a station for the Asian communities in the United Kingdom; and

- BBC7, broadcasting classic and new comedy, drama and children's programmes.

Regulation of broadcast media

In December 2003, under the provisions of the *Communications Act 2003*, Ofcom became the single regulator for broadcast media, assuming the responsibilities of five individual regulators: the Broadcasting Standards Commission (BSC); the Independent Television Commission (ITC); the Office of Telecommunications (Oftel); the Radio Authority; and the Radiocommunications Agency. Although the BBC is subject to Ofcom's regulation concerning programme standards and economic regulation, the BBC's Board of Governors is responsible for managing its public service remit.

Ofcom has a range of responsibilities inherited from the five regulators it replaced. It monitors standards and fairness on terrestrial, cable and satellite TV and radio, considers complaints, and adjudicates on claims of unfair treatment in broadcasts and of unwarranted infringement of privacy in programmes or in their preparation.

Another responsibility is licensing and regulating all commercial television services (including BBC commercial services) operating in, or from, the United Kingdom, including those delivered by non-terrestrial platforms. Ofcom must ensure that a wide range of commercial television services is available throughout the United Kingdom and that they are of high quality and appeal to a variety of tastes and interests. It must also ensure fair competition in the provision of these services, and compliance with the rules on media ownership. The various television services are regulated through licence conditions, codes and guidelines. The codes cover programme content, advertising, sponsorship and technical standards. If a licensee does not comply with the conditions of its licence or the codes, Ofcom can impose financial penalties.

Ofcom's licensing and regulatory remit covers all independent radio services including national, local, cable, satellite and restricted services. Its three main tasks are to plan frequencies, appoint licensees with a view to broadening listener choice, and to regulate programming and advertising. Licensees must adhere to Ofcom codes covering engineering, programmes, news and current affairs, and advertising and sponsorship. Satellite radio services must be licensed by Ofcom if they are transmitted from the United Kingdom for general reception within the country, or if they are transmitted from outside but are managed editorially from within the United Kingdom.

Ofcom is also responsible for managing the UK radio spectrum, although the Government retains some overriding powers of direction. This involves international representation, commissioning research, and allocating radio spectrum and licensing its use.

The press

On an average weekday just over 50 per cent of adults in the United Kingdom read a national newspaper and nearly 27 per cent read a regional daily paper. Each week nearly 28 per cent of adults read a paid-for local weekly title. The United Kingdom has a long tradition of a free (and often outspoken) press. While newspapers are almost always financially independent of any political party, they can express obvious political leanings in their editorial coverage, which may derive from proprietorial and other non-party political influences.

In addition to sales revenue, newspapers earn considerable amounts from advertising. The press is the largest advertising medium in the United Kingdom, with total advertising spending in 2003 of around £8.4 billion (see page 265).

The national press

The national press consists of 11 morning daily papers and 11 Sunday papers. In the six months to March 2004, more than 12.7 million national newspapers were sold every weekday and over 14 million on Sunday. The biggest-selling daily paper is the *Sun*, which sells around 3.4 million copies.

At one time London's Fleet Street area was the centre of the industry, but now all the national papers have moved their editorial and printing facilities to other parts of London or away from the capital altogether. Editions of many papers are also printed in other countries.

National newspapers are often described as broadsheet or tabloid papers on the basis of differences in format, style and content, although one broadsheet, *The Times*, is available in a 'compact' tabloid size as well as the traditional broadsheet and another, the *Independent*, is only available in compact format. Many newspapers have colour pages and most produce extensive supplements as part of their Saturday or Sunday editions, with articles on the arts, personal finance, travel, gardening, home improvement, food and wine, fashion and other leisure topics. Increasing competition from other media in the delivery of news, information and entertainment has contributed to a gradual decline in circulation for many titles.

Regional newspapers

There are more than 1,300 regional and local newspaper titles and 98 regional press publishers, the top 20 of which account for 85 per cent of all UK regional and local newspaper titles. Most towns and cities throughout the United Kingdom have their own regional or local newspaper. These range from morning and evening dailies to papers that are published once a week. They mainly cover stories of regional or local interest, but the dailies also cover national and international news. In addition, they provide a valuable medium for advertising. Between July and December 2003, nearly 41 million regional papers were sold each week, and 29 million free titles distributed each week.

London has one paid-for evening paper, the *Evening Standard*. Its publisher also produces a free daily morning newspaper, *Metro*, launched in 1999. *Metro*'s London edition had a circulation of nearly 450,000 between July and December 2003. There are local weekly papers for every district in Greater London; these are often different local editions of one centrally published paper.

About 650 free distribution newspapers, mostly weekly and financed by advertising, were published in the United Kingdom in 2003. Top free weekly titles include the *Manchester Metro News* and the *Glaswegian*.

There is a broad-based daily and weekly newspaper industry in Scotland covering local, Scottish and UK as well as international issues. The *Daily Record* is the biggest-selling weekday paper, and the *Sunday Mail* the most popular Sunday paper. There are also broadsheet newspapers including the *Scotsman* (based in Edinburgh) and the *Herald* (in Glasgow). The press in Wales includes Welsh-language and bilingual papers; Welsh community newspapers receive an annual grant as part of the Government's wider financial support for the Welsh language. Newspapers from the Republic of Ireland, as well as the British national press, are widely read in Northern Ireland. Regional newspapers include the *Belfast Telegraph*, the *Irish Times* and the *News Letter* in Ulster.

The minority ethnic press

There are several newspapers and magazines produced by minority ethnic communities in the United Kingdom. Most are published weekly, fortnightly or monthly, although there are some daily titles including the Chinese newspaper, *Sing Tao*, the Urdu *Daily AUSAF* and the Arabic *Al-Arab*. Afro-Caribbean newspapers include the *Gleaner*, the *Voice, New Nation* and *Caribbean Times*, each published weekly. The *Asian Times* is an English language weekly for people of Asian descent. Publications also appear in other languages, particularly Bengali, Gujarati, Hindi and Punjabi.

The periodical press

There are nearly 8,500 separate periodical publications that carry advertising. In 2003, advertising expenditure in the sector was more than £1.8 billion. Periodicals are generally classified as either 'consumer' titles, offering readers leisure-time information and entertainment, or 'business and professional' titles, which provide people with material relevant to their working lives. Within the former category, there are general consumer titles, which have a wide appeal, and specialist titles, aimed at people with particular interests, such as motoring, sport or music. A range of literary and political journals appears monthly or quarterly, and there are also many in-house and customer magazines produced by businesses or public services.

Electronic newspapers

Most national newspaper groups have set up websites, providing access to articles from their printed titles or on-line versions of their papers. Some offer additional special interest sites. The audience for on-line papers is growing fast: in August 2004, the *Sun*'s on-line version had just over 4.1 million visitors (up from 3 million in August 2003).

The Talking Newspaper Association of the United Kingdom is a registered charity whose members supply newspapers and magazines in alternative formats, primarily audio cassette, for blind, partially sighted and disabled people. Its national service, which acts as a newsagent for the visually impaired, records over 250 titles on to audio cassette and supplies over 100 titles in electronic formats. The Association reaches more than 250,000 visually impaired listeners across the United Kingdom.

Press Complaints Commission

A policy of press self-regulation, rather than statutory control or a law of privacy, operates in the United Kingdom. The Press Complaints Commission (PCC) deals with complaints about the content and conduct of newspapers and magazines, and operates a Code of Practice agreed by editors, which covers inaccuracy, invasion of privacy, harassment and misrepresentation by the press. The PCC's jurisdiction also extends to on-line versions of newspaper and magazine titles by publishers that already subscribe to the Code. It is a non-statutory body whose 17 members are drawn from both the public and the industry. In January 2004, the PCC created a Charter Compliance Panel to scrutinise the way it deals with complaints.

In 2003 the PCC received 3,649 complaints, a 39 per cent increase on the previous year. The PCC has taken action to make lodging a complaint as straightforward as possible. Around 42 per cent of the complaints related to national newspapers, 41 per cent to regional newspapers, 9 per cent to newspapers specific to Scotland, 7 per cent to magazines and the rest to publications in Northern Ireland and to agencies. Most complaints breaching the Code – 96 per cent in 2003 – are resolved by editors.

The press and the law

There is no state control or censorship of the newspaper and periodical press, and newspaper proprietors, editors and journalists are subject to the law in the same way as any other citizen. However, certain statutes include sections that apply to the press. There are laws governing the extent of newspaper ownership in television and

radio companies (see below) and mergers involving newspapers. Press representatives have a legal right to be supplied with agendas and reports of meetings of local authorities.

There is a requirement to reproduce the printer's imprint (the printer's name and address) on all publications, including newspapers. Publishers are legally obliged to deposit copies of newspapers and publications at the British Library (see page 247).

Publication of advertisements is governed by wide-ranging legislation, including public health, copyright, financial services and fraud legislation. Legal restrictions are imposed on certain types of prize competition.

Laws on contempt of court, official secrets and defamation are also relevant to the press. A newspaper might be in contempt of court if it published something that created a substantial risk that the course of justice in active legal proceedings would be seriously impeded or prejudiced. The unauthorised publication of protected official information in areas such as defence and international relations, where unauthorised disclosure would be damaging, is an offence under the *Official Secrets Acts*. These are restrictions on publication generally, not just through the printed press. Most legal proceedings against the press are libel actions brought by private individuals.

Media ownership

The *Communications Act 2003* simplified UK media ownership rules. The new rules aim to promote competition and attract new investment, while encouraging a range of different viewpoints and maintaining specific limits on the ownership of media assets. The changes mean that individuals and organisations from outside the European Economic Area (see page 104) and local authorities can now own Broadcasting Act licences. Ofcom (see page 262) will be reviewing the rules at least every three years. New public interest tests will allow the Secretary of State for Trade and Industry to intervene in media mergers where there are public interest considerations.

There are also changes to the rules governing cross-media ownership. The new '20 per cent' rule means that no one controlling more than 20 per cent of the national newspaper market can hold an ITV licence or hold more than a 20 per cent stake in any ITV service. No one owning a regional ITV licence can own more than 20 per cent of the local or regional newspaper market in the same region.

Advertising and sponsorship

Total UK expenditure on advertising rose by 2.5 per cent to £17.2 billion in 2003. Press advertising accounted for nearly 49 per cent (see page 262), while television accounted for a further 25 per cent (see page 257).

Increasingly, companies are using new technology such as the Internet to advertise their products. Although Internet advertising accounted for only 2 per cent of total expenditure in 2003, this was an increase of £143 million or nearly 62 per cent on 2002.

Broadcast media

Advertising and sponsorship are allowed on all commercial television and radio services, subject to controls. Ofcom (see page 262) oversees the codes governing advertising standards and programme sponsorship previously operated by the ITC and the Radio Authority and can impose penalties on broadcasters that do not comply.

In 2003 there were 8,835 complaints to the ITC about advertisements broadcast on UK television (Table 17.5). Following consultation, Ofcom is seeking parliamentary approval for its proposals to contract out the regulation of broadcast advertising. The new system is expected to begin in November 2004.

Advertisements on independent television and radio are broadcast in breaks during programmes as well as between programmes, and must be distinct and separate from them. Advertisers are not allowed to influence programme content.

Political advertising and advertisements for betting (other than the National Lottery, the football pools, bingo and amusement arcades) are prohibited. All tobacco advertising is banned on television and radio. Religious advertisements may be broadcast on commercial radio and television, provided they comply with the Ofcom guidelines.

The BBC may not raise revenue from broadcasting advertisements or from commercial sponsorship

Table 17.5 Reasons for complaints about television advertising, 2003, UK

	Complaints received	Advertisements complained about	Advertisements where complaint was upheld[1]
Misleading	1,875	474	91
Offensive	5,499	548	30
Harmful	1,038	302	28
Miscellaneous	423	95	25
All complaints	**8,835**	**1,419**	**174**

1 Where complaint was upheld wholly or in part.
Source: Ofcom

of programmes on its public service channels. It must not give publicity to any firm or organised interest except when this is necessary in providing effective and informative programmes. It does, however, cover sponsored events.

Non-broadcast media

Advertising in non-broadcast media, including newspapers, magazines, posters, sales promotions, cinema, direct mail, and electronic media (such as paid-for Internet advertising and text messages) is regulated by the Advertising Standards Authority (ASA).

The ASA is an independent body set up to ensure that advertisers conform to the Committee of Advertising Practice (CAP) Code (the British Code of Advertising, Sales Promotion and Direct Marketing). This requires that advertisements and promotions are legal, decent, honest and truthful; are prepared with a sense of responsibility to the consumer and society; and respect the principles of fair competition generally accepted in business.

The ASA monitors compliance with the Code and investigates complaints received. In 2003 it received 14,277 complaints. Pre-publication advice is available to publishers, agencies and advertisers from the CAP Copy Advice Team. If an advertisement is found to be misleading or offensive, the ASA can ask the advertiser to change or remove it. Failure to do so can result in damaging adverse publicity from the ASA's weekly publication of its judgements, the refusal of advertising space by publishers, and the loss of trading privileges. The ASA can also refer misleading advertisements to the Office of Fair Trading (see page 358), which has the power to seek an injunction to prevent their publication.

Further reading

Department for Culture, Media and Sport: Annual report 2004. Cm 6220. The Stationery Office, 2004.

Ofcom Annual Plan 2004–05. Ofcom, 2004.

BBC Annual Report 2003/2004. BBC, 2004.

ITV1 2003 Review and 2004–05 Statement. ITV, 2004.

Websites

Department for Culture, Media and Sport
www.culture.gov.uk

Department of Trade and Industry
www.dti.gov.uk

British Broadcasting Corporation (BBC)
www.bbc.co.uk

Channel 4
www.channel4.com

Five
www.channel5.co.uk

ITV (Channel 3)
www.itv.com

National Statistics
www.statistics.gov.uk

Office of Communications (Ofcom)
www.ofcom.gov.uk

Press Complaints Commission
www.pcc.org.uk

Royal Mail Group plc
www.royalmailgroup.com

UK government portal
www.direct.gov.uk

www.

18 Sport

The United Kingdom has a long tradition of sporting invention, participation and achievement. In 2003, UK sportsmen and sportswomen held over 50 world titles in a variety of sports, including athletics, professional boxing, sailing, water skiing, snooker and swimming. In the same year able-bodied UK athletes won 88 medals at world and European championships, while disabled athletes won 99 medals at this level.

Major sporting events in 2003/04

In December 2003, the European Cross Country Championship took place in Edinburgh, and for the second consecutive year the winner of the women's race was Great Britain's Paula Radcliffe.

Nearly 31,700 runners completed the London Marathon in April 2004. The event, which started in 1981, is the one of the largest marathons in the world (only the New York and Chicago Marathons had more finishers in 2003). Each year around three-quarters of the runners are sponsored, raising about £30 million for charities and other good causes. Tracey Morris, a 36-year-old optician from Leeds, was the first British woman home, finishing in 2 hours, 33 minutes and 52 seconds, which won her a place in the British team for the Olympic Games in Athens. The oldest runner to take part was 93-year old Fauja Singh, who ran his first marathon at the age of 89. He improved his record in 2004, finishing in 6 hours, 7 minutes and 13 seconds.

On 15 May 2004 the Arsenal football team ended its 2003–04 season with a 2–1 win over Leicester City. With 90 points, Arsenal was the clear winner of the Premiership title. It did not lose any of the 38 matches in the season, becoming the first team in the top division to go through a whole league season unbeaten since Preston in 1888–89.

Rugby Union World Cup winners

On 22 November 2003 the England team won the Rugby Union World Cup after a hard-fought final against the host nation, Australia. The match was decided in the last minute of extra time by a drop kick from Jonny Wilkinson, resulting in a score of 20–17 to England. It was the first time a team from the northern hemisphere had won the world title.

To celebrate the win a victory parade from Marble Arch to Trafalgar Square was held on 8 December 2003, with the team travelling in two open-topped buses before an estimated crowd of 750,000 fans.

In June and July 2004 Portugal hosted the Euro 2004 football championship. England was the only team from the United Kingdom to qualify for the competition and reached the quarter-finals, losing to the eventual runners-up, Portugal, on penalties. Greece beat Portugal 1–0 in the final and became European Champions for the first time.

The national cricket sides of New Zealand, the West Indies and India visited England during summer 2004. England equalled its best ever run in Test cricket by winning seven consecutive Test matches: three against New Zealand and four against the West Indies. This was the first time for 75 years that England had managed this feat and only the third time ever.

The United Kingdom also hosts a number of successful annual world sporting events – for example the British Open (golf), Wimbledon (tennis) and the Embassy World Championship (snooker).

In April 2004, Manchester hosted the UCI World Cup Classic in track cycling. The event took place

Olympic successes for Team GB

Team GB won 30 medals (9 gold, 9 silver and 12 bronze) at the Olympic Games in Athens in August 2004 (Table 18.2), placing the team tenth in the medals table. Over 270 men and women from 22 sports represented Great Britain during the two weeks of the Games.

Sailing was the most successful sport for Team GB, with five medals: two gold, one silver and two bronze. Kelly Holmes won two gold medals. Her victories in the 800 and 1500 metres were the first time that a British athlete had achieved this middle-distance double since 1920. The gold medal won by Matthew Pinsent in the coxless four was his fourth gold medal in Olympic rowing, while Bradley Wiggins' three medals in cycling – one gold, one silver and one bronze – were the most won by a Briton at a single Olympics since 1964.

at the Manchester Velodrome, which will also be hosting the event in 2005 and 2006. In July and August 2004, Ayrshire in Scotland hosted the World Bowling Championship and also in July, Lilleshall in Shropshire staged the Junior Outdoor Target Archery World Championships.

England has been chosen to host the UEFA European Women's Championships in football. This means that England qualifies automatically for the eight-nation final that will be held in summer 2005.

Results of some of the regular sporting events held in the United Kingdom are given in Table 18.1.

Participation

Watching and participating in sport are two of the most popular forms of leisure activity. In 2002 *Game Plan*, a report published jointly by the Cabinet Office Strategy Unit and the Department for Culture, Media and Sport (DCMS), included a target for increasing the proportion of the population in England that were reasonably active[1]

1 30 minutes physical activity on at least five days a week.

by 2020. It also set out a strategy to increase the percentage of schoolchildren (aged 5–16) who spend a minimum of two hours each week on physical education (PE) and school sport within and beyond the curriculum from 25 per cent in 2002 to 75 per cent by 2006.

Sporting Britain, a report outlining the progress made towards achieving these targets was published by the DCMS in April 2004. It reported that:

- 31 per cent of adults achieve the target of 30 minutes physical activity on at least five days a week. The Government's goal is to increase this by at least 1 per cent a year;
- 62 per cent of pupils spend at least two hours a week on PE and school sport within and beyond the curriculum;
- 44 per cent of pupils are doing their two hours within the curriculum.

The 2002 General Household Survey indicated that 59 per cent of adults in Great Britain had taken part in a sport, game or physical activity (including walking 2 miles or more) in the four weeks before interview. In every age group, males were more likely than females to engage in a sport

European Year of Education through Sport

With the Euro 2004 football championship taking place in Portugal and the Olympic Games in Greece, the European Union (EU) chose 2004 as European Year of Education through Sport (EYES). The main aim of EYES is to raise awareness of the importance of sport in developing personal and social skills, and to reinforce the links between sport and education. Its slogan was 'Move your body, stretch your mind'.

The Clean Start programme, coordinated by UK Sport, is one of the projects that are being promoted by EYES 2004. Its objective is to teach 13- to 17-year-olds about drug-free sport. Cross-curricular activities aim to help pupils to improve their self-confidence, respect for health and well-being, commitment to personal achievement and problem-solving, and analytical and communication skills.

Table 18.1 Winners of major sporting events, 2003/04 UK[1]

Athletics
Flora London Marathon (April 2004): *Men* – Evans Rutto
(Kenya); *Women* – Margaret Okayo (Kenya); *Men's wheelchair*
– Saul Mendoza (Mexico); *Women's wheelchair* – Francesca
Porcellato (Italy)

Badminton
YONEX All England Open Championships (March 2004):
Men – Dan Lin (China); *Women* – Ruir Gong (China)

Cricket
Test matches (summer 2004) – England v New Zealand 3–0,
England v West Indies 4–0
Frizzell County Championship – Warwickshire
Cheltenham & Gloucester Trophy – Gloucestershire
Twenty20 Cup – Leicestershire
Norwich Union League – Glamorgan

Equestrianism
Mitsubishi Motors Badminton three-day event (May 2004) –
William Fox-Pitt riding Tamarillo
Hickstead Derby (June 2004) – John Whitaker riding
Buddy Bunn

Football
FA Barclaycard Premiership – Arsenal
Bank of Scotland Premier League – Celtic
Carling Cup Final – Middlesbrough beat Bolton 2–1
(February 2004)
CIS Insurance Cup Final – Livingston beat Hibernian 2–0
(March 2004)
FA Cup Final – Manchester United beat Millwall 3–0
(May 2004)
Tennents Scottish Cup Final – Celtic beat Dunfermline 3–1
(May 2004)

Golf
HSBC World Matchplay Championship (October 2003) – Ernie
Els (South Africa)
Open Golf Championship (July 2004) – Todd Hamilton (USA)

Horse racing
Martell Grand National (April 2004) – Amberleigh House,
ridden by Graham Lee (Ireland), trained by Ginger McCain
Vodaphone Epsom Derby (June 2004) – North Light, ridden by
Kieren Fallon (Ireland), trained by Sir Michael Stoute

Motorcycling
World Superbike Championship, British Round 1 (June 2004) –
Race 1: Noriyuki Haga (Japan); Race 2: Chris Vermeulen
(Australia); British Round 2 (August 2004) – Race 1: Noriyuki
Haga (Japan); Race 2: Noriyuki Haga (Japan)
FIM Fiat Vans Speedway – British Grand Prix (June 2004) –
Greg Hancock (USA)
Cinzano British Motorcycle Grand Prix (July 2004) – 500 cc:
Valentino Rossi (Italy); 250 cc Daniel Pedrosa (Spain); 125 cc
Andrew Dovizioso (Italy)

Motor racing
Wales Rally of Great Britain (November 2003) – Petter Solberg
(Norway)
Formula 1 British Grand Prix (July 2004) – Michael
Schumacher (Germany)

Rowing
University Boat Race (March 2004) – Cambridge

Rugby league
Tetley's Super League Final (October 2003) Bradford Bulls beat
Wigan Warriors 25–12.
Powergen Challenge Cup Final (April 2004) – St Helens beat
Wigan 32–16

Rugby union
RBS Six Nations Championship (March 2004) – France
Powergen Cup Final (April 2004) – Newcastle beat Sale
37–33
Zurich Premiership Final (May 2004) – Wasps beat Bath 10–6
Celtic League (May 2004) – Llanelli Scarlets beat Ulster Rugby
23–16
WRU Konica Minolta Cup Final (May 2004) – Neath beat
Caerphilly 36–13

Snooker
UK Championship Final (December 2003) – Matthew Stevens
beat Stephen Hendry 10–8
Embassy World Championship Final (May 2004) – Ronnie
O'Sullivan beat Graeme Dott 18–8

Tennis
Wimbledon Finals (July 2004): *Men's singles* – Roger Federer
(Switzerland) beat Andy Roddick (USA) 4–6 7–5 7–6 6–4;
Women's singles – Maria Sharapova (Russia) beat Serena
Williams (USA) 6–1 6–4

1 UK sportsmen and sportswomen unless otherwise indicated.

Table 18.2 British Olympic Medallists, August 2004, Athens

Gold

Athletics
Kelly Holmes – 800 m, 1500 m
Jason Gardner, Darren Campbell,
Marlon Devonish, Mark Lewis-Francis – 4 x 100 m relay

Cycling track
Bradley Wiggins – individual pursuit
Chris Hoy – 1 km time trial

Equestrian eventing
Leslie Law – mixed individual

Rowing
Ed Coode, James Cracknell,
Matthew Pinsent, Steve Williams – coxless four

Sailing
Shirley Robertson, Sarah Webb, Sarah Ayton – Yngling class
Ben Ainslie – Finn class

Silver

Badminton
Gail Emms, Nathan Robertson – mixed doubles

Boxing
Amir Khan – lightweight class

Canoe/kayak slalom
Campbell Walsh – K-1

Cycling track
Steve Cummings, Rob Hayles,
Paul Manning, Bradley Wiggins
Chris Newton, Bryan Steel – team pursuit 4000 m

Diving
Leon Taylor, Peter Waterfield – synchronised 10 m platform

Equestrian eventing
Jeanette Brakewell, William Fox-Pitt, Pippa Funnell,
Mary King, Leslie Law – mixed team

Rowing
Cath Bishop, Katherine Grainger – coxless pair
Debbie Flood, Frances Houghton,
Alison Mowbray, Rebecca Romeo – coxless four

Sailing
Joe Glanfield, Nick Rogers – 470 class

Bronze

Archery
Alison Williamson – individual (70 m)

Athletics
Kelly Sotherton – heptathlon

Canoe/kayak flatwater
Ian Wynne – K-1 500 m

Canoe/kayak slalom
Helen Reeves – K-1

Cycling track
Rob Hayles, Bradley Wiggins – Madison

Equestrian eventing
Pippa Funnell – mixed individual

Modern pentathlon
Georgina Harland

Rowing
Elise Laverick, Sarah Winckless – double sculls

Sailing
Chris Draper, Simon Hiscocks – mixed 49er
Nick Dempsey – Windsurfing Mistral (board)

Swimming
Stephen Parry – 200 m butterfly
David Davies – 1500 m freestyle

or physical activity. For both males and females, participation decreased with age (Figure 18.3).

Walking 2 miles or more was the form of sport or physical activity most likely to have been done by adults of both sexes over the four-week period before interview (Table 18.4). It was also the most popular activity across all age groups. Participation rates for swimming were relatively high for both men and women. Cue sports were more popular among men, whereas keep fit/yoga was more popular among women.

Football

A survey carried out by Sport England in 2002 showed that 57 per cent of boys and 18 per cent of girls aged 6–16 played football (outside school hours) on at least ten days over a 12-month period. Between 2000 and 2004, the Government invested, through the Football Foundation, a total of £62 million in the development of grass-roots football, community and education initiatives, and essential stadium safety work. The Football Association of Wales Trust aims to encourage

Figure 18.3 Participation[1] in a sport, game or physical activity,[2] by age, 2002/03, Great Britain

Percentages

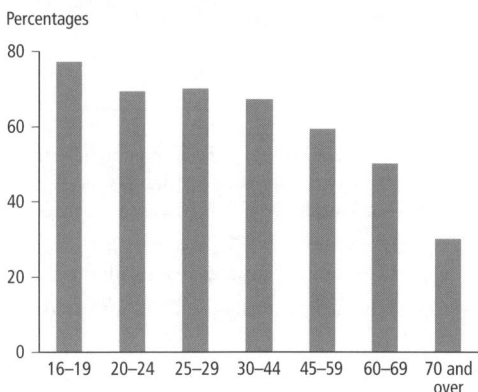

1 Percentage participating in the four weeks before interview.
2 Includes walking.
Source: General Household Survey, Office for National Statistics

Table 18.4 'Top ten' sports, games or physical activity undertaken[1] by adults, 2002

Percentages

	Men	Women
Walking	36	34
Snooker/pool/billiards	15	4
Cycling	12	6
Swimming	12	15
Football[2]	10	.
Golf[2]	9	.
Weight training	9	3
Keep fit/yoga	7	16
Running	7	3
Tenpin bowling	4	3
Horse riding[3]	.	2
Tennis[3]	.	2

1 People aged 16 and over reporting participation in the four weeks prior to the survey.
2 Not in top ten for women.
3 Not in top ten for men.
Source: General Household Survey; Office for National Statistics

more boys and girls of school age to take part in football and raise the standards of play in Wales.

Women's football is one of the fastest growing sports. The number of girls' teams in England increased from 80 in 1993 to 6,209 in 2003/04, and the number of women's teams from 400 to 1,013 over the same period.

In England, 308 clubs are affiliated to the Football Association (FA) and about 40,000 clubs to regional or district associations. In Scotland, there are 79 full and associate clubs and nearly 6,000 registered clubs under the jurisdiction of the Scottish Football Association. In Wales there are 155 clubs affiliated to the Football Association of Wales (FAW) and 1,653 clubs affiliated to areas. The Irish Football Association (covering Northern Ireland) has 838 affiliated clubs.

Figures for the English Barclays Premier League for 2003–04 show that the average attendance at each game was 35,000. In comparison, in the German Bundesliga 1 it was 37,000; in Primera Division 1 in Spain it was 28,600; and in Serie A in Italy it was 25,600, while in the Scottish Premier League it was about 15,200.

The Football League is the governing body for the 72 clubs in Divisions 1, 2 and 3 (renamed the Coca-Cola Football League Championship, Coca-Cola Football League 1 and Coca-Cola Football League 2 in 2004). These clubs attracted a total of 15.4 million supporters to league matches during the 2003–04 season – the biggest aggregate attendance generated for 40 years. In 2003–04, the Coca-Cola Championship had an average attendance of 15,303, which is 50 per cent higher than the equivalent divisions in Germany and Italy and more than double those in France and Spain.

Horse racing

Over 6 million people attended race meetings in Great Britain in 2003, the highest figure recorded. There were 1,220 race meetings and 13,000 horses in training. The cumulative television audience was over 500 million. Horse racing is second to football as the most televised sport on terrestrial channels. In 2003, about £9 billion was bet off-course on horse racing, most of it in licensed betting offices. The sport had record levels of overall income and prize money in 2003. In June 2004, the sport's governing authority, the British Horseracing Board, reached agreement with the Office of Fair Trading on proposals for the modernisation of the sport over the next few years.

Tennis

The Lawn Tennis Association (LTA) estimated that about 2.9 million people aged four and upwards played tennis in Great Britain in 2003. All the

profits generated by the Wimbledon
Championships – £25.8 million in 2003 – are
invested by the LTA in British tennis for the
development of the game. The LTA's strategy
focuses on three priorities: making the game
appealing to juniors and keeping them in the sport;
developing a network of accessible clubs that are
welcoming to young people; and identifying and
developing the most talented players.

Sports policy

A 'Sports Cabinet' identifies priorities for sport in
the United Kingdom. Its membership comprises
the Secretary of State for Culture, Media and Sport
(who chairs the 'Cabinet') and the ministers with
responsibility for sport in England, Wales,
Scotland and Northern Ireland. The heads of the
five Sports Councils are also invited as observers.

The Government's Plan for Sport, an action plan for
delivery of the strategy for England set out in
A Sporting Future for All, was published in 2001. An
update, published in April 2003, gave objectives for
sport and education and sport in the community,
to be achieved by 2006.

In 2002, the Government's sport and physical
activity objectives in England, entitled *Game Plan*,
was published by the DCMS and the Cabinet
Office Strategy Unit. The first *Game Plan Delivery*
report was published in April 2004.

Achievements include:

- an Activity Coordination Team (ACT), jointly
chaired by the Minister for Sport and the
Minister for Public Health, which has brought
together seven other government
departments, local government, health
organisations and sport funding bodies to
coordinate the drive to improve health by
increasing participation in sport and physical
activity. This work will contribute to the
public health White Paper due to be
published in autumn 2004;

- of total funding of £581 million to improve
the community use of facilities in schools and
other educational establishments in England
over 2002–06, £270 million had been
committed to 1,494 projects by the end of
June 2004;

- a total of £119 million had been committed
under the Space for Sport and Arts
Programme to improve primary school

facilities in 65 deprived areas across England.
At 30 June 2004, 168 projects had been
completed and a further 78 were on site;

- from July 2004 the public has had access to
a database of sports facilities called Active
Places, covering venues such as sports halls,
swimming pools, synthetic turf pitches, golf
courses, ice rinks and athletics tracks.

Sport 21 2003–2007 Shaping Scotland's Future, the
updated strategy for sport in Scotland, was
published in March 2003. It is founded on three
visions of a Scotland where:

- sport is more widely available to all;

- sporting talent is recognised and nurtured;
and

- world-class performance is achieved and
sustained.

It contains 11 targets for 2007 and a key challenge
for 2020. Six implementation groups have been set
up to prepare target strategies. The National
Implementation Forum, chaired by the Minister
for Tourism, Culture and Sport, meets biannually
to monitor strategies, assess their implementation
at local level, and evaluate their impact.

In July 2003 the Welsh Assembly Government
launched a consultation strategy, entitled *Sport
and Active Recreation in Wales: Climbing Higher,
Dringo'n Uwch*, covering the period to 2023. The
priorities of the strategy include:

- to encourage people in Wales to be more
physically active;

- to maximise the links between sport, active
recreation and the natural environment;

- to encourage the development of agility,
balance, coordination and skill across a range
of activities; and

- to achieve sporting success.

Organisation and administration

Sports Councils

Government responsibilities and funding for sport
and recreation are largely channelled through five
Sports Councils:

- the United Kingdom Sports Council,
operating as UK Sport;

- the English Sports Council, operating as Sport
England;

- the Sports Council for Wales;
- the Scottish Sports Council, operating as **sport**scotland; and
- the Sports Council for Northern Ireland.

UK Sport takes the lead on those aspects of sport that require strategic planning, administration, coordination or representation for the United Kingdom as a whole. Its main functions include:

- coordinating support to sports in which the United Kingdom competes internationally (as opposed to the four home countries separately);
- tackling drug misuse in sport;
- coordinating policy for bringing major international sports events to the United Kingdom; and
- representing UK sporting interests overseas at international level.

All the Sports Councils distribute government and Lottery funds. UK Sport focuses on elite sportsmen and sportswomen, while the individual Sports Councils are more concerned with the development of sport at the community level by promoting participation, giving support and guidance to providers of sports facilities, and supporting the development of talented sportsmen and women, including disabled people. They also manage the National Sports Centres.

Sports governing bodies

Individual sports are run by independent governing bodies. Some have a UK or Great Britain structure, others are constituted on a regional basis. In Northern Ireland almost half of the sports are part of an all-Ireland structure that covers both Northern Ireland and the Republic of Ireland. The functions of governing bodies include drawing up rules, holding events, regulating membership, selecting and training national teams, and producing plans for their sports. There are also organisations representing people who take part in more informal physical recreation, such as walking. Most sports clubs in the United Kingdom belong to, or are affiliated to, an appropriate governing body.

Governing bodies that receive funding from the Sports Councils are required to produce Whole Sports Plans (WSPs), from the grass roots to the highest competitive levels. WSPs provide a blueprint for each sport that indicates how agreed

sporting outcomes can be achieved. At UK level there are ten Olympic sports with which the five Sports Councils have agreed to adopt a 'One Stop Plan' approach to help them to deliver sporting success in elite competitions. A number of international federations have their headquarters in the United Kingdom: the Commonwealth Games Federation and federations for badminton, billiards and snooker, bowls, cricket, curling, golf, netball, sailing, squash, tennis and wheelchair sports.

Other sports organisations

Central Council of Physical Recreation

The Central Council of Physical Recreation (CCPR) is the representative body for 270 national sporting organisations, covering an estimated 150,000 voluntary sports clubs and 8 million members. It aims to lead the development of a sustainable and effective non-governmental and voluntary sector for sport and recreation by:

- representing the interest of voluntary sport and recreation;
- working in partnership with the Government and its agencies; and
- providing high-quality services for its members.

The Scottish Sports Association, the Welsh Sports Association and the Northern Ireland Sports Forum are equivalent associations to the CCPR. Their primary aim is to represent the interests of their members to the appropriate national and local authorities, including the Sports Councils, from which they may receive some funding.

British Olympic Association

The British Olympic Association (BOA) comprises representatives of the 35 national governing bodies of Olympic sports. It organises the participation of British teams in the Olympic Games, sets standards for selection and raises funds. It is supported by sponsorship and by donations from the private sector and the general public, and works closely with UK Sport.

The BOA contributes to the preparation of competitors in the period leading up to the Games, by arranging training camps and programmes to support national governing bodies and their athletes in areas such as acclimatisation,

London's Olympic bid

In May 2003 the Government announced its support for London's bid to host the 2012 Olympic and Paralympic Games. The proposal will include the building of sports facilities near Stratford in east London. Transport links will be improved by the completion of the second section of the Channel Tunnel Rail Link, scheduled for 2007, and the extension of the Docklands Light Railway to the nearby City Airport (scheduled for completion by the end of 2005). London will also make use of venues such as Wimbledon, Lords, ExCeL and Wembley Stadium (see page 276).

In May 2004, the International Olympic Committee (IOC) announced a shortlist of five cities – London, Madrid, Moscow, New York and Paris – to host the 2012 Olympic and Paralympic Games. The London Bid Company will submit London's bid to the IOC by November 2004. The IOC will announce the result in July 2005.

psychology and physiology. Its Olympic Medical Institute at Northwick Park Hospital in Harrow provides medical services for competitors before and during the Olympics. Its educational arm aims to educate youngsters about the Olympic Games and the Olympic movement. The BOA will celebrate its 100th anniversary in 2005.

Women in sport

UK Sport organises a UK Coordinating Group on Women in Sport that aims to raise participation by women in sport at all levels, and increase the number of women involved in coaching, managing and administering sport. The Foundation promotes opportunities for women and girls in sport and active recreation across the United Kingdom. It is primarily funded by Sport England and private sponsors, but remains autonomous. Its activities include:

- providing advice and information on up-to-date research, policy and strategy development, sources of funding, and national and regional initiatives;

- influencing national and regional government, and sports council strategy and policy to make sure that all policies, strategies and programmes are equitable; and

- collecting, developing and sharing examples of best practice.

Sport for disabled people

Sport for disabled people is organised by a wide range of agencies in the United Kingdom. Some organisations promote the needs of people with a particular type of disability across a range of sports. These include the British Amputee and Les Autres Sports Association, British Blind Sport, British Wheelchair Sports Foundation, Cerebral Palsy Sport and the United Kingdom Sports Association for People with Learning Disability. The British Deaf Sports Council organises sporting opportunities for people with hearing impairment and coordinates British interests at the World Deaf Games.

In addition, the English Federation of Disability Sport, Disability Sport Cymru, Scottish Disability Sport and Disability Sport Northern Ireland are responsible for the general coordination and development of sport for disabled people. A number of sports already have a degree of integration: archery, athletics, cricket, cycling, equestrianism, football, judo, powerlifting and weightlifting, rugby union, sailing, swimming and wheelchair tennis and table tennis. The Commonwealth Games in Manchester in 2002 was the first major sports event in the world to include an integrated programme for disabled people.

The British Paralympic Association (BPA) was established in 1989. It comprises 26 national governing bodies and disability sport organisations. It ratifies selection, and funds and manages the Great Britain Paralympic Team in the winter and summer Paralympic Games. The BPA's games programme is funded through sponsorship, fundraising, Lottery funding, and donations from the public and private sectors.

The separate World Class Performance Programme of the BPA helps support the preparation of Britain's elite disabled athletes. It provides sport science and medicine advice and develops leading research into performance preparation. In May 2002 UK Sport announced a £1.7 million investment programme to support the British team for the 2004 Paralympic Games in Athens in September, including multi-sport preparation camps, to be held twice a year, to help the athletes experience similar conditions and climate to those expected in Athens.

Funding

National Lottery

Of every pound spent on the National Lottery, 4.7 pence goes to sport. Between 1994, when the National Lottery started, and July 2004 the Sports Councils awarded 26,383 grants worth around £2.5 billion. Money has gone to improve sporting opportunities, provide new sporting facilities in schools and elsewhere, support current and potentially future elite performers, and to stage major events. In projects to improve sporting opportunity, over £1.4 billion of Lottery funds have been invested in over 3,900 community facilities in England since 1995; in Scotland, over 6,660 awards totalling more than £208 million have been made by sportscotland to April 2004. The Sports Council for Northern Ireland has made about 1,800 awards, worth over £70 million.

Sponsorship

Many sports benefit from sponsorship, which may take the form of financing specific events or championships, such as cricket leagues or horse races, or support for sports organisations or individual performers. Football and motor sport receive the largest amounts of private sponsorship. Sponsorship is encouraged by a number of bodies, including the Institute of Sports Sponsorship, which comprises some 100 UK companies involved in sponsoring sport. Sponsors in the United Kingdom now invest more than £1 billion annually in sport.

SportsAid

SportsAid raises funds to help encourage and support young people and disabled people with sporting talent. It receives a grant from Sport England to cover administration costs, and has regional branches throughout England as well as sister organisations in Wales, Scotland and Northern Ireland. Financial grants are provided on an individual basis, with each application being assessed on the criteria of talent and need. Those receiving funds must usually be aged between 12 and 18; there is no age limit for disabled people. Between 1975 and 2004, the charity distributed over £20 million in grants.

From October 2004, SportsAid will be raising additional funds to support the DCMS Talented Athlete Scholarship Scheme (TASS). TASS will provide scholarships and bursaries for young

people between the ages of 16 and 25 and develop sporting links with higher and further education institutions.

The Scottish Sports Aid Foundation, SportsAid Cymru/Wales and the Ulster Sports and Recreation Trust have similar functions.

Foundation for Sport and the Arts

The Foundation for Sport and the Arts, set up by the football pools promoters in 1991, has made awards totalling nearly £350 million to schemes benefiting over 100 sports, mainly for small-scale projects. The Foundation is keen to promote the interest and engagement of all, particularly the young, in inclusive sporting and artistic pursuits.

Sports facilities

The United Kingdom has a range of sporting facilities including 13 National Sports Centres, operated by the individual Sports Councils. A number of major facilities have been improved in recent years, including the Millennium Stadium in Cardiff, the Wimbledon tennis complex and several football grounds. New facilities were built in Manchester for the 2002 Commonwealth Games.

United Kingdom Sports Institute

The Sports Institutes of England, Wales, Scotland and Northern Ireland work together to form the United Kingdom Sports Institute (UKSI) network, which aims to deliver world-class services and facilities to athletes throughout the United Kingdom. UK Sport plays a strategic lead role and works closely with governing body performance directors to discover and introduce the latest performance-enhancing technology and equipment through research and innovation. In February 2004, it launched a Performance Lifestyle programme, which is designed to help athletes balance sport and personal commitments more effectively.

The English Institute of Sport (EIS) provides a network of training facilities in nine regional multi-sport centres together with 35 satellite sites. The network has been fully operational since the end of 2003 and is currently helping athletes drawn from 30 sports.

Wembley Stadium

The construction and operation of the new national stadium at Wembley in London is the responsibility of Wembley National Stadium Ltd, a wholly owned subsidiary of the FA. The new 90,000-seat stadium will host events for football, rugby league and athletics, as well as concerts. It is scheduled for completion in 2006. The project is estimated to cost about £757 million, of which £161 million will come from public funding.

The design includes a 7,000-tonne retractable roof that will be supported by a steel arch weighing 1,750 tonnes, thus avoiding the need for columns inside the stadium and improving views for spectators. The arch is 133 metres high and 315 metres long – said to be the longest single roof structure in the world.

The UKSI network supported by **sports**cotland comprises the Scottish Institute of Sport, which opened its new base at Stirling in 2002, and six area institutes. The centre of the UKSI network in Wales is the Welsh Institute of Sport in Cardiff, which is the premier venue in Wales for top-level training and for competition in many sports.

The Sports Council for Northern Ireland is working in partnership with the University of Ulster to develop a Northern Ireland network centre of the UKSI.

Services for high-performance athletes have been provided through the Sports Institute for Northern Ireland since July 2001. These include strength and conditioning advice, physiotherapy and injury management, sports medicine, sports science, athlete career, and education and high-performance planning. A capital investment programme was being finalised in summer 2004 that will include facilities for athletes from a wide range of sports.

Local facilities

Local authorities are the main providers of basic sport and recreation facilities for the local community, including indoor sports centres, parks, lakes, playing fields, playgrounds, tennis courts, natural and artificial pitches, golf courses and swimming/leisure pools. Commercial facilities include health and fitness centres, tenpin bowling centres, ice-skating and roller-skating rinks, squash courts, golf courses and driving ranges, riding stables and marinas.

Many amateur clubs cater for indoor recreation, but more common are those providing outdoor sports facilities, particularly for bowls, cricket, football, golf, hockey, rugby, and tennis. The Government has enabled clubs to apply for charitable status. For those clubs that cannot, or do not wish to, become charities, the 2002 Budget included a package of tax measures giving clubs access to tax reliefs similar to those available to charities if they register as Community Amateur Sports Clubs (CASCs) with the Inland Revenue. The 2004 Budget expanded the benefits available to CASCs to include the 80 per cent relief on business rates that charities already receive.

The Government is allocating £60 million to provide new or refurbished community sports facilities in England through the Community Club Development Programme over the period 2003/04 to 2005/06; £20 million of this comes from the Capital Modernisation Fund, which is aimed at improving the delivery of public services. New rules governing the sale of playing fields mean that £540 million has been invested in new sports facilities since 2001. The Big Lottery Fund (formed following a merger between the New Opportunities Fund and the Community Fund in early 2004) and Sport England are investing almost £800 million in facilities for school and community sport.

Support services

Coaching

The organisation SportsCoach UK provides a comprehensive range of services for coaches in all sports. Supported by the Sports Councils, it works closely with sports governing bodies, local authorities, and higher and further education institutions. In 2003 some 36,000 coaches and schoolteachers participated in its programmes.

In July 2002 the Coaching Task Force recommended increasing the pool of talented coaches in England and introducing a national coaching certificate. The DCMS is taking forward these recommendations by investing £28 million over 2003/06 to establish a five-level UK Coaching

Certificate and introducing 45 coach development officers and 3,000 community sports coaches across England.

Volunteering

Nearly 6 million people volunteer in sport in the United Kingdom and many clubs would not be able to function without them. Sport England's Volunteer Investment Programme helps to improve the management of the volunteer workforce in sport through encouraging best practice. The DCMS leadership and volunteering in school and community sport programme, known as Step into Sport, is investing £15 million between 2002/03 and 2005/06 in volunteering and leadership programmes for young people. By the end summer 2004, the DCMS expected 69,000 young people aged 14–25 would have taken Sports Leadership awards, 21,000 would have run sports festivals for primary school children and over 5,500 would have started mentored community volunteering.

In Scotland, one of the key targets of *Sport 21 2003–2007* is that Scotland should have 150,000 volunteers who are contributing to the development and delivery of Scottish sport. An implementation group that includes Volunteer Development Scotland, the Scottish Council for Voluntary Organisations, **sport**scotland, the Scottish Executive, the Convention of Scottish Local Authorities, SkillsActive Scotland and the Scottish Sports Association has been established. It has prepared a draft strategy that consists of seven 'steps to success' to recruit these volunteers, which has been endorsed by Scottish ministers. A number of sub groups have been established to deliver specific actions in the strategy in, for example, education and training, research, and communication.

The recruitment and development of volunteers is also one of the main priorities of Dragon Sport, a Sports Council for Wales initiative aimed at increasing extra-curricular and sports club membership among 7- to 11-year-olds. Since the scheme began, 423 schools have signed up and 132 extra-curricular clubs have been established.

Sports medicine

The UKSI provides medical services – principally sports medicine and sports physiotherapy – along with sports science, strength and conditioning and Performance Lifestyle advice for athletes on the World Class Programmes.

Boat Race anniversary

The famous 6.8-kilometre Boat Race on the River Thames between crews from Oxford and Cambridge Universities was run for the 150th time in March 2004. The first race was held in 1829 in Henley. It then moved to London, initially from Westminster to Putney, but due to overcrowding in the centre of the capital the universities found a new location between Putney and Mortlake. Since 1856 it has been held every year, except during the two World Wars.

The race has an estimated worldwide television audience of 500 million. In 2004 the score stood at 78 to Cambridge, 71 to Oxford, and one dead heat in 1877. Cambridge won the 2004 race and also holds the fastest time of 16 minutes and 19 seconds, achieved in 1998.

The Department of Health (DH), in partnership with the DCMS, is proposing to develop and recognise a new speciality – sport and exercise medicine (SEM). SEM will consist of multi-disciplinary teams of specialists who:

- promote a holistic approach to addressing medical conditions and injuries in those who wish to exercise;
- prevent further injuries by providing advice on the safe use of physical exercise in the treatment and prevention of illness; and
- promote general wellness through the increased use of exercise and physical activity.

The DH plans to issue a consultation document with proposals for establishing and recognising this new speciality in autumn 2004.

Sports science

In addition to the medical services, the UKSI also provides support in sports science through the traditional three disciplines of physiology, psychology and biomechanics, as well as through support and advice in nutrition, technology, performance analysis, and sociology.

Drug misuse

Sporting governing bodies and national governments are working to eradicate drugs and doping methods in sport under the auspices of the World Anti-Doping Agency (WADA). The UK Government is committed to the fight against drugs in sport, and signed the Copenhagen Declaration on Anti-Doping in Sport in March 2003, in which it committed to adopting the World Anti-Doping Code into sport's rules and regulations.

The World Anti-Doping Code will harmonise anti-doping activities and processes across different countries and different sports, creating one definitive set of anti-doping rules and regulations covering testing procedures, banned substances and disciplinary sanctions.

As part of its overall sporting excellence remit, UK Sport acts as the UK national anti-doping organisation, and is committed to promoting ethically fair and drug-free sport that is delivered through a drug testing programme.

Between 1999 and 2004, UK Sport has undertaken 29,114 tests across 50 sports. These showed that 98.5 per cent of athletes in the United Kingdom tested clean of prohibited substances.

In February 2004, UK Sport launched a new on-line database for reporting positive test results. The database includes all findings that have been through the entire disciplinary process from April 2003, and over time this will develop into a full

historical record of the testing programme. There is also a drug information database which provides guidance to athletes on any prohibited substances that UK licensed medications may contain.

Further reading

The Framework for Sport in England. Sport England, 2004.

First Game Plan Delivery Report. Department for Culture, Media and Sport, 2004.

Sporting Britain. Department for Culture, Media and Sport, 2004.

The Government's Plan for Sport: 2nd Annual Report. Department for Culture, Media and Sport, 2003.

Game Plan: A strategy for delivering Government's sport and physical activity objectives report. Department for Culture, Media and Sport and Cabinet Office Strategy Unit, 2002.

Sport 21 2003–2007 Shaping Scotland's Future. sportscotland, 2003.

Sport and Active Recreation in Wales: Climbing Higher, Dringo'n Uwch. Welsh Assembly Government, 2003.

Websites

Department for Culture, Media and Sport
www.culture.gov.uk

Department of Culture, Arts and Leisure (Northern Ireland)
www.dcalni.gov.uk

British Olympic Association
www.olympics.org.uk

UK Sport
www.uksport.gov.uk
(Site has links to individual governing bodies)

Sport England
www.sportengland.org

sportscotland
www.sportscotland.org.uk

Sports Council for Northern Ireland
www.sportni.org

Sports Council for Wales
www.sports-council-wales.co.uk

Central Council of Physical Recreation
www.ccpr.org.uk

Scottish Sports Association
www.scottishsportsassociation.org.uk

Women's Sports Foundation
www.wsf.org.uk

www.

19 The environment

The United Kingdom has around 75,000 separate species of plants and animals (excluding micro-organisms). The indigenous vegetation of much of the country is deciduous forest dominated by oak, lime, ash and beech, with pine locally important in highland and some lowland areas. However, almost all the vegetation in the UK landscape has been affected in some way by human activity stretching over thousands of years (Table 19.1).

All native large carnivores, such as wolves and bears, are now locally extinct, but small carnivores such as foxes and stoats are common in most rural areas, while many small mammals and birds are widespread. The United Kingdom has six native amphibian and six native reptile species, plus nine introduced species. Both fresh and salt water ecosystems contain a wide variety of fish. Data on many species are being collected on a national database – the National Biodiversity Network (*www.searchnbn.net*).

The Government launched its sustainable development strategy, *A Better Quality of Life*, in 1999 (see page 114). *Changing Patterns*, published in September 2003, sets out the Government's framework for breaking the link between economic growth and environmental degradation and thus achieving sustainable consumption and production. *Changing Patterns* was accompanied by a consultation paper with proposals for 12 'decoupling' indicators.

Land

Protecting countryside and wildlife

The Department for Environment, Food and Rural Affairs (Defra) is responsible for policy on the environment, wildlife and the countryside in England. It sponsors the Environment Agency (see page 300), the Countryside Agency, English Nature and the Forestry Commission (see

Table 19.1 Land by agricultural and other uses, 2002, UK

Percentages

| | Agricultural land | | | Forest and woodland | Urban land and land not otherwise specified[3] | Total land[4] (=100%) (thousand hectares) |
	Crops and bare fallow	Grasses and rough grazing[1]	Other[2]			
England	30	36	5	8	21	12,972
Wales	3	73	1	13	10	2,064
Scotland	7	67	2	17	8	7,710
Northern Ireland	4	77	1	6	12	1,348
United Kingdom	**19**	**51**	**4**	**11**	**16**	**24,094**

1 Includes grasses, and sole right and common grazing.
2 Set-aside and other land on agricultural holdings such as farm roads, yards, buildings, gardens and ponds. Woodland on agricultural holdings is included in 'Forest and woodland'.
3 Figures are derived by subtracting land used for agricultural and forestry purposes from the land area. Figures include: land used for transport and recreation; non-agricultural, semi-natural environments such as sand dunes, grouse moors and non-agricultural grasslands; and inland waters.
4 As at January 2002. Includes inland waters.
Source: Department for Environment, Food and Rural Affairs; Forestry Commission; Forest Service

page 419). It also sponsors the Joint Nature Conservation Committee (JNCC), a committee of English Nature, the Countryside Council for Wales and Scottish Natural Heritage, and administers the England Rural Development Programme (see page 411).

The Countryside Agency is the statutory body in England that aims to improve the quality of life for people in the countryside and improve the quality of the countryside itself. The Agency has an annual budget of about £90 million and is structured around six priority areas – villages, services, enterprise, wider welcome (recreation opportunities in the countryside), living landscapes, and countryside for towns. English Nature promotes the conservation of wildlife and natural features, and provides advice to the Government on nature conservation. Its total budget in 2003/04 was £82 million.

In *Rural Strategy 2004*, issued in July, the Government announced that a new integrated agency for resource management, nature conservation, biodiversity, landscape, access and recreation would be established in England. It will bring together elements of the work done by the Countryside Agency, Defra's Rural Development Service and English Nature. As its establishment will require primary legislation, the component parts will operate in a confederation from April 2005, with each organisation responsible for fulfilling its own statutory duties within that partnership.

The devolved administrations in Wales and Scotland sponsor similar bodies to those in England. The Countryside Council for Wales (CCW) has responsibilities for landscape and nature conservation, and for countryside recreation. Scottish Natural Heritage (SNH) has both the countryside and landscape powers of the Countryside Agency and the nature conservation duties and powers of English Nature. Like English Nature, CCW and SNH are responsible for providing advice and information to the Government and the public on nature conservation, for notifying land as being of special interest due to its wildlife and geological features, and for establishing National Nature Reserves. In Northern Ireland, responsibility rests with the Environment and Heritage Service (EHS), an agency within the Department of the Environment (DoE). The EHS protects and manages the natural and built environment.

The JNCC is the statutory committee through which English Nature, CCW and SNH exercise their joint nature conservation functions. These include: providing advice on the development and implementation of policies that affect nature conservation, both in Great Britain and internationally; establishing common standards for the monitoring of, and research into, nature conservation; and analysis of the information produced. At the international level, the JNCC provides technical advice to the Government and others to aid implementation of global and European conservation obligations.

Voluntary organisations

Voluntary organisations are well represented in conservation work. Although they are funded largely by subscription, private donations and entrance fees, many receive government support.

The National Trust, a charity established in 1895, had over 3 million members in 2003/04. It owns and protects places of historic interest and natural beauty for the benefit of the nation. The Trust cares for 248,000 hectares of land in England, Wales and Northern Ireland and 965 kilometres of coastline. The separate National Trust for Scotland, also a charity, has over 250,000 members.

National Parks

National Park status recognises the national importance of the area concerned in terms of landscape, biodiversity and as a recreational resource. The name National Park does not signify national ownership – most of the land in such parks is owned by farmers and other private landowners. Each park is administered by an independent National Park Authority.

The first National Parks – the Lake District and the Peak District in England, and Snowdonia in Wales – were designated in 1951. In 2004 there were 12 such parks in England, Wales and Scotland (see map in colour section); the Broads area of East Anglia has equivalent status. The largest is the Cairngorms, at 380,000 hectares, which was opened in 2003.

In June 2004, the Government announced that the New Forest will be designated a National Park; the South Downs is being considered for designation. A consultation leaflet was published in June 2004 to consider whether the Mountains of Mourne

area should become Northern Ireland's first
National Park.

National Parks and Areas of Outstanding Natural
Beauty (AONBs) in England and Wales are
designated by the Countryside Agency and the
CCW, subject to confirmation by the Secretary of
State for Environment, Food and Rural Affairs or
the National Assembly for Wales. SNH advises the
Scottish Executive on the designation of National
Parks in Scotland.

Areas of Outstanding Natural Beauty

The purpose of AONBs in England, Wales and
Northern Ireland is the conservation and
enhancement of the natural beauty of the
landscape, although many also fulfil a wider
recreational purpose. Designation started in
1956 with the Gower peninsula in south Wales;
the most recent addition was the Tamar Valley in
Cornwall in 1995. There are 50 AONBs covering
2.4 million hectares. Two new areas – Erne
Lakeland and Fermanagh Caveland – have been
proposed in Northern Ireland.

National Scenic Areas

In Scotland the 40 National Scenic Areas (NSAs)
are broadly equivalent to AONBs and cover 1
million hectares. They give special attention to the
best scenery in Scotland when new development is
being considered. Certain developments in these
areas are subject to consultation with SNH, which
can refer matters to the Scottish Executive in the
event of a disagreement.

Forest, regional and country parks

There are 18 forest parks in Great Britain, covering
nearly 300,000 hectares, which are administered by
the Forestry Commission. There are over 270
country parks in England recognised by the
Countryside Agency, 35 in Wales recognised by
CCW, and 36 in Scotland. Scotland also has four
regional parks. Country and regional parks in
Great Britain are administered by local authorities.
Northern Ireland has 11 country parks,
administered by the EHS or by local authorities. It
also has eight forest parks, three forest drives and
over 40 minor forest recreation sites, all of which
are administered by the Forest Service, an agency
of the Department of Agriculture and Rural
Development (DARD – see page 420).

Tree preservation

Tree Preservation Orders enable local authorities
to protect trees and woodlands. Once a tree is
protected, it is generally an offence to cut it down
or carry out most types of work to it without
permission. Courts can impose substantial fines
for breaches of such Orders. Replacement trees
must be planted where protected trees are felled in
contravention of an Order or are removed because
they are dying, dead or dangerous.

Over 100,000 hectares of woodland are included in
Sites of Special Scientific Interest (SSSIs – see page
283). Organisations involved in protecting existing
woods and planting new areas of woodland include
English Nature, SNH and voluntary bodies such as
the Woodland Trust, which owns over 1,100 woods
across the United Kingdom covering 18,300
hectares.

Public rights of way and open country

England has about 190,000 kilometres of rights of
way,[1] including 146,600 kilometres of footpaths
and 32,400 kilometres of bridleways. There are
15 long-distance walking routes in England and
Wales, designated as National Trails, and five Long
Distance Routes in Scotland (see map in the
colour section).

In England and Wales, local highway authorities
are responsible for asserting and protecting the
rights of the public to use and enjoy public rights
of way, and to ensure any obstructions occurring
on them are removed. In Scotland, this is done by
planning authorities.

Registered common land[2] in England and Wales
totals nearly 550,000 hectares.[3] The open character
of commons has made them popular for informal
recreation, although significant areas (particularly
in the uplands) remain important for agriculture.
Around 80 per cent of common land is privately
owned. The Countryside and Rights of Way Act
2000 (see page 282) gives the public a right of
access on foot to nearly all registered common land
in England and Wales.

1 Where the general public has legal title to go across someone
  else's property.
2 The term 'common land' derives from the fact that certain people
  held rights of common over the land. The different types of rights
  of common signified different entitlements to the products of the
  soil of the common – for example to the pasture, or to sand,
  gravel or peat.
3 This total does not include some common land excluded from
  registration such as the New Forest and Epping Forest.

Commons are largely unimproved and therefore have high amenity and wildlife value; many are protected by law and by nature conservation designations. For example, around half of the common land in England is found within National Parks and about half is designated as SSSIs (see page 283). Ministerial consent is usually required to undertake work on commons or to enclose areas by fencing.

The *Common Land Policy Statement* published by Defra and the National Assembly for Wales in 2002 contained proposals for legislation relating to the registration and protection of common land and village greens. Defra plans to consult on a draft Bill as soon as parliamentary time allows.

In England and Wales, the *Countryside and Rights of Way Act 2000* created a public right of access to mountain, moor, heath, down and also to registered common land. The Countryside Agency and the CCW are preparing maps of the areas affected. The phased introduction of the new right of access started on a regional basis in September 2004. When they come fully into force at the end of 2005, it is estimated that some 1.2 to 1.8 million hectares of land will have been opened up. An updated Countryside Code was launched in July 2004 to reflect the new rights of access. The *Land Reform (Scotland) Act 2003* established a right of responsible access to land and inland water for recreation and passage. Part one of the Act places duties on local authorities to uphold the exercise of access rights, to plan for a system of core paths, and to establish local access forums for their areas. The SNH has produced a Scottish Outdoor Access Code setting out guidance on the rights and responsibilities of landowners and those taking access. The Scottish Parliament approved the Code in July 2004.

The coast

Great Britain has approximately 17,820 kilometres of coastline, including 163 estuaries, and is very indented: nowhere is more than 125 kilometres from tidal waters. Northern Ireland's coastline is approximately 539 kilometres. About 75 per cent of Europe's chalk coasts are in the United Kingdom.

Local planning authorities are responsible for planning land use at the coast; they also aim to safeguard and enhance the coast's natural attractions, and have responsibilities for conservation of areas of scientific interest. The policy for managing coastal erosion and flooding is determined by Defra and the devolved administrations. Operational responsibility lies with local authorities and, in England and Wales, the Environment Agency.

Certain stretches of undeveloped coast of particular beauty in England and Wales are defined as Heritage Coast. There are 46 Heritage Coasts, protecting 32 per cent (1,027 kilometres) of the English coastline and 33 per cent (499 kilometres) of the coastline of Wales (see map in the colour section).

The National Trust (see page 280), through its Neptune Coastline Campaign, raises funds to acquire and protect stretches of coastline of great natural beauty and recreational value in England, Wales and Northern Ireland. The Coastal and Maritime Partnership also brings together a wide range of interests in Wales. The National Trust for Scotland cares for more than 400 kilometres of the Scottish coastline and protects other stretches through conservation agreements.

Flood and coastal defence

Nearly 2 million properties in floodplains along rivers, estuaries and coasts in the United Kingdom are potentially at risk of flooding. A further 80,000 properties are at risk in towns and cities from flooding caused by heavy downpours that overwhelm urban drains. The United Kingdom spent £800 million on flood management in 2003/04. The Environment Agency operates a flood warning system to over 1.2 million properties in England and Wales, which aims to give people at least two hours' notice of impending flooding.

During 2002/03, Defra coordinated an appraisal of the effect of all government policies on flood risk. A new strategy for flood and coastal erosion risk management will be launched in late 2004 or early 2005, to take a 10- to 20-year perspective.

Wildlife protection

All wild bird species in Great Britain, except for a few pest and quarry species, are protected under the *Wildlife and Countryside Act 1981*. Certain birds may be killed or taken at specific times of year, or under a licence issued under the Act.

Other species of animals and plants are protected under the Act when they are considered in danger of extinction, or likely to become so endangered unless conservation measures are taken, or when protection is needed to comply with international legislation. Similar provisions apply under the Wildlife (Northern Ireland) Order 1985. The *Nature Conservation (Scotland) Act 2004* amended the 1981 Act in Scotland in respect of measures for such species. The JNCC (see page 280) is required to review Schedules 5 and 8 (protected animals and plants, respectively) of the 1981 Act every five years and to consult on the level of protection given to these species.

Bird populations are good indicators of the state of wildlife in the countryside, since they are widely distributed and are near the top of the food chain. There are concerns about the declines in certain bird species, as modern land management practices (particularly in agriculture) have altered their habitats and reduced the food supply they need for breeding or surviving the winter.

Defra is providing funding up to 2007 for agri-environment schemes to restore farmland habitats (see page 411) and for the development of wild bird indicators using information from annual surveys run by the British Trust for Ornithology (BTO) and other UK bird conservation agencies.

The UK Biodiversity Action Plan (see page 284) includes targets to reverse declines in bird population. Twenty-six species are considered to require action. The wild bird population index is part of a set of biodiversity indicators while the populations of UK woodland and farmland birds (Figure 19.2) are a headline indicator of sustainable development (see page 114).

Wildlife crime

Wildlife crime takes many forms, including theft of eggs from birds of prey, illegal shooting, trapping, poisoning, digging up of wild plants, and the illicit trade in endangered species. Between 1998 and 2002, seizures under the Convention on International Trade in Endangered Species (CITES, see opposite) in the United Kingdom increased by 8 per cent.

Defra and the Scottish Executive together manage a team of around 100 wildlife inspectors. Their main roles are to verify information submitted in support of applications to keep or trade in wildlife

Figure 19.2 Population of wild birds,[1] UK

Indices (1970=100)

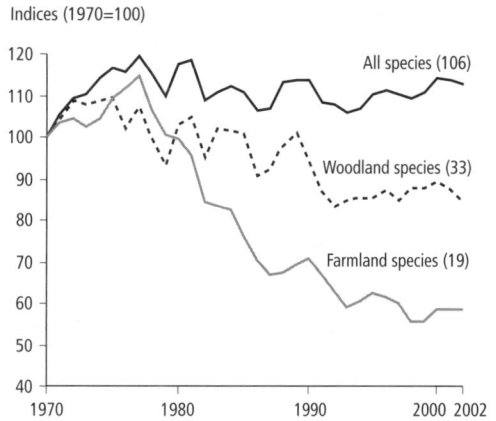

1 The Breeding Birds Survey was not completed in 2001. Estimates for that year are based on the average for 2000 and 2002 for individual species.
Source: British Trust for Ornithology; Royal Society for the Protection of Birds; Department for Environment, Food and Rural Affairs

species, and to check that people are complying with the administrative controls contained in wildlife legislation. There are also specialist wildlife officers in almost every UK police force.

The Partnership for Action against Wildlife Crime, chaired by the police and Defra, provides a forum for communication and co-operation between the statutory enforcement authorities and non-governmental organisations (NGOs) with an active interest in wildlife law enforcement.

The National Wildlife Crime Intelligence Unit, within the National Criminal Intelligence Service (see page 205), provides law enforcement agencies with the information they need to target and disrupt wildlife crimes and the criminals involved. It also acts as a focal point for the gathering and analysing of intelligence on serious wildlife crime at regional, national and international levels.

Much of UK law in relation to wildlife crime is shaped by international regulations. CITES prohibits trade in around 900 species and controls that of a further 32,600. CITES is implemented in the United Kingdom by the Control of Trade in Endangered Species (Enforcement) Regulations 1997.

Habitat protection

Habitat protection is mainly achieved through the networks of SSSIs in Great Britain, and Areas of

Special Scientific Interest (ASSIs) in Northern
Ireland. Sites are protected for their plants, animals
or geological or physiographical features. Some
SSSIs and ASSIs are of international importance
and have been designated for protection under the
EC Wild Birds and Habitats Directives or the
Ramsar Convention (see page 285). In March
2004, 63 per cent of assessed SSSIs in England
were in a favourable or recovering condition.

Conservation agencies in England and Wales have
powers to refuse consent for damaging activities
on SSSIs, to develop management schemes (in
consultation with owners and occupiers of SSSIs),
and to serve a management notice to require
works to be done where necessary. The maximum
penalty for deliberate damage to an SSSI is
£20,000 in a magistrates' court, and unlimited
fines in the Crown Court. Under the *Nature
Conservation (Scotland) Act 2004*, the maximum
penalty in Scotland is £40,000. The Environment
(Northern Ireland) Order 2002 gives the EHS
similar powers in relation to ASSIs.

Charities play an important role in protecting
wildlife throughout the United Kingdom. The
Wildlife Trusts care for over 2,560 nature reserves
covering 82,000 hectares. Over 560,000 people
belong to the 47 independent trusts, which are
mainly based in England and Wales; Scotland is
covered by the Scottish Wildlife Trust. The Royal
Society for the Protection of Birds (RSPB), with
over 1 million members, manages 188 nature
reserves covering 127,911 hectares.

Biodiversity, species recovery and reintroduction

The United Kingdom is one of 187 Parties to the
UN Convention on Biological Diversity Treaty,
agreed at the Rio Earth Summit in 1992 (see page
293). The Parties have agreed to develop national
strategies and programmes for the conservation
and sustainable use of biological diversity and to
ensure the fair and equitable sharing of benefits
from the use of genetic resources. The seventh
meeting of the Conference of the Parties took
place in Kuala Lumpur in February 2004. Issues
discussed included the role of protected areas in
the preservation of biological diversity, the transfer
of technology and the measures to achieve – by
2010 – a significant reduction in the rate of loss of
biodiversity.

The UK Biodiversity Action Plan (UKBAP) is the
Government's response to the Convention. It has
391 species action plans, 45 habitat action plans
and 162 local biodiversity action plans. A review
of UKBAP will be completed in 2005.

Defra published England's biodiversity strategy,
Working with the Grain of Nature, in 2002. A
set of biodiversity indicators to monitor its
implementation, measure progress towards, and
contribute to international targets was published
in December 2003, together with the first annual
stocktake from the England Biodiversity Group.
The delivery of the Northern Ireland Biodiversity
Strategy, published in 2002, is coordinated by the
Northern Ireland Biodiversity Group. The strategy

Table 19.3 Protected areas, 31 March 2004, UK

Type of site[1]	Number of sites	Area (thousand hectares)
National Nature Reserves (NNRs)	395	234
Local Nature Reserves (LNRs)	1,046	45
Sites of Special Scientific Interest (SSSIs) (Great Britain)	6,569	2,341
Areas of Special Scientific Interest (ASSIs) (Northern Ireland)	211	93
Marine Nature Reserves (MNRs)	3	19
Special Protection Areas (SPAs)	242	1,470
Candidate Special Areas of Conservation (SACs)	605	2,501
Ramsar wetland sites	144	759
Environmentally Sensitive Areas (ESAs)[2]	43	3,190
Areas of Outstanding Natural Beauty (AONBs)	50	2,407
National Scenic Areas (Scotland)	40	1,002

1 Some areas may be included in more than one category.
2 As at 31 March 2002.
Source: JNCC, Department for Environment, Food and Rural Affairs

developed by the Scottish Biodiversity Forum for the Scottish Executive was launched in May 2004. In Wales, the Assembly is advised by the Wales Biodiversity Group.

The Royal Botanic Gardens at Kew (see page 399) has been successful for many years in the reintroduction of species. In August 2004, its Millennium Seed Bank at Wakehurst Place, West Sussex, held 13,000 species secured from around the world. It also held seeds of all UK flora species.

The Royal Botanic Garden Edinburgh (RBGE, see page 399) promotes conservation programmes for rare plants in Scotland and for coniferous trees worldwide, maintaining genetically diverse populations in cultivation at many sites as pools for eventual reintroduction to the wild.

International action

In addition to the Convention on Biological Diversity (see page 284), the United Kingdom is a party to many international wildlife conventions and EC Directives. The 1992 EC Habitats Directive aims to promote biodiversity through the conservation of natural habitats, wild flora and non-avian fauna. Its key obligations are to select and designate a network of sites – Special Areas of Conservation (SACs) – and to provide stringent protection for habitats and species linked to the Directive. It is envisaged that these sites will make a significant contribution to conserving the 169 habitat types and 623 species identified by the Directive as being most in need of conservation in a European context. In the United Kingdom, 76 of the habitat types have been identified, as have 51 species. Along with the similar Special Protection Areas (SPAs) set up under the earlier Birds Directive, SACs form the UK component of the Europe-wide Natura 2000 network.

Advice to the Government on which sites should be SACs or SPAs has been provided by the statutory conservation agencies (see page 280) and coordinated by the JNCC. At 31 March 2004, 605 candidate SACs covering 2.5 million hectares had been submitted and 242 SPAs covering 1.5 million hectares had been classified.

The Convention on Wetlands of International Importance (the Ramsar Convention) is an intergovernmental treaty covering all aspects of wetland conservation and use. At April 2004, there were 144 designated and 8 proposed Ramsar sites

in the United Kingdom. CITES seeks to ensure, through a permit system, that trade in threatened species is legal and not detrimental to the conservation of the species concerned. The Convention on the Conservation of Migratory Species of Wild Animals (the Bonn Convention) coordinates international action on a range of endangered migratory species.

The United Kingdom is a member of the IUCN (the World Conservation Union), the largest nature conservation body in the world with a membership of nearly 1,000 governmental and non-governmental organisations. It helps societies to conserve the integrity and diversity of nature and to ensure that use of natural resources is equitable and ecologically sustainable.

Land quality

Land quality in the United Kingdom is relatively good, but faces pressure from a range of factors including contamination, urbanisation, localised erosion and declining organic content. Contaminated land is the legacy of an industrial age that generated wealth but also caused much pollution. Government policy emphasises the importance of voluntary action to clean up contaminated land, and most attempts to clean up sites occur when they are redeveloped. The proportion of new homes built on previously developed land is a headline indicator of sustainable development (see page 114).

Under the *Environmental Protection Act 1990*, local authorities are working to identify contaminated land, and by June 2004, 73 sites in England and Wales had been identified. Of these, 20 were designated as special sites where the Environment Agency is the lead regulator. The most common pollutants at the sites were organic compounds and metals. By March 2004, Scottish local authorities had identified two sites as contaminated; neither were special sites.

Many of the species identified in UKBAP depend on the right type and quality of soil for their survival, and a good balance of soil types is required to support the existing range of ecosystems, landscapes and agriculture. The Government is committed to ensuring that soil protection receives the same priority as air and water. Defra published the *First Soil Action Plan for England* in May 2004. This sets out a three-year programme designed to ensure that soil will be used and looked after in ways that get the best from this resource. It was complemented by a report on soils and a consultation on a strategy for soil protection in England and Wales, published by the Environment Agency in the same month.

Waste and recycling

Defra estimates that the United Kingdom produces over 400 million tonnes of waste a year, the majority of which comes from agricultural, industrial and construction sources. Households produce a considerable amount of waste – 88 per cent of the estimated 29.3 million tonnes of municipal waste in England in 2002/03.

Municipal and household waste were 1.8 per cent and 1.0 per cent lower, respectively, in 2002/03 than in 2001/02. The proportion of household waste that is recycled increased from 9 per cent in 1998/99 to 14.5 per cent in 2002/03. Household waste (amount and proportion recycled) and all controlled waste[4] are covered by a headline indicator of sustainable development (see page 114). All English local authorities have targets for household waste recycling and composting, and Defra is offering grants totalling £20 million to help them in 2004/05. Wales, Scotland and Northern Ireland have each developed their own national strategies and specific targets.

The Environment Agency has begun a second survey of industrial and commercial waste production, with results expected by spring 2005. The first survey, in 1998/99, reported annual arisings of such waste of 75 million tonnes in England and Wales.

Nearly half of waste from households, commerce and industry is disposed of to landfill, a method that makes little practical use of waste (although landfill gas from some sites is used for energy generation). In the case of municipal waste (Table 19.5), 16 per cent was recycled or composted in England in 2002/03, but the majority, 75 per cent, was disposed of in landfill.

Recent legislation is intended to improve the amount of waste recycled:

- the *Household Waste Recycling Act 2003* places a duty upon local authorities in England and

Map 19.4 Household waste recycling by area, 2002/03 England and Wales

Percentage of household waste recycled

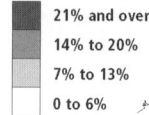

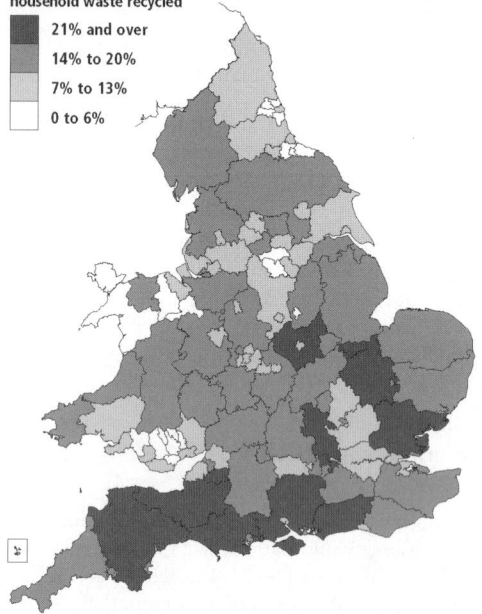

- 21% and over
- 14% to 20%
- 7% to 13%
- 0 to 6%

1 Data for Wales are for 2001–02.
Source: Department for Food, Environment and Rural Affairs; Welsh Assembly Government

Wales to provide a collection of at least two types of recyclable waste from every household by the year 2010; and

- the *Waste and Emissions Trading Act 2003* aims to help the United Kingdom deliver its commitments to both the Kyoto Protocol (see page 293) and the EC Landfill Directive. The Act provides a legislative framework for trading schemes that allow the required reductions – whether in biodegradable[5] municipal waste going to landfill or in emissions of greenhouse gases to the atmosphere – to be made where it is most cost effective to do so.

By 2005, the Government aims to reduce the amount of UK industrial and commercial waste disposed of in landfill sites to 85 per cent of 1998 levels. In England, it aims to recycle or compost at least 25 per cent of household waste by 2005/06, increasing this to 33 per cent by 2015. Meeting these targets would go some way towards fulfilling

---

4 Controlled waste comprises municipal/household waste, industrial and commercial waste, and construction and demolition waste. Non-controlled waste comes from agriculture, mining and quarrying.

5 Biodegradable waste consists of material such as paper, food and green waste, which produce methane – a powerful greenhouse gas – as they degrade.

Table 19.5 Management of municipal waste, England

	1997/98		2002/03	
	Thousand tonnes	%	Thousand tonnes	%
Landfill	21,765	85	21,969	75
Incineration with energy recovery	1,624	6	2,607	9
Refuse-derived fuel manufacture	156	1	87	-
Recycled/composted	2,063	8	4,577	16
Other	102	-	69	-
Total	**25,711**	*100*	**29,308**	*100*

Source: Department for Environment, Food and Rural Affairs

the Government's obligation under the EC Landfill Directive, which requires the United Kingdom to reduce the landfilling of biodegradable municipal waste to 35 per cent of its 1995 level by 2020.

The Waste and Resources Action Programme (WRAP) aims to overcome market barriers to the recovery and recycling of waste. In 2003, it gained additional responsibilities following the review of waste policy *Waste not, Want not*. The review concluded that waste volumes in England would double and costs increase by £1.6 billion a year between 2002 and 2020. WRAP is a not-for-profit company limited by guarantee by Defra, the Department of Trade and Industry (DTI) and the devolved administrations. The Waste Implementation Programme was also set up by Defra in response to the recommendations made in *Waste not, Want not*. It aims to divert biodegradable municipal waste away from landfill. In February 2004, it launched two programmes, worth £32 million, to encourage the take up of new technologies for treating biodegradable municipal waste.

The landfill tax credit scheme enables landfill site operators in the United Kingdom to channel up to 6 per cent of their landfill tax liability into environmental bodies for use in approved projects. Examples include reclamation of polluted land, research and education activities to promote reuse and recycling, provision of public parks, and restoration of historic buildings.

Wales

The Welsh Assembly Government's waste strategy includes targets for public bodies to reduce their waste arisings by at least 10 per cent from the 1998 level by 2010, and targets for local authorities to have 40 per cent of waste recycled/composted by

Recycling electrical equipment

At least 1 million tonnes of waste electrical and electronic equipment (WEEE) from domestic and commercial sources is discarded in the United Kingdom every year and the Environment Agency estimates that this waste stream is growing by 4 to 8 per cent a year. There are also concerns about the high level of hazardous materials in such waste.

The EC Waste Electrical and Electronic Equipment Directive requires the United Kingdom to provide collection facilities for such equipment. From August 2005, producers will be responsible for ensuring that the collected WEEE is treated and that specified recycling targets are met. The related EC Restriction of the Use of Certain Hazardous Substances in Electrical and Electronic Equipment Directive bans the sale, from July 2006, of new electrical and electronic equipment containing more than agreed levels of lead, mercury, cadmium, hexavalent chromium and two classes of flame retardants.

The Directives aim to reduce the disposal of WEEE to landfill and to increase levels of recovery and recycling by removing hazardous components during treatment and ultimately during manufacture. They cover a wide range of equipment including televisions, power tools, computers, kitchen appliances, electronic toys and monitoring and control equipment.

Legislation is planned to implement the Directives in the United Kingdom.

the same date. Municipal waste arisings in 2002/03 were 1.79 million tonnes, up by 4 per cent from 2001/02. The proportion that was recycled or composted increased from 8.4 per cent in 2001/02 to 12.6 per cent in 2002/03. Twelve per cent of household waste was collected for recycling/ composting. The Assembly-backed Strategic Recycling Scheme has funds of £30 million for reuse, recycling and composting projects in Welsh communities. Between 2001 and 2005, the Assembly gave grants of £63.5 million to local authorities to help them develop sustainable waste management practices.

Scotland

Scotland produced around 9 million tonnes of waste in 2002/03. In 2001/02, 92 per cent of municipal waste was landfilled and 7 per cent was recycled. The *National Waste Plan 2003* contains targets to recycle or compost 25 per cent of municipal waste by 2006, rising to 55 per cent by 2020 and, by the same date, to reduce the proportion of waste sent to landfill from 90 to 30 per cent. It also includes plans for segregated kerbside recycling collection for nine out of ten Scottish homes by 2020. A Strategic Waste Fund of £230 million over the three years 2003 to 2006 will assist local authorities implement Area Waste Plans.

Northern Ireland

The Department of the Environment's *Waste Management Strategy for Northern Ireland* sets out a number of targets. These include: recovering 25 per cent of household waste by 2005, rising to 40 per cent by 2010; reducing the landfilling of industrial and commercial wastes to 85 per cent of 1998 levels by 2005; and reducing the quantities of biodegradable waste being landfilled to 75 per cent of 1995 levels by 2010, rising to 50 per cent by 2013 and 35 per cent by 2020. In June 2004, the independent Waste Management Advisory Board published a review of the Strategy commissioned by the DoE, with recommendations for the implementation of its next phase.

Packaging

The EC Directive on Packaging and Packaging Waste set targets that at least 50 per cent of UK packaging waste should be recovered and at least 25 per cent recycled by 2001. Revised EU targets have been set for 2008; the Government has responded by setting new targets for 2004 to 2008 for regulated businesses. In 2003, the United

Kingdom recovered 5.37 million tonnes of packaging waste – a recovery rate of 53.4 per cent.

Recycling facilities

Across the United Kingdom, recycling banks are available for the public to deposit various waste materials, including bottles, cans, clothes, paper and plastics. In addition, some local authorities provide kerbside collection of recyclable materials. In 2003, 69 per cent of newsprint was recycled. In comparison, 42 per cent of aluminium cans, 34 per of container glass and 6 per cent of plastics were recycled in 2001, the most recent year for which data are available for these materials.

Hazardous waste

There is an extensive framework of national and EU legislation on the manufacture, distribution, use and disposal of hazardous chemicals. Since 1996, the EC Hazardous Waste List that defines the scope of the Hazardous Waste Directive has been refined and increased in length.

International movements of hazardous waste are controlled by the Basel Convention on the Control of Transboundary Movements of Hazardous Wastes and their Disposal. The United Kingdom is a signatory of the Basel Convention Protocol on Liability and Compensation.

The Hazardous Waste Forum was set up by the Government in December 2002 to consider the demands on industry made by existing and forthcoming legislation and to consider targets for hazardous waste reduction and recovery. In December 2003, the Forum published an action plan for the reduction and environmentally sound management of hazardous waste.

A three-month consultation on the proposed Hazardous Waste Regulations, covering the movement of hazardous waste from the producer to the disposal or treatment facility, was launched in July 2004 in England. If adopted, the new Regulations will replace the Special Waste Regulations 1996 and introduce simpler procedures for the management of hazardous waste, while meeting the requirements of the EC Hazardous Waste Directive. Similar consultations are planned in Wales and Northern Ireland. The Scottish Executive consulted on the revised Regulations in 2003, and the Special Waste Amendment (Scotland) Regulations 2004 came into force in July.

EC End-of-life Vehicles Directive

Around 1.8 million end-of-life vehicles (ELVs) are scrapped in the United Kingdom each year, generating about 2 million tonnes of waste material. About 74 to 80 per cent of the weight of a typical ELV is reused or recycled. The requirements of the EC ELV Directive include:

- producers to limit the use of certain hazardous substances in vehicles and promote recyclability;

- ELVs to be treated before dismantling, recycling or disposal;

- permits for facilities treating ELVs that have not had pollutants removed; and

- recovery and recycling targets to be met in 2006 and 2015.

In June 2003, the UK Government announced that, until 2007, the 'last owner' of the vehicle (and not the 'producer') would continue to have responsibility for the cost of its treatment and disposal. Parts of the Directive, including the treatment provisions, were implemented in the United Kingdom in regulations introduced in November 2003. The Government is continuing to consult on how to implement the Directive's other requirements.

Managing hazardous waste

From July 2004, the Landfill Directive makes it illegal to dispose of hazardous waste with other types of waste in the same section of a landfill (greatly reducing the number of sites that can accept hazardous waste). It also requires hazardous waste to be pre-treated prior to disposal and, from July 2005, this pre-treatment must meet EC waste acceptance criteria. Replacement of the Special Waste Regulations with the Hazardous Waste Regulations will increase the types and quantities of waste classed as hazardous. Implementation of the ELV, WEEE and RoHS Directives (see box opposite and page 287) will also affect hazardous waste management in the United Kingdom. Defra and other organisations launched a new website in July 2004 to provide information to those affected by the changes.

Litter and dog fouling

It is a criminal offence to leave litter in any public place in the open air or to dump rubbish except in designated places. Local authorities have a duty to keep public land free of litter and refuse, including dog excrement, as far as is practicable. In 2002/03, local authorities in England spent £456 million on street cleansing and litter. They can issue £50 Fixed Penalty Notices (FPNs) for litter and dog fouling offences (£40 for dog fouling offences in Scotland); the maximum fine, upon successful prosecution if FPNs are not paid, is £2,500 for littering and £1,000 for dog fouling (£500 in Scotland). The *Dog Fouling (Scotland) Act 2003* makes it an offence to fail to clear away and dispose of the excrement appropriately.

ENCAMS is a charity that runs the Keep Britain Tidy campaign and tackles issues such as litter,

fly-tipping, abandoned vehicles, dog fouling, gum, graffiti and vandalism in the United Kingdom. It is part-funded by the Government and works in collaboration with local authorities and the private sector. It conducts a continuous survey of local environmental quality in England. Findings from the second survey published in 2003 included a 27 per cent reduction in dog fouling in 2002/03 compared with 2001/02, a marked increase in chewing gum deposits and a significant rise in fast food litter. Some 40 per cent of sites examined were classed as either good or satisfactory, but 54 per cent of sites were considered unsatisfactory and 6 per cent were poor.

Monitoring by the environment agencies, local authorities, police and ENCAMS shows that the incidence of fly-tipping (the illegal dumping of waste) has increased since the introduction of the landfill tax in 1996. The Environment Agency estimates that fly-tipping incidents cost the local authorities over £100 million a year to clear. Household rubbish, food and drink containers, vehicles and tyres were the most commonly dumped materials.

The maximum penalty on successful prosecution for fly-tipping (and other offences relating to waste) is a fine of up to £20,000 in a magistrates' court and up to five years' imprisonment and/or an unlimited fine in the Crown Court. In 2002/03, the Environment Agency won 186 successful prosecutions against fly-tippers. Similar penalties exist in Scotland, where prosecutions normally proceed before the sheriff courts. Defra is developing a fly-tipping strategy to help improve local environmental quality in line with the new powers available to the authorities under the *Anti-Social Behaviour Act 2003* (see also page 302). The Act requires local authorities and the Environment Agency to submit monthly data on the type and quantity of fly-tipping they deal with. The Agency's Internet-based reporting system, Flycapture, went live in April 2004 and, by July, over 94 per cent of local authorities in England and Wales had registered to use it.

Historic buildings and monuments

In England, lists of buildings of special architectural or historic interest are compiled by the Department for Culture, Media and Sport (DCMS) with advice from English Heritage. In Wales and Scotland, buildings are listed by Cadw (the Welsh Historic Monuments executive agency) and Historic Scotland (an agency of the Scottish Executive) respectively. In Northern Ireland, the EHS has responsibility for historic buildings, following consultation with the advisory Historic Buildings Council and the local district council.

It is a criminal offence to demolish a listed building, or alter or extend it in a way that affects its character, without prior consent from the local planning authority or – on appeal or following call-in – the appropriate government minister. A local planning authority can issue a building preservation notice to protect for six months an unlisted building that it considers to be of special architectural or historic interest and that is at risk, while a decision is taken on whether it should be listed.

There are proposals for a new system of heritage protection which will create a single list of historic sites and buildings in England. The new system is being piloted by English Heritage at 15 sites, including York's Roman Walls, the Weld Estate in Dorset, and at several Piccadilly Line Stations on the London Underground.

English Heritage assesses known archaeological sites in order to identify those that should be afforded statutory protection. It makes its recommendations to the DCMS, which maintains

the schedule of ancient monuments.[6] The number of entries tends to fluctuate as some of those sites considered less important may be 'descheduled', while others are added.

Similar arrangements exist to identify buildings and ancient and historic monuments eligible for statutory protection in Wales and Scotland. In Northern Ireland, the EHS assesses all known archaeological sites to identify those that should be protected. It then makes recommendations to the Historic Monuments Council and also maintains the schedule.

English Heritage is responsible for the maintenance, repair and presentation of 410 historic properties in public ownership or guardianship. It gave grants of £39 million in 2002/03 for the repair of other important ancient monuments and historic buildings. Most English Heritage properties are open to the public, and there were nearly 5.5 million visits to staffed properties in 2002/03. Government funding for English Heritage in 2004/05 is £122 million.

Cadw and Historic Scotland, which perform similar functions, care for 129 and over 330 monuments respectively. There were nearly 3 million visitors to Historic Scotland's properties where admission is charged in 2003/04 and over 1 million visitors to monuments in Wales in 2002/03. The DoE in Northern Ireland has 181 historic monuments in state care or guardianship, managed by the EHS. These received an estimated 150,000 visits in 2002.

Local planning authorities have designated more than 8,000 conservation areas of special architectural or historic interest in England and there are 513 in Wales, around 600 in Scotland and 58 in Northern Ireland. These areas receive additional protection through the planning system, particularly over the proposed demolition of unlisted buildings.

The National Heritage Memorial Fund helps towards the cost of acquiring, maintaining or preserving land, buildings, objects and collections that are of outstanding interest and of importance to the national heritage. In addition, its trustees

---

6 The word 'monument' in this context covers the whole range of archaeological sites. Scheduled monuments are not always ancient, or visible above ground.

are responsible for distributing the heritage share of the proceeds from the National Lottery (see page 275). By March 2004, the Heritage Lottery Fund had made more than 14,500 decisions across the United Kingdom, worth over £2.9 billion.

Many of the royal palaces and all the royal parks are open to the public; their maintenance is the responsibility of the DCMS and Historic Scotland. Historic Royal Palaces, the Royal Household and the Royal Parks Agency carry out this function on behalf of the Secretary of State in England.

World Heritage sites

The World Heritage List was established under the United Nations Educational, Scientific and Cultural Organisation's (UNESCO) 1972 World Heritage Convention in order to identify and secure lasting protection for sites of outstanding universal value.

There are 26 UK World Heritage sites (see map at the end of the first colour section), including three in Overseas Territories – St George in Bermuda, Henderson Island, and Gough Island wildlife reserve. The latest area to gain World Heritage status in the United Kingdom was Liverpool's waterfront and commercial centre, in July 2004.

Great Britain's historic canal network

There are over 4,820 kilometres of fully navigable inland waterways in Great Britain. British Waterways (see page 341) is responsible for caring for and managing 75 per cent of them. Its network of canals and rivers includes 2,555 listed structures and buildings, and 69 scheduled ancient monuments, including three sites on English Heritage's Buildings at Risk register.

In 2002/03, British Waterways spent £83.6 million on major repairs and renovation of its canals. Projects included the restoration of a unique counterweighted lift bridge on the Huddersfield Broad Canal.

Air and the atmosphere

Air quality

Air quality in the United Kingdom has improved considerably since the infamous London smogs of the 1950s, due to the replacement of coal by electricity and natural gas for domestic heating, tighter regulation[7] and structural changes in industry, and the introduction of progressively more stringent standards for vehicle exhaust emissions. For example, emissions of carbon monoxide (CO) fell by 56 per cent between 1990 and 2002, while those for sulphur dioxide (SO_2) fell by 73 per cent.

Under the provisions of the *Environment Act 1995*, the Government is required to publish an Air Quality Strategy setting out its policies for managing ambient air quality in the United Kingdom, particularly in relation to reducing air pollution and any remaining risks to people's health and the natural and built environment. The current strategy contains air quality standards and objectives for nine pollutants of particular concern to human health: nitrogen dioxide, PM_{10} (particulate matter less than 10 microns in diameter), SO_2, CO, ozone, lead, benzene, 1,3-butadiene and polycyclic aromatic hydrocarbons (PAHs).

In February 2003, Defra and the devolved administrations introduced tighter objectives for benzene, CO and PM_{10}, and an objective for PAHs for the first time. These are the same throughout the United Kingdom except for benzene and PM_{10}. A tougher PM_{10} objective than elsewhere was proposed for Scotland because air quality there is generally better; conversely, a less stringent objective was proposed for London. Similarly, tighter benzene objectives were set for Scotland and Northern Ireland than for England and Wales.

Monitoring air quality

The United Kingdom has an automatic air quality monitoring network with 120 sites in both urban and rural areas (as at March 2004) covering much of the country. In general there has been a long-term decline in the number of air pollution days, largely because of the reduction in particles and

7 Information on air pollution legislation is given on page 302.

SO_2, but fluctuations from one year to another can occur because of differences in weather conditions. In 2003, air pollution in the United Kingdom was recorded as moderate or higher on an average of 50 days per monitoring site in urban areas; this compared with 20 days in 2002, and 59 days when the series started in 1993. In rural areas, air pollution was recorded as moderate or higher on 61 days on average per site in 2003 compared with 30 days in 2002. Days of moderate or heavy air pollution are a headline indicator of sustainable development – see page 114.

The main causes of moderate or higher air pollution at urban sites are ground level ozone and PM_{10}. Ground level ozone is formed from photochemical reactions of other pollutants such as nitrogen oxides (NO_x) and volatile organic compounds (VOCs) – for example solvents used in industry, domestic products and dry cleaning, fumes at petrol pumps, and paints. Pollution caused by PM_{10} and SO_2 has fallen significantly since 1993, leaving ozone as the principal cause of pollution in urban areas.

Air Quality Bulletins provide the public with hourly updates of air pollution data from the national monitoring network. These give the concentrations of the main pollutants, together with a forecast. The information features on television and radio weather reports, and appears in many national and local newspapers. Information can also be accessed through the United Kingdom's Air Quality Archive website (*www.airquality.co.uk*).

Vehicle emissions

Measures to reduce pollution from road transport are seen as vital to achieving the objectives set out in the UK Air Quality Strategy. Progressively tighter standards for fuels and vehicle emissions mean that urban road transport emissions of CO, NO_x and particulates are projected to fall by around 70 per cent between 1995 and 2015.

Vehicle emissions standards are governed by a series of EC Directives enforced in the United Kingdom under the Motor Vehicles Construction and Use and Type Approval Regulations. All new petrol-engine passenger cars are fitted with catalytic converters, which typically reduce emissions by over 75 per cent. These measures to reduce emissions from new vehicles have been accompanied by improvements in fuel quality with, for instance, reductions in components such as benzene and sulphur and the phasing out of leaded petrol.

Compulsory testing of vehicle emissions is a key element in the UK strategy for improving air quality. Metered emission tests and smoke checks feature in the annual 'MoT' roadworthiness test. Enforcement checks carried out at the roadside or at operators' premises also include a check for excessive smoke. Local councils in England and Wales with designated Air Quality Management Areas have the power to use roadside testing to enforce vehicle exhaust emissions standards in those areas. Similar powers are available to all Scottish local authorities and the National Assembly for Wales is consulting on extending them to local authorities there.

Transboundary air pollution

The pollutant gases SO_2 (mainly from power stations), NO_x (from road transport and power stations), and ammonia (NH_3 – mainly from livestock) can be carried over long distances before being deposited directly onto vegetation and soil or being washed out as acid rain. Acidification results when sensitive ecosystems are not capable of neutralising the deposited acidity. In the United Kingdom, the ecosystems that are most sensitive to acidification are located in the northern and western uplands. High levels of acid deposition have a damaging effect on soils, freshwater, trees and buildings.

The United Kingdom is a party to the UNECE (United Nations Economic Commission for Europe) Convention on Long Range Transboundary Air Pollution, set up in 1979 in response to evidence that acidification of lakes in Scandinavia was linked to emissions of SO_2 from other countries in Europe, including the United Kingdom. Under the Convention, there have been a number of protocols to reduce emissions of acidifying pollutants.

The latest Gothenburg Protocol, signed in 1999, tackles the problems of acidification, eutrophication[8] and ground-level ozone (photochemical or summer smog). Under the Protocol, the United Kingdom agreed annual emission ceilings, to be achieved by 2010, of 625 kilotonnes for SO_2, 1,181 kilotonnes for NO_x, 297 kilotonnes for NH_3, and 1,200 kilotonnes for VOCs. Emission levels for 2002 are given in Table 19.6.

---

8 The process by which pollution from sewage or fertilisers stimulates excessive growth of algae. Death and decomposition of the algae depletes the oxygen content of the water, resulting in the death of fish and other animals.

Table 19.6 Emissions of selected air pollutants, UK

	1992	2002
		Kilotonnes
Carbon monoxide	6,872	3,238
Nitrogen oxides	2,566	1,582
Volatile organic compounds[1]	2,430	1,364
Sulphur dioxide	3,463	1,003
Ammonia[1]	359	306
PM10[2]	298	161

1 Excludes emissions from 'natural' sources such as forests, which are outside the scope of international reporting conventions.
2 Excludes resuspension.
Source: Department for Environment, Food and Rural Affairs

Alongside the Gothenburg Protocol, the EC National Emission Ceilings Directive is intended to tackle the harmful effects to human health and the environment from transboundary air pollution. Regulations came into force in the United Kingdom in January 2003, setting ceilings for 2010 for the same four pollutants. The United Kingdom is committed to further cuts in SO_2 and NO_x emissions, reducing the ceilings to 585 kilotonnes and 1,167 kilotonnes respectively.

Road transport and power stations are two of the most important sources of air pollutants in the United Kingdom. In 2002, road transport accounted for 59 per cent of CO emissions and 45 per cent of NO_x emissions, while power stations accounted for 68 and 24 per cent of SO_2 and NO_x emissions respectively.

Climate change

Several gases naturally present in the atmosphere keep the Earth at a temperature suitable for life by trapping energy from the Sun – the 'greenhouse' effect. However, emissions from human activities are increasing the atmospheric concentrations of several greenhouse gases, causing global warming and climate change.

Global climate data analysed by the Hadley Centre (part of the Met Office) shows that 2003 was the third warmest year after 1998 and 2002 in the 143-year records. The ten warmest years on record have all occurred since the beginning of the 1990s. On the hottest day of 2003, the temperature reached 38.5°C at Brogdale, near Faversham in Kent, breaking the previous UK record by 1.4°C.

During 2002/03, Defra's Global Atmosphere Division commissioned research worth £12 million on climate change and stratospheric ozone depletion. Research at the Hadley Centre is focused on improving climate predictions and investigating the causes of climate change. Recent results from its climate model suggest that if greenhouse gas emissions remain high, there will be a rise in average global temperature of 4.5°C over the next 100 years; but if emissions fall sufficiently, the temperature rise will be 2°C.

The first international action dealing with climate change dates from the Rio Earth Summit in 1992. The resulting UN Framework Convention on Climate Change (UNFCCC) was adopted in 1994 and called for the stabilisation of greenhouse gas concentrations in the atmosphere at a level that would prevent dangerous man-made interference with the climate system. By 2004, 188 governments (including the European Union) were Parties to the Convention. The tenth Conference of the Parties (COP) will be held in Buenos Aires, Argentina, in December 2004.

At the third COP held at Kyoto in 1997, Parties agreed legally binding targets for developed countries to reduce emissions of the basket of six main greenhouse gases: carbon dioxide (CO_2), methane (CH_4), nitrous oxide (N_2O), hydrofluorocarbons (HFCs), perfluorocarbons (PFCs) and sulphur hexafluoride (SF_6). The Kyoto Protocol committed developed nations to a 5.2 per cent reduction in greenhouse gas emissions below 1990 levels by 2008–12. The European Union subsequently agreed to a collective reduction of 8 per cent by that date, which was shared out by Member States to reflect national circumstances.

The UK Government and the devolved administrations intend to move towards a domestic goal of a 20 per cent cut in CO_2 emissions between 1990 and 2010. The energy White Paper published in February 2003 (see page 440) accepted the Royal Commission on Environmental Pollution's recommendation that the United Kingdom should aim to reduce CO_2 emissions by 60 per cent from current levels by about 2050.

The United Kingdom is on course to meet its target under the Protocol of a reduction of 12.5

per cent by 2008–12. The baseline used is the sum of the 1990 totals for CO_2, CH_4, N_2O and the 1995 totals for HFCs, PFCs and SF_6. Emissions of the basket of greenhouse gases, weighted by global warming potential, fell by 14 per cent between the 1990 baseline and 2003 (Figure 19.7). The most significant greenhouse gas emitted by the United Kingdom is CO_2, followed by CH_4 and N_2O. Total emissions of CO_2 in the United Kingdom in 2003 were provisionally estimated at 152.5 million tonnes. This is about 7 per cent lower than in 1990, but 1.5 per cent higher than in 2002, largely due to greater use of coal for electricity generation and a decrease in net imports of electricity from the continent. The increase partly reverses the 3.5 per cent reduction in the previous year. Emissions of CO_2 and the basket of greenhouse gases together form one of the headline indicators of sustainable development.

Figure 19.7 Emissions of greenhouse gases, UK

Million tonnes carbon equivalent

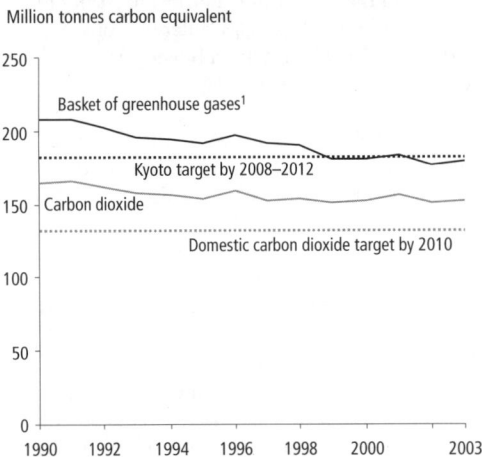

1 Emissions of the basket of greehouse gases (CO_2, CH_4, N_2O, HFCs, PFCs, SF_6) are presented based on their global warming potential.
Source: NETCEN

The integrated package of policies and measures contained in the UK climate change programme includes the climate change levy, which applies to sales of electricity, coal, natural gas and liquefied petroleum gas to the non-domestic sector (see page 441). This aims to encourage business energy efficiency and is expected to save at least 5 million tonnes of carbon emissions by 2010. The package also includes a target to deliver 10 per cent of the United Kingdom's electricity from renewable sources of energy by 2010.

Emissions trading

Emissions trading schemes – another key element of the European Union and United Kingdom climate change programmes – are designed to allow businesses to reduce their emissions of greenhouse gases in the most economically efficient way. The UK scheme, launched in 2002, was the world's first economy-wide greenhouse gas emissions trading scheme. It works by giving individual companies and installations a cap, which when added together forms an overall emissions cap for the trading scheme. Participating companies can meet their individual obligation by:

Transport and climate change

Transport contributes about a quarter of CO_2 emissions in the United Kingdom. Road transport accounts for 85 per cent of this, with cars providing around half of all transport emissions. Between 1970 and 2002, road traffic increased by 142 per cent, outstripping growth in the economy – gross domestic product increased by 107 per cent over the same period. Carbon dioxide emissions attributable to road transport were 130 per cent higher in 2001 than in 1970.

The Royal Commission on Environmental Pollution's special report on the environmental effects of civil aircraft in flight, published in 2002, stressed that emissions from aircraft are likely to be a major contributor to global warming if the present increase in air traffic continues unabated. Passenger-kilometres flown from UK airports more than doubled from 125 billion in 1990 to 260 billion in 2000. By 2050, the International Panel on Climate Change believes that aviation will produce up to 15 per cent of man-made global warming. The Government is seeking to balance the economic benefits of air transport against the environmental impact and a White Paper, *The Future of Air Transport* (see page 341), was published in December 2003.

- reducing their own emissions to the target level;
- reducing their emissions below their target and selling or banking the excess 'emissions allowances';
- letting their emissions remain above target and buying emissions allowances from other participants.

Across the whole scheme, those with low-cost emission reduction opportunities tend to sell allowances to those with higher cost options, thereby minimising the overall cost of delivering a set of environmental benefits.

Thirty-two organisations, including some of the largest businesses, participate directly in the UK scheme and have legally binding targets to reduce their emissions against 1998–2000 levels. The scheme is also open to around 5,000 further companies with Climate Change Agreements. The *Waste and Emissions Trading Act 2003* (see page 286) contains provisions to develop the statutory framework for emissions trading schemes.

The ozone layer

Stratospheric ozone is a layer of gas about 15 to 50 kilometres above the Earth's surface, which protects it from the more harmful effects of solar radiation. UK scientists first discovered ozone losses over much of the globe – including a 'hole' in the ozone layer over Antarctica – in 1985. The hole has been growing, reaching a record 29 million square kilometres in 2000; after a slight decrease to 27 million square kilometres in 2001, it increased almost to the 2000 level in 2003 (the variation in size is due to meteorological factors). Similar, but less dramatic, thinning of the ozone layer occurs over the North Pole each year. Ozone depletion is caused by man-made chemicals containing chlorine or bromine, such as chlorofluorocarbons (CFCs), hydrochlorofluorocarbons (HCFCs), methyl bromide, carbon tetrachloride and halons.

In an effort to repair this damage, over 170 countries have ratified the Montreal Protocol, an international treaty for the protection of the stratospheric ozone layer. This is enforced in the United Kingdom by an EC Regulation. The implementation of the Protocol has reduced the emissions of ozone depleting substances, although it will be some time before the full impact is felt.

EU Emissions Trading Scheme

The EU Emissions Trading Scheme will commence on 1 January 2005. The first phase runs from 2005–07 and the second phase from 2008–12 (to coincide with the first Kyoto Commitment Period). Over 1,000 installations within the United Kingdom are covered by the Scheme and all are required to hold a greenhouse gas emissions trading permit. Each Member State must set a 'cap' on emissions of CO_2 and permitted installations will be allocated allowances (similar to quotas) that they can trade to help them meet their emissions reduction targets.

Full compliance with the Protocol is likely to result in the recovery of the ozone layer within the next 50 years.

Noise

Local authorities have a duty to inspect their areas for 'statutory nuisances' including noise nuisance from domestic premises, vehicles, machinery or equipment in the street, industrial/commercial premises, road works, and construction and demolition sites. They must take reasonable steps to investigate complaints and serve a noise abatement notice where it is judged to be a statutory nuisance.

According to the Chartered Institute of Environmental Health, domestic premises were the most common source of noise complaints, accounting for some 224,500 such incidents out of a total of 305,090 reported to local authorities in 2002/03 in England and Wales. From 9,230 notices served in this period, there were 665 prosecutions and 452 convictions.

Defra is responsible for developing government policy on neighbourhood noise (noise other than in the workplace) and other statutory nuisance. This includes developing a national ambient noise strategy and implementing the EC Environmental Noise Directive. Other government departments are responsible for reducing emissions from specific noise sources and for other noise and nuisance issues – for example, the Department for

Transport covers noise emissions from civil aviation, vehicles and railways.

Radioactivity

Most radiation to which the UK population is exposed occurs naturally (for example from the radon gas given off by some rock formations, particularly granite). Man-made radiation represents about 15 per cent of the total exposure, mostly from medical sources such as X-rays. The keeping and use of radioactive materials are subject to stringent control by the Environment Agency, the Scottish Environment Protection Agency (SEPA) or the Chief Radiochemical Inspector in Northern Ireland. The Health and Safety Executive (HSE – see page 158) is responsible for regulating safety at civil nuclear installations. The National Radiological Protection Board (NRPB) advises on health risks posed by radiation and how to guard against them.

Radioactive waste management

The United Kingdom has over 100,000 tonnes of solid, long-lived radioactive waste in storage. This will rise to over 500,000 tonnes over the next century as nuclear reactors and other facilities come to the end of their lives and are decommissioned. All solid radioactive waste in the United Kingdom is either disposed of in suitable facilities on land or safely stored pending a decision on how it is to be managed.

Radioactive waste varies widely in nature and level of activity, and the methods of current management reflect this. Most solid waste of low radioactivity is disposed of at the shallow disposal facility at Drigg in Cumbria. Small quantities of very low-level waste are disposed of at authorised landfill sites. Some intermediate-level waste is stored at nuclear licensed sites (usually where it is generated), but most of the UK inventory is at Sellafield in Cumbria. High-level or heat-generating waste is stored in either raw (liquid) or vitrified (glass-like) form.

In 2001, the Government and the devolved administrations started a major programme of consultation and research, *Managing Radioactive Waste Safely*, to decide policy for the management of higher activity wastes in the United Kingdom. After a consultation exercise, the Government set up an independent body, the Committee on Radioactive Waste Management (CoRWM), in 2003 to oversee a review of the long term options.

This review will include a programme of public debate backed by research and CoRWM will make its recommendations to the Government in 2006.

International commitments

An EC Directive lays down basic standards for the protection of the health of workers and the public against the dangers arising from ionising radiation. The provisions of the Directive are implemented in the United Kingdom through a number of Acts. The *Radioactive Substances Act 1993* provides the legislative framework for the regulation of radioactive waste. The United Kingdom is also a contracting party to the International Joint Convention on the Safety of Spent Fuel Management and on the Safety of Radioactive Waste Management.

The contracting parties to the Oslo and Paris Convention on the Protection of the Marine Environment of the North East Atlantic (OSPAR), including the United Kingdom, have agreed to reduce radioactive discharges to the North East Atlantic in the period to 2020. The *UK Radioactive Discharge Strategy 2001–2020* sets out how the United Kingdom will implement this agreement.

Water

Freshwater environment

Freshwater habitats in the United Kingdom include rivers, lakes and ponds, and wetlands such as fens, bogs and reedbeds. Many invertebrates and all amphibians native to the United Kingdom are dependent on these habitats, and there are 38 native species of freshwater fish. A comprehensive survey of the fish populations in the rivers, streams and lakes in England and Wales, *Our nations' fisheries*, was published by the Environment Agency in May 2004. Two threatened mammals, the European otter and the water vole, depend on aquatic habitats as do a large number of bird species, including the bittern (a UKBAP priority species).

Despite rainfall being fairly well distributed throughout the year in the United Kingdom (see page 3), there are limited natural and man-made capacities for storage, and the high population density means there is relatively little water per person. Available resources of water include rivers, reservoirs and underground aquifers.[9] The Environment Agency's strategy for water resource management considers both environmental and socio-economic factors (see chapter 28).

Marine environment

The seas around the United Kingdom support a wide variety of plants and animals, and are a source of both food and fuel. It is estimated that around 50 per cent of the United Kingdom's biodiversity is to be found in the sea. However, marine life and the food chain can be put at risk by pollution, overfishing and other activities. Defra and the devolved administrations have responsibility for protecting the United Kingdom's seas and coastal waters.

Publication of the Government's first marine stewardship report, *Safeguarding our Seas,* was followed later in 2002 by a consultation document *Seas of Change.* This formed the basis for discussion on how to provide a conservation and sustainable development approach to managing the seas. The Government expects to produce further marine stewardship reports every three to five years. English Nature is developing a maritime strategy to help implement the Government strategy set out in *Safeguarding our Seas* and the biodiversity strategy for England, *Working with the Grain of Nature* (see page 285).

In July 2004, the Government published *Review of Marine Nature Conservation,* which recommends an integrated framework for the management of the UK marine environment. Coastal and marine SACs around the United Kingdom have been identified and forwarded to the European Commission for approval. The Scottish Executive is consulting on a framework for Scotland's marine environment.

Government policy is not to permit any deposit of waste in the sea when there is a safe land-based alternative, unless it can be demonstrated that sea disposal is the best practicable option. The only wastes routinely considered for deposit in the sea are dredged material from ports and harbours, and small quantities of fish waste.

The Maritime and Coastguard Agency (see page 339) is responsible for dealing with spillages of

oil or other hazardous substances from ships at sea. The Agency has an Enforcement Unit at its headquarters in Southampton for apprehending ships making illegal discharges of oil and other pollutants off the UK coast. In England, the maximum fine for pollution from ships is £250,000 in cases heard in magistrates' courts.

Water quality

River water quality is a headline indicator of sustainable development (see page 114). The United Kingdom is changing the way quality is measured to ensure consistency with the new challenge of improving the ecological quality of water in the United Kingdom under the EC Water Framework Directive.

The chemical and biological quality of UK rivers has improved significantly in the past 10 to 15 years, primarily due to reduced pollution from point sources such as sewage treatment works and industry. However, the rate of improvement has levelled off and threats to the ecological quality of rivers and other water bodies from excess nutrients, siltation, and organic pollution from agricultural (see page 299) and non-agricultural diffuse sources are difficult to track and control.

Using water quality assessment criteria, it is estimated that 95 per cent of rivers in the United Kingdom were of good or fair chemical quality in 2002, and 75 per cent of monitored rivers in 2002 were of good chemical quality.[10] Only 3.2 per cent of Scottish rivers were classed as poor quality in 2003, but the reduction of 155 kilometres in the net length of poor quality rivers was partly due to unusually dry weather.

There has been some progress in addressing nutrient pollution. In 2002, 54 per cent of rivers in England and Wales had high concentrations of phosphate compared with 64 per cent in 1990, while 29 per cent of rivers had high concentrations of nitrate compared with 32 per cent in 2000 and 30 per cent in 1995.

The *Water Act 2003* updates the framework for abstraction licensing, promotes greater water conservation and planning for the future by water companies, and makes changes to the regulatory

---

9 Layers of rock that are able to hold or transmit large quantities of water.

10 These estimates are approximate because the classification scheme in Scotland differs from that in England, Wales and Northern Ireland.

environment (see page 457). Apart from certain exceptions, the Act applies to England and Wales. Its implementation is subject to Commencement Orders (the first one was signed in March 2004), with different provisions becoming effective at different times. For example, licensing changes take effect by 1 April 2005, drought plans to be produced by each company providing water services become statutory in 2005 and water resources plans become statutory in 2007/08.

In Scotland, the *Water Environment and Water Services (Scotland) Act 2003* introduced a 'source-to-sea' planning framework for river basin management designed to reduce levels of pollution and protect water resources and habitats associated with rivers and lochs. It includes provision for the protection of the environment through regulations on water pollution, the abstraction of water, engineering works and fish farming.

About 96 per cent of the UK population live in properties connected to a sewer, and the waste water from the majority of these properties is given secondary treatment[11] or better. Investment in the sewerage system and improving sewage treatment standards continue to build on the treatment improvements in the largest sewage works, and are expected to deliver further improvements, including at least secondary treatment for smaller remaining significant discharges, by the end of 2005.

Discharges to inland, coastal and groundwaters

All discharges to water in the United Kingdom are regulated. In England and Wales, the Environment Agency controls water pollution by issuing legally binding documents, known as consents, for all effluent discharges into controlled waters (groundwaters, inland and coastal waters). The effluent quality is monitored against the conditions set within the consents.

The Agency maintains public registers containing information about water quality, performance and compliance, consents, authorisations and

11 The preliminary treatment of sewage involves screening to remove rags, grit and other solids. Primary treatment involves a physical and/or chemically enhanced settlement of suspended solids not removed by preliminary treatment. Secondary treatment involves 'biological' treatment – using bacteria to break down the biodegradable matter in waste water.

monitoring. Trade effluent discharges to public sewers are controlled by the water companies.

In 2003, the Environment Agency substantiated almost 30,000 pollution incidents to water, land and air in England and Wales. Of these, 779 incidents had a serious impact on water, a decrease of 10 per cent on the previous year (see Table 19.8). The sewage and water industry, and agriculture are the most common sources of such serious water pollution incidents.

Table 19.8 Water pollution incidents[1] by source, England and Wales

	2002	2003
Sewage and water industry	168	198
Agriculture	150	98
Industry	105	92
Domestic/residential	43	38
Transport	36	27
Waste management facilities	18	20
Other	346	306
Total	**866**	**779**

1 Incidents where the source was identified. Category 1 (most serious) and Category 2 (serious) incidents.
Source: Environment Agency

In Scotland, controlling water pollution is the responsibility of SEPA: appeals are dealt with by the Scottish Executive and trade effluent discharges to the public sewer are controlled by Scottish Water. In 2002/03, SEPA recorded and investigated 1,409 water pollution incidents, of which 335 were classified as significant; although the number of incidents fell by 30 per cent from 2001/02, significant incidents increased by 79 per cent

The EHS is responsible for pollution prevention and control in Northern Ireland, including issuing discharge consents for trade effluent and sewage discharges not connected to the public sewer. Discharges from waste water treatment works are controlled by the Department for Regional Development's Water Service. The EHS also undertakes pollution incident response in Northern Ireland. A total of 2,500 reports of water pollution were made to the EHS in 2003, of which 1,552 were substantiated.

Under the Groundwater Regulations 1998 certain listed dangerous substances may be disposed of to land only after investigation and authorisation.

The Regulations also give the Environment Agency and SEPA powers to control or stop activities that might indirectly cause groundwater pollution. Similar legislation applies in Northern Ireland, where the prior investigation and authorisation of disposals is undertaken by the EHS.

Diffuse pollution from agriculture

Diffuse pollution from agriculture is seen as the single biggest problem facing water quality in the United Kingdom over the next ten years. Agricultural nutrients, pesticides, veterinary medicines, microbes from livestock manure, and soil erosion from farmland can all cause water pollution. Defra and the devolved administrations are considering measures to tackle this problem as part of the improvements to the quality of inland and coastal waters needed to meet the requirements of the EC Water Framework Directive.

One aspect of this wider problem is nitrate pollution arising from the application of inorganic fertiliser, livestock manures and other organic wastes on farmland. Approximately 70 per cent of nitrate enters water from agricultural land. The designation of Nitrate Vulnerable Zones (NVZs), under the EC Nitrates Directive, is intended to reduce or prevent this pollution. An area is designated as an NVZ when the nitrate concentrations in its ground or surface water exceed, or are likely to exceed, 50 mg/litre or where eutrophication is a (potential) problem.

Farmers in NVZs are required to implement an Action Programme of measures that promote best practice in the use and storage of fertiliser and manure, and build on the guidelines set out in the *Code for Good Agricultural Practice for the Protection of Water*.

In 2002, 55 per cent of England, 3 per cent of Wales and 14 per cent of Scotland were designated as NVZs. In 2003, Northern Ireland announced four new NVZs to address elevated nitrate levels in groundwaters. In view of the widespread eutrophication of its surface waters, Northern Ireland is consulting on a proposal to apply an Action Programme.

Bathing waters and coastal sewage discharges

Bathing water quality is influenced by natural factors (such as temperature, salinity and

sunlight), discharges from coastal sewerage treatment works, storm water overflows, river-borne pathogens (that is, pollutants that could affect human health), and run-off from urban and agricultural land. Over recent years, the overall quality of UK bathing waters has continued to improve and, in 2003, 98 per cent of coastal bathing waters and all inland bathing water complied with the EC Bathing Waters Directive's imperative standards for coliforms.

The Scottish Executive aims to meet European standards at all 60 Scottish bathing waters. It has identified nine bathing waters as sensitive under the EC Urban Waste Water Treatment Directive. The National Assembly for Wales has identified 24 Welsh bathing waters, Defra has declared 180 such coastal areas in England, and there are 16 identified bathing waters in Northern Ireland.

The identification confirms that advanced treatment has been or will be provided to discharges into the bathing waters from local sewage treatment works. In 2004, ENCAMS (see page 289) gave Seaside Awards to 375 UK beaches for meeting appropriate standards of water quality and beach management compared with 317 in 2003. The Awards are given to beaches that: comply with the EC Bathing Waters Directive mandatory standards; are clean, safe and well managed; and provide appropriate information about water quality.

The European Blue Flag Campaign is an initiative of the Foundation of Environmental Education in Europe and is administered in the United Kingdom by ENCAMS. To be considered, a beach must have attained the guideline standard of the EC Bathing Waters Directive before being assessed for 24 other criteria, including beach cleanliness, dog control, wheelchair access, the provision of life-saving equipment and other facilities. In 2004, 123 UK beaches were awarded a Blue Flag, compared with 105 in 2003.

Total inputs to the sea from rivers and discharges are reported to OSPAR (see page 296) and there are international commitments to reduce the loads of hazardous substances and nutrients.

Business and the consumer

Business has an important role to play in environmental matters. A Defra survey found that

UK industry[12] spent an estimated £2.6 billion on environmental protection in 2002, representing approximately 0.4 per cent of total turnover, or just over £700 per employee. This is spending by companies where the primary aim is to reduce environmental pollution caused during normal operations, for example reducing emissions to air or water, to dispose of waste materials, to protect soil and groundwater or to prevent noise.

Envirowise is a government-funded programme offering free, independent advice to UK companies on practical ways to minimise waste and increase profit. It works in partnership with the Carbon Trust (see page 454), which supports energy efficiency measures.

Other government initiatives to encourage environmentally sound practices include:

- the Advisory Committee on Business and the Environment, which provides a forum for government and business to discuss environmental issues;

- the DTI's Technology Programme, which aims to help businesses exploit technologies by providing some of the funding and sharing some of the risk in taking new and innovative technologies to market; and

- the Advisory Committee on Consumer Products and the Environment, which advises the Government on policies to reduce the environmental impacts associated with the production and consumption of goods and services.

Environmental management systems

An environmental management system provides organisations with a means to help them control and minimise the impact of their products, services and activities on the environment. Recognised models include the international management system ISO 14001, and the EU Eco-Management and Audit Scheme (EMAS). The latter is based on ISO 14001, but additionally requires the reporting of environmental performance. Both require auditing by an accredited independent third party. In the United Kingdom, accreditation is provided by the UK Accreditation Service.

---

12 Results relate to spending by extractive, manufacturing and energy supply industries. They do not include spending by the environment industries such as waste management, water and sewerage.

In 2003, the British Standards Institution (see page 391) published a new British Standard, BS8555, designed primarily for small and medium-sized enterprises. It allows companies to implement environmental management in stages, to eventually achieve full certification under ISO 14001 or EMAS.

Environmental labelling

UK consumers often rely on the information given on product labels when trying to choose environmentally friendly goods. To help them, the Government encourages accurate and relevant environmental labelling, as part of an integrated approach to reduce the environmental impact of consumer products. The mandatory EU A–G energy label on household appliances indicates how efficient a product is, with 'A' being most energy efficient and 'G' least energy efficient. Through Defra, the Government also administers the voluntary EU ecolabelling award scheme. The voluntary Green Claims Code sets out guidance for businesses that make environmental claims about their products, and provides an introduction to the international standard on environmental labelling, ISO 14021. Defra's Market Transformation Programme aims to encourage the take-up of more energy efficient domestic appliances. Among other areas, it covers technical standards, consumer product information, and minimum standards.

Responsibility for environmental affairs

General government expenditure on environmental protection increased by 2.8 per cent in 2003, to £5.4 billion. This included £3.2 billion on waste management (mainly through local authorities), £0.6 billion on nature conservation, and £0.3 billion on waste water management.

The Environment Agency is a non-departmental public body, accountable to ministers, which aims to protect and improve the environment in England and Wales. With a budget of about £800 million in 2003/04, it is responsible for regulating and controlling pollution, managing water resources, and improving flood defence. It also carries out conservation work, and manages and maintains fisheries and some waterways. SEPA carries out many of the same responsibilities in

Scotland, while in Northern Ireland, environmental protection is the responsibility of the Environment and Heritage Service. The three agencies work closely together – for example, producing joint technical guidance.

Many local authorities, voluntary organisations and charities are also involved in environmental conservation and protection.

Pollution control

Central government and the devolved administrations make policy, promote legislation and advise pollution control authorities on policy implementation. Local authorities are responsible for:

- collecting and disposing of domestic waste;
- keeping the streets clear of litter;
- controlling air pollution from domestic premises and, in England and Wales, from many industrial premises;
- reviewing, assessing and managing local air quality; and
- controlling noise and general nuisance.

Environmental legislation

Conservation and the countryside

The primary conservation legislation in Great Britain is the *Wildlife and Countryside Act 1981*, which provides for a range of measures to protect plants and animals from damage and destruction. Similar provisions apply under the Wildlife (Northern Ireland) Order 1985.

The 1981 Act was strengthened by the *Countryside and Rights of Way Act 2000*, which gave ministers and departments in England and Wales a statutory duty to have regard to the conservation of biological diversity in carrying out their functions, and contained new measures for the conservation and protection of habitats and wildlife. The *Nature Conservation (Scotland) Act 2004* placed a duty on public organisations to promote biodiversity, strengthened the protection of SSSIs (see page 283) and provided for new measures to tackle wildlife crime and protect fossils in Scotland.

Waste management

Waste management (see pages 286–89) in Great Britain is governed by the *Environmental Protection Act 1990* (as amended) and the Waste Management Licensing Regulations 1994 – similar legislation exists in Northern Ireland. A licence is required by anyone wanting to deposit, recover, or dispose of waste. Licences are issued by the Environment Agency, SEPA and EHS. A duty of care requires waste producers, and anyone else with responsibility for waste, to take all reasonable steps to keep their waste safe. If they give their waste to someone else, they must be sure that those people are authorised to take it and can transport, recycle or dispose of it safely. Failure to comply with either the licensing requirements or a duty of care is an offence.

Local authorities are responsible for the collection and disposal of all household waste and some commercial waste. In 'two-tier' areas (see page 9), district councils are responsible for collection, and county councils for disposal, while in unitary areas the council has both roles.

The disposal of radioactive waste in the United Kingdom is regulated by the *Radioactive Substances Act 1993*. This Act makes the Environment Agency in England and Wales and SEPA in Scotland responsible for regulating the safe use and storage of radioactive materials and the management of waste. The DoE regulates radioactive waste in Northern Ireland.

Industrial pollution control

Certain industrial processes require authorisation from the appropriate regulator before they can operate. The Pollution Prevention and Control (PPC) regime, which implements the EC Integrated Pollution Prevention and Control (IPPC) Directive, is being phased in and will be fully established by 2007. It replaces Integrated Pollution Control (IPC). Under both systems, regulators are required to ensure that pollution from industry is prevented or reduced through the use of best available techniques, subject to assessment of costs and benefits. Less polluting processes are regulated only in respect of their emissions to air. Under the new PPC regime, Local Air Pollution Prevention and Control (LAPPC) is replacing Local Air Pollution Control (LAPC). Similar, but slightly different systems for implementing the IPPC Directive apply in the different parts of the United Kingdom.

Under PPC, the issuing of integrated permits will apply to more industrial activities than previously. These include animal rendering, the food and drink industry, and intensive livestock installations. Regulators are also required to take into account a wider range of environmental impacts (including noise, energy efficiency and site restoration) when issuing integrated permits.

The IPPC Directive requires the publication of the European Pollutant Emission Register (EPER), an inventory of chemical emissions and sources from across Europe. The Pollution Inventory for England and Wales, administered by the Environment Agency, and the Scottish Pollution Release Inventory provide Internet-based data for the EPER.

Air pollution

Ambient air pollution (see pages 291–95) is controlled and regulated by several different pieces of legislation, depending on the source of emissions. Industrial processes with the potential for producing pollutants are subject to regulation under IPC and IPPC (see above). Processes with a significant but lesser potential for air pollution require approval, in England and Wales from local authorities, in Scotland from SEPA, and in Northern Ireland from the Industrial Pollution and Radiochemical Inspectorate or relevant district council, depending on the process. Local authorities also control emissions of dark smoke from commercial and industrial premises, and implement smoke control areas to deal with emissions from domestic properties.

Noise

In Great Britain, the primary legislation used to take action against the producers of noise (see pages 295–96) that causes nuisance is the *Environmental Protection Act 1990*. Under the *Housing Act 1996*, local authorities in England and Wales have powers to deal with anti-social

behaviour by tenants, including noise. In Scotland, action against noisy neighbours is taken under earlier legislation. The *Crime and Disorder Act 1998* introduced Anti-Social Behaviour Orders (see page 290) in England, Scotland and Wales, which can be used against any person who is causing harassment, alarm or distress to others, including noise nuisance. An EC Directive specifies the maximum noise level of certain new equipment for use outside.

Further reading

e-Digest of Environmental Statistics. Defra. Available only on the Internet: *www.defra.gov.uk/environment/statistics/index.htm*

Environment in your Pocket 2003. Defra, 2003.

Rural Strategy 2004. Defra, 2004.

Heritage Counts 2003. English Heritage, 2003.

Changing Patterns: UK Government Framework for Sustainable Consumption and Production. DTI and Defra, 2003.

The State of the Countryside 2003. Countryside Agency, 2003.

Municipal Waste Management Survey 2002–2003. Defra, 2004.

Sustainable Development Indicators in your Pocket 2004. Defra, 2004.

Achieving a Better Quality of Life 2003. Defra, 2004.

Quality of Life Counts. Defra, 2004. Available only on the Internet: *www.sustainable-development.gov.uk/indicators/national/index.htm*

Indicators of Sustainable Development for Scotland: Progress Report 2004. Scottish Executive, 2004.

Sustainable Development Indicators for Wales, 2004. National Assembly for Wales, 2004.

Websites

England

Department for Environment, Food and Rural Affairs (Defra)
www.defra.gov.uk

Environment Agency
www.environment-agency.gov.uk

Government Sustainable Development Unit
www.sustainable-development.gov.uk

Wales

Welsh Assembly Government
www.wales.gov.uk

Environment Agency Wales
www.environment-agency.gov.uk/regions/wales/

Sustainable Development Team, Welsh Assembly Government
www.wales.gov.uk/themessustainabledev/

Scotland

Scottish Executive Environment and Rural Affairs Department (SEERAD)
www.scotland.gov.uk

Scottish Environment Protection Agency (SEPA)
www.sepa.org.uk

Sustainable Development Team, Scottish Executive
www.sustainable.scotland.gov.uk

Northern Ireland

Department of the Environment (DoE)
www.doeni.gov.uk

Department of Agriculture and Rural Development (DARD)
www.dardni.gov.uk

Environment and Heritage Service (EHS)
www.ehsni.gov.uk

WWW.

20 Housing, planning and regeneration

The United Kingdom is a relatively densely populated country with 246 people per square kilometre in 2003. At the time of the 2001 Census there were almost 24.5 million households. Compared with 1991, the average household size had declined from 2.51 to 2.36 people.

Increasing demand for housing and a period of relatively low interest rates have led to a buoyant UK housing market. In 2003, the average UK dwelling price was £155,500, 16 per cent higher than in the previous year and almost two and a half times the average price ten years earlier.

The combination of a growing population and the declining size of households places increasing pressure on land use. Throughout the United Kingdom a number of programmes continue to work to regenerate areas which have been in decline and are in need of investment.

Housing

The Office of the Deputy Prime Minister (ODPM) has responsibility for determining housing policy in England and supervising the housing programme. Responsibility for housing policy in Wales, Scotland and Northern Ireland rests with the devolved administrations. They work with local authorities, or the Northern Ireland Housing Executive (NIHE) in Northern Ireland, and with the private and voluntary sectors. Local authorities and the NIHE are responsible for preparing local housing strategies. Social housing (housing at below market rent) is provided by local authorities, registered social landlords (RSLs, see page 310) – most of which are housing associations – and registered housing associations (RHAs) in Northern Ireland. RSLs are registered by the Housing Corporation (in England), the Welsh Assembly Government and Communities Scotland, through which bodies they also receive

government funding. In Northern Ireland, the Housing Division of the Department for Social Development registers RHAs, funds the NIHE and the housing association movement, and has regulatory powers over both.

The Sustainable Communities Plan (*Sustainable Communities: Building for the Future*), published in February 2003, set out a 15- to 20-year programme of action that included £22 billion of investment to improve housing and communities in England between March 2004 and May 2006. In July 2004 the Government announced a further £16 billion for the Plan during the period 2006/07 to 2007/08.

To meet the demand for affordable housing in the South East, the Plan identified four growth areas where land can be accessed relatively inexpensively so that large numbers of homes can be built. The areas are Ashford in Kent; Milton Keynes and the South Midlands; the corridor from London to Stansted and Cambridgeshire; and the Thames Gateway, a 64-kilometre strip of land covering parts of east London, south Essex and north Kent. In July 2003, the Government committed £446 million over three years for projects in priority areas within the Thames Gateway. This is expected to generate additional funds and to help produce an extra 200,000 homes by 2016.

The ODPM estimates that almost 1 million homes in the North of England and the Midlands are affected by low housing demand, leading in some areas to homes being abandoned. Low demand areas are characterised by limited market choice, the departure of economically active households, poor facilities and inadequate local services. Both social and private sector housing are affected. Nine such areas have been identified as 'market renewal pathfinders'. The Plan will provide £500 million to these areas between 2003/04 and 2005/06 as the first stage of a long-term programme to tackle failing housing markets through widespread demolition and rebuilding. The level of funding will increase beyond 2006 and the Government has announced that over £450 million will be invested in the pathfinders and other areas of low demand in 2007/08.

A new Key Worker Living programme was introduced in April 2004, to help key workers obtain housing within a reasonable distance of their workplace in areas of England where high house prices are undermining recruitment and retention. Eligible workers include teachers, police officers, nurses and other essential health workers, social workers and staff in the prison and probation services. The scheme offers four options to help key workers into home ownership or shared ownership, upgrade to family homes, or rent at affordable levels. The programme replaces the Starter Home Initiative, which helped over 10,000 key workers to buy their first home during the three years it operated. Key Worker Living has a two-year budget of £690 million and is expected to help up to 16,000 key workers over

three years.

In December 2003 a Housing Bill was introduced. The main areas of legislation for England and Wales set out in the Bill are:

- replacing the existing housing fitness standard with a new Housing Health and Safety Rating System (see page 311);

- introducing a mandatory licensing scheme for larger, higher-risk houses in multiple occupation and discretionary powers for local authorities to license smaller multi-occupied properties;

- providing local authorities with new powers to license private landlords in areas experiencing low housing demand or anti-social behaviour;

- requiring sellers of residential property, or their agents, to assemble a home information pack for buyers and sellers which is available when the property is marketed;

Review of housing supply

A review was set up in 2003 by the Chancellor of the Exchequer and the final report, *Delivering Stability: Securing our Future Housing Needs*, was published in March 2004. It concluded that the number of homes being built in the United Kingdom is not keeping pace with demand and is adversely affecting the local economy. Only 175,000 dwellings were built in 2001, the lowest number since the Second World War. Between 1971 and 2001, UK house prices rose by 2.4 per cent a year in real terms, compared with the European Union average of 1.1 per cent. Housing supply has remained unresponsive and, as a result, growing numbers of new households cannot afford to buy. Weak supply has also reduced labour mobility and contributed to an increase in homelessness.

The review suggested that the number of private sector homes built in England each year would need to be 70,000 above the current level in order to reduce the trend in real house prices to 1.8 per cent. An increase of 17,000 in the annual supply of social housing would be needed to keep pace with the needs of new households, and up to 9,000 above

this rate to reduce the backlog of existing need. The review recommended that:

- the Government should set a goal for improved market affordability (using, for example, a ratio of house prices to earnings or incomes);

- planning bodies should take account of market signals, such as prices and affordability, when setting housing targets and allocating land;

- regional planning boards and housing boards should be merged into regional planning executives;

- local authorities should be given incentives to support development; and

- the housebuilding industry should invest more in skills, improve customer satisfaction and develop sites more quickly.

The Government has accepted the need for an affordability goal and is weighing the need for increased development against the social and environmental implications. It has announced that by 2007/08 there will be 10,000 extra social rented homes built each year compared with 2004/05.

- tightening some of the rules relating to the Right to Buy scheme (see page 309); and
- enabling the Housing Corporation and National Assembly for Wales to pay grants to developers and housebuilders to develop affordable housing.

Supporting People

Supporting People programmes were introduced across the United Kingdom in April 2003. They are designed to deliver housing-related support services to vulnerable people, such as the homeless, older people, people with mental health problems or physical disabilities, and victims of domestic violence. The aim is to prevent crises such as hospitalisation, institutional care or homelessness, by providing early support when it is most effective, so that vulnerable people can live independently in the community.

In England, 150 administering authorities received £1.8 billion in Supporting People grants in the first year. These authorities run the programmes through partnerships with local housing and social services, as well as the health and probation services. The programmes provide housing-related support to over 1.2 million vulnerable people.

In Wales, local authorities administer Supporting People funds for the elderly and those people receiving a care service. The Welsh Assembly Government retains a grant scheme to pay for other forms of supported housing.

The Scottish Executive allocated £421 million to local authorities for the Supporting People programme in 2003/04. Housing support services are monitored through registration by the Scottish Commission for the Regulation of Care.

In Northern Ireland the Supporting People programme is administered by the NIHE, in partnership with the four Health and Social Services Boards and the Probation Board. It has an annual budget averaging £51.5 million from 2004/05 to 2006/07.

Housing stock and housebuilding

In 1951 there were 14.1 million dwellings in the United Kingdom. By 2003 the number had increased to 25.6 million. Housebuilding peaked in 1968 when total completions amounted to 426,000 dwellings, 53 per cent by private enterprises and 47 per cent by the social sector (primarily local

Extra care housing

Funding was allocated for 16 schemes providing 1,420 extra care housing places in England during 2004/05, the first year of the Extra Care Housing Fund. The Fund makes available £87 million over two years. Extra care housing offers flexible care, with 24-hour support from social care and health teams. People living in these facilities have their own private flat or bungalow with access to meals, domestic support, leisure facilities, and nursing care where necessary.

authorities). By comparison there were 183,900 dwellings completed in 2002/03, of which 89 per cent were by private enterprise. RSLs (predominantly housing associations) now dominate building in the social sector, and in 2002/03 accounted for 99 per cent of such completions (see Figure 20.1). Local authorities and the NIHE are no longer major developers of new social housing, but they still play an important role as landlords.

The types of dwelling built have changed over the last century. Terraced housing was the norm before the First World War and over a third of the current stock of this type of housing dates from before 1919. Between 1919 and 1944 there was an expansion in the number of semi-detached dwellings. After 1965 the private sector began to build more detached houses, while large numbers of purpose-built flats were provided in the public sector. Figure 20.2 illustrates the mix of accommodation in 2002/03.

To minimise greenfield development (that is, building on land that has not previously been developed) and to encourage urban regeneration, the Government wishes to see unoccupied homes brought back into use. The number of empty homes in England fell from 869,000 in 1993 to 720,000 in 2003. Eighty-five per cent of vacant dwellings are privately owned, with about half of these vacant for at least six months. In May 2004 the Government announced that it would introduce amendments to the Housing Bill (see page 305) aimed at bringing the 300,000 long-term empty homes in England back into productive use. The proposed changes would allow councils to apply to make Empty Homes Management Orders on long-term empty

Figure 20.1 Housebuilding completions,[1] by sector, UK

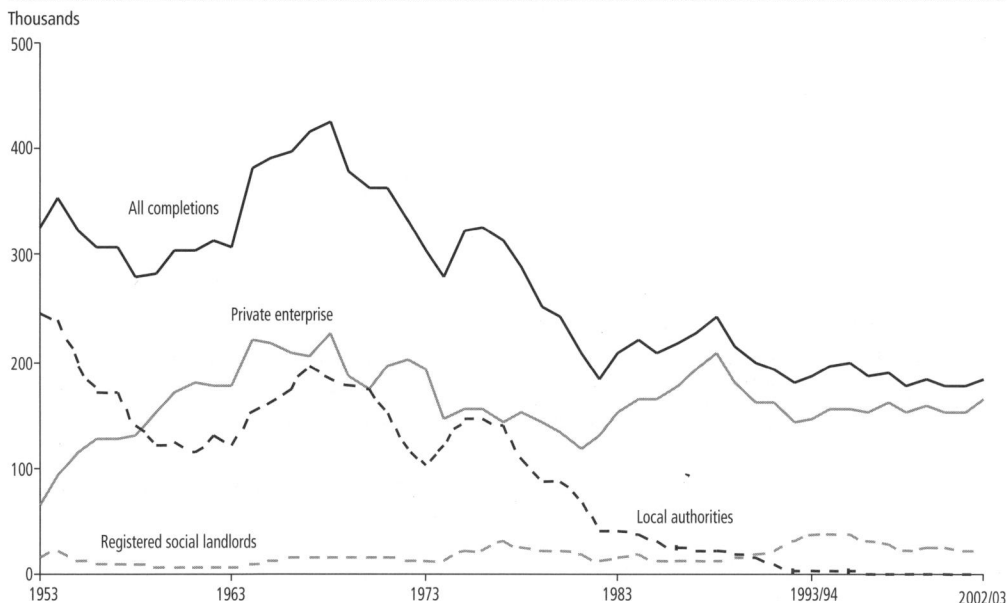

1 From 1990/91 data are for financial years.
Source: Office of the Deputy Prime Minister; National Assembly for Wales; Scottish Executive; Northern Ireland Department of the Environment

Figure 20.2 Households, by type of dwelling, 2002/03, UK

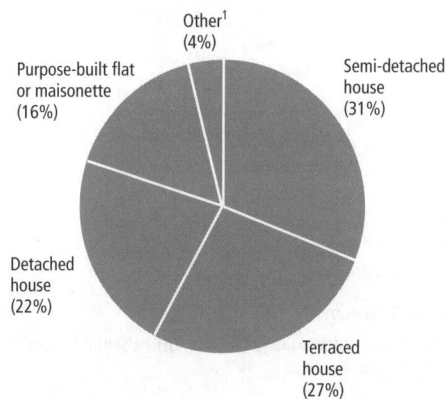

1 Includes converted flats.
Source: General Household Survey, Office for National Statistics; Continuous Household Survey, Northern Ireland Statistics and Research Agency

properties where there is a strong case for doing so. The owner of the property would retain legal ownership and be entitled to any rental income generated by the local authority after deduction of its relevant costs, for example in carrying out renovation work.

Home ownership

Between 1991 and 2003 the number of owner-occupied dwellings in the United Kingdom increased by 33 per cent to 18.0 million, while the number of rented dwellings increased by around 15 per cent to 7.6 million. Northern Ireland had the highest proportion of owner-occupied dwellings in 2003, and Scotland the lowest (Table 20.3).

The average price of dwellings bought and sold in the United Kingdom in 2003 was £155,500 (Figure 20.4), although there were marked regional variations, with buyers in London and the South East paying the most. However, in 2003, the North East and the East Midlands recorded the largest percentage increases (Table 20.5).

Mortgage loans

A feature of UK home-ownership is the relatively high proportion of homes purchased with a mortgage. About three-quarters of house purchases are financed in this way. In 2003, 71 per cent of such loans were obtained through banks and 14 per cent through building societies, with 15 per cent through other specialist mortgage lenders.

Table 20.3 Tenure of dwellings, 2003,[1] UK

Percentages

	Owner-occupied[2]	Rented from local authority[3]	Rented privately or with job or business	Rented from registered social landlord
England	71	11	10	8
Wales	73	14	9	4
Scotland	64	22	8	6
Northern Ireland	75	16	5	3
United Kingdom	**70**	**13**	**10**	**7**

1 As at 31 March for England and Northern Ireland, and 1 April for Wales. Figures for Scotland are for 31 December 2002.
2 Including dwellings purchased with a mortgage or loan as well as those owned outright.
3 Including the Northern Ireland Housing Executive.
Source: Office of the Deputy Prime Minister; National Assembly for Wales; Scottish Executive; Department for Social Development, Northern Ireland

Figure 20.4 Average dwelling prices, UK

£ thousand

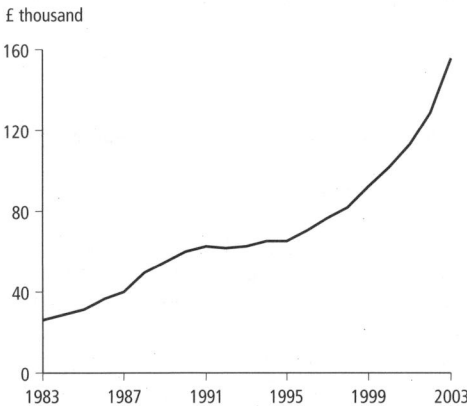

Source: Survey of Mortgage Lenders, Office of the Deputy Prime Minister

There are a variety of types of mortgage, the two most common being repayment and interest-only. With repayment mortgages, the debt and the interest are both repaid during the life of the mortgage (typically 25 years). Around 71 per cent of all new mortgages were standard repayment mortgages in 2003. Interest-only mortgages, usually involving endowment policies, ISAs (individual savings accounts, see page 469) or personal pensions, account for the bulk of other mortgages. Since the late 1980s there has been a decrease in the popularity of endowment mortgages because of the possibility that investments may not grow fast enough to repay the capital borrowed. In 1988, 83 per cent of new mortgages for house purchase were endowment mortgages, by 2003 this had fallen to 5 per cent.

Table 20.5 Average dwelling prices, 2003, UK

£

	All dwellings	% increase on 2002
North East	94,590	22.5
North West	108,956	18.1
Yorkshire & the Humber	107,325	20.4
East Midlands	133,215	22.5
West Midlands	132,898	18.0
East	181,494	17.8
London	236,476	9.1
South East	213,115	15.1
South West	170,560	18.0
England	165,834	15.8
Wales	104,140	20.3
Scotland	92,006	13.8
Northern Ireland	102,348	8.7
United Kingdom	**155,485**	**15.7**

Source: Survey of Mortgage Lenders; Office of the Deputy Prime Minister

Flexible mortgages are a type of repayment mortgage designed to respond to changing working patterns and incomes over the lifetime of the loan. Borrowers are given the options of making overpayments or underpayments, as well as taking payment breaks. Flexible mortgages have been growing in popularity and 73 per cent of new mortgages in 2003 had at least one flexible feature.

In the first quarter of 2003 UK base rates (see page 346) fell to their lowest level since the early 1960s.

However, due to rising house prices, first-time buyers accounted for 33 per cent of loans for house purchases during this period, the lowest since records began in 1969. By the fourth quarter of 2003 first-time buyers accounted for 28 per cent of loans, illustrating the affordability gap for would-be homeowners. In response to rising house prices, the base rate was increased during 2004 reaching 4.75 per cent by August 2004.

There were over 25,000 new equity release mortgages advanced in the United Kingdom in 2003, 55 per cent more than in the previous year. These funds are commonly used by elderly homeowners to pay for day-to-day living expenses, home repair and improvement, or episodes of care.

Low-cost home ownership

Since the 1980s the increase in the proportion of dwellings that are owner-occupied has in part been due to government schemes aimed at helping lower-income households into home ownership. In England these include the Right to Buy, Right to Acquire and Voluntary Purchase Grants, which offer tenants in social housing a discount against the market value of the homes they rent if they are eligible and wish to buy them. More than 650,000 local authority dwellings were sold into home ownership between 1990/91 and 2002/03. In order to tackle exploitation and profiteering, particularly in areas of high demand and rising prices, the Housing Bill (see page 305) proposes some changes to the Right to Buy scheme, including extending to five years both the qualification period and the period after sale during which landlords can require repayment of discount. This follows a reduction in the maximum discount available to tenants in 41 areas in March 2003.

A number of other schemes support low-cost home ownership by enabling people to part buy and part rent a home (shared ownership), providing equity loans or making grants available to tenants of social housing who wish to buy a home in the private sector. The Home Ownership Task Force, which reported in November 2003, was set up by the Government to examine how people in housing need in England could be helped to meet their aspirations to own their own home. The Government has accepted most of the recommendations and they are being implemented. These include better information and advice and changes to existing schemes to meet purchasers' needs.

The Miles Review

Only a quarter of mortgage lending in the United Kingdom is on fixed (as opposed to variable) rates, a much lower proportion than in many other countries. Very few of these mortgages are fixed for more than two or three years. In April 2003, the Chancellor of the Exchequer announced a review to identify the factors underlying the low take-up of fixed rate mortgages. Reporting in March 2004, the Miles Review recommended that:

- lenders should make their full range of mortgage products available to all borrowers;

- mortgage advisers should help people assess risk by presenting 'what if' calculations, indicating the scale of variability in interest rates; and

- lenders should include a leaflet setting out the current mortgage rates on all their products when issuing annual statements.

The review considered that these proposals, combined with the removal of certain legislative and regulatory barriers for banks and building societies, would help shift the balance away from short-term deals to ten-year fixed rate loans.

In Wales, local authorities and housing associations operate a low-cost home ownership scheme allowing purchasers to buy a home for 70 per cent of its value (50 per cent in rural areas). The balance is secured as a charge on the property.

Communities Scotland administers a Housing Association Grant for low-cost home ownership. This is used to bridge the shortfall between the cost of provision and locally assessed market value. Communities Scotland also administers a Grant for Rent and Owner Occupation, the purpose of which is to widen the choice of housing for those seeking to become homeowners. The grants are targeted at areas of wholly social sector housing and areas of high demand.

In Northern Ireland, over 108,000 NIHE tenants had bought their homes between October 1979 and March 2003. The Northern Ireland Co-ownership Housing Association administers a 'buy half, rent half' (shared ownership) scheme which, between April 1978 and June 2003, had helped 17,600 people become homeowners.

Rented housing

In 2003, 20 per cent of UK dwellings were rented from the social sector (local authorities and housing associations), while 10 per cent were rented privately (Table 20.3, page 308).

Social housing

Much of the Government's expenditure on social housing is provided as subsidies to UK local authorities to help pay for the costs of nearly 3.5 million rented council homes. More than 2,000 housing associations provide a further 1.7 million units of social housing.

Since the late 1980s, Government policy has aimed to promote a wider range of social landlords through stock transfers. In England, a Large Scale Voluntary Transfer (LSVT) Programme has been running since 1988. By April 2004, almost 820,000 dwellings had been transferred from local authorities to RSLs with the support of tenants and the approval of the Secretary of State.

RSLs are the major providers of new subsidised homes for those in housing need. They range from almshouses to large housing associations managing thousands of homes. They include LSVT and local housing companies set up to own and manage council homes transferred from local authorities.

The Housing Corporation, which regulates housing associations in England, gives capital grants to provide homes for rent and for sale, primarily from the Approved Development Programme (ADP). The Planned ADP budget for 2004/05 is £1.6 billion.

The Housing Inspectorate, based at the Audit Commission, is responsible for inspecting the housing services of local authorities and housing associations in England. It reports the results of its housing association inspections to the Housing Corporation, as the statutory regulator.

Local authorities in Wales own around 200,000, or about 14 per cent, of all Welsh homes. By law they have to manage their own stock efficiently and, in consultation with their tenants, address housing

Housing and Employment Mobility Service

A new Housing and Employment Mobility Service (HEMS) will be introduced in 2005, with the aim of improving housing and employment mobility throughout the United Kingdom. It will help tenants move around the country by providing information about jobs and housing opportunities in other areas. There will be three elements:

- services for social landlords, their tenants and applicants, to help people find new homes;
- website information about local areas, covering access to housing, neighbourhoods and jobs; and
- web access to information on vacancies in social housing.

HEMS is a joint project between the ODPM, Jobcentre Plus, the Scottish Executive, the Welsh Assembly and the Northern Ireland Assembly. Existing housing mobility services run by LAWN (London Alliance West and North), which helps tenants to move out of London, and HOMES (Housing Mobility and Exchange Services) will continue to operate until HEMS is in place.

needs and demands. The Housing Bill (see page 305) provides for a Social Housing Ombudsman for Wales, to investigate complaints against RSLs.

Communities Scotland is responsible for the regulation and inspection of both RSLs and local authority landlords. In 2004/05 it plans to invest £284 million in housing projects, helping to complete more than 4,600 new and improved homes and allowing work to start on another 5,350, mainly for rent through housing associations.

The NIHE, the strategic housing authority, is the landlord of 102,000 properties, nearly one-third of rented properties in Northern Ireland. It assesses the need for, and arranges the supply of, social housing. The Government's contribution to housing of £370 million in 2004/05, supplemented by rental income and capital receipts, meant that gross resources available were £710 million. An additional £25 million was available from private finance to build new social housing. The NIHE has continued to transfer its new-build programme to registered housing associations. The 2004/05 programme will provide 1,300 new homes.

Private renting

During the past 60 years the size and nature of the UK private rented sector has changed. Before the Second World War 57 per cent of the population lived in private rented accommodation. Most tenancies were unfurnished, subject to rent control and occupied by the same tenants for many years. For many people today, private renting is a more temporary tenure, occupied by those such as students and young professionals who may need to move frequently, and by people who are saving to buy. There are, in addition, people who have no other option because they cannot afford to buy and do not qualify for social rented accommodation. In 2002/03 just over a fifth of households in the private rented sector in England received rent assistance in the form of housing benefit.

'Assured' and 'shorthold' (in Scotland, 'short assured') tenancies are the most common forms of arrangement for letting houses and flats by private landlords. If the tenancy is shorthold, the landlord can regain possession of the property six months after the beginning of the tenancy (or at the end of an agreed fixed term if that is longer than six months), provided that he or she gives the tenant two months' notice requiring possession. If the tenancy is assured, the tenant has the right to remain in the property unless the landlord can prove to the court that he or she has grounds for possession, and the landlord does not have an automatic right to repossess the property when the tenancy comes to an end. In both types of tenancy the landlord can charge a full market rent.

The National Approved Lettings Scheme is a voluntary accreditation scheme for private sector landlords in England that aims to promote best practice among lettings agencies. It sets minimum standards for service and financial probity of agents in handling clients' money.

Improving existing housing

The Government defines a decent home as one that:

- meets the current statutory minimum standard for housing, which at present is the 'fitness standard';

- is in a reasonable state of repair;
- has reasonably modern facilities; and
- provides a reasonable degree of thermal comfort through effective insulation and efficient heating.

The 2001 English House Condition Survey found that 7.0 million dwellings (33 per cent) failed to meet the decent home standard in 2001. This had fallen from 9.4 million (46 per cent) in 1996. Households that rent privately, people who live alone, ethnic minorities and households with no one in full-time employment are most likely to be living in non-decent homes.

The Government intends to reform the legislation on housing fitness for England and Wales. The current statutory housing fitness standard (set out in the *Housing Act 1985*) is based in part on criteria first introduced approximately 80 years ago. To reflect a more modern approach to health and safety hazards in the home, the Government has developed the Housing Health and Safety Rating System (HHSRS) and included measures in the Housing Bill (see page 305). Subject to legislation, local housing authorities will in future base enforcement decisions on assessments of 29 categories of housing hazard covered by the HHSRS.

Disabled people in all tenures can apply for grants so that they can continue to live independent lives in their own homes. The Disabled Facilities Grant (DFG) is allocated to eligible applicants through local authorities in England and Wales, and pays for essential adaptations to the home.

Following recommendations from the Housing Improvement Task Force (see page 312) and a consultation paper on *Modernising Scotland's Social Housing* (see page 312) Scottish ministers announced the Scottish Housing Quality Standard in February 2004. To meet this standard a house must be energy efficient; free from serious disrepair; healthy, safe and secure; provided with modern facilities and services; and comply with the existing statutory tolerable standard.

Private housing

Local authorities in England and Wales have wide discretionary powers to help homeowners and tenants to repair, improve and adapt their properties and to assist in the regeneration of communities. Assistance can include grants, loans and equity release schemes. In 2002/03, local authorities in England used these powers to fund around £259 million of repairs for some 68,000 homeowners and tenants.

Local authorities have similar powers in Scotland. In October 2003 the grants system was modified to target help to people on the lowest incomes and encourage homeowners to carry out priority work. The Scottish Executive set up a Housing Improvement Task Force in 2001 to examine the issues affecting the condition and quality of private sector housing and the process of buying and selling houses in Scotland. Its final report, *Stewardship and Responsibility: A Policy Framework for Private Housing in Scotland*, was published in March 2003.

In Northern Ireland, funding is allocated through the house renovation grants scheme, administered by the NIHE, on a similar basis to that in England. In rural areas of Northern Ireland, financial assistance to replace isolated dwellings that cannot be restored is also available.

Social housing

Most capital expenditure on local authority housing goes towards major repairs and renovations. The number of non-decent homes in the social sector in England fell from 2.3 million in 1996 to 1.6 million in 2001. The main reason why these homes failed the standard was a failure to provide a reasonable degree of thermal comfort. In 2000 the Government set a target to bring all social housing in England up to the decent standard by 2010.

The Government is adopting three ways of securing additional investment in council-owned housing:

- stock transfer to RSLs (see page 310);
- management companies set up by local authorities, but operating independently, with responsibility for management of their housing stock; and
- private finance initiatives (PFI, see below).

The Sustainable Communities Plan (see page 304) announced funding of £2.8 billion over three years from 2003/04 to improve council housing and £685 million of PFI credits. The PFI for local authority housing uses private sector funding to refurbish or re-provide council houses and thereafter to provide housing services, with tenants remaining tenants of the local authority. By September 2003 there were two signed Housing

Revenue Account PFI 'pathfinders' and 14 at various stages of procurement, with the aim of refurbishing a total of 25,000 council houses across England.

In 2003 the Scottish Executive published a consultation paper, *Modernising Scotland's Social Housing*. The main proposals included:

- developing a national social housing standard to deliver minimum quality standards to all tenants of social landlords in Scotland;
- continuing commitment to community ownership to ease the transfer of further council stock to RSLs and release money for future investment; and
- extending the 'prudential borrowing regime' to local authority housing capital investment.

When it announced the Scottish Housing Quality Standard in February 2004 (see page 311), the Executive set a target date of 2015 for local authorities and RSLs to meet the Standard.

Rural housing

The Housing Corporation finances a special rural programme in England to build houses in villages with a population of 3,000 or less. The Sustainable Communities Plan (see page 304) included a government target for the Corporation to provide 3,500 affordable homes in small villages between 2004/05 and 2005/06. This was in addition to the target of 1,600 for 2003/04. The plan also included measures to make it easier for local authorities to limit the resale of ex-council housing in rural areas so that it is reserved for local people.

The National Assembly for Wales supports the development of housing in rural areas if it is a strategic priority for the local authority.

The Scottish Executive's Rural Housing Investment Programme provided 1,450 new and improved homes across Scotland in 2003/04 and aims to approve a further 1,400 in 2004/05. A £10 million Special Rural Development Programme for affordable housing was announced in 2003. Funding will be allocated over 2004/05 and 2005/06.

In Northern Ireland, between 2001/02 and 2003/04, 363 new social rented homes were provided in rural areas outside district and larger towns. Disrepair and housing unfitness in the private sector is tackled through the house renovation grants scheme (see page 312). During 2003/04, just over 900 properties outside the main cities benefited from renovation grant assistance, while around 200 private dwellings were provided through replacement grant aid.

Growing numbers of people are buying second homes or purchasing property as an investment (see box), and this has contributed to rising house prices in some rural areas, leading to concern that many young people and those on low incomes are unable to buy. Local authorities in England have been given powers to reduce the council tax discount on second homes. From April 2004 they can charge up to 90 per cent council tax for second homes and up to 100 per cent for long-term empty homes. Welsh local authorities can levy 100 per cent council tax on second homes. Scottish local authorities will be able to charge up to 90 per cent from April 2005.

Second homes

In 2002/03 an estimated 175,000 households in England had a second home that was also in England. Most of these households (89 per cent) owned rather than rented the second home. Although around half had acquired it for holidays, weekends or retirement, there were other uses such as working or studying away from the main home. An estimated additional 81,000 households held a second home purely as an investment. Such properties are often let to holidaymakers or full-time tenants.

Homelessness

Local housing authorities in England and Wales have a statutory duty to ensure that suitable accommodation is available for applicants who are eligible for assistance, have become homeless through no fault of their own, and who fall within a priority need group (this is the 'main homeless duty'). Priority need groups include families with children, and households that include someone who is vulnerable, for example because of pregnancy, domestic violence, old age, or physical or mental disability.

Where applicants are homeless but not owed the main duty (for example, because they do not fall

within a priority need group) the housing authority must assess their needs and ensure that they are provided with advice and assistance in their own attempts to find accommodation. Authorities also have a general duty to ensure that advice about homelessness and the prevention of homelessness is available free of charge to everyone in their district. In most areas, such advice is available from housing aid centres, Shelter (a charity that offers housing advice to homeless and badly housed people), Citizens Advice and other local agencies.

Local authorities in England and Wales also have a duty to carry out reviews of homelessness within their area at least every five years and produce strategies for tackling and preventing it. The first strategies were published in July 2003.

The number of households accepted as homeless by local authorities in England increased by 5 per cent to 137,000 during 2003/04. Figure 20.6 shows the trend in the number of homeless households in temporary accommodation in recent years. There were just over 97,000 such households at the end of 2003/04, about 7 per cent of which were in bed and breakfast (B&B) accommodation.

Figure 20.6 Homeless households[1] in temporary accommodation, England

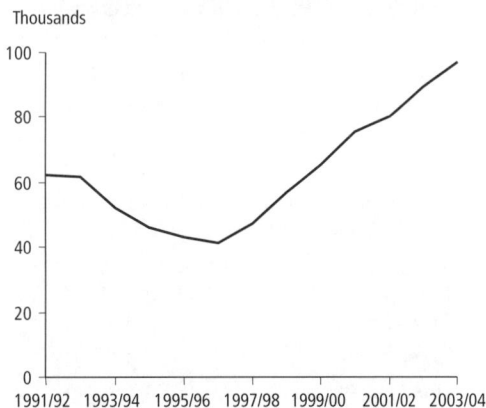

Thousands

1 Excludes 'homeless at home' cases who have remained in their existing accommodation after acceptance but have the same rights to suitable alternative accommodation as those in accommodation arranged directly by local authorities. Data are at 31 March and include households awaiting the outcome of homeless enquiries.
Source: Office of the Deputy Prime Minister

Some £260 million is being invested over the three years to 2005/06 to help English local authorities sustain reductions in rough sleeping; end the use of B&B hotels as a form of temporary accommodation for homeless families with children; and develop new ways of tackling homelessness. The Homelessness (Suitability of Accommodation) Order 2003 means that local authorities can no longer place families with children in B&B for longer than six weeks.

Domestic violence accounted for 13 per cent of local authority homelessness acceptances in England in 2003/04. Funding of £18.8 million was provided to build and develop more refuges to help women and children fleeing violent partners. The money was used in partnership with local refuge groups, RSLs and local authorities. There

Moving home

According to the 2001 Census, one in eight people in England and Wales had moved house during the previous year. Mobility was highest in the south-east of England, particularly Inner London where 4 per cent of the population had moved in from other parts of the United Kingdom, 5 per cent had left, and almost 9 per cent had moved within the area.

Private rented accommodation is by far the most transient form of tenure, favoured by students, under-25s, and single people. Data from the 2002/03 Survey of English Housing showed that over half of all tenants renting private furnished accommodation had been in their home for less than a year. In contrast more than half of those who owned their homes outright had been in the same home for over 20 years.

The most common reason why established households move is larger accommodation (19 per cent). Other reasons are job-related (12 per cent), to go to a better area (12 per cent), and divorce or separation (9 per cent). While 32 per cent of those in privately rented furnished accommodation moved 50 miles or more, or abroad, only 4 per cent of those in accommodation rented from a council did so. To make it easier for those in social sector housing to move, a Housing and Employment Mobility Service will be launched in 2005 (see page 310).

will be further funding totalling £13.3 million in 2004/05 and 2005/06.

In Wales, the National Homelessness Strategy and action plan were published in 2003. The strategy identified 23 objectives to be covered within local homelessness strategies. Assembly funding for voluntary sector schemes aimed at tackling homelessness and rooflessness in Wales has increased from £650,000 in 1999/2000 to £4.9 million in 2004/05.

Scotland and Northern Ireland have similar legislation on homelessness to that in England and Wales. The Scottish Executive allocated funds of £127 million for the period 2003/04 to 2005/06 to deliver the recommendations of the Homelessness Task Force that reported in 2002. The *Homelessness (Scotland) Act 2003* took forward the legislative recommendations and set a target that by 2012 all homeless people will be entitled to permanent accommodation. The Act widened the priority need categories, relaxed the local connection requirement and introduced greater help to intentionally homeless people. It also requires landlords to inform local authorities of repossession cases so that early action can be taken to prevent homelessness.

In Northern Ireland there were 17,150 applications under the homeless persons legislation during 2003/04, and almost 8,600 acceptances, much the same as the previous year. The *Homelessness Strategy for Northern Ireland*, published by the NIHE in 2002, focuses on helping people avoid homelessness, helping people out of homelessness and supporting people when they get a home.

People sleeping rough

The Rough Sleepers Unit (RSU), established in 1999, was set the target of reducing rough sleeping in England from a baseline of 1,850 in 1998 to as near to zero as possible – and by at least two-thirds – by 2002. By December 2001 the latter target had been met. The Homelessness and Housing Support Directorate at ODPM, which has taken on the work of the RSU, works with local authorities to sustain the reduction. In June 2003 an estimated 500 people were sleeping out on any single night – the lowest level recorded.

Over the three years to 2004, £3.5 million was made available to support projects whose aim was to reduce the number of people sleeping rough in

Wales. In Scotland, the number of rough sleepers fell by a third between May 2001 and October 2003. This programme was allocated £4 million in capital funding between 2002 and 2004 and will also receive £9.5 million a year in revenue funding up to 2006. Between 2003 and 2006 investment of £100 million will fund the replacement of Glasgow's outdated homeless hostels with more suitable accommodation and support services.

Asylum seekers

Asylum seekers may be able to obtain housing through the National Asylum Support Service while their claim is being processed. People who are subsequently granted refugee status or humanitarian protection or discretionary leave to remain are entitled to claim housing benefit (see page 173) and to apply for social housing.

Land use planning

In Great Britain land use planning is the direct responsibility of local authorities. They prepare development plans and determine most planning applications. The ODPM and the devolved administrations have responsibility for the operation of the system. They issue national planning policy guidance, approve structure plans (except in Wales where unitary authorities have this role), decide planning appeals and determine planning applications that raise issues of national importance. In England the ODPM operates through the Government Offices for the Regions (GOs, see page 12) and the Planning Inspectorate.

In Northern Ireland, the Department of the Environment (DoE) functions as the single planning authority. The Planning Service, an executive agency within the DoE, is responsible for operational planning, issuing policy and guidance, determining planning applications and preparing development plans.

England

There are just over 400 planning authorities in England – including county councils, district councils, unitary authorities and National Park authorities. The first planning laws were enacted in 1909 and the modern system dates from the *Town and Country Planning Act 1947* and subsequent legislation in 1990 and 1991. The Government's national policy is set out in 25

Planning Policy Guidance notes (PPGs) – covering issues such as housing, transport, sport and recreation – and in 15 Minerals Policy Guidance notes (MPGs) as well as in other guidance. The PPGs are gradually being revised and replaced with Policy Planning Statements (PPSs).

There are several tiers to the planning system. Central government issues national planning guidance to local authorities and also Regional Planning Guidance (RPG) based on advice from regional planning conferences. In two-tier local authorities (see page 9) the upper-tier (county councils) produce 'structure plans', indicating where development should be focused, while the lower-tier (such as district councils) produce 'local plans' with more detailed and site-specific information. Local authorities decide individual planning applications with reference to these plans. In London the Mayor has responsibility for production of a 'spatial development strategy' covering development, regeneration and transport issues in the capital.

The *Planning and Compulsory Purchase Act 2004* is intended to make the planning system fairer, faster and more predictable by simplifying the way decisions are made. The Act applies to Wales as well as England, with specific sections for the different development planning arrangements in the two countries.

Provisions included in the Act aim to:

- simplify planning development with a new two-tier system whereby Regional Spatial Strategies are prepared by each English region and Local Development Frameworks (see page 317) by unitary and district councils;

- introduce a requirement for local planning authorities to consult with local communities;

- speed up the process for major infrastructure projects requiring a decision by central government;

- introduce Business Planning Zones to aid regeneration by encouraging investment and fast-tracking developments in areas where jobs are needed most; and

- make the compulsory purchase system faster and clarify local authority powers to acquire land for planning and regeneration.

Most of these provisions will come into force in late 2004.

A draft Planning Policy Statement 1 (PPS1 – *Creating Sustainable Communities*) was issued in February 2004 for consultation. It states the policies and principles that will support the reformed planning system. It urges planners to integrate economic, social, environmental and resource factors; to support development proactively rather than simply regulate and control; to set clear visions for communities; and to promote community participation. The Statement sets out the importance of building well-designed homes, offices, factories and leisure facilities that will benefit the community and stand the test of time.

Planning Policy Guidance Note 3: Housing (PPG3) sets out the Government's planning policies for housing in England. It encourages planning authorities to recycle brownfield (previously developed) sites within urban areas, bring empty homes back into use and convert existing buildings in preference to the development of greenfield sites. It also encourages planning authorities to use land more efficiently; assist with the provision of affordable housing in both rural and urban areas; and promote mixed-use developments that integrate housing with shops, local services and transport.

The Government's national target is that, by 2008, 60 per cent of additional housing in England should be provided on brownfield land or by re-using existing buildings. In 2003, 66 per cent of new housing was built on such land.

Sustainable development for rural areas

A draft PPS for rural areas (PPS7) was published in September 2003. It describes how planning policies can help raise the quality of rural life by:

- revitalising country towns and villages;
- supporting wide-ranging economic activity;
- improving the availability and viability of community services and facilities;
- meeting rural needs for affordable housing;
- assisting farmers and equestrian enterprises;
- providing tourism and leisure facilities so that rural areas can be enjoyed by everyone; and
- protecting the landscape, wildlife and biodiversity.

Wales

Issues covered in *Planning Policy Wales*, published in 2002, include: keeping development away from flood risk areas; the possible establishment of the first Green Belt areas; development of land and buildings in a way that creates a more accessible environment, particularly for people with limited mobility; guidance on the sustainable use of previously developed land beyond housing needs alone; encouraging both rural and farm diversification; and proposals to relax the control of developments in the open countryside so that development on farm complexes can be permitted in certain circumstances.

In 2002, the Minister for Environment launched a programme to improve the planning system in Wales. Based on proposals in *Planning: Delivering for Wales*, the programme involves the Welsh Assembly Government working with the 25 local planning authorities and the Planning Inspectorate in Wales to ensure that the planning system is open, fair and transparent; delivers improved quality and speed; and integrates with other plans and processes.

Scotland

There are 33 planning authorities in Scotland comprising 32 local authorities and the Loch Lomond and Trossachs National Park Authority. The Cairngorms National Park is also a planning authority in relation to certain functions.

Legislation for planning policy in Scotland is contained in the *Town and Country Planning (Scotland) Act 1997*. Scottish Planning Policies (SPPs) provide statements of Scottish Executive policy on nationally important land use and other planning matters, supported where appropriate by a locational framework. SPPs will gradually replace National Planning Policy Guidelines (NPPGs) by 2007. By August 2004 there were five: on the planning system, economic development, housing, flooding, and transport and parking.

Following a review of strategic planning (see also page 317), Scotland's first *National Planning Framework* was published in April 2004. It aims to guide the spatial development of Scotland and provide a context for development plans and planning decisions. In particular, it covers:

- the impact of Scotland's position at the north-west corner of Europe;

- the need for coordinated action in the West Edinburgh and Clyde Corridor;

- the importance of investment in the East Coast transport infrastructure;

- the role of Ayrshire and the South West as a gateway; and

- promoting economic diversification and environmental stewardship in rural areas.

Northern Ireland

The Planning Service in Northern Ireland has embarked on a programme of change. In 2002, *Modernising Planning Processes*, presented proposals for improving the planning system. The Implementation Plan, launched in February 2003, identifies specific issues and actions the Planning Service intends to take by the end of 2005 to modernise and improve the development control process, the formulation of planning policy for Northern Ireland and the preparation of development plans for local council areas.

Development plans

Development plans help to shape land use and provide a framework for consistent decision-making. Planning applications are determined in accordance with relevant development plan policies unless 'material considerations' indicate otherwise. Provisions in the *Planning and Compulsory Purchase Act 2004* (see also page 315) require unitary and district councils in England to prepare Local Development Frameworks (LDFs). LDFs will replace structure plans, local plans and unitary development plans and contain:

- a statement of core policies setting out the local authority's approach to development;

- a statement of community involvement setting out the planning authority's policy for involving the community in the development and revision of LDFs and in significant development control decisions;

- site-specific policies and proposals, including area action plans for smaller local areas; and

- a map showing designations such as conservation areas, sites for particular future land uses or developments and locations of any proposed or actual area action plans.

Local planning authorities will be able to produce, by agreement, joint LDFs between two or more districts and between two or more districts and counties, under a joint committee. The continuous updating and review of LDFs will become a requirement for all local authorities.

To ensure that all local authorities have LDFs in place, the Government is providing £350 million between 2003/04 and 2005/06 through the Planning Delivery Grant. The grant is performance-based and from 2004/05 is being allocated to local authorities that have made significant improvements in their handling of development control planning applications, plan making, housing delivery in high demand areas, location of Enterprise Areas, and appeals. These criteria build on those for 2003/04, which included additional funding for the growth areas and areas of high housing demand. Funding is also being allocated to the regional planning bodies for their work on new regional spatial strategies and reviews of existing planning guidance.

The Act includes specific clauses for Wales covering the introduction of Local Development Plans (LDPs), which will replace Unitary Development Plans. LDPs will be subject to independent examination, with local planning authorities being obliged to act on any recommendations of the inspector before formally adopting the plan. The Welsh Assembly Government will have the power to intervene in the production of an LDP, before adoption, if it felt the plan was unsatisfactory.

In Scotland, development plans are prepared by local authorities and consist of structure and local plans. In the case of National Parks, the Park Authorities have responsibility for the preparation of a National Park Plan and for local planning, and are statutory consultees on structure planning for the area. Following the Review of Strategic Planning (see page 316), the Scottish Executive outlined a new approach to development planning. It proposed that in the four main cities (Aberdeen, Dundee, Edinburgh and Glasgow), there should be two tiers of development plan: a City Region Plan (CRP) and an LDP. Elsewhere there should be a single tier LDP. Councils not involved in a CRP should include an explanation of their strategy in the LDP. Certain aspects of the modernisation programme will require legislative change that will be taken forward through a Planning Bill.

The Scottish Executive's Planning Audit Unit works with planning authorities to establish best practice in development control and development planning, and to highlight areas where improvements could be made to processes and services. By August 2003 two-thirds of Scottish councils had conducted a planning audit.

In Northern Ireland, the *Modernising Planning Processes Implementation Plan* of February 2003 (see page 317) will reduce the number of development plans by grouping local council areas together, and will provide complete development plan coverage by the end of 2006.

The Planning Portal

The Planning Portal (*www.planningportal.gov.uk*) is a website for all aspects of planning in England and Wales. Users can:

- read planning news;
- see if planning permission is needed and how to obtain it;
- access development plans, regulations and guidance notes on which application and appeals procedures are based;
- find out about planning in their area; and
- make on-line planning applications to some local authorities.

A national e-government project, PARSOL (Planning and Regulatory Services Online), is being funded by the Government to help local authorities ensure that they can receive and process planning applications online by 2005.

Development control

Development control is the process for regulating the development of land. Most forms of development, such as the construction of new buildings, alterations to existing buildings or changes of land use, require permission from the relevant planning authority. Applications are dealt with on the basis of the development plans and other material considerations, including national and regional guidance.

In 2003/04 district planning authorities in England received 675,000 applications for permission, and made 625,000 decisions, granting permission to 84 per cent of applications. Householder developments accounted for 54 per cent of all decisions in 2003/04, compared with 12 per cent for new dwellings and 15 per cent for commercial and industrial developments. Other decisions involved listed buildings or conservation areas, advertisements, or change of use.

Planning authorities in Scotland received 51,330 applications for permission in 2003/04 and granted permission to 94 per cent of these.

In 2003/04, 75 per cent of all planning decisions in England were made within the statutory eight-week period. The Government's target is for 80 per cent of applications to be dealt with within this period. Similar targets apply in Wales, Scotland and Northern Ireland.

In England, Wales and Scotland, certain planning applications are referred for decision to the Secretary of State, the Welsh Assembly, or Scottish ministers, rather than being decided by the local planning authority. In general, this only occurs where the planning issue is of more than local importance. A small number are referred to a public inquiry, such as the Terminal 5 inquiry at London Heathrow Airport, which concluded with government approval for the project.

If a local authority refuses to grant planning permission, grants it with conditions attached or fails to decide an application within eight weeks (or two months in Scotland), the applicant has a right of appeal to the Secretary of State, the Welsh Assembly or Scottish ministers.

The Planning Inspectorate serves both the Deputy Prime Minister in England and the National Assembly for Wales on appeals, development plans and other casework on planning, housing, the environment, highways and related legislation. It provides information and guidance to appellants and other interested parties about the appeal process. In 2003/04, nearly 19,000 planning appeal cases were determined in England and Wales.

The Scottish Executive Inquiry Reporters Unit is responsible for the determination of most planning appeals and organises public local inquiries into planning proposals and related matters. Just under 1,000 cases were determined in Scotland in 2003/04. The Executive is consulting on proposals to broaden the right of appeal and is considering measures to improve the inquiry process. In Northern Ireland, the applicant has the right of appeal to the Planning Appeals Commission. Major planning applications can be referred to a public inquiry in certain circumstances.

Green Belts

Green Belts are areas of land that are protected from development. The aim is to control the sprawl of large built-up areas, prevent towns from merging with one another, preserve the heritage of historic towns and encourage the recycling of derelict and other urban land, thereby encouraging urban regeneration. Not all Green Belt land is countryside. It can cover small villages comprising a mixture of residential, retail, industrial and recreational land as well as fields and forests. Development on Green Belts is only permitted under exceptional circumstances.

In 2003, there were 14 separate designated Green Belt areas in England, amounting to 16,700 square kilometres (about 13 per cent of the land area). This is an increase of 190 square kilometres since 1997. The Sustainable Communities Plan (see page 304) includes a government commitment to maintain or increase the area of land designated as Green Belt in each English region.

In Scotland there are seven Green Belt areas totalling 1,590 square kilometres. A further three are approved in principle at St Andrews, Dunfermline and Perth. Following research showing a high degree of support for Green Belts, a new SPP is being prepared and will be published in draft form in 2005.

There are 2,450 square kilometres of Green Belt in Northern Ireland, about 18 per cent of the total land area. There are no Green Belts at present in Wales, but their creation is under consideration.

Regeneration

Regeneration policies aim to enhance both the economic and social development of communities through a partnership between the public and private sectors, with a substantial contribution from the latter. They support and complement other programmes tackling social and economic decline, and initiatives such as Sure Start (see page 167), the Crime and Disorder Reduction

Partnerships (see page 206) and the work of the Social Exclusion Unit (see page 112). Run-down areas in the United Kingdom benefit from European Union (EU) Structural Funds, which assist a variety of projects in the least prosperous industrial, urban and rural areas of the EU. Over £10 billion of Structural Funds, including £3 billion covering Objective 1 areas (see page 358), have been allocated to the United Kingdom for the period 2000–06.

England

In England, the nine Regional Development Agencies (RDAs, see page 13) set out priorities for regeneration and ensure that new programmes enhance and complement those already in place. RDA strategies, alongside RPG overseen by GOs, provide a regional framework for economic development and regeneration.

The Department of Trade and Industry is the lead sponsor of the RDAs, with the GOs responsible for day-to-day issues. The ODPM, with a number of other departments, is responsible for financing RDAs and ensures that they consider regeneration when implementing their regional strategies. RDAs will support regeneration schemes from a single budget worth £2 billion in 2005/06. They are required to deliver targets set collectively by government departments.

English Partnerships (EP) is sponsored by the ODPM. EP and the RDAs form the Government's main regeneration agencies. EP is a key contributor to delivering the Sustainable Communities Plan (see page 304) and seeks to create new jobs and investment through sustainable economic regeneration and development in the English regions. EP's funding programme increased from £163 million in 2003/04 to £179 million in 2004/05 and 2005/06.

EP has responsibility for: the Greenwich Peninsula; the National Coalfields Programme; Millennium Communities; support for urban regeneration companies (URCs, see page 320); the English Cities Fund; the National Land Use Database; the production and maintenance of a national brownfield strategy; and a register of surplus public sector land. It worked alongside the Forestry Commission and the Environment Agency to create a Land Restoration Trust, operating from 2004, to provide for the long-term sustainable management of cleaner and safer public open space and forestry across England.

Neighbourhood renewal

In 2001, *New Commitment to Neighbourhood Renewal: A National Strategy Action Plan* set out the Government's plans for delivering economic prosperity, safe communities, high-quality education, decent housing and better health to the poorest parts of the country. At the national level the plan is implemented by the Neighbourhood Renewal Unit in the ODPM.

Funding is provided through a number of programmes, including the Neighbourhood Renewal Fund (NRF) and the New Deal for Communities. By 2008, the NRF will have provided £2.9 billion extra resources for 88 of the most deprived local authority districts in England.

New Deal for Communities has been operating since 1998 and since 1999 has covered 39 neighbourhoods across England. It is a ten-year programme with funding of £2 billion. In each area, partnerships have been established between local communities, service providers and other agencies. Each partnership covers a neighbourhood of between 1,000 and 4,000 households and has between £30 million and £60 million to spend over ten years.

Urban renaissance

In February 2004 the Government announced measures to bring about a renaissance in cities in the North of England and to spread growth into the wider regional economy. *Making it Happen: The Northern Way* contains plans to develop the concept of a 'Northern Growth Corridor' and to work with RDAs and regional planning bodies to make the most of the transport infrastructure and to bring economic performance in the North up to the national average. The Government is providing finance through the Housing Market Pathfinder Fund, the Coalfields Enterprise Fund, and money for urban parks and green spaces.

A Tale of Eight Cities, published in April 2004, reported on progress in revitalising the eight 'core' English cities: Birmingham, Bristol, Leeds, Liverpool, Manchester, Newcastle, Nottingham and Sheffield. A full report is planned in 2005.

Urban regeneration companies

The first URCs were formed in England in 1999. They are independent partnerships established by local authorities, RDAs, EP and the private sector to produce strategies on physical and economic regeneration. Although the emphasis is on physical and economic regeneration, each URC has produced a strategy that covers more, and that reflects local circumstances. By May 2004 16 URCs had been established in England, and one each in Wales and Northern Ireland. Three URCs were announced in Scotland in June 2004.

Parks and open spaces

Published in 2002, *Living Places – Cleaner, Safer, Greener*, highlighted litter, graffiti and fear of crime as the reasons people do not always make use of public spaces. These issues are the subject of a five-year improvement programme. Additionally, in February 2003, the Government announced funding of £201 million to improve parks and public spaces. The Commission for Architecture and the Built Environment (CABE) is receiving £18 million of this funding over three years; part has been used to set up a green spaces unit (CABE space) with the aim of ensuring good quality design, management and maintenance of public spaces.

Rural regeneration

Although most problems arising from dereliction and unemployment occur in urban areas, some rural areas have also been affected by declining employment in traditional sectors such as mining, agriculture and defence establishments. Even in areas that appear relatively prosperous, some individuals are disadvantaged by poor local services, poor public transport and low wages or seasonal unemployment.

The RDAs outside London are responsible for rural regeneration. The Countryside Agency (see also page 280) promotes and advises on conserving and enhancing the countryside, on access to the countryside for recreation, and on the economic and social development of England's rural areas. It also administers a number of grants designed to help meet village needs for transport, shops or other services.

Wales

Following the reduction in steelmaking capacity and consequent redundancies, announced in 2001, the Welsh Assembly Government provided funding of £76 million to help stimulate the regeneration of the affected communities. Projects include the reopening of the Ebbw Vale railway line to passengers, a Community Learning Network and a URC for Newport.

23 March 2004 UK adventurer, David Hempleman-Adams, reached over 40,000 feet, (12,192 metres) in a balloon with an open wicker basket at Greeley, Colorado, USA, breaking the existing record of 35,626 feet (10,859 metres).

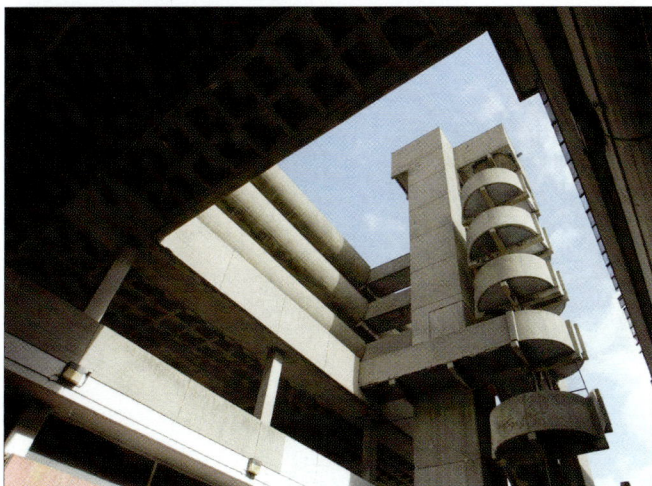

© PA PHOTOS

24 March 2004 The 1960s Tricorn Shopping Centre in Portsmouth is demolished to the sound of Tchaikovsky's *1812 overture*, the piece of music that it was likened to by one of its admirers when it was first built. Although it won a Civic Trust award for 'its exciting visual composition' in 1967, it was voted Great Britain's fourth ugliest building in a poll of 500 designers in 1968, and 'most hated building' in a BBC Radio 4 poll in 2001. The Centre has been empty for nearly 30 years, and derelict for 15.

27 March 2004
A decommissioned warship HMS *Scylla* is sunk in Whitsand Bay, off the Cornish coast, to create Europe's first artificial diving reef. Web cameras have been attached to the 2,500-tonne vessel.

© PA PHOTOS

28 March 2004 150th anniversary of UK entry into the Crimean War (1853–56). *(Above left)* Florence Nightingale (1820–1910) organised a unit of female nurses during the Crimean War and is often considered the founder of modern nursing.

Above right: Members of the 8th Hussars gather at the cookhouse in camp, photographed by Roger Fenton, the world's first official war photographer. The Crimean War was also the first to be reported on by a civilian correspondent, William Russell, writing for *The Times.*

Centre: Lithograph after the Charge of the Light Brigade in the Battle of Balaclava, by William Simpson.

Below: Mary Seacole, awarded a medal in recognition of her work in the Crimean War, came first in an Internet poll of the 100 Great Black Britons in February 2004. The poll highlighted the contribution that Black people have made to UK society since Roman times. The website for the poll received more than 1 million hits and 10,000 people voted.

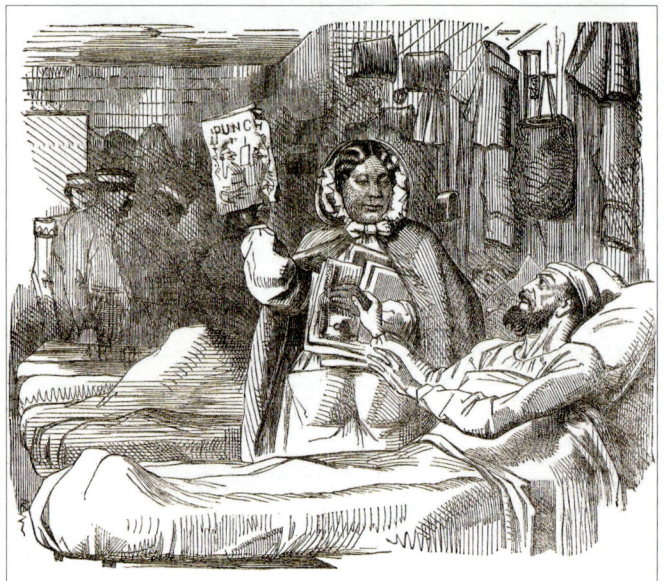

5 April 2004 HM The Queen is greeted by wellwishers on the platform at Gare du Nord station in Paris, at the start of her two-day state visit to France to celebrate the 100th anniversary of the *Entente Cordiale*.

5 April 2004 The National Railway Museum in York announces that it has raised the £2.5 million it needed to buy the *Flying Scotsman*, the first steam engine to achieve 100 mph. Here crowds welcome the *Flying Scotsman* as it arrives for RailFest 2004 in May. Afterwards, it will haul excursion trains between York and Scarborough.

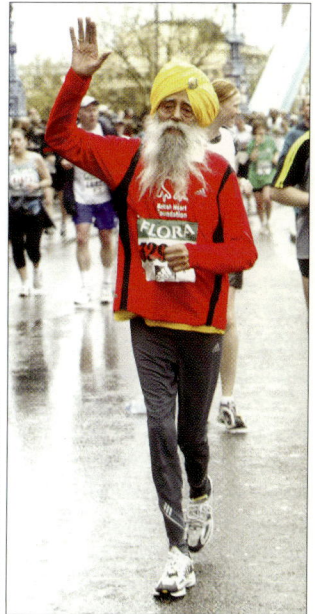

18 April 2004 The oldest runner taking part in the Flora London marathon, 93-year-old Fauja Singh, crosses Tower Bridge. He finished the 42.2-kilometre course in 6 hours, 7 minutes and 13 seconds.

27 April 2004 The Swiss Re Tower, nicknamed the Gherkin, is opened at 30 St Mary Axe in the City of London. The glass lens cap on the top is the only piece of curved glass in the building. Construction workers used advanced abseiling techniques to complete the 40-storey, 180-metre high glass-clad tower.

© FOSTER AND PARTNERS

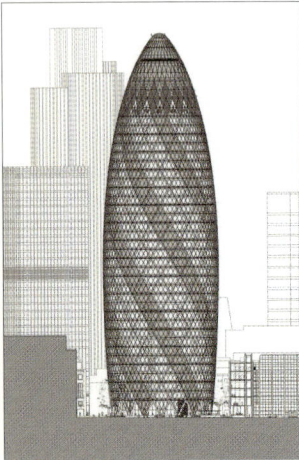

© FOSTER AND PARTNERS

29 April 2004 A total of 106 buildings in Birmingham's historic Jewellery Quarter are listed on the advice of English Heritage. The area is home to over 500 businesses involved in the jewellery trade, and to Birmingham's Assay Office, which tests between 40,000 and 80,000 items a day.

© MARKETING BIRMINGHAM

Wales is receiving up to £1.3 billion from the EU to fund a variety of programmes until 2006. These include Objective 1 Funds (see page 358) for West Wales and the Valleys. By March 2004 some £700 million had been allocated to over 1,000 projects in Wales. The programmes are aimed at developing a stronger, more sustainable economy, better infrastructure, a more highly skilled workforce, and the regeneration of urban and rural communities.

Communities First is an area-based regeneration programme in the 100 most deprived electoral wards, and in other communities with pockets of deprivation. The programme emphasises the involvement of local people in decision-making through a community-based partnership. The Welsh Assembly Government has allocated £152 million to this programme between 2001 and 2006.

The Welsh Development Agency's (WDA's) regeneration programmes include physical and environmental regeneration activities, such as land reclamation and environmental improvements; activities to provide site development work to assist with business infrastructure; and support for community initiatives, such as the Market Towns Initiative and the Small Towns and Villages programmes.

North Pembrokeshire and South Ceredigion

The North Pembrokeshire and South Ceredigion Regeneration Plans were announced in March 2003. Both areas suffered major job losses with the closures in 2002 of clothing factories in Fishguard and Cardigan. The plans aim to boost the long-term prosperity of the area, and are being taken forward by a range of public and private sector partners including Pembrokeshire and Ceredigion County Councils, the WDA, Education and Learning Wales, the Welsh Tourist Board and local business and community groups. In total, £60 million, including £10 million from the Welsh Assembly, will be invested over three years. The plans include the redevelopment of Fishguard and Cardigan town centres and the establishment of a research and technology park at Aberporth.

Scotland

The Social Inclusion Partnership (SIP), established in 1999, involves 48 local partnerships tackling the problems that disadvantaged groups and communities face across Scotland. The SIPs are multi-agency partnerships, consisting of all relevant local public agencies, the voluntary and private sectors, and representatives from the community. They were supported over three years from 2001/02 by £169 million from the Social Inclusion Partnership Fund. From March 2005, SIPs will be integrated with Community Planning Partnerships.

Scottish Enterprise is the main economic development agency for lowland Scotland. It consists of a national office and 12 local enterprise companies. Highlands and Islands Enterprise and its ten local enterprise companies cover the rest of Scotland. Communities Scotland (see page 309) also has a responsibility for regeneration. It works closely with a number of partners, in particular local authorities.

Northern Ireland

The Department for Social Development (DSD) has a lead role in addressing social need and social inclusion in Northern Ireland. It does this through its main business areas – housing, social security, child support, urban regeneration and community development – using a combination of public and private sector investment as well as contributions from EU Structural Funds (see page 357) and the International Fund for Ireland.

Physical development schemes are the main elements of urban regeneration policy in Northern Ireland. Frequently used initiatives are:

- Urban Development Grants, which aim to encourage physical and economic regeneration in targeted areas and seek to promote job creation, inward investment and environmental improvement through the development of vacant, derelict or underused land and buildings;

- Comprehensive Development Schemes, which contribute to the regeneration of disadvantaged areas through development or redevelopment; and

- Environmental Improvement Schemes, which help to improve the appearance of public spaces in town and city centres across Northern Ireland.

The Neighbourhood Renewal Strategy, which started in June 2003, sets out a long-term plan for the renewal of the most deprived neighbourhoods in urban areas of Northern Ireland.

The *Heart of the City* (August 2003) is an integrated urban design strategy for Londonderry, which will inform the future planning and design of key development sites. The strategy places an emphasis on high-quality architecture, public open spaces and landscaped areas.

The *Belfast City Centre Regeneration Policy Statement*, published in April 2004, sets out the overall approach and objectives for maximising the regeneration potential of investment in the city centre for the benefit of Belfast and Northern Ireland as a whole. The Laganside Corporation has been a model for brownfield regeneration in Belfast and has successfully transformed the waterfront area. Outside these cities the Community Regeneration and Improvement Special Programme has regenerated run-down town and village centres.

Further reading

ODPM Annual Report 2004. Cm 6206. The Stationery Office, 2004.

The Housing Corporation: Annual Review. The Housing Corporation.

2001 English House Condition Survey. Office of the Deputy Prime Minister. The Stationery Office, 2003.

Scottish House Condition Survey 2002. Communities Scotland, 2003.

English Partnerships: Annual Report and Financial Statements. English Partnerships, 2004.

Housing in England 2002/03. Office of the Deputy Prime Minister. The Stationery Office, 2004.

Housing Statistics (annual). Office of the Deputy Prime Minister. The Stationery Office.

Sustainable Communities: Building for the Future. Office of the Deputy Prime Minister, 2003.

Social Trends (annual). Office for National Statistics. The Stationery Office.

Websites

Office of the Deputy Prime Minister
www.odpm.gov.uk

National Assembly for Wales
www.wales.gov.uk

Scottish Executive
www.scotland.gov.uk

Northern Ireland Executive
www.nics.gov.uk

English Partnerships
www.englishpartnerships.co.uk

Housing Corporation
www.housingcorp.gov.uk

Communities Scotland
www.communitiesscotland.gov.uk

Northern Ireland Housing Executive
www.nihe.gov.uk

Northern Ireland Planning Service
www.planningni.gov.uk

WWW.

21   Transport

British residents travelled on average 11,000 kilometres within Great Britain in 2003, 53 per cent further than in the early 1970s. Although the number of trips[1] has increased slightly – from 956 a year in 1972/1973 to 990 in 2003 – the average trip length has grown by almost 50 per cent, from 7.6 kilometres to 11.1 kilometres. In Northern Ireland, residents travelled on average about 9,310 kilometres in 2001–2003, each person making an average of 960 journeys every year.

Travel by car or van accounts for the majority of passenger mileage in Great Britain – 85 per cent in 2002 (Table 21.1). In 2003, 46 per cent of households had access to one car, 26 per cent to two or more cars, whereas 27 per cent had no car. In Northern Ireland, 83 per cent of the total distance travelled was by car or van in 2001–2003: 44 per cent of households had access to one car, 29 per cent to two or more cars, while 27 per cent had no car.

Leisure was the most common reason for travel in Great Britain in 2003, accounting for 31 per cent of all trips and 41 per cent of total distance travelled. Shopping accounted for 20 per cent of trips and 12 per cent of total distance travelled, while commuting accounted for 15 per cent of trips but 19 per cent of distance travelled. In Northern Ireland, leisure accounted for 26 per cent of all journeys made and 31 per cent of the total distance travelled in 2001–2003. Shopping represented 20 per cent of journeys and 15 per cent of total distance travelled, while for commuting and business travel the figures were 19 and 29 per cent, respectively. There have been reductions in the fatality rates of accidents involving most forms of transport since the 1980s (Table 21.2).

---

1 A trip is defined as a one-way course of travel having a single main purpose. Outward and return halves of a return trip are treated as two separate trips. A trip cannot have two separate purposes, so if this involves a mid-way change of purpose then it is split into two trips.

Table 21.1 Passenger transport, by mode,[1] Great Britain

Billion passenger-kilometres

	1992	2001	2002
Road			
Buses and coaches	43	46	47
Cars, vans and taxis	583	622	634
Motorcycles, mopeds			
and scooters	5	5	5
Pedal cycles	5	4	4
Road total	635	678	690
Rail[2]	38	47	48
Air[3]	5	8	8
All modes[4]	**678**	**733**	**746**

1 Since 2000 figures have been produced on a different basis and are not directly comparable with earlier years.
2 Financial years. Includes urban rail systems and underground railways.
3 Excludes air taxis, private flying and passengers paying less than 25 per cent of the full fare. Includes Northern Ireland and the Channel Islands.
4 Excludes travel by water within Great Britain.
Source: Department for Transport

Roads

The length of the road network in Great Britain in 2003 was 392,321 kilometres. Motorways accounted for 3,476 kilometres (0.9 per cent of the total), and trunk roads (which have been affected in England since 2001 by the 'detrunking' programme) for 9,340 kilometres, or 2.4 per cent. However, motorways carried 19 per cent of all traffic, and trunk roads another 14 per cent. Combined, they carried 62 per cent of all goods vehicle traffic in Great Britain. In Northern Ireland the road network totalled 24,887 kilometres in April 2004, of which 114 were motorway.

Table 21.2 Death rates, by mode, Great Britain

Rate per billion passenger-kilometres

	1982	1992	2002
Motorcycle[1,2]	108.0	97.3	111.0
Walk	77.0	74.6	44.1
Pedal cycle[1,2]	46.0	43.4	29.4
Car[1,2]	6.4	3.6	2.7
Van[1,2]	3.1	2.1	1.0
Water[3,4]	0.9	0.0	0.0
Bus or coach[2]	0.6	0.4	0.4
Rail[5]	0.6	0.4	0.3
Air[3]	0.0	0.1	0.0

1 Driver and passenger fatalities.
2 Figures revised back to 1993 due to revision in traffic estimates and methodology. Consequently the data are not directly comparable with earlier years.
3 Data are for the United Kingdom.
4 Passenger fatalities on UK-registered merchant vessels.
5 Financial years. Includes train accidents and accidents occurring through movement of railway vehicles.
Source: Department for Transport

Figure 21.4 Passenger cars, 2001, EU comparison

Number per 1,000 inhabitants

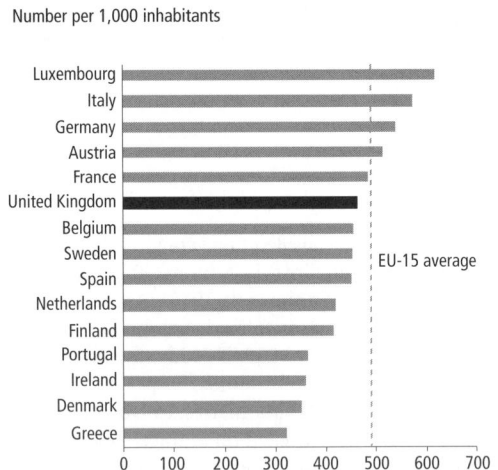

Source: Eurostat

Motor vehicles

The number of licensed vehicles on Great Britain's roads at the end of 2003 was 31.2 million, an increase of 2.1 per cent on 2002, with private cars accounting for 80 per cent of the total (Table 21.3). There were 794,000 licensed vehicles on Northern Ireland roads at the end of 2002, a 3.3 per cent increase on 2001.

Despite the increase in the number of cars in recent years, in 2001 there were fewer passenger cars per 1,000 population in the United Kingdom than the European Union (EU) average (Figure 21.4) – 464 compared with 488.

Table 21.3 Motor vehicles licensed at end year, Great Britain

Thousands

	1983	1993	2003
Private cars	15,543	20,102	24,985
Goods vehicles	488	428	426
Motorcycles	1,290	650	1,005
Buses[1]	113	107	96
Total[2]	**20,209**	**24,826**	**31,207**

1 Includes privately owned and operated vehicles.
2 Total includes Crown and exempt vehicles, and other vehicles.
Source: Department for Transport

Driver and vehicle licensing

The Driver and Vehicle Licensing Agency in Great Britain and Driver and Vehicle Licensing Northern Ireland are responsible for issuing driving licences and for registering and licensing vehicles. All vehicles must be licensed before they can be driven on public roads and drivers must hold either a full or (in the case of learner drivers) a provisional licence. There were 32.1 million driving licence holders in Great Britain in 2002, representing 71 per cent of all adults.

Driving standards

Driving tests in Great Britain are conducted by the Driving Standards Agency (DSA), the national driver testing authority. In 2002/03, 1.3 million car tests were conducted. To obtain a full driving licence, new drivers of motor vehicles must pass a computer-based touch screen theory test and a practical test. The pass rate for the driving test has fallen, from 50 per cent in 1992 to 43 per cent in 2002/03. The DSA also supervises a statutory register for approved driving instructors, compulsory basic training for all learner moped and motorcyclists, and a voluntary register for instructors of large goods vehicles. In Northern Ireland, the Driver and Vehicle Testing Agency (DVTA) is responsible for driving tests. Almost 50,000 tests were taken in 2002/03, with an overall

🚆🚗⛴

100th anniversary of registration and licences

The *Motor Car Act 1903*, which came into force on 1 January 1904, required all motor vehicles in the United Kingdom to be registered and to carry number plates, displayed in a prominent position, and for all drivers to be licensed annually. County councils and county borough councils were made registration and licensing authorities. The vehicle registration fee was 20 shillings (£1) and the driver's licence fee 5 shillings (25p).

pass rate of 48 per cent. For the theory test, the pass rate was 68 per cent.

The minimum ages for driving in the United Kingdom range from 16 for invalid carriages and mopeds to 21 for medium/large sized vehicles, minibuses and buses.

Vehicle standards

Before most new cars and goods vehicles are allowed on the roads, they must meet safety and environmental requirements, based primarily on standards drawn up by the EU. The Vehicle Certification Agency is responsible for ensuring these requirements are met through a process known as 'type approval'.

Vehicles are subject to annual roadworthiness, or 'MOT', tests, which in Great Britain are the responsibility of the Vehicle and Operator Service Agency (VOSA). VOSA also uses roadside and other enforcement checks to ensure that drivers and vehicle operators comply with legislation. In Northern Ireland the DVTA is responsible for vehicle testing.

New vehicle and fuel technologies

Road transport accounts for around 85 per cent of the transport sector's carbon emissions, which in turn account for about 21 per cent of total UK emissions. The *Powering Future Vehicles* (PFV) strategy, launched by the Government in 2002, and the 2003 energy White Paper, *Our energy future – creating a low carbon economy* (see chapter 28), both seek to reduce the negative effects of traffic.

The PFV strategy sets out the twin objectives of promoting the development, introduction and take-up of low-carbon vehicles and fuels, and ensuring the involvement of industry in the new technologies. It also sets government targets for sales of low-carbon vehicles. The strategy provides fiscal and grant incentives for consumer and business take-up of cleaner, more efficient vehicles and fuels; and research, development and demonstration funding for new technologies. The Energy White Paper built on this strategy, highlighting the significant contribution that vehicle and fuel technologies, such as renewable hydrogen and biomass-based fuels, could make to long-term reductions in emissions of carbon dioxide.

Traffic and congestion

Road traffic is one of the Government's headline indicators of sustainable development (see page 114). In 2003 motor vehicle traffic levels in Great Britain were an estimated 0.8 per cent higher than in 2002, reaching 490 billion vehicle-kilometres (Table 21.5). Figure 21.6 shows road traffic by vehicle type. Since 1993 total motor vehicle traffic volumes have increased by nearly 19 per cent. Road traffic intensity, however, fell by 12 per cent between 1990 and 2003.

The Department for Transport (DfT) has been improving its congestion monitoring capability through developing more detailed and varied data sources. Journey time information is being gathered from a variety of data sources, such as MIDAS induction loops on the most congested motorways, TrafficMaster Automatic Number Plate Recognition cameras on all-purpose trunk roads, roadside sensors, and data from global positioning systems (GPS) tracking devices in vehicles. The data sources being developed will

Table 21.5 Motor vehicle traffic, by road class, Great Britain

Billion vehicle-kilometres

	1993	2002	2003
Motorways	68.2	92.6	92.9
Urban major roads[1]	77.3	82.1	81.6
Rural major roads	113.3	136.5	139.4
Minor roads	153.5	175.3	176.4
All roads	**412.3**	**486.6**	**490.3**

1 Urban roads are those within an urban settlement with a population of more than 10,000 people.
Source: Department for Transport

Figure 21.6 Motor vehicle traffic, by vehicle type, 2003, Great Britain

Total: 490 billion vehicle-kilometres

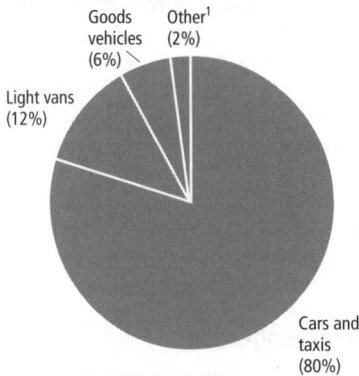

Goods vehicles (6%)
Other[1] (2%)
Light vans (12%)
Cars and taxis (80%)

1 Buses and coaches, and motorcycles.
Source: Department for Transport

enable the DfT to produce detailed reports on the pattern and location of congestion, identify congestion hot-spots and assess the impact of efforts to tackle the problems. The information will be available for use by the DfT, the Highways Agency (see page 331), Transport Direct (see under traffic information) and local authorities.

Traffic management schemes aim to reduce congestion by means of bus lanes and other bus priority measures, 'red routes' with special stopping controls, and parking controls. The DfT is developing indicators of congestion taking into account delay, journey time reliability and severe congestion. Targets based on these indicators will be in place by July 2005. The *Traffic Management Act 2004* creates measures to tackle congestion caused by incidents on motorways and badly managed work by utility companies and local authorities. The Act will help local councils and the Highways Agency to manage roads more effectively, and cut out some of the unnecessary disruption that holds up people's journeys.

Congestion charging

Under the *Transport Act 2000*, local authorities in England and Wales can introduce road user charging or workplace parking levy schemes to help manage congestion. For at least the first ten years of a scheme, the net revenue must be used to fund local transport improvements. Authorities must consult local people and businesses, make

improvements to local transport and obtain ministerial approval before a scheme can start.

The first UK congestion charging scheme began in 2002, in the historic centre of Durham. After one year's operation, vehicle traffic in the zone had fallen by 85 per cent. The revenue is being used to fund improvements to the city's bus services.

The Mayor of London introduced a congestion charging scheme in central London in 2003. The charging zone covers 21 square kilometres, with 174 entry and exit points around its boundary. Extension of the scheme to parts of west London is under consideration.

After the first year of operation:

- there were some 110,000 congestion payments a day;
- congestion within the zone had fallen by 30 per cent, meeting the original aim of the scheme;
- traffic levels entering the zone had fallen by 18 per cent during charging hours, with a 33 per cent reduction for cars;
- disruption to bus services in and around the charging zone had fallen by up to 60 per cent; and
- there had been a year-on-year increase of 29,000 bus passengers entering the zone during the morning peak period.

Traffic information

The Highways Agency's national Traffic Control Centre (TCC), based in Birmingham, became operational in 2004. It collects information on the strategic road network, setting the on-road variable message signs to give drivers route advice, and keeping the travel news on radio, television, the Internet and other organisations updated in real time. During 2004, further services were added including the relaunch of the Highways Agency's website (*www.highways.gov.uk*) and the introduction of a real time traffic information site called Traffic England. An automated telephone service is also planned to provide the latest information on traffic conditions across the strategic road network. Transport Direct, a comprehensive, user-friendly travel information service, is due to be formally launched towards the end of 2004. It will provide travellers with integrated travel planning, live travel news and links to Internet retailers and ticketing services.

The initial service will cover travel by car, train, coach, bus and tram, and domestic flights, with walking links between interchanges. Further enhancements are planned. Under a three-year contract worth £15 million, an Atos Origin-led consortium is responsible for overall project management including the design, build and managed service operation of the portal.

In Northern Ireland, the Roads Service, an executive agency of the Department for Regional Development, operates the Traffic Information and Control Centre, providing real time and travel information, and strategic management and control of traffic on both urban and inter-urban networks.

Road safety

The number of people killed on roads in Great Britain was 2 per cent higher in 2003 than in 2002, but 2 per cent lower than the baseline average for 1994–98 (Table 21.7). The number of people seriously injured in 2003 was 6 per cent lower than in 2002 and 24 per cent lower than in 1994–98.

Table 21.7 Road casualties, Great Britain

	Average 1994–98	2002	2003
Killed	3,578	3,431	3,508
Seriously injured	44,078	35,976	33,707
Slightly injured	272,272	263,198	253,392
All casualties	**319,928**	**302,605**	**290,607**

Source: Department for Transport

Northern Ireland has the highest rate of road traffic accident casualties in the United Kingdom. In 2002 the rate per 100,000 population was 702, compared with rates of 543, 490 and 381 respectively in England, Wales and Scotland. In 2002/03, 158 people were killed on roads in Northern Ireland, five more than in 2001/02; however, the number of people seriously injured was 1,487, 9 per cent fewer than in 2001/02.

Total casualties fell by 8 per cent in 2002/03 to 11,546 and road traffic injury accidents by 8 per cent to 6,569.

Government targets for improving road safety by 2010, compared with the average level for 1994–98, are:

- a 40 per cent reduction in the number of people killed or seriously injured in road accidents;

- a 50 per cent reduction in the number of children killed or seriously injured; and

- a 10 per cent reduction in the slight casualty rate (expressed as the number of people slightly injured per 100 million vehicle-kilometres).

To help meet these targets, more 20 mph (32km/h) zones around schools and in residential areas have been created and road safety education is provided, for example through a network of child pedestrian training schemes.

Home Zones are residential streets where the road space is shared between drivers of motor vehicles and other road users, with the wider needs of residents (including people who walk or cycle, and children) in mind. Their aim is to change the way that streets are used and to improve the quality of life for local residents by making them for people as well as for traffic. There were initially eight pilot projects in England, one in Wales, four in Scotland and one in Northern Ireland. Subsequently, a £30 million Home Zones Challenge fund was established in England in April 2001 and 61 schemes were selected from 237 bids received in January 2002. These included wholly new zones as well as extensions to the pilot schemes.

The 'Dealing with Disadvantage' initiative forms part of the Government's response to the revised target set to reduce road deaths in areas of social exclusion. For the first phase of the project in 2002, ten authorities were selected in the Greater Manchester area that have particularly acute child pedestrian accident problems, and are classified as deprived districts according to Neighbourhood Renewal Unit (see page 320). Comprehensive strategies are being developed to reduce casualty rates in disadvantaged areas faster than across the local authority as a whole. Authorities have been encouraged to consider broad-based solutions and to work in partnership with a range of local interested parties. Funding of £17.6 million was made available nationally over three years.

Under the first phase of an EC Directive, new cars and car-derived vans up to 2.5 tonnes will need to have approved pedestrian protection from 2005. They will be subjected to a series of technical tests which would indicate how they would interact with a pedestrian in an accident. Further measures are expected to apply to new models from 2010. The aim of the Directive is to reduce serious and fatal pedestrian injuries by up to 20 per cent, once both phases have been fully implemented.

Motoring offences

Police, traffic wardens and parking attendants dealt with a record 11.8 million motoring offences in England and Wales during 2002, 11 per cent higher than in 2001. This represented 425 offences per 1,000 licensed vehicles, compared with 343 per 1,000 in 1992. The previous highest rate over the last decade was in 1997, at 403 per 1,000 vehicles. Of the total offences in 2002, 55 per cent were penalty charge notices issued by local authority parking attendants, 26 per cent were fixed penalty notices issued by the police (including traffic wardens) while a further 18 per cent were dealt with by court proceedings.

Obstruction, waiting and parking offences together accounted for 7.6 million offences in 2002, while speed limit offences accounted for 1.7 million.

Traffic cameras provided evidence for 1.5 million motoring offences dealt with in England and Wales in 2002, 40 per cent higher than in 2001, of which 94 per cent were speeding offences. Research carried out for the DfT suggests that between April 2000 and March 2002 there was an average 35 per cent reduction in people killed or seriously injured in road accidents at sites where speed cameras were in operation. The number of vehicles speeding at camera sites was on average 67 per cent lower than at comparable sites without cameras.

Road haulage

Most freight in Great Britain is carried by road, which in 2002 accounted for 82 per cent of goods by tonnage and 62 per cent in terms of tonne-kilometres.

An operator's licence is required for heavy goods vehicles (HGVs) in the United Kingdom – these are vehicles over 3.5 tonnes gross weight. There were 426,000 licensed HGVs in Great Britain at the end of 2003, 16 per cent of which had gross weight of over 38 tonnes. About 84 per cent of the 105,000 operator licences in issue are for fleets of

five or fewer vehicles. In Northern Ireland, 20,000 HGVs were registered in 2002.

Freight traffic by HGVs in Great Britain amounted to 152 billion tonne-kilometres in 2003, the same as in 1998, but 18 per cent higher than in 1993. By commodity, 28 per cent of this traffic was identified as food, drink and tobacco. Road hauliers are tending to use larger vehicles carrying heavier loads – 88 per cent of traffic (tonne-kilometres) in 2003 was moved by vehicles of over 25 tonnes gross weight. In Northern Ireland, freight traffic by HGVs in 2002 amounted to over 48 million tonnes, up almost 7 million tonnes since 1998.

International road haulage has continued to grow steadily. In 2003 almost 2.6 million road goods vehicles or unaccompanied trailers – 471,000 of which were powered vehicles registered in the United Kingdom – travelled to mainland Europe by ferry or the Channel Tunnel, 2.6 per cent more than in 2002. Almost 60 per cent of traffic was from Dover Strait ports (Dover, Folkestone, Ramsgate and the Channel Tunnel), with a further 34 per cent from North Sea ports. In total, international road haulage by UK-registered HGVs amounted to 11.7 billion tonne-kilometres in 2003, 94 per cent of which was with the EU.

The Government's aims for the freight industry are to facilitate the continuing development of a competitive and efficient sector, while reducing the impact that moving freight has on congestion and the environment. This includes encouraging freight traffic to be shifted from road to rail or water where this makes sense, offering financial support where appropriate. Water freight grants are designed to encourage a shift of freight currently travelling by road to water, or to prevent freight on water from switching to road. The grants assist companies with the costs of new or improved freight handling facilities or other capital investments.

Bus and coach services

In 2002/03 travel on buses and coaches in Great Britain increased by 1 per cent to 46.9 billion passenger-kilometres – 22.9 billion were on local buses and 24.0 billion on non-local buses and coaches. Over 4.4 billion passenger journeys were made on local bus services, 3 per cent more than in the previous year and 5 per cent above the low point of 4.2 billion in 1998/99. The number of bus passenger journeys in London has grown substantially since the mid-1990s, reaching 1.5 billion in 2002/03, an 8 per cent increase on the previous year, 21 per cent higher than in 1998/99 and 38 per cent higher than in 1993/94. Nearly 35 per cent of all passenger journeys on local buses occurred in London. Outside London, however, there was a slight fall in the number of passenger journeys in England in 2002/03. There was increased bus use in the rest of the United Kingdom in 2002/03. In Scotland, passenger journeys rose by 1 per cent to 445 million, in Wales, they grew by 5 per cent to 109 million, and in Northern Ireland, 66 million bus passenger journeys were made, 1 per cent more than in the previous year.

The Government's target for local public transport use (buses and light rail) in England, as amended by the 2004 Spending Review, is to increase use by more than 12 per cent from 2000 levels by 2010, with growth in every region.

In 2002/03 there were 16,400 double-deck buses in the Public Service Vehicle (PSV) fleet in Great Britain, 22 per cent fewer than in 1992/93 and 32 per cent fewer than in 1987/88, although there was a small increase of 400 in 2002/03. The number of single-deck buses also increased slightly to 43,200. Vehicles of low-floor design accounted for 14,100 PSVs in 2002/03 compared with only 5,100 five years earlier. There were 19,700 coaches in stock. In Northern Ireland there were around 1,450 buses in service with 'Translink' in 2002/03.

Operators

Almost all bus services in Great Britain are provided by private sector concerns, apart from 17 local authority owned bus companies. Transport for London (TfL) coordinates bus sevices in the capital and manages over 700 bus routes operated by about 25 private sector companies under contract as well as its own bus company, trading as East Thames Buses.

The five largest bus operators in Great Britain also run rail services and some have expanded into transport services in mainland Europe as well as in North America, Australia and New Zealand.

In Northern Ireland almost all road passenger services are operated by subsidiaries of the publicly owned Northern Ireland Transport

Holding Company (NITHC), under the brand name 'Translink'. Citybus operates services in Belfast, with Ulsterbus running most of the services in the rest of Northern Ireland.

Services

Most local bus services are provided commercially, although local authorities may subsidise services that are not commercially viable but are considered socially necessary, such as those operating in the evenings and on Sundays. Outside London, nearly 19 per cent of local bus services in Great Britain (in terms of vehicle-kilometres operated) were subsidised in 2002/03. Local bus fares in Great Britain increased by 1 per cent in real terms (after allowing for inflation) in 2002–03. Average fares in London, however, fell by 4 per cent as TfL maintained its flat-fare structure with no fare rises in real terms. Overall, bus fares have risen by 19 per cent in Great Britain over the ten years to 2002/03, while those in London have risen by 7 per cent.

Local authorities in England and Wales are required to develop bus strategies as part of their Local Transport Plans (LTPs, see page 342). Outside London, statutory backing also exists for 'bus quality partnerships' and 'quality contracts' between local authorities and bus operators. Authorities have powers to promote joint ticketing and to work with Train Operating Companies on bus/rail ticketing. In Scotland, local authorities are expected to set out their plans for bus services in their Local Transport Strategies.

Bus priority measures, such as bus lanes, are becoming more extensive, and in some areas guided busways (with buses travelling on segregated track) are being adopted. Park and ride schemes – in which car users park on the outskirts of towns and travel by bus to the centre – are increasingly being used to relieve congestion, with around 70 new or improved schemes envisaged in England in the period 2003/04 to 2005/06.

A number of schemes provide funds for improving local bus services. The Rural Bus Subsidy Grant (RBSG) in England has funding of £51 million for 2004/05. Introduced in 1998/99, it supported around 2,000 rural bus services in 2004 and can be used to operate new and enhanced services in rural areas with populations of less than 25,000. The Welsh Assembly Government is allocating more than £8 million to local authorities in 2003/04 under its Local Transport

Services Grant to increase the number and range of subsidised bus services and to support community transport projects, while in Scotland, the Executive's Rural Transport Fund has provided for over 400 new or improved rural bus services since its introduction in 1998/99.

In January 2004 the annual Rural Bus Challenge, in which local authorities bid for project funding, resulted in awards totalling £20 million to 42 projects proposed by local authorities throughout rural England, while the Urban Bus Challenge competition also awarded £20 million to 40 urban schemes, in order to help tackle urban deprivation and social exclusion.

Local authorities in England are required by law to offer, as a minimum, half-price bus travel concessionary schemes for the elderly and disabled. Nearly all (94 per cent in 2001) offered a half-fare concessionary scheme. The remainder either had flat-fare schemes or schemes offering free travel, such as in London. Local authorities generally require proof of residency in the area before issuing a concessionary fare permit. Travel on local bus services in Wales is free for pensioners and disabled people, while in Scotland, there is a national minimum standard of free off-peak local bus fares for elderly and disabled people. Travel on public transport in Northern Ireland is free for blind people and for everyone over the age of 65, while people with a range of specified disabilities travel at half fare. Concessionary fare reimbursement for local bus services in Great Britain amounted to £495 million in 2002/03, compared with £2,599 million in payments by passengers.

Coaches account for much of the non-local mileage operated by PSVs, which in total amounted to 1,590 million vehicle-kilometres in 2001/02. Organised coach tours and holiday journeys account for about 60 per cent of coach travel in Great Britain. High-frequency scheduled services, run by private sector operators, link many towns and cities, and commuter services run into London and some other major centres each weekday. National Express has the only scheduled national coach network. It carries more than 12 million passengers every year to over 1,200 destinations throughout Great Britain.

Taxis and private hire vehicles

There were an estimated 72,500 licensed taxis in Great Britain at the end of 2002, and 6,900 in

Northern Ireland. In London (which has over 20,000 'black cab' taxis) and several other major cities, taxis must be purpose-built to conform to strict requirements. In many districts, taxi drivers have to pass a test of their knowledge of the area.

Private hire vehicles (PHVs or 'minicabs') have increased in number in recent years and there were an estimated 89,000 PHVs in Great Britain, and around 2,500 in Northern Ireland in 2002. PHVs can only be pre-booked through a licensed operator and cannot ply for hire in the street. In London, the role of the Public Carriage Office (PCO) has been extended to include the licensing of private hire operators, drivers and vehicles as a result of the *Private Hire Vehicles (London) Act 1998*, implementation of which began in January 2001. Over 2,000 operators have applied for licences and it is estimated that there are about 40,000 drivers and a similar number of vehicles. All PHV drivers now have to meet PCO licensing standards to trade legally in the capital.

Cycling and motorcycling

After decades of decline, the use of two-wheeled transport in Great Britain has stabilised, albeit at a low level. In 2002, motorcycles and pedal cycles each accounted for 1 per cent of total passenger-kilometres travelled in Great Britain. Following a revival of interest in motorcycling, the number of licensed motorcycles, scooters and mopeds was just over 1 million at the end of 2003. This was the highest figure since 1986 and compares with a low of 594,000 in 1995. Northern Ireland had 17,600 licensed motorcycles, scooters and mopeds at the end of 2002.

The National Cycle Network, including links, provided over 13,000 kilometres of cycling and walking routes throughout the United Kingdom in 2003. By 2005 this will be extended to 16,000 kilometres. About one-third of the Network is on paths that are free from motor traffic, with the remainder using quiet lanes or traffic-calmed roads in towns and cities. An estimated 126 million trips were made on the Network in 2003, representing a year-on-year increase of 10 per cent in cycle use. Around 46 per cent of users were cyclists and 53 per cent pedestrians. The network is coordinated by the transport charity Sustrans.

Walking

People in the United Kingdom are walking less than in the past, with fewer journeys on foot and many more by car. The UK Government and devolved administrations wish to reverse this trend, and expect local authorities to give more priority to walking. Almost all local authorities include walking strategies in their LTPs and Strategies (see page 342). Many have set targets to encourage walking by means of a variety of initiatives, for example improving pavement and footway maintenance, removing obstructions, improving pedestrian crossings and creating 20 mph (32 km/h) zones.

The average distance walked per person in Great Britain in 2003 was 309 kilometres, a 3 per cent fall from the figure in 1992/1994, and now accounts for 2.8 per cent of the total distance travelled. The number of walking trips per person in 2003 was 245 – 172 of these were under 1.6 kilometres – averaging just over 1 kilometre per trip; this compares with 306 trips with an average length of just under 1 kilometre in 1992/1994. Since 1992/1994 the proportion of primary-aged children walking to school has declined from 61 to 53 per cent, with an increase from 30 to 39 per cent in the numbers being driven to school. For secondary school pupils there was a similar shift from walking to car use.

Safe routes to school projects (www.saferoutestoschool.org.uk) aim to make it easier for children to walk and cycle to school. They combine practical measures, such as redesigns of roadspace to provide for cyclists and pedestrians and 20 mph speed limits near schools, with educational measures, for example cycle training for children, and an emphasis on the health benefits of walking and cycling.

The road programme

The Highways Agency is an executive agency of the DfT and is responsible for operating, maintaining and improving the road network of motorways and trunk roads in England. In London, responsibility for all major roads except motorways lies with the Greater London Authority (see page 10). In Wales and Scotland, responsibility for the motorway and trunk road network rests with the devolved administrations.

The Highways Agency managed 8,255 kilometres of motorway and trunk roads in 2003/04. This figure is declining and reflects the ongoing transfer of 'non-core' roads – those carrying mainly local traffic – to local highway authorities, a process

which is expected to be completed by March 2006. In addition, local authorities have a budget of £2.7 billion in 2004/05 for maintaining non-trunk roads. The Welsh Assembly Government is the highway authority for 1,708 kilometres of motorways and trunk roads in Wales. Three major projects are due for completion in 2004/05. In Scotland, the motorway and trunk road network extends to almost 3,500 kilometres, around 6 per cent of the total road network, but carries almost a third of the total vehicle mileage. The motorway and trunk road programme for 2004/05 will cost £254 million for a number of major improvement projects, including the completion of the M74 in Glasgow, trunk road maintenance and structural repairs.

The Highways Agency's 2004/05 programme includes expenditure of £730 million on maintaining the network and £508 million on major improvements to the network. A £5.5 billion package of major national and local transport measures was announced for England in December 2002. A further £7 billion (£4 billion of which is allocated ten-year plan money – see page 342) of funding for improvements to some of England's most congested roads was announced in July 2003. This funding is intended to ensure that better use is made of existing roads, for example by building new capacity along particularly busy stretches and making improvements to public transport. Key elements include widening sections of the M25, M1 and M6 motorways.

The M6 Toll, the first toll motorway in the United Kingdom, opened in December 2003. Operated by Midland Expressway, a private sector company, the 43-kilometre, three-lane road bypasses the busiest section of the existing M6 in the West Midlands, one of the most congested roads in Western Europe. Average daily traffic was over 55,000 vehicles by July 2004. In August 2004, the Toll road reached its landmark 10 millionth customer triggering the end to introductory discounted toll rates. A new option for relieving congestion on the M6 between Birmingham and Manchester in the form of a second toll Expressway, as an alternative to widening the M6, was announced in July 2004.

Railways

Network Rail is responsible for operating all railway track and infrastructure in Great Britain. It owns and maintains 34,000 kilometres of track used by the train and freight operating companies. Its assets also include 40,000 bridges and tunnels, 2,500 stations, 1,000 signal boxes and 9,000 level crossings. It is a company limited by guarantee, that is, a private company operating along commercial lines, but without shareholders. It aims to make surpluses from its operations that are reinvested into maintaining and upgrading the rail infrastructure. Northern Ireland Railways, operating as part of the 'Translink' brand, serves 58 passenger stations and operates a network of about 342 kilometres of track.

Most railway services in the United Kingdom are operated by the private sector, although Northern Ireland Railways is a wholly owned subsidiary of the NITHC (see page 329). Apart from 17 major stations operated directly by Network Rail, nearly all stations and passenger depots are leased to the 25 passenger Train Operating Companies (TOCs) that run passenger services under franchise. There are also a number of small open-access operators, such as Hull Trains, running passenger services not provided under franchise agreements. Franchise lengths vary from two to fifteen years. The standard duration of new franchises is seven to ten years. Most of the TOC franchisees are large transport concerns also operating bus and coach services (see page 329).

The TOCs, such as Virgin West Coast/ CrossCountry, Midland Mainline and ScotRail, lease their rolling stock from three rolling stock companies: Angel Trains, HSBC Rail and Porterbrook Leasing. Freight services are run by four companies (see page 334), and there are a number of infrastructure maintenance companies.

Rail regulation and strategy

Great Britain's railways are currently regulated by two organisations: the Strategic Rail Authority (SRA) and the Office of Rail Regulation (ORR). The two bodies have common statutory purposes but different powers to achieve them. The SRA is subject to directions and guidance from the Government, while the ORR is independent.

As well as providing overall strategic direction and leadership to the rail industry, the SRA lets and manages passenger franchises, develops and sponsors major infrastructure projects, manages freight grants, and is responsible for some aspects of consumer protection. Government support to

Bicentenary of the railway

There were several important railway anniversaries in 2004. These have been celebrated at events throughout 2004 with the centrepiece being 'RailFest', a nine-day festival held in May/June at the National Railway Museum in York. Among the anniversaries were:

- 400 years since the construction of the first recorded tramway system in Great Britain – a wagonway for transporting coal – in Nottinghamshire;

- 200 years since the construction of the first steam-powered locomotive by Cornish engineer Richard Trevithick. The engine was used to transport iron from the Penydarren Ironworks in Merthyr Tydfil, south Wales to the local canal;

- 100 years since the steam locomotive *City of Truro* unofficially exceeded 100 mph (162 km/h) on a stretch of line in Somerset;

- 100 years since the first electric main line service opened, between Liverpool and Southport;

- 50 years since British Rail opened its first electrified inter-city main line service, between Manchester and Sheffield; and

- 50 years since the last express steam locomotive was built in the United Kingdom.

the rail industry amounted to approximately £3.8 billion in 2003/04.

The ORR was established in July 2004 as successor to the Office of the Rail Regulator. Its principal function is to regulate Network Rail's stewardship of the national network. It also licenses operators of railway assets, approves agreements for access by operators to track, stations and light maintenance depots, and enforces domestic competition law.

Rail safety

Although there were a number of fatal rail accidents between 1997 and 2002, there is evidence that overall trends in railway safety are improving (Table 21.2). Health and Safety Executive (HSE,

Rail review

In July 2004 the Government published a White Paper, *The Future of Rail*, following a review of the structure of Great Britain's railways. The review considered the structural and organisational changes needed to enable the rail industry to deliver for its customers, as well as looking at the regulation of safety and the progress being made by the industry in improving performance and controlling costs.

The key changes outlined in the White Paper are:

- the Government will take charge of setting the strategy for the railways – it will set the level of public expenditure and take the strategic decisions on what this should buy. This means that the SRA will be wound up, and its strategic responsibilities and financial obligations will pass to the Secretary of State for Transport;

- Network Rail will be given clear responsibility for operating the network and for its performance;

- track and train companies will work more closely together. The number of franchises will be reduced and they will be aligned more closely with Network Rail's regional structure;

- there will be increased local decision-making and more clarity of roles and responsibilities;

- the ORR will cover safety as well as performance and cost, and will acquire responsibility for safety regulation from the Health and Safety Executive; and

- a deal for freight that will enable the industry and its customers to invest for the long term.

The Government will implement these changes as quickly as possible, working in partnership with the industry.

see page 158) figures for Great Britain show that in 2002/03 there were 75 significant train incidents (that is, most collisions and derailments occurring on, or affecting, passenger trains), 17 fewer than in 2001/02. However, ten people were killed in train accidents in 2002/03 – seven as a result of the derailment of a passenger train at Potters Bar (Hertfordshire) in May 2002 – compared with five in 2001/02. Measures being taken to improve the safety of the railway network include:

- establishment of the Rail Safety and Standards Board to lead and facilitate the railway industry's work to achieve continuous improvement in health and safety performance;

- fitting the train protection and warning system (TPWS) to the national network by the end of 2003;

- fitting the new European automatic train protection (ATP) system to lines on the European high-speed network as they are upgraded;

- investment in new rolling stock, enabling the withdrawal of all remaining slam-door trains by 2005; and

- the development of a new national safety plan to improve safety management and ensure best practice.

Passenger services

The passenger network (see map in the colour section) comprises an inter-city network, linking the main city centres of Great Britain; local and regional services; and commuter services in and around the large conurbations, notably London and the South East. Passenger traffic continues to grow (Table 21.8) and on the national railways

Table 21.8 Passenger traffic on rail,[1] underground and selected light rail services, Great Britain

Million passenger-kilometres

	1992/93	2001/02	2002/03
National railways	31,700	39,100	39,700
London Underground	5,758	7,451	7,367
Glasgow Underground	39	44	43
Docklands Light Railway (London)	33	207	232
Greater Manchester Metro	53	161	165
Tyne and Wear Metro	271	238	275
Croydon Tramlink (London)	.	99	100
Centro (West Midlands)	.	50	50
Stagecoach Supertram (Sheffield)	.	39	40

1 Excludes Heathrow Express.

Source: Department for Transport

rose by 3 per cent to 40.9 billion passenger-kilometres in 2003/04, representing 1,014 million passenger journeys, the highest number since the 1960s. In Northern Ireland, the main routes run from Belfast to Londonderry and from Belfast south to the border with the Republic of Ireland and on to Dublin. Northern Ireland Railways handled 6.5 million passenger journeys in 2003/04.

According to the SRA's Public Performance Measure, an average of 81 per cent of scheduled services arrived on time in 2003/04, 2 percentage points higher than in 2002/03.

Freight

Rail freight traffic in Great Britain grew by 1 per cent in 2003/04 to 18.9 billion tonne-kilometres, representing 88.9 million tonnes of freight lifted (by weight). There were 416,000 freight train journeys in 2003/04, 11 per cent more than in the previous year. Most traffic by volume is in bulk commodities, mainly coal, coke, iron and steel, building materials and petroleum. The two largest operators are EWS (English, Welsh & Scottish Railway), which also runs trains through the Channel Tunnel; and Freightliner, which operates container services between major ports and inland terminals. The other two operators are Direct Rail Services (DRS) and GB Railfreight.

The Government and the devolved administrations are keen to encourage more freight to be moved by rail, to relieve pressure on the road network and to bring environmental benefits. Grants are available to encourage companies to move goods by rail or water rather than by road. The Welsh Assembly Government operates the Freight Facilities Grant scheme in Wales and provided funds for two schemes in 2003/04.

The Royal Train

A new locomotive responsible for hauling the Royal Train was unveiled on 18 February 2004. Painted in the official Royal Train colour, Royal Claret, it was named *The Queen's Messenger*. The first Royal Train ran on 13 June 1842, transporting Queen Victoria from Slough to London (Paddington) on a journey taking 25 minutes.

Channel Tunnel

The Channel Tunnel, which had its tenth anniversary in 2004, is operated by the Anglo-French group Eurotunnel, under a concession from the UK and French Governments. As well as managing the infrastructure of the Channel Tunnel – tunnels, terminals and track – Eurotunnel operates a drive-on, drive-off shuttle train service, with separate shuttles for passenger and freight vehicles, between terminals near Folkestone (Kent) and Calais. In 2003 the service carried nearly 2.3 million cars (down 2 per cent on 2002), nearly 1.3 million goods vehicles (up by 4 per cent) and 72,000 coaches (unchanged). Volumes of cars and coaches have been falling in recent years, while goods vehicle numbers have continued to increase.

Eurostar high-speed train services are operated jointly by Eurostar (UK) Ltd, SNCF (French National Railways) and SNCB (Belgian National Railways) under the commercial direction of Eurostar Group Ltd. Services connect London (Waterloo) and Paris or Brussels. Trains also serve Ashford International (Kent), Calais, Lille, Disneyland Paris, Moutiers and Bourg St Maurice in the French Alps (in the winter) and Avignon (in the summer). Eurostar carried 6.3 million passengers in 2003.

Channel Tunnel Rail Link

The first section of the 109-kilometre Channel Tunnel Rail Link (CTRL), between the Channel Tunnel terminal and Fawkham Junction (Kent), opened in September 2003. Eurostar trains are now able to travel in the United Kingdom at speeds of up to 186 mph (300 km/h). This has reduced the fastest journey between London and Paris to 2 hours 35 minutes, and between London and Brussels to 2 hours 15 minutes.

Construction work on the second section, to a new international terminal at London St Pancras, is due for completion in 2007. When this section is complete, Eurostar journey times to and from the continent will be reduced by a further 20 minutes. High-speed domestic services will also operate from Kent to London and new international stations will be built at Stratford (east London) and Ebbsfleet (Kent). The total cost of the CTRL project is forecast to be £5.2 billion.

Underground railways

The world's first underground railway opened in London in 1863, and the 'Tube' network serves 275

UK rail speed record

The UK rail speed record was broken on 30 July 2003 when a Eurostar test train reached 208 mph (335 km/h) on section 1 of the Channel Tunnel Rail Link. The previous record of 162 mph (261 km/h) was set in 1979 by British Rail's Advanced Passenger Train.

Table 21.9 Modern tram and light rail systems, 31 March 2004, UK

	Number of stations	Length of route (km)
Tyne and Wear Metro	58	78
Manchester Metrolink	37	39
Stagecoach Supertram (Sheffield)	48	29
Croydon Tramlink (London)	38	28
Docklands Light Railway (London)	34	27
Midland Metro (West Midlands)	23	20
Nottingham Express Transit	23	14

Source: Department for Transport

stations on over 408 kilometres of track. It is run by London Underground Ltd (LUL), which is part of TfL (see page 342). In 2003/04, 948 million passenger journeys were made on the network. The Glasgow Underground, the only other such UK system, and the world's third oldest, opened in 1896 with 15 stations, and operates on a 10-kilometre circle in central Glasgow.

Responsibility for maintaining and upgrading LUL's infrastructure is with the private sector under a public-private partnership (PPP – see page 370), while LUL continues to have responsibility for safety and for operating passenger services across the network. Under the PPP, three infrastructure companies (Infracos) – Tube Lines, Metronet Rail BCV and Metronet SSL – work under contract to LUL for a 30-year period starting in April 2003. Ownership of LUL's assets – trains, stations, track and tunnels – remains in the public sector; the Infracos lease these assets for the period of the contracts. The PPP will enable many billion pounds to be invested in the Underground's infrastructure over the 30 years.

Light railways and tramways

In spring 2004 seven modern tram and light rail services were in operation (Table 21.9). A 4.4-kilometre extension to the Docklands Light Railway in London is expected to be completed by late 2005, and a further 2.5-kilometre extension under the River Thames to Woolwich has won government approval.

As well as the modern tram networks there are much older systems still in operation, including Blackpool (Lancashire), which opened in 1885, and the Great Orme tramway at Llandudno (north Wales), dating back to 1902. Heritage tramways run at Beamish (Co Durham), Crich (Derbyshire) and Seaton (Devon).

Heritage railways

There are over 100 passenger heritage railways, often connected with the preservation of steam locomotives. Services are mostly operated by volunteers and cater mainly for tourists and railway enthusiasts. Some run on the tracks of closed British Rail routes. Examples include:

- the Snowdon Mountain Railway in north Wales, opened in 1896, which carries visitors to within 20 metres of the summit;

- the Romney, Hythe and Dymchurch Railway in Kent, opened in 1927, using the 15-inch gauge (38 centimetres) and running for 22 kilometres. In its early years it was known as the 'Smallest Public Railway in the World';

- the Strathspey Railway in the Central Highlands of Scotland, which uses existing standard gauge track. The first stage between Aviemore and Boat of Garten opened in 1978 and an extension to Grantown-on-Spey is being explored; and

- the 3-foot narrow gauge (just under 1 metre) Giant's Causeway & Bushmills Railway in Antrim, Northern Ireland, which opened in 2002. A little over 3 kilometres long, it links the World Heritage site with the Old Bushmills whiskey distillery.

Air travel

Between 1993 and 2003 the number of passengers joining or leaving aircraft at UK airports increased by 77 per cent to 176.9 million. Cargo (excluding mail and passengers' luggage) rose by 62 per cent to 2.15 million tonnes. Aircraft landings and take-offs increased by 44 per cent to 1.67 million. These figures exclude double counting of domestic passengers, so that those who take off from one UK airport and land at another UK airport are only counted once.

According to the DfT, these trends look set to continue; the number of air passengers is forecast to grow by around 4 per cent a year over the next decade, and the freight market by 7 per cent (see page 337). The number of UK residents going abroad by air has grown rapidly (Figure 21.10), from 25.4 million visits in 1993 to 47.2 million in 2003.

There were 50 UK airlines at the end of 2003, all in the private sector, as are most of the major

airports. Day-to-day responsibility for the regulation of civil aviation rests with the Civil Aviation Authority (CAA); this includes air safety, economic and airspace regulation, consumer protection, and environmental research and consultancy.

Airlines

British Airways is one of the world's largest international airlines. In August 2004 its worldwide network covered 158 destinations in 74 countries. Its main operating bases are London's two main airports, Heathrow and Gatwick.

Traffic on UK-owned airlines, 2003

Aircraft-kilometres flown	1.6 billion
Passengers uplifted[1]	110 million
Passenger-kilometres flown	257 billion
Cargo and mail uplifted (tonnes)[1]	1.0 million
Cargo- and mail-kilometres flown	6.3 billion

1 Passenger and cargo movements are counted every time an aircraft takes off, that is, on every stage of a journey rather than once for the whole journey.

The longest established UK air route

On 29 March 2004 Southampton Airport celebrated 70 years of air services between Southampton and Jersey. This air link is believed to be the longest established UK air route still in existence. In 1934, Commander Charles Eckersley-Maslin piloted the first flight to Jersey. The plane was a de Havilland Dragon Rapide DH84 aircraft, operated by Jersey Airways. Passengers were charged £3 for the return Southampton/Portsmouth and Jersey flight.

Figure 21.10 Trips abroad by air, UK residents

Millions

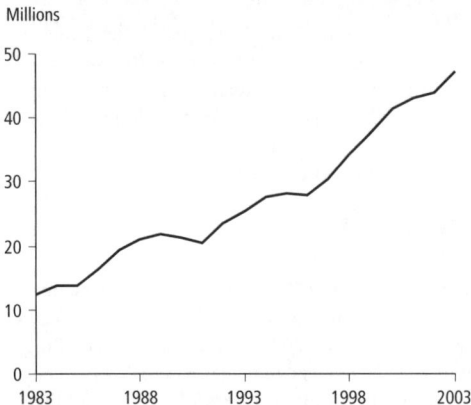

Source: International Passenger Survey, Office for National Statistics

British Airways was one of the founders of the 'Oneworld' alliance of nine airlines, offering customers an extensive worldwide route network and a wide range of benefits. Together, in August 2004, these airlines offered travel to 562 scheduled destinations in 131 countries, with over 8,500 flights every day.

At the end of 2003 there were 921 aircraft in service in the UK airline fleet, 27 per cent more than in 1993.

Airports

There are about 140 licensed civil aerodromes in the United Kingdom, and 35 handled more than 100,000 passengers in 2003. The total number of passengers at UK civil airports was a record 200.0 million in 2003, a 6 per cent increase on 2002 and 78 per cent higher than in 1993. Freight handled amounted to 2.2 million tonnes, with

Table 21.11 Passenger numbers uplifted by main UK airlines

Millions

	Airline type	2002	2003
British Airways plc[1]	Scheduled	31.4	33.2
easyJet Airline Company Ltd	Low-cost	9.1	18.1
bmi British Midland[2]	Scheduled	8.0	9.2
Britannia Airways[3]	Charter	8.0	8.0
My Travel Airways UK	Charter	7.5	7.9

1 Includes CitiExpress Ltd and, in 2002, Euro Ops (Gatwick) services.
2 Includes bmi Regional.
3 Being rebranded as Thomson.
Source: Civil Aviation Authority

Table 21.12 Passenger traffic at main airports,[1] UK

Million passengers

	1993	2002	2003
London Heathrow	47.6	63.0	63.2
London Gatwick	20.1	29.5	29.9
Manchester	12.8	18.6	19.5
London Stansted	2.7	16.0	18.7
Birmingham	4.0	7.9	8.9
Glasgow	5.0	7.8	8.1
Edinburgh	2.7	6.9	7.5
London Luton	1.8	6.5	6.8
East Midlands	1.4	3.2	4.3
Belfast International	2.2	3.6	4.0
Newcastle	2.1	3.4	3.9
Bristol	1.1	3.4	3.9
Other UK airports	8.8	18.9	21.3
Total	**112.3**	**188.8**	**200.0**

1 Terminal passengers, excluding double counting and those in transit.
Source: Civil Aviation Authority

Concorde's last flight

Thousands of people witnessed three Concordes land consecutively at London Heathrow on their last day of commercial service on 24 October 2003. Concorde's final flight was on 26 November 2003, from London Heathrow to Airbus UK headquarters in Filton, Bristol, the factory where it was built in the 1960s and 1970s.

mail accounting for a further 0.2 million tonnes. Heathrow is the world's busiest international airport and accounted for 63.2 million passengers (excluding those in transit) in 2003, 32 per cent of UK passengers in 2003, while Gatwick, the world's busiest single runway airport, accounted for 29.9 million passengers, 15 per cent.

All UK airports used for public transport must be licensed by the CAA for reasons of safety. Stringent requirements, such as adequate firefighting, medical and rescue services, have to be satisfied before a licence is granted.

Ownership and control

BAA is the largest global commercial airport operator. It handled 131 million passengers at its seven UK-owned airports – Heathrow, Gatwick, Stansted, Glasgow, Edinburgh, Aberdeen and Southampton – in 2003. Overseas, it has management contracts or stakes in ten airports

and retail management contracts at two others. The second largest UK operator is TBI, with three UK airports – London Luton, Cardiff International and Belfast International – and interests in 38 others around the world.

In Scotland, Highland and Islands Airports Ltd (HIAL) manages and maintains ten airports and in 2003 handled around 864,000 passengers. These airports receive considerable investment from the Scottish Executive to ensure the continued provision of 'lifeline' services to remote areas.

Airport development

Following extensive public consultation, a White Paper, *The Future of Air Transport*, was published in December 2003. This set out the framework for the development of air transport over the next 30 years in the regions of England as well as in Wales, Scotland and Northern Ireland, aiming to balance the economic benefits against the environmental impact. Since the 1970s there has been a fivefold increase in air travel; half the population now flies at least once a year, and many fly more often. Forecasts suggest that demand could be between two and three times current levels by 2030. In addition, air freight has doubled in the last ten years; one-third by value of all goods exported goes by air. The key conclusions of the White Paper are:

- two new runways to be built in the South East of England by 2030, the first at Stansted (by 2011 or 2012) and the second at Heathrow (within the 2015 to 2020 period), provided they meet strict environmental conditions;

- growth to take place at other UK airports, including extending existing runways, providing additional runways, and developing terminal and other facilities; but

- no new airports to be constructed in central Scotland, south-east Wales, the Midlands, the South East or the South West, although existing facilities in these areas should be expanded.

BAA is investing £8.6 billion of capital expenditure in its three airports in the South East of England over an 11-year period up to 2014. Around £7 billion of this will be at Heathrow, including £4.2 billion on the Terminal 5 project. The new terminal is on schedule to open in 2008 and will increase Heathrow's passenger handling capacity by 30 million passengers a year. At Gatwick, BAA is spending about £840 million on infrastructure to raise current traffic levels by a third to 40 million a year by 2014. This includes the £100 million Pier 6 project which contains the world's biggest air passenger bridge, large enough to allow a Boeing 747-400 to pass underneath. BAA is also investing £660 million to cater for the rapid growth of low-cost carriers at Stansted Airport. An application will be submitted in 2005 to allow expansion from the current limit of 25 million to around 35 million passengers a year.

Air traffic control

National Air Traffic Services (NATS) provides air traffic control services to civil and military aircraft flying in UK airspace, and in the eastern North Atlantic and western North Sea. It operates under contract to the airport operators at 14 UK airports, including all seven BAA airports, and also provides an approach radar service to three others. In addition NATS provides air control services to QinetiQ (the greater part of the former Defence Evaluation and Research Agency) at the Larkhill (Wiltshire) and Aberporth (Ceredigion) Ministry of Defence test ranges. NATS is a PPP (see page 370), in which the Government's partners are a consortium of seven UK airlines known as the Airline Group, and BAA. The CAA retains

responsibility for air safety regulation, and also regulates NATS air traffic control charges.

Figures for 2003 indicate that NATS handled a record number of flights, with proportionately fewer delays. A total of 2.08 million flights used UK airspace in 2003, an increase of 4 per cent on 2002. Over 95 per cent of flights experienced no traffic control delay, up from 87 per cent in 2002. The average delay fell from 2.58 minutes in 2002 to 0.74 minutes in 2003.

En route air traffic management services to aircraft flying over the United Kingdom are provided from the following centres:

- London Area Control Centre at Swanwick, Hampshire;

- London Terminal Control Centre at West Drayton, Middlesex;

- Scottish Area Control Centre and Oceanic Control Centre at Prestwick, Ayrshire; and

- Manchester Area Control Centre at Manchester Airport.

The Oceanic Area Control Centre provides services to aircraft flying the North Atlantic.

In the long term, all NATS' en route operations will be carried out from Swanwick and a new centre at Prestwick, which is expected to be in full operational service by 2009.

The first phase of a £1 billion investment plan – the replacement of its entire UK radar network – was announced by NATS in 2003. The planned investment will replace much of the UK air traffic control infrastructure, and is intended, among other things, to enable the company to handle a projected 50 per cent increase in flights, from 2 to 3 million, by 2010/11.

Air safety

The Safety Regulation Group of the CAA is responsible for the day-to-day safety regulation of UK airlines, airports and air traffic control, and for issuing airworthiness and maintenance approvals on behalf of the European Aviation Safety Agency. On the basis of either European or UK law, it must be satisfied that aircraft are properly designed, manufactured, operated and maintained; that airlines are competent; that flight crews, air traffic controllers and aircraft maintenance engineers are fit and competent; that licensed aerodromes are safe to use; and that air traffic services and general aviation activities meet required safety standards. All aircraft registered in the United Kingdom must be granted a certificate of airworthiness by the CAA before being flown. Of the 17,012 registered on 1 January 2004, 32 per cent were not currently certificated, 26 per cent had transport category passenger status, 24 per cent permit to fly status and 15 per cent private status.

The Air Accidents Investigation Branch (AAIB) is part of the DfT and is responsible for the investigation of civil aircraft accidents and serious incidents within UK airspace and those that occur overseas to aircraft registered or manufactured in the United Kingdom. In 2003 the AAIB was involved in the investigation of 467 civil aviation accidents or incidents worldwide and provided technical assistance to military aircraft accident investigations on six occasions.

Shipping and ports

An estimated 95 per cent by weight (75 per cent by value) of UK foreign trade is carried by sea. The UK-registered fleet declined considerably in tonnage terms between 1975 and 1997, but strategies to promote UK shipping have resulted in a threefold increase in tonnage since then. Total international revenue earned by the UK shipping industry in 2003 was £5.0 billion. Freight revenue accounted for £3.7 billion (£2.9 billion on dry cargo and passenger vessels and £0.8 billion on tankers and liquefied gas carriers). The remaining revenue came from passengers and from charter receipts.

There were 649 UK-owned trading vessels of 100 gross tonnes and over at the end of 2003, with a total deadweight of 15.0 million tonnes, an increase of 2.7 million tonnes on 2002. There were 149 vessels totalling 5.5 million deadweight tonnes used as oil, chemical or gas carriers, and 453 vessels totalling 9.3 million deadweight tonnes employed as dry-bulk carriers, container ships and other types of cargo ship. In addition, there were 47 passenger ships with deadweight of 0.1 million tonnes. In all, 77 per cent of UK-owned vessels are registered in the United Kingdom, the Channel Islands, the Isle of Man (see page 7)or UK Overseas Territories (see page 77) such as Bermuda.

Cargo services

Nearly all scheduled cargo-liner services from the United Kingdom are containerised. UK tonnage

serving these trades is dominated by a relatively small number of companies. Besides the carriage of freight by liner and bulk services between the United Kingdom and the rest of Europe, many roll-on, roll-off services carry cars, passengers and commercial vehicles.

Passenger services

Provisional figures for 2003 show that there were 26.5 million international[2] sea passenger journeys to and from the United Kingdom, 8 per cent fewer than in 2002. There were 14.6 million journeys through Dover (55 per cent of the total) with a further 3.1 million through Portsmouth, the second largest port for international sea passenger traffic, and 2.3 million through Holyhead. Domestic[3] sea passenger journeys totalled 3.8 million. It is estimated that a further 18 million passengers were carried on ferry services to offshore islands such as the Isle of Wight, Orkney, Shetland, and the islands off the west coast of Scotland.

Branson sets cross-Channel record

On 14 June 2004 Sir Richard Branson set the record for the fastest ever crossing of the English Channel by an amphibious vehicle, crossing the Channel in 1 hour, 40 minutes and 6 seconds, beating the previous record of six hours set by two Frenchmen.

P&O Ferries is the largest UK ferry operator, with a fleet of over 40 ships operating on 15 routes around the UK coast. Cross-Channel services are operated by roll-on, roll-off ferries, high-speed catamarans and high-speed monohulls.

Maritime safety

The Maritime and Coastguard Agency (MCA) is an executive agency of the DfT and is responsible throughout the United Kingdom for implementing the Government's maritime safety policy. This includes coordinating search and rescue at sea through HM Coastguard (see below),

2 International routes to Belgium, Denmark, Finland, France, Germany, Republic of Ireland, The Netherlands, Norway, Spain and Sweden.
3 Domestic routes between Great Britain and Northern Ireland, the Isle of Man and the Channel Islands.

Queen Mary 2

Following its naming by The Queen on 8 January 2004, the maiden voyage of the *Queen Mary 2* took place on 12 January, when the liner sailed from Southampton to Fort Lauderdale in the United States. At 345 metres long, 72 metres high and with accommodation for 2,620 passengers on 19 decks, it is the world's biggest ever passenger ship.

and checking that ships meet UK and international safety rules. It works to prevent loss of lives at the coast and at sea, to ensure that ships are safe, and to prevent coastal pollution. During 2003/04, 112 foreign ships were under detention in UK ports after failing safety inspection, compared with 132 in 2002/03.

HM Coastguard is one of the four emergency services in the United Kingdom and is divided into three regions – Eastern, Wales and West of England, and Scotland and Northern Ireland. Each region has a number of Maritime Rescue Coordination Centres and Sub Centres, from which it coordinates the response to maritime incidents. HM Coastguard can call upon its own helicopters, cliff and mud rescue teams; lifeboats of the Royal National Lifeboat Institution (see page 114) and other volunteer lifeboats; aircraft, helicopters and ships from the Armed Forces; and merchant shipping and commercial aircraft. In 2003 a total of 5,689 persons were rescued and 316 lives were lost (including suicides and bodies recovered where the actual cause of death was unknown), indicating that 94.4 per cent of persons involved in life threatening situations were rescued.

Several locations in UK waters are potentially hazardous to shipping. There are around 1,300 marine aids to navigation around the UK coast,[4] including 350 lighthouses and over 700 buoys. Responsibility for these rests with three lighthouse authorities. Measures to reduce the risk of collision include the separation of ships into internationally agreed shipping lanes. This applies,

for example, in the Dover Strait, one of the world's busiest seaways, which is monitored by radar from the Channel Navigation Information Service at the MCA's Dover base.

The Marine Accident Investigation Branch (MAIB) is part of the DfT and examines and investigates all types of marine accidents to or on board UK ships worldwide, and other ships in UK territorial waters. In 2003 the MAIB received 1,522 accident and incident reports, of which 689 were accidents to ships, 631 accidents to people and 202 hazardous incidents (near misses). During the year, 15 full investigations were started.

Ports

There are over 100 ports of commercial significance in the United Kingdom, while several hundred small harbours cater for local cargo, fishing vessels, island ferries or recreation. Ports fall into three categories: those owned and run by boards constituted as trusts; those owned by local authorities; and company-owned facilities.

The largest UK ports group, Associated British Ports (ABP), owns and operates 21 ports in England, Wales and Scotland, including the major ports of Grimsby and Immingham, Southampton, Hull, Port Talbot, Ipswich, Newport, Cardiff, Goole and Fleetwood. Other major facilities owned by private sector companies include Felixstowe, Harwich and Medway. Northern Ireland has four main ports, at Belfast, Larne, Londonderry and Warrenpoint. With the exception of Larne, which is privately owned, they are all public trust ports.

The Government aims to assist ports in maintaining competitiveness; to develop nationally agreed safety standards; to promote environmental best practice; and to build on the approach detailed in its 2000 ten-year plan for transport, which recognises the importance of port hubs within integrated transport systems.

Port traffic

Freight traffic at UK ports was 555 million tonnes in 2003, a 1 per cent fall compared with 2002. Traffic through the 52 major UK ports (generally those handling over 1 million tonnes a year) accounted for 538 million tonnes (97 per cent) of the total. Inwards traffic, 58 per cent of the total, increased by 2 million tonnes to 323 million

---

4 These figures include the Republic of Ireland, the Isle of Man, the Channel Islands and Gibraltar.

tonnes, while outward traffic fell by 6 million tonnes to 231 million tonnes.

The principal ports, in terms of total tonnage handled, are shown in Table 21.13. Forth, Milford Haven and Sullom Voe mostly handle oil, while the main destinations for non-fuel traffic are London, Felixstowe, Grimsby and Immingham, Tees and Hartlepool, and Liverpool. In 2002 crude oil accounted for 32 per cent of all major ports traffic.

Table 21.13 Traffic through principal ports, UK

Million tonnes

	1993	2002	2003
Grimsby and Immingham	41.3	55.7	55.9
Tees and Hartlepool	42.7	50.5	53.8
London	50.9	51.2	51.0
Forth	26.4	42.2	38.7
Southampton	30.9	34.2	35.8
Milford Haven	35.7	34.5	32.7
Liverpool	30.5	30.4	31.7
Sullom Voe	39.4	29.4	26.4
Felixstowe	20.3	25.1	22.2
Dover	13.8	20.2	18.8

Source: Department for Transport

Felixstowe is the most important port for container and conventional services, handling 38 per cent of this type of traffic in 2002. Dover handled 30 per cent of total road goods vehicles and unaccompanied trailers, and is also the major arrival and departure point for sea passengers (see above). The top four UK ports are among the ten largest ports in northern Europe. Northern Ireland ports handle some 95 per cent of its trade.

Inland waterways

Although UK inland waterways are now used mainly for leisure and general recreation, they have a number of other important roles: as a heritage and environmental resource, as a catalyst for regeneration, and in land drainage and water supply. Some continue to carry freight.

In 2002, UK inland waters traffic[5] carried goods amounting to 49.0 million tonnes, a fall of 8 per

5 This covers internal non-seagoing traffic and seagoing traffic that crosses into inland waterways.

cent on the previous year and 18 per cent lower than in 1992. The volume of goods moved was 1.7 billion tonne-kilometres, down from 1.8 billion tonne-kilometres in 2001. The River Thames was the busiest inland waterway, carrying 19.3 million tonnes of traffic in 2002, followed by the River Forth with 8.5 million tonnes.

British Waterways is the leading UK navigation authority, with responsibility for some 3,200 kilometres of canals, rivers and docks, over half the UK total. It is a public sector body, sponsored by the Department for Environment, Food and Rural Affairs and the Scottish Executive. There are about 30 other navigation authorities in the United Kingdom.

The Pontcysyllte aqueduct

As one of the seven 'Wonders of the Waterways', and the highest and biggest in the British Isles, the Pontcysyllte aqueduct carries the Llangollen canal across the River Dee in north Wales. It is 37 metres high and over 300 metres long. The first stone was laid in July 1795 and construction took ten years, at a cost of around £47,000. It is currently being cleaned, in time to celebrate its 200th anniversary in 2005.

In the last few years British Waterways has completed Great Britain's largest programme of waterway restorations, in which over 350 kilometres of canals and waterway structures were restored or built, with funding coming from a range of partnerships and public support. The organisation is working towards self-sufficiency for Great Britain's inland waterways through innovative commercial ventures and has the objective of attracting twice as many people to its canals and rivers in 2012 compared with 2003. The cross-border body Waterways Ireland manages, maintains, develops and restores the inland navigable waterway systems throughout the island of Ireland, principally for recreational purposes.

Transport policy

In July 2004 the Government published a transport strategy White Paper, *The Future of*

Transport: a network for 2030. The strategy builds on the long-term approach to transport planning established in the ten-year plan for transport, published in 2000 and which came into effect in April 2001. The White Paper incorporates the 2004 Spending Review (see page 368), which rolled forward the original ten-year plan public spending package to 2014/15.

Spending by the DfT will rise by an annual average of 4.5 per cent in real terms between 2005/06 and 2007/08. This includes a £1.7 billion transport reform package for the railways over and above the original ten-year plan provision. The Spending Review also increased forecast ten-year plan spending by £0.5 billion each year from 2006/07. This higher level of spending will grow in real terms (by 2.25 per cent each year) through to 2015. Further details of how the revised spending package will be broken down between transport modes will be published in autumn 2004. Public spending by the DfT in 2003/04 is shown in Figure 21.14.

Under the *Transport Act 2000*, local transport authorities in England (excluding London) and Wales have drawn up five-year Local Transport Plans (LTPs). Most English authorities are expecting to publish their second LTPs in July 2005. In Scotland all local authorities have produced Local Transport Strategies and Strathclyde Passenger Transport has a public transport strategy.

Every year, capital allocations to English local authorities are made in the LTP capital settlement. This funding has been used by authorities to invest in capital road maintenance works and schemes to improve local road networks and infrastructure, public transport, walking and cycling. The 2004 Spending Review established a Transport Innovation Fund (TIF), additional to the LTP funding stream, to support authorities that pursue measures aimed at key shared national and local priorities such as congestion reduction and improving public transport services. Mechanisms for deciding on allocations from the TIF will be published in the 2005 Budget alongside regional guideline budgets, with a view to making the first allocations in 2006.

The Mayor of London (see page 10) is responsible for transport in the capital except for main line rail. The Mayor's Transport Strategy recognises that increasing the capacity of London's transport system cannot be based on the private car. It aims

Figure 21.14 Department for Transport public spending, by main activity, 2003/04[1]

Total: £14.5 billion

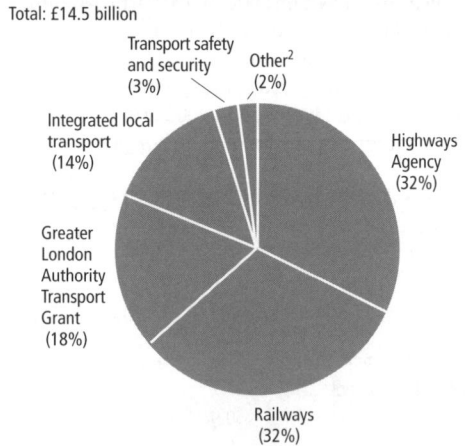

1 Resource and capital expenditure, estimated outturn.
2 Includes logistics and maritime, transport strategy and delivery, aviation and central administration.
Source: Department for Transport

to increase bus capacity by around 40 per cent and to increase total rail capacity by up to 40 per cent between 2002 and 2011.

With these additional improvements, total rail capacity, including CrossRail – a new east-west route planned through central London – and Thameslink 2000 – an upgrade of the existing Thameslink cross-London north-south route – could be increased by up to 50 per cent by 2016. Authorities in London produce local implementation/borough spending plans in line with the Strategy, which is delivered by TfL.

The *Railways and Transport Safety Act 2003* set up a new Rail Accident Investigation Branch (RAIB), on similar lines to the AAIB and MAIB (see pages 339 and 340). This is in response to recommendations made in Lord Cullen's report into the Ladbroke Grove rail crash of 1999, in which 31 people died. Other measures in the Act include introducing alcohol limits in relation to shipping and civil aviation (broadly replicating the drink driving legislation that applies to motorists and railway workers); establishing a new police authority for the British Transport Police (see also page 205), and restructuring the Office of the Rail Regulator, which will now have a statutory board and has become the ORR (see page 332).

Wales

The *Transport Framework for Wales* sets the context within which the Welsh Assembly Government makes decisions relating to transport. It aims to provide a better coordinated and sustainable system, including improved public transport. Programmes have been set out under the framework for rail, roads and local transport.

The Welsh Assembly Government Transport Directorate had an annual budget of £326 million in 2004/05. It is responsible for the maintenance and improvement of motorways and trunk roads in Wales, and the administration of grants to local authorities and other bodies to fund a range of capital transport schemes and transport services.

In 2004 the Welsh Assembly Government announced a Transport Grant of £85 million for 2004/05. The total includes £36 million to support integrated transport solutions such as bus-rail interchanges, £34 million to improve the local road network, and £8 million each to help develop the rail network and to encourage walking and cycling, including Safe Routes to Schools (see page 331).

Scotland

In June 2004 the Scottish Executive issued a White Paper, *Scotland's Transport Future*, setting out its vision of a safe, integrated and reliable transport system that supports economic growth and provides opportunities for all. It plans to achieve this through investing in infrastructure and services, and reforming delivery at a national and regional level. Major projects include new rail links, for example to Edinburgh and Glasgow International airports, a route development fund to stimulate new or existing bus services and road improvements, such as the M74 completion and the Aberdeen bypass. The White Paper proposes reforming transport delivery through the creation of a national transport agency and statutory regional transport partnerships, comprising local authorities and representatives from business and other organisations in the region.

Total planned expenditure on transport of £1.3 billion in 2004/05 includes £643 million for motorways and trunk roads (of which £338 million is a cost of capital charge), £211 million for rail services, £28 million for ferries and £22 million for Highlands and Islands airports.

The Scottish Executive is also taking a long-term view of financial planning for public transport infrastructure, and funding of £3 billion is planned over the next ten years.

The first piece of private rail legislation to go before the Scottish Parliament since devolution was introduced in May 2003 and passed in July 2004. The *Stirling-Alloa-Kincardine Railway and Linked Improvements (Scotland) Act 2004* gives permission for the re-opening of this link, part of the Scottish Executive's proposed improvements to the Scottish rail network.

Northern Ireland

The *Regional Transportation Strategy for Northern Ireland 2002–2012* identifies strategic investment priorities and considers potential funding sources and the affordability of planned initiatives over the ten years. Funding of £3.5 billion is envisaged over the lifetime of the strategy. The principal initiatives include:

- upgrading existing rail network and services, and providing new, modern trains and increased rail capacity;

- quality bus routes on all main Belfast commuter routes and providing new, modern accessible buses;

- building a rapid transit system in the Belfast metropolitan area; and

- strategic highway improvements to provide, for example, up to 13 bypasses and about 85 kilometres of dual carriageway.

Further reading

Department for Transport Annual Report 2004. Cm 6207. The Stationery Office, 2004.

Maritime Statistics, annual report. The Stationery Office.

National Travel Survey, annual bulletin. Department for Transport.

Northern Ireland Transport Statistics, annual report. Northern Ireland Department for Regional Development.

Public Transport Statistics, Great Britain, annual report. Department for Transport.

Road Traffic Statistics for Great Britain, annual bulletin. Department for Transport.

Scotland's Transport Future. White Paper. Scottish Executive, 2004.

The Future of Air Transport. White Paper. Cm 6046. Department for Transport. The Stationery Office, 2003.

The Future of Rail. White Paper. Cm 6233. Department for Transport. The Stationery Office, 2004.

The Future of Transport: a network for 2030. Cm 6234. Department for Transport. The Stationery Office, 2004.

Transport Statistics Great Britain, annual report. The Stationery Office.

Transport Trends, annual bulletin. Department for Transport.

Travel Survey for Northern Ireland, annual report. Northern Ireland Department for Regional Development.

Websites

Department for Transport
www.dft.gov.uk

Welsh Assembly Government
www.wales.gov.uk

Scottish Executive
www.scotland.gov.uk

Northern Ireland Department for Regional Development
www.drdni.gov.uk

Transport for London
www.tfl.gov.uk

Strategic Rail Authority
www.sra.gov.uk

The Office of Rail Regulation
www.rail-reg.gov.uk

WWW.

22 Economic framework

Growth in the UK economy continued for the 12th consecutive year in 2003 (Figure 22.1). The chained volume measure of gross domestic product (GDP) (see glossary) rose by 2.2 per cent. This was slightly above the 1.8 per cent growth in 2002, but slightly below its post-war average of around 2½ per cent a year.

Figure 22.1 Annual change in GDP at market prices,[1] UK

Percentages

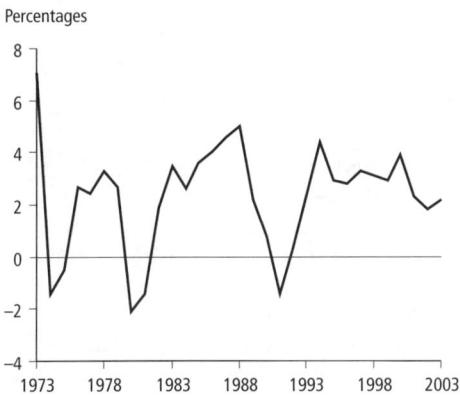

1 Chained volume measure, reference year 2001.
Source: Office for National Statistics

In recent decades the service sector (see chapter 29) has dominated growth. In 2003 it grew by 2.5 per cent, slightly below the 2.7 per cent achieved in 2002. The real estate sector, hotels and restaurants, post and telecommunications, and health and social work all showed above average rates of growth. The construction sector also grew strongly in 2003, by 4.9 per cent, following growth of 3.8 per cent in 2002. After declining by 2.5 per cent in 2002, output of production industries was broadly unchanged in 2003. Increases of 2.2 per cent in electricity, gas and water supply and 0.4 per cent in manufacturing – following two successive years of decline – offset a 5.4 per cent fall in mining and quarrying (including oil and gas extraction). The agriculture, forestry and fishing industry declined by 2.6 per cent in 2003 following an 11.9 per cent increase in the previous year.

In 2003 the rate of growth in expenditure by households slowed to 2.3 per cent, compared with 3.2 per cent in 2002, while general government expenditure rose by 3.5 per cent, slightly less than the 3.8 per cent in the previous year. Gross fixed capital formation (see glossary) increased by 2.2 per cent in 2003, less than the 2.7 per cent increase in the previous year. On the trade side, volumes were weaker than in recent years. Exports of goods and services rose only marginally in both 2002 and 2003. Imports grew by 1.3 per cent in 2003, following a 4.1 per cent rise in 2002.

Economic strategy

The main elements of the Government's economic strategy, designed to deliver high and stable levels of economic growth and employment, are as set out in the 2004 Budget:

- maintaining macroeconomic stability;
- raising the sustainable rate of productivity growth;
- increasing employment opportunity for all;
- building a fairer society;
- delivering high-quality public services; and
- protecting the environment.

HM Treasury is the department with prime responsibility for macroeconomic policy – in particular, taxation and spending – and setting the inflation target that the independent Monetary Policy Committee of the Bank of England is required to meet (see page 348). It is also responsible for wider economic policy, which it carries out in conjunction with other government departments, such as Trade and Industry, Education and Skills, Work and Pensions, and Transport.

Economic and monetary union (EMU)

Government policy on EMU (see page 69) was originally set out by the Chancellor of the Exchequer in October 1997. The Government is in favour of UK membership providing the economic conditions are right. The determining factor is the national economic interest and whether the economic case for joining is clear and unambiguous. The Government has set out five economic tests, which must be met before any decision to join can be made. The five tests are:

- sustainable convergence between the United Kingdom and the economies of a single currency;

- whether there is sufficient flexibility to cope with economic change;

- the effect on investment;

- the impact on the UK financial services industry; and

- whether it is good for employment.

The most recent assessment of the five economic tests in June 2003 concluded that at that time a decision to join EMU would not be in the national economic interest. The Treasury will review progress on whether it is in the United Kingdom's economic interest to join EMU, and will announce the results of the review in the 2005 Budget. If a decision to recommend joining is taken by the Government, it will be put to a vote in Parliament and then to a referendum of the UK people.

Economic stability

The Government has established frameworks for the operation of both monetary and fiscal policy with the aim of achieving low and stable inflation and sound public finances. It seeks to ensure the coordination of monetary and fiscal policy by setting mutually consistent objectives for both.

The Bank of England's Monetary Policy Committee (see page 348) sets the base rate for interest rates to meet the Government's new inflation target (see page 353). As interest rate changes take some time to be fully effective, the Committee must consider its inflation forecast and the impact of other factors some two years ahead and beyond. Since the introduction of the new monetary framework in 1997, official interest rates peaked at 7½ per cent in 1998, compared with a peak of 15 per cent in 1989 in the previous economic cycle. From the beginning of 2001

The Allsopp Review

The final report of a wide-ranging review of economic statistics, conducted by Christopher Allsopp, was published in March 2004. The report, *Review of Statistics for Economic Policymaking – Final report to the Chancellor of the Exchequer, the Governor of the Bank of England and the National Statistician*, made over 60 recommendations aimed at improving national and regional statistics. It focused mainly on whether the changing UK economic structure is being properly reflected in the nature, frequency and timeliness of official economic statistics. The main recommendations included:

- a National Accounts framework that responds better to the economic structure of the United Kingdom;

- updating the surveys and methodology that underpin the National Accounts;

- better short-term estimates of output;

- improving the estimates of expenditure components;

- developing better measures of the labour market and productivity;

- developing Regional Accounts to provide better quality, more timely annual baseline estimates; and

- improving existing labour market and population data and estimating regional price levels.

The Office for National Statistics will be implementing these recommendations in full.

onwards the Bank cut interest rates by 2½ percentage points reaching a low of 3½ per cent in July 2003. Since then interest rates have been gradually increased and were 4¾ per cent in August 2004.

The United Kingdom has a freely floating exchange rate and no capital controls: in the last ten years the only official intervention against sterling was conducted in September 2000 by the Bank of England as part of concerted support by the G7 group of countries (see chapter 7) for the euro. In recent years there have been significant fluctuations in bilateral exchange rates, but sterling's effective exchange rate measured against a weighted basket of currencies has been relatively stable. In early 2003 there was a small depreciation in the sterling effective exchange rate index (ERI) but this was reversed in early 2004, since when the ERI has remained close to its average since 1997. Figure 22.2 shows sterling's exchange rate against other major currencies since 1999.

Figure 22.2 Selected exchange rates[1] against sterling

Indices 1999 Q1=100

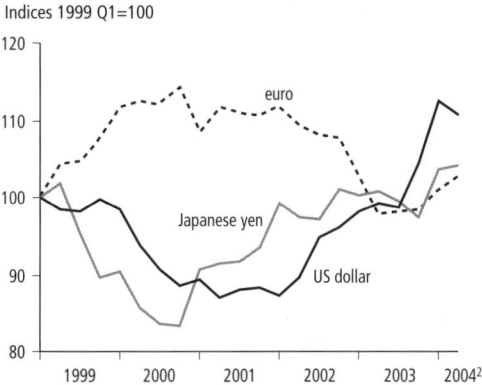

1 Quarterly average spot exchange rates.
2 Data is shown up to Quarter 2 only.
Source: Bank of England

Fiscal policy framework

The *Code for Fiscal Stability* sets out the five key principles of fiscal management at the heart of the Government's fiscal policy framework:

- transparency in the setting of fiscal policy objectives, the implementation of fiscal policy and the publication of the public accounts;

- stability in the fiscal policy-making process and in the way fiscal policy impacts on the economy;

- responsibility in the management of the public finances;

- fairness, including between generations; and

- efficiency in the design and implementation of fiscal policy and in managing both sides of the public sector balance sheet.

The Code also requires the Government to state both its objectives and the rules through which policy will be operated. These objectives are:

- over the medium term, to ensure sound public finances and that spending and taxation impact fairly within and between generations; and

- over the short term, to support monetary policy and, in particular, to allow the 'automatic stabilisers' to help smooth the path of the economy.

These objectives are implemented through the Government's two fiscal rules, against which the performance of fiscal policy can be judged:

- the golden rule – over the economic cycle, the Government will borrow only to invest and not to fund current spending; and

- the sustainable investment rule – public sector net debt as a proportion of GDP will be held over the economic cycle at a stable and prudent level. Other things being equal, net debt will be maintained below 40 per cent of GDP over the economic cycle.

The fiscal rules are designed to ensure sound public finances in the medium term. They allow flexibility in two key respects:

- the rules are set over the economic cycle, allowing fiscal balances to vary between years in line with the cyclical position of the economy; and

- the rules work together to promote capital investment while ensuring sustainable public finances in the longer term.

The fiscal rules are the foundation of the public spending framework (see chapter 23) and have important consequences for the structure of the budgeting regime.

The Budget

The Budget is presented annually by the Chancellor of the Exchequer in a major speech to Parliament. Budget day in 2004 was on 17 March and the 2004 Budget Report comprised two documents:

- the Economic and Fiscal Strategy Report, setting out the Government's long-term goals and the comprehensive strategy it is pursuing to achieve them, the progress that has been made so far, and the further steps the Government is taking in the 2004 Budget to advance its long-term goals; and

- the Financial Statement and Budget Report, providing a summary of each of the main Budget measures and how they affect the Budget arithmetic, and updated forecasts of the economy and the public finances. See text box on page 371 on Budget tax measures.

Pre-Budget Report

Under the Code for Fiscal Stability (see page 347), the Government is committed to publishing a Pre-Budget Report (PBR) at least three months before the Budget (usually in the previous November, although the PBR for the 2004 Budget was published in December 2003). The PBR sets out updated forecasts for the economy and the public finances, reports on how the Government's policies are helping to deliver its long-term goals, and describes the reforms that the Government is considering ahead of the Budget and on which it will be consulting in the months ahead.

Key announcements in the December 2003 PBR included:

- an updated economic forecast, which stated that growth in the UK economy is expected to continue strengthening and that the Government is on track to meet its fiscal rules for sound public finances over the economic cycle;

- new measures to raise productivity, including improving access to finance for small business and reducing red tape for business;

- further reforms to promote employment opportunity across the United Kingdom;

- additional help for pensioners and for families with children from April 2004;

- measures to promote fairness in the tax system; and

- further steps to protect and enhance the environment.

Bank of England

The Bank of England (see also page 461) was founded in 1694 and nationalised in 1946. It gained operational independence in 1997 when it was given responsibility for setting the United Kingdom's official interest rate (see page 346). It is the United Kingdom's central bank and is responsible for ensuring both monetary and

financial stability – which constitute its two core purposes. The Bank also plays its part in promoting an open and internationally competitive financial centre in the United Kingdom.

Under the *Bank of England Act 1998*, the Court of Directors is responsible for managing the affairs of the Bank, apart from the formulation of monetary policy. The Court comprises the Governor, two Deputy Governors and 16 non-executive directors. It is required to report annually to the Chancellor of the Exchequer.

Monetary policy framework

The Bank's monetary policy objective is to deliver price stability and, subject to that, to support the Government's economic policy, including its growth and employment objectives. Price stability is defined by the Government's inflation target (see page 353).

Responsibility for meeting this target and for setting interest rates rests with the Bank's Monetary Policy Committee (MPC), comprising the Governor, the two Deputy Governors, two further Bank executives and four external members appointed by the Chancellor of the Exchequer. The Committee meets every month and decisions on interest rates are announced at noon immediately after the meeting; minutes of the meetings, including a record of each member's vote, are normally published on the second Wednesday after each meeting. The Committee is accountable to the Bank's Court of Directors, to government and to the public through Parliament.

Financial stability

The Bank's financial stability objective is to maintain the stability of the financial system as a whole. The Bank seeks to identify and analyse issues concerning the structure and functioning of both UK and overseas financial markets and the operation of the international financial system, and to encourage changes designed to increase their overall safety and effectiveness. The Bank also undertakes work on the arrangements for handling financial crises should they occur and, in exceptional circumstances, acts as the financial system's 'lender of last resort'. In discharging its financial stability remit, the Bank works closely with HM Treasury and the Financial Services Authority – through the Joint Standing

Committee established under the 1997 Memorandum of Understanding – and with other central banks and international organisations. Internally, guidance on priority setting is provided by the Bank's high-level Financial Stability Board. Public understanding of issues relating to financial stability is promoted through, for example, the Bank's biannual *Financial Stability Review*.

Other main functions

As the economy grows, demand for central bank money – notes and coin – increases. The banking system has to buy the notes from the Bank, but lacks the funds to do so. The Bank, through its operations in the sterling money markets, distributes these funds at rates which implement the MPC's interest rate decisions. These operations influence the general level of short-term interest rates, as the rates at which the Bank deals are quickly passed on through financial markets. This in turn affects the whole pattern of interest rates across the UK economy.

Structure and performance

The value of all goods and services produced in the UK economy for final consumption (see glossary) is measured by GDP. In 2003, the chained volume measure of GDP at market prices amounted to £1,035 billion (Table 22.3). The economy's trend rate of growth between 1997 and 2001 was 3 per cent a year, compared with 2¹/₂ per cent over the previous economic cycle between 1982 and 1993.

According to the Organisation for Economic Co-operation and Development (OECD), the United Kingdom experienced lower economic growth than all its major competitors in the 1970s and, apart from Germany and France, in the 1980s. In the 1990s, UK growth was the same as the European Union (EU) average but below that of the United States (Table 22.4). Over the ten years to 2002, relative UK performance improved considerably. Although annual average growth still lagged behind the United States, it was above the EU and G7 averages.

In the 2004 Budget, HM Treasury forecast GDP to grow by between 3 and 3¹/₂ per cent in both 2004 and 2005, with the economy returning to its long-term trend rate of growth of between 2¹/₂ per cent and 3 per cent by 2006.

Spending on transport

According to the ONS Expenditure and Food Survey, the average UK household spent £59 a week on transport in 2002/03. This included buying and running vehicles as well as transport services (fares and other transport costs). In contrast, households spent £56 a week on recreation and culture and £43 on food and non-alcoholic drink.

The proportion of transport spending devoted to the purchase of vehicles increases with income, from around 30 per cent in lower income groups to around 50 per cent in higher groups. In terms of age, spending on purchases of new vehicles as a proportion of total spending is highest in the 50 to 64 age group. Households in London spent the most on transport services at £17.90 a week, more than double the UK average of £8.40.

UK living standards, as measured by the chained volume measure of GDP per head, have grown steadily over the last 30 years. Between 1993 and 2003, GDP per head increased from £13,417 to £17,426, an average increase of 2.6 per cent a year.

Output

The service sector's contribution to gross value added (GVA, see glossary) at current basic prices has continued to grow (Table 22.5), reaching 73 per cent in 2003. Within this sector, real estate, renting and business activities contributed 25 per cent of total GVA, with the wholesale and retail trade accounting for a further 13 per cent.

Production industries had a 20 per cent share of GVA in 2003, down from 26 per cent ten years earlier. The manufacturing sub-sector contributed only 16 per cent to GVA in 2003, compared with 21 per cent in 1993.

The contribution of agriculture, forestry and fishing to GVA fell from 2 to 1 per cent between 1993 and 2003. The construction industry's share of GVA increased from 5 to 6 per cent over the same period.

Table 22.3 Gross domestic product and gross value added, UK

£ million

	1993	1998	2001	2002	2003
Chained volume measures (reference year 2001)					
Final consumption expenditure					
Households	483,154	564,239	635,583	655,865	671,013
Non-profit institutions	19,042	23,300	24,345	25,818	26,593
General government	166,871	174,546	189,724	196,862	203,674
Gross capital formation					
Gross fixed capital formation	111,652	153,202	165,504	169,928	173,623
Changes in inventories	362	4,905	6,189	2,513	2,467
Acquisitions less disposals of valuables	−8	57	396	226	9
Total exports	160,712	232,057	272,369	272,635	272,949
Gross final expenditure	**931,391**	**1,152,018**	**1,294,110**	**1,323,847**	**1,350,328**
less Total imports	165,333	242,789	299,801	311,955	315,911
Statistical discrepancy	0	0	0	0	201
GDP at market prices	**773,805**	**909,819**	**994,309**	**1,011,892**	**1,034,618**
less Basic price adjustment	87,946	100,366	113,146	117,857	123,309
Gross value added at basic prices	**686,032**	**809,585**	**881,163**	**894,035**	**911,309**
Chained volume index					
GDP at market prices (2001 = 100)	77.8	91.5	100.0	101.8	104.1

Source: Quarterly National Accounts, Office for National Statistics

Table 22.4 Annual average percentage change in GDP, G7 countries and EU

Percentages

	Decades			Economic cycles	
	1970s	1980s	1990s	1982–1993	1993–2002[1]
United Kingdom	2.4	2.3	2.1	2.4	2.8
United States	3.3	3.0	3.0	2.9	3.2
Japan	5.2	3.7	1.7	3.6	1.1
Germany	3.2	1.9	3.3	3.3	1.3
France	3.7	2.2	1.7	2.0	1.9
Italy	3.3	2.4	1.5	1.9	1.6
Canada	4.4	3.0	2.4	2.2	3.5
G7 average	3.6	2.9	2.4	2.2	2.0
EU average	3.4	2.2	2.1	2.7	2.4

1 Not a complete cycle.
Source: National Accounts of OECD countries

Table 22.5 also shows changes in the chained volume measure of output since 1993. Agriculture, public administration and defence, and manufacturing have grown only slightly, whereas transport, storage and communication, and real estate, renting and business activities have increased by between a half and three-quarters.

Household income and expenditure

In 2003, the chained volume measure of UK household final expenditure — spending by the household sector on products or services to satisfy immediate needs or wants – rose by 2.3 per cent to £671 billion, representing 74.5 per cent of the total

Table 22.5 Output by industry – gross value added,[1] UK

	1993 (£ million)	% contribution 1993	2003 (£ million)	% contribution 2003	% change 1993–2003, chained volume measure[2]
		Current basic prices			
Agriculture, hunting, forestry and fishing	10,544	1.8	9,476	1.0	2.1
Production industries					
Mining and quarrying	13,526	2.4	27,500	2.8	11.5
Manufacturing[3]	120,989	21.0	152,803	15.7	8.7
Electricity, gas and water supply	16,271	2.8	14,924	1.5	22.7
Total production industries	150,786	26.2	195,227	20.0	10.1
Construction	29,166	5.1	61,538	6.3	24.7
Service industries					
Wholesale and retail trade	68,325	11.9	123,630	12.7	41.6
Hotels and restaurants	15,737	2.7	33,222	3.4	27.4
Transport, storage and communication	46,408	8.1	75,634	7.7	74.8
Financial intermediation[4]	39,289	6.8	52,041	5.3	36.1
Adjustment for financial services	−19,569	−3.4	−45,294	−4.6	76.9
Real estate, renting and business activities	102,712	17.9	242,717	24.9	56.2
Public administration and defence	39,223	6.8	50,489	5.2	4.2
Education	31,900	5.5	55,752	5.7	16.2
Health and social work	36,677	6.4	71,294	7.3	40.6
Other services	23,625	4.1	50,421	5.2	42.5
Total service industries	384,329	66.9	709,907	72.7	42.7
Total gross value added	**574,825**	**100**	**976,148**	**100**	**32.7**

1 Represents the difference between the value of the output of goods and services produced by a company and its intermediate consumption – the value of the goods and services or raw materials used up in the production of such output.
2 Reference year 2001.
3 See Table 27.2 for an industry breakdown.
4 The activity by which an institutional unit acquires financial assets and incurs liabilities on its own account by engaging in financial transactions on the market.
Source: Quarterly National Accounts and *United Kingdom National Accounts 2004 – the Blue Book*, Office for National Statistics

£901 million final consumption expenditure. Expenditure on semi-durable and durable goods rose by 5.7 per cent and 4.7 per cent respectively, while growth in services was limited to 0.8 per cent.

Table 22.6 shows the pattern of household final consumption expenditure. Since 1993, using the chained volume measure, growth has been strongest in the semi-durable and durable goods categories, and weakest in services and non-durable goods. By purpose, communication (postal services and telephone and telefax equipment and services), recreation and culture, and clothing and footwear have shown the most significant growth. Household spending on alcohol and tobacco and education have increased the least.

Total resources (income) of the household sector – including non-profit institutions serving households[1] – rose by 4.3 per cent in 2003 to £1,097 billion. Gross disposable income – after deductions, including taxes and social contributions – totalled £753 billion. Real household disposable income (see glossary) rose by 2.1 per cent to £728 billion. Wages and salaries increased by 3.5 per cent during 2003 to £523 billion, accounting for almost 60 per cent of household primary income. The household saving ratio[2] increased to 6.0 per cent in 2003 from 5.8 per cent in 2002. The net worth[3] of the household

1 These include bodies such as charities, universities, churches and trade unions.
2 The percentage of total available resources saved during the year.
3 The value of assets after deducting for any liabilities.

Table 22.6 Household final consumption expenditure, UK

	2003 (£ billion)	Chained volume measures[1] % contribution 2003	% change 1993–2003
UK domestic			
Food and drink	61.8	*9.2*	16.8
Alcohol and tobacco	26.0	*3.9*	3.5
Clothing and footwear	44.0	*6.6*	97.9
Housing	116.7	*17.4*	11.5
Household goods and services	38.8	*5.8*	50.4
Health	11.1	*1.7*	18.0
Transport	95.9	*14.3*	35.2
Communication	15.2	*2.3*	157.1
Recreation and culture	84.5	*12.6*	101.5
Education	8.5	*1.3*	5.7
Restaurants and hotels	76.1	*11.3*	22.7
Miscellaneous	81.5	*12.1*	23.7
Total	**660.0**	***98.4***	**35.7**
of which:			
Durable goods	84.4	*12.6*	94.8
Semi-durable goods	88.9	*13.2*	111.5
Non-durable goods	159.7	*23.8*	14.3
Services	327.1	*48.7*	22.0
Net tourism	11.0	*1.6*	
Total UK national	**671.0**	***100***	**38.9**

1 Reference year 2001.
Source: Quarterly National Accounts, Office for National Statistics

sector has shown strong growth in recent years, more than doubling between 1995 and 2003. It increased by 11.7 per cent in 2003 to £5,448 billion. Of the total, non-financial assets increased by 11.5 per cent to £3,424 billion, while financial assets rose by 12.1 per cent to £2,024 billion.

Investment

The chained volume measure of gross fixed capital formation grew by 2.2 per cent in 2003, with business investment accounting for 10.8 per cent of GDP, slightly down from the 11.1 per cent recorded in 2002. General government investment grew by 24.4 per cent in 2003, following a 5.6 per cent rise in 2002.

In 2003, by asset type, there were increases of 9.9 per cent in dwellings and 4.8 per cent in both other buildings and structures and in intangible

fixed assets; in contrast, transport equipment fell by 5.7 per cent, while other machinery and equipment declined by 2.7 per cent.

UK whole economy investment has accounted for a smaller share of GDP than for other industrialised countries – 16.3 per cent of GDP (at current prices) in 2003, compared with a G7 average of 17.8 per cent.

International trade

According to the OECD, the United Kingdom was the fifth largest trading nation in 2003 (behind the United States, Germany, Japan and France) with exports of goods and services accounting for 25 per cent of GDP at current prices. See chapter 24 for information on the UK balance of payments.

Mergers and acquisitions

In 2003 expenditure on acquisitions abroad by UK companies continued to fall, declining by 22 per cent. This follows a drop of 36 per cent in 2002 and was far below the record level of £181 billion established in 2000. One of the significant transactions in 2003 was the purchase of US-based Household International by banking group HSBC Holdings for a reported value of around £9.1 billion. Expenditure on acquisitions in the United Kingdom by foreign companies fell very sharply – by nearly 45 per cent – and again far below the record level of £65 billion in 2000.

Table 22.7 Mergers and acquisitions involving UK companies

	1993	1998	2003
Acquisitions abroad by UK companies			
Number	521	569	243
Value (£ billion)	9,213	54,917	20,756
Acquisitions in the UK by foreign companies[1]			
Number	267	252	129
Value (£ billion)	5,187	32,413	9,309
Acquisitions in the UK by UK companies			
Number	526	635	558
Value (£ billion)	7,063	29,525	18,679

1 Includes acquisitions by foreign companies routed through their existing UK subsidiaries.
Source: Office for National Statistics

A significant acquisition in 2003 was of the retail businesses of brewing group Scottish & Newcastle by Spirit Amber Bidco – an international consortium of investors – for a reported value of £2.5 billion. Expenditure on acquisitions in the United Kingdom by UK companies fell by nearly 26 per cent in 2003, although the number of acquisitions was 30 per cent higher than in 2002. A significant transaction recorded during 2003 was the acquisition of Debenhams by Baroness Retail Ltd – a consortium of investors – for a reported value of £1.7 billion.

Prices

Two main measures of consumer price inflation are used in the United Kingdom:

- the Consumer Prices Index (CPI), formerly known as the UK Harmonised Index of Consumer Prices (HICP), is the main UK domestic measure of inflation for macroeconomic purposes. HICPs are calculated in each Member State of the European Union for the purposes of European comparisons; they are also used by the European Central Bank as the measure of price stability across the euro area (see also text box below); and

- the all items Retail Prices Index (RPI), a general purpose measure of inflation whose uses include indexation of pensions, state benefits and index-linked gilts.

The inflation target

In his Pre-Budget Report statement in December 2003, the Chancellor of the Exchequer changed the UK inflation target so that it was based on the UK HICP, which the National Statistician has renamed the CPI. The CPI inflation target was set by the Government at 2 per cent, applying from 10 December 2003, although the Bank of England has the task of meeting the target. Formerly the Bank was required to meet an inflation target of 2¹/₂ per cent based on the RPI excluding mortgage interest payments (RPIX) measure of inflation. The change in target does not affect pensions or benefits, which will continue to be linked to changes in the RPI.

Both the CPI and RPI measure the average change from month to month in the prices of goods and services purchased in the United Kingdom, although there are differences in coverage and methodology. In particular, the CPI excludes a number of items that are included in the RPI, mainly related to housing, including council tax and mortgage interest payments.

The CPI and RPI are compiled using a large and representative 'basket' of over 650 goods and services sampled each month to see how prices are changing. Each year the composition of this basket is reviewed, so that it remains representative of consumer spending patterns. For example, items may be added to represent new or increasing areas of spending, while other items may be deleted as spending on them falls. For the 2004 review, new items included digital cameras, dishwasher tablets, fresh turkey steaks, fishing rods and basic manicure, while mini-disc players, dishwasher powder, frozen turkey and gin were removed from the basket.

Figure 22.8 Annual change in consumer prices, UK

Percentages

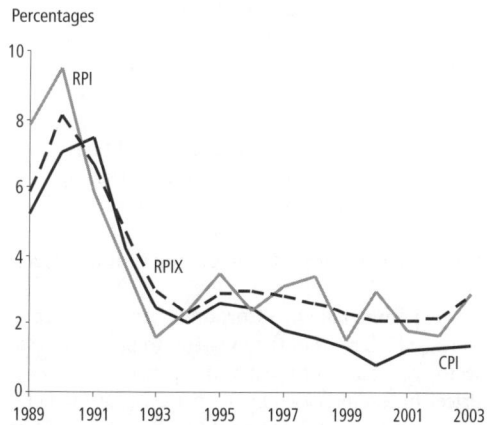

Source: Office for National Statistics

Annual RPI inflation has fluctuated considerably in the last 25 years or so, peaking at 21.9 per cent in the year to May 1980. However, it was much lower in the 1990s, and since 1993 has been in a relatively narrow range, from around 1¹/₂ per cent to 3¹/₂ per cent. In 2003, it averaged 2.9 per cent, up from 1.7 per cent in the previous year. RPIX,

Table 22.9 Consumer and producer price indices, UK

	1993	1998	2003
Consumer prices			
CPI (1996 = 100)	93.2	103.4	109.8
RPI (January 1987 = 100)	140.7	162.9	181.3
RPIX (January 1987 = 100)	140.5	160.6	180.0
Producer prices (2000 = 100)			
Output prices			
Manufactured products	88.8	98.1	101.3
of which:			
Food, beverages and tobacco	88.2	97.8	104.7
Petroleum products	60.6	76.8	95.4
Input prices[1]			
Materials purchased	102.2	93.6	95.2
Fuels purchased	120.0	103.8	102.1

1 Includes Climate Change Levy from April 2001.
Source: Monthly Consumer Price Indices and Producer Prices, Office for National Statistics

on which the previous inflation target was based, averaged 2.2 per cent in 2002, increasing to 2.8 per cent in 2003, above the Government's former target of 2½ per cent – set in May 1997.

The Government's new target measure of inflation, the CPI, averaged 1.4 per cent during 2003. The equivalent average index for the European Union, HICP, was 2.0 per cent.

The input price index for materials and fuels purchased by manufacturing industry rose by 1.3 per cent in 2003 following a 4.5 per cent fall in 2002. Producer output price inflation was 1.5 per cent, compared with 0.1 per cent in 2002.

The experimental ONS Corporate Services Price Index, which aims in the long run to be the service sector equivalent of the manufacturing Producer Prices Index, increased by 3.0 per cent (at the net sector level) in 2003 compared with 1.9 per cent in 2002. The price of banking services showed the greatest increase in 2003, rising by 7.7 per cent.

Labour market

UK employment reached 28.3 million in spring 2004, 206,000 higher than in the same period a year earlier, and representing a working age employment rate of 74.7 per cent. Unemployment was 1,432,000, 52,000 less than a year earlier. The rate of 4.8 per cent was well below the averages of

Long-run Composite Price Index

In February 2004, the Office for National Statistics launched a new long-run Composite Price Index that tracks the path of UK consumer price inflation since 1750. It found that consumer prices increased about 140-fold between 1750 and 2003, with most of the increase occurring since the Second World War. Between 1750 and 1938, prices rose by a little over three times, but since 1938, they have increased more than fortyfold.

The United Kingdom has experienced periods of significant inflation in earlier times. During the Napoleonic Wars, prices jumped 50 per cent in ten years reflecting poor harvest quality and the impact of war. Since 1934 prices have increased every year, with particularly rapid increases taking place between 1973 and 1981 when oil price rises impacted badly on the industrialised world.

8.1 per cent for the EU-15 and 9.0 per cent for the EU-25.

Industrial and commercial policy

The Department of Trade and Industry (DTI) aims to increase UK competitiveness and scientific excellence to generate higher levels of sustainable growth and productivity.

Competitiveness

UK performance in improving productivity is assessed in the DTI's Productivity and Competitiveness Indicators. The latest full update of indicators was published in November 2003 and is available on the DTI website. The indicators measure UK performance in five key areas – investment, innovation, skills, enterprise and competition – against other G7 members and the OECD. The 2003 indicators show that:

- the United Kingdom had the fastest average growth rate of GDP per head in the G7 between 1989–2002, largely due to strong labour market performance;

- UK macroeconomic stability had improved;

- UK unemployment was the lowest in the G7; and

- the United Kingdom has an excellent science base, with more published papers and citations per head of population than any G7 country.

On the other hand, there are areas where UK performance could improve, including:

- investment, which continues to lag behind that of its competitors;

- innovation, where many aspects of UK performance remain around or below average; and

- skills, where too few adults have the basic vocational skills that allow them to engage effectively in the economy.

In spring 2004 the DTI and HM Treasury published a consultation document reviewing the set of indicators used to monitor UK productivity performance. The results of the consultation are due to be published later in 2004.

In 2003 UK whole economy productivity growth (measured by output per worker) was 1.0 per cent, slightly higher than the 0.7 per cent recorded in 2002. An alternative measure, output per hour worked, showed a 1.6 per cent increase in 2003, compared with 1.8 per cent in 2002. Productivity has increased more in production industries than in the rest of the economy over the last ten years (Table 22.10).

Enterprise, innovation and business support

In September 2003 the DTI published its strategy for raising productivity in the United Kingdom, focusing on five key priorities: transferring knowledge from the science base and between businesses; maximising potential in the workplace; extending competitive markets; strengthening regional economies; and forging closer links with key economic players at home and overseas. The strategy includes increasing funding for science; creating a new business-focused Technology Strategy; implementing the new Skills Strategy (see page 149); promoting diversity, flexible working and partnership in the workplace; and launching Consumer Direct (see page 480).

The Government believes that productivity is the key to securing long-term growth in living

Table 22.10 Productivity and unit wage costs, UK

	1993	1998	2001 = 100 2003
Output per worker			
Whole economy	85.1	94.8	101.8
Output per job			
Whole economy	85.0	94.5	101.9
Production industries	80.4	87.2	106.4
Manufacturing industries	82.6	87.0	106.6
Output per hour worked			
Whole economy	84.3	93.6	103.5
Production industries	81.0	87.1	107.6
Manufacturing industries	83.0	86.7	107.9
Unit wage costs			
Whole economy	84.9	91.4	104.7
Manufacturing industries	85.5	101.2	100.5

Source: Office for National Statistics

standards. The DTI aims to promote enterprise and innovation by encouraging business start-ups, and by increasing the capacity of business, including small and medium-sized enterprises (SMEs) to grow, invest, develop skills, adopt best practice, and exploit opportunities abroad. It provides a range of grants, loan guarantees and subsidised consultancy to address a range of business issues through its Business Support Solutions programmes.

Business Link is the national business advice service, delivering independent advice, business information and access to a wide network of business support organisations throughout England. It reports to the Small Business Service, an agency of the DTI, which is responsible for organising the delivery of help to SMEs. Similar business support arrangements apply in other parts of the United Kingdom, via Scottish Enterprise's Business Gateway for lowland Scotland, Highlands and Islands Enterprise, Business Eye for Wales and Invest Northern Ireland.

Business finance

The Government is working in partnership with the private sector to help address weaknesses in the finance market for SMEs. Nine DTI products, grouped into four themes, reflect the areas in which businesses are most likely to need help:

innovation, best practice, raising finance and regional financial support. These products include the Grant for Investigating an Innovative Idea, Grant for Research and Development, and Selective Finance for Investment in England (see page 357). In many cases similar schemes are offered by the appropriate organisations in Wales, Scotland and Northern Ireland. Products available across the United Kingdom include Collaborative Research and Development and the Small Firms Loan Guarantee.

The Queen's Awards for Enterprise

The Queen's Awards for Enterprise are the top UK annual awards for business performance. Successful organisations are entitled to use the Queen's Award emblem on their stationery, packaging, goods and advertising. Valid for five years, they are awarded for outstanding achievement in three categories: international trade, innovation and sustainable development. All UK organisations operating regularly as a 'business unit', and that can meet the criteria, are eligible to apply. In 2004 a total of 112 Awards were conferred – 66 for international trade, 39 for innovation and 7 for sustainable development.

Information and communication technology (ICT)

The e-Government Unit within the Cabinet Office, works with departments to deliver efficiency savings while improving the delivery of public services by coordinating electronic government services around the needs of customers. It also provides sponsorship of Information Assurance and is responsible for ensuring that all government services will be available electronically by 2005 with key services achieving high levels of use. The e-Government Unit has taken on the majority of the work previously undertaken by the Office of the e-Envoy.

By the end of the first quarter of 2004, 74 per cent of 664 government services identified were online. The Government's new online service, Directgov (*www.direct.gov.uk*), replaced UK online in May 2004. The new service is designed around the needs of the user, with the intention of making it easy to find and access government information and services electronically. The new site contains extensive content for motorists, parents, disabled people and carers, together with broader information for other groups, such as UK citizens

abroad and the over-50s. This will be expanded to include content for householders, jobseekers and adult learners. As well as government departments, the site links to relevant third parties which can offer additional advice and support.

According to the ONS e-commerce survey, 59 per cent of businesses had access to the Internet in 2002, compared with 51 per cent in the previous year. Larger businesses had greater ICT usage – 99 per cent of firms with 1,000 or more employees had Internet access in 2002 compared with 56 per cent of those with fewer than ten. Other key findings for 2002 from the survey included:

- 29 per cent of UK businesses had a website, compared with 25 per cent in 2001;
- broadband was the main type of Internet connection for 14 per cent of UK businesses;
- 4 per cent of UK businesses sold via the Internet and 13 per cent bought via the Internet; and
- 66 per cent of UK companies had PCs and 51 per cent had email – both little changed from 2001.

UK businesses in the non-financial sector sold £23.3 billion over the Internet in 2002, a rise of 39 per cent on the previous year (Table 22.11). Other results from the 2002 ONS e-commerce survey included:

- the total sold online represented 1.2 per cent of total sales both online and offline;
- of the total sold online, £6.4 billion was to households;
- the share of total online sales by UK businesses to households rose from 24 per cent in 2001 to 27 per cent in 2002; and
- goods continued to represent the largest share of the value of Internet sales by UK businesses (£15.4 billion). The sale of services online accounted for the second largest share, at £6.8 billion.

In addition:

- UK businesses, excluding financial businesses, bought £22.9 billion online – up 14 per cent from £20.1 billion in 2001; and
- the value of orders received over other information and communication technologies (that is, excluding the Internet) was £169.1 billion in 2002 – a 6 per cent decrease on 2001.

Table 22.11 Online sales by UK businesses in the non-financial sectors, by broad sector

£ billion

	2001	2002
Manufacturing, electricity, gas and water supply, construction	4.4	6.2
Wholesale, retail, catering, travel, telecommunications	11.3	15.9
Computing, other business services	0.8	0.7
Other services	0.2	0.5
Total	**16.8**	**23.3**

Source: Office for National Statistics

Regional policy and development

Government regional policy aims to build economic success in the regions and boost regional capacity for innovation and enterprise. The Office of the Deputy Prime Minister (ODPM) has overall responsibility for regional policy in England, while responsibility for the nine Regional Development Agencies in England rests with the DTI (see also chapter 2).

The DTI provides direct financial assistance to business. Until the end of March 2004 the DTI channelled funds via the Regional Selective Assistance programme and Enterprise Grants. However, from April 2004, they were replaced in the English Assisted Areas by Selective Finance for Investment in England.

The new scheme aims to secure employment opportunities and increase regional competitiveness and prosperity in areas where

there are significant disparities from the national average in unemployment, the employment rate, or in the area's dependency on manufacturing. It also seeks to secure growth in productivity (measured by GVA per workforce job) compared with the sector and national averages; and higher skills, with the majority of new jobs required to be at National Vocational Qualification level 2 (or equivalent) and above.

As an indicator of competitiveness within the manufacturing, services and other sectors, GVA per workforce job in 2001 ranged from £33,000 in Scotland to £23,500 in Northern Ireland, averaging £30,600 in the United Kingdom as a whole.

The headline figure of GVA per head (workplace basis) in 2002 ranged from £15,600 in England to £12,000 in Wales (Table 22.12). England, however, had the smallest increase in GVA in 2002, growing by 4.7 per cent on a per head basis, compared with 5.1 per cent in Northern Ireland. In these figures, GVA allocates the income of commuters to where they work, rather than where they live, so this may artificially inflate the GVA per head estimates for regions with a high level of inward commuting, such as London.

EU regional funding

Structural Funds, which account for over one-third of the European Union budget, are the main instruments for supporting social and economic restructuring across the EU. The UK allocation for the period 2000–06 is over £10 billion. Regions may have access to up to four funds, depending on their Objective status (see below). These funds comprise the European Regional Development Fund (ERDF), European Social Fund (ESF), the guidance section of the European Agricultural

Table 22.12 Gross value added at current basic prices, UK

	£ billion Gross value added			£ thousand Gross value added per head		
	2000	2001	2002	2000	2001	2002
England	699.8	737.7	775.3	14.3	14.9	15.6
Wales	31.9	33.4	35.1	11.0	11.5	12.0
Scotland	67.1	69.6	73.0	13.3	13.7	14.4
Northern Ireland	18.5	19.4	20.5	11.0	11.5	12.1
United Kingdom[1]	**817.3**	**860.1**	**903.8**	**13.9**	**14.6**	**15.3**

1 Excludes compensation of employees and gross operating surplus (which cannot be assigned to regions) and statistical discrepancy.
Source: Office for National Statistics

Guidance and Guarantee Fund, and the Financial Instrument for Fisheries Guidance.

The ERDF aims to improve economic prosperity and social inclusion by investing in projects to promote development and encourage the diversification of industry into other sectors. It is available in Objective 1 and 2 areas. The ESF funds training, human resources development and equal opportunities schemes in both Objective 1 and 3 areas. In Objective 2 areas it can be used to complement the ERDF activities.

Objective 1 status is the highest level of regional funding available from the EU. Eligible areas are those with less than 75 per cent of EU average GDP. Funding is aimed at promoting development and structural adjustment. In the United Kingdom, the qualifying areas are Cornwall and the Isles of Scilly; Merseyside; South Yorkshire; and West Wales and the Valleys.

In addition, the United Kingdom has two transitional[4] Objective 1 areas: the Scottish Highlands and Islands, and Northern Ireland (which also qualifies for a unique PEACE programme – see page 37). In total, the United Kingdom will receive over £3.9 billion of Objective 1 money between 2000 and 2006.

Objective 2 status is the second highest level of funding available from the EU. It aims to support the economic and social conversion of areas facing structural difficulties. Areas qualify under four main strands – industrial, rural, urban and fisheries. This objective covers nearly 14 million people in the United Kingdom and a further 5 million are covered by transitional programmes. The United Kingdom will receive over £3.1 billion for Objective 2 (including transitional arrangements) over the period 2000–06.

Objective 3, which applies to all areas, involves only the ESF and operates outside Objective 1 and 2 areas.

Between March and July 2003 the DTI, HM Treasury and ODPM held a joint UK-wide consultation on the future of the Structural Funds after 2006. In December 2003, the Secretary of State for Trade and Industry announced the Government's proposed approach to the reform of the funds, advocating in particular a substantial devolution and

decentralisation of EU regional policy. In July 2004 the European Commission published its draft regulations for the operation of the Structural and Cohesion Funds from 2007 to 2013.

Competitive markets

Enterprise Act 2002

The *Enterprise Act 2002* included a range of measures designed to strengthen UK competition law and consumer enforcement frameworks, transform its approach to bankruptcy and corporate rescue, and benefit consumers. The Act built on the *Competition Act 1998*, insolvency reforms and measures already implemented from the 1999 White Paper *Modern Markets: Confident Consumers*. The Office of Fair Trading (OFT) became a corporate body in April 2003 and a new statutory board took on the role of Director General of Fair Trading. The Act also established an independent Competition Appeal Tribunal. Most of the substantive consumer and competition provisions of the 2002 Act came into force on 20 June 2003.

Office of Fair Trading

The OFT plays a leading role in promoting and protecting consumer interests throughout the United Kingdom, while ensuring that businesses are fair and competitive.

Its work is structured into three areas:

- markets and policy initiatives – where there are doubts that markets or market practices are working well, it will carry out market studies, consider super-complaints made by designated consumer bodies, liaise regularly with interested parties, gather information and market intelligence, and provide advice on new legislation and policy initiatives;

- consumer regulation enforcement – tackling rogue traders, eliminating unfair trading practices, approving consumer codes of practice and licensing certain traders; and

- competition enforcement – safeguarding competition by enforcing legislation, including action under the *Competition Act 1998* against anti-competitive behaviour and agreements, and decisions on mergers.

4 Areas that were eligible in 1994–99 but which are no longer eligible in the period 2000–06.

Each quarter, around 200 UK trading standards departments provide data to the OFT on the number of complaints received; the main complaint categories are shown in Table 22.13. The house fittings and appliances group generated the most complaints in 2003.

Table 22.13 Consumer complaints received by trading standards departments, UK

	2002	2003
House fittings and appliances	309,269	308,707
Other household requirements	103,773	103,926
Personal goods and services	122,915	120,083
Professional and financial services	64,507	79,973
Transport	136,169	141,859
Leisure	97,810	99,587
Total	**834,443**	**854,135**

Source: Office of Fair Trading

Sectoral regulators

A number of bodies regulate particular industries or sectors formerly in public ownership, including Ofgem (see page 450), OFWAT (see page 456), Ofcom (see page 262) and ORR (see page 332). Each regulator has the power to apply and enforce the *Competition Act 1998* to deal with anti-competitive agreements or abuse of market dominance relating to relevant activities in their designated sector.

Since May 2004, the OFT and utility regulators have been applying EC competition law as well as national competition law in the United Kingdom. To ensure consistency, the OFT and the utility regulators are members of the European Competition Network (together with the European Commission and all the competition authorities in other Member States which have been designated to apply EC competition law).

Competition Commission

The Competition Commission is an independent public body established under the *Competition Act 1998*. It conducts in-depth inquiries into:

- mergers (both anticipated and completed);
- markets (the successor to monopoly inquiries); and
- the regulation, including price regulation, of the major regulated industries.

The OFT and those utility regulators that have concurrent powers also examine markets and may make a reference to the Competition Commission to decide whether a feature or combination of features of a market in the United Kingdom for goods and services prevents, restricts or distorts competition.

The *Enterprise Act 2002* (see page 358) has enhanced the role of the Commission in most merger and market investigation inquiries, making it responsible for decisions on competition questions and for making and implementing decisions on appropriate remedies. Every inquiry the Commission undertakes is in response to a reference made to it by another authority. Since the Act was implemented this is usually the OFT, but references may also be made by the Secretary of State for Trade and Industry, or by sectoral regulators. The Commission has no power to conduct inquiries on its own initiative. During 2003/04, it completed work on eight merger references and one monopoly reference.

Mergers and markets

The OFT has a duty to make a reference to the Commission if it believes there is or may be a relevant merger situation[5] that has resulted or may be expected to result in a substantial lessening of competition within any market or markets in the United Kingdom for goods and services.

Exceptionally, the Secretary of State can intervene in the consideration of a merger if this might raise a 'public interest consideration' specified by the *Enterprise Act 2002*, such as national security. The Secretary of State can serve a European intervention notice in cases where the competition issues have an EC dimension and fall under the EC Merger Regulation. This might occur if measures were being considered to protect legitimate interests such as public security.

The special provisions for newspaper mergers were changed by the *Communications Act 2003* (see chapter 17). This Act defined mergers involving newspapers and broadcasting enterprises as media mergers and set out specific public interest considerations. The Commission will now consider media mergers as it does other mergers

---

5 A merger qualifies for investigation if either the value of the UK turnover of the enterprise acquired (or to be acquired) exceeds £70 million or if the share of supply of goods or services in the United Kingdom (or a substantial part of the United Kingdom) is at least 25 per cent as a result of the merger.

unless the Secretary of State intervenes to apply the media public interest considerations.

Corporate affairs

There were an estimated 4.0 million private sector enterprises in the United Kingdom at the start of 2003 (Table 22.14). The 6,075 large companies (those with 250 or more employees) accounted for an estimated 42 per cent of private sector employment, and for 48 per cent of private sector turnover.

According to a *Financial Times* survey of the world's 500 largest companies published in May 2004, 36 of the companies are UK-owned and they have a combined market capitalisation of US$1,439 billion. Of the top ten UK companies by market capitalisation, three were banks and there were two each in oil and gas, and in pharmaceuticals and biotechnology (Table 22.15). BP, the biggest UK company, was the ninth largest in the world and the second largest oil and gas company. In the other most valuable sectors, by market capitalisation:

■ the United Kingdom had two representatives in the world's top ten banks – HSBC Holdings and Royal Bank of Scotland;

Table 22.15 Top ten UK companies by market capitalisation, 2004[1]

Company/business sector	Market capitalisation (US$ billion)[2]
BP/oil & gas	174.6
HSBC Holdings/banks	163.6
Vodafone/telecommunication services	159.2
Shell Transport & Trading/oil & gas	158.8
GlaxoSmithKline/pharmaceuticals & biotechnology	115.5
Royal Bank of Scotland/banks	88.8
AstraZeneca/pharmaceuticals & biotechnology	76.9
Unilever/food producers & processors	65.6
Barclays/banks	56.9
BHP Billiton/mining	54.7

1 As at end March.
2 Market capitalisation represents the number of shares issued multiplied by their market value.
Source: FT 500 Survey

■ GlaxoSmithKline was the world's fourth largest pharmaceuticals and biotechnology company, and AstraZeneca ranked seventh; and

■ Vodafone was the world's largest telecommunication services company.

Table 22.14 UK business enterprises,[1] start 2003

	Number of enterprises	% of enterprises	% of employment	% of turnover[2]
Enterprises with employees	1,155,210	28.7	85.4	92.1
Number of employees:				
1–4	759,650	18.9	10.3	9.3
5–9	202,965	5.0	6.6	6.3
10–19	105,845	2.6	6.8	6.9
20–49	54,800	1.4	7.8	8.0
50–99	16,230	0.4	5.2	5.9
100–199	8,045	0.2	5.2	6.2
200–249	1,600	0.0	1.6	1.9
250–499	3,065	0.1	4.9	7.4
500+	3,010	0.1	36.9	40.2
Enterprises with no employees[3]	2,866,175	71.3	14.6	7.9
All enterprises	**4,021,390**	*100*	*100*	*100*

1 Private sector. For statistical purposes public corporations and nationalised bodies are included. Around 76,000 central and local government enterprises and non-profit organisations are excluded.
2 Excludes financial intermediation, where turnover is not available on a comparable basis.
3 Sole proprietorships and partnerships comprising only the self-employed owner-manager(s), and companies comprising only an employee director.
Source: Small Business Service

Over 3,000 UK enterprises employed 500 or more people (Table 22.14), accounting for just 0.1 per cent of total enterprises, but representing 37 per cent of total employment and 40 per cent of turnover.

Small firms play an important part in the UK economy. Around 46 per cent of the private sector workforce in 2003 worked in companies employing fewer than 50 people. Nearly 2.9 million enterprises were sole proprietorships or partnerships without employees, while a further 760,000 enterprises employed one to four people. Together these 3.6 million enterprises accounted for 90 per cent of enterprises, 25 per cent of employment and 17 per cent of turnover.

The number of enterprises in the United Kingdom registering for value added tax (VAT) increased by 1,200 or 0.7 per cent between 2001 and 2002, while those de-registering increased by 8,900 or 5.3 per cent (Table 22.16). In 2002, in most sectors there was a slight increase or no change in the number of new registrations compared with 2001. Manufacturing, transport and communications, finance and other services all experienced small falls. The largest net losses were in wholesale, retail and repairs where de-registrations exceeded registrations by 5,400, and in manufacturing, where there was a net loss of 5,000 businesses. The largest net gain was in business services where the number of VAT-registered businesses rose by 6,200. This industry sector grew by almost 190,000 in the nine years to 2002 to 494,000, or 28 per cent of all UK VAT-registered businesses at the start of 2003.

Table 22.16 Business start-ups and closures,[1] UK

		Thousands and rate per 10,000 resident adults	
	2000	2001	2002
Registrations			
Number	184	175	176
Rate	39	37	37
De-registrations			
Number	165	167	176
Rate	35	35	37
Businesses registered at end year	1,755	1,762	1,762

1 Those registering and de-registering for VAT. There are separate registration and de-registration thresholds.
Source: Small Business Service

Company profitability

Company profitability for all UK private non-financial companies, in terms of the net rate of return on capital employed, was 13.0 per cent in 2003, above the 12.1 per cent recorded in 2002 (Figure 22.17). Among the individual sectors:

- manufacturing companies' net rate of return increased to 7.0 per cent, compared with 6.6 per cent in the previous year;

- service companies' net rate of return was 15.9 per cent, compared with 15.4 per cent in 2002; and

- the net rate of return of UK Continental Shelf companies was 29.9 per cent, compared with 30.7 per cent in 2002.

Corporate structure

At the end of August 2004 there were 1,792,918 companies on the Companies House active business register in England and Wales, with a further 102,152 companies in Scotland. This includes companies incorporated overseas with a place of business or branch in Great Britain. Most

Figure 22.17 Profitability of UK private non-financial corporations – net rate of return

Percentages

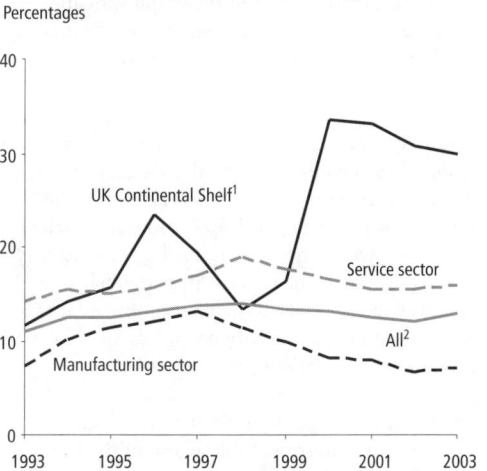

1 Those involved in the exploration for, and production of, oil and natural gas from the UK Continental Shelf.
2 Includes other sectors (such as construction, electricity and gas supply, agriculture, mining and quarrying).
Source: Office for National Statistics

corporate businesses are 'limited liability' companies – the liability of members is restricted to contributing an amount related to their shareholding (or to their guarantee where companies are limited by guarantee). Businesses can also be incorporated as limited liability partnerships, with the organisational flexibility and tax status of a partnership but with limited liability for their members.

Companies may be either public or private. Certain conditions must be satisfied before they can become plcs – they must be limited by shares and meet specified minimum capital requirements. Private companies are generally prohibited from offering their shares to the public.

Company law and corporate governance

Company law is designed to meet the need for proper regulation of business, to maintain open markets and to create safeguards for those wishing to invest in companies or do business with them. It takes account of EC Directives on company law, and on company and group accounts and their auditing.

A quoted company is required, as part of the annual reporting cycle, to publish a report on directors' remuneration. This must include full details, including the performance criteria for share options and long-term incentive schemes, a justification of any compensation payments when a contract is terminated, and a graph showing company performance. A company must put a resolution to shareholders on this remuneration report at each annual general meeting.

A fundamental revision of company law in Great Britain has been under way following an independent three-year review. The aim of the review was to develop a simple, modern, efficient and cost-effective framework for business activity in Great Britain. The Government published its response to the review's major recommendations and set out in 2002 its core proposals for reform in a White Paper, *Modernising Company Law*.

The Companies (Audit, Investigations and Community Enterprise) Bill was published in December 2003. It aims to improve confidence in companies and financial markets, following recent corporate failures, and to promote social enterprise. Part one of the Bill strengthens the system of regulating auditors, the enforcement of

accounting and reporting requirements and the company investigations regime. Part two provides for community interest companies (CICs). These would be a new type of company, designed for social enterprises that want to use their profits and assets for the public good.

In 2002 the Government commissioned an independent review of the role and effectiveness of company non-executive directors. The Higgs Review reported in January 2003. It recommended changes to the 'Combined Code' on corporate governance to require a greater proportion of independent, better-informed individuals on a company's board. The new Code requires greater transparency and accountability in the boardroom, formal performance appraisal, and closer relationships between non-executive directors and shareholders. The report calls for boards to put in place a more rigorous appointments process. The Financial Reporting Council agreed the final text of the new Code, which came into effect for reporting years beginning after 1 November 2003.

Insolvency

The Insolvency Service, an executive agency of the DTI, deals with insolvency matters in England and Wales and some limited insolvency matters in Scotland. Its role is to ensure fair, dynamic and competitive markets in which everyone can be confident in participating. It does this by ensuring that financial failure is dealt with fairly and effectively and by detecting and deterring fraud and financial misconduct. In Scotland, Accountant in Bankruptcy is an executive agency of the Scottish Executive Justice Department. The Northern Ireland Insolvency Service operates within the Department of Enterprise, Trade and Investment.

There was a 13 per cent fall in company insolvencies in England and Wales in 2003; in Scotland, where insolvencies are defined differently, the decline was 20 per cent. The number of individual insolvencies in England and Wales rose by 19 per cent (Table 22.18).

The *Enterprise Act 2002* contained provisions to modernise insolvency law in England and Wales in the areas of both individual and corporate insolvency. These provisions included.

- reducing the discharge period for most bankrupts and removing outdated statutory restrictions;

Table 22.18 Insolvencies, Great Britain

Numbers

	2002	2003
England and Wales		
Company insolvencies[1]		
Compulsory liquidations	6,230	5,234
Creditors' voluntary liquidations	10,075	8,950
Total	16,305	14,184
Individual insolvencies		
Bankruptcy orders	24,292	28,021
Individual voluntary arrangements[2]	6,295	8,307
Total	30,587	36,328
Scotland		
Companies		
Compulsory liquidations	556	436
Creditors' voluntary liquidations	232	195
Total	788	631
Individuals		
Sequestrations	3,215	3,328

1 Including partnerships.
2 Including deeds of arrangement.
Source: Insolvency Service

- introducing tighter restrictions on bankrupts whose conduct has been irresponsible or reckless;

- changing the provisions relating to the treatment of the bankrupt's home;

- for companies, restricting administrative receivership and streamlining administration;

- abolishing the Crown's right to recover unpaid taxes ahead of other creditors; and

- modernising the financial regime of the Insolvency Service.

Similar legislation covering bankruptcy and diligence is currently being introduced in Scotland. This is intended to modernise the bankruptcy laws to reduce the stigma of bankruptcy, encourage business restarts and improve oversight of culpable debtors.

Regulation of business

The Cabinet Office's Regulatory Impact Unit (RIU) aims to ensure all new and existing regulation is necessary, to meet the principles of better regulation, and to impose the minimum burden. The RIU reports to the Minister for the Cabinet Office and assists government ministers to ensure that regulations are fair and effective. It takes an overview of regulations affecting business, the voluntary sector, charities and the public sector.

The Unit's work involves promoting the principles of good regulation; removing unnecessary or over-burdensome legislation under the *Regulatory Reform Act 2001*; improving assessment, drawing up and enforcement of regulation; taking account of the needs of business; identifying risk and assessing options to deal with risk; responsibility for the Cabinet Office Code of Practice on Consultation; and supporting the Better Regulation Task Force. This Task Force is an independent body that makes recommendations to Government on the quality of existing or proposed regulations, and carries out studies of particular regulatory issues.

Industrial associations

Trade associations represent companies that produce or sell a particular product or group of products. They exist to supply common services, regulate trading practices and represent their members in dealings with government departments. A range of other organisations exists to represent the views of business and to provide advice and assistance.

The CBI (Confederation of British Industry) was founded in 1965 and is the largest business organisation in the United Kingdom. Membership is corporate, comprising companies and trade associations – its direct corporate members employ over 4 million people, and its trade association membership represents over 6 million people in some 200,000 firms. The CBI's objective is to help create and sustain the conditions in which business can compete and prosper, both in the United Kingdom and overseas. It is the UK member of the Union of Industrial and Employers' Confederations and has offices in Brussels and Washington as well as 12 UK regional offices.

The British Chambers of Commerce (BCC) is the national network for chambers of commerce, which are local, independent, non-profit-making organisations funded by membership subscriptions. In June 2004 over 135,000 businesses were members of Chambers in its accredited network. With over 2,500 staff covering more than 100 locations, the network provides a support team to businesses throughout the United Kingdom. The BCC represents business views to the Government at local, regional and national levels and is also part of the global network of Chambers of Commerce. It publishes a quarterly economic survey of UK businesses.

The Institute of Directors (IoD) provides advice on matters affecting company directors, such as corporate management, insolvency and career counselling, and represents the interests of members to authorities in the United Kingdom and EU. It had almost 53,500 members at the end of 2003.

The Federation of Small Businesses (FSB) is the largest campaigning pressure group promoting and protecting the interests of the self-employed and owners of small firms. It has over 185,000 members, and provides them with information and guidance on subjects such as taxation, employment, health and safety, and insurance.

Enterprise Insight is a government-supported initiative and a joint venture between the BCC, CBI, FSB and IoD. It aims to encourage more positive attitudes to enterprise among young people aged 5 to 30 and to develop their entrepreneurial skills. It will be holding the first national Enterprise Week during November 2004.

Further reading

Budget 2004. Prudence for a purpose: A Britain of stability and strength. Economic and Fiscal Strategy Report and Financial Statement and Budget Report March 2004. HM Treasury. The Stationery Office, 2004.

Companies in 2003–2004. Department of Trade and Industry. The Stationery Office, 2004.

Modernising Company Law. Cm 5553. 2 vols. Department of Trade and Industry. The Stationery Office, 2002.

Pre-Budget Report – The Strength to take the long-term decisions for Britain. Cm 6042, HM Treasury. The Stationery Office, 2003.

The Challenge of Culture Change: Raising the Stakes. Better Regulation Task Force Annual Report 2004. The Stationery Office, 2004.

Trade and Industry: Departmental Report 2004. Cm 6216. The Stationery Office, 2004.

United Kingdom National Accounts – the Blue Book (annual). Office for National Statistics. The Stationery Office.

Websites

Department of Trade and Industry
www.dti.gov.uk

HM Treasury
www.hm-treasury.gov.uk

National Statistics
www.statistics.gov.uk

23 Public finance

Total UK government spending is expected to be around £488 billion in 2004/05, and public sector current receipts are forecast to be £455 billion (Table 23.1). Social protection (see chapter 12) is the biggest single element of public spending, involving expenditure of £138 billion (28 per cent of total public spending) in 2004/05, followed by spending on health of £81 billion, and by spending on education of £63 billion.

In 2003/04 there was a deficit of £20.3 billion on the public sector current budget, compared with a deficit of £13.9 billion in 2002/03 (Table 23.2). Public sector net borrowing was £34.0 billion in 2003/04, 35 per cent higher than in 2002/03. Public sector net investment rose by 21 per cent in 2003/04 to £13.7 billion.

Fiscal policy framework

The fiscal policy framework is designed to ensure sound public finances, which are a prerequisite for sustainable investment in public services. The *Code for Fiscal Stability* sets out the five key principles of fiscal management – transparency, stability, responsibility, fairness and efficiency – and government objectives are implemented through two fiscal rules that are the foundation of the spending framework and are designed to promote economic stability:

- the golden rule: over the economic cycle, the Government will borrow only to invest and not to fund current spending; and

- the sustainable investment rule: public sector net debt as a proportion of gross domestic product (GDP) will be held over the economic cycle at a stable and prudent level – generally below 40 per cent of GDP.

The fiscal framework recognises that projections of public finances involve a considerable element of uncertainty. Projections are therefore based on cautious assumptions for key economic variables,

Table 23.1 Government expenditure and revenue, 2004/05, UK

	£ billion	Per cent
Expenditure by function		
Social protection	138	28
Health	81	17
Education	63	13
Law and protective services	29	6
Defence	27	6
Debt interest	25	5
Other health and personal social services	22	5
Industry and agriculture	20	4
Housing and environment	17	3
Transport	16	3
Other[1]	49	10
Total Managed Expenditure	**488**	**100**
Receipts		
Income tax	128	28
National Insurance	78	17
VAT	73	16
Excise duties	40	9
Corporation tax	35	8
Council tax	20	4
Business rates	19	4
Other[2]	62	14
Total receipts	**455**	**100**

1 Other expenditure includes spending on general public services; recreation, culture and religion; international co-operation and development; public service pensions; spending yet to be allocated; and some accounting adjustments.
2 Other receipts include capital taxes; stamp taxes and duties; vehicle excise duties; and some other tax and non-tax receipts.
Source: *Budget Report 2004*, HM Treasury

including the trend rate of growth, oil prices and the level of unemployment. This minimises the need for unexpected changes in taxation or spending. The assumptions are audited by the Comptroller and Auditor General (see page 369) under a three-year rolling review to ensure they remain reasonable and cautious.

Table 23.2 Key fiscal indicators, UK

	1998/99	1999/2000	2000/01	2001/02	2002/03	2003/04
Public sector						
Surplus on current budget (£ billion)	10.0	19.6	20.5	9.4	−13.9	−20.3
Net investment (£ billion)	6.4	4.4	5.2	9.9	11.3	13.7
Net borrowing (£ billion)	−3.6	−15.2	−15.4	0.5	25.2	34.0
Net debt (£ billion)	348.9	341.3	307.2	311.7	341.9	375.7
Net debt as a percentage of GDP	*39.1*	*36.3*	*31.3*	*30.2*	*31.5*	*32.8*

Source: *Financial Statistics*, Office for National Statistics

Public spending framework

Public expenditure is measured across the whole public sector using aggregate Total Managed Expenditure (TME). TME is the sum of public sector current expenditure, public sector net investment and public sector depreciation. For budgeting purposes, TME is split into:

- Departmental Expenditure Limits (DELs), which are three-year spending limits for government departments; and

- Annually Managed Expenditure (AME), which covers those elements of spending that cannot reasonably be subject to firm multi-year pre-set limits and are instead subject to scrutiny twice a year as part of the Budget process (see chapter 22).

To improve long-term planning and protect capital investment, DELs are further divided into capital and resource (current) budgets, and these are managed separately.

The framework for managing public expenditure includes incentives for departments to plan for the long term and to ensure that resources are used as effectively and efficiently as possible. Features of the framework include:

- firm three-year plans for public spending, which are reviewed every two years;

- flexibility to allow departments to carry over unspent resources into future financial years, so reducing wasteful end-of-year spending surges;

- Public Service Agreements, through which each department is committed to achieve challenging targets;

- Resource Accounting and Budgeting (RAB), with public expenditure planned, controlled and reported on a full resource basis, in line with best commercial practice, and departmental investment strategies, with an emphasis on asset management and estate rationalisation in departments; and

- administration cost limits for government departments.

Public expenditure

TME rose in terms of constant (2004/05) prices from £253.4 billion in 1973/74 to £469.6 billion in 2003/04 (Table 23.3). During this period TME peaked as a proportion of GDP at 49.9 per cent in 1975/76. By 1999/2000 this had fallen to 37.4 per cent, before rising to 41.1 per cent in 2003/04.

UK local authorities are estimated to have spent nearly £120 billion in 2003/04, around a quarter of TME. The main categories of local government current and capital expenditure are education and

Table 23.3 Trends in Total Managed Expenditure, UK

	1973/74	1983/84	1993/94	1998/99	2002/03	2003/04
In nominal terms (£ billion)	33.2	148.7	284.6	332.7	419.1	459.0
In real terms (£ billion)[1]	253.4	327.4	373.4	383.3	440.7	469.6
Percentage of GDP	*44.5*	*48.2*	*43.6*	*38.3*	*39.6*	*41.1*

1 Cash figures adjusted to 2004/05 price levels.
Source: *2004 Spending Review*, HM Treasury

Table 23.4 Components of Total Managed Expenditure, UK

Plans £ billion

	2004/05	2005/06	2006/07	2007/08
Resource DEL	263.9	284.5	302.0	317.4
Capital DEL	26.3	29.1	31.5	34.9
less depreciation	−11.0	−11.7	−12.1	−11.8
Departmental Expenditure Limits	**279.3**	**301.9**	**321.4**	**340.5**
Annually Managed Expenditure	**208.3**	**218.9**	**227.8**	**239.5**
of which:				
Social security benefits	123.1	127.7	132.9	140.0
Tax credits	13.8	14.3	14.4	14.5
Locally financed expenditure	24.2	26.0	27.9	30.0
Central government gross debt interest	23.9	25.4	26.5	27.4
Total Managed Expenditure	**487.6**	**520.8**	**549.2**	**580.0**

Source: *2004 Spending Review*, HM Treasury

Table 23.5 Main Departmental Expenditure Limits, UK[1, 2]

£ billion

	Baseline[3]		Plans	
	2004/05	2005/06	2006/07	2007/08
Total Departmental Expenditure Limits	**278.7**	**300.8**	**321.4**	**340.5**
of which:				
Education and Skills	27.6	31.1	32.9	35.2
Health	71.5	78.5	86.0	94.4
of which: National Health Service	69.4	76.4	83.8	92.1
Transport	10.4	11.0	13.6	12.9
Office of the Deputy Prime Minister[4]	7.0	7.5	7.8	8.4
Local government	43.7	46.2	48.6	51.0
Home Office	12.7	13.2	14.2	14.9
Defence	29.7	30.8	32.1	33.4
International Development	3.8	4.5	5.0	5.3
Trade and Industry	5.0	6.1	6.5	6.6
Work and Pensions	8.2	8.3	8.2	8.1
Chancellor's departments	4.9	5.2	5.3	5.5
Scotland[5]	21.3	22.8	24.2	25.5
Wales[5]	11.0	11.8	12.8	13.6
Northern Ireland Executive[5,6]	7.0	7.4	7.9	8.3

1 Resource and net capital DELs on a full resource budgeting basis, net of depreciation.
2 Figures for some departments include DELs for related departments or other bodies. For example, Health covers the Department of Health and the Food Standards Agency.
3 Excludes one-off and time-limited expenditure.
4 Excludes local government.
5 Allocations within DEL totals may be subject to final decisions in allocation by the devolved administrations.
6 There is a separate DEL for the Northern Ireland Office.
Source: *2004 Spending Review*, HM Treasury

2004 Spending Review

The 2004 Spending Review, published in July 2004, sets public spending plans in the United Kingdom for the three years to 2007/08 within the overall spending limits set in the Budget in March 2004. These allow:

- current spending to increase by an annual average of 2.5 per cent in real terms in 2006/07 and 2007/08; and
- public sector net investment to rise from 2 per cent of GDP in 2004/05 to $2\frac{1}{4}$ per cent by 2007/08.

The growth rate of overall public spending and departmental spending is lower than in the 2002 Spending Review. However, the Government's objective is to maintain the growth in front-line public services, and it plans to achieve this through cutting administration costs in real terms and achieving planned efficiency gains of 2.5 per cent a year over the period of the 2004 Spending Review (see below and page 58).

The allocation of resources in the 2004 Spending Review is intended to:

- deliver world-class public services that enhance opportunity for all;
- equip the United Kingdom to meet the challenges of the global economy;
- strengthen communities and build a fairer society; and
- enhance the United Kingdom's security, and promote stability and prosperity around the world.

Taking into account locally financed expenditure, spending on the key priorities of education, health, social services, transport, housing and criminal justice will account for about three-quarters of the total extra planned spending. The 2004 Spending Review includes:

- greater investment in learning and skills, with, for example, total spending on education in England £12 billion higher in 2007/08 than in 2004/05;
- confirmation of the increased resources for health announced in the 2002 Budget, with UK health spending growing by an annual average of 7.2 per cent in real terms between 2002/03 and 2007/08;
- investment in transport, with additional resources to put the railways on a sustainable footing;
- a major programme of investment in affordable and decent housing, including a 50 per cent increase in new building in the social sector;
- spending on crime and justice to be £3.5 billion higher in 2007/08 than in 2004/05;
- spending on science to grow by an average of 5.8 per cent a year in real terms – a ten-year investment framework for science and innovation (see page 389) was published alongside the Spending Review;
- additional resources to support the Government's commitment to tackling global poverty, with development spending rising to nearly £6.5 billion in 2007/08, representing a ratio of official development assistance to Gross National Income of 0.47 per cent; and
- over £1 billion more for counter-terrorism by 2007/08.

training, social protection, public order and safety, transport, environmental protection, general public services, and housing and community amenities.

Public expenditure is planned and controlled on a departmental basis, except where devolved responsibility lies with the Scottish Parliament, the National Assembly for Wales, the Northern Ireland Assembly (when it is sitting) or local authorities. Table 23.6 shows expenditure in 2002/03 when

non-devolved expenditure has been allocated. England accounted for 80.7 per cent of identifiable expenditure in the United Kingdom, Scotland 9.9 per cent, Wales 5.6 per cent and Northern Ireland 3.7 per cent.

Public sector efficiency

The 2004 Spending Review announced further steps designed to improve the efficiency of the public services taking account of an independent

Table 23.6 Identifiable expenditure[1] on services, 2002/03, UK

	Expenditure (£ billion)	£ per head
England	270.3	5,453
Scotland	33.3	6,579
Wales	18.9	6,479
Northern Ireland	12.3	7,267
UK identifiable expenditure	334.8	5,652
Outside UK	7.7	
Total identifiable expenditure	342.5	
Non-identifiable expenditure,[2] UK	58.1	
Total expenditure on services	400.5	
Accounting adjustments	18.4	
Total Managed Expenditure	**418.9**	

1 Identifiable expenditure is that which can be recognised as having been incurred for the benefit of individuals, enterprises or communities within particular regions.
2 Expenditure on services delivered collectively to the United Kingdom as a whole, such as on defence.
Source: *Public Expenditure Statistical Analyses 2004*, HM Treasury

review of public sector efficiency by Sir Peter Gershon:

- agreed departmental targets for achieving annual efficiencies of over £20 billion a year by 2007/08;

- departmental plans for meeting these agreed targets, including proposals for a gross reduction of over 84,000 Civil Service posts and the relocation of 20,000 other Civil Service posts away from London and the South East (see page 58);

- administration budgets for departments that will reduce administration costs as a proportion of spending to a record low; and

- a framework under the leadership of the chief executive of the Office of Government Commerce (OGC) for implementing, measuring and monitoring the Government's efficiency programme.

The OGC, an independent office of HM Treasury, will play a key role in delivering efficiency improvements. It works with central civil government as a catalyst to achieve best value for money (VFM) in commercial activities. The OGC achieved VFM gains of £1.6 billion up to March 2003. Between 2003/04 and 2005/06 its target is to deliver £3 billion of VFM gains in central civil government procurement. A new target has been set of delivering a further £3 billion saving by 2007/08 in central government civil procurement. The OGC also has a key role in helping departments and other government bodies to implement the property, estate management, and other locational and workspace issues arising from the Lyons Review of the scope for relocating Civil Service posts out of London and the South East (see page 58).

Examination of public expenditure

Examination of public expenditure is carried out by select committees of the House of Commons. The committees study in detail the activities of particular government departments and question ministers and officials. The Public Accounts Committee considers the accounts of government departments, executive agencies and other public sector bodies, and examines reports by the Comptroller and Auditor General (C&AG) on the way in which they have used their resources.

Audit of government spending is conducted by the C&AG, an officer of the House of Commons and head of the National Audit Office (NAO), the principal state audit body in the United Kingdom. The C&AG and the NAO are independent of government. The C&AG certifies the accounts of all government departments and executive agencies, and those of many other bodies receiving public funds. The C&AG also has statutory authority to report to Parliament on the economy, efficiency and effectiveness with which departments and other public bodies have used their resources. In 2003/04 the NAO audited over £700 billion of government expenditure and revenue.

The Audit Commission is responsible for appointing the auditors for local authorities and health service bodies in England and Wales and for promoting VFM in these sectors. There are separate audit bodies dealing with the expenditure of the devolved administrations:

- The Auditor General for Scotland, supported by Audit Scotland, is responsible for auditing the expenditure of the Scottish Parliament and Executive.

- Under the *Public Audit (Wales) Act 2004* there will be a single public audit body for Wales, headed by the Auditor General for Wales in charge of a new Wales Audit Office. The Office will be responsible for the financial and performance audit of the National Assembly for Wales, its sponsored bodies, and the health bodies. The Auditor General for Wales will be responsible for appointing auditors for local government bodies (which are currently audited by the Audit Commission).

- In Northern Ireland the Comptroller and Auditor General for Northern Ireland and the Northern Ireland Audit Office report on the accounts of public sector bodies.

Public-private partnerships

The Government sees public-private partnerships (PPPs) as an important part of the delivery of high-quality public services. PPPs cover a variety of arrangements, including:

- the Private Finance Initiative (PFI), in which the public sector contracts to purchase services, such as the construction and operation of public services infrastructure on a long-term basis;

- the introduction of private sector ownership and enterprise into state-owned businesses; and

- the sale of government services into wider markets, using private sector expertise and capital to exploit the commercial potential of government assets.

Among the largest PPPs are a £16 billion infrastructure investment programme for the London Underground (see page 335) and the PPP for air traffic control (see page 338), which is providing around £1 billion for investment in new technology. In Scotland the Scottish schools PPP programme is providing some £2.4 billion of new and modernised schools.

Debt and reserves management

The Government meets its borrowing needs by selling debt to the private sector. At the end of the financial year 2003/04 the stock of UK public sector net debt was £376 billion (see Table 23.2), nearly £34 billion higher than at the end of 2002/03. Net debt was 32.8 per cent of GDP at the end of 2003/04. In 2003 the United Kingdom had the lowest debt of any Group of Seven (G7) country in terms of general government net financial liabilities as a percentage of nominal GDP.

The objective of the Government's debt management policy is to minimise, over the long term, the cost of meeting the Government's financing needs, taking into account risk while ensuring that debt management policy is consistent with the aims of monetary policy. Operational responsibility for managing government debt rests with a Treasury agency, the UK Debt Management Office (DMO).

Gilt-edged stock

A gilt is a UK Government security issued by HM Treasury. The term 'gilt' (or 'gilt-edged') is a reference to the security of the investment; the UK Government has never failed to make interest or principal payments on gilts. Gilts include 'conventionals', which represent a guarantee by the Government to pay the holder a fixed cash payment (coupon) every six months until the maturity date, when the holder receives the final coupon payment and the return of the principal; and index-linked stocks, on which both principal and interest payments are adjusted in line with movements in the Retail Prices Index (see page 353). The DMO, on behalf of the Government, is aiming for gilts sales of about £47 billion in 2004/05. Gilts are issued primarily by auction, and the DMO plans to hold 15 auctions of conventional gilts and ten of index-linked gilts in 2004/05.

At the end of March 2004 holdings of central government marketable securities were estimated at £340.3 billion: £240.5 billion of conventional gilts, £80.5 billion of index-linked gilts and £19.3 billion of Treasury Bills (short-term securities issued as part of the DMO's cash management operations). Insurance companies and pension funds held 63.5 per cent of gilts at the end of March 2004, other UK financial institutions 7.8 per cent, UK households 8.3 per cent, local authorities and public corporations 0.9 per cent and holders in the rest of the world 19.4 per cent.

Official reserves

The United Kingdom holds official reserves of gold, foreign currency assets and International Monetary Fund (IMF) Special Drawing Rights (SDRs). Apart from SDR assets that constitute the UK reserve tranche position at the IMF, these are held in the Exchange Equalisation Account (EEA). The Bank of England, acting as the Treasury's agent, manages the EEA by carrying out day-today tasks, such as foreign exchange dealing and portfolio investment, within the framework of an annual remit set by the Treasury.

At the end of June 2004 UK gross official holdings of international reserves totalled US$44.9 billion, including US$17.4 billion of euro, US$12.5 billion of US dollars, US$6.0 billion of SDRs, US$5.1 billion of Japanese yen and US$4.0 billion of gold. After deducting liabilities of US$27.3 billion, the net reserves totalled US$17.6 billion, US$1.2 billion higher than a year earlier.

Main sources of revenue

Government revenue is forecast to be £455 billion in 2004/05. The main sources (Table 23.1) are:

- taxes on income (together with profits), which include personal income tax, corporation tax and petroleum revenue tax (see page 372);

- taxes on expenditure, which include VAT (value added tax) and customs and excise duties;

- National Insurance contributions (NICs); and

- taxes on capital, which include inheritance tax, capital gains tax, council tax and business rates (also known as non-domestic rates).

Taxation policy

The Government is committed to a modern and fair tax system that encourages work and saving, keeps pace with developments in business practice

Budget tax measures

Among the measures contained in the Budget in March 2004 were:

- action to protect tax revenues and modernise the tax system (see page 372);

- simplification of the tax regime for pensions (see page 373);

- acceptance of the recommendations of a review to integrate the Inland Revenue and HM Customs and Excise (see page 372); and

- further measures to protect the environment.

and the global economy, and raises sufficient revenue to fund the Government's objective to build world-class public services.

Collection of taxes and duties

Most taxes and duties are collected by the Inland Revenue and HM Customs and Excise (Tables 23.7 and 23.8). Local authorities collect the main local taxes: council tax and business rates.

Table 23.8 Main Customs and Excise taxes and duties, UK

£ billion

	1998/99	2002/03	2003/04
Payments by HM Customs and Excise into the Consolidated Fund[1]			
VAT	52.3	63.5	69.1
Duties on:			
hydrocarbon oils	21.6	22.1	22.8
tobacco	8.2	8.1	8.1
spirits	1.6	2.3	2.4
beer	2.7	2.9	3.0
wine and made wine	1.5	1.9	2.0
cider and perry	0.1	0.2	0.2
betting, gaming and lottery	1.5	1.3	1.3
air passengers	0.8	0.8	0.8
Customs duties and agricultural levies	2.1	1.9	1.9
Insurance premium tax	1.2	2.1	2.3
Landfill tax	0.3	0.5	0.6
Climate change levy	.	0.8	0.8
Aggregates levy	.	0.2	0.3
All payments	**94.0**	**108.7**	**115.7**

1 Excluding shipbuilder's relief.
Source: HM Customs and Excise

Table 23.7 Inland Revenue taxes and duties, UK

£ billion

	1998/99	2002/03	2003/04
Net receipts by Board of Inland Revenue			
Income tax and capital gains tax combined[1]	88.5	111.1	116.5
Corporation tax	30.0	29.3	28.2
Inheritance tax	1.8	2.4	2.5
Stamp duties	4.6	7.5	7.6
Petroleum revenue tax	0.5	1.0	1.2
Windfall tax	2.6	.	.
Total	**128.1**	**151.3**	**155.9**

1 From October 1999 until April 2003 receipts are net of payments of Working Families' Tax Credit and Disabled Person's Tax Credit.
Source: Inland Revenue

Under the self-assessment system for collecting personal taxation, around 9.3 million people – primarily higher-rate taxpayers, the self-employed and those receiving investment income – are required to complete an annual tax return for the Inland Revenue. Such taxpayers may calculate their own tax liability, although they can choose to have the calculations done by the Inland Revenue if they return the form by the end of September. About 1.1 million people submitted their tax returns to the Inland Revenue electronically in 2003/04. A shorter self-assessment tax return is being introduced for those with simple tax affairs.

The United Kingdom has agreements governing double taxation with over 100 countries. They are intended to avoid double taxation arising, to deal with cross-border economic activity, and to prevent fiscal discrimination against UK business interests overseas. They also include provisions to counter tax avoidance and evasion.

Protecting tax revenues

The 2004 Budget contained measures to tackle tax avoidance, protect revenue and maintain the integrity of the tax system including:

- the closure of loopholes in partnerships, finance leasing and VAT, and a new requirement for accountancy firms and others involved in promoting certain tax avoidance

schemes to register the schemes with the Inland Revenue or, for VAT avoidance schemes, with HM Customs and Excise;

- measures to tackle complex schemes using trusts for the purposes of avoiding taxes (such as avoiding inheritance tax by giving away an asset while continuing to enjoy its benefits);

- a new minimum rate of corporation tax on distributed profits (see page 373), designed to deter the self-employed from adopting a corporate legal form for tax reasons rather than as a step to expansion; and

- the introduction from 2006 of a system of duty stamps for spirits, designed to prevent losses from fraud on spirits.

Taxes on income

Income tax

Income tax is charged on all income originating in the United Kingdom – although some forms, such as child benefit, are exempt – and on all income arising abroad of people resident in the United Kingdom. Income tax is imposed for the year of assessment beginning on 6 April. The tax rates and bands for 2003/04 and 2004/05 are shown in Table 23.9. In 2004/05 there are an estimated 29.9 million income taxpayers, including 3.4 million at

---

Integration of the Inland Revenue and HM Customs and Excise

In March 2004 the Government announced that it had accepted in full recommendations to integrate the Inland Revenue and HM Customs and Excise. The two departments employed nearly 100,000 people in 2003/04 and handled almost £325 billion of tax collected in 2002/03: 86 per cent of UK net tax and social security contributions.

The Inland Revenue is responsible for collecting income tax; corporation tax; capital gains tax; inheritance tax; petroleum revenue tax; and stamp duties, and is responsible for NICs and tax credits. HM Customs and Excise collects VAT; customs duties; insurance premium tax; excise duties on fuel, alcohol, tobacco, and betting and gaming; and a range of environmental taxes. It also has a frontier protection role, which makes it responsible for controlling imports and exports.

The Government plans to introduce legislation for the creation of the new department, which will be known as HM Revenue and Customs (HMRC). A new executive chairman has been appointed jointly to head both departments from September 2004. There are separate plans to transfer counter-drugs work from the new department to the new Serious Organised Crime Agency (see page 206). Development of strategic tax policy will become the responsibility of HM Treasury (supported by HMRC), while HMRC will lead on policy maintenance and delivery issues. The integration of the two departments and proposed efficiency reforms could create scope for overall savings of up to 16,000 jobs by the end of 2007/08. Some 3,500 of these jobs would be redeployed within HMRC, producing a net reduction in posts of 12,500.

the starting rate of 10 per cent, 22.3 million at the basic rate of 22 per cent, 3.4 million at the higher rate of 40 per cent (32.5 per cent on dividends) and about 840,000 with a marginal rate at the 20 per cent lower rate for savings income or the 10 per cent ordinary dividend rate.

Allowances and reliefs reduce an individual's income tax liability. All taxpayers are entitled to a personal allowance against income from all sources, with a higher allowance for the elderly (see Table 23.9).

One of the most significant reliefs, which is designed to encourage people to save towards their retirement, covers contributions to pension schemes. The *Finance Act 2004* includes provisions to implement the Government's arrangements for simplifying the taxation of pensions, which will take effect in April 2006. A single set of rules will replace the eight different sets of tax rules, and there will be a single lifetime allowance on the amount of pension savings that can benefit from tax relief. This allowance will initially be £1.5 million, rising to £1.8 million by 2010.

Table 23.9 Income tax allowances and bands, UK

	£	
	2003/04	2004/05
Income tax allowances		
Personal allowance		
age under 65	4,615	4,745
age 65–74	6,610	6,830
age 75 and over	6,720	6,950
Married couple's allowance[1]		
age 65 before 6 April 2000	5,565	5,725
age 75 and over	5,635	5,795
Income limit for age-related		
allowances	18,300	18,900
Blind person's allowance	1,510	1,560
Bands of taxable income[2]		
Starting rate of 10 per cent	0–1,960	0–2,020
Basic rate of 22 per cent	1,961–30,500	2,021–31,400
Higher rate of 40 per cent	over 30,500	over 31,400

1 Tax relief for this allowance is restricted to 10 per cent. The minimum amount for the allowance is £2,210 in 2004/05 (£2,150 in 2003/04).
2 The rate of tax applicable to savings income in the basic rate band is 20 per cent. For dividends the rates applicable are 10 per cent for income below the basic rate upper limit and 32.5 per cent above that.
Source: Inland Revenue

Corporation tax

Corporation tax is payable by companies on their income and capital gains. The main rate of corporation tax in the United Kingdom is 30 per cent, which is levied on companies with annual profits of over £1.5 million. The small companies' rate is 19 per cent, levied on firms with annual profits of between £50,001 and £300,000. There is a zero starting rate, so that companies with annual profits of up to £10,000 do not pay corporation tax. A sliding scale of relief is allowed for companies with annual profits of between £10,001 and £50,000 and between £300,001 and £1.5 million, so that the overall average rate paid by these firms is up to 19 per cent and between 19 per cent and 30 per cent respectively. In the March 2004 Budget the Government announced that there would be no change in these rates, but from 1 April 2004 there would be a minimum rate of 19 per cent on profits distributed to individuals; businesses reinvesting their profits or with taxable profits of over £50,000 are not affected by this measure.

Some capital expenditure – on plant and machinery, industrial buildings and agricultural buildings, for example – may qualify for relief in the form of capital allowances, and there are tax credits to encourage research and development. In the March 2004 Budget the first-year allowance of 40 per cent for expenditure on plant or machinery by small or medium-sized businesses was increased to 50 per cent for one year from 1 April 2004. This is intended to assist the cash flow of small businesses and to provide higher funding for new investment.

Taxes on capital

Capital gains tax

Capital gains tax (CGT) is payable by individuals, personal representatives of deceased people, and trusts on gains realised from the disposal of assets. It is payable on the amount by which total chargeable gains for a year exceed the exempt amount (£8,200 for individuals and £4,100 for most trusts in 2004/05, up from £7,900 and £3,950 respectively in 2003/04). Subject to conditions, gains on some types of asset are exempt from CGT, including the principal private residence, a private car, UK government gilt-edged securities, and gains on assets held in a Personal Equity Plan or an Individual Savings Account (see page 469). For individuals, CGT in 2004/05 will be payable at

10, 20 or 40 per cent, depending on a person's marginal income tax rate.

CGT taper relief reduces the amount of the chargeable gain depending on how long an asset has been held, with a higher rate of relief for business assets than for non-business assets.

Inheritance tax

Inheritance tax is essentially charged on estates at the time of death and on gifts made within seven years of death; most other lifetime transfers are not taxed. There are several important exemptions from inheritance tax, including transfers between spouses, and gifts and bequests to UK charities, major political parties and heritage bodies. In general, business assets and farmland are exempt from inheritance tax, so that most family businesses can be passed on without a tax charge.

Tax is charged at a single rate of 40 per cent above a threshold (£263,000 in 2004/05, up from £255,000 in 2003/04). About 5 per cent of estates each year become liable for an inheritance tax bill.

National Insurance contributions

Most people who work pay NICs. There are four main classes of NICs: Class 1 (paid by employees and their employers); Class 2 (paid by the self-employed); Class 3 (voluntary contributions paid to safeguard the rights to some benefits); and Class 4 (paid by the self-employed on their taxable profits above a set lower limit and paid in addition to their Class 2 contributions).

Employees with earnings below £79 a week in 2004/05 do not pay Class 1 contributions. There are rebates where employees are in their employer's pension scheme and this is contracted out of the State Second Pension (see page 164).

Taxes on expenditure

Value added tax (VAT)

VAT is a tax on consumer expenditure and is collected at each stage in the production and distribution of goods and services. The final tax is payable by the consumer. The standard rate is 17.5 per cent. Certain goods and services are relieved from VAT, either by being charged at a zero rate or by being exempt, and there is a reduced rate of 5 per cent on certain goods and services:

Table 23.10 National Insurance contributions, main rates, 2004/05, UK

£

Class 1	
Employees (primary contribution)	11% of £91.01 a week to £610 a week, and 1% of earnings above £610 a week
Employers (secondary rate)	12.8% above £91 a week
Class 2[1,2]	£2.05 a week
Class 3	£7.15 a week
Class 4	8% of £4,745 a year to £31,720 a year, 1% above £31,720 a year

1 The self-employed may claim exemption from paying Class 2 contributions if their earnings are below the small earnings exception limit: £4,215 in 2004/05.
2 There are special rates for share fishermen (who are paid from a share of their boat's profits and are not employees) and for volunteer development workers, of £2.70 and £3.95 a week respectively in 2004/05.
Source: Inland Revenue

- Under zero rating, a taxable person does not charge tax to a customer but reclaims any VAT paid to suppliers. Among the main categories where this applies are goods exported to other European Union (EU) countries; most foods; water and sewerage for non-business use; passenger transport; books, newspapers and periodicals; construction of new residential buildings; young children's clothing and footwear; drugs and medicines supplied on prescription; specified aids for handicapped people; and certain supplies by or to charities.

- For exempt goods or services, a taxable person does not charge any VAT but is not entitled to reclaim the VAT on goods and services bought for his or her business. The main categories where this applies are many supplies of land and buildings; financial services; postal services; betting and gaming (apart from some exceptions); lotteries; much education and training; health and welfare; and, since 1 June 2004, admission charges to many cultural attractions, such as theatres, galleries, zoos and museums.

The reduced rate of 5 per cent applies to a number of goods and services, including domestic fuel and power, certain types of property conversion, children's car seats, women's sanitary products, and the installation of energy-saving materials in homes.

From April 2004 the annual level of turnover above which traders must register for VAT was raised from £56,000 to £58,000. Other measures in the 2004 Budget included raising the turnover limit for the annual accounting scheme, which allows businesses to make one VAT return each year instead of the usual four, from £600,000 to £660,000 a year.

Environmental and transport taxes

There are a number of environmental and transport taxes:

- Vehicle excise duty (VED): since March 2001 VED for new cars has been determined according to the carbon dioxide (CO_2) emissions of the vehicle and the type of fuel used. There are six VED bands for new cars (Table 23.11). For cars registered before 1 March 2001, VED is determined according to engine size. The standard rate is £165, with a lower rate of £110 for cars up to 1,549 cc. VED for goods vehicles ranges from £165 to £1,850 a year (£160 to £1,350 for lorries with reduced pollution certificates). Duty on buses varies according to seating capacity.

Table 23.11 Vehicle excise duty rates for cars registered on or after 1 March 2001, UK

£

CO_2 emissions (g/km)	Petrol car	Diesel car	Cars using alternative fuels
100 and below	65	75	55
101 to 120	75	85	65
121 to 150	105	115	95
151 to 165	125	135	115
166 to 185	145	155	135
186 and over	160	165	155

Source: *Budget Report 2004*, HM Treasury

- Road fuel duties: see box on page 376.
- Air passenger duty: for flights within the United Kingdom and for those to destinations in the European Economic Area (EEA, see page 104), countries applying to join the EU (Bulgaria, Romania and Turkey, see page 71) and Switzerland, the duty is £5 for the lowest class and £10 for any other class; the

equivalent rates to other destinations are £20 and £40 respectively. All flights from airports in the Scottish Highlands and Islands are exempt from duty in recognition of their remoteness and dependence on air travel.

- Landfill tax: this is levied on active waste at the standard rate of £15 a tonne, with a lower rate of £2 a tonne for inert waste. The standard rate will be increased by £3 a tonne in 2005/06 and by at least £3 a tonne in the following years to reach a medium- to long-term rate of £35 a tonne. The introduction of the tax was accompanied by a reduction in employers' NICs and future increases will be introduced in a way that is revenue neutral to business.

- Aggregates levy: this is levied at £1.60 a tonne on virgin aggregate commercially exploited in the United Kingdom. To enhance the levy's environmental impact in Northern Ireland, in April 2004 the Government extended the scope and duration of relief on aggregate used in processed products, so that it now also covers virgin aggregate in its raw state. The levy has been accompanied by a new Aggregates Levy Sustainability Fund, which provides support to businesses affected by environmental extraction, and a reduction in employers' NICs.

- Climate change levy: this is levied on the non-domestic use of energy and, together with associated measures, is designed to encourage businesses to use energy more efficiently and reduce emissions of CO_2. All revenues are recycled back to business through a reduction in employers' NICs introduced at the same time as the levy and additional support for energy efficiency measures (see page 454).

Other indirect taxes and duties

As well as duties on tobacco, beer, wines and spirits, other indirect taxes and duties include:

- Insurance premium tax: this is levied at 5 per cent on most general insurance, with a higher rate of 17.5 per cent on travel insurance and on insurance sold by suppliers of cars and domestic appliances.

- Betting and gaming duties: these are charged on off-course betting, pool betting, gaming in casinos, bingo and amusement machines. Rates vary with the particular form of gambling. On the National Lottery there is a 12 per cent duty

Transport and the environment

The Government has introduced a number of measures designed to improve the efficiency of the transport system, while safeguarding the environment. As well as the changes to VED (see page 375), fuel duty differentials have been introduced to encourage the take-up of less environmentally damaging fuels.

The March 2004 Budget announced that sulphur-free petrol and diesel would benefit from a 0.5 pence per litre differential relative to the rates for ultra-low sulphur fuels. This differential is expected to lead to sulphur-free fuels becoming the standard specification for road fuels in the United Kingdom. The Chancellor of the Exchequer will review the date of the introduction of this differential at the time of the 2004 Pre-Budget Report. Among other transport-related measures in the 2004 Budget was the continuation of a 20 pence per litre duty incentive in favour of biodiesel until at least 2007. A duty incentive of the same amount for bioethanol will be introduced from 1 January 2005.

In April 2002 the Government reformed the system of taxation on company cars, so that the tax charge was linked to vehicle emissions. An initial evaluation of the change, published in May 2004, found that the system had reduced business mileage and brought lower CO_2 emissions as a result of more fuel-efficient cars.

on gross stakes, but no tax on winnings. The Government has modernised the structure of gambling taxation, including replacing general betting duty and the duty on bingo by a 15 per cent tax on the gross profits of bookmakers and bingo companies.

Stamp taxes and duties

Under a major reform of stamp duty on UK property transactions, stamp duty land tax replaced stamp duty on UK land and buildings in December 2003. The reform is intended to modernise administrative arrangements, close

loopholes, remove distortions and pave the way for the introduction of e-conveyancing systems. The tax is payable at 1 per cent of the total price when above £60,000 (£150,000 for non-residential land and buildings), 3 per cent above £250,000 and 4 per cent above £500,000. However, in the most disadvantaged areas in the United Kingdom, no tax is payable on certain non-residential transfers, while transfers of residential property of up to £150,000 are exempt.

Some other transfers are subject to stamp duty. Transfers of shares generally attract duty at 0.5 per cent of the cost, while certain types of document, such as declarations of trust, generally attract a small fixed duty of £5. Transfers by gift and transfers to charities are exempt.

Local authority taxation

Domestic property in Great Britain is subject to the council tax, one of the main sources of income for local authorities (see page 61). Each dwelling is allocated to one of eight valuation bands, based on its capital value (the amount it might have sold for on the open market) in April 1991. In Wales new valuation bands, based on property values in April 2003, will take effect in April 2005, with a ninth band for properties over £424,000.

In 2004/05, in England, the average council tax for a Band D dwelling (occupied by two or more adults) is £1,167 (£1,119 in London, £1,143 in other metropolitan areas and £1,185 in shire areas). In Scotland the average Band D council tax is £1,053 and in Wales £887.

Discounts are available for dwellings with fewer than two resident adults and those on low incomes may receive council tax benefit of up to 100 per cent of the tax bill (see page 173). In the March 2004 Budget the Government announced a one-off payment of £100 to each pensioner household with someone aged 70 or over to help with their council tax bills. Under the *Local Government Act 2003*, local authorities in England can reduce the 50 per cent discount for second homes. They can also remove or reduce the 50 per cent discount for long-term empty property. Local authorities in Wales and Scotland also have these powers.

Business rates (also known as non-domestic rates) are a tax on the occupiers of commercial property. The rateable value is assessed by reference to annual rents and reviewed every five years. Separate business rates are set for England, Wales

Review of local government funding

The report of a review of local government funding in England – *Balance of Funding Review Report,* published in July 2004 – concluded that council tax should be retained but that it should be reformed.

The Government has agreed that council tax should be retained. It has set up an independent inquiry to:

- make recommendations for the reform of council tax in England, taking into account the revaluation in 2007 of domestic property;

- assess the case for giving local authorities more flexibility to raise additional revenue;

- analyse the options for changing the balance of funding, including local income tax, reform of business rates, and other possible local taxes and charges;

- consider the implications for financing elected regional assemblies (see page 13); and

- consider any implications of its recommendations for other parts of the United Kingdom.

The Welsh Assembly Government has undertaken a separate review in Wales. An independent review of local government finance in Scotland was announced in June 2004.

In Northern Ireland proposals to reform the domestic rating system were published in July 2004 and are planned to take effect from April 2007. They include the replacement of domestic rental values with individual assessments of the capital value of every residential property in Northern Ireland.

and Scotland, and collected by local authorities. They are paid into separate national pools and redistributed to local authorities in proportion to their population.

In Northern Ireland, rates – local taxes on domestic and non-domestic properties – are based on the value of the property. For 2004/05 the average domestic rates bill in Northern Ireland is £509.

Further reading

2004 Spending Review: New Public Spending Plans 2005–2008. Cm 6237. HM Treasury. The Stationery Office, 2004.

Balance of Funding Review Report. Office of the Deputy Prime Minister, 2004.

Budget 2004. Prudence for a purpose: A Britain of stability and strength. Economic and Fiscal Strategy Report and Financial Statement and Budget Report March 2004. HM Treasury. The Stationery Office, 2004.

Debt and Reserves Management Report. Annual report. HM Treasury.

Financing Britain's Future: Review of the Revenue Departments. Cm 6163. HM Treasury. The Stationery Office, 2004.

Inland Revenue Statistics. Available only on the Internet at *www.inlandrevenue.gov.uk/stats*

Public Expenditure Statistical Analyses. Annual report. HM Treasury. The Stationery Office.

Websites

HM Treasury
www.hm-treasury.gov.uk

Inland Revenue
www.inlandrevenue.gov.uk

HM Customs and Excise
www.hmce.gov.uk

United Kingdom Debt Management Office
www.dmo.gov.uk

WWW.

24   International trade and investment

The United Kingdom's open economy is more dependent upon international trade than many other countries. It is the sixth largest exporter of goods in the world and the second largest exporter of services. In 2003, exports were equivalent to 25 per cent of gross domestic product (GDP). Furthermore the United Kingdom has the highest ratio of inward and outward investment to GDP of any leading economy. As a result, the Government is committed to the continuing liberalisation of global trade and investment.

Table 24.1 shows how the UK balance of trade in goods and services compares with other G7 countries.

Table 24.1 International balance of trade in goods and services, G7 countries

		US$ billion	
	1993	1998	2003
Canada	0.0	12.3	35.4
France	19.4	38.8	20.6
Germany	3.4	32.1	102.7
Italy	32.1	40.6	7.9
Japan	97.0	72.4	69.1
United Kingdom	−9.8	−14.1	−53.0
United States	−65.0	−160.0	−494.9

Source: OECD Economic Outlook

Balance of payments

The balance of payments (Table 24.2) provides a record of the transactions between the residents of the United Kingdom and the rest of the world. It records inward and outward transactions, the overall net flow of transactions between UK residents and the rest of the world, and how that flow is funded. Economic transactions include:

- exports and imports of goods, such as oil, finished manufactured goods, and chemicals;

- exports and imports of services, such as international transport, travel, and financial and business services;

- income flows, such as dividends and interest earned by non-residents on investments in the United Kingdom and by UK residents investing abroad;

- financial flows, such as investment in shares, debt securities, loans and deposits; and

- transfers, such as payments to, and receipts from, EU institutions, foreign aid and funds brought by migrants to the United Kingdom.

The balance of payments is divided into four main categories:

- the current account – trade in goods (on a balance of payment basis, see glossary) and services (Table 24.3), income (investment income and compensation of employees – for example, locally engaged staff in UK embassies and military bases abroad) and current transfers (such as food aid);

- the capital account – capital transfers and the acquisition and disposal of non-produced, non-financial assets (such as copyrights);

- the financial account – the flow of direct, portfolio and other investment and reserve assets; and

- the international investment position – the United Kingdom's stock of external financial assets and liabilities.

Table 24.2 summarises the UK balance of payments position. The current account for 2003 was in deficit by £20.4 billion compared with a

Table 24.2 Balance of payments summary,[1] UK

£ million

	1993	1998	2001	2002	2003
Current account					
Trade in goods and services	−6,485	−8,504	−27,432	−31,098	−32,673
Income	−191	12,906	11,652	21,475	22,097
Current transfers	−5,243	−8,374	−6,611	−8,599	−9,854
Current balance	−11,919	−3,972	−22,391	−18,222	−20,430
Capital account	309	516	1,206	868	1,243
Financial account	11,330	2,219	23,816	8,849	17,455
Net errors and omissions[2]	280	1,237	-2,631	8,505	1,732

1 Balance of payments basis.
2 Amount necessary to bring the sum of all balance of payments entries to zero.
Source: *Balance of Payments*, Office for National Statistics

deficit of £18.2 billion in 2002. The deficit in trade on goods and services also increased – to £32.7 billion in 2003 from £31.1 billion in 2002. However, the surplus on the income account rose to a record £22.1 billion. The surplus on the capital account also increased, rising to £1.2 billion in 2003 from £0.9 billion in 2002.

The current account deficit with EU-15 countries widened sharply in 2003, reaching a record £22.7 billion compared with £12.9 billion in 2002. The balance on all current account components fell from the 2002 levels, with particularly sharp falls for both trade in goods and income. Over the same period, the balance with non-EU countries moved from a deficit of £5.3 billion to a surplus of £2.2 billion. This was due to a lower deficit on trade in goods, combined with higher surpluses on trade in services and income.

Trade in goods and services

Table 24.3 summarises UK trade in goods and services at current prices and Figure 24.4 shows the balances over the past 30 years. The deficit on the balance in goods increased in 2003 and the surplus on the balance in services decreased, leading to an overall increase in the shortfall in the balance of goods and services.

Commodity composition of goods

UK exports of goods are dominated by manufactures (Figure 24.5) – finished manufactures and semi-manufactured goods – which accounted for about the same proportion (82 to 83 per cent) of exports in 2003 as they did in 1973. Oil, which had risen as a proportion of total exports from

Table 24.3 External trade in goods and services,[1] UK

£ million

	1993	1998	2001	2002	2003
Exports of goods	122,229	164,056	190,055	186,517	187,846
Exports of services	41,411	66,278	82,314	87,203	89,693
Exports of goods and services	163,640	230,334	272,369	273,720	277,539
Imports of goods	135,295	185,869	230,703	233,192	235,136
Imports of services	34,830	52,969	69,098	71,626	75,076
Imports of goods and services	170,125	238,838	299,801	304,818	310,212
Balance of trade in goods	−13,066	−21,813	−40,648	−46,675	−47,290
Balance of trade in services	6,581	13,309	13,216	15,577	14,617
Balance of trade in goods and services	**−6,485**	**−8,504**	**−27,432**	**−31,098**	**−32,673**

1 Balance of payments basis.
Source: *Balance of Payments*, Office for National Statistics

Figure 24.4 Balance of payments in goods and services, UK

£ billion

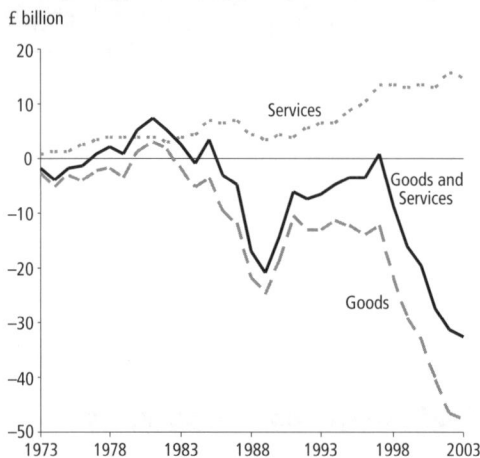

Source: *Balance of Payments*, Office for National Statistics

5 per cent in 1973 to 21 per cent in 1984, subsequently declined to under 8 per cent in 2003.

Historically the United Kingdom was predominantly an importer of foods and basic materials. Over the last 30 years, however, imports of manufactures have grown rapidly. Between 1973 and 2003 the share of finished manufactures rose from 32 per cent of total imports to 59 per cent. The United Kingdom has not recorded a surplus on manufactured goods since 1982. Basic materials fell from 12 per cent of total imports by value in 1973 to 3 per cent in 2003. Food, beverages and tobacco accounted for 19 per cent of imports in 1973, compared with 9 per cent in 2003. Intermediate goods, such as car parts, computer chips and semi-conductors, accounted for 20 per cent of exports and 17 per cent of imports in 2003.

Sectors with significant positive trade balances in 2003 included chemicals and crude oil, while those with large negative balances included consumer goods (including cars), food, beverages and tobacco, and capital goods (such as heavy engineering machinery). The deficit on trade in motor cars was over £7 billion.

Geographical breakdown of goods

UK trade in goods is mainly with other developed countries (Figure 24.6). In 2003, 84 per cent of UK

Figure 24.5 Trade in goods, 2003,[1] UK

£ billion

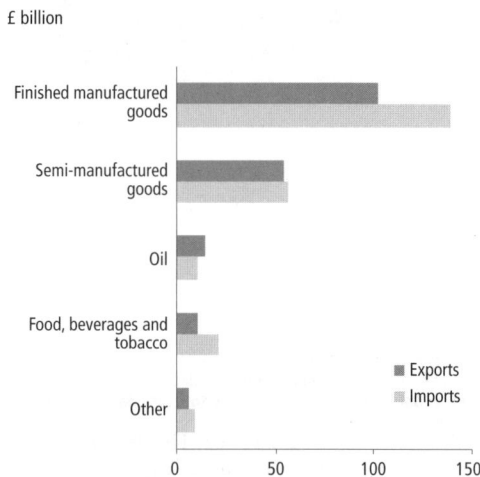

1 Balance of payments basis.
Source: *Balance of Payments*, Office for National Statistics

exports were to fellow member countries of the Organisation for Economic Co-operation and Development (OECD), and 80 per cent of imports came from these countries.

The United States remained the largest single UK export market in 2003, accounting for over 15 per cent of all exports. Germany remains the largest

Figure 24.6 Distribution of trade in goods, 2003,[1] UK

£ billion

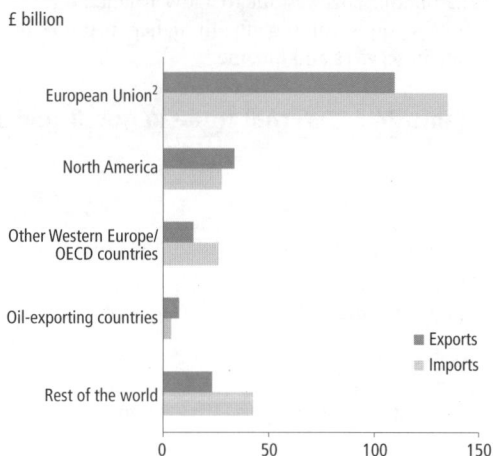

1 Balance of payments basis.
2 Data have been recalculated to reflect EU enlargement from 1 May 2004.
Source: *Balance of Payments*, Office for National Statistics

single supplier (Table 24.7). The majority of the main UK trading partners are EU Member States.

On 1 May 2004, ten countries joined the EU – Cyprus, the Czech Republic, Estonia, Hungary, Latvia, Lithuania, Malta, Poland, Slovakia and Slovenia. They accounted for exports worth £4.7 billion and imports worth £6.0 billion in 2003.

Table 24.7 Trade in goods – main export and import markets, 2003, UK[1]

	Value (£ million)	% share of UK trade in goods
Main export markets		
United States	29,005	15.4
Germany	20,656	11.0
France	18,747	10.0
Netherlands	13,502	7.2
Republic of Ireland	12,153	6.5
Belgium and Luxembourg	11,283	6.0
Italy	8,868	4.7
Spain	8,538	4.5
Sweden	3,800	2.0
Japan	3,710	2.0
Main import markets		
Germany	33,433	14.2
United States	22,820	9.7
France	20,105	8.6
Netherlands	16,561	7.0
Belgium and Luxembourg	13,056	5.6
Italy	11,399	4.8
Republic of Ireland	9,834	4.2
Spain	9,114	3.9
China	8,291	3.5
Japan	8,045	3.4

1 Balance of payments basis.
Source: *Balance of Payments*, Office for National Statistics

Trade in services

A surplus has been recorded for trade in services (see glossary) in every year since 1966. In 2003 the surplus declined to £14.6 billion from the record £15.6 billion reached in 2002. Exports of services rose by £2.5 billion in 2003, while imports increased by £3.5 billion. Business services accounted for over 30 per cent of exports in services. In percentage terms, the largest increases between 2002 and 2003 in both imports and exports were in the computer and information services sector (Table 24.8).

The travel sector recorded its largest ever deficit in 2003. In the early 1990s exports in this sector accounted for between 24 and 27 per cent of the total trade in services, compared with 16 per cent in 2003. Imports of travel services have increased by 2 or 3 percentage points over the same period, accounting for 40 per cent of trade in services in 2003. Increasing numbers of UK citizens travelling abroad, and a slow recovery in US visitors to the United Kingdom after the 11 September 2001 attacks, have contributed to this deficit.

Income and transfers

The surplus on the income account grew to a record £22.1 billion in 2003 from £21.5 billion in 2002. A sharply reduced deficit on the 'other investment' category more than offset a lower surplus on direct investment, which fell to £31.4 billion in 2003 from a record £33.8 billion in 2002.

Earnings on UK direct investment abroad increased to £55.7 billion in 2003. A strong rise in dividends received, which rose to a record £31.9 billion, more than offset a decline in reinvested earnings, which fell to £18.2 billion. Earnings on direct investment in the United Kingdom reached their highest level since 2000. Total earnings on equity rose to £17.4 billion in 2003, from £14.4 billion in 2002, while earnings on debt rose to £6.8 billion in 2003 from £4.5 billion in 2002.

The deficit on current transfers widened to £9.9 billion in 2003 from £8.6 billion in 2002.

Outward and inward investment

With an open economy, the United Kingdom has no restrictions on the outward flow of capital.

The continuing current account deficit was largely funded in 2003 by net inward investment in UK-issued debt securities. The attractiveness of UK debt to foreign investors may have reflected the higher sterling interest rates compared to dollar or euro-denominated issues.

Overall the financial account recorded net inflows of £17.5 billion in 2003 compared with £8.8 billion in 2002. Total UK net investment[1] abroad rose to

---

1 Comprises direct, portfolio and other investment. UK net investment abroad also includes financial derivatives (net) and reserve assets.

Table 24.8 Trade in services, ranked by exports, 2003, UK

	Value (£ million)			% change on 2002	
	Exports	Imports	Balance	Exports	Imports
Business services[1]	27,400	12,288	15,112	1.5	−3.1
Travel	13,928	29,740	−15,812	2.4	7.4
Financial services	13,417	3,481	9,936	−1.3	8.0
Transport	12,958	17,194	−4,236	10.4	3.4
Insurance	6,419	789	5,630	−3.0	4.1
Royalties and licence fees	6,055	4,516	1,539	4.6	−2.0
Computer and information services	4,268	1,779	2,489	22.5	48.7
Communications	1,957	1,898	59	−11.8	−7.0
Government	1,892	2,630	−738	19.9	38.6
Personal, cultural and recreational services	1,294	685	609	−7.8	−14.1
Construction	105	76	29	−46.2	−26.9
Total	**89,693**	**75,076**	**14,617**	**2.9**	**4.8**

1 Includes merchanting, operational leasing and consultancy services such as advertising, engineering and legal services.
Source: *Balance of Payments*, Office for National Statistics

£337 billion in 2003, from £121 billion in 2002, a position only exceeded in 2000. Net foreign investment in the United Kingdom rose to £354 billion in 2003 from £130 billion in 2002. Net direct investment abroad increased to £32.1 billion in 2003 from £24.4 billion in the previous year, while net direct investment in the United Kingdom fell from £19.3 billion to £9.8 billion. This latter figure is well below the peak achieved in 2000 but comparable to figures reported in the mid-1990s. Net portfolio investment abroad recovered strongly in 2003, amounting to £34.7 billion, following net investment of £1.0 billion in 2002. The UK stock of external liabilities amounted to £3,602 billion at the end of 2003 and its stock of assets abroad to £3,550 billion so that external liabilities amounted to £52 billion.

International direct investment

According to the United Nations Conference on Trade and Development *World Investment Report 2003*, the United Kingdom was ranked seventh at attracting inward investment in 2002 and fourth in its outward investment.

Recent inward investment announcements have included:

- Suzuki GB, the UK subsidiary of Japan's Suzuki Motor Corporation, is to develop a new national parts, training and technical centre at Milton Keynes, Buckinghamshire involving investment of over US$22 million;

- Hüco Lightronic, the UK subsidiary of Hüco electronic GmbH of Germany, opened a new 2,045 square metre manufacturing facility at Limavady, Northern Ireland; and

- leading US financial services firm Lehman Brothers opened its new European headquarters in Canary Wharf, London.

International trade policy

The Department of Trade and Industry (DTI) represents UK interests in international trade policy, working closely with EU partners and drawing on UK bilateral relations and membership of international organisations such as the World Trade Organisation.

A DTI White Paper on trade and investment, *Making Globalisation a Force for Good*, was published in July 2004. It deals with the questions of how globalisation can be controlled throughout the world, especially in developing countries, and how a world trading system can be fair as well as free.

European Union

The free movement of goods, people, services and capital is a fundamental principle of the EU. These four freedoms, set out in the Treaties of Rome, form the basis of the Single European Market (see page 69). A further ten countries joined the EU on

1 May 2004 (see page 381), boosting the size of the Single Market.

The EU Common Commercial Policy (CCP) establishes uniform principles covering trade between all Member States. These include changes in tariff rates, the conclusion of tariff and trade agreements with non-member countries, uniformity in trade liberalisation measures, export policy, and instruments to protect trade such as anti-dumping measures and subsidies.

Since 1993, the EU has formed a single territory – enlarged since May 2004 – without internal borders within which the free movement of goods is guaranteed. It applies a common external tariff to imports from third countries. However, the EU has also signed preferential trade agreements with a number of countries. These include:

- the European Economic Area (with Norway, Iceland and Liechtenstein);

- Association Agreements with the countries of central and eastern Europe (see page 75);

- agreements with the Mediterranean countries;

- bilateral agreements with South Africa, Mexico and Chile; and

- the Cotonou Agreement with the African, Caribbean and Pacific (ACP) countries.

In May 2003 the European Commission published the new Internal Market Strategy for 2003 to 2006 to make the internal market work better and build on the jobs and wealth that have been created since the free movement of goods within the EU took effect. The Strategy aims to take account of the effects of enlargement (see page 71) and of an ageing population, and aims for the EU to become the world's most competitive economy by 2010. Particular priorities include implementing the free movement of services, removing the remaining obstacles to trade in goods, and improving the regulatory framework.

In January 2004 the Commission issued a report on the implementation of the Internal Market Strategy. It found that too many European industries still operate in fragmented markets due to trade obstacles and differences in standards and regulations. It reported that only 27 of the 45 measures due to be implemented before the end of 2003 to improve the working of the Single Market had been delivered on time. Others were on the verge of being completed, but many of the

measures that had been delayed were important legislative initiatives.

EU initiatives for simplifying national and Community rules include SLIM (simpler legislation for the internal market) and the European Business Test Panel, which allows for consultation with business during the drafting stage of new legislation.

The SOLVIT dispute mechanism, which operates through a network of centres based in each Member State, aims to find an informal and speedy solution to problems arising from the misapplication of EU rules, without the need for legal action. Details are held on an online database system. In the United Kingdom, the DTI's Action Single Market/UK SOLVIT Centre acts not only as a contact point for UK business and citizens but also as a first port of call for similar centres in other Member States when single market problems arise.

World Trade Organisation (WTO)

The WTO was established in 1995 to succeed the General Agreement on Tariffs and Trade. Its main functions are to act as a forum for trade negotiations, administer trade agreements and handle disputes. The key principle is non-discrimination, ensuring that similar products from different countries must be treated in the same way. By April 2004 there were 147 member countries, with 29 negotiating to join. In November 2001, WTO members agreed an agenda – the Doha Development Agenda – to introduce a new round of trade negotiations. All members agreed to place developing country concerns at the heart of these negotiations. However, the Ministerial Conference in Cancun, Mexico, in September 2003, failed to agree negotiating frameworks for key issues such as agriculture. In August 2004 WTO members agreed a deal that made it more likely that trade liberalisation could be completed by the end of 2005. Key WTO members accepted proposals to cut the subsidies wealthy countries give their farmers for exports.

The WTO provides an arbitration service for countries involved in trade disputes through its dispute settlement system – ideally, the countries concerned should discuss their problems and settle any dispute mutually. The trade policy review mechanism within the WTO allows members to discuss an individual country's trade regime. By August 2004 the WTO had recorded 314 disputes.

Although the United Kingdom is a member of the WTO in its own right, for all practical purposes it works through membership of the EU, as required by the CCP (see page 383).

Developing countries

The DTI works closely with the Department for International Development and other government departments to ensure that developing countries participate in, and benefit from, the world trade system. Close collaboration between government departments, coordinated by the DTI, ensures consistency of approach.

The Generalised System of Preferences (GSP) exists to promote the better integration of developing countries into the world trading system. It aims to encourage them to increase exports by allowing their products preferential access to the markets of developed countries. The United Kingdom is party to the EC GSP, operated by all Member States. The European Commission is developing a new scheme which will operate from 2005.

The Cotonou Agreement, signed in June 2000 in Cotonou, Benin, replaced the Lomé Convention. This had provided a framework for trade, aid and political relations between the EU and the 77 ACP countries. Under the Cotonou Agreement, the ACPs have unrestricted access to the EU market for substantially all industrial goods and for a wide range of agricultural products. One of the Agreement's main objectives is the integration of ACP states into the global economy. The current preferential access for the ACP countries is incompatible with WTO rules and operates under a waiver, due to expire at the end of 2007. Negotiations for WTO-compliant Economic Partnership Arrangements with the ACP regions are under way and new agreements will come into force by 2008. They will progressively remove barriers to trade between the EU and ACP countries and will aim to put trade relations with the ACP countries on a secure and sustainable footing.

Controls on trade

Import controls

In addition to EU-wide restrictions, certain goods are prohibited from import into the United Kingdom or are restricted for reasons of health and safety, or to protect the environment.

> ### Freight movements in and out of the UK
>
> - UK airports handled 2.2 million tonnes of freight in 2003. The busiest airport was Heathrow, which handled 1.2 million tonnes.
>
> - UK ports handled 555 million tonnes of freight in 2003. Grimsby and Immingham was the busiest port, handling 56 million tonnes.
>
> - In 2003, 1.3 million trucks passed through the Channel Tunnel.

Prohibited goods include unlicensed drugs; offensive weapons; indecent and obscene material; counterfeit and pirated goods and goods that infringe patents; and meat, milk and their products from outside the EU (with some exceptions).

Restricted goods, which cannot be imported without authority such as a licence, include firearms, explosives and ammunition; animals outside the Pet Travel Scheme (see page 415); live birds; endangered species and derived products (under the CITES Convention, see page 284); certain plants and their produce; and radio transmitters not approved for use in the United Kingdom.

The DTI's Import Licensing Branch (ILB) is responsible for issuing import licences in accordance with UK and EC law. In 2003/04 it issued 338,000 licences.

Export controls

Governments control the export of goods and technology for a variety of reasons. Licences for goods subject to strategic export control are issued by the DTI acting through its Export Control Organisation (ECO). These controls apply to a wide range of goods, components and spare parts, and technology, including:

- military equipment such as arms, ammunition, bombs, tanks, imaging devices, military aircraft and warships;
- nuclear-related items including nuclear materials, nuclear reactors and processing plant;

30 April 2004 The Annual Report of the Marine Conservation Society reveals that Northern Ireland has the lowest level of litter on beaches in the United Kingdom. Pictured is Portrush East Strand in County Londonderry, one of ENCAMS Blue Flag Beaches.

© MARK HARTWELL, EHS

2 May 2004 Nicola Benedetti, a 16-year-old violinist from Ayrshire, Scotland, wins the 26th BBC Young Musician of the Year award with a performance of Szymanowski's Violin Concerto No 1.

6 May 2004 50th anniversary of Roger Bannister, then a 25-year-old medical student, breaking the 4-minute mile.

© BBC PHOTO LIBRARY

© MARY EVANS PICTURE LIBRARY

11 May 2004 The Scottish National Gallery of Modern Art wins the £100,000 Gulbenkian Museum of the Year prize for its *Landform* landscape structure designed by Charles Jencks.

17 May 2004 Michael Landy's life-sized reproduction of his childhood home, entitled *Semi-Detached, 2004,* goes on show at Tate Britain.

24–25 May 2004 Firefighters check the area after extinguishing a fire at a warehouse in East London owned by Momart, one of the leading UK art handlers and storers. Works destroyed in the blaze include Patrick Heron's *Vertical Light* and Tracey Emin's *Tent, Everyone I Have Ever Slept With*.

26 May 2004 An exhibition of art installations by contemporary fashion designers including Paul Smith, Zandra Rhodes and Alexander McQueen opens in the 14th century castle and grounds of Belsay Hall, Northumberland. Pictured is Stella McCartney with her crystal chandelier in the form of a leaping horse, made from more than 3,000 crystal spheres, suspended from the rafters of the Great Hall.

26 May 2004 Daniel Radcliffe, the actor who plays Harry Potter, faces the photographers at the UK premiere of *Harry Potter And The Prisoner of Azkaban* at the Odeon Leicester Square. This is the third film from author JK Rowling's series of books on the boy wizard.

6 June 2004 World leaders and thousands of veterans gather to commemorate the 60th anniversary of D-Day in Normandy, when allied troops landed in France to start the successful liberation of Europe.

(Top) UK veterans watch a parachute drop over Normandy ahead of the D-Day anniversary.

(Left) A Canadian veteran on Juno beach.

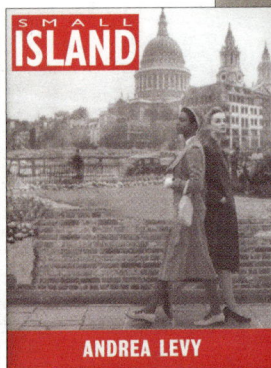

8 June 2004 Andrea Levy wins the 2004 Orange Prize for Fiction for her fourth book *Small Island*. Set in 1948, *Small Island* captures the lives of a Jamaican couple in post-war London.

- dual-use items – goods designed for civil use but which can be used for military purposes;

- chemical weapons precursors, and related equipment and technology;

- certain micro-organisms, biological equipment and technology; and

- goods used in programmes involved in weapons of mass destruction and missiles used for their delivery.

The ECO also issues licences for the export or supply of goods and certain activities subject to control as a result of the imposition of UN trade sanctions or a UN embargo against particular countries or regions.

The *Export Control Act 2002* (ECA) sets out a new legislative framework for the control of strategic goods and technology, and provides for a more transparent framework and increased parliamentary accountability. The ECA came into force in May 2004. Exports subject to control under legislation other than that administered by the ECO include: certain live animals and protected species of wildlife and flowers (under CITES); antiques and works of art; and drug precursors.

Government services

The Government provides a wide range of advice and practical support to meet the needs of overseas inward investors and exporters. UK Trade & Investment is responsible for trade development and inward investment. The Export Credits Guarantee Department (ECGD) helps UK exporters win business and helps firms to invest overseas.

UK Trade & Investment

UK Trade & Investment is the government organisation that supports both UK companies trading internationally and overseas enterprises seeking to locate in the United Kingdom. The organisation's staff work throughout the English regions, London, Glasgow and in embassies and diplomatic missions across the world. It seeks to help businesses exporting for the first time and those experienced in international trade who wish to expand into new markets, by providing expert advice, reliable data, and professional research.

UK Trade & Investment also works closely with the English Regional Development Agencies and the national development agencies in Wales, Scotland and Northern Ireland, in order to assist businesses seeking to set up or expand in the United Kingdom. Information is provided in a single package containing details of locations, financial incentives, product sectors, availability of labour, employee costs, skills and tax. UK Trade & Investment can also help companies find suppliers, deal with utilities and planning regulations, and advise on immigration, staff recruitment and training, financial incentives, site issues, regulatory issues and links with centres of excellence such as universities.

Figures for 2003/04 on inward investment decisions notified to UK Trade & Investment by its national and regional development agency partners, and new jobs expected to be created, are shown in Table 24.9. New investments accounted for 42 per cent of these projects and expansions for a further 35 per cent. Investment in industries linked to the knowledge-driven economy – computer software, IT, Internet, e-commerce, electronics and telecommunications sectors – formed the largest category of inward investment, with 243 projects (30 per cent). Other major sectors for UK inward investment were pharmaceuticals and biotechnology, management, the automotive sector, and food and drink.

Table 24.9 Top ten UK Trade & Investment inward investment decisions notified, 2003/04

Country	Projects	% of total	New jobs[1]
United States	314	39	10,668
France	54	7	1,318
Japan	52	6	2,344
Canada	51	6	562
Germany	49	6	2,876
Republic of Ireland	30	4	1,126
Norway	30	4	314
India	28	3	646
Sweden	24	3	417
China	23	3	324
Rest of EU	69	9	2,462
Rest of world	87	11	2,406
Total	**811**	*100*	**25,463**

1 Jobs expected to be created.
Source: UK Trade & Investment

Export Credits Guarantee Department (ECGD)

ECGD is the official UK export credit agency. Its role is to help UK manufacturers and investors trade overseas by providing them with insurance and/or backing for finance to protect against non-payment. It complements the insurance that is available from the private sector. ECGD insurance is available both for UK exporters of goods and services, and investors in overseas projects. The largest part of its operation involves underwriting finance packages to support the sale of capital goods, such as aircraft, machinery and services, and to help UK companies take part in overseas projects such as hospitals, airports and power stations.

Including overseas investment insurance and reinsurance, the total business supported by ECGD in 2003/04 was £2,991 million.

ECGD's main civil business in 2003/04 was in the water and power generation and transmission

Table 24.10 Top ten markets for ECGD guarantees, 2003/04

	Value (£ million)	% share of total market
Saudi Arabia	1,026	34.3
United States	184	6.1
Chile	180	6.0
Bahrain	158	5.3
South Africa	141	4.7
Turkey	101	3.4
Indonesia	89	3.0
Mexico	84	2.8
Philippines	83	2.8
Azerbaijan	82	2.7
Sub-total	2,126	71.1
World	2,991	100

Source: ECGD

sectors, accounting for 46 per cent of all such business.

Further reading

Export Credits Guarantee Department. Annual Review and Resource Accounts 2003/04. The Stationery Office, 2004.

Liberalisation and globalisation, maximising the benefits of international trade and investment. Economics Paper No. 10. Department of Trade and Industry, 2004.

Making Globalisation a Force for Good. Cm 6278. The Stationery Office, 2004.

Trade and Industry. Departmental Report 2004. Cm 6216. The Stationery Office, 2004.

Trade and the global economy, the role of international trade in productivity, economic reform and growth. HM Treasury and Department of Trade and Industry, 2004.

United Kingdom Balance of Payments – the Pink Book (annual publication). Office for National Statistics. The Stationery Office.

UK Trade & Investment. Departmental Report 2004. Cm 6215. The Stationery Office, 2004.

Websites

National Statistics
www.statistics.gov.uk

Department of Trade and Industry
www.dti.gov.uk

HM Customs and Excise
www.hmce.gov.uk

WWW.

25 Science, engineering and technology

The United Kingdom has been at the forefront of many world-class advances in science, engineering and technology. Notable areas of UK achievement include aerospace, biomedicine, biotechnology, chemicals, electronics and materials. Achievements by UK scientists in the last 30 years include the development of in-vitro fertilisation (1978) and DNA fingerprinting (1985); the invention of the World Wide Web address system and layout (1990); the birth of the world's first cloned mammal (1996); and the UK contribution to the human genome project (completed in 2003).

Research and development expenditure

Gross domestic expenditure in the United Kingdom on research and development (R&D) in 2002 was £19.6 billion, or 1.9 per cent of gross domestic product (GDP, see glossary). Of this, £17.6 billion was on civil R&D, with the rest going to defence projects. In real terms, gross domestic expenditure on R&D increased by 3 per cent between 2001 and 2002.

Business enterprise is the largest source of funding, providing 47 per cent of expenditure in 2002 (see Figure 25.1). Contract research organisations often carry out R&D for companies and are playing an increasingly important role in the transfer of technology to UK industry. Business enterprise also supports university research and finances contract research at government establishments. Some charities have their own laboratories as well as offering grants for research.

Nobel Prizes for UK scientists

In October 2003, Sir Peter Mansfield was awarded the Nobel Prize in Physiology or Medicine, sharing the award with the US scientist Paul C. Lauterbur, for their discoveries concerning magnetic resonance imaging (MRI – see page 395).

Anthony J. Leggett of the United Kingdom and the United States was awarded the Nobel Prize in Physics, sharing the 2003 Prize with Alexei A. Abrikosov (United States and Russia) and Vitaly L. Ginzburg (Russia), for pioneering contributions to the theory of superconductors and superfluids. Superconducting material is used, for example, in MRI for medical examinations and in particle accelerators in physics. Knowledge about superfluid liquids gives an insight into the ways in which matter behaves in its lowest and most ordered state.

UK economist Clive W.J. Granger shared the 2003 Nobel Prize in Economic Sciences with US economist Robert F. Engle. He demonstrated that statistical methods used for stationary time series could give wholly misleading results when applied to the analysis of non-stationary data. His significant discovery was cointegration – that specific combinations of non-stationary time series may exhibit 'stationarity' thereby allowing for correct statistical inference.

Figure 25.1 Gross domestic expenditure on R&D, 2002, UK

Total: £19.6 billion

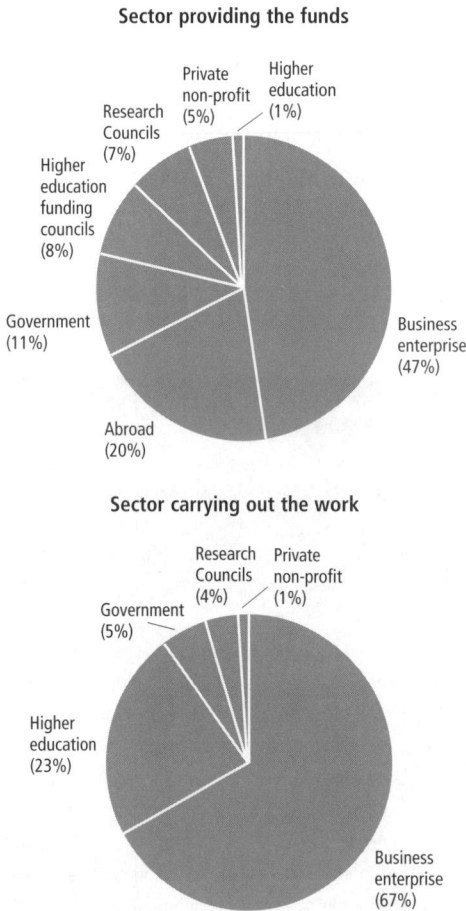

Sector providing the funds

Private non-profit (5%)
Higher education (1%)
Research Councils (7%)
Higher education funding councils (8%)
Government (11%)
Abroad (20%)
Business enterprise (47%)

Sector carrying out the work

Research Councils (4%)
Private non-profit (1%)
Government (5%)
Higher education (23%)
Business enterprise (67%)

Source: Office for National Statistics

Business enterprise carried out work worth some £13.1 billion in 2002, an increase of 3 per cent on 2001 in real terms. Business enterprises' own funds accounted for 66 per cent of this work, with 27 per cent coming from overseas, and most of the remaining 7 per cent from government.

Government role

The Secretary of State for Trade and Industry, assisted by the Minister for Science, has overall responsibility for science, engineering and technology (SET). They are supported by the Office of Science and Technology (OST), part of the Department of Trade and Industry (DTI, see

The R&D scoreboard is an international benchmarking tool for investment in R&D. The scoreboard contains details of investment, sales, profits and employee numbers for 700 UK-based companies (39 from the FTSE 100, see page 470) and 700 international companies. The 2003 scoreboard showed UK-based companies with R&D investments totalling £16 billion, and the international companies with R&D investments totalling £207 billion.

The 2003 scoreboard suggests that the challenges facing the United Kingdom are to:

- maintain its leading position in pharmaceuticals, biotechnology, health, aerospace and defence;
- increase R&D investment as a percentage of sales in other sectors; and
- encourage medium-sized companies (those with an annual turnover of up to £500 million) in all sectors, but particularly high R&D sectors, to increase their R&D investment.

pages 389 and 390). The Ministerial Committee on Science Policy provides the framework for the collective consideration of, and decisions on, major science policy issues.

The OST, headed by the Government's Chief Scientific Adviser, is responsible for policy on SET, both nationally and internationally, and coordinates science and technology policy across government departments. The Chief Scientific Adviser also reports directly to the Prime Minister.

An independent Council for Science and Technology advises the Prime Minister and the First Ministers of Scotland and Wales on the strategic policies and framework for science and technology in the United Kingdom. Its members are drawn from academia, business and charitable foundations and institutions.

Strategy and finance

The DTI/OST publication *The Forward Look 2003: Government-funded science, engineering and technology* sets out government spending on science, engineering and technology for 2002–05. *Forward Look* contains reports and financial data from departments, Research Councils, learned bodies and the devolved administrations.

The science and engineering base is mainly financed through two funding streams, known as the Dual Support system. One stream is provided by the education departments through their higher education funding councils. The other is provided by the DTI/OST through the Research Councils, which award programme and project grants for specific research programmes, both to universities and to their own institutions. The OST is examining ways to implement changes to the Dual Support system recommended by the review of science and research.

Planned total government expenditure on SET in 2004/05 (both civil and defence and including the science budget) is £9.3 billion (Figure 25.2).

Figure 25.2 Planned net government expenditure on SET, 2004/05, UK

Total: £9.3 billion

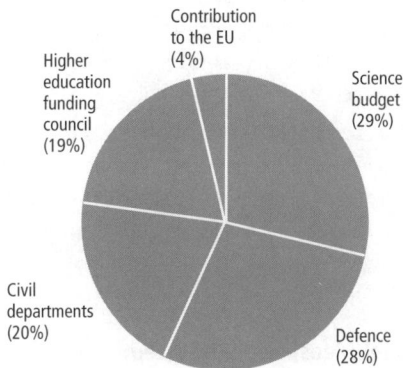

Higher education funding council (19%)
Contribution to the EU (4%)
Science budget (29%)
Civil departments (20%)
Defence (28%)

Source: Office for National Statistics

Departmental responsibilities

Office of Science and Technology

The OST, through the Director General of Research Councils, has responsibility for the allocation of the UK science budget and for the

Science and innovation investment framework

As part of the 2004 Spending Review (see page 368), the Government published the *Science and innovation investment framework 2004–14*. It envisages an annual real growth in public science funding for R&D of 5.8 per cent. Total science funding will rise by £1 billion in real terms between 2004/05 and 2007/08 to nearly £5 billion. The Framework plan is for R&D as a proportion of GDP to increase from 1.9 per cent to 2.5 per cent over ten years.

The Framework aims to:

- maintain or improve the ranking of the United Kingdom against the United States and the rest of the OECD, and build world-class centres of research;

- improve the responsiveness of the publicly funded research base to the needs of the economy and public services;

- increase business investment in R&D from 1.2 per cent of GDP to 1.7 per cent over the next decade;

- ensure a strong supply of scientists, engineers and technologists;

- achieve sustainable levels of research activity and investment in universities and public laboratories; and

- increase confidence in and awareness of scientific research and its applications.

government-financed Research Councils (see pages 393–96). Through the Research Councils, the science budget supports research by:

- awarding research grants to universities, other higher education establishments and some other research units;

- funding Research Council establishments to carry out research or provide facilities;

- paying subscriptions to international scientific facilities and organisations; and

- supporting postgraduate research students and postdoctoral fellows.

Foresight programme

The Government's Foresight programme encourages the public and private sectors to work together to identify opportunities in markets and technologies likely to emerge over the next 10 to 20 years. The programme is coordinated by a joint industry/academic steering group, headed by the Chief Scientific Adviser.

Foresight operates through a rolling programme that looks at three or four areas at any one time. The starting point for a project area is either a key issue where science holds the promise of solutions, or an area of science where the potential applications and technologies have yet to be considered and articulated.

Projects in the latest Foresight programme are being carried out in the following areas: flood and coastal defence; cyber trust (relating to computers and the Internet) and crime prevention; exploiting the electromagnetic spectrum; and brain science and drugs. The project on cognitive systems was concluded in November 2003.

The science budget also funds programmes of support to the science and engineering base through the Royal Society (see page 402) and the Royal Academy of Engineering (see page 403). The other main sources of funds for universities are the higher education funding councils (see page 396).

Department of Trade and Industry

In 2004/05, the DTI's planned expenditure (excluding the OST) on SET is £376 million. This expenditure covers innovation and technology for a number of industrial sectors, including aeronautics, biotechnology, chemicals, communications, engineering, environmental technology, IT, space, and nuclear and non-nuclear energy.

Funding for innovation may include the development, design and financing of new products, services and processes, exploitation of new markets, creation of new businesses and associated changes in the management of people and in organisational practices. Through its Innovation Unit, a mixed team of business secondees and government officials, the DTI seeks to promote a culture of innovation in all sectors of the economy.

Technology and knowledge transfer

The DTI is involved in a number of programmes to increase collaboration and the flow of knowledge between the science and engineering base and businesses, including:

- LINK (*www.ost.gov.uk/link*), which promotes partnership in pre-commercial research between companies and the research base. Government departments and Research Councils fund up to 50 per cent of the cost of research projects, with companies providing the balance;

- the International Technology Service (*www.globalwatchonline.com*), which helps UK companies to benefit from technological expertise around the world;

- Knowledge Transfer Partnerships (managed by the Small Business Service – see page 355) that facilitate technology and knowledge transfer between businesses and universities, colleges or research organisations; and

- a network of 24 Faraday Partnerships that aim to improve co-operation between the science, engineering and technology base and industry in the exploitation of SET in the United Kingdom.

National Measurement System

The DTI is responsible for the National Measurement System (NMS), which funds science and technology programmes in measurement science, including materials metrology. In 2004/05 DTI expects to invest nearly £70 million in the NMS.

Measurement standards and calibration facilities provided by the NMS enable businesses and public authorities to make accurate measurements that are nationally and internationally accepted. Most of the work is carried out at the National Physical

Laboratory, LGC (formerly the Laboratory of the Government Chemist), NEL (formerly the National Engineering Laboratory) and the National Weights and Measures Laboratory.

British Standards Institution

The DTI works closely with the British Standards Institution (BSI), the national standards body that is independent of the Government, to promote UK trade and technology interests. DTI support for BSI is directed towards European and international standards, which account for over 90 per cent of the Institution's work. It also provides support for the United Kingdom Accreditation Service (UKAS), the sole national body recognised by the Government to accredit organisations that test, calibrate, inspect and certify against standards. The DTI contribution to BSI and UKAS was £6.5 million in 2003/04.

Intellectual property

The Patent Office, an executive agency of the DTI, is responsible for granting patents and registering designs and trade marks. In 2002 it received almost 30,000 applications for patents and over 60,000 applications for trade marks.

The Patent Office works towards the worldwide harmonisation of rules and procedures, and the modernisation and simplification of intellectual property law. International patenting arrangements include the European Patent Convention and the Patent Co-operation Treaty. For trade marks the European Community Trade Mark System and the Madrid Protocol provide a way to acquire rights beyond UK borders. The Patent Office Central Enquiry Unit and its website (*www.patent.gov.uk*) offer detailed information about intellectual property rights. To raise awareness of the value and importance of intellectual property throughout the United Kingdom, the Patent Office runs seminars and workshops for business advisers, small and medium enterprises and academics.

Ministry of Defence

Planned net expenditure by the Ministry of Defence (MoD) on R&D in 2004/05 is around £2.6 billion. The MoD invests about £450 million a year in research, managed by the Chief Scientific Adviser, to ensure that UK Armed Forces stay ahead of threats from potential adversaries. The MoD has a research budget and an equipment

procurement budget (see chapter 8). MoD research is principally carried out by two organisations: the Defence Science and Technology Laboratory (Dstl) and QinetiQ plc, although a growing amount of research is being let by competitive tendering. Dstl is government-owned and carries out research in key areas that must be conducted within government. It provides a high-level overview of defence science and technology, acts as an in-house source of impartial advice and manages international research collaboration.

A third of QinetiQ was sold to the Carlyle Group in 2002. The MoD plans to sell its entire stake in QinetiQ before 2008.

Department of Health

The Department of Health (DH) supports R&D to inform policy and practice in public health, healthcare and social care. This includes:

- National Health Service (NHS) R&D funding, which supports projects funded by other non-commercial R&D sources (including charities) carried out in the NHS, and also specific health and social care projects meeting the identified research needs of the DH and the NHS;
- a Policy Research Programme (PRP), directly commissioned by the DH; and
- ad hoc project funding from other DH R&D budgets and support for non-departmental public bodies (NDPBs).

The DH expects to spend some £611 million on research in 2004/05: £549 million on NHS R&D, £32 million on the PRP and about £30 million involving the NDPBs and ad hoc budgets.

Home Office

Some scientific and medical research, as well as the regulatory safety and efficacy testing of new drugs and other substances, involves the use of live animals. In Great Britain this is regulated through a licensing system administered by the Home Office under the *Animals (Scientific Procedures) Act 1986*, and in Northern Ireland the system is regulated by the Department of Health, Social Services and Public Safety, under the same Act. Animals may only be used for specified permitted purposes, when the benefits are judged likely, on expert assessment, to outweigh the cost to their welfare. There also has to be full application of the '3Rs':

- replacement of animals with non-animal alternatives whenever practicable;
- where animals have to be used, reducing their number to the minimum; and
- refinement of the procedures to minimise their suffering.

Prescribed standards of animal housing and care also have to be maintained in the establishments concerned.

In 2003, 2.9 million procedures were performed, mostly on mice and other rodents. Breeding of genetically modified animals is also regulated, and is included in the above figure, accounting for about a quarter of the total. The number of regulated procedures is lower than in 1987 (when the current legislation was introduced), when 3.6 million procedures were performed.

Scottish Executive

The Scottish Higher Education Funding Council disburses the majority of the Scottish Executive's support for the science base. This amounts to some £212 million for 2004/05 – £161 million for research and £51 million to support the strategic development of the sector. The Executive is also spending about £169 million directly on research in agriculture and fisheries, health, and the biological, environmental, economic and social sciences. A large proportion of this goes to the Scottish Agricultural and Biological Research Institutes, the Fisheries Research Service and the Scottish Agricultural College. In addition, the UK Research Councils contribute around £210 million to Scottish research institutions.

The Executive has established an independent Scottish Science Advisory Committee to advise it on strategic science matters.

Northern Ireland

In Northern Ireland the Support Programme for University Research (SPUR) is a public-private partnership that invests in the research infrastructure. The first phase, SPUR 1, is investing some £44 million over the period 2001/02 to 2004/05. The second phase, SPUR 2, will invest £50 million between 2003 and 2007. About two-thirds of the programme expenditure is for science-related projects.

Invest NI has a similar role to that of DTI's Innovation Unit, supporting industrial R&D, technology transfer and innovation.

Space activities

The UK civil space industry has an estimated workforce of around 6,000 people. The civil space programme is brought together through the British National Space Centre (BNSC), a partnership of government departments and the Research Councils. BNSC's policy and aims were set out in *Space Strategy 2003–2006 and beyond*. It gives UK space activity three objectives:

- to enhance UK standing in astronomy, planetary and environmental sciences;
- to stimulate increased productivity by promoting the use of space in government, science and commerce; and
- to develop innovative space technologies and systems to deliver sustainable improvement in the quality of life.

Galileo

The United Kingdom has taken a leading role in the development of Galileo, the joint European Union (EU)/European Space Agency programme to develop and operate its own civil satellite system for navigation, positioning and timing applications. It will offer long-term improvements to traffic management systems for all forms of transport and in commercial, industrial and other strategic areas. The first experimental satellite is due to be launched in 2005.

Through BNSC, the Government spends around £190 million a year on space activities. Nearly 60 per cent of this is channelled through the European Space Agency (ESA) for collaborative programmes such as Earth observation, telecommunications, and space science. Much of this expenditure returns to the United Kingdom through contracts awarded to UK industry. The remainder of the space budget is spent on international meteorological programmes carried out through the European Meteorological Satellite Organisation (EUMETSAT); developing experiments for ESA satellites; and on the national programme, which is aimed at complementing R&D supported through ESA. Almost half of the UK space programme is concerned with satellite-based Earth observation (remote sensing) for commercial and environmental applications.

The United Kingdom is a major contributor to ESA's Earth observation satellite, ENVISAT, launched in 2002. This carries a new generation of radar and radiometer systems as well as other scientific environmental instruments, some of which were either designed or constructed in the United Kingdom. A third of the UK space budget is devoted to space science led by the Particle Physics and Astronomy Research Council (see page 396), in support of astronomy, planetary science and geophysics. The United Kingdom is contributing substantially to the SOHO mission to study the Sun; to the Cluster mission launched in 2000 to study solar-terrestrial relationships; to the Infrared Space Observatory, which is investigating the birth and death of stars; and to the Cassini Huygens Mission (see page 396) to send a probe to Saturn and its moon Titan, launched in 1997.

The United Kingdom is also participating in XMM, ESA's X-ray spectroscopy mission to investigate X-ray emissions from black holes, and ESA's SMART-1 Mission (Small Missions in Advanced Research Technology). This is the first European spacecraft to travel to and orbit the Moon. *Beagle 2*, the space lander designed and built in the United Kingdom to look for life on Mars, successfully detached from the ESA's Mars Express spacecraft in December 2003. However, it failed to make contact and was presumed lost or damaged. The instruments developed for *Beagle* were especially light and efficient and could be developed for future missions.

Research Councils

The UK Research Councils are independent public bodies responsible to the OST (see page 389). They are funded largely through the Government Science Vote,[1] and have a total budget of

£2.4 billion in 2004/05. There are seven Research Councils in the United Kingdom, each with members of its governing council drawn from universities, the professions, industry and government. The Councils support research, study and postgraduate training in universities and other higher education institutions. They also carry out or support research, through their own institutes and at international research centres, often jointly with other public sector bodies and international organisations. They provide awards to about 15,000 postgraduate students in science, social sciences, engineering and technology.

The Research Councils have a range of initiatives to encourage academics to commercialise their findings, to work with industry and to enhance the entrepreneurial culture in the UK research base. They also work with the public, promoting awareness and listening to their views on issues where research plays a part. The Arts and Humanities Research Board (AHRB, see below) will become the eighth Research Council in 2005.

Research Councils UK

Research Councils UK (RCUK) is the strategic partnership of the seven UK Research Councils and the AHRB. The partnership aims to:

- create a common framework for research, training and knowledge transfer;
- provide a single focus for dialogue with organisations involved with research;
- channel independent scientific advice from the Research Councils to the Government;
- promote collaboration to deliver scientific and strategic goals; and
- harmonise procedures to give organisations involved with research a more efficient service.

Arts and Humanities Research Board

The AHRB supports research in the arts and humanities, from archaeology and English literature to design and dance. It funds research and postgraduate study within the United Kingdom's higher education institutions and provides funding for museums, galleries and collections that are based in or attached to higher education institutions in England. An Arts and Humanities Research Council will be established in 2005.

---

1 The Director General of Research Councils, located in the OST, has overall responsibility for advising ministers on the resources needed by the Research Councils, the Royal Society and the Royal Academy of Engineering (the Science Vote).

Biotechnology and Biological Sciences Research Council (BBSRC)

BBSRC is the principal UK public funding agency for basic and strategic research in non-clinical biosciences. The scientific themes of its research committees are biomolecular sciences; genes and developmental biology; biochemistry and cell biology; plant and microbial sciences; animal sciences; agri-food; and engineering and biological systems. As well as funding research in universities and other research centres, BBSRC sponsors eight research institutes.

Integrative systems biology

BBSRC funds a number of projects in which disciplines are coming together to provide predictive approaches to bioscience research, for example understanding the spread of disease and epidemiology, identifying gene and protein functions, and modelling whole cell behaviour.

BBSRC has provisionally allocated up to £15 million a year to establish new Centres for Integrative Systems Biology. These will bring together biological experimentation, insight from the physical sciences and the power of modern computational and mathematical science.

Council for the Central Laboratory of the Research Councils (CCLRC)

The CCLRC has two functions: it works with the other Research Councils to provide access to large scale experimental facilities and it advises the Government on future large scale facilities so that the United Kingdom can maintain its place at the forefront of SET. It is responsible for the Rutherford Appleton Laboratory in Oxfordshire, the Daresbury Laboratory in Cheshire and the Chilbolton Observatory in Hampshire.

The CCLRC's large scale facilities include ISIS, the world's brightest pulsed neutron and muon source, which is used to study the atomic structure of materials; the Central Laser Facility, which enables research into fundamental and applied science and engineering; and the synchrotron radiation source, the brightest UK source of ultraviolet light and X-rays, which is used for

materials and life science. Other areas of specialism include particle physics, e-science, high capability computing, space science, instrumentation, atmospheric and radio research, and accelerator science. Commercial applications for CCLRC science are actively exploited through its own knowledge transfer company, CLIK.

On behalf of the Government, the CCLRC is also the main shareholder in Diamond Light Source Limited, the largest science facility to be built in the United Kingdom for more than 30 years, which is due to start operations in 2007. Diamond will produce pinpoint ultra-violet and X-ray beams of exceptional brightness, that will enable scientists and engineers to probe deep into the basic structure of matter.

Upgrading Astra

Following a £3 million grant in March 2004, the CCLRC's Astra laser will be upgraded to a unique dual-beam laser. Each of the two beams in the new laser will deliver a 0.5 petawatt (10^{15} W) pulse as short as 30 femtoseconds (10^{-15} s) every few minutes. Each focused beam will attain an intensity of 10^{22} Wcm^{-2}. Astra can already generate temperatures and pressures matched by those found inside the Sun. Increasing the intensity by three orders of magnitude is expected to have considerable impact in the field of astrophysics. Nuclear physics researchers will also be able to investigate and modify nuclear processes in an unprecedented manner as the electric field of the laser radiation will be sufficiently high to perturb the energy levels of an atomic nucleus. The upgrade is expected to take three years.

Economic and Social Research Council

The Economic and Social Research Council (ESRC) supports basic, strategic and applied research and related postgraduate training in the social sciences. Research funded by the ESRC is conducted in higher education institutions or independent research establishments. It aims to focus economic and social research on scientific and national priorities; enhance the capacity for

Centre on Migration, Policy and Society (COMPAS)

COMPAS, launched in October 2003, provides data and analysis on issues ranging from labour migration to asylum seekers and political refugees. One of the Centre's aims is to work closely with immigrant groups. The £3.4 million Centre has begun work on five major research programmes, all of which aim to have a significant impact on not only policymakers, but migrants and asylum seekers themselves.

the highest quality in social science research; and increase the impact of research on policy and practice.

Engineering and Physical Sciences Research Council (EPSRC)

EPSRC invests in basic, strategic and applied research and related postgraduate training to help the United Kingdom meet the next generation of technological change. Its remit includes areas such as mathematics, materials science, information technology and structural engineering. It also promotes public awareness of science and engineering and manages programmes in basic technology and e-science on behalf of all the Research Councils.

Fusion

EPSRC awarded £48 million towards research into fusion during 2003/04. Fusion involves forcing atoms together to make heavier atoms, a process which is accompanied by the release of large amounts of energy: one kilogram of fusion fuel produces the same amount of energy as 10,000 tonnes of coal. The grant, awarded to the UK Atomic Energy Authority, will underpin UK involvement in JET, the Joint European Torus – the largest tokamak reactor in the world. It will also enable development of a UK fusion device, MAST (Mega-Amp Spherical Tokamak) and a major expansion of research on materials.

Medical Research Council (MRC)

The Medical Research Council, see also chapter 13, page 199) is the main source of public funds for biomedical, health services and related research and training aimed at maintaining and improving public health. The Council has three major institutes: the National Institute for Medical Research, the Laboratory of Molecular Biology and the Clinical Sciences Centre. There are also 26 smaller MRC Units, an MRC Health Services Research Collaboration based in the Department of Social Medicine in Bristol University and involving groups in seven other universities, and seven grant-funded centres. Most of these are attached to higher education institutions or hospitals throughout the United Kingdom. The MRC also has laboratories overseas in The Gambia and Uganda.

About half of the MRC's research expenditure is allocated to its own institutes and units, with the rest going mainly on grant support and research training awards to teams and individuals in higher education institutions. The Council works closely with the health departments, major charities, industry and international collaborators.

Magnetic resonance imaging

Sir Peter Mansfield (see page 387) was funded for more than 20 years by the MRC. His work was instrumental in harnessing the natural phenomenon of magnetic resonance for clinical use. MRI scanning produces exact images of internal organs without using invasive techniques and is widely regarded as one of the most important diagnostic advances of the 20th century. MRI scans are now routinely used in thousands of hospitals worldwide to monitor injury and disease, and the technique and its offshoot, functional MRI, are helping scientists to gain their first real understanding of how the human brain works.

Natural Environment Research Council (NERC)

NERC funds and carries out scientific research in the environmental sciences. A strategy document,

Science for a sustainable future 2002–2007, identified priority areas for NERC, including:

- Earth life-support systems – water, biogeochemical cycles and biodiversity;
- predicting and mitigating the effects of climate change; and
- sustainable economies – identifying and providing sustainable solutions to the challenges associated with energy, land use and the effects of natural hazards.

NERC provides training for the next generation of environmental scientists. It also provides a range of facilities for use by the wider environmental science community, including a marine research fleet. Its wholly owned research centres are the British Geological Survey, the British Antarctic Survey, the Centre for Ecology and Hydrology, and the Proudman Oceanographic Laboratory. NERC also supports 15 collaborative centres in UK universities.

European Ice Core Project in Antarctica (EPICA)

An international project involving scientists from the British Antarctic Survey has shown how temperature changed in the past and how the concentrations of gases and particles in the atmosphere varied. The first results confirm that over the last 740,000 years the Earth experienced eight ice ages, when its climate was much colder than today, and eight warmer periods (interglacials). By comparing the pattern of this past climate with global environmental conditions today, the scientists conclude that, without human influence, the present warm period could last at least another 15,000 years.

Particle Physics and Astronomy Research Council (PPARC)

PPARC directs, coordinates and funds research, education and postgraduate training in four broad areas of science – particle physics, astronomy, cosmology and space science.

PPARC provides researchers with access to world-class facilities and funds UK membership of international bodies such as the European Organisation for Nuclear Research (CERN), ESA

and the European Southern Observatory (ESO). PPARC directly manages three scientific establishments in support of its ground-based astronomy programme: the UK Astronomy Technology Centre at the Royal Observatory, Edinburgh; the Isaac Newton Group of telescopes on La Palma in the Canary Islands; and the Joint Astronomy Centre in Hawaii. It also contributes money for the UK involvement in telescopes in Australia, Hawaii and Chile as well as the MERLIN/VLBI National Facility – an array of radio telescopes distributed around Great Britain.

PPARC operates a comprehensive support programme to industry to encourage knowledge transfer and exploitation of the novel technologies developed for its science programme. Its developing e-science programme, designed to handle the massive data requirements of new facilities, is expected to have applications extending far beyond particle physics.

Cassini Huygens mission

UK scientists funded by PPARC are providing critical instrumentation for the joint NASA/ESA Cassini Huygens mission, which successfully entered Saturn's orbit on 1 July 2004, having travelled 2 billion miles during its seven-year journey to the ringed planet. The Cassini spacecraft has now begun a four-year tour of Saturn and its mysterious rings, providing a wealth of scientific data. On 25 December 2004 the Huygens probe will separate from the Cassini mother ship to descend onto the surface of Titan, Saturn's largest moon, to conduct in-situ experiments of Titan's atmosphere and surface which is thought to resemble primitive Earth 4 billion years ago. The combined Cassini Huygens spacecraft will increase understanding of planetary systems and how life may have formed on Earth.

Research in higher education institutions

Universities carry out most of the United Kingdom's strategic and basic research in science and technology. The higher education funding councils provide the main general funds to support research in universities and other higher education institutions in Great Britain. These funds pay the salaries of permanent academic staff (who usually teach as well as undertake research) and contribute to the infrastructure for research. The quality of research performance is a key element in the allocation of funding. In Northern Ireland institutions are funded by the Department for Employment and Learning. In 2001/02, UK universities and colleges received £3.5 billion in research funding

The Research Councils finance basic and strategic research in higher education institutions as well as funding specific research projects. The other main channels of support are industry, charities, government departments and the EU.

Science parks

Science parks encourage and support the start-up, incubation and growth of knowledge-based businesses. They have formal or operational links to a higher education institution or other major research centre. In 2004 there were around 100 science parks in the United Kingdom, 75 of which were members of the UK Science Park Association, hosting over 2,200 firms and employing over 47,000 people.

Public engagement in science

The Government supports activities such as the annual Festival of Science and National Science Week – both organised by the British Association for the Advancement of Science (see page 402). It also offers grants to science communicators through a scheme administered by the Royal Society.

Science and Engineering Ambassadors

The Science and Engineering Ambassadors (SEAs) project was launched by the Department for Education and Skills (DfES) and the DTI in 2002. Individuals with backgrounds in science, engineering, technology and mathematics go into schools to help teachers develop the curricula and to act as role models for the young. SEAs are administered across the United Kingdom by SETNET – the Science, Engineering, Technology and Mathematics Network, – and delivered through a network of 53 SET points.

Science festivals in 2004

The British Association for the Advancement of Science's annual Festival of Science was held in September in Exeter, on the theme of the responsibility of being a scientist. Around 300 leading UK scientists discussed their research with the public and an estimated 15,000 people took part.

The Edinburgh International Science Festival was held in April and attended by an estimated 69,000 people in 20 venues across the city. Its aim was to communicate science and technology, and the wonder of discovery to the widest possible audience.

The third Cheltenham Festival of Science was held over five days in June and attended by an estimated 27,000 people. The theme was perception, including events such as the science of whiskey and the science of perfume. The festival also included discussions on genetic modification, nuclear power, society's obsession with food, and the future of zoos.

The Wrexham Science Festival was held in March and attracted audiences from north Wales, Cheshire and Shropshire. Topics included killer whales, astronomy, working horses, coral reefs and willow weaving.

The transit of Venus

On the morning of 8 June 2004, the planet Venus passed between the Earth and the Sun and was observed by spectators across the United Kingdom. Transits occur in pairs eight years apart, at intervals of 122 years. Over 100 astronomers celebrated the transit in Much Hoole, the Lancashire village where 20-year-old Jeremiah Horrocks first correctly predicted and then observed the transit in 1639. The transit helped 18th century astronomers to estimate the distance of the Earth to the Sun – a distance now known as one astronomical unit (nearly 150 million kilometres).

National Science Week

The 11th National Science Week, coordinated by the British Association for the Advancement of Science and held throughout the United Kingdom, took place in March 2004. Organisations participating included hospitals, schools, industry and museums, and events included 'Spring into science', a national project to record the arrival of spring, and the Ig Nobel Prizes tour (see box).

The Ig Nobels

The Ig Nobel Prizes tour of the United Kingdom took place as part of National Science Week. The awards are intended to celebrate the unusual and imaginative, as well as spur people's interest in science.

The 2003 prize for medicine was awarded to a team from University College London. They demonstrated that the hippocampus, the part of the brain associated with navigation and spatial memory, was enlarged in the brains of London taxi drivers compared with other people. The scientists also found that part of the hippocampus grew larger as the taxi drivers spent more time in the job.

Scientific museums

The Natural History Museum is one of the most popular UK visitor attractions. It has exhibitions devoted to the Earth and the life sciences and is also a leading centre in the fields of taxonomy and biodiversity. It is founded on collections of 70 million specimens from the natural world, and has 500,000 historically important original works of art. The museum employs 350 scientists, and is active in research projects in 60 countries. The museum also offers an advisory service to foreign institutions. It won 'Large Visitor Attraction of the Year' at the Excellence in England Awards in 2004.

The Science Museum promotes public understanding of the history of science, technology, industry and medicine. The collections contain many of the icons of the scientific age with objects as diverse as Crick and Watson's DNA model and Stephenson's *Rocket* (see page 399).

These two museums are in South Kensington, London. Other important collections include those at the Museum of Science and Industry in Manchester, the Museum of the History of Science in Oxford, and the Royal Scottish Museum, Edinburgh.

Aventis Prize for Science Books 2004

The winner of the 16th international science book prize, managed by the Royal Society, was Bill Bryson for *A Short History of Nearly Everything*. Mr Bryson, an American based in England and more usually associated with travel writing, was awarded the prize in recognition of the exposure the book had given to science.

The prize for the best science book for children under 14 was awarded to author Nick Arnold and illustrator Tony De Saulles for *Really Rotten Experiments*. It is the second time the pair have won the award.

Discovery centres

There are over 80 science and discovery centres in the United Kingdom, attracting over 11 million visits each year. The Science and Discovery Centre Network was set up in 2001 to support and promote the centres, and is funded by the OST and the Wellcome Trust (see page 401).

At-Bristol comprises three attractions: Explore-At-Bristol – a hands-on science centre with more than 150 exhibits and a planetarium; Wildwalk-At-Bristol – a natural history centre featuring interactive displays; and the IMAX Theatre-At-Bristol.

Techniquest Science Discovery Centre in Cardiff has over 100 hands-on exhibits and by 2004 had welcomed over 2.5 million people since it opened in 1986. Events in 2004 included Animalympics, exploring how humans would do in a battle with animals when running and jumping.

Scotland has four interactive science centres – in Aberdeen, Dundee, Edinburgh and Glasgow – which in 2003 together attracted 584,000 paying visitors and 109,000 pupils on school visits. The Glasgow Science Centre is the largest such centre in the United Kingdom and, like Stratosphere in Aberdeen, has a range of exhibits. Dynamic Earth in Edinburgh specialises in the earth sciences and Sensation in Dundee in biological sciences.

In Belfast, the W5 Interactive Discovery Centre is located within Northern Ireland's Millennium project, Odyssey. It has over 100 hands-on, high-technology exhibits and attracted 222,000 visitors in 2003/04.

Zoological gardens

The Zoological Society of London (ZSL), an independent conservation, science and education charity founded in 1826, runs London Zoo in Regent's Park. It also owns and runs Whipsnade Wild Animal Park in Bedfordshire. ZSL is responsible for the Institute of Zoology, which carries out research in support of animal conservation. The Institute's work covers topics such as ecology, reproductive biology and conservation genetics. ZSL also operates in overseas projects concerned with practical field conservation, primarily in East and Southern Africa, the Middle East and parts of Asia. Other zoos in the United Kingdom include those in Edinburgh, Bristol, Chester, Dudley and Marwell (near Winchester).

Botanic gardens

The Royal Botanic Gardens, Kew, founded in 1759, are based at Kew in south-west London and at Wakehurst Place, Ardingly in West Sussex (see also page 285). They contain one of the largest collections of living and dried plants in the world. Research is conducted into all aspects of plant life, including physiology, biochemistry, genetics, economic botany and the conservation of habitats and species.

The Royal Botanic Garden in Edinburgh was established in 1670 and is the national botanic garden of Scotland. Together with its three associated specialist gardens, it has become an internationally recognised centre for taxonomy; for the conservation and study of living and preserved plants and fungi; and as a provider of horticultural education.

A National Botanic Garden and research centre for Wales was opened in 2000 on a site on the Middleton Hall estate near Carmarthen.

The Rainhill Trials

October 2004 marks the 175th anniversary of the Rainhill Trials, a competition held by the Liverpool and Manchester Railway Company to find the best locomotive engine for a railway line that was being built to serve the two cities.

The competition was notable for the participation of the *Rocket*, considered by many to be the forerunner of all steam passenger locomotives, and a key factor in the advance of the Industrial Revolution. The engine was designed and built by George Stephenson with the help of his son, Robert, and Henry Booth.

The success of the *Rocket* was due to several new design features. It was the first locomotive to have a multi-tube boiler – with 25 copper tubes rather than a single flue or twin flue. The blast pipe also increased the draught to the fire by concentrating exhaust steam at the base of the chimney, generating more power.

The *Rocket* is on display at the Science Museum (see page 398).

The SET workforce

The term 'science and engineering base' is used to describe the research and postgraduate training capacity based in the universities and colleges of higher education and in establishments operated by the Research Councils (see pages 393–96). Also included are the national and international central facilities (such as CERN – see page 400) supported by the Research Councils and available for use by UK scientists and engineers. There are also important contributions from private institutions, chiefly those funded by charities. The science and engineering base is the main provider of basic research and much of the strategic research carried out in the United Kingdom. It also collaborates with the private sector in the conduct of specific applied research.

According to the 2002 ONS Business R&D Survey, the number of staff employed on R&D in UK businesses in 2002 had increased to 167,000, 10 per cent more than in 2001 and 22 per cent more than a low point in 1997. Scientists and engineers accounted for almost two-thirds.

In 2001/02 there were over 87,000 full-time SET staff employed in higher education, including nearly 48,500 in teaching and research and just over 35,500 working only in research. In all, 33 per cent were women.

In 2003 the Government published *A Strategy for Women in Science, Engineering and Technology*. The aim of the strategy is to improve the participation of women in employment, education and policy making in the United Kingdom and it is aimed equally at academia, industry and public service.

International collaboration

European Union

The EU's Sixth Framework Programme for Research and Technical Development (FP6), published in June 2002, has a budget of €17.5 billion for the four years to 2006. Framework programmes are the EU's main instrument for funding research. There are seven key areas within FP6: research in genomics and biotechnology for health; information society technologies; nanotechnologies and nanosciences; aeronautics and space; food safety; sustainable development; and economic and social sciences. Framework programmes also provide support for mobility, fellowships, infrastructures and the continuation of nuclear research under Euratom.

FP6 is a key mechanism in realising a European Research Area, which aims to regroup EU support

Rosalind Franklin Award

The second Rosalind Franklin Award, promoting women in science, was awarded to Professor Carol Robinson in May 2004. The award commemorates the scientist whose work contributed to the discovery of the double helix structure of DNA and rewards excellence in SET. Professor Robinson, of Cambridge University, is a world leader in the field of mass spectrometry and has applied the process to study the interactions of proteins.

for better coordination of research and innovation policies, at national and EU levels. The United Kingdom is actively engaged in the development of a common European Space Strategy involving ESA, the EU and others.

The six grant-giving Research Councils (see pages 393–96), in association with UK universities, maintain the UK Research Office in Brussels, which promotes UK participation in European research programmes. The CCLRC (see page 394) receives funds from the EU to make its facilities available to researchers from other Member States.

The Government is in consultation for FP7 covering the four years from 2006, and plans to outline its position in 2005.

Other international activities

The COST programme (European co-operation in the field of scientific and technical research) is a multilateral agreement involving 34 countries. Its purpose is to encourage co-operation in national research activities across Europe, with participants from industry, academia and research laboratories. The United Kingdom participates in the majority of COST actions and in the management of the programme.

Another example of international collaboration is CERN, home to the European Laboratory for Particle Physics, based in Geneva, where the Large Hadron Collider is due to be completed by 2007. Scientific programmes at CERN aim to test, verify and develop the 'standard model' of the origin and structure of the Universe. There are 20 member states. PPARC (see page 396) leads UK participation in CERN, and the CCLRC (see page 394) coordinates several aspects of research community involvement. The CCLRC provides the UK contribution to the costs of access by UK researchers to the high-flux neutron source at the Institute Laue-Langevin and to the European Synchrotron Radiation Facility, both in Grenoble.

The United Kingdom is a member of the European Space Agency, providing PPARC researchers entry to the Cosmic Vision 2020 space mission programme. In 2002 it also joined the multinational European Southern Observatory, giving PPARC-funded scientists access to a suite of 8-metre VLTs (Very Large Telescopes) in Chile.

PPARC is a partner in the European Incoherent Scatter Radar Facility within the Arctic Circle, which conducts research on the ionosphere. NERC has a major involvement in international programmes of research into global climate change, organised through the World Climate Research Programme and the International Geosphere-Biosphere Programme. It also supports the UK subscription to the Ocean Drilling Programme.

The MRC (see page 395) pays the UK subscription to the European Molecular Biology Laboratory (EMBL), which has its home research base in Heidelberg, Germany. The European Bioinformatics Institute, an outstation of the EMBL, at Hinxton, near Cambridge, provides access to important molecular biology, sequencing and structural databases. The MRC is also responsible for UK subscriptions to the International Agency for Cancer Research, Lyon.

BBSRC (see page 394) and MRC pay the UK subscription to the Human Frontiers Science Program, which promotes international collaboration in molecular level approaches to brain function and other biological functions.

The Research Councils have a number of bilateral arrangements to promote international collaboration. For example, the BBSRC has agreements with its equivalent organisations in Canada, China, France, India, Japan, the Republic of Korea, the Netherlands and the United States, and supports travel, workshops and other activities to encourage international links.

The United Kingdom is a member of the science and technology committees of many international organisations, including the OECD and NATO (see page 67), and various specialised agencies of the United Nations, including UNESCO. The Research Councils and the Royal Society are members of the European Science Foundation – an association of 76 major national funding agencies in 29 European countries. The UK Government also enters into bilateral agreements with other governments to encourage closer collaboration in SET.

The Foreign & Commonwealth Office has established a network of Science & Technology (S&T) attachés in 45 posts in 22 countries. These aim to:

- inform UK science policy development, benchmarking UK performance against other nations and using S&T in international negotiations;
- promote the United Kingdom as the international partner of choice for collaboration, and attract overseas expertise in areas which complement existing or potential UK strengths; and
- to help companies access overseas innovation and technology, facilitate high technology trade and attract foreign investment.

The British Council (see page 81) promotes 'cutting edge' UK science through events, partnership programmes, seminars, exhibitions and information provision.

Other organisations

Charitable organisations

Medical research charities are a major source of funds for research in the United Kingdom. According to the Association of Medical Research Charities (AMRC), its members spent more than £660 million in support of medical research in the United Kingdom in 2002/03. The two largest contributors are the Wellcome Trust and Cancer Research UK.

The Wellcome Trust is an independent charity, established under the will of Sir Henry Wellcome in 1936. Its mission is 'to foster and promote research with the aim of improving human and animal health'. To this end, it supports 'blue sky' research and applied clinical research, and encourages the exploitation of research findings for medical benefit. The Trust also seeks to raise awareness of the medical, ethical and social implications of research and to promote dialogue between scientists, the public and policy makers.

In 2002/03, the Wellcome Trust spent £552 million. It will be committing £1.5 billion over five years to complement the programme of resources announced in the 2004 Spending Review.

Cancer Research UK is the largest volunteer-supported cancer research organisation in the world, supporting the work of around 3,000 scientists across the United Kingdom. Its annual scientific expenditure is more than £190 million, most of which is raised through donations.

Professional and learned institutions

There are numerous technical institutions, professional associations and learned societies in the United Kingdom, which promote their own disciplines or the education and professional well-being of their members. The Council of Science and Technology Institutes has ten member institutes representing biochemistry, biology, chemistry, the environment, food science and technology, geology, hospital physics and physics.

Science

The Royal Society, founded in 1660, had 11,272 Fellows and 129 Foreign Members in 2004. The Society has three roles: as the national academy of science, as a learned society and as a funding agency for the scientific community. It offers independent advice to government on science matters, acts as an international forum for discussion of ground-breaking scientific research, supports many of the best young scientists and engineers in the United Kingdom, facilitates dialogue between scientists and the public, and promotes science education. Its government grant for 2004/05 is £31 million.

In Scotland the Royal Society of Edinburgh, established in 1783, promotes science by offering postdoctoral research fellowships and studentships, awarding prizes and grants, organising meetings and symposia, and publishing journals. It also acts as a source of independent scientific advice to the Government and others.

Three other major institutions publicise scientific developments by means of lectures and publications for specialists and schoolchildren. Of these, the British Association for the Advancement of Science, founded in 1831, is mainly concerned with the sciences, while the Royal Society of Art, dating from 1754, deals with the arts and commerce as well as science. The Royal Institution, founded in 1799, arranges a large and varied public programme of events to bring science to a wider audience, including the *Christmas Lectures* and the *Friday Evening Discourses*. Over 100 events are organised each year, attracting around 70,000 visitors of all ages. The *Christmas Lectures* (started by Michael Faraday) have been running since 1825. As well as being broadcast in the United Kingdom, the lectures are transmitted to other parts of Europe, Japan and Korea.

Colossus

The 60th anniversary of Colossus, now generally recognised as the world's first programmable electronic computer, took place in 2004. Built by Tommy Flowers at the Post Office research laboratory, it was designed to break the codes of the German military in World War Two. It went into operation at Bletchley Park in February 1944 and, once running, it was not turned off until the end of the war, in order to help prevent its 1,500 vacuum valves from blowing. Reading 5,000 teleprinted characters a second, it helped cut code breaking from weeks to hours, which was to prove vital for the D-Day preparations (see page 99).

Engineering

EC^{UK} – the Engineering Council (UK) – is responsible for the Register of Chartered

Airplane engines

Rolls-Royce delivered the first of its Trent 900 engines designed for Airbus's A380 double-decked 'super-jumbo' in February 2004. The engine will provide 70,000 lb of thrust at take-off and its makers claim it is the world's cleanest large turbofan engine, as measured by emissions per pound of thrust. The manufacturer has also been working to reduce noise emissions from the engine in order to meet regulations for departure at London airports. The Trent 900's Quick system, which provides constant data on how the engine performs in-flight, helps maintenance teams anticipate problems before they become aggravated. In previous tests at Rolls-Royce test beds, the engine coped successfully with the simulated ingestion of a bird and with a 'blade off' test, in which a fan blade is deliberately fired loose. The A380 can seat around 555 people, about 155 more than current jumbo jets, and is due to enter service in spring 2006.

Engineers, Incorporated Engineers and Engineering Technicians. EC[UK] is supported by 35 professional engineering institutions and 14 professional affiliates. In partnership with the institutions, the Council accredits higher and further education courses in engineering and technology and advises the Government on academic, industrial and professional issues.

The Engineering and Technology Board promotes SET in order to support the supply of appropriately skilled individuals to meet present and future needs in the United Kingdom. It works in partnership with business and industry, government, education and the engineering profession, and is financially supported by professional partners, the registration fees of 250,000 registered engineers, and industry sponsorship. It also receives core funding from the DTI.

The national academy of engineering in the United Kingdom is the Royal Academy of Engineering, which has just over 1,300 Fellows including around 90 Foreign Members. It assists the development of national policy on engineering issues by submitting expert evidence to parliamentary and government bodies. The Academy's programmes seek to enhance UK engineering capabilities, inspire the next generation of engineers, raise awareness of the importance of engineering to society and develop links between industry and higher education. It had a government grant of £5.3 million in 2003/04.

Further reading

The Forward Look 2003: Government-funded science, engineering and technology. Department of Trade and Industry/Office of Science and Technology. The Stationery Office, 2003.

Invest in Innovation – A strategy for science, engineering and technology. Department of Trade and Industry/HM Treasury/Department for Education and Skills, 2002.

Science and innovation investment framework 2004–2014. HM Treasury, 2004.

SET for success, the supply of people with science, technology, engineering and mathematics skills. HM Treasury, 2002.

A Strategy for Women in Science, Engineering and Technology. Department of Trade and Industry, 2003.

Websites
Office of Science and Technology
www.ost.gov.uk

Research Councils UK
www.rcuk.ac.uk

Council of Science and Technology
www.cst.gov.uk

WWW.

26 Agriculture, fishing and forestry

In terms of gross value added (GVA – see glossary), agriculture accounted for only 0.8 per cent of the total UK economy in 2003, unchanged from the previous three years. Its share of the total economy has declined from 2.9 per cent in 1973 and 1.6 per cent in 1995, mainly because of a long-term fall in agricultural prices. Issues such as the continuing debate on genetically modified food (see page 408), however, mean that its profile across the United Kingdom is greater than its contribution to the economy would suggest.

The United Kingdom was 64 per cent self-sufficient for all food and 77 per cent for indigenous food in 2003. This represented a small increase from the previous year, when the lowest level of self-sufficiency was recorded since 1988, the year in which the current method of calculation was first applied.

Although the UK agricultural industry accounts for the lowest proportion of national GVA of any country in the European Union (EU), it is more efficient than most, with the fourth highest GVA per annual work unit (full-time equivalents) (Table 26.1).

Agriculture

In 2003 UK agriculture contributed £7.9 billion to the economy and employed some 533,000 people. Agricultural land represents 77 per cent of the total UK land area, compared with around 40 per cent for the EU as a whole. Most agricultural land in the United Kingdom is grassland or rough grazing, with only a quarter used to grow crops (Figure 26.2).

In June 2003 there were 304,000 farm holdings in the United Kingdom, with an average area of 56.4 hectares. Over half were smaller than the minimum size considered by the EU to be necessary for full-time holdings. About two-thirds of all agricultural land was owner-occupied; the rest was tenanted or rented.

Table 26.1 Comparison of agricultural industries, 2002, EU-15

	Agriculture as a percentage of		GVA per AWU[3]
	GVA at market prices[1,2]	National employment	(thousand euro[4])
Denmark	1.7	3.5	46.1
Netherlands	2.1	3.2	43.6
Belgium	1.0	1.9	39.9
United Kingdom	0.4	1.4	34.7
France	1.8	3.9	32.0
Luxembourg	0.5	2.4	31.0
Germany	0.7	2.5	28.2
Italy	2.2	4.8	24.7
Spain	3.2	6.2	23.7
Sweden	0.5	2.4	21.9
Greece	4.7	16.5	17.3
Ireland	1.8	7.6	16.6
Finland	0.5	5.0	16.0
Austria	1.0	5.9	15.9
Portugal	2.0	11.9	6.4
EU-15	**1.4**	**4.0**	**24.8**

1 Excludes directly paid subsidies and therefore differs from contribution to total economy GVA.
2 Data for 2000.
3 Annual work units (full-time equivalents).
4 At current prices.
Source: Eurostat

Total income from farming in 2003 rose in real terms for the third successive year, by 28 per cent to £3.2 billion, 50 per cent below its peak in 1995 but 77 per cent above the low point in 2000. The value of output (including subsidies directly related to products) rose by 6.2 per cent, or £963 million. Output volume was 1.7 per cent lower, but prices received were generally higher, due in part to exchange rate movements. There were notable increases in the value of output of livestock and cereals. Income per full-time worker

Migrant agricultural workers

As Table 26.1 shows, the United Kingdom has the lowest proportion of its workforce employed in agriculture of any EU country. However, the sector does employ a large number of migrant and seasonal workers. The Home Office runs the Seasonal Agricultural Workers' Scheme, which allows workers from outside the European Economic Area (see page 104) to enter the United Kingdom to undertake seasonal agricultural work for farmers and growers. There will be 16,250 places on this scheme in 2005.

The *Gangmasters (Licensing) Act 2004* followed a tragedy in which 21 Chinese workers were drowned by the incoming tide when picking cockles in Morecambe Bay, Lancashire, in February 2004. The Act applies to labour providers in the agricultural, shellfish-gathering and associated processing and packaging sectors, and aims to stop the exploitation of workers by setting up a licensing scheme. This will enable everyone in the food supply chain to distinguish between legal and illegal operators.

from agriculture in the United Kingdom increased by 32 per cent in real terms.

Since 1973 the productivity of the UK agriculture industry has increased by 45 per cent. Total factor productivity increased by 0.8 per cent in 2003 as labour inputs continued to fall.

Prices received by agricultural producers for their products were 17 per cent lower in 2003 compared with the peak in 1995 (see Figure 26.3). The largest falls were in the prices of root crops (52 per cent), cereals (37 per cent) and seeds (35 per cent). The main reason for the overall fall has been the relatively high level of sterling since the mid-1990s, which made exports more expensive and imports cheaper. Reform of the Common Agricultural Policy (see page 413), which cut commodity prices and compensated with direct payments to farmers, also had an effect. The 5 per cent rise in product prices during 2003 was mainly due to the higher prices of fresh fruit, up 14 per cent; fresh vegetables, up 13 per cent; eggs, up 22 per cent; and cereals, up 11 per cent.

Figure 26.2 Agricultural land use, June 2003, UK

Total: 18.4 million hectares

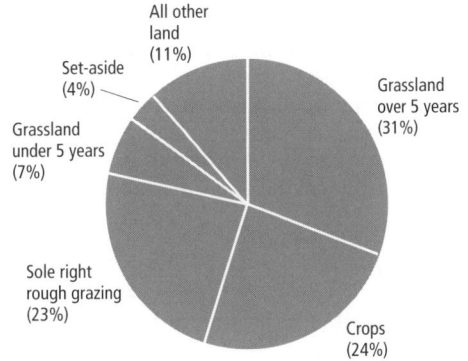

Source: Department for Environment, Food and Rural Affairs

Figure 26.3 Producer prices for agricultural products,[1] UK

Index (1995=100)

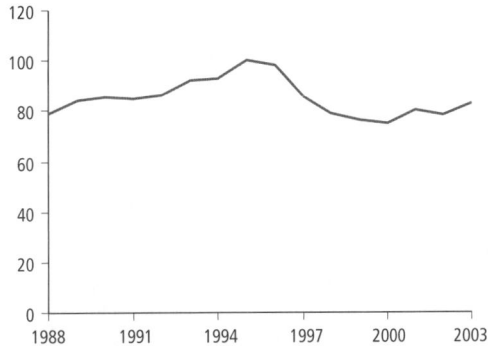

1 Index reflects prices received by producers but excludes direct subsidies.
Source: Department for Environment, Food and Rural Affairs

Agricultural tenure

About 35 per cent of agricultural land (excluding common rough grazing) in England and 21 per cent in Wales is rented. There is a similar proportion of rented land in Scotland, some of it under crofting tenure.

Crofting is a system of land tenure regulated through the *Crofting Acts* and found only in the Highlands and Islands of Scotland. A croft is a unit of land subject to these Acts; there are around 17,700 in total, and croft land covers almost

130,000 hectares (not including common grazing land). The *Land Reform (Scotland) Act 2003* gave crofting communities the right to acquire and control land where they live and work, together with sporting rights associated with that land.

Most farms in Northern Ireland are owner-occupied, but the conacre system allows owners not wishing to farm all their land to let it to others on what are nominally short-term lettings (for 11 months or 364 days). Conacre land, about 34 per cent of agricultural land, is used mainly for grazing.

Production

Home production of the principal foods is shown in Table 26.4.

Livestock

About 40 per cent of UK farms are devoted mainly to dairy farming, beef cattle or sheep. Most of the beef animals and sheep are reared in uplands where agriculture is largely related to grassland and moorland areas. Among world-famous UK livestock are the Hereford, Welsh Black and Aberdeen Angus beef breeds; the Jersey, Guernsey and Ayrshire dairy breeds; the Large White pig breed; and Suffolk and Romney Marsh sheep. The United Kingdom has more than 60 native sheep breeds and many cross-bred varieties. Data on livestock products are given in Table 26.5.

Cattle and sheep constitute 35 per cent of the value of UK gross agricultural output. Dairy production is the largest of the sector, followed by cattle and calves, and then sheep and lambs.

In 2002 the average size of dairy herds was 87 in England, 66 in Wales, 95 in Scotland and 61 in Northern Ireland. The average milk yield for each dairy cow in the United Kingdom in 2003 was 6,620 litres. The total value of production of milk and milk products for human consumption rose by 7 per cent, to £2.6 billion. This was primarily due to an increase in the value of milk sold for processing to dairy companies, which in turn arose mainly from an increase in the average price of milk received by farmers.

More than half of home-bred beef production originates from the national dairy herd, in which the Holstein-Friesian breed predominates. The remainder derives from suckler herds producing

Table 26.4 Home production as a percentage of total new supply[1] for use in the UK

Percentages

	Average 1992–94	2002	2003
Oats	110	120	124
Wheat	121	102	121
Barley	123	117	119
Oilseed rape	86	92	119
Linseed	124	57	107
Potatoes	90	84	81
Sugar (as refined)	62	65	77
Vegetables	79	64	63
Fruit	17	9	8
Poultrymeat	93	91	91
Mutton and lamb	111	85	87
Pork	104	74	72
Beef and veal	103	71	70
Bacon and ham	48	42	42
Milk[2]	101	102	102
Eggs	96	87	87
Butter	67	64	67
Cheese	68	65	61

1 Total new supply is home production plus imports less exports.
2 Includes milk used in the production of dairy products.
Source: Department for Environment, Food and Rural Affairs

high-quality beef calves. In the year to June 2003 the UK cattle population increased by 1.1 per cent to 10.5 million. The value of production of cattle and calves rose only slightly in 2003, by 0.4 per cent to £2.1 billion, due primarily to an increase in the value of home-fed production of beef and veal.

The number of sheep and lambs in the United Kingdom was 35.8 million in June 2003, unchanged from a year earlier. The value of production in 2003 rose by 12 per cent to £1 billion, mainly due to a 13 per cent increase in the value of home-fed production and a 6.1 per cent increase in subsidy payments.

In the year to June 2003 the total number of pigs in the United Kingdom fell by 9.7 per cent, to 5.0 million. The value of production fell by 0.5 per cent in 2003 to £678 million, the lowest since 1977 and half the peak value of £1.4 billion in 1996. The main reason was a 0.4 per cent fall in the value of home-fed production of pigmeat, to £686 million, the lowest since 1988.

The UK poultry population in June 2003 comprised 117 million chickens and other table fowls; 29 million birds in the laying flock; 11 million fowls for breeding; and 10 million turkeys, ducks and other poultry. The size of the breeding flock fell by 2.8 per cent in the year to June 2003. The value of production of poultrymeat rose by 2.1 per cent to £1.3 billion in 2003 as average prices generally rose.

Table 26.5 Livestock products, UK

Thousand tonnes

	Average 1992–94	2002	2003
Beaf and veal	936	694	687
Mutton and lamb	399	307	316
Pork	819	624	577
Bacon and ham	214	200	200
Poultrymeat	1,283	1,537	1,566
Milk (million litres)[1]	14,098	14,179	14,370
Eggs (million dozen)[2]	795	858	879

1 For human consumption; includes milk used in the production of dairy products.
2 For human consumption only; does not include eggs for hatching.
Source: Department for Environment, Food and Rural Affairs

Crops

Farms devoted primarily to arable crops are found mainly in eastern and central southern England and eastern Scotland. The main crops are shown in Figure 26.6 and Table 26.7. In 2003, 3.1 million hectares were planted to cereals – predominantly wheat and barley – a reduction of 5.7 per cent on 2002, and 8.6 per cent less than in 2000. In particular, there was a fall in the area of wheat planted in 2003 due to wet weather conditions in the autumn in some important growing regions. The total volume of cereal production fell by 6 per cent, while the total value rose by 10 per cent.

The value of production of oilseed rape increased by 42 per cent in 2003. The volume of production rose by 21 per cent to 1.8 million tonnes, one of the largest ever recorded for this crop. Prices remained strong throughout the year and subsidy payments rose by 48 per cent. The value of sugar beet production was unchanged from 2002.

Large-scale potato and vegetable cultivation takes place on fertile soils throughout the United Kingdom. The total area for all potato cultivation fell by 8.4 per cent in 2003, while the value of production rose by 1.0 per cent as prices paid to producers rose.

Horticulture

Table 26.8 gives details of the main horticultural products. In June 2003 the total area devoted to horticulture (excluding mushrooms, potatoes and peas for harvesting dry) amounted to 176,000 hectares, virtually unchanged from the previous year. This area relates to field area and does not take into account the number of crops in the year.

The overall value of production of vegetables increased by 1 per cent to £962 million in 2003. The value of production of ornamentals, such as flowers and shrubs, also rose, by 3 per cent to £772 million, and the value of fruit increased by 16 per cent to £285 million as increased demand for some crops coincided with lower yields to produce higher prices.

Genetically modified crops

The year 2003 witnessed the final phases of a four-year UK programme of farm-scale evaluations (FSEs) of genetically modified (GM) crops, in which independent researchers studied the effects that the management of such crops might have on farmland wildlife when compared

Figure 26.6 Area under crops, June 2003, UK

Total: 4.5 million hectares

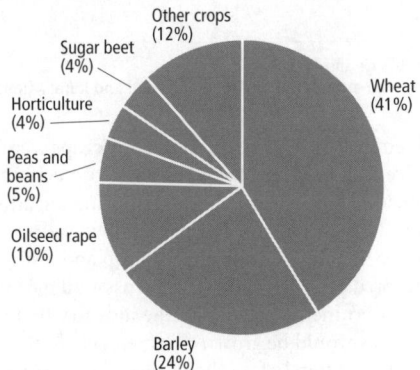

Source: Department for Environment, Food and Rural Affairs

Table 26.7 Cereals and other crops in the UK

	Average 1992–94	2002	2003
Cereals			
Wheat			
Production ('000 tonnes)	13,434	15,973	14,288
Yield (tonnes per hectare)	7.2	8.0	7.8
Value of production (£ million)	1,729	1,480	1,572
Barley			
Production	6,452	6,128	6,370
Yield	5.4	5.6	5.9
Value	849	628	735
Oats			
Production	526	753	749
Yield	5.2	6.0	6.2
Value	70	67	79
Total for cereals[1]			
Production	20,507	22,965	21,511
Yield	6.4	7.1	7.0
Value	2,654	2,182	2,394
Other crops			
Oilseed rape			
Production	1,180	1,468	1,771
Yield	2.7	3.4	3.3
Value	363	298	423
Sugar beet			
Production	9,511	9,557	9,296
Yield	48.4	56.5	57.3
Value	361	283	283
Potatoes			
Production	7,143	6,966	5,918
Yield	41.5	44.0	40.7
Value	545	478	483

1 Includes rye, mixed corn and triticale.
Source: Department for Environment, Food and Rural Affairs

Table 26.8 Horticulture in the UK

	Average 1992–94	2002	2003
Vegetables[1,2]			
Area ('000 hectares)	168	121	124
Value of production (£ million)	950	951	962
Fruit			
Area	43	31	31
Value	269	245	285
of which:			
Orchard fruit			
Area	30	22	22
Value	125	85	104
Soft fruit			
Area	13	9	9
Value	141	137	155
Ornamentals[2]			
Area	19	22	21
Value	566	749	772

1 Includes peas harvested dry for human consumption.
2 Areas relate to field areas multiplied by the number of crops in the year.
Source: Department for Environment, Food and Rural Affairs

with equivalent non-GM crops. Four crops were involved, all modified to be resistant to specific herbicides: oilseed rape (both spring and autumn sown), beet and maize. The project involved between 60 and 75 fields of each crop and also monitored gene-flow, including cross-pollination. The Government agreed with the industry that no GM crops would be grown commercially in the United Kingdom before the results of the FSEs had been fully assessed.

Results from three of the crops were published in October 2003. The FSEs found that growing conventional beet and spring oilseed rape was better for many groups of wildlife than growing the GM herbicide-tolerant strains. In contrast, GM herbicide-tolerant maize was better than conventional varieties for many groups of wildlife. Results from autumn oilseed rape are expected to be published in 2005.

In addition to the FSE, the Government instigated a wide-ranging review and consultation process on GM agriculture. The three main elements were:

- a UK-wide public debate on GM issues, which reported general unease among the public about GM crops and food, and little support for commercialisation of GM crops;

- a review of GM science, conducted by the Royal Society, which found that the science behind the FSEs was sound; that GM is not a single technology and applications should be assessed on a case-by-case basis; and that there is no scientific case for ruling out all GM crops or products; and

- a study of costs and benefits, conducted by the Cabinet Office Strategy Unit, which concluded that the GM crops currently available offer only limited benefits to UK farmers, although future developments could offer benefits of greater value and significance.

The Government announced in March 2004 that it would not allow commercial planting of GM beet and spring oilseed rape strains, while agreeing, in principle and subject to conditions, to the commercial planting of GM maize. Commercial planting of the GM maize will only be allowed if certain restrictions are imposed on its EU marketing consent. In addition, in response to concerns about the banning of the herbicide atrazine (which was used in the FSEs), the Government envisages that if the relevant company wishes to renew the existing EU consent beyond October 2006 it will need to submit new evidence comparing the GM maize with whatever herbicide practice is in operation with conventional maize at that time.

Also in March 2004, the Government published guidance covering new regulations on genetically modified organisms (GMOs), on tighter labelling of GM products and on monitoring for environmental effects. The rules also extend the range of products requiring traceability, labelling and other controls.

Non-food uses of crops

The Industrial (Non-food) Crops section in the Department for Environment, Food and Rural Affairs (Defra) is responsible for the development of crops which provide renewable raw materials for energy and industry. Such crops can help meet sustainable development, climate change and renewable energy targets, as well as providing new commercial opportunities for the agriculture sector. Defra also provides the secretariat for a government/industry forum on non-food uses of crops, and supports the National Non-Food Crops Centre, an independent centre of expertise on industrial uses of agricultural products. Crops for the production of heat and power are supported through the Energy Crops Scheme, part of the England Rural Development Programme (see page 411). A new Bioenergy Infrastructure Scheme provides support for biomass energy supply chains.

Food safety

The Food Standards Agency (FSA, see page 199) aims to ensure that the food consumers eat is safe, and to offer independent, balanced advice to government throughout the United Kingdom. The Meat Hygiene Service, an executive agency of the FSA, is responsible for enforcing legislation on meat hygiene, inspection, animal welfare at slaughter and the control of specified risk materials in all licensed abattoirs and cutting premises in Great Britain. In Northern Ireland this role is carried out by the Department of Agriculture and Rural Development (DARD) on behalf of the FSA.

The FSA conducts an annual Consumer Attitudes to Food survey. The 2003 survey found that there have been changes in the levels of concern over food safety in recent years – in 2003, 42 per cent of respondents (aged 16 and over) said that they were 'very' or 'fairly' concerned about BSE, compared with 61 per cent in 2000. For GM food these figures were 38 per cent and 43 per cent, respectively. Around half of those interviewed in 2003 expressed concern about the amount of fat, salt and sugar in food.

Pesticides

The Pesticides Safety Directorate (PSD), an executive agency of Defra, administers the regulation of agricultural, horticultural, forestry, food storage and home garden pesticides. Its principal functions are to evaluate and process applications for approval of pesticide products for use in Great Britain and provide advice to government on pesticides policy. The PSD aims to:

- ensure the safe use of pesticides, both for people and the environment;

- reduce negative effects of pesticides, encourage reductions in their use, and encourage the development and introduction of alternative control measures; and

- harmonise pesticide regulation in Europe.

Organic farming

Organic farming requires farmers to operate a system based on ecological principles, which imposes strict limitations on the use of inputs from outside the organic system. Anyone involved in the production, processing or import (from outside the EU) of organic food must be registered with one of the United Kingdom's 11 approved organic certification bodies, and subject to at least annual inspections by them. The EC regulation controlling the industry sets out the principle that organic farming aims to be self-sufficient, and fertility should come principally from the farm itself, for example through the use of animal and plant manures and crop rotation systems.

The area of land organically farmed in the United Kingdom grew rapidly in the late 1990s, in response to a number of factors, including a drop in farm incomes, the extension of the scope of organic farming to include livestock, and increases in subsidy rates. In January 2004 the total area of organic land (including land in the process of conversion) was 695,600 hectares, representing about 4 per cent of the total UK agricultural area (excluding common grazing). Of the total, 53 per cent was in Scotland, 37 per cent in England, 8 per cent in Wales, and 1 per cent in Northern Ireland. Permanent and temporary pasture accounted for 86 per cent of organic land, while 6 per cent was used to grow cereals, 2 per cent vegetables and 3 per cent other crops.

The Organic Conversion Information Service, funded by Defra in England, provides free advice to farmers and growers considering conversion to organic farming. Similar services operate in Wales through the Farming Connect Organic Development Centre, and in Scotland SEERAD funds the Scottish Agricultural College to operate a telephone helpline. The Committee on Organic Standards advises on standards of organic food production, set by Defra in consultation with the other UK agricultural departments.

Exports, marketing and promotion

Exports of food, animal feed and drink were around £9.9 billion in 2003, compared with £20.9 billion for imports. EU countries accounted for 63 per cent of all UK food and drink exports; the main markets were the Republic of Ireland (£1.6 billion) and France (£1.2 billion).

Imports and exports of food, animal feed and drink both increased by 11 per cent between the fourth quarter of 2002 and the fourth quarter of 2003. However, this represents a larger increase in imports than exports in absolute terms, and the trade deficit in this area widened by 12 per cent over the period. The largest import categories in 2003 were fruit and vegetables (£4.9 billion), meat (£3.4 billion) and drink (£3.3 billion). Drink was the largest export category, worth £3.5 billion, with the majority of this coming from sales of whisky (see page 425).

Food from Britain (FFB), an organisation funded by Defra and the food and drink industry on behalf of the four UK agricultural departments, provides marketing and international business development services to the industry. It has a network of nine international offices, each with local food industry expertise and trade contacts. The FFB has been awarded £3 million over the three years to 2006 to help promote the regional food sector in England. The funding is being used for a programme of activities aimed at trade development, increasing competitiveness and raising consumer awareness.

The British Farm Standard red tractor logo, administered by Assured Food Standards and owned by the National Farmers' Union, identifies food that has been independently verified as having been produced in accordance with assurance standards covering food safety, animal welfare and environmental issues.

The Food Chain Centre is a government-supported industry-led body, established in 2002 to research and promote ways in which the food chain can be made to operate more efficiently. It also seeks to publicise best practice and encourage information sharing within the food chain.

Agricultural shows

Several major agricultural shows are held each year across the United Kingdom, including:

- the Balmoral Show, Belfast (May);
- the Royal Highland Show, Edinburgh (June), with more than 5,000 animals on show and the largest trade exhibition of agricultural machinery in Great Britain;
- the Royal Show, Stoneleigh, Warwickshire (early July), where visitors can see the latest techniques and improvements in UK agriculture;
- the Royal Welsh Show, Llanelwedd, Builth Wells (late July – the centenary show was held in 2004);
- the Royal Welsh Agricultural Winter Fair, Llanelwedd, Builth Wells, for livestock and carcases (December); and
- the Royal Smithfield Show, London (every other year), for agricultural technology, machinery, services, supplies, livestock and carcases.

Farmers' markets

In June 2004 there were around 470 farmers' markets operating in the United Kingdom, selling produce direct to consumers. Of these, 150 were accredited to FARMA, a body formed from the amalgamation of the Farm Retail Association and the National Association of Farmers' Markets. Accredited markets must follow these rules:

- food must be locally produced (each market has a definition of local);
- all produce sold must be grown, reared or otherwise produced by the stallholder; and
- information should be available to customers about the rules of the market and the production methods of the producers.

Government role

Defra has responsibility for agriculture, fisheries, food, animal welfare issues, environmental protection, and wildlife and the countryside in general. It also administers support policies agreed in Brussels which provide around £3 billion a year to UK agriculture from the EU budget.

The Scottish Executive Environment and Rural Affairs Department (SEERAD), the Welsh Assembly Government's Agriculture and Rural

Regional foods

In 2004, both Arbroath Smokies (haddock) and Scottish Farmed Salmon joined Roquefort (a French cheese), Gorgonzola (an Italian cheese) and Prosciutto de Parma (an Italian ham) on the list of products recognised by the EU for their quality and regional identity.

Both the UK products have been registered by the European Commission as a protected geographical indication under the EU's protected food name scheme. The aim of the scheme is primarily to provide consumers with a guarantee of the geographical origin and methods of production of the products they are buying.

Among 35 UK products protected under the scheme are Dorset Blue cheese, Cornish clotted cream, Scotch beef and lamb, and Welsh lamb.

Transporting agricultural products

Agricultural products, foodstuffs and beverages in the United Kingdom are usually transported by road. A total of 106 million tonnes of agricultural products were moved by heavy goods vehicles within Great Britain in 2003, with an average haul of 107 kilometres. In terms of tonne-kilometres, nearly 58 per cent of such agricultural products were moved more than 150 kilometres, and 22 per cent more than 300 kilometres.

Affairs Department (ARAD), and the Department of Agriculture and Rural Development in Northern Ireland (DARD) have varying degrees of responsibility for agriculture and fisheries.

Each of the four UK administrations has produced its own agricultural strategy setting out its aims and ambitions for the industry and outlining mechanisms to help achieve these objectives. While the detailed approach varies, reflecting the different needs of farmers, each strategy is intended to help the farming industry to become more economically viable, while promoting environmental and public health benefits.

Rural Development Programmes (RDPs)

RDPs have the general aims of conserving and improving the environment; creating productive and sustainable rural economies; and developing more diverse and competitive rural industries. The RDPs run from 2001 to 2006, and will invest nearly £3 billion in the UK rural economy.

The England RDP is investing £1.6 billion in rural development and agri-environment measures. These include the Environmentally Sensitive Areas (ESAs) and Countryside Stewardship Schemes; the Rural Enterprise Scheme; the Energy Crops Scheme; the Processing and Marketing Grant; and the Vocational Training Scheme.

The Scottish Rural Development Programme (SRDP) concentrates on complementing the Common Agricultural Policy (see page 413) and provides support for less favoured areas (LFAs), agri-environment measures, and afforestation. Around £685 million is being spent over the lifetime of the programme. In addition, the Agricultural Business Development Scheme provides support to farmers and crofters and their families in the Highlands and Islands. SEERAD will provide £50 million towards supporting diversification elsewhere in Scotland between 2001 and 2006.

The Rural Development Plan for Wales involves investment of around £450 million. The programme makes funds available for schemes such as the Tir Gofal (Land in Care) whole farm agri-environment scheme and the Processing and Marketing Grant Scheme. It includes support for hill farming and a range of forestry and farm woodland initiatives.

The Rural Development Regulation Plan for Northern Ireland, which runs from 2000 to 2006, is worth £266 million. It includes the LFA support scheme and an enhanced agri-environment programme. DARD also manages a RDP targeted at the broader rural community that is expected to be worth about £80 million between 2001 and 2007.

Land based schemes

Land based schemes are a major part of the RDPs. Within them, agri-environment schemes make payments for the management of land to maintain, enhance and extend wildlife habitats; conserve historic or geological features; encourage public access; and restore traditional aspects of the countryside. Agri-environment schemes are funded by the EU and the Government, and include:

- the ESA scheme,[1] which offers incentives to farmers to adopt agricultural practices that will safeguard and enhance parts of the country of particularly high landscape, wildlife or historic value. The scheme operates as Tir Gofal in Wales;

- the Countryside Stewardship Scheme, which is the main scheme for the wider countryside in England. Farmers and land managers enter ten-year agreements to manage land in an

environmentally beneficial way in return for annual payments. The Countryside Management Scheme fulfils a similar role in Northern Ireland;

- the Rural Stewardship Scheme in Scotland, which has replaced both the ESA and Countryside Premium Scheme as the main means of encouraging environmentally friendly farming practice;

- organic farming schemes, which offer payments to farmers to aid them in converting to organic farming and thereafter to continue to manage their land in an environmentally beneficial way; and

- simplified 'entry level' agri-environment schemes, which are being developed in England, Wales and Northern Ireland. A pilot for the English scheme was launched in four areas in 2003.

In England, the entry level scheme will form part of a new, integrated agri-environment scheme to be known as 'Environmental Stewardship'.

Other land based schemes include the Farm Woodland Premium scheme (partly funded by the EU), which aims to encourage farmers to convert productive agricultural land to woodland by providing payments to help offset consequent falls in agricultural income (the Scottish Forestry Grants Scheme and Farmland Premium fulfil a similar role); and the Hill Farm Allowance Scheme, which provides support to hill farmers in the English LFAs, in recognition of the difficulties they face and the vital role they play in maintaining landscape and community in upland areas. This scheme operates as Tir Mynydd in Wales, while in Scotland, the Less Favoured Area Support Scheme supports environmentally sustainable farming in remote and disadvantaged areas.

Project based schemes

These schemes are intended to benefit the wider rural economy. Those operating in England are the Rural Enterprise Scheme, which helps farmers and other rural businesses adapt to changing markets; the Vocational Training Scheme, which is aimed at improving the occupational skills of farmers and foresters; and the Processing and Marketing Grant.

1 The ESA and Countryside Stewardship Schemes closed to new applicants on 31 March 2004. Subject to EU approval, they will be replaced in 2005 by the new Environmental Stewardship Scheme.

Common Agricultural Policy (CAP)

The CAP was introduced in 1962, driven by a need to ensure food security in Europe. However, recent reforms emphasise a more market-oriented approach to agriculture. Total UK expenditure under the CAP and on national grants and subsidies (less levies) in 2003 increased by 8 per cent from 2002, to £2.8 billion (Figure 26.9).

To prevent and detect fraud, expenditure under the CAP arable and livestock schemes is protected through the Integrated Administration and Control System (IACS). The controls include verification checks of claimed land and animals, via both on-the-spot inspections and remote sensing by satellites.

EU legislation permits Member States to recycle, or 'modulate', a proportion of payments made direct to farmers under CAP commodity regimes. Modulation, to help fund the RDP, was introduced in 2001 at an initial flat rate of 2.5 per cent, rising to 3 per cent in 2002 and 3.5 per cent in 2003 and 2004. This means a proportion of subsidy payments is reallocated to agri-environment and forestry schemes such as Countryside Stewardship, Tir Gofal, and ESAs. The Government is matching the sum reallocated to provide further funding for the RDPs.

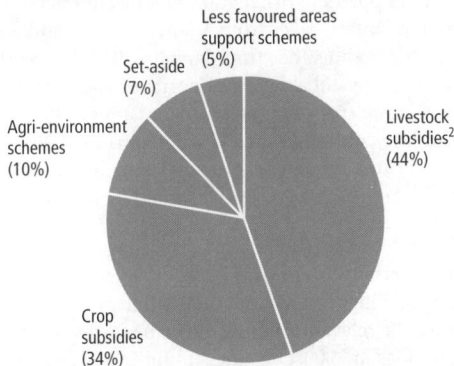

Figure 26.9 Public expenditure under the CAP and on national grants and subsidies, 2003, UK

Total:[1] £2.9 billion

Less favoured areas support schemes (5%)
Set-aside (7%)
Agri-environment schemes (10%)
Livestock subsidies[2] (44%)
Crop subsidies (34%)

1 Total is gross of taxes (including vehicle licences).
2 Includes animal disease compensation.
Source: Department for Environment, Food and Rural Affairs

In June 2003, and again in April 2004, the Council of Agriculture Ministers agreed proposals to reform the CAP. These reforms break the link between most subsidies and what and how much farmers produce, and make subsidy dependent on meeting environmental and other standards. They are intended to reduce environmental damage, make European agriculture more competitive and market-oriented, promote simplification of the CAP, facilitate the EU enlargement process (see page 71) and increase flexibility while guaranteeing farmers income stability.

A major part of the CAP reform process will be the introduction of the Single Payment Scheme in 2005. It will replace a large number of the subsidies farmers receive with a single payment that will not be linked to what they produce. The new scheme is intended to reduce the environmental impact of farming by removing an incentive to intensify production, and by linking payment of the subsidy to compliance with environmental, food safety, animal health and other standards. It will be implemented on a regional basis across the United Kingdom.

Livestock subsidies

Five direct subsidies are currently available to livestock producers. These include the Beef Special Premium, a subsidy for male cattle; the Suckler Cow Premium, a subsidy for female cattle which form part of a suckler breeding herd used for rearing calves for meat production; and the Sheep Annual Premium, a subsidy for breeding ewes. These subsidies will be replaced by the Single Payment Scheme in 2005.

Arable Area Payments Scheme (AAPS)

Under this scheme – part of the CAP – farmers may claim area payments on cereals, oilseeds, proteins and linseed, and on flax and hemp for fibre. A condition for claiming is that farmers (excluding small producers) must 'set aside', and not use, a certain percentage of their land, thereby avoiding overproduction, and must comply with the strict rules for managing set-aside. The minimum rate for set-aside for 2004 was 5 per cent of the total area claimed (down from 10 per cent in 2003).

In 2003 there were around 55,000 claims for area payments in the United Kingdom in respect of 4.5 million hectares of land. After allowing for modulation, payments for claims made in 2003 are expected to total about £1.1 billion. The AAPS will be replaced by the Single Payment Scheme.

Professional, scientific and technical services

A number of organisations provide professional, scientific and technical services:

- the Rural Development Service of Defra provides services for the England RDP, relating to the enhancement and protection of the environment, including biodiversity and rural development;

- in Wales, similar services are provided by Farming Connect and ARAD's divisional offices;

- in Scotland, SEERAD agricultural staff provide professional and technical scheme implementation services, and the Scottish Agricultural College (SAC) provides professional, business, scientific and technical services in the agriculture, rural business, food and drink, and environmental markets;

- DARD has a similar remit in Northern Ireland;

- the Farm Business Advice Service aims to help farmers increase profitability and examine the possibility of diversification; and

- Lantra, which is the UK Sector Skills Council (see page 136) for the industry, receives government support under contracts from Defra and the Scottish Executive.

Animal health and welfare

Professional advice and action on the statutory control of animal health and the welfare of farm livestock are the responsibility of the State Veterinary Service in Great Britain. It is supported in England and Wales by the Veterinary Laboratories Agency (*www.defra.gov.uk/corporate/vla*), which also offers its services to the private sector on a commercial basis. Similar support is provided in Scotland by the SAC. In Northern Ireland, DARD's Veterinary Service carries out a similar role to the State Veterinary Service, supported by its Veterinary Sciences Division.

The Welsh Assembly Government will take over residual animal health and welfare powers in Wales from Defra by the end of 2004. A Veterinary Policy Unit will be created, based within the Assembly's

Environment Planning and Countryside Division. Defra, the Scottish Executive and the Welsh Assembly Government launched an Animal Health and Welfare Strategy for Great Britain in June 2004. The Strategy aims to make improvements in the health and welfare of kept animals while protecting society, the economy and the environment from the effect of animal diseases.

Defra published a draft Animal Welfare Bill in July 2004. It covers the welfare of all farmed, wild or exotic animals in captivity, domestic animals, and animals in entertainment and sport, and proposes a new statutory duty of care on owners. The Bill applies to England and Wales. Similar legislation is being considered in Scotland.

The United Kingdom enforces controls on imports of live animals, genetic material, and products of animal origin, including checks on all individual consignments originating from outside the EU and frequent checks on those from other EU Member States. Measures can be taken to prevent the import of diseased animals and genetic material from regions or countries affected by disease.

Imports of poultry from Thailand were suspended by the EU in January 2004 in response to an outbreak of Highly Pathogenic Avian Influenza (HPAI – 'bird flu'). This supplemented an existing UK ban on the import of live poultry and hatching eggs. Outbreaks of HPAI had already been confirmed elsewhere in South East Asia, but occurrence of the disease in Thailand was of more concern as the EU imports large quantities of Thai poultrymeat.

An EC Directive on welfare standards for laying hens stopped the installation of conventional barren battery cages from 1 January 2003, and will ban them altogether from January 2012. Currently farmers are still able to use 'enriched cages', which have more space for each bird and a nest, perch and litter, although the EC will report in 2005 on the various systems for rearing laying hens, and make proposals as to which should be allowed.

The Pet Travel Scheme allows cats, dogs and ferrets from certain countries to enter or re-enter the United Kingdom without quarantine provided they meet the relevant rules. The scheme started for cats and dogs in 2000, covering a number of European countries only. It has since been extended to cover certain other countries, for example Jamaica, Australia, Japan, the United States and Canada. An

EC regulation on the non-commercial movement of pets came into force in 2003 and applied from July 2004. This has changed the documentation required for animals to travel, and also added ferrets and some additional countries to the scheme. The UK scheme will continue broadly unchanged until at least 2008.

Movement of live animals

The British Cattle Movement Service (BCMS) was set up in 1998 to record the births, movements and deaths of the 10 million cattle in Great Britain. There is a legal requirement to notify the BCMS of all births, deaths and movements between holdings, and around 13 million such movements are notified each year. In Northern Ireland, all cattle and cattle movements are recorded on the Animal and Public Health Information System (APHIS).

The United Kingdom was one of 12 European countries to sign up to the new Council of Europe Convention on the Protection of Animals during International Transport in November 2003. The Convention will extend animal welfare standards beyond the borders of the EU.

Tuberculosis (TB) in cattle

In response to the 1996 Krebs report, a scientific review into the links between bovine tuberculosis and badgers, the Government set out a five-point plan of action to tackle bovine TB. One element is research to find out how the disease is spread among cattle and wildlife, including research into improved diagnostic tests and the development of a TB vaccine. An on-farm epidemiological survey, known as TB99, is starting to provide data to help understand the disease and focus future research. Another important element of the Government's strategy in Great Britain is designed to establish the contribution that badger culling strategies could make in reducing the spread of TB to cattle. However, reactive culling (in areas where there have been recent outbreaks of TB) under the trial was suspended in November 2003 when evidence emerged that there was actually an increase in the number of cases of bovine TB occurring in reactive culling areas compared with areas in which no culling took place. Proactive culling (where all badgers in an area are killed regardless of whether or not there has been an outbreak of TB) and control surveying will continue until results can be obtained.

In Northern Ireland, DARD is implementing revised control measures aimed at bringing about a reduction in the incidence of bovine TB.

Fur farming

Keeping animals solely or primarily for slaughter for their fur is illegal across the United Kingdom.

Veterinary medicinal products

The Veterinary Medicines Directorate, an executive agency of Defra, aims to protect public health, animal health and the environment, and to promote animal welfare, by ensuring the safety, quality and efficacy of all aspects of veterinary medicines in the United Kingdom. The Government is advised by the independent scientific Veterinary Products Committee on scientific issues arising from the authorisation procedures for veterinary medicines.

Plant Health Service

The Plant Health Service aims to prevent the introduction or spread of serious plant pests and diseases which threaten agriculture, horticulture and the environment. During 2003/04 the service dealt with the first outbreak of potato ring rot in the United Kingdom. Tests were carried out on over 165,000 potato tubers to trace the origin of the outbreak of the infection and also to check there had been no spread to other farms. The outbreak was contained by February 2004.

The fishing industry

The United Kingdom has a major interest in sea fisheries, reflecting its geographical position in the North East Atlantic, and is one of the EU's largest fishing countries, taking about a fifth of the total catch in major species. It has an interest in more than 100 'Total Allowable Catches' set by the European Commission (see page 64). In 2003 total UK fish supplies amounted to some 586,000 tonnes, with the UK fishing industry supplying around 73 per cent by quantity. Household consumption of fish in the United Kingdom in 2003 was estimated at 476,000 tonnes. Fisheries Departments, in partnership with the European Commission, are responsible for the administration of legislation concerning the fishing industry, including fish and shellfish farming. The Sea Fish Industry Authority, a largely industry-financed body, undertakes research and development, provides training and promotes the marketing and consumption of sea fish. There are also two government laboratories specialising in fisheries research – one in Aberdeen and one in Lowestoft.

The Cabinet Office Strategy Unit published a report into the UK fishing industry in March 2004. It concluded that the industry could be profitable and sustainable in the future, provided that it modernises to deal with global competition. Key recommendations of the report include:

- removal of at least a further 13 per cent of the whitefish fleet to ensure long-term profitability and stock recovery;
- improving the industry's compliance with rules and regulations;
- regionalisation of the Common Fisheries Policy (see page 417) within the United Kingdom, while strengthening the EU's role in ensuring fairness; and
- reducing the volatility in stock by adopting a 'large stock' strategy, which would mean reducing the amount of fish caught in the short term to achieve long-term benefits.

Fish caught and the fishing fleet

UK fishing industry statistics are shown in Table 26.10. Altogether, some 550,600 tonnes of sea fish, with a total value of £481 million, were landed into the United Kingdom by both the UK fleet and foreign fishing vessels in 2003. Another major source of supply is the bulk import of fish caught by other countries.

In 2003 demersal fish (those living on or near the bottom of the sea) accounted for 32 per cent by weight of total landings by UK fishing vessels into the United Kingdom. Pelagic fish (those living in mid water) accounted for 39 per cent and shellfish for the remaining 29 per cent. Landings of all types of fish (excluding salmon and trout) by UK fishing vessels into the United Kingdom totalled 444,600 tonnes. Haddock and cod represented 28 and 11 per cent, respectively, of the total value of demersal fish landed. The quayside value of landings of all sea fish, including shellfish, by UK vessels into the United Kingdom in 2003 was £392 million.

Catches of crabs, lobsters, nephrops (for example langoustines) and other shellfish have increased

to supply a rising demand. In 1985 UK fishermen landed 75,000 tonnes of shellfish worth about £65 million but by 2003 landings into the United Kingdom by UK vessels were 129,000 tonnes, worth £171 million.

Some of the species caught by UK fishing vessels find a more favourable market overseas and these species are usually exported or landed directly abroad. In 2003 UK vessels landed 186,700 tonnes of sea fish directly into non-UK ports, with a value of £129 million.

The United Kingdom is contributing to the EU objective of reducing its fishing fleet by both cutting numbers and limiting the time some vessels spend at sea. At the end of 2003 the UK fleet consisted of 7,271 vessels (including 340 greater than 24.39 metres or 80 feet), and there were 11,774 professional fishermen (Table 26.10).

There is a substantial fish processing industry in the United Kingdom. Based on a survey of the sector in 2004, there are around 560 businesses which employ some 18,500 people.

At the retail level, there are approximately 1,400 fishmongers. An increasing proportion of all fish (87 per cent by volume and 88 per cent by value, excluding canned produce) is sold through supermarkets. A small proportion of the catch is used to make fish oils and animal feeds.

Cetacean by-catch

An estimated 300,000 whales, dolphins and porpoises worldwide are killed each year by being trapped in fishing nets. In March 2004 the EU Agriculture and Fisheries Council reached agreement on a new regulation to reduce the level of by-catch caused by fishing fleets from EU countries. The regulation sets out a number of actions to be taken, including the compulsory fitting of acoustic devices ('pingers') to fishing vessels over 15 metres using fixed gear in the North Sea, English Channel and Celtic Sea, and a programme of pilot projects to monitor the impact of fisheries where pingers are used and compare the results with by-catch from vessels under 15 metres long. This research will be used to help in reviewing the regulations.

8 June 2004 The Royal Geographical Society, with the Institute of British Geographers, opens a study centre at its South Kensington headquarters. The *Unlocking the Archives* project gives the public access to resources collected from 500 years of geographical research and exploration. The items are not on display.

Above: *Endurance* frozen in the ice in Antarctica, 1914–16. The RGS holds most of the surviving photographs taken by Frank Hurley of Shackleton's Trans-Antarctic Expedition.

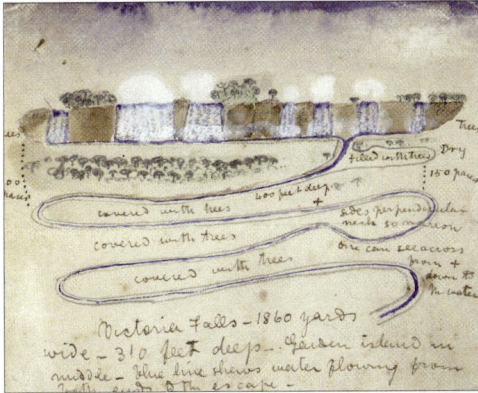

Left: Watercolour sketch map of the Victoria Falls and the downstream gorge, with manuscript notes by David Livingstone, 1860. The Society has an extensive collection of material from 19th century exploration.

Left: Watercolour of Keerung town, Nepal by Dr H A Oldfield, 1855. Oldfield was the surgeon to the British Residency in Kathmandu (1850–63); his paintings of people, architecture and landscapes were the first non-religious images of Nepal (photography did not reach Nepal until 1869 at the earliest).

14 June 2004 Richard Branson breaks the record for crossing the English Channel in an amphibious vehicle. Using an Aquada, which can reach speeds of more than 100 mph on land and 30 mph on water, he made the crossing to Calais in 1 hour, 40 minutes and 6 seconds.

20 June 2004 Cyclists on Clapham Common begin the 87-kilometre British Heart Foundation London to Brighton Bike Ride. The event raised more than £2.5 million for the BHF's fight against heart disease, and 27,000 cyclists took part.

24 June 2004 Festival-goers at Glastonbury music festival take time out to watch the England–Portugal football match in the Euro 2004 quarter-finals, shown on a big screen. They are pictured celebrating Michael Owen's goal.

26 June 2004 Sylvia Disley, a British Olympian from the 1948 Games, holds aloft the Olympic flame at Heathrow Airport surrounded by children from Lampton School, Hounslow. The flame has been relayed around the world through cities that have previously hosted, are due to host, or are bidding to host the Olympic Games. It returned to Athens in time for the 2004 Games.

28 June 2004 The New Forest is to be designated England's eighth National Park, the first to be designated in England for almost 50 years. With an area of about 570 square kilometres, it will be England's smallest.

28 June 2004 An information consultation leaflet is published to answer some commonly asked questions about the process of establishing a proposed National Park in the Mourne area – potentially Northern Ireland's first National Park.

www.ehsni.gov.uk

A Mourne National Park?

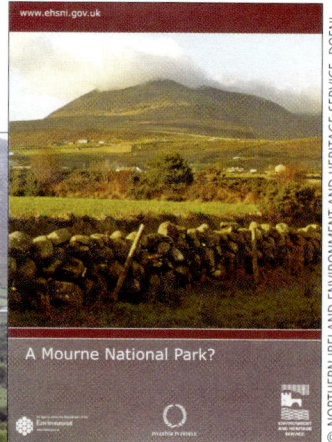

Table 26.10 UK fishing industry: summary table

	1991	1996	2001	2002	2003
Fleet size at end of year					
Number of vessels	11,411	8,667	7,721	7,578	7,271
Employment					
Number of fishermen	n/a	19,044	14,645	12,746	11,774
Total landings by UK vessels[1]					
Quantity ('000 tonnes)	787	892	738	685	631
Value (£ million)	496	635	574	546	521
Household consumption					
Quantity ('000 tonnes)	418	471	492	491	476

1 Figures relate to landings both in the United Kingdom and in other countries.
Source: Department for Environment, Food and Rural Affairs

Aquaculture

Fish farming is a significant industry in remote rural areas on the west coast of Scotland, as well as in Orkney, Shetland and Eilean Siar, primarily producing salmon. In addition, species such as cod, halibut and turbot are entering commercial production. Trout is also farmed as a freshwater species, and various shellfish species are produced all round the UK coast. In Scotland, the industry directly employs about 2,000 people, and generates over £500 million a year, accounting for around 50 per cent of all Scottish food exports by value.

Aquaculture is subject to a comprehensive regulatory regime covering such issues as fish and shellfish health and disease control, control of discharges into the marine and riverine environment, site leasing and planning, and the use of medicines and other chemicals.

Common Fisheries Policy (CFP)

Management of UK sea fisheries is subject to the EU Common Fisheries Policy (CFP). Under this policy, UK vessels have exclusive rights to fish within 6 miles of the UK coast. Certain other EU Member States have historic rights in UK waters between 6 and 12 miles. UK vessels have similar rights in other Member States' 6 to 12 mile belts. Between 12 and 200 miles, EU vessels may fish wherever they have access rights. Non-EU countries' vessels may fish in these waters if they negotiate reciprocal fisheries agreements with the EU. UK fishery limits extend to 200 miles or the median line (broadly halfway between the UK coast and the opposing coastline of another state).

The primary aim of the CFP is to ensure rational and sustainable exploitation of fish stocks through conservation and management policies designed to protect resources and reflect the needs of the fishing industry. The CFP aims to improve the balance between catching capacity and available resources by regulating the amount of fishing and the quantities of fish caught, through a system of Total Allowable Catches (TACs), based on scientific advice, which are then distributed to Member States.

The EU Fisheries Council is seeking to improve the CFP by developing a more long-term approach to fisheries management, including the setting of 'multi-annual' catch limits to replace the previous annual allocations and introducing recovery plans for depleted stocks. State aid for building fishing vessels will cease from the end of 2004, as will aid for the transfer of EU fishing vessels to third countries. New Regional Advisory Councils are being set up under the CFP in order to introduce a more regional approach to fisheries management.

Conservation of fish stocks

Stocks of some fish in EU waters, notably cod and hake, have been depleted through a combination of overfishing, low numbers of fish surviving to a size where they are taken commercially, and possible environmental factors.

Measures have been put in place that aim to halt and ultimately reverse the decline in EU cod stocks, which is recognised as a serious problem. A long-term plan for cod recovery began in 2004, including limiting the number of days each month fishermen can spend at sea catching cod.

Fish quotas

EU fisheries ministers set TACs for a wide range of stocks each year, and the TACs are divided into quotas for each Member State. UK quotas are then allocated between various groups within the UK fishing fleet. Some allocations are managed by fishermen's organisations, known as producer organisations. However, overall responsibility for managing UK quotas rests with Defra and the other UK Fisheries Departments. Quotas, technical conservation and other management measures aim to restore balance to fish populations and allow them to renew themselves.

In December 2003 there were increases in a number of TACs including the quota for haddock, in order to allow boats to take advantage of an abundance of the species.

Restrictive licensing system for fishing vessels

A restrictive licensing system is operated by the UK Fisheries Departments, controlling the activities of the UK fishing fleet in accordance with the EU and UK objectives on fleet and catch management. All engine-powered UK-registered vessels which fish for profit for sea fish (other than salmon, migratory trout and eels) are required to hold a licence issued by one of the Departments. To constrain the size of the fleet, additional licences are not granted. Licences may, however, be transferred or aggregated in accordance with detailed rules. A national licensing scheme for shellfish was introduced in 2004, limiting the number of vessels permitted to catch crabs, lobsters and crayfish.

Sea Fisheries Committees

The 12 Sea Fisheries Committees (SFCs) and the Environment Agency (see page 300) regulate local sea fisheries around the entire coast of England and Wales out to 6 miles. SFCs were established in the 19th century and are empowered to make by-laws for the management and conservation of their districts' fisheries, and to control fishing for environmental purposes. In Scotland, inshore

fisheries are primarily regulated by Scottish legislation, and the system is being reformed with the intention of delegating management responsibilities to local area management groups.

Forestry

The area covered by woodland at the end of March 2004 amounted to 17 per cent of total land area in Scotland, 14 per cent in Wales, 9 per cent in England and 6 per cent in Northern Ireland. This gives a total of 12 per cent for the United Kingdom, or 2.8 million hectares, double the cover in 1947, and compares with 36 per cent for the EU as a whole.

Table 26.11 Area of woodland by ownership and type, 31 March 2004, UK

Thousand hectares

	Conifers	Broadleaves[1]	Total productive woodland
Forestry Commission/ Forestry Service			
England	154	52	205
Wales	98	11	110
Scotland	440	25	465
Northern Ireland	58	4	62
United Kingdom	**749**	**93**	**842**
Private woodland[2]			
England	217	692	909
Wales	64	112	176
Scotland	611	254	865
Northern Ireland	10	14	24
United Kingdom	**902**	**1,072**	**1,974**
Total			
England	370	744	1,114
Wales	162	123	286
Scotland	1,051	280	1,330
Northern Ireland	68	18	86
United Kingdom	**1,651**	**1,165**	**2,816**

1 Broadleaves include coppice and coppice with standards.
2 Private woodland figures for England, Scotland and Wales are based on the 1995–99 National Inventory of Woodland and Trees (NIWT) adjusted to reflect subsequent changes (although at present no adjustment is made for woodland converted to another land use). The NIWT did not include Northern Ireland.
Source: Forestry Commission

In 2003/04, 23,664 hectares of trees were planted in Great Britain, including both new planting and restocking. This total included 8,600 hectares of new broadleaf planting and 2,800 hectares of new conifer planting (Figure 26.12). Since the early 1990s, incentives for planting broadleaves and native pinewood, and for planting on former agricultural land, have led to a growth in the number of broadleaved trees planted; previously, timber production was the key priority, resulting in the planting mainly of fast-growing conifer trees.

Tree planting is sponsored through various grant schemes which encourage the planting of species native to the United Kingdom, including the Forestry Commission's Woodland Grant Scheme and the agricultural departments' Farm Woodland Premium Scheme. In Scotland these grants were replaced in June 2003 with two new schemes – the Forestry Grant Scheme and the Farmland Premium Scheme, operated by the Forestry Commission and SEERAD respectively. Changes to the grants made in England and Wales are expected to be made in 2005.

Woodland Grants are components of the RDPs (see page 411). In England, expenditure of £139 million between 2000 and 2006 is provided for Forestry Commission schemes and in Scotland, £95 million.

The United Kingdom uses a large amount of timber, paper, board and other wood products each year, equivalent to about 50 million cubic metres under bark. Around 85 per cent of this has to be imported, at a cost of about £9 billion a year. The timber industry, using wood from sustainable forests, has received considerable investment in recent years. The volume of wood supplied from Great Britain's forests each year has more than doubled from 4 million cubic metres over bark standing in the 1970s to 9.5 million in 2002. This is forecast to increase to over 16 million cubic metres by 2020.

The National Forest covers 520 square kilometres of the English Midlands, covering parts of Derbyshire, Leicestershire and Staffordshire. The aim is to increase woodland cover, from 6 per cent at its inception in 1994, to about 33 per cent of the total area, with another third remaining in agriculture. Over 5 million trees had been planted by the end of March 2004, raising woodland cover to some 15 per cent.

Figure 26.12 New woodland creation,[1] Great Britain

Thousand hectares

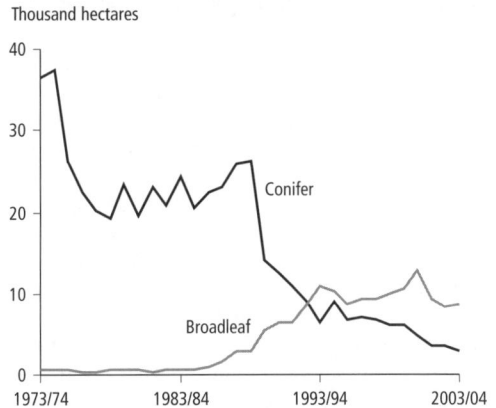

1 Excludes areas of new private woodland created without grant aid.
Source: Forestry Commission

Major afforestation projects involving the Forestry Commission, the Countryside Agency and 58 local authorities include the creation of 12 Community Forests in and around major cities in England, with a total designated area of 450,000 hectares. These forests help to restore areas marked by industrial dereliction, provide new habitats for wildlife and create sites for recreation and environmental education. In 2002/03, 983 hectares of new woodlands were created in Community Forest areas, bringing the total created since 1990 to 10,041 hectares.

The Forestry Commission and forestry policy

The Forestry Commission operates as a cross-border public body within Great Britain (for Northern Ireland see page 420). It serves as the forestry department of the administration, advising on forestry policies and, working with partners, putting those policies into practice. In particular, it gives grant aid for the stewardship of existing woodlands and woodland expansion in the private sector, and manages the national forests of England, Wales and Scotland.

The work of the Commission in each part of Great Britain is overseen by a National Committee that has responsibility for giving strategic direction to the Commission's activities. The Forestry

Ministers' Group discusses matters of common interest, such as the UK Forestry Standard, which sets out the criteria and standards for the management of all UK forests and woodland.

Forestry Commission England is responsible for leading implementation of the Government's England Forestry Strategy. Some of the key targets for the Commission for 2003–06 are planting 15,000 hectares of new woodland (6,700 hectares had been planted by the end of March 2004), harvesting 38 per cent of annual timber growth each year to promote the sustainable use of the woodland resource, and creating 2,700 hectares of new woodland in coalfield areas and deprived wards to encourage economic regeneration. Forest Enterprise England, an executive agency of Forestry Commission England, is responsible for managing the public forest estate, which amounts to 257,400 hectares and contains 19 per cent of England's woodlands. Forestry Commission Scotland manages the national forests of Scotland, which total 660,000 hectares, and gives grant aid for woodland expansion and stewardship in the private sector through the Scottish Forestry Grants Scheme. Forestry Commission Wales manages the 113,000 hectares of woodland owned by the Assembly.

Progress on sustainable forest management is measured by the UK Indicators of Sustainable Forestry. The 40 indicators were first published in October 2002, and are grouped into six themes: woodland; biodiversity; condition of forest and environment; timber and other forest products; people and forests; and economic aspects.

Forest Research is the principal organisation in the United Kingdom involved on forestry and tree-related research. An agency of the Commission, it produces scientific research and surveys, both to inform the development of forestry policies and practices and to promote high standards of sustainable forest management. The priorities for forestry research are agreed at the meetings of the forestry ministers.

Forestry in Northern Ireland

The Forest Service is an executive agency within DARD and promotes the interests of forestry through sustainable management and expansion of state-owned forests. It encourages private forestry through grant aid for planting. It manages over 61,500 hectares of forest land. The Service offered 423,000 cubic metres of timber for sale in 2003/04, with receipts of £5.4 million, and there were some 446,000 paying visitors to its forests. Forestry and timber processing employ about 1,000 people in Northern Ireland.

Further reading

Agriculture in the United Kingdom 2003. Defra, SEERAD, DARD and NAW. The Stationery Office, 2004.

Department for Environment, Food and Rural Affairs and Forestry Commission: Departmental Report 2004. Cm 6219. The Stationery Office, 2004.

Forestry Statistics (annual publication). Forestry Commission.

Scottish Agriculture Facts and Figures 2003. Scottish Executive, 2004.

Statistical Review of Northern Ireland Agriculture 2003. DARD, 2004.

United Kingdom Sea Fisheries Statistics. Defra. The Stationery Office.

Websites

Department for Environment, Food and Rural Affairs
www.defra.gov.uk

National Assembly for Wales
www.wales.gov.uk

Scottish Executive Environment and Rural Affairs Department
www.scotland.gov.uk/seerad

Department of Agriculture and Rural Development (Northern Ireland)
www.dardni.gov.uk

The Forestry Commission
www.forestry.gov.uk

The Forest Service
www.forestserviceni.gov.uk

27 Manufacturing and construction

Manufacturing overview

The manufacturing sector's share of the UK economy was 16 per cent (£153 billion) of gross value added (GVA – see glossary) at current basic prices in 2003, compared with 21 per cent in 1993. It accounted for 13 per cent of employment (3.4 million jobs) in December 2003. The regions with the highest proportion of employees in manufacturing were the East Midlands and West Midlands (at 19 and 18 per cent respectively). London had the lowest at 6 per cent.

The recession in the early 1990s led to a decline in manufacturing output. It began to rise between 1993 and 2000, before declining again in 2001 and 2002. Output rose slightly in 2003. Productivity (measured by output per job) was 29 per cent higher in 2003 than in 1993.

Manufacturing Strategy

In May 2002 the Government published a *Manufacturing Strategy* for the United Kingdom. It identified seven key issues for Government, companies and the workforce:

- macroeconomic stability;
- investment;
- science and innovation;
- best practice;
- raising skills and education levels;
- modern infrastructure; and
- the right market framework.

As part of the Strategy, the Department of Trade and Industry (DTI) established the Manufacturing Advisory Service (MAS), providing manufacturers with advice on how to improve productivity. MAS operates through:

- ten regional centres of manufacturing excellence, providing advice to small and medium enterprises;
- a national network of centres of expertise in manufacturing that companies can turn to for advice. The network consists of accredited bodies such as trade associations, university departments and Research Councils (see page 393); and
- a website, providing access to all parts of MAS and to other complementary sources of information and advice.

The second annual report of MAS showed that, in 2003, it delivered a total value added of £39 million to UK manufacturers, an average of £104,000 for every company assisted. It also responded to nearly 11,000 enquiries from firms seeking advice, visited over 4,400 companies to carry out an initial diagnostic health check and completed almost 1,000 in-depth consultancies.

A further report, *The Manufacturing Strategy Two Years On*, was published in July 2004 and covers the progress made and what more needs to be done, and identifies the priorities that need to be focused on to achieve a high value, highly skilled and competitive manufacturing sector.

Manufacturing size and output

The number of manufacturing enterprises fell by 1.5 per cent in 2002 and total turnover was 2.5 per cent lower than in 2001 (Table 27.1). Over half of all manufacturing businesses had an annual turnover of less than £250,000 in 2003 and employed fewer than five people. In contrast, there were 1,140 enterprises with turnover of at least £50 million and 925 employing 500 or more people.

Table 27.1 Manufacturing industry, UK

	Number of enterprises (thousand)	Total turnover (£ billion)
1998	169.4	460.7
1999	170.2	461.8
2000	167.3	469.1
2001	164.7	461.9
2002	162.2	450.1

Source: Annual Business Inquiry, Office for National Statistics

GVA, output and productivity are shown in Tables 27.2, 27.3 and 27.4. Output of the chemicals and man-made fibres industry has grown by 36 per cent since 1993 and output of the transport equipment industry (which includes aerospace and defence) by 19 per cent. Electrical and optical equipment, although 39 per cent higher in 2003 than in 1993, has shown a marked short-term decline – it fell by 20 per cent between 2000 and 2003. Output of some sectors continued to decline – leather and leather products, for example, were 44 per cent lower than in 1993 and textiles and textile products fell by 35 per cent.

An outline of the major manufacturing sectors follows, in order of their significance to the UK economy in terms of GVA. Based on 2003 data, food, drink and tobacco is the largest sector, with transport equipment (including aerospace and defence) moving up from fifth to third place compared with equivalent 2002 data. For each sector a table shows the number of enterprises and turnover at current prices for the latest available three years. These data are collected by the ONS Annual Business Inquiry (ABI), which in 2002 sampled about 74,000 businesses. Occasionally, statistics come from sources other than National Statistics, such as trade associations. Any variations usually reflect differences in coverage of the industry concerned.

Food, drink and tobacco

In 2002 there were 7,560 enterprises in the UK food and drink manufacturing and processing industry, with a combined turnover of £76.7 billion (Table 27.5).

The largest concentration of enterprises is in the production of bread, fresh pastry goods and cakes, followed by those engaged in the production, processing and preserving of meat and meat products. Spirits production gives Scotland the highest concentration of employment in the alcoholic and soft drinks manufacturing industry.

Table 27.2 GVA at current basic prices in manufacturing, 2003, UK

1992 Standard Industrial Classification (SIC) category	£ million	% contribution
Food, drink and tobacco	22,232	14.5
Textiles, leather and clothing		
Textiles and textile products	5,519	3.6
Leather and leather products	593	0.4
Wood and wood products	2,523	1.7
Pulp, paper and paper products; publishing and printing	20,343	13.3
Coke, refined petroleum products and nuclear fuel	3,012	2.0
Chemicals, chemical products and man-made fibres	15,409	10.1
Rubber and plastic products	7,914	5.2
Other non-metallic mineral products	5,499	3.6
Basic metals and fabricated metal products	15,210	10.0
Engineering and allied industries		
Machinery and equipment not elsewhere classified	12,022	7.9
Electrical and optical equipment	16,874	11.0
Transport equipment	18,133	11.9
Other manufacturing not elsewhere classified	7,520	4.9
Total manufacturing	**152,803**	**100**

Source: *United Kingdom National Accounts 2004 – the Blue Book*, Office for National Statistics

Table 27.3 Index of manufacturing output, UK

2001 = 100

1992 SIC category	1993	1998	2003
Food, drink and tobacco	97.1	100.0	100.8
Textiles, leather and clothing			
Textiles and textile products	143.5	126.1	92.9
Leather and leather products	128.9	116.6	71.7
Wood and wood products	107.8	101.4	102.1
Pulp, paper and paper products; publishing and printing	95.3	99.0	98.6
Coke, refined petroleum products and nuclear fuel	112.4	111.8	95.8
Chemicals, chemical products and man-made fibres	74.6	86.3	101.1
Rubber and plastic products	90.4	104.2	96.6
Other non-metallic mineral products	98.8	96.6	102.8
Basic metals and fabricated metal products	95.8	102.5	93.6
Engineering and allied industries			
Machinery and equipment not elsewhere specified	101.5	104.3	95.5
Electrical and optical equipment	62.4	85.0	86.7
Transport equipment	85.9	103.1	102.5
Other manufacturing not elsewhere classified	93.7	99.9	101.0
Total manufacturing	**89.5**	**98.2**	**97.3**

Source: Office for National Statistics

Table 27.4 Output per job in manufacturing industries, UK

2001 = 100

1992 SIC category	1993	1998	2003
Food, drink and tobacco	89.7	94.4	107.2
Textiles, leather and clothing	81.6	83.4	117.6
Pulp, paper and paper products; publishing and printing	88.6	88.3	100.2
Chemicals, chemical products and man-made fibres	67.2	77.7	102.7
Rubber and plastic products	99.5	91.5	99.5
Other non-metallic mineral products	86.8	89.9	112.1
Basic metals and fabricated metal products	85.6	90.8	102.8
Engineering industries			
Machinery and equipment not elsewhere classified	89.7	90.3	108.4
Electrical and optical equipment	65.2	75.7	107.8
Transport equipment	89.0	94.1	112.1
Wood and wood products; coke, refined petroleum products and nuclear fuel; manufacturing not elsewhere classified	107.0	96.6	103.2
Total manufacturing	**82.6**	**87.0**	**106.6**

Source: Office for National Statistics

The biggest food and drink export category in 2003 was alcoholic beverages, with exports valued at £2.9 billion, accounting for 33 per cent of the total value of food and drink sales overseas. The largest food-exporting sectors, each worth over £500 million, were dairy products and cheeses, processing and preserving of fish products, and cocoa, chocolate and confectionery.

Organic foods are a growing sector of the market. According to the Soil Association, retail sales between April 2002 and April 2003 were worth just

Table 27.5 Food products, drink and tobacco, UK

	Number of enterprises	Total turnover (£ billion)
2000	7,888	73.9
2001	7,706	74.7
2002	7,560	76.7

Source: Annual Business Inquiry, Office for National Statistics

over £1 billion, 10 per cent higher than in the previous year. This makes the United Kingdom the third biggest outlet for organic food in the world. Organic baby food accounted for 41 per cent of all baby food sold.

Bread and morning goods

The bread and morning goods (such as rolls, baps, scones, teacakes and croissants) market is worth over £3 billion a year and is one of the largest sectors in the UK food industry. Total volume is about 2.9 million tonnes, the equivalent of over 9 million large loaves every day. In 2002, 73 per cent of bread in the United Kingdom (by value) was produced by plant bakers, of which British Bakeries, Allied Bakeries and Warburtons accounted for 53 per cent. In-store bakeries (within supermarkets) accounted for around 19 per cent of sales, with high street retail (craft) bakers producing the remaining 9 per cent. Of bread sold, 69 per cent is white, 19 per cent is brown or wholemeal and the remaining 12 per cent is accounted for by the more than 200 varieties of specialist bread available to the UK consumer. The UK sandwich market accounts for around 50 per cent of bread eaten (although most sandwiches are still made at home) and was worth £3.3 billion in 2002.

Dairy products

In Great Britain, 83 per cent of household purchases of milk were bought from retail outlets in 2003, with the remaining 17 per cent delivered to the doorstep. This latter proportion has been declining for some time – in 1998 the figure was 35 per cent. Household consumption of liquid milk per head in the United Kingdom – 2.15 litres a week in 2002 – is among the highest in the world. Semi-skimmed (containing between

1.5 and 1.8 per cent fat) and skimmed milk (not more than 0.5 per cent fat) consumption accounted for 70 per cent of total milk sales in 2002.

The UK dairy industry accounted for 69 per cent of butter and 68 per cent of cheese supplies to the domestic market in 2002, and achieved significant sales overseas. Over 400 different types of cheese are produced in the United Kingdom. Cheddar has the highest sales but other well-known varieties include Caerphilly, Cheshire, Double Gloucester, Stilton and Wensleydale.

Beer

UK consumers spent £3.1 billion on beer in the retail sector in 2003, 7 per cent more than in 2002; a further £15.7 billion was spent in restaurants and hotels. Beer (including lager) production in 2003, at 58.0 million hectolitres, was 2.4 per cent higher than in 2002; beer released for home consumption in the United Kingdom amounted to 60.3 million hectolitres, 1.5 per cent higher than in 2002 (Table 27.6). Exports were valued at £231 million in 2003, amounting to 3.5 million hectolitres.

Lager accounted for 48 per cent of all draught beer sales in 2003, but there is still a strong demand for traditional cask-conditioned and brewery-conditioned ales and stouts. The UK brewing industry has six major national brewery groups,

Table 27.6 Alcoholic drink industry, UK

		Thousand hectolitres	
	1993	1998	2003
Production			
Beer	56,746	56,652	58,014
Potable spirits			
Home-produced whisky	3,570	4,576	3,937
Other	404	569	616
Released for home consumption			
Beer	59,177	58,835	60,301
Wine of fresh grapes			
Still	6,806	8,349	10,943
Sparkling	296	416	640
Made wine	990	1,651	762
Cider and perry	4,496	5,548	5,876
Spirits			
Home-produced whisky	374	289	318
Other[1]	504	505	744

1 Includes imported spirits.
Source: HM Customs and Excise

42 regional/family brewers and about 430 micro-breweries. Throughout the world brewers use UK malt, made almost entirely from home-grown barley.

Spirits

Home-produced whisky production in 2003 was 3.9 million hectolitres, an increase of 1 per cent on 2002. The Scotch whisky industry is one of the top UK export earners, with overseas sales up 4 per cent in 2003 to nearly £2.4 billion. The United States remained the largest market by value, with sales worth £329 million. The industry exports to 200 countries worldwide – the top five overseas markets are shown in Table 27.7. In September 2003 some 10,000 people worked in the Scotch whisky industry and a further 30,000 were employed in Scotland in associated sectors. There are around 90 malt and grain whisky distilleries in Scotland, the majority in Speyside and in the Highlands, with seven on Islay and three in the Lowlands. Most Scotch consumed is a blend of malt and grain.

Table 27.7 Top five overseas markets for Scotch whisky

Million bottles

Country	2002	2003	% share in 2003
France	148.1	133.7	13.6
United States	108.2	124.4	12.7
Spain	109.2	122.0	12.4
South Korea	46.6	44.6	4.5
Germany	31.5	42.8	4.4
Total exports	**942.0**	**980.7**	*100*
of which:			
European Union	416.6	404.2	41.2

Source: Scotch Whisky Association

Welsh whisky

More than 100 years after the end of whisky production in Wales, a new whisky was launched in March 2004. Penderyn single malt is made by the independent Welsh Whisky Company (*Y Cwmni Wisgi Cymreig*) producing 75,000 bottles a year at its distillery in the village of Penderyn in the Brecon Beacons.

Gin and vodka production are also important parts of the spirits industry, with 16 distilleries and compounders in the United Kingdom. Some 70 per cent is now bottled in Scotland. Around 80 per cent of UK-produced gin and 20 per cent of vodka were exported in 2003, worth over £250 million – 24 per cent higher than in the previous year. The largest export market was the United States, worth £97 million.

Wine, cider and perry

There were 333 commercial vineyards in the United Kingdom at the end of 2002, covering 812 hectares of land, nearly all in the southern half of England and Wales. Most of the home production is white wine, mainly from Germanic vines. Cider and perry are made predominantly in the west and south-west of England, notably in Herefordshire, Somerset and Devon. Bulmers, one of the two biggest UK producers, is the world's largest cider maker.

Tobacco

The Tobacco Manufacturers' Association estimates that UK spending on legitimate tobacco products in 2003 was £12.3 billion, of which £9.8 bilion was paid in tax (£8.0 billion in excise duty and £1.8 billion in VAT). Sales in recent years have been affected by the growth of smuggling. Government estimates of revenue lost through tobacco smuggling in 2002/03 were £3.0 billion, compared with £3.2 billion in 2001/02; revenue lost through cross-border shopping amounted to £1.4 billion in 2002/03.

The industry's export sales were £901 million in 2003 – with Europe, the Middle East and Africa important markets. The UK tobacco industry remains one of the top ten balance of payments earners in the UK economy. In 2003 around 6,700 people were directly employed in tobacco manufacturing, with a further 81,000 jobs

Table 27.8 Tobacco production, UK

	1993	1998	2003
Cigarettes (billion)	134	164	108
Cigars (million)	1,109	823	675
Handrolling tobacco (tonnes)	3,866	6,673	3,729
Pipe tobacco (tonnes)	1,850	1,159	1,025

Source: Tobacco Manufacturers' Association

indirectly supported in supplier industries and associated employment in distribution and retailing. Three major manufacturers supply the UK market: Gallaher, Imperial Tobacco and British American Tobacco.

Paper, printing and publishing

In 2002 the UK pulp, paper and paper products industry had a turnover of £11.5 billion and the publishing and printing industry a turnover of £33.9 billion. Total industry output fell by 1.5 per cent in 2003, although it was 3.5 per cent higher than in 1993. Exports in 2003 were £5.1 billion – the largest contributors were paper and paperboard (27 per cent), publishing of books (25 per cent), and publishing of journals and periodicals (10 per cent).

Table 27.9 Pulp, paper and paper products, publishing and printing, UK

	Number of enterprises	Total turnover (£ billion)
2000	32,588	45.3
2001	32,492	44.9
2002	32,334	45.4

Source: Annual Business Inquiry, Office for National Statistics

Paper

The paper and board sector is dominated by a small number of medium and large firms. In 2003 there were 80 pulp, paper and board mills in the United Kingdom, employing around 15,800 people and concentrated in north Kent, Lancashire, the West Country and central Scotland. These mills produce hundreds of different grades of paper and board, which are converted into a wide range of products for use in industry, commerce, education, communications, distribution and in the home. They also produce a host of speciality papers for industrial use, for example material that is subsequently coated, sensitised or laminated.

UK papermaking production in 2003 was 6.2 million tonnes, about the same as in 2002, and 15.3 per cent higher than in 1993. Exports in 2003 grew to 1.3 million tonnes, 5.4 per cent more than in 2002 and 19 per cent higher than in 1993. Exports to the European Union (EU) rose for the first time since 1999 by 4.9 per cent to 0.9 million tonnes. There has been a trend towards producing waste-based packaging grades. Recycled paper (including imports) made up 68.6 per cent of the raw material for UK newspapers in 2003, up from 65.1 per cent in 2002 and 63.5 per cent in 2001.

Printing and publishing

Unlike the paper and board sector, the UK printing and publishing industry has many small businesses – only 3.4 per cent of enterprises employed 50 or more people and over 91 per cent employed fewer than 20 people in 2003. Many publishing and printing firms are based in south-east England. Mergers have led to the formation of large groups in newspaper, magazine and book publishing. The main export categories for the printing and publishing industry are shown in Table 27.10.

The UK book-publishing industry is a major exporter, with exports of £1.3 billion in 2003, 6 per cent higher than in 2002 (Table 27.11). The United States remained the largest export market, with just over one-sixth of the total; the Republic of Ireland was again in second place.

The UK printing industry had a turnover of £14.2 billion and employed an average of 191,000 people in 2002. It continued to take advantage of technological changes. The use of digital technology has improved both automation and personalisation. Direct exports were worth £501 million in 2003.

Table 27.10 Printing and publishing industry: top ten export categories, UK

£ million

	2002	2003
Books, booklets and brochures	1,025	993
Newspapers and periodicals	487	553
Single sheets	135	224
Trade advertising	99	104
Printed labels	70	83
Cartons, boxes, etc	80	79
Postcards and greetings cards	64	71
Dictionaries and encyclopedias	31	40
Security printing	41	32
Maps and charts	23	30

Source: HM Customs and Excise

Table 27.11 Top ten export destinations for books, UK

	£ million		% share
	2002	2003	in 2003
United States	214	224	17.1
Republic of Ireland	93	94	7.2
Germany	83	88	6.7
Australia	61	72	5.5
Netherlands	69	71	5.4
France	53	62	4.7
Japan	46	44	3.4
Spain	60	43	3.3
Italy	39	41	3.2
South Africa	31	41	3.1
Total exports	**1,234**	**1,306**	**100**

Source: Department of Trade and Industry

Table 27.12 Transport equipment, UK

	Number of enterprises	Total turnover (£ billion)
2000	4,934	43.4
2001	4,897	44.0
2002	4,934	46.4

Source: Annual Business Inquiry, Office for National Statistics

Transport equipment

This sector covers the production of cars and commercial vehicles, vehicle components, shipbuilding and marine engineering, and railway equipment (all included in Table 27.12) and aerospace and defence (included in Table 27.14).

Motor vehicles

UK car production in 2003, at 1.66 million, was 2 per cent higher than in 2002, and 21 per cent higher than in 1993. Traditional home markets no longer dominate production – exports accounted for 69 per cent of production in 2003 compared with 39 per cent a decade earlier. There were 1.14 million passenger cars produced for export in 2003, 9 per cent more than in 2002, with significant growth at BMW MINI, Honda, Nissan and Peugeot. Commercial vehicle production in 2003 fell by 1 per cent to 189,000; 54 per cent, or 103,000 units, were for export. The sector is dominated by light commercial vehicles (mainly vans and minibuses). In total, UK motor vehicle exports were worth £14.6 billion in 2003, 7 per cent more than in 2002.

In 2003 about 243,000 people were employed in vehicle and component production and manufacturing activities in the United Kingdom. This was around 3,000 fewer than in 2002, a trend similar to UK manufacturing as a whole, and driven mainly by improvements in manufacturing efficiency.

Half a million Minis

The 500,000th new-style Mini rolled off the production line at BMW's Oxford plant in August 2004. The original Mini first went on sale in 1959 and more than five million were sold up to October 2000 when Rover, then owned by BMW, ceased production at Longbridge in Birmingham. BMW revived the marque in 2001, and the plant now produces 174,000 cars a year.

The United Kingdom is an important location for car and commercial vehicle manufacture (Table 27.13). In addition to the independent MG Rover, there are eight other global car manufacturers in the United Kingdom: Nissan, Toyota, Peugeot, Honda, BMW (MINI and Rolls-Royce), Ford PAG (Aston Martin, Land Rover and Jaguar Daimler), General Motors (Vauxhall) and Volkswagen (Bentley). Nissan's Sunderland plant is the most productive in Europe in terms of vehicles produced per employee, with Honda and Toyota also in the top ten. Nissan is also the largest UK producer at present, with 332,000 cars made in 2003.

A range of smaller producers, such as Morgan, Noble, Bristol and TVR, target specialist markets such as sports and luxury cars. London Taxis International produces the famous London 'black cab' in Coventry. About 3,000 taxis were produced there in 2003, one-sixth of them for export.

The main UK truck manufacturer is Leyland Trucks, based in Lancashire. Medium-sized vans are manufactured by LDV at Birmingham, Ford at Southampton and by the General Motors/Renault/Nissan joint venture at the IBC

427

Table 27.13 Car and commercial vehicle production, UK

Percentages

	2001	2002	2003
Passenger cars			
Total production ('000s)	1,492	1,630	1,658
of which:			
1,000 cc and under	6	5	1
1,001 cc to 1,600 cc	42	44	45
1,601 cc to 2,500 cc	43	44	45
2,501 cc and over	9	7	9
Production for export ('000s)	894	1,047	1,144
of which:			
1,000 cc and under	6	3	1
1,001 cc to 1,600 cc	37	42	44
1,601 cc to 2,500 cc	45	45	45
2,501 cc and over	12	9	10
Commercial vehicles			
Total production ('000s)	193	191	189
of which:			
Light commercial vehicles	88	88	88
Rigid trucks	6	6	6
Motive units	1	1	1
Buses, coaches and minibuses	4	5	5
Production for export ('000s)	96	114	103
of which:			
Light commercial vehicles	91	92	92
Rigid trucks	5	4	4
Motive units	–	–	–
Buses, coaches and minibuses	4	4	4

Source: Motor Vehicle Production Inquiry, Office for National Statistics

Shipbuilding and marine engineering

In 2002, there were about 760 enterprises employing 25,000 people in the UK shipbuilding and ship repair industry, with a turnover of £1.9 billion. Exports in 2003 were worth £268 million. Strong competition from Eastern Europe and the Far East has made commercial shipbuilding a highly challenging market for European shipyards operating in the commercial sector. The United Kingdom also has large naval yards in Portsmouth, Plymouth and on the Clyde.

There were around 770 enterprises in the UK boat building (pleasure and sporting boats) industry in 2002, with turnover of £662 million. Exports in 2003 were worth £455 million. The industry covers both sail and motor vessels. These range from small day boats to super yachts (private ocean-going leisure craft over 24 metres in length). This sector is becoming increasingly important to the marine industry, as it is an expanding, high value added market.

The UK marine leisure industry is a distinct group of about 3,210 firms and 1,450 sole traders, providing specialised products and services to marine leisure users around the world. According to the British Marine Federation, the export market grew by 10 per cent in 2003 to £794 million, the EU and North America accounting for 72 per cent of the total. Boat exports were worth £498 million. Just over 30,000 people were employed in the industry in 2003, 5 per cent more than in 2002. About 30 per cent were involved in boat building and a further 16 per cent in equipment manufacture.

The UK marine equipment industry is diverse, ranging from propulsion and navigation

Boat Show golden anniversary

The London Boat Show celebrated its 50th anniversary in January 2004 at its new venue, the ExCeL exhibition centre in London's Docklands. An estimated 210,000 visitors attended, compared with 145,000 in 2003 at its former Earls Court Exhibition Centre venue. The other major UK boat show was held in Southampton in September 2004.

plant in Luton, Bedfordshire. Alexander Dennis is the leading bus manufacturer. Accessibility is an important issue and the company is one of the world leaders in the design of low-floor chassis and variable height suspension.

Engine production is increasing in the United Kingdom and is currently estimated at a little below 3 million units a year. Ford is producing diesel engines at Dagenham and petrol engines at Bridgend, and BMW's new Hams Hall (West Midlands) plant is producing engines for several BMW models including the new BMW 1 series. The other principal UK engine makers are Honda, MG Rover, Nissan and Toyota.

equipment to generators and safety equipment. It provides equipment for commercial vessels, naval ships and leisure boats. Faced with a diminishing home market, this sector has been successful in targeting the Korean, Japanese and Chinese markets.

Railway equipment

A number of UK enterprises are engaged in manufacturing railway equipment for both domestic and overseas markets, mainly producing specialist components and systems for use in rolling stock, signalling, track and infrastructure applications. Employment in the industry averaged 14,000 in 2002, with a turnover of £1.8 billion, over £400 million higher than in 2001. In 2003, exports were worth £151 million. About 4,000 firms are involved in the supply chains, and UK expertise extends to technical consultancy and project management.

The largest company in this sector is the Canadian-owned Bombardier Transportation, which assembles and maintains UK passenger rolling stock. Most new trains now being introduced in the United Kingdom have a number of foreign-made components, and UK input varies from 5 to 75 per cent of total value. Privatised train operating companies have placed orders for around 5,000 new passenger carriages since 1997, while many older trains have been refurbished. An extensive programme of infrastructure modernisation is also being undertaken.

Aerospace and defence

The UK aerospace industry is one of the few in the world with a complete capability across the whole spectrum of aerospace products and technology. Exports grew by 8 per cent to £12.5 billion in 2003.

Table 27.14 Aerospace and defence, UK

	Number of enterprises	Total turnover (£ billion)
2000	811	17.1
2001	769	17.4
2002	716	15.9

Source: Annual Business Inquiry, Office for National Statistics

Industry activities cover design and manufacture of airframes and structures, aeroengines, guided weapons, simulators and space satellites, materials, flight controls including automatic electronic signalling (fly-by-wire) and fibre optics (fly-by-light) equipment, and avionics and complex components, with their associated services. The United Kingdom also has one of the largest defence manufacturing industries in the Western world.

Among the leading companies are BAE Systems and Rolls-Royce. BAE Systems is a global company engaged in the development, delivery and support of advanced defence and aerospace systems for air, land, sea and space. The company designs, manufactures and supports military aircraft, ships, submarines, radar, avionics, communications, electronics and guided weapons systems. It had global sales of £12.6 billion in 2003, compared with £12.1 billion in 2002, and an order book of £46.0 billion.

Engines

Rolls-Royce is one of the world's leading manufacturers of power systems. Rolls-Royce engines power over 30 civil aircraft types. It is also responsible for 11,000 helicopter engines in commercial service. Its group turnover in 2003 was £5.6 billion, including £2.7 billion in civil aerospace and £1.4 billion in defence aerospace, and it had an order book worth £18.7 billion. In civil aerospace, it delivered 746 engines to 48 airlines and 68 corporate customers in 2003. In defence aerospace, Rolls-Royce has the world's largest military engine customer base, serving over 160 armed forces worldwide, with 24,000 engines in current military service.

Civil aircraft

Airbus is jointly owned by the European Aeronautic Defence and Space Company (EADS) and BAE Systems (with 80 and 20 per cent stakes, respectively). Airbus UK designs and manufactures the wings for the whole range of Airbus airliners at its two sites in Filton (Bristol) and Broughton (Chester). By the end of June 2004, 5,000 Airbus aircraft had been ordered and over 3,000 were in service with more than 200 operators worldwide. Airbus is now engaged in the design and manufacture of the wings for the new A380 'super jumbo' – the world's first twin-deck, four-aisle airliner, with capacity for 555 passengers – which is due to enter service in 2006.

Bombardier Aerospace of Canada, the third largest civil aircraft manufacturer in the world, produces a wide range of turboprop and regional jet aircraft and business jets. At its Belfast site, Bombardier Aerospace Northern Ireland designs and manufactures major civil aircraft sub-assemblies, advanced engine nacelles and flight controls, as well as providing aviation support services.

Military aircraft and missiles

BAE Systems, along with EADS and Alenia of Italy, has developed the Eurofighter Typhoon, a multi-role aircraft for the RAF and for the German, Italian and Spanish air forces. Of 620 aircraft presently on order, 232 will be built in the United Kingdom. The company is also a partner with Lockheed Martin of the United States in the F-35 Joint Strike Fighter (JSF) aircraft. Three variants are being developed, with requirements for around 3,000 aircraft. The RAF and Royal Navy will use a short takeoff and vertical landing (STOVL) version. The first JSF is expected to be operational in 2010. BAE Systems also developed the Harrier jump-jet, latterly as part of the US-UK AV-8B programme, and the European joint venture Tornado combat aircraft. The Hawk fast-jet trainer remains in production with new versions planned for RAF service and export.

Europe's main guided weapons business, MBDA, is jointly owned by BAE Systems (37.5 per cent), EADS and Italy's Finmeccanica. The French-owned Thales, including Thales Air Defence in Belfast, is another major company operating in the UK guided weapons sector.

Helicopters

AgustaWestland, currently jointly owned by GKN and Finmeccanica, produces the multi-role EH101 medium-lift helicopter for civilian and military markets. There are two UK variants for the Royal Navy and for the RAF. It also manufactures the Super Lynx 300 light battlefield and naval helicopter, and has produced under licence from Boeing the Apache AH Mk1 attack helicopter for the UK Armed Forces. It has a joint venture with Bell in the United States to produce the Bell Agusta AB139 helicopter.

Space equipment and services

The UK space industry includes companies that provide space technology (the upstream sector) and those exploiting this technology (the downstream sector). The upstream sector

employed 5,900 people and generated turnover of £501 million in 2002/03, 2 per cent less in real terms than in 2001/02; space prime business accounted for 49 per cent of the total. UK participation in the European Space Agency, and the British National Space Centre's (BNSC) role in coordinating UK space policy (see page 392), has enabled UK-based companies to participate in many leading space projects. The industry's strengths are in the development and manufacture of civil and military communications satellite systems, small satellites, radar and antennae, and software. In the field of Earth observation, BNSC has played a major role in programmes which have led to the development of platforms, space radar and meteorological satellite hardware, and in the exploitation of space data imaging products.

EADS Astrium is Europe's leading space company. Its satellite business activities cover civil and military communications and Earth observation, science and navigation programmes, avionics and equipment. In the United Kingdom it operates from two sites in Portsmouth, Hampshire and Stevenage, Hertfordshire, together employing over 2,000 people.

Electrical and optical equipment

In 2002, 29 per cent of turnover in this industry was in the radio, TV and communications equipment sector; 26 per cent in electrical machinery; 23 per cent in medical, precision and optical equipment and watches; and 22 per cent in office machinery and computers.

Total output rose sharply up to 2000, but then fell 20 per cent by 2003. It remained 39 per cent higher than in 1993. Between 1993 and 2003, production of office machinery and computers nearly trebled, while radio, TV and communications equipment output, which peaked in 2000, was up by 52 per cent. However, production of medical and optical instruments was only 1 per cent higher than in 1993, while that of electrical machinery and apparatus fell by 13 per cent over the same period.

Total exports fell by 18 per cent in 2003 to £36.6 billion. Computers and process equipment accounted for £8.9 billion, TV and radio transmitters £6.5 billion, measuring instruments £4.5 billion, and electronic components £4.1 billion.

Table 27.15 Electrical and optical equipment, UK

	Number of enterprises	Total turnover (£ billion)
2000	16,418	69.1
2001	16,141	63.2
2002	15,914	53.1

Source: Annual Business Inquiry, Office for National Statistics

A substantial proportion of employment in these sectors (especially sales and administrative jobs) is based in southern England, with Scotland and Wales important areas for inward investors. In 2002, electrical and instrument engineering accounted for Scottish exports worth £6.7 billion, 39 per cent less than in 2001, but worth 46 per cent of Scotland's total manufactured exports.

Many leading overseas-based multinational electronics firms have substantial manufacturing investment in the United Kingdom. The main electronic consumer goods produced are television sets – 1.6 million were manufactured in 2003. UK production is concentrated in the high-value market, increasingly in widescreen and digital sets.

The UK computer industry produces an extensive range of systems for all uses – 10 million personal computers were produced in 2003. Many multinational computer manufacturers operate in the United Kingdom, though between 2000 and 2003 production of computers declined by about 32 per cent. In 2002 there were 1,630 enterprises involved in the manufacture of computers and other information processing equipment, with turnover of £10.8 billion, although this was down 18 per cent on the previous year.

Both UK and foreign companies produce a range of other electrical machinery and apparatus in the United Kingdom. These include electric motors, generators and transformers; electricity distribution and control apparatus; insulated wire and cables (including optical fibre cables for telecommunications); and lighting equipment. There were nearly 5,500 enterprises in this sector in 2002, with turnover of £13.9 billion.

Communications equipment

Domestic telecommunications equipment manufacturers have invested heavily in facilities to meet rapidly increasing demand for telecommunications services (see chapter 17). The main products are switching and transmission equipment, telephones and terminals. Transmission equipment and cables for telecommunications and information networks include submarine and high-specification data-carrying cables, such as fibre optics.

Another sector of the industry manufactures radio communications equipment, radar, radio and sonar navigational aids for ships and aircraft, thermal imaging systems, alarms and signalling apparatus, public broadcasting equipment and other capital goods.

Medical electronics

The high demand for advanced medical equipment in the United Kingdom stems from its comprehensive healthcare system and extensive clinical research and testing facilities in the chemical, biological, physical and molecular sciences. UK scientists and engineers have made important contributions to basic research and development (R&D) in endoscopy, computerised tomography scanning, magnetic resonance imaging (pioneered in the United Kingdom), ultrasonic imaging, coronary artery diagnosis and renal analysis. Total exports in this sector were £2.0 billion in 2003. Turnover amounted to £3.0 billion and the sector employed an average of 34,000 people in 2002.

Instrumentation and control

The UK instrumentation and control sector is diverse, with around 3,350 enterprises, employing 77,000 people in 2002 and with turnover of £8.1 billion. The sector covers the design, development and manufacture of scientific and industrial equipment and systems for analysis, measurement, testing and control.

Chemicals and chemical products

The chemicals industry is one of the primary UK manufacturing sectors and accounted for 10 per cent of manufacturing industry GVA in 2003. Around 37 per cent of turnover in 2002 was in the manufacture of basic chemicals, with a further 32 per cent in pharmaceutical products. Soap and detergents, cleaning and polishing preparations, and perfumes and toilet preparations accounted for 11 per cent of industry turnover.

The sector underpins the UK manufacturing industry, with chemicals being essential supplies for most other industrial processes. Although output only grew by 1 per cent in 2003, it was still 36 per cent higher than in 1993. The industry is a leading UK exporter, and had a trade surplus in 2003 of £5.6 billion. Exports totalled £31.3 billion, of which 40 per cent were pharmaceuticals and 31 per cent basic chemicals.

Table 27.16 Chemicals, chemical products and man-made fibres, UK

	Number of enterprises	Total turnover (£ billion)
2000	3,952	47.5
2001	3,865	48.9
2002	3,817	48.7

Source: Annual Business Inquiry, Office for National Statistics

The UK chemicals industry is diverse, with important representation in all principal chemical sectors – ranging from bulk petrochemicals to low-volume, high-value specialised organics. It includes key industrial materials, such as plastics and synthetic rubber (both in primary forms), and other products such as man-made fibres, soap and detergents, cosmetics, adhesives, dyes and inks, and intermediate products for the pharmaceutical and a range of other downstream industries.

Bulk chemicals

North Sea oil and gas provide accessible feedstock for the large UK organics sector, including products such as ethylene, propylene, benzene and paraxylene. These provide the building blocks for the manufacture of many chemical products, including plastics that are strong, durable and lightweight, and are increasingly used in transport and packaging applications; and synthetic fibres such as nylon and polyester used in textiles, clothing and home furnishings.

There is substantial inorganics production, including sulphuric acid, chlorine and caustic soda, based on minerals such as salt, sulphur, and phosphate ores, or on reaction between gases. These also serve many other chemical processes.

Formulated products

The United Kingdom produces many formulated consumer products, such as decorative paint, home laundry and cleaning products, and personal care items like toothpaste, shampoos and skincare products, as well as a wide range of industrial speciality products, such as adhesives, inks and lubricants.

Fine chemicals

Fine chemicals meet specific needs through highly sophisticated product and process development. Active ingredients for the pharmaceuticals and agrochemical sectors are at the forefront of this kind of innovation. In recent years, the application of chirality[1] in synthesis has allowed firms to make drugs and agrochemicals more closely tailored to specific targets. Leading-edge research by international pharmaceutical and agrochemical companies in the United Kingdom is supported both by a strong academic research capability and a network of specialist manufacturers of 'fine' chemicals. The latter specialise in the highly skilled processes needed to produce commercial quantities of the complex molecules identified by the pharmaceutical and agrochemical companies' research.

Pharmaceuticals

The UK pharmaceuticals industry had record exports worth £12.4 billion and a trade surplus of £3.2 billion in 2003, making it the world's fourth largest pharmaceuticals sector earner by trade surplus. It is largely based in the South East, East (Hertfordshire/Essex), North West and North East of England. Research-driven, it is one of the most dynamic UK industries, and is of key importance to the economy. Principal overseas markets are Western Europe, North America and Japan. Recently, the largest growth has been in medicines acting on the cardiovascular system, followed by central nervous system and alimentary tract remedies. The UK pharmaceuticals sector had an estimated total UK market value of £13.2 billion in 2003, of which prescription medicines accounted for 85 per cent.

There are 365 pharmaceutical companies operating in the United Kingdom, with indigenous

---

1 Chiral compounds are mirror images of each other, analogous to left- and right-handed forms. One form may be more effective, or safer, than the other.

and US-owned multinationals dominating production. In terms of total market sales, Pfizer (United States) was the leading company in 2003, with an 11.4 per cent market share. UK-based GlaxoSmithKline and AstraZeneca (Anglo-Swedish) were in second and third place, accounting for 9.7 and 5.1 per cent respectively of market sales.

About 83,000 people were employed in the UK pharmaceuticals industry in December 2002 with a further 250,000 jobs in downstream/related sectors. The industry's investment in UK-based R&D exceeded £3.5 billion in 2003, nearly a quarter of all UK industrial R&D. AstraZeneca and GlaxoSmithKline are the top two UK-based companies in terms of R&D expenditure.

Of the world's top 100 medicines, 25 were discovered and developed in the United Kingdom. Among more than 20 new medicines launched in the United Kingdom in 2003 were treatments for HIV, pneumonia, rheumatoid arthritis, heart disease, diabetes, prostate hyperplasia, hormone deficiency, asthma, eczema, osteoporosis, Crohn's disease, medicines used in bone marrow transplantation and for surgical pain, and the first UK contraceptive patch. The top ten UK pharmaceutical products are shown in Table 27.17 below.

Table 27.17 Top ten UK pharmaceutical products, 2003

Product	Manufacturer	Total sales £ million
Lipitor	Pfizer	325
Zoton	Wyeth	271
Simvastatin	generic	200
Istin	Pfizer	193
Zocor	Merck, Sharp & Dohme	187
Seretide	GlaxoSmithKline	165
Zyprexa	Eli Lilly	148
Tritace	Aventis	142
Lipostat	Bristol-Myers Squibb	128
Efexor	Wyeth	127

Source: The Association of the British Pharmaceutical Industry

Significant UK manufacturing R&D investment in 2003 included:

- Eli Lilly announced in May a four-year, £220 million UK manufacturing and R&D investment package for its Speke, Merseyside

(biomanufacturing), Earlswood, Surrey (R&D), and Basingstoke, Hampshire (manufacturing) sites;

- AstraZeneca inaugurated a £90 million manufacturing expansion at its Avlon Works (Bristol) facility in May; and

- GlaxoSmithKline announced investment of £76 million in a clinical imaging centre at Imperial College, London.

Biotechnology

Biotechnology is the application of knowledge about living organisms, and their components, to industrial products and processes. The United Kingdom has companies developing and exploiting biotechnology in all areas: from pharmaceuticals and diagnostics, through speciality chemicals, food and agriculture, to the environment.

In 2002 the United Kingdom had over 480 specialist biotechnology companies, estimated to employ almost 26,000 people. A further 1,100 companies were involved in broader bioscience/healthcare related activities. Companies are clustered particularly around Cambridge, Oxford and London, as well as in parts of the South East, the North West and Scotland. Research laboratories of many leading pharmaceutical multinationals are based in the United Kingdom. The industry benefits from the strong science base in UK universities and the large number of leading research institutes in the United Kingdom (see chapter 25). UK companies account for 40 per cent of products in clinical trials by European public companies. In addition, 41 per cent of new biotechnology drugs in late stage clinical trials in Europe are from the United Kingdom.

Basic metals and fabricated metal products

Steel

The Industrial Revolution in the United Kingdom (c.1760s–1830s) was largely based on the manufacture of iron and steel and heavy machinery. These sectors remain important, accounting for 10 per cent of manufacturing GVA in 2002, but are declining, with the exception of products for the construction industry. Output of basic metals and fabricated metal products fell by 2.5 per cent in 2003, but exports increased by 8 per cent to £11.1 billion.

Table 27.18 Basic metals and fabricated metal products, UK

	Number of enterprises	Total turnover (£ billion)
2000	32,058	41.0
2001	31,630	40.7
2002	31,167	38.5

Source: Annual Business Inquiry, Office for National Statistics

Steel production is concentrated in south Wales and northern England, with substantial processing in the Midlands and Yorkshire. Major restructuring in the steel industry has taken place since the 1980s, including the closure of steelmaking at the Corus Llanwern site in south Wales in 2001 and Corus investment plans leading to the rationalisation of engineering steels production (Rotherham and Sheffield) and of east coast facilities (Teesside and Scunthorpe). The former ASW's plants in Cardiff and Sheerness, Kent, which closed in 2002, resumed production under new ownership in 2003. Similarly, Alphasteel in Newport re-started steelmaking late in 2002 and, following a change in ownership, has embarked on a major expansion plan.

UK crude steel production increased by 13 per cent to 13.3 million tonnes in 2003, reversing five consecutive years of decline. Production was boosted by the resumption of normal working at Port Talbot, south Wales, following a major accident at the Corus plant in 2002. The UK steel industry exported 6.2 million tonnes in 2003, 10 per cent more than in 2002. Most export gains took place in markets outside the EU, principally China and the Middle East. The EU market share of exports fell from 75 per cent in 2002 to 60 per cent in 2003.

Corus is Europe's second largest steelmaker and the seventh biggest in the world. It employed 24,600 people in the United Kingdom at the end of December 2003, almost 50 per cent of its total employees, and produced 89 per cent of total UK crude steel in 2003. It produces carbon steel by the basic oxygen steelmaking method at its plants in Port Talbot, Teesside and Scunthorpe and engineering steels by the electric arc furnace method at its Rotherham and Stocksbridge (Sheffield) plants. It also manufactures a wide range of other products at sites across Great Britain.

Products manufactured by other UK steel companies include reinforcing bars for the construction industry, wire rods, hot rolled bars, bright bars, tubes, and wire and wire products. Production of special steels is centred on the Sheffield area and includes stainless and alloy special steels for the aerospace and offshore oil and gas industries.

Steel has had a notable success in the UK construction industry, with its market share in building frames of two or more storeys increasing from 30 per cent in the early 1980s to more than 69 per cent in 2003. It has 95 per cent of the single-storey market. The market mix is changing, with a fall in the construction of London multi-storey offices and a national increase in hospitals, schools, shops and high-rise residential accommodation. Total iron and steel sales to the construction sector were £2.7 billion in 2003. Consumption of constructional steelwork was over 1.2 million tonnes with an additional 2.2 million tonnes of other steel used by the construction sector.

Steel is a fully recyclable product and may be recycled any number of times without loss of quality. The UK steel recycling industry reclaimed 10.3 million tonnes of steel scrap in 2003, 3.1 million tonnes of which were sold to UK steelmakers and foundries and 7.2 million tonnes exported to steelmakers overseas. In a typical year in the United Kingdom, the steel industry saves enough energy through recycling to provide electricity for several million households.

Non-ferrous and fabricated metals

Non-ferrous metals in the United Kingdom are produced from both primary and recycled raw materials. They are extremely recyclable without loss of quality and have always made significant contributions to sustainability. Including precious metals, exports totalled £3.1 billion in 2003, about the same as in 2002.

The aluminium sector supplies the packaging, transport, building and construction, and general and electrical industries. It had a turnover of £2.1 billion in 2002, with exports in 2003 worth £1.0 billion. In 2003, 750,000 tonnes of aluminium were recycled, two-thirds back into wrought products and one-third into cast products.

Precious metals had a turnover of £532 million in 2002, and exports worth £930 million in 2003.

Copper and copper alloys are used for electrical wire and cables, power generation and electrical and electronic connectors, automotive components, plumbing and building products, and components for industrial plant and machinery. In 2002 this sector had a turnover of £704 million, with exports worth £502 million in 2003. About 50 per cent of the raw material feed to the semi-finished sector is sourced from the recycling of secondary material, both process scrap and life-expired components.

Lead is used for lead acid batteries and roofing, and zinc used for galvanising to protect steel. Including tin production, this sector had a turnover of £446 million in 2002, with exports worth £104 million in 2003.

Nickel is used principally as an alloying element to make stainless steel and high-temperature turbine alloys, and titanium is used for high-strength, low-weight aerospace applications. In 2002 turnover in this sector was £636 million and exports were valued at £596 million in 2003.

Fabricated metal products include those made by forging, casting, pressing, stamping and roll forming of a wide variety of metals. Many of these products are subjected to surface engineering processes, which improve their working performance. These include electroplating, galvanising, anodising and heat treatment. In 2002 turnover in this sector was £25.7 billion (67 per cent of the basic metals and fabricated metal products total), with structural metal products having the largest individual share at £7.0 billion.

Construction

The UK construction industry accounted for 6 per cent of GVA in 2003. Output has recovered from the recession that affected the industry in the early 1990s, and was 9 per cent higher in 2003 than in the previous peak in 1990. The growth in output in 2003 was 4.9 per cent. The number of workforce jobs in the industry grew between December 2002 and 2003 by 6 per cent to 2,088,000, 14 per cent higher than in 1993.

In 2003 the total value of work done in the construction industry in Great Britain was £92.7 billion, of which £49.8 billion was new work and £42.9 billion repair and maintenance (Table

Table 27.19 Construction industry, UK

	Number of enterprises (thousand)	Total turnover (£ billion)
1998	179.9	102.4
1999	188.3	111.4
2000	190.6	121.5
2001	193.0	130.1
2002	195.6	142.5

Source: Annual Business Inquiry, Office for National Statistics

Table 27.20 Value of construction output by type of work, current prices, Great Britain

£ billion	2001	2002	2003
New work			
New housing			
Public	1.4	1.7	2.0
Private	8.8	10.4	13.2
Other new work			
Infrastructure	7.1	8.1	7.3
Other public	5.3	6.9	8.8
Other private industrial	3.7	3.4	3.6
Other private commercial	13.6	15.0	14.9
Total	40.0	45.4	49.8
Repair and maintenance			
Housing			
Public	6.6	6.4	7.5
Private	11.0	12.8	14.0
Other work			
Public	6.1	6.7	7.9
Private	11.0	12.3	13.6
Total	34.7	38.2	42.9
All work	**74.7**	**83.6**	**92.7**

Source: Department of Trade and Industry

27.20). There was an additional £2.6 billion of work done in Northern Ireland, of which £2.1 billion was new work and £0.5 billion repair and maintenance.

The volume of output in Great Britain at constant prices grew by 4 per cent in 2003, the highest annual increase since 1989. New work increased by 3 per cent and repair and maintenance by 7 per cent. In Northern Ireland, the volume of output also grew by 4 per cent in 2003, with new work increasing by 3 per cent and repair and maintenance by 7 per cent. The main areas of activity within the UK construction industry covered by these statistics are:

- building and civil engineering – ranging from major private sector companies with diverse international interests to one-person enterprises carrying out domestic repairs; and

- specialist work – companies or individuals undertaking construction work ranging from structural steelwork and pre-cast concrete structures to mechanical and electrical services (including the design and installation of environmentally friendly building control systems).

Other areas of construction work not covered in the above statistics include:

- the supply of building materials and components (Table 27.21 has production details) – ranging from large quarrying companies, and those engaged in mass production of manufactured items, to small, highly specialised manufacturers; and

- consultancy work – companies or individuals engaged in the planning, design and supervision of construction projects. Estimated earnings by engineering consultants on projects in the United Kingdom in 2003 were £3.7 billion. This figure accounts for 30 per cent of all income earned by UK professional services firms.

Table 27.21 Production of building materials and components, Great Britain

	2001	2002	2003
Bricks (billion)	2.75	2.75	2.77
Concrete building blocks (million sq m)	87.9	91.5	95.5
Cement (million tonnes)[1]	11.1	11.1	11.2
Sand and gravel (million tonnes)[2]	88.2	82.7	82.5
Ready mixed concrete (million cu m)[1,3]	23.0	22.6	22.3
Slate (thousand tonnes)[4]	93.1	95.0	79.1
Concrete roofing tiles (million sq m)	24.8	25.0	21.4

1 UK figures.
2 Sales.
3 Deliveries.
4 Excluding slate residue used for fill.
Source: *Construction Statistics Annual 2004*, Department of Trade and Industry

In 2003 the value of new orders in Great Britain was £34.0 billion, of which £10.8 billion was new housing and £23.1 billion other new work (Table 27.22). The volume of new orders at constant prices fell by 5 per cent over the year.

Table 27.22 Value of new orders by type of work, current prices, Great Britain

			£ billion
	2001	2002	2003
New housing			
Public and housing association	1.1	1.1	1.3
Private	6.5	8.1	9.5
Total	7.6	9.2	10.8
Other new work			
Infrastructure	5.2	5.6	4.9
Public	4.1	5.9	6.1
Private industrial	2.5	2.2	2.4
Private commercial	10.2	10.5	9.7
Total	22.0	24.2	23.1
All new work	**29.6**	**33.4**	**34.0**

Source: Department of Trade and Industry

Housing

The volume of new housing orders in Great Britain in 2003 rose by 5 per cent at constant prices, with the private sector accounting for 87 per cent of the total. Construction started on 193,800 dwellings: 177,300 by the private sector; 16,200 by registered social landlords; and 300 by local authorities. New dwellings completed by sector are shown in Table 27.23. For more information on housing, see chapter 20.

Table 27.23 Permanent dwellings completed by sector, Great Britain

			Thousands
	1993	1998	2003
Private enterprise	141	146	158
Registered social landlords	35	23	17
Local authorities	3	–	–
Total	**179**	**170**	**175**

Source: Office of the Deputy Prime Minister

Major construction projects in the United Kingdom

Some recently completed projects include:

- the Birmingham Bull Ring redevelopment, including the new Selfridges 'Armadillo' store, which opened in September 2003;

- Swiss Re headquarters 'the Gherkin', City of London, on the former site of the Baltic Exchange, officially opened in April 2004. The building is 180 metres tall, on 40 floors, and has 46,450 square metres (net) of office accommodation; and

- the M6 Toll Road, 43 kilometres long, bypassing the M6 motorway in the congested West Midlands, which opened in December 2003.

Current projects include:

- the Docklands Light Railway 4.4 kilometre extension to London City Airport and North Woolwich, due for completion by late 2005;

- the new Wembley Stadium, featuring a 130 metre arch supporting the retractable roof, due to be completed in 2006;

- Terminal 5, Heathrow Airport, due to open in spring 2008; and

- the Channel Tunnel Rail Link – section 1 (74 km) from the Channel Tunnel to Fawkham Junction, north Kent, opened in September 2003, and section 2 (39 km) to London St Pancras is due to open in early 2007.

Overseas contracting and consultancy

UK companies operate internationally and in any one year UK consultants work in almost every country in the world.

UK contractors have pioneered management contracting and design and build, and also the financing mechanisms developed in the domestic market through innovations such as the Private Finance Initiative (see page 370). They won new international business in 2002 worth £4.3 billion, 9 per cent less than in 2001. Contractors were particularly successful in North America, the most valuable market, which accounted for 48 per cent of all new contracts.

The main categories of work in which UK consultants are involved include structural commercial (roads, bridges, tunnels and railways); electrical and mechanical services; chemical, oil and gas plants; and water supply.

Further reading

The Manufacturing Strategy Two Years On. Department of Trade and Industry, 2004.

Websites

National Statistics
www.statistics.gov.uk

Department of Trade and Industry
www.dti.gov.uk

Office of the Deputy Prime Minister
www.odpm.gov.uk

WWW.

28 Energy and natural resources

The energy industries in the United Kingdom play a central role in the economy by producing, transforming and supplying energy in its various forms to all sectors.

In 2003, they accounted for 3.3 per cent of gross domestic product (GDP, see glossary). They are also major contributors to the UK balance of payments through the export of crude oil and oil products; in 2003, the United Kingdom's trade surplus in fuels was £5.4 billion.

Figure 28.1 Production of primary fuels, UK

Million tonnes of oil equivalent

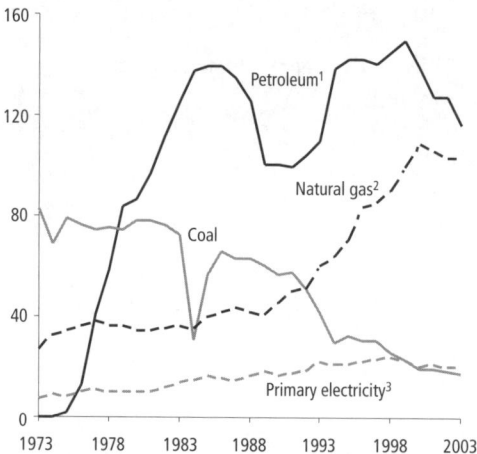

1 Includes crude oil, natural gas liquids and feedstocks.
2 Includes colliery methane.
3 Nuclear, natural flow hydro-electricity and, from 1988, generation at wind stations.
Source: Department of Trade and Industry

Production and resources

Production of primary fuels (Figure 28.1) was 4.6 per cent lower in 2003 than in 2002, at 260.4 million tonnes of oil equivalent (including electricity generated from renewables and waste sources). Petroleum production was 116.3 million tonnes of oil equivalent, down by 8.5 per cent, while production of gas (including gaseous renewables) was 102.9 million tonnes of oil equivalent, 0.7 per cent lower than in 2002. Although ten new fields started production in 2003 (see page 443), the 2 per cent they contributed to total production was insufficient to make up the decline in production from older established fields. Stocks of crude oil and petroleum products were 3 per cent higher at the end of 2003 than a year earlier.

Coal production continued its long-term downward trend, with a fall of 6.0 per cent in 2003. Despite this, coal still supplies a significant proportion of the country's primary energy needs: 34.6 per cent of the electricity supplied in 2003 was from coal compared with 32.0 per cent in 2002. Gas remains a major fuel for generating electricity, accounting for 38.1 per cent of supply in 2003 – a fall of 2.1 percentage points from 2002. Nuclear energy supplied 21.5 per cent of electricity in 2003, a fall of 0.4 percentage points from 2002.

The United Kingdom had a trade surplus in fuels of 21.7 million tonnes of oil equivalent in 2003. In volume terms, imports of fuel in 2003 were 7.0 per cent higher than in 2002, while exports were 9.6 per cent lower. The United Kingdom became a net importer of gas in the fourth quarter of 2003 as its reserves started to deplete. However, it remains a net exporter of oil and oil products despite declining production. Most UK production of crude oil and natural gas liquids (NGLs) is exported, primarily because the product is generally lighter and more valuable than that produced in other areas of the world.

The United Kingdom has an obligation under EU law to maintain stocks of key oil products at or above a certain level, to ensure adequate supplies would exist for any international oil supply emergency. These obligations are based on the UK annual consumption of the key products such as motor spirit (petrol), diesel-engined road vehicle (DERV) fuel and other gas diesel oils, aviation fuel and other kerosenes, and fuel oils. These obligations are updated every July as consumption data for the previous year are finalised. The UK obligation, based on 2002 consumption data, is to hold a total of 11 million tonnes of these products, equal to 67.5 days of consumption. At the end of 2003 the United Kingdom held stocks equal to 78.8 days of consumption.

Consumption

Total UK primary energy consumption rose by 0.9 per cent in 2003, to 232.7 million tonnes of oil equivalent (based on primary fuel input, Table 28.2). On a temperature-corrected basis, which shows what annual intake might have been if the average temperature during the year had been the same as the average for 1971–2000, consumption rose by 0.1 per cent. Also on a temperature-corrected basis, consumption of coal increased by 8 per cent in 2003, while consumption of oil and gas fell by 0.7 per cent and 1.6 per cent respectively.

Final energy consumption, that is, consumption by the final user rather than that which is used for transformation into other energy, shows a strong seasonal pattern with more energy being consumed in the winter months and less in the summer, particularly in the domestic and service sectors. Final consumption by sector is shown in Figure 28.3. Each day, the domestic sector uses 1,060 Gigawatts (GWh) of gas and 317 GWh of electricity, while industry uses 470 GWh of gas and 310 GWh of electricity.

In 2003, energy consumption in the industry, transport and domestic sectors rose by 0.6 per cent, 1.2 per cent and 0.2 per cent respectively, but

Table 28.2 Inland consumption for energy use (in terms of primary sources), UK[1]

Million tonnes oil equivalent

	1993	2002	2003
Natural gas	62.9	94.7	94.5
Oil	78.1	74.1	74.1
Coal	55.0	37.8	40.4
Nuclear electricity	21.6	20.1	20.0
Hydro electricity[2]	0.5	0.5	0.4
Renewables and waste	1.2	2.8	3.2
Net electricity imports	1.4	0.7	0.2
Total[3]	**220.7**	**230.6**	**232.7**

1 Not corrected for temperature (see text).
2 Excludes pumped storage.
3 Total includes losses of electricity during transmission and distribution.
Source: Department of Trade and Industry

consumption in the service sector fell by 2.1 per cent. There has been a rise in household energy use per person since 1970 from 0.66 to 0.81 tonnes of oil equivalent per person in 2003.

Transport energy use

Transport has been the biggest energy user in the United Kingdom for the past 17 years, accounting for 35 per cent of final energy use in 2003. Overall

Figure 28.3 Final energy consumption by final user,[1] 2003, UK

Total: 158 million tonnes of oil equivalent

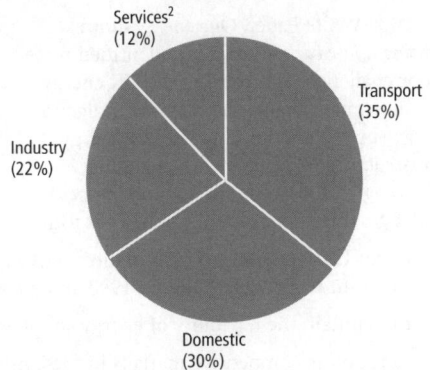

Services[2] (12%)
Transport (35%)
Industry (22%)
Domestic (30%)

1 Excluding non-energy use of fuels.
2 Includes agriculture, public administration and commerce.
Source: Department of Trade and Industry

energy consumption in the transport sector almost doubled between 1970 and 2003, with most of the increase taking place during the 1980s. Fuel consumption in the air transport sector nearly trebled (Figure 28.4).

Fuel use by road passenger vehicles has increased by 77 per cent since 1970; the distance travelled by passengers has increased by 89 per cent, while energy consumption per passenger-kilometre fell slightly (Figure 28.5).

Figure 28.4 Transport energy consumption, UK

Million tonnes of oil equivalent

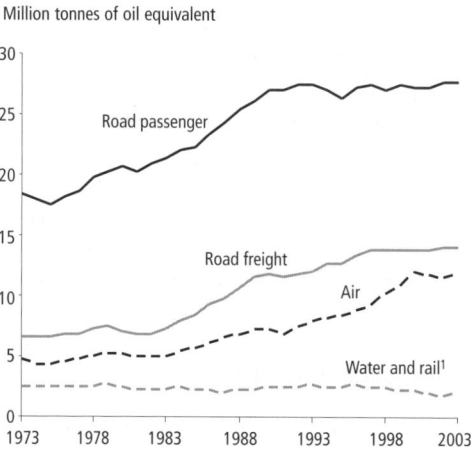

1 For rail transport, electricity consumed at transport premises is included from 1990 onwards.
Source: Department of Trade and Industry; Department for Transport

Energy policy

The 2003 White Paper, *Our energy future – creating a low carbon economy*, identified three major challenges confronting the UK energy system: climate change; a declining indigenous energy supply; and keeping the UK energy infrastructure up to date with changing technologies and needs. To address these challenges, the Government's policy has four goals:

- to cut UK emissions of carbon dioxide (CO_2) by about 60 per cent between 1990 and 2050;
- to maintain the reliability of energy supplies;
- to promote competitive markets in the United Kingdom and beyond, helping to raise the rate of sustainable economic growth and improve productivity; and

Figure 28.5 Energy consumption and distance travelled by road passengers, UK

Index (1970=100)

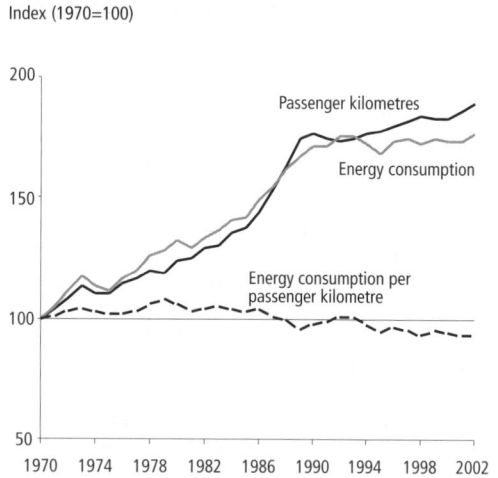

Source: Department of Trade and Industry; Department for Transport

- to ensure that every home is adequately and affordably heated.

The *Sustainable Energy Act 2003* imposes various duties on the Secretary of State for Trade and Industry, the National Assembly for Wales, Ofgem (the Office of Gas and Electricity Markets – see page 450) and local authorities in order to help achieve these four goals.

The Department of Trade and Industry (DTI) and the Department for Environment, Food and Rural Affairs (Defra) published *Creating a low carbon economy – first annual report on implementation of the Energy White Paper* in April 2004. This describes the progress made in meeting the White Paper's four goals; 56 out of 112 milestones set as a first step towards achieving the White Paper's long-term commitments had been completed by the end of March 2004 (each milestone has its own target date – the latest is December 2010).

The Government believes that energy efficiency is likely to be the cheapest and safest way of addressing all four goals, and that renewable energy will play an important part in reducing carbon emissions, while also strengthening energy security and improving industrial competitiveness. In December 2003, it announced plans to increase the level of the Renewables Obligation (see page

452) in stages from 10.4 per cent in 2010/11 to 15.4 per cent in 2015/16.

The *Energy Act 2004* contains provisions designed to exploit the United Kingdom's renewable energy potential (see pages 453–54), together with measures relating to the integrity and security of the electricity and gas supply. New planning policies aimed at encouraging the development of renewable energy in England were published by the Office of the Deputy Prime Minister (ODPM) in August 2004. Recognising that additional ways of reducing CO_2 emissions will be needed to meet its 2050 target, the Government is also drawing up a Carbon Abatement Technologies (CAT) Strategy.

The Sustainable Energy Policy Network (SEPN) is taking forward the implementation of the White Paper. SEPN members are drawn from government departments, the devolved administrations, regulators and other key organisations. SEPN groups meet at all levels of government, including an ad hoc ministerial committee and a management board attended by senior civil servants from key departments.

The Government has sought views on the most appropriate indicators with which to monitor progress annually. *UK energy sector indicators 2004*, published in April 2004, presents four key

indicators (greenhouse gas and CO_2 emissions, reliability, competitiveness, and fuel poverty), 27 supporting indicators, and a range of background energy indicators.

Climate change levy

The climate change levy (CCL) was introduced in April 2001 as an environmental tax on the use of energy by business and the public sector. Its purpose is to encourage the efficient use of energy, in order to help meet UK targets for cutting emissions of greenhouse gases.

The revenue raised by the levy is recycled back to business, primarily through a 0.3 percentage point reduction in employers' National Insurance contributions. Revenue from the levy also provides support for investment in energy efficiency measures by businesses through 100 per cent enhanced capital allowances (ECAs), and support for the Carbon Trust (see page 454), which provides energy efficiency advice for business and supports the development of low carbon technologies. The levy and package of associated measures form part of the Government's strategy for moving the burden of tax from 'beneficial' activity, such as employment, to 'detrimental' activity, such as pollution. The levy package is expected to reduce emissions by the equivalent of at least 5 million tonnes of carbon by 2010.

Between the introduction of CCL and June 2004, 44 eligible energy-intensive sectors of industry have entered into Climate Change Agreements (CCAs) to improve their energy efficiency and reduce carbon emissions, in return for an 80 per cent discount from the levy. The 88 per cent of industrial sites certified by Defra as having met their 2003 milestone targets can continue to benefit from the levy discount between April 2003 and March 2005. Eligibility for a CCA is currently limited to those sectors whose processes are controlled by the Prevention Pollution Control Regulations 2000, but the Government is planning to extend the eligibility criteria for CCAs to sectors that meet a specific energy-intensity threshold.

International developments

The EU's Sixth Framework Programme of Research and Technological Development is the focus for research, development and demonstration of energy technologies in the EU. The Programme has a budget for the years 2002 to 2006 of €17.5 billion.

Hydrogen buses in London

In January 2004, three hydrogen fuel cell buses were introduced as part of a two-year EU project to reduce air pollution and noise. CUTE (Clean Urban Transport for Europe) involves nine other European cities and is the largest project of its type in the world. The London trial is a joint venture between London Buses, DaimlerChrysler, BP, First (the United Kingdom's largest surface transport company), the Energy Saving Trust (see page 454) and the Department for Transport.

The single-decker buses, which cost £750,000 each and can travel 200 kilometres before they need refuelling, are the first buses in the United Kingdom to run with no harmful emissions. They run off hydrogen gas contained in six cylinders on their roofs; the fuel cell turns the gas into electrical power and the only emission is water.

The European Commission's energy action programme, Intelligent Energy for Europe, began in August 2003 and will run to 2006. It supports EU policies in the field of energy and aims to support sustainable development in an energy context. The programme has four areas: the promotion of renewable energies (ALTENER); improved energy efficiency (SAVE); energy aspects of transport (STEER); and the promotion of renewable energy sources and energy efficiency in developing countries (COOPENER).

The International Energy Agency (IEA), based in Paris, is an autonomous agency linked with the Organisation for Economic Co-operation and Development (OECD). It monitors world energy markets on behalf of industrialised countries and promotes reform of energy markets, both among its members and internationally. The IEA is the energy forum for member countries, including the United Kingdom. IEA member governments are committed to taking joint measures to meet oil supply emergencies and agree to share information, co-ordinate their energy policies and co-operate in the development of rational energy programmes.

Energy Products Directive

The EC Energy Products Directive came into force on 1 January 2004 and provides an EU framework for taxation on energy products, increasing the existing minimum rates of duty on hydrocarbon oils and introducing minimum rates of duty on other energy products, including electricity, natural gas, coal and other solid fuels. The minimum rates in the Directive do not affect any of the United Kingdom's existing rates or exemptions, but will require increases in some other Member States, in order to provide environmental benefits across the EU.

Oil and gas exploration and production

In 2003, oil and gas accounted for about three-quarters of total UK energy consumption, either through direct use or as a source of energy for electricity generation. Total UK production of crude oil and NGLs in 2003 was 8.5 per cent lower than in 2002, at 106.1 million tonnes. Total indigenous UK production of natural gas in 2003 was 0.7 per cent lower than in 2002 and, in 2003, imports of gas accounted for 8.4 per cent of gas

available for consumption. The United Kingdom is beginning to become more dependent on gas imports as reserves in the UK Continental Shelf (UKCS) start to decline.

The UKCS comprises those areas of the seabed and subsoil up to and beyond the territorial sea over which the United Kingdom exercises sovereign rights of exploration and exploitation of natural resources. Exports from the UKCS rose by 17.5 per cent in 2003 to 16.0 billion cubic metres (bcm). About 7.7 bcm were imported from Norway and from Belgium via the UK–Belgium interconnector, representing 8.4 per cent of total supplies in 2003, compared with 5.8 per cent in 2002.

Table 28.6 Oil statistics, UK

Million tonnes

	1993	2002	2003
Oil production			
Land	3.7	2.7	2.2
Offshore	96.5	104.8	95.6
Refinery output	89.6	78.4	79.1
Deliveries	75.8	69.6	71.5
Exports			
Crude, NGL, feedstock	64.4	87.1	79.4
Refined petroleum	23.0	23.4	23.3
Imports			
Crude, NGL, feedstock	61.7	57.0	54.2
Refined petroleum	10.1	15.3	17.3

Source: Department of Trade and Industry

Taxation

The North Sea fiscal regime is a major mechanism for gaining economic benefit for the United Kingdom from its oil and gas resources. The Government grants licences to private sector companies to explore for, and exploit, oil and gas resources (see box, page 443). Its main sources of revenue from oil and gas activities are petroleum revenue tax, levied on profits from fields approved before 16 March 1993, and corporation tax, charged on the profits of oil and gas companies. Companies pay a 10 per cent supplementary charge on North Sea profits and receive a 100 per cent first-year allowance for capital expenditure in the North Sea.

Licensing

The main type of offshore licence is the traditional Seaward Production Licence, which covers the life of a field from exploration to decommissioning.

To increase oil and gas production in the North Sea, a new type of licence called 'Promote' was introduced in 2003, which offers opportunities to smaller business.

The 'Frontier' licence was introduced in February 2004 to boost exploration by allowing companies to apply for relatively large amounts of acreage at significantly reduced costs, and then relinquish three-quarters of that acreage after a screening period. It applies to blocks in the Atlantic Margin, west of the Shetland Isles. Onshore production licences are called Petroleum Exploration and Development Licences (PEDLs), and are similar to the offshore production licences.

New licensing rounds

In March 2004 the Secretary of State for Trade and Industry invited applications for licences in the 22nd offshore and 12th onshore licensing rounds. These were the most extensive rounds of their kind since 1965; they opened all of the UK onshore area and 1,039 blocks and part blocks in the offshore area for oil and gas licensing opportunities.

Under these rounds, traditional offshore licences applied to all regions of the UKCS, with Frontier licences only available in the challenging West of Shetland region and Promote licences in areas excluding the West of Shetland. Twenty of the 68 companies that applied are potential new entrants to the North Sea.

Production and reserves

There were 259 offshore fields in production at the end of 2003: 131 oil, 104 gas and 24 condensate (a lighter form of oil). During 2003, ten new field developments (all offshore) were approved, consisting of three oilfields, five gas fields and two condensate fields. In addition, approval for four incremental offshore developments and one incremental onshore development was granted.

Only 204 development wells were drilled offshore during 2003 compared with 249 in 2002, although the number of exploration and appraisal wells started offshore increased slightly, from 44 to 45. In 2003, 17 development wells were drilled onshore, compared with 18 in 2002, and only four exploration and appraisal wells were started onshore, compared with 14 in 2002.

Oil and gas production from the UKCS peaked in 1999. It is expected to continue to decline as remaining reserves are depleted, and was estimated at just over 4 million barrels of oil equivalent per day (mboepd) in 2003.

The value of the United Kingdom's recoverable oil and gas reserves mainly depends upon the estimated physical amounts remaining, the current rate of extraction and the assumed future price per unit of oil and gas, net of the cost of extraction. Since 1993, the estimated stock of reserves has fallen as a result of extraction, but the value of reserves has generally risen, as oil prices have increased. By the end of 2002, oil reserves were valued at £59 billion while gas reserves were estimated to be worth £51 billion.

Offshore gas

Natural gas now accounts for some 40 per cent of total inland primary fuel consumption in the United Kingdom. In 2003, indigenous production fell by 0.5 per cent to 108.4 bcm.

The first significant discovery of offshore gas in the United Kingdom was in 1965, and cumulative gross gas production to the end of 2003 was 1,933 bcm. Maximum possible remaining gas reserves in present discoveries now stand at 1,206 bcm.

Pipelines

Some 10,928 kilometres of submarine pipelines transport oil, gas and condensate from one field to another and to shore. Nine landing places on the North Sea coast bring gas ashore to supply a national and regional high- and low-pressure pipeline system some 273,000 kilometres long, which transports natural gas around Great Britain.

A 40-kilometre pipeline takes natural gas from Scotland to Northern Ireland; exports to the Irish Republic are conveyed by the Britain–Ireland interconnector. The pipeline from Bacton in Norfolk to Zeebrugge in Belgium (232 kilometres), which was opened in 1998, has an annual export capacity of 20 bcm of gas, or about 15 per cent of UK peak demand. Although a smaller volume of gas can flow into the United Kingdom at present, the interconnector's owners are proceeding with plans to increase import capacity from the current 8.5 bcm to 16.5 bcm a year in 2005 and 23.5 bcm a year in 2006.

Economic and industrial aspects

Since 1965, the UK oil and gas production industry has generated operating surpluses of some £325 billion, of which about £119 billion (including £25 billion of exploration and appraisal expenditure) has been reinvested in the industry, £110 billion paid in taxation, and about £96 billion retained by the companies. Total annual income of the oil and gas sector fell slightly to just under £25 billion in 2003.

In 2003, the average price received by producers from sales of UKCS oil was £130 per tonne, compared with £124 per tonne in 2002. Total revenues from the sale of production from the UKCS in 2003 fell slightly compared with 2002, with revenue from oil (including NGLs) at some £14.5 billion and revenue from gas at £7.6 billion. Taxes and royalty receipts attributable to UKCS oil and gas fell to some £4.4 billion in 2003/04.

The PILOT initiative promotes co-operation between industry and the Government to develop recovery of the United Kingdom's oil and gas resources and prolong indigenous supplies. One of its targets is that production should not decline below 4 mboepd in 2005 and 3 mboepd by 2010. Two initiatives it has helped to develop are the DEAL Data Registry (www.ukdeal.co.uk), which catalogues well and seismic survey data for the UKCS, and the National Hydrocarbon Data Archive (NHDA, www.bgs.ac.uk/nhda), which will be a repository for some of the more valuable geoscientific data collected during exploration of the UKCS.

Production investment in the oil and gas extraction industry in 2003 fell slightly from that in 2002 to some £3.7 billion, including exploration and appraisal investment of just over £0.3 billion. It formed just over 16 per cent of total UK industrial investment. In 2003, some 30,000 people were engaged in extraction, while the industry supported some 230,000 in other sectors.

The offshore environment

All new developments are assessed under the Offshore Petroleum Production and Pipelines (Assessment of Environmental Effects) Regulations, the Environmental Impact Assessment (EIA) Regulations and the Offshore Petroleum Activities (Conservation of Habitats) Regulations. The EIA Regulations apply to the drilling of wells, the installation of pipelines, extended well tests and the development of new fields. Environmental Statements are required for projects that could have a significant impact on the marine environment. The Habitats Regulations additionally apply to activities that are not covered by the EIA Regulations, such as offshore oil and gas surveys, well abandonment and decommissioning operations.

In addition to these assessment procedures, permits are required for a number of offshore activities. The Offshore Combustion Installations (Prevention and Control of Pollution) Regulations 2001 control emissions from offshore combustion installations, that is, gas turbines and diesels burning natural gas or diesel fuel which are predominantly used to generate electricity. Permits are also required for the use and discharge of chemicals during all offshore operations under the Offshore Chemicals Regulations 2002. By 2005, operators will be able to use the UK Oil and Gas Portal (www.og.dti.gov.uk/portal.htm) to apply online for environmental consents.

The amount of oil spilled around the United Kingdom and offshore is small in relation to production, amounting to 96 tonnes in 2002. The number of spills recorded increased from 349 in 1997 to 481 in 2002. About 96 per cent of reports were for a spill of less than 1 tonne.

Since 1986, the United Kingdom has carried out surveillance flights in accordance with international obligations under the Bonn Agreement. These flights are unannounced and cover all offshore installations on the UKCS. The DTI uses a computer link to the aircraft, which transmits photographic images of possible pollution incidents and enables it to investigate these as they happen. In 2003, a total of 61 dedicated or operational over-flights were flown, surveying 2,243 installations; the installations in the southern North Sea and Irish Sea (Morecambe Bay) were covered during designated shipping flights. The total amount of oil observed from unreported spills was 2.4 tonnes from 26 separate detections. DTI works closely with the Scottish Fisheries Protection Agency, Defra and the Maritime and Coastguard Agency (see page 339), which all routinely over-fly UK waters.

Decommissioning

The *Petroleum Act 1998* places a decommissioning obligation on the operators of every offshore installation and the owners of every offshore pipeline on the UKCS. Companies have to submit a decommissioning programme for ministerial approval and ensure that its provisions are carried out. The OSPAR Convention (see page 296) has agreed rules for the disposal of defunct offshore installations at sea. There is a ban on the dumping and leaving in place of such installations, but derogations are possible for concrete platforms and the footings of steel installations with a jacket weight above 10,000 tonnes.

All installations put in place after 9 February 1999 must be removed completely. The Government encourages the re-use of facilities and expects operators to show that they have investigated such a course. It also encourages free trade in mature offshore oil and gas assets, as a means of extending field life and maximising economic recovery.

By August 2004, 25 decommissioning programmes, covering 30 redundant installations, had been approved by the DTI. The DTI is working with the United Kingdom Offshore Operators Association to identify best environmental practice for dealing with drill cuttings[1] at the decommissioning stage. OSPAR's Offshore Industry Committee agreed in March 2004 to UK proposals for action.

Offshore safety

Offshore health and safety are the responsibility of the Health and Safety Executive (HSE, see page 158). Its Offshore Division (OSD) ensures that risks to people who work in oil and gas extraction are properly controlled. OSD's regulatory tasks range from providing advice and guidance on operational and technical matters to working with industry on reducing releases of hydrocarbons.

Suppliers of goods and services

As the UK offshore oil and gas sector matures, UK supply and manufacturing companies have increasingly turned to work in other industrial sectors and in overseas hydrocarbon-producing areas. The Oil and Gas Industry Development Group in the DTI works with PILOT (see page 444) and takes other action to help the industry realign to changing market circumstances. The UK supply chain database (*www.og.dti.gov.uk/portal.htm*), maintained by the DTI, contains contact details of over 3,000 companies in the UK oil and gas supply chain, and is available for global buyers who seek information on the capabilities and contact details of UK-based companies in this sector.

Gas supply industry

Structure

Working in a fully competitive market, the holder of a gas transporter's[2] licence in Great Britain may not also hold licences for supply or shipping. National Grid Transco plc (NGT) is the owner, operator and developer of the majority of Britain's gas transport system. Its network supplies 40 per cent of the country's energy needs and it is responsible for dealing with gas leaks and emergencies. It has also had a monopoly in gas metering, which the energy regulator (Ofgem) opened to competition in July 2004 following extensive consultation through its review of gas metering arrangements.

Shippers participate in balancing supply and demand in the pipeline network, within a regime partly driven by commercial concerns, and utilising gas trading arrangements, which include a screen-based on-the-day commodity market for trading in wholesale supplies of gas. In addition, there are auctions for the allocation of entry capacity into the high-pressure national transmission system and commercial incentives for NGT to operate and balance the system efficiently.

In Northern Ireland, natural gas has been available since 1996 when the Scotland to Northern Ireland

---

1 Rock fragments, sometimes contaminated with drilling mud, which can accumulate on the seabed around drilling installations.

2 Suppliers sell piped gas to consumers; public gas transporters (PGTs) operate the pipeline system through which gas will normally be delivered and shippers arrange with PGTs for appropriate amounts of gas to go through the pipeline system.

gas pipeline was put into operation. Phoenix
Natural Gas Ltd has a combined licence for the
conveyance and supply of gas in Greater Belfast.
Bord Gais Eireann (BGE – based in the Republic
of Ireland) is responsible for the development and
maintenance of the whole of Ireland's natural gas
transport network. The company intends to
complete a gas transmission pipeline to the
north-west of Northern Ireland by autumn 2004
and a connecting South–North pipeline by 2006.
Piped natural gas should be available to 80 per cent
of the population of Northern Ireland by 2012.

Competition

Since deregulation of the industry in 1994,
wholesale gas has been traded like most other
commodities. At the end of 2003, around 50
companies were active in the UK gas market, but
some companies owned or partly owned more
than one supplier.

By March 2004, 40 per cent of gas customers
(8.2 million)[3] had changed from British Gas to one
of 20 other companies in the domestic market. In
2003, when 3.1 million domestic gas customers
changed suppliers, a standard credit[4] customer
who had not switched was paying, on average,
£46 more on a standard bill of £289 a year.

Only companies that have been granted a
supplier's licence are allowed to sell gas. Licence
conditions include providing gas to anyone who
requests it and is connected to the mains gas
supply. Special services must be made available for
elderly, disabled and chronically sick people.
Suppliers must offer customers a range of
payment options, and although they set their own
charges, they must publish their prices and other
terms so that customers can make an informed
choice. Domestic gas prices fell by 1.1 per cent in
real terms (including VAT) in 2003, continuing
the trend of a 16 per cent fall since 1995.

Ofgem acts to ensure that Great Britain's
competitive retail market works for all customers
and that anti-competitive practices do not take
place. It is also working to prevent continuing
problems caused by doorstep selling, which
undermine customer confidence.

3 Excludes customers who changed suppliers and then returned to
British Gas.
4 Paying monthly in advance by cheque or cash, at a bank or post
office.

Consumption and the market

In the United Kingdom, gas was traditionally used
as a fuel for the domestic, commercial and
industrial markets. During the 1990s, a market
opened up for the use of gas for power generation.
This offers higher generation efficiency, fewer
carbon emissions and lower fuel costs than
conventional coal-fired technology. The increase
of gas-fired generation caused rapid growth in UK
gas use. In 2003, gas represented around 47 per
cent of UKCS hydrocarbon production, 40 per
cent of UK energy production and around 4 per
cent of world gas production, making the United
Kingdom the fourth largest gas producer.

UK demand for natural gas in 2003 was 0.3 per
cent higher than in 2002. Final consumption rose
in all sectors but 1.7 per cent less gas was used for
electricity generation because high gas prices
meant that some generators found it more
profitable on occasions to sell gas rather than use
it for generation. Prices paid by industry
(excluding the CCL) increased slightly in 2003 by
0.7 per cent in real terms, having fallen by 20 per
cent over the last decade.

The effect of the stable demand for gas and the
decline in indigenous gas production is that the
United Kingdom is expected to become a net
importer of gas (on an annual basis) by around
2006 (it already imports gas during the winter).
The dependence on imports is expected to
increase sharply to 40–50 per cent by 2010,
and 80–90 per cent by 2020. This will require
additional import infrastructure; a number
of commercial projects are under discussion
including expanded and new interconnectors with
continental Europe, a major new pipeline from the
Norwegian Continental Shelf and new liquefied
natural gas (LNG) terminals. There are plans to
increase gas storage capacity within Great Britain
to help meet demand peaks. The first long-term
deal to import LNG was signed in August 2004.

Downstream oil

Oil consumption

Deliveries of petroleum products for inland
consumption (excluding refinery consumption)
in 2003 included 19.9 million tonnes of petrol for
motor vehicles, 17.7 million tonnes of DERV fuel,
10.5 million tonnes of aviation turbine fuel,

6.1 million tonnes of gas oil (distilled from petroleum) and 1.6 million tonnes of fuel oils (blends of heavy petroleum).

Oil refineries

In 2003, the United Kingdom's 13 refineries processed 84.5 million tonnes of crude and process oils, slightly less than in 2002. About two-thirds of UK output by weight is in the form of lighter, higher-value products such as gasoline, DERV and jet kerosene. Petrol production is more important in the United Kingdom than in its European counterparts, accounting for about a third of each barrel of crude oil compared with the European average of just over a fifth.

In 2003, UK exports of refined petroleum products rose by 4.2 per cent to £4.9 billion. Virtually all exports went to partners in the EU and in the IEA (especially France, Germany and the United States).

The importance of petroleum in transport

Transport accounted for 70 per cent of all petroleum energy and non-energy use in the United Kingdom in 2003. Road transport used 37.6 million tonnes of petrol (unleaded and lead replacement petrol) and DERV fuel. Water transport used 1.1 million tonnes (mainly gas oil and diesel) and railways used 0.3 million tonnes (mainly gas oil, diesel and fuel oil). Most of the use of petrol (95 per cent) was by cars and taxis, with goods vehicles (mainly light vans) accounting for 4 per cent and motorcycles most of the remaining 1 per cent. Goods vehicles, however, accounted for 68 per cent of the use of DERV fuel, with coaches accounting for 7 per cent, and the remaining 25 per cent mainly used by diesel cars and taxis.

Coal

The UK coal industry is entirely in the private sector. The main deep mine operator in the United Kingdom is UK Coal plc. UK Coal, Scottish Coal Company Ltd, H J Banks and Company and Celtic

Energy (which operates in Wales) are the main opencast operators. In May 2004, there were 38 opencast sites in production and 11 major deep mines. A number of deep mines have closed over the years, including the Selby complex in north Yorkshire, which closed in summer 2004. The coal industry employed just over 7,900 people in May 2004, of whom around 73 per cent were employed at deep mines. Opencast production accounts for most of the relatively low-sulphur coal mined in Scotland and South Wales.

UK coal production fell by 6.0 per cent to 27.8 million tonnes in 2003, a new record low for deep-mined coal (down 4.6 per cent to 15.6 million tonnes) and the lowest level since 1976 for opencast coal (12.1 million tonnes, down 7.8 per cent on the year).

Market for coal

Imports of coal in 2003 were 31.9 million tonnes, some 11 per cent higher than in 2002 and the second highest annual volume on record, 35.5 million tonnes in 2001. Very little UK coal is exported – only 542,000 tonnes in 2003.

UK demand for coal in 2003 was 6.4 per cent higher at 62.4 million tonnes, with consumption by electricity generators up 11.2 per cent. This was mainly due to high gas prices leading to coal-fired generation in preference to gas-fired, but it was also prompted by a reduced output from nuclear power stations in the fourth quarter of the year. Electricity generators accounted for 85 per cent of total coal use in 2003, compared with 81 per cent in 2002. Coal use in coke ovens and blast furnaces in the steel industry was very slightly higher than in 2002, at 6.6 million tonnes.

Cleaner coal

Cleaner coal technologies reduce the environmental impact of coal used for power and industrial applications by increasing the efficiency of its conversion to energy and reducing harmful emissions (one of the causes of acid rain). Improvements in the efficiency of coal-fired power stations lead to reductions in carbon dioxide emissions, a major contributor to climate change.

The DTI is supporting research and development (R&D) into cleaner coal technology, covering a number of technologies in advanced power generation and emissions reduction. In the longer run, it should be possible for UK project developers to benefit from carbon credits through international trading under the Kyoto Protocol (see page 293) clean development mechanism.

Other sources of funding for cleaner coal R&D for UK companies include the British Coal Utilisation Research Association (BCURA), the Engineering and Physical Sciences Research Council (see page 395) and the EU's Sixth Framework Programme (see page 441).

Coal Authority

The Coal Authority is a public body sponsored by the DTI. Its responsibilities include:

- licensing coal-mining operations and granting leases to exploit coal reserves;

- coal subsidence damage claims not falling on coal mining companies;

- managing property in coalfield areas;

- managing minewater pollution and other environmental problems associated with coal mining; and

- providing geological and other information on past and future coal-mining activity to house buyers, other purchasers of property and local authorities.

Nuclear power

Nuclear power substantially reduces the use of fossil fuels that would otherwise be needed for electricity generation. It generates about one-sixth of the world's energy and over a third of Europe's. Calder Hall, in Cumbria, which was connected to the national grid in 1956 and operated until the end of March 2003, was the first nuclear power station in the world to provide electricity commercially. No new nuclear reactors have been ordered or built in the United Kingdom since Sizewell B in Suffolk, which began to generate electricity in 1995. In 2003, the United Kingdom had 31 operating reactors at 13 nuclear power stations. Nuclear stations generated 89 terawatt hours (TWh) in 2003 and contributed 22.2 per cent of total electricity generation.

Existing nuclear stations are expected to continue to contribute to the country's energy requirements provided they do so to the high safety and environmental standards currently observed.

Government projections suggest that nuclear power generation could represent about 17 to 18 per cent of total generation by 2010 and about 7 per cent by 2020. These projections assume no new stations will be built, and recognise that plant lifetimes are dependent on safety and economic factors. The energy White Paper (see page 440) did not rule out the possibility that, at some point in the future, the construction of new nuclear power stations might be necessary if the United Kingdom is to meet its carbon targets. However, in the Government's view, the economics of nuclear power make it an unattractive option for new generating capacity and there are still important issues concerning nuclear waste to be resolved.

British Energy

The private sector company British Energy (BE) owns and operates seven advanced gas-cooled reactor stations and the pressurised water reactor (PWR) at Sizewell B. BE's reactors have a declared net capacity of 9,580 megawatts (MW).

Following financial difficulties in 2002, BE received a short-term government loan, which it repaid in March 2003. The Government agreed to continue to fund BE's operation while its restructuring plan was agreed and implemented, and extended the credit facility on a contingency basis to September 2004 or the date on which the restructuring plan became effective. The maximum amount to be made available was £275 million. The *Electricity (Miscellaneous Provisions) Act 2003* is designed to facilitate the Government's response to BE's financial difficulties and to allow it to plan for a smoother path through administration should BE be unable to deliver its restructuring plan.

British Nuclear Fuels (BNFL)

BNFL operates four magnox power stations, while seven others are being defuelled or decommissioned. BNFL is the primary UK provider of nuclear products and services including spent fuel management, recycling, reprocessing oxide fuel, decommissioning and cleaning up redundant nuclear facilities, and treating historic wastes for both UK and international customers. The company's turnover in 2003/04 was £2.32 billion. BNFL comprises four business groups: British Nuclear Group; Westinghouse; Nuclear Sciences and Technology Services; and Spent Fuel Services.

29 June 2004 The Met Office's £80 million new headquarters in Exeter wins Major Project of the Year and Best Office Building of the Year in awards organised by *Building Services Journal* and the *Electrical and Mechanical Contractor*.

2 July 2004 Liverpool is awarded UNESCO World Heritage status. The area covered includes the waterfront, the pier head and docks, the commercial district – an area of warehouses and merchant's houses around Duke Street – and the cultural quarter around William Brown Street.

2 July 2004 The Royal Society for the Protection of Birds reports that ospreys have nested for the first time in Wales. The birds, with a five-foot wingspan, returned to Scotland in the late 1950s after a century of extinction as a British breeding bird. Their return to the Lake District in 2001 was the result of several years of conservation work. Ospreys tend to return to their nests year after year.

6 July 2004 Racing veteran Martin Brundle drives a Jaguar along Regent Street, as part of a Formula One demonstration in the capital. Thousands of fans gathered for the unprecedented sight of Formula One cars 'racing' on London's streets.

7 July 2004 The huge arch that will be the centrepiece of the new Wembley stadium is slowly raised into place. The 133-metre high arch weighs 1,750 tonnes.

19 July 2004 Liverpool's Anglican Cathedral celebrates the 100th anniversary of the laying of its foundation stone. The Cathedral is the largest in Great Britain. It was designed by architect Gilbert Scott, designer of the distinctive telephone kiosk.

27 July 2004 *The Source*, a 32-metre high sculpture made up of 729 moving spheres suspended on metal cables, is activated to mark the opening of the London Stock Exchange's new building at Paternoster Square. *The Source* marks the start and end of each day's trading with an arrow indicating whether the markets have opened or closed up or down and giving the opening and closing price of the FTSE 100.

14–29 August 2004 The Olympic Games are held in Athens. The Great Britain team won 9 gold medals, 9 silver medals and 12 bronzes.

20 August Chris Hoy wins the Men's 1 kilometre time trial in a time of 1 minute and 0.711 seconds, the fastest time ever at sea level.

21 August Great Britain finished the Olympic regatta with two gold medals, one silver and two bronzes to emulate the five-medal haul from Sydney in 2000. *(Front from left)* Sarah Webb, Shirley Robertson and Sarah Ayton won gold for Yngling. *(Back left)* Nick Rogers and *(back right)* Joe Glanfield won silver in the Men's 470; Ben Ainslie *(back centre)* won gold for Men's Finn.

23 and 28 August Kelly Holmes wins gold for the Women's 800 metres and the Women's 1,500 metres, the first Briton for 84 years to achieve the Olympic middle-distance double.

28 August *(from left)* Mark Lewis-Francis, Marlon Devonish, Darren Campbell, and Jason Gardener win the Men's 4x100 metres relay.

Managing the nuclear legacy

The *Energy Act 2004* (see page 441) provides for
the creation of the Nuclear Decommissioning
Authority (NDA), a non-departmental public
body that will take responsibility for discharging
the historic liabilities in the United Kingdom
owned and managed by BNFL and the UK Atomic
Energy Authority (see below). It is estimated that
the costs of cleaning up this legacy, which are
already being met by the taxpayer, will amount to
£48 billion over the next century.

The NDA is a cross-border public authority
reporting to both the Secretary of State for Trade
and Industry, and Scottish ministers. It is
responsible for developing a long-term strategy for
decommissioning and cleaning up designated sites.
In doing so, it will work closely with the nuclear
regulators (Environment Agency, Scottish
Environment Protection Agency, HSE Nuclear
Installations Inspectorate and the Office for Civil
Nuclear Security) to ensure that its clean-up plans
are carried out in line with environmental and
international obligations. The new authority is
expected to be fully operational by 1 April 2005.

UK Atomic Energy Authority (UKAEA)

UKAEA manages the decommissioning and
environmental restoration of its former nuclear
research sites at Dounreay (Caithness), Windscale
(Cumbria), Harwell (Oxfordshire) and Winfrith
(Dorset). It also manages the UK contribution to
the fusion energy programme at Culham,
Oxfordshire. UKAEA is a non-departmental public
body, funded mainly by the DTI.

By summer 2003, UKAEA had dismantled 18
major radioactive facilities including six research
reactors. It has also produced plans for the
restoration of all its sites. The estimated cost of its
liabilities is £9.7 billion.

Fusion research

Nuclear fusion research in the United Kingdom is
funded by the Engineering and Physical Sciences
Research Council (EPSRC, see page 395) and
Euratom (the European Atomic Energy
Community). The main focus of government
spending in this area is magnetic confinement,
which is based at Culham in Oxfordshire. The
UKAEA operates Europe's leading fusion facility
– JET (Joint European Torus) on behalf of its
European partners in the European Fusion
Development Agreement – as well as the UK
domestic programme. Through the EU, the
Euratom/UKAEA Fusion Association contributes
to International Thermonuclear Experimental
Reactor – the international partnership between
China, Europe, Japan, Russia, South Korea and the
United States – to demonstrate the principle of
power production from fusion.

Nuclear safety

The safety of nuclear installations is the
responsibility of the nuclear operators within a
system of regulatory control enforced by the HSE.
Regulation of nuclear safety is primarily achieved
through a system of licensing. The HSE assesses
and inspects sites to satisfy itself that the licensees
meet their responsibilities for safety.

The International Convention on Nuclear Safety
has been ratified by 53 countries (including the
United Kingdom and other members of the EU)
and the European Commission. Each signatory is
required to submit a report showing how it meets
the articles of the Convention, and such reports
are the subject of peer review by the other parties.
The most recent UK report for the Convention on
Nuclear Safety was prepared in 2002.

The Nuclear Safety Directorate, acting for the HSE
(see page 158), gives specialist assistance to the
International Atomic Energy Agency (IAEA), the
OECD's nuclear energy agency, and Euratom. The
main UK contribution to the international effort
to improve safety in Central and Eastern Europe
and the former Soviet republics is channelled
through the EU nuclear safety programmes.

Electricity

The *Energy Act 2004* provides for the creation of
a single wholesale electricity market in Great
Britain. The British Electricity Trading and
Transmission Arrangements (BETTA) are
scheduled to be introduced in April 2005. The
Government hopes that extending the New
Electricity Trading Arrangements (NETA) to
Scotland will increase competition in Scotland and
across Great Britain more generally.

England and Wales

In December 2003, 43 companies held generation
licences in England and Wales. The largest

generating companies are RWE Innogy, Powergen (now called E.ON UK), British Energy and Centrica. National Grid Transco owns and operates the transmission system, and is responsible for balancing electricity supply and demand. Its appointment as the GB System Operator under BETTA was confirmed in August 2004.

The 12 Distribution Network Operators (DNOs) are responsible for transferring electricity from the high-voltage National Grid to consumers via local distribution networks. Supply – the purchase of electricity by end users from electricity suppliers – has been fully open to competition since 1999.

Cross-border acquisitions and takeovers have become a feature of the European power market and most of the companies involved in distribution and supply are now overseas-owned. All but one of the main UK generators also now own supply businesses.

NETA came into effect in England and Wales in 2001, replacing the Electricity Pool that had operated since privatisation in 1990. NETA was designed to introduce more competition into wholesale electricity trading and to create a commodity-based market. Participants are free to trade electricity for any half-hour period until one hour ahead of real time ('gate closure'). From that point until real time, the market operates through the Balancing Mechanism, run by NGT, because of the need to balance the system on a second-by-second basis.

Scotland

Scottish Power and Scottish and Southern Energy transmit and distribute electricity within their respective franchise areas, and generate and supply electricity throughout the United Kingdom. They are also contracted to buy all the output from British Energy's two Scottish nuclear power stations (Hunterston B and Torness) until BETTA becomes operative or April 2006, whichever is the later. Under BETTA, transmission assets in Scotland will continue to be owned by the two companies.

Northern Ireland

Three private sector companies generate electricity in Northern Ireland from power stations: AES Kilroot Power Ltd, Premier Power Ltd and Coolkeeragh Power Ltd. Most of the output is sold to Northern Ireland Electricity plc (NIE), which

has a monopoly of transmission and distribution, and a licence to supply.

The electricity market has been gradually opened up to competition since 1999. From April 2004, the right to choose a supplier was extended to 36 per cent of the total market (mainly large industrial consumers). In addition to NIE, a number of second-tier suppliers are operating.

Three interconnectors link the electricity system of Northern Ireland with that of the Republic of Ireland. The main North–South interconnector has a capacity to trade 2 x 600 MW of electricity – enough to power several major towns. The interconnectors enable trade of electricity between Northern Ireland and the Republic of Ireland and, through the Moyle interconnector (Northern Ireland–Scotland), with Great Britain.

Regulation and other functions

The electricity and gas markets in Great Britain are regulated by Ofgem, according to policies set by the Gas and Electricity Markets Authority. Ofgem's principal objective is to protect the interests of gas and electricity customers, wherever appropriate, by promoting effective competition. Other duties and objectives include ensuring that reasonable demands for electricity are met and that electricity and gas licensees are able to finance their statutory obligations. Ofgem is responsible for setting performance standards for gas and electricity companies, and for price regulation of companies where competition has not yet fully emerged or where there is a natural monopoly.

The Northern Ireland Authority for Energy Regulation, a non-ministerial government department, regulates electricity and natural gas industries in Northern Ireland. It is supported by the Office for the Regulation of Electricity and Gas.

Consumption

In 2003, final consumption of electricity in the United Kingdom rose by 1.3 per cent to 337 TWh. The major users were the domestic sector and industry (around 34 per cent each). Commerce, public administration, transport and agriculture together accounted for 32 per cent. Sales of electricity through the public distribution system in the United Kingdom were 325 TWh in 2003.

Electricity prices for industrial customers fell by 6.8 per cent in real terms during 2003, continuing the downward trend of the previous ten years. Domestic consumer prices for electricity fell by 1.9 per cent in real terms (including VAT) during 2003 and have fallen by 29 per cent in real terms (including VAT) since 1995.

Since deregulation in 1998, around 10.5 million[5] domestic customers (42 per cent) have switched suppliers, including 4.2 million in 2003. These customers saved an average of £21 on their annual bill. The average annual domestic electricity bill in the United Kingdom for a customer paying by standard credit was estimated at £237 in 2003.

Energywatch

Energywatch was established under the *Utilities Act 2000* as an independent adviser for consumers in the gas and electricity markets in Great Britain. The Government is working with Ofgem, Energywatch and the industry to ensure that the market works better and to improve consumers' confidence. Energywatch also seeks to ensure that both the industry as a whole and individual companies improve their performance in a range of other areas including customer contact, administration and the management of accounts. It receives a grant from the DTI, which is derived from the licence fee that energy companies have to pay to the Government.

Generation

Non-nuclear power stations owned by the major UK power producers consumed 58 million tonnes of oil equivalent in 2003, of which coal accounted for 55 per cent and natural gas for 42 per cent. Other power companies (for which gas is the most widely used fuel) and over 2,000 small autogenerators (which produce power for their own use) have equal access with the major generators to the grid transmission and local distribution systems.

Combined cycle gas turbines (CCGTs)

In 2003, CCGT stations accounted for 33 per cent of the electricity supplied by major power producers, compared with 7 per cent in 1993. CCGT stations, favoured by the smaller, independent producers and using natural gas, offer cheap generation and give out almost no sulphur dioxide and some 55 per cent less CO_2 per

unit of electricity than coal-fired plant. At the end of December 2003, the United Kingdom had 29 CCGT stations, with a total registered capacity of 23.5 gigawatts (GW).

Combined heat and power (CHP)

CHP is a highly fuel-efficient technology, which puts to use the waste heat produced as a by-product of the electricity generation process. It can convert more than 75 per cent of fuel input into useful energy, while conventional generation wastes around half the energy content of the fuel and emits considerably more CO_2 per kilowatt hour (kWh) of useful output. CHP thus benefits the environment and contributes to UK climate change targets by reducing emissions of greenhouse gases. It is also used for cooling and chilling.

CHP can be fuelled by a variety of energy sources. It offers particular benefits where there is a regular need for heat as well as electricity on a local scale, such as in hospitals, leisure centres and new housing developments. About 83 per cent of CHP plants are less than 1 MW capacity; however, large-scale plant (above 10 MW) constitutes 81 per cent of total CHP capacity.

Between 1991 and 2003, the electricity generation capacity of CHP plants more than doubled. In 2003, 1,506 CHP schemes with a combined capacity of 4,879 MW produced a total of 24.2 TWh. This represents just over 6 per cent of the total electricity generated in the United Kingdom (and 11 per cent of electricity consumption in the commercial and industrial sectors).

EU strategy is to double CHP's share of the EU electricity market from 9 per cent in 2001 to 18 per cent by 2010. The UK Government is committed to having at least 10,000 MW of Good Quality CHP[6] generating capacity by 2010, but recent modelling work suggests that capacity is likely to fall short of this target. The *Strategy for combined heat and power to 2010*, published in April 2004, sets out a range of measures to support the long-term growth of CHP and its capacity to meet the target, including CCL exemptions, enhanced capital allowances to stimulate investment and working with Ofgem to ensure a level playing field under NETA.

---

6 Good Quality CHP refers to CHP generation that achieves a designated level of operational efficiency as defined under the UK Combined Heat and Power Quality Assurance (CHPQA) programme (*www.chpqa.com*).

---

5 Excludes those customers who have returned to their original supplier.

Trade

NGT and Electricité de France run a 2,000 MW cross-Channel cable link, allowing transmission of electricity between the two countries. The link has generally been used to supply 'baseload' power – which needs to be generated and available round the clock – from France to England. Imports met just 0.7 per cent of the United Kingdom's electricity needs in 2003.

Scotland has a peak winter demand of under 6 GW and generating capacity of over 9 GW. The additional available capacity is used to supply England and Wales through transmission lines linking the Scottish and English grid systems. This interconnector's capacity has been upgraded from 1,600 MW to 2,200 MW. The 60-kilometre 500 MW undersea Moyle interconnector between Scotland and Northern Ireland allows exports of power from Scotland.

Renewable energy

Renewable electricity can be generated from wind (both offshore and onshore), water (hydro, wave and tidal power), sunlight (the direct conversion of solar radiation into electricity, called photovoltaics or PV), biomass (energy from forestry, crops or biodegradable waste) and from the earth's heat (geothermal energy). None of these forms of generation, except biomass, involves the production of carbon, and biomass generation produces only the carbon that the material has absorbed from the atmosphere while growing. Emissions arising from the management, handling and transport of the biomass are small relative to its energy content. The exposed coastline of the United Kingdom offers particularly strong potential for the expansion of wind, wave and tidal power. Table 28.7 gives details of UK renewable energy sources. Renewables and wastes provided 2.9 per cent of the electricity generated in the United Kingdom in 2003 compared with 3 per cent in 2002.

Heat, as well as electricity, can be generated from renewable sources. Solar energy can heat water directly, either for hot water or for space heating in buildings. Heat from the ground, river water, sewage and the air can be extracted via a heat exchanger for both water and space heating. Biomass can be used to generate heat in either heat-only developments or in CHP units.

Table 28.7 Total use of renewables, UK

	1993	2002	2003
Active solar heating and photovoltaics	0	1	1
Wind and wave	1	3	3
Hydro (small and large scale)	24	12	8
Landfill gas	10	27	31
Sewage gas	10	5	5
Wood (domestic and industrial)	28	14	12
Waste combustion	15	24	23
Other biofuels	10	13	17
Total (million tonnes of oil equivalent) (=100%)	**1.6**	**3.3**	**3.6**

Source: Department of Trade and Industry

Growth in the proportion of electricity generated from renewable sources has a vital role to play in government efforts to exceed the UK Kyoto commitment to reduce emissions of greenhouse gases by 12.5 per cent below 1990 levels by 2008–12 (see page 294). The Government's target is to obtain 10 per cent of UK electricity sales from sources eligible for the Renewables Obligation (see below) by 2010, rising to 15 per cent by 2015. Measures to meet this target will help the United Kingdom meet EU targets for 2010 – 12 per cent of national gross energy consumption from renewables and 22 per cent of green electricity in total electricity consumption.

The Renewables Obligation is the Government's key measure to encourage renewable energy generation. Orders came into force in 2002 that oblige all licensed electricity suppliers in Great Britain to ensure that a specified and growing proportion of their electricity comes from renewable sources. Initially set at 3.0 per cent for 2002/03, the level of the Obligation rose to 4.3 per cent for 2003/04 and will rise by annual steps to 15.4 per cent in 2015/16. Suppliers may meet their Obligation by supplying eligible renewable electricity to customers in Great Britain, by buying Renewable Obligation Certificates (ROCs) reflecting renewable generation by others, or by paying a buy-out price to the electricity regulator, Ofgem, rather than supplying renewable electricity. The buy-out price is set at a level intended to make this option unattractive. In September 2004, the Government issued a consultation paper on limited changes to the Renewables Obligation Order, and expects to complete the 2005/06 review of the Renewables Obligation by December 2005.

The Scottish Executive published a renewable energy strategy for Scotland in May 2003 and set a target that 40 per cent of electricity generated in Scotland by 2020 should be from renewables.

The *Strategic Energy Framework for Northern Ireland*, published in June 2004, requires renewables to contribute 12 per cent of all electricity consumed by 2012. There are plans to introduce a Northern Ireland Renewables Obligation from 1 April 2005. It is intended that Northern Ireland ROCs will be fully tradeable with those issued in Great Britain. By 2010, it is estimated that support from the Renewables Obligation and the benefit of exemption from the climate change levy will be worth around £1 billion a year to the UK renewable energy industry.

Renewables UK, a unit within the DTI, seeks to help UK manufacturers of renewable equipment and technology overcome barriers to renewables projects in the United Kingdom and to benefit from the expanding global renewables market. It aims to raise awareness of the industry and to take advantage of transferable skills from the established oil and gas industry. The Renewables Advisory Board, an independent non-departmental public body sponsored by the DTI, provides advice to the Government on renewable energy issues. The DTI supports collaborative R&D in renewables technologies through its Technology Programme.

Wind energy

Wind energy generated at both onshore and offshore installations is expected to make the largest contribution to the expansion of renewable energy in the United Kingdom between 2004 and 2010. At the end of 2003, UK wind generating capacity was 742 MW, up from 534 MW at the end of 2002. This is equivalent to an annual generation of 1.29 GWh or 0.5 per cent of UK electricity supply, and was produced by 1,043 turbines operating at 84 sites, two of which were offshore. The British Wind Energy Association (BWEA) expects 22 new wind projects will be built in the United Kingdom in 2004, representing some 474 MW of new capacity. These include a new offshore wind farm at Scroby Sands, off the

coast at Great Yarmouth. Total installed wind capacity by 2005 is predicted to be around 1,700 MW, equivalent to the generation of about 4.49 TWh – sufficient to meet the needs of just under 1 million UK households.

The first round of leasings of areas of the UK seabed for offshore wind farms, announced in December 2000, resulted in 18 proposals from developers and could result in more than 500 turbines, generating 1.5 GW. A second round of offshore leasings, on a much larger scale than the first, was announced in July 2003; each farm is expected to comprise hundreds of turbines and the energy produced will be sufficient to provide electricity for over 3.5 million households.

Three strategic areas of shallow coastal waters – the Thames Estuary, the Greater Wash and the North West of England – have been identified as appropriate for development. In December 2003, 15 new sites were announced in these areas. They include the world's largest proposed offshore wind farm off the Lincolnshire coast, which could have over 250 turbines and provide up to 1.2 GW of generating capacity.

The DTI estimates that, by 2010, UK offshore wind farms could provide up to 6 GW of energy, enough to power 15 per cent of all households in the United Kingdom. Under the *Energy Act 2004* (see page 441), developers can now build wind farms more than 12 nautical miles out to sea, beyond territorial waters.

Biomass and waste

Agricultural biomass includes both agricultural wastes such as straw and poultry litter, and energy crops such as short rotation coppice and *Miscanthus* (a perennial woody grass) grown specifically for energy generation. Forest biomass includes material direct from the forests (such as small roundwood and harvesting residues) and sawmill products (such as wood chips and sawdust). Other sources of clean woody biomass include arboricultural arisings.

Elean power station at Sutton (Cambridgeshire) is the United Kingdom's first straw-fired power plant. With a potential output of 36 MW, it burns 200,000 tonnes of straw a year and generates enough power for 80,000 homes. The power station at Thetford in Norfolk burns over 450,000 tonnes of poultry litter and other agricultural biomass each year, producing 38.5 MW of electricity – enough for around 93,000 homes.

The Government is supporting biomass projects through a £29 million Energy Crops Scheme running from 2000 to 2006 and, subject to European Commission approval, a £3.5 million Bio-energy Infrastructure Scheme.

Wave and tidal power

The DTI's Renewables Innovation Review, published in December 2003, recognised the large UK wave and tidal resource and predicts that wave and tidal stream power could develop into a significant global market by 2050. As the current leader in this field, the United Kingdom is well placed to exploit this. Research and development are supported through the DTI's Technology Programme and a number of technologies have already been demonstrated at full scale. A new £50 million Marine Research Development Fund was announced in August 2004 and the *Energy Act 2004* allows the development, for the first time, of marine renewable energy sources outside UK territorial waters.

The world's first free-standing tidal energy turbine system began trials at Lynmouth, north Devon in August 2003, while a new floating wave power machine, Pelamis, which is capable of generating enough electricity to power 500 homes, began trials off Orkney in August 2004. Successful trials of a prototype tidal stream generator took place off Shetland in 2002 and those for a prototype marine current turbine off the Devon coast in 2004.

Solar energy

Solar radiation can be converted directly into electricity using PV cells. The costs of solar PV technology have fallen substantially over the last 25 years and are expected to fall further as global markets expand and as its use increases to meet electricity requirements in areas without access to grid supplies.

PV integrated into or attached to houses and other buildings can deliver clean, silent electricity at the point of use, but requires government support because of its current high cost. The Large Scale Photovoltaic Demonstration scheme has £25 million available to help raise awareness of the technology in the public and private sectors, reduce technology costs and stimulate demand.

The Government also supports the development of active solar heating and passive solar design. Active solar heating systems convert solar radiation into heat that can be used directly, stored for use in the future, or converted to electricity. The UK climate means that the technology is best suited to low temperature heating applications, which do not require direct sunlight. The most common of these is the provision of heat for domestic hot water systems. Government grants for the installation of solar water heating systems for households or communities are available under the £10 million Clear Skies Scheme (*www.clear-skies.org*). Additional funding of £2.5 million will extend the scheme to March 2006.

Passive solar design uses the fabric and orientation of a building to capture the sun's energy and thus reduce the need for artificial heating, cooling and lighting. Significant progress has been made in the United Kingdom in the non-domestic buildings sector, but uptake in the housebuilding sector has been slower.

Energy efficiency

Energy efficiency is an essential part of the UK climate change programme (see page 293) and the Government funds a number of programmes.

The Carbon Trust is a government-backed, non-profit organisation that seeks to help UK business and the public sector reduce carbon emissions. The Trust's funding is around £50 million a year from the Government – partly from recycled receipts from the climate change levy (see page 441). It works in partnership with the Research Councils and others to support low carbon technology innovation across all sectors, and offers free energy efficiency information and advice to business and public sector organisations.

The Energy Saving Trust is a non-profit organisation funded by government and the private sector whose initiatives cover energy efficiency, renewable energy and clean fuels. Its network of advice centres across the United Kingdom provide free and impartial energy efficiency advice to households and small businesses, including advice on grants available locally as well as general advice on how to make homes more energy efficient. It also offers an information service for local authorities.

Energy efficiency – the Government's plan for action, published in April 2004, contains a package of measures which could deliver over 12 million tonnes of carbon savings by 2010. These measures include a doubling of the level of current Energy Efficiency Commitment activity from 2005 to 2008, with a possible extension to 2011. Under the Commitment, electricity and gas suppliers must meet targets for the promotion of improvements in domestic energy efficiency. They do this by encouraging and assisting consumers to take up energy efficiency measures, such as insulation and heating measures, and energy-efficient appliances and light bulbs.

The Market Transformation Programme, a Defra initiative, aims to promote products and services which do less harm to the environment by using less energy, water and other resources. It focuses on improving the delivered energy performance of domestic and non-domestic products, especially energy-consuming appliances, equipment and components.

Fuel poverty

A household is considered to be living in fuel poverty when it needs to spend more than 10 per cent of its income on household fuel use in order to keep warm. Fuel poverty is generally more significant in the United Kingdom than in the rest of Europe, where homes have traditionally been built to higher energy efficiency standards.

The *UK Fuel Poverty Strategy*, published in 2001, sets out policies for ending fuel poverty by 2010 in vulnerable[7] households. The second annual progress report, published in April 2004, estimates that the number of UK households in fuel poverty has declined from 5.5 million in 1996 (of which 4 million were vulnerable) to 2.25 million in 2002 (of which 1.75 million were vulnerable). Falling fuel prices and increases in incomes, especially for the most vulnerable, are thought to be the main factors for the reduction, with a smaller contribution from improved energy efficiency.

The Fuel Poverty Advisory Group (FPAG) is a non-departmental public body jointly sponsored by Defra and the DTI. Its primary task is to advise the Government on practical measures needed to achieve its target of eradicating fuel poverty in England. In its 2004 annual report, FPAG

---

7 A vulnerable household is one containing children or someone who is elderly, sick or disabled.

Household energy efficiency

Existing energy efficiency measures, such as greater loft insulation and more efficient central heating boilers, have already delivered a considerable improvement in household energy efficiency. However, the demand for energy continues to rise due to the growing number of households and higher levels of 'energy service' (warmer and better lit homes using more appliances). Around 11 million of the estimated 17 million dwellings with wall cavities in the United Kingdom do not have insulation. Government programmes have increased the rate of uptake of cavity wall insulation towards 280,000 a year, but this rate will have to treble before 2009 in order to meet the target energy savings. Further R&D is also needed to develop cost-effective and compatible methods of improving the energy efficiency of the estimated 7 million homes with solid walls.

estimates that the number of vulnerable fuel-poor households needs to be reduced to 400,000 by March 2008 to be on track to meet the Government's 2010 target.

Warm Front is the Government's main programme to tackle fuel poverty in England and is targeted specifically at vulnerable households in the private sector in receipt of an income-related or disability benefit. Between April 2001 and February 2004, the scheme assisted some 670,000 households with measures such as insulation, replacement boilers, new gas and electric central heating systems, and gas central heating repairs. The forthcoming Fuel Poverty Implementation Plan will set out the future for Warm Front and outline how fuel poverty targets will be met.

The overall target dates for ending all fuel poverty in Scotland and Wales are 2016 and 2018 respectively. Warm Deal, the Scottish Executive's insulation grant scheme, provided energy efficiency packages to over 180,000 households between 1999 and February 2004. The National Assembly for Wales's fuel poverty programme, the Home Energy Efficiency Scheme (HEES), made £13.3 million available in 2003/04. The Assembly expects HEES to have assisted a total of 95,000 households by March 2007.

The target dates for Northern Ireland are to end fuel poverty in vulnerable households and social housing by 2010, and to end all fuel poverty by 2016. *Towards a fuel poverty strategy for Northern Ireland* was published for consultation by the Department for Social Development in October 2003. The interim target is to have assisted at least 40,000 households by 2006, from an estimated 203,000 households in fuel poverty.

Water supply

About three-quarters of the United Kingdom's water supply is obtained from upland lakes, reservoirs and river intakes, while a quarter is from underground sources (stored in layers of porous rock). Parts of East Anglia, South West, South East and southern England are more dependent on groundwater than the rest of the United Kingdom. Northern England, Scotland and Wales have a relative abundance of unpolluted water from upland sources. Northern Ireland also has plentiful supplies for domestic use and for industry.

Water put into the public water supply system (including industrial and other uses) in England and Wales averaged 15,394 megalitres a day (Ml/d) in 2002/03. An average of 2,387 Ml/d was supplied in Scotland, and 710 Ml/d in Northern Ireland. Some 58,489 Ml/d were abstracted from all sources in England and Wales in 2001, of which public water supplies accounted for 16,231 Ml/d. The electricity supply industry took 32,263 Ml/d and agriculture 108 Ml/d (excluding spray irrigation which accounted for a further 259 Ml/d). Abstractions for the public water supply were 13 per cent higher in 2001 than in 1971, but 8 per cent lower than in 1991. Electricity supply industry abstractions have varied greatly since 1990, but have recently increased and in 2001 were very similar to the 1971 level. Total abstractions for all other purposes fell during the 1970s, but have since increased again.

Despite improved efficiency in the use of water, public demand continues to increase. Household water consumption per person in England and Wales grew from 140 litres a day in 1992/93 to 150 litres a day in 2003, due to the increasing numbers of households, increasing use of domestic appliances and warmer weather.

England and Wales

The Environment Agency regulates the amount of water that can be abstracted from each resource under the *Water Resources Act 1991* by issuing abstraction licences. There is a charging scheme for abstraction of water.

The 26 water companies across England and Wales have statutory responsibilities for public water supply, including quality and sufficiency. Ten of these companies are also responsible for sewage treatment.

The average household bill in 2004/05 is £249 (£117 for water and £132 for sewerage). Since privatisation in 1989, average household bills for water and sewerage have increased by 25 per cent in real terms.

The *Water Industry Act 1999* prohibits water companies from disconnecting households and other premises deemed vital to the community. It also makes provision for the protection of water customers on metered supplies who are vulnerable to hardship because of high usage for essential household purposes. These include a large number of low-income families, and elderly and disabled people. These provisions are laid down in the Vulnerable Groups Regulations and their amendments.

WaterVoice provides independent representation for all customers of the water and sewerage companies in England and Wales. Operating through regional committees, it represents the interests of customers in respect of price, services and value for money, and investigates complaints. The ten regional committee chairmen form the WaterVoice Council, which deals with issues at national and European levels.

The Director General of Water Services, who heads the Office of Water Services (Ofwat), is the economic regulator of the water industry in England and Wales. The Director set price limits for water and sewerage services for 2000–05, which assumed water companies would deliver a capital investment programme of £15.6 billion at May 1999 prices during this period. This investment is intended to maintain the water and sewerage systems, improve customer services, and cope with growth in demand. It includes £7.4 billion to improve drinking water and environmental water quality, to meet new EU and national standards.[8]

The 2004 price review will set water and sewerage price limits for 2005–10 and a revised capital investment target. Ofwat published its draft decisions in August 2004 and plans to finalise these in December 2004. Its decisions will be based partly on the water companies' water resource plans for 2004. These annual plans of water supply and demand are reviewed each year by the Environment Agency.

About a quarter of households and around 90 per cent of commercial and industrial customers were charged for water on a metered basis in 2003. Most homes are still charged according to the rateable value of their property. All water companies supply and install free meters to households on request. In 2004/05, the average unmeasured bill for water is £122 and, for sewerage, it is £136. The average measured bill is £101 for water and £121 for sewerage.

The Drinking Water Inspectorate (DWI) is responsible for ensuring that water companies in England and Wales supply safe wholesome water, and comply with the requirements of the relevant Water Supply (Water Quality) Regulations. New Regulations were introduced in 2000 for England and 2001 for Wales, and came fully into force on 1 January 2004. In 2003 (the final year of reporting against the previous Regulations), 99.88 per cent of the 2.9 million tests carried out on drinking water samples taken in England and Wales met national and EU quality standards. The new Regulations were introduced to reflect the requirements of an EC Directive on drinking water quality, which included meeting new and revised standards by December 2003.

The UN World Water Development Report, published in March 2003, found that the United Kingdom had the fourth best water quality of 122 selected countries, behind Finland, Canada and New Zealand.

New regulatory arrangements

The *Water Act 2003* (see page 298) commits the Government to the sustainable management and use of water resources in England and Wales. It updates the framework for abstraction licensing, and aims to promote greater water conservation and planning for the future by water companies. Licensing changes will be introduced in 2005, drought plans are expected to become statutory in 2005, and water resources plans in 2007/08. A new regime for competition in the water industry will allow licensees to supply non-household customers who use more than 50 megalitres a year.

The Act establishes a new regulatory authority for the water industry in England and Wales, which will be known as the Water Services Regulation Authority (WSRA) and will be set up on 1 April 2006. The post of Director General of Water Services will be abolished, though the new Authority may still commonly be known as Ofwat. The Act also abolishes existing customer services committees, which will be replaced by a new independent Consumer Council for Water (CCW). This will begin work on 1 October 2005.

Water conservation

Targets are set each year for water companies in England and Wales to reduce leakage. In 2003/04, 3,650 Ml/d of water put into the supply were lost through leakage – 30 per cent lower than in the peak year of 1994/95, but about the same as in 2002/03.

The Enhanced Capital Allowance scheme for water technologies was launched in July 2003 to provide tax incentives for companies investing in designated technologies that save water and improve water quality, while the Market Transformation Programme (see page 300) encourages products that use less water. Envirowise (see page 300) offers free advice and information on reducing water use in business.

Scotland

Scottish Water was created from the merger of the three former water authorities in Scotland as a result of the *Water Industry (Scotland) Act 2002*. It is the fourth largest water service provider in the United Kingdom, supplying about 2.4 billion litres of water a day and serving just under 5 million customers with drinking water. It also provides sewerage services.

Scottish Water is a public sector organisation accountable to three regulatory bodies: the Water Industry Commissioner for Scotland; the Scottish

---

8 The 2000–05 programme includes tightening sewage effluent quality standards to improve river estuaries and coastal waters, reducing the impact of storm overflows from the sewerage system and renovating iron water mains to reduce discoloured water.

Map 28.8 Non-energy minerals, UK

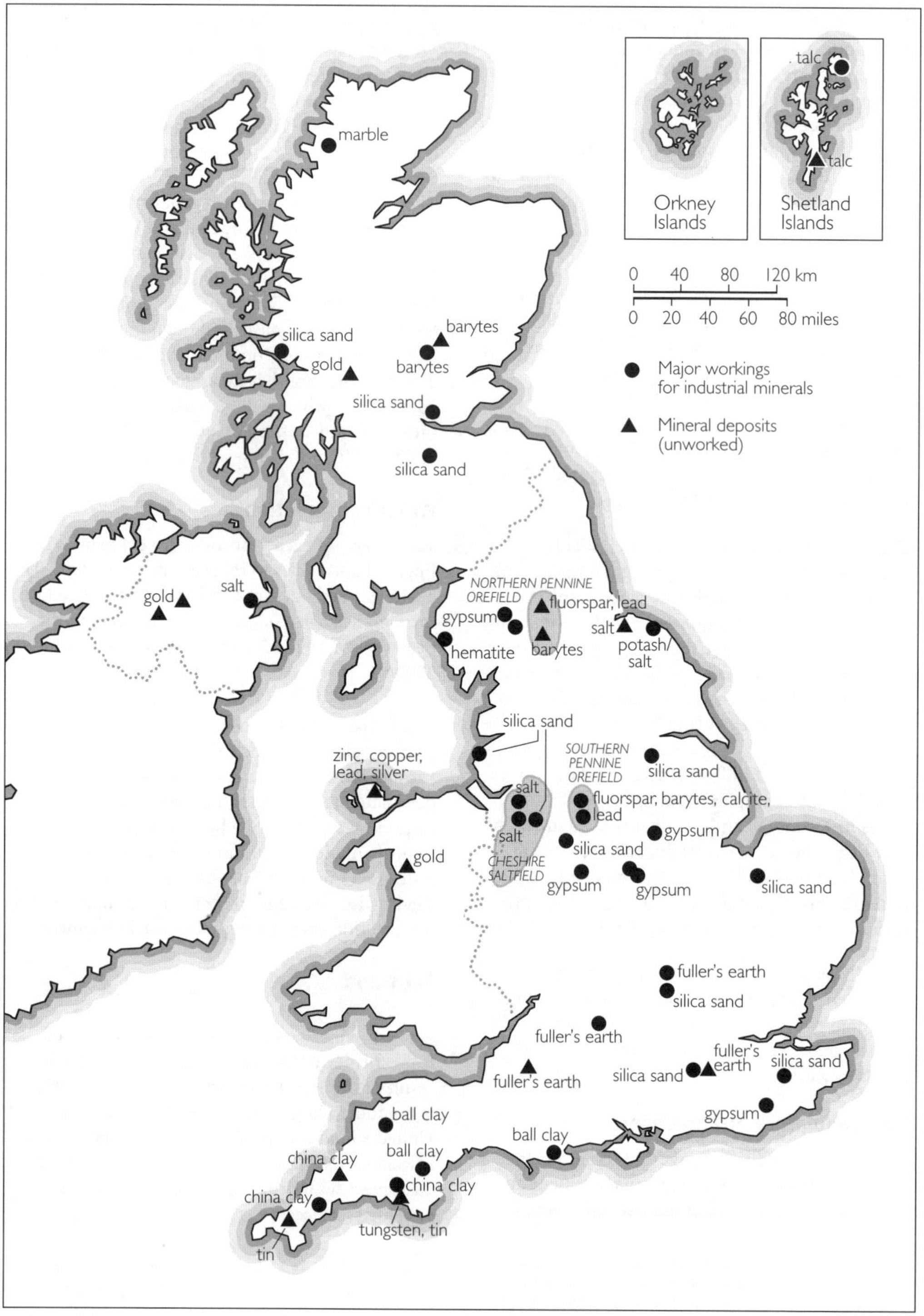

talc
talc

Orkney
Islands

Shetland
Islands

| 0 | 40 | 80 | 120 km |

| 0 | 20 | 40 | 60 | 80 miles |

● Major workings
for industrial minerals

▲ Mineral deposits
(unworked)

marble

silica sand
gold
barytes
barytes
silica sand
silica sand

gold salt

NORTHERN PENNINE
OREFIELD
gypsum ▲fluorspar, lead
salt
hematite barytes potash/
salt

silica sand

zinc, copper,
lead, silver
SOUTHERN
PENNINE
OREFIELD silica sand
salt
fluorspar, barytes, calcite,
lead
salt gypsum
gold
CHESHIRE
SALTFIELD
silica sand
gypsum silica sand
gypsum gypsum

fuller's earth
silica sand

fuller's earth
fuller's
silica sand earth silica sand
fuller's earth
gypsum

ball clay
china clay ball clay ball clay
china clay china clay
tin
tungsten, tin

Environment Protection Agency; and the Drinking Water Quality Regulator for Scotland.

Northern Ireland

The Water Service is an executive agency of the Department for Regional Development (DRD). It is responsible for the supply and distribution of drinking water and the provision of sewerage services to over 765,000 domestic, agricultural, commercial and business customers.

The Water Service envisages that expenditure of around £3 billion will be required over 15 to 20 years to bring water and sewerage services up to standard and to meet increasing demand. It plans to invest £590 million over the three-year period to 2006. In 2003, 99.31 per cent of the 98,920 tests carried out on drinking water in Northern Ireland met national and EU quality standards.

A major programme of reform will move Northern Ireland's water and sewerage services onto a fully self-financing basis by the end of the decade and relocate responsibility for the delivery of these services outside central government. New

arrangements for the economic regulation of the Northern Ireland water industry and consumer representation on water and sewerage issues are also planned.

Non-energy minerals

Output of non-energy minerals in 2002 was 294.1 million tonnes, valued at £2.5 billion. The total number of employees in the extractive industry in Great Britain was around 24,000.

The United Kingdom is virtually self-sufficient in construction minerals, and produces and exports several industrial minerals, notably china clay, ball clay, potash and salt. Over 90 per cent of non-energy minerals extracted in Great Britain each year are used to supply the construction industry with materials. Production of china clay (or kaolin), the largest export, was 2.1 million tonnes in 2003, of which 89 per cent was exported. The Boulby potash mine in north-east England is the most important UK non-energy mineral operation. Production in 2003 was a record 1.04 million tonnes, of which some 62 per cent was exported.

Table 28.9 Production of some of the main non-energy minerals, UK

	Million tonnes			Production value 2002
	1992	2001	2002	(£ million)
Sand and gravel	98.9	101.4	94.4	707
Silica sand	3.6	3.8	3.8	53
Igneous rock	57.7	51.5	51.2	336
Limestone and dolomite	107.9	102.6	93.6	670
Chalk	9.2	8.2	8.6	72
Sandstone	14.9	20.0	18.4	108
Gypsum	2.5	1.7	1.7	17
Salt comprising rock salt, salt in brine and salt from brine	6.1	6.1	5.7	148
Common clay and shale[1]	12.2	10.4	10.3	19
China clay[2]	2.5	2.2	2.2	192
Ball clay	0.7	1.0	0.9	44
Fireclay[1]	0.6	0.5	0.5	6
Potash	0.9	0.9	0.9	68
Fluorspar	0.1	0.1	0.1	5
Fuller's earth[2]	0.2	0.1	0.0	5
Slate	0.3	0.6	0.7	30

1 Great Britain only.
2 Moisture-free basis.
Source: *United Kingdom Minerals Yearbook 2002*, British Geological Survey

The largest non-energy mineral imports are non-metallic mineral products (£5.7 billion, of which rough diamonds accounted for £3.1 billion), refined non-ferrous metals (£3.4 billion), iron and steel (£2.4 billion) and ores, concentrates and scrap (valued at £1.6 billion in 2002).

Aggregates levy

The aggregates levy is an environmental tax on the commercial exploitation of aggregates in the United Kingdom. It was introduced in 2002 at £1.60 a tonne on the extraction of sand, gravel and rock. The object is to reduce the demand for such aggregates and encourage the use of recycled materials, thereby reducing the environmental costs associated with quarrying operations.

The Government has recognised the special position of processed product manufacturers in Northern Ireland – due to the land boundary with the Republic of Ireland – by introducing the Aggregates Levy Credit Scheme. Provided they adhere to a code of good environmental practice, operators may be eligible for an 80 per cent relief from the full rate of the levy for virgin materials and processed products until March 2011. The scheme is administered by the Department of the Environment for HM Customs and Excise.

Further reading

e-digest of environmental statistics. Defra. Available only on the Internet: *www.defra.gov.uk/environment/statistics/index.htm*

Digest of United Kingdom energy statistics. DTI. The Stationery Office.

UK energy sector indicators. DTI.

Energy report (the Blue Book). DTI. The Stationery Office.

United Kingdom minerals yearbook. British Geological Survey.

Creating a low carbon economy – first annual report on the implementation of the Energy White Paper. DTI and Defra, 2004.

Energy efficiency – the Government's plan for action. Cm 6168. Defra. The Stationery Office, 2004.

Our energy future – creating a low carbon economy. Cm 5761. DTI. The Stationery Office, 2003.

Strategy for combined heat and power to 2010. Defra, 2004.

The economic importance of minerals to the UK. British Geological Survey, 2004.

Websites

Department of Trade and Industry
www.dti.gov.uk

Department for Environment, Food and Rural Affairs
www.defra.gov.uk

National Assembly for Wales
www.wales.gov.uk

Scottish Executive
www.scotland.gov.uk

Northern Ireland Executive
www.northernireland.gov.uk

Sustainable Energy Policy Network
www.dti.gov.uk/energy/sepn/index.shtml

Office of Gas and Electricity Markets
www.ofgem.gov.uk

Office of Water Services
www.ofwat.gov.uk

BGS Minerals
www.bgs.ac.uk/mineralsuk

European Commission energy website
www.europa.eu.int/comm/energy

WWW.

29 Services

This chapter covers the UK service sector, although some areas, such as public services and telecommunications, are covered in other chapters. The sector is the main contributor to economic growth in the United Kingdom, accounting for 73 per cent of gross value added (GVA – see glossary) at current basic prices in 2003. The sector expanded by 2.5 per cent during the year (Table 29.1), slightly below the 2.7 per cent growth in 2002. There were over 23.5 million workforce jobs in the sector in December 2003, representing 79 per cent of all jobs.

Financial services and the economy

The financial services sector accounted for over 5 per cent of GVA in the United Kingdom in 2003 and for 1.05 million employee jobs.

London is one of the three main financial centres in the world, along with New York and Tokyo, and is the premier financial centre in Europe. Major financial institutions and markets include the Bank of England, the London Stock Exchange and Lloyd's insurance market. Scotland (Edinburgh and Glasgow) is the second financial centre in the United Kingdom, and one of the main European centres for institutional fund management – £327 billion of funds were under management in Scotland at the end of 2003. Other sizeable UK financial centres are Birmingham, Bristol, Leeds and Manchester. International Financial Services London (IFSL) promotes the international activities of UK-based financial institutions and professional and business services. It also seeks to raise awareness of the leading UK role in international financial markets and highlight the major contribution of financial services to the UK economy.

Bank of England

The Bank of England (see also page 348 and 466) has close links with financial markets and institutions, and is responsible for maintaining

Table 29.1 Gross value added chained volume measures¹ at basic prices, service industries, UK

	2002	2003	% change in 2003
			2001 = 100
Wholesale and retail trade	105.0	107.3	2.2
Hotels and restaurants	103.7	109.2	5.3
Transport and storage	101.3	100.8	−0.5
Post and telecommunication	101.2	105.9	4.6
Financial intermediation²	98.8	100.6	1.8
Real estate, renting and business activities	103.3	110.2	6.7
Ownership of dwellings	101.7	103.3	1.6
Public administration, defence and social security	102.7	104.8	2.0
Education	101.2	101.6	0.4
Health and social work	103.8	107.7	3.8
Other services	102.8	101.9	−0.9
Adjustment for financial services	102.9	114.1	10.9
Total service industries	102.7	105.3	2.5

1 See glossary.
2 Operations of institutions such as banks, building societies, insurance companies, pension funds and trusts.
Source: Office for National Statistics

stability in the financial system. It analyses and promotes initiatives to strengthen the system, monitors developments to try to identify potential threats to stability, and undertakes work on the arrangements for handling financial crises should they occur. It is also the financial system's 'lender of last resort' in exceptional circumstances. In this work, the Bank co-operates closely with HM Treasury and the Financial Services Authority (FSA, see page 471).

In addition, the Bank provides banking services to its customers, principally the Government, the banking system and other central banks. It plays a key role in payment and settlement systems, and manages the country's foreign exchange reserves on behalf of HM Treasury.

Banking

The UK banking sector is the third largest in the world after the United States and Japan. In addition to having one of the largest commercial banking industries, the United Kingdom is also a major international centre for investment and private banking. The substantial presence of foreign banks underlines the banking sector's international outlook. Its assets and liabilities totalled £4,160 billion at the end of 2003, nearly three times the level in 1993. Foreign banks accounted for over half of the banking sector's assets, and 287 of the 382 banks operating in the United Kingdom in 2003 were foreign-owned.

'Retail' banking primarily caters for personal customers and small businesses. Nearly all banks also engage in some 'wholesale' activities, which involve taking larger deposits, deploying funds in money-market instruments, and making corporate loans and investments, while some concentrate on wholesale business. Banks feature among the United Kingdom's top companies (see page 360) – three of the top ten companies by market capitalisation in March 2004 were banks: HSBC, Royal Bank of Scotland and Barclays.

Retail bank services include current accounts, savings accounts, loan arrangements, credit and debit cards, mortgages, insurance, investment products, share-dealing services and 'wealth management' services. Around 92 per cent of households in the United Kingdom have at least one adult member with a bank or building society or other savings account (Table 29.2).

Table 29.2 Households by type of saving in 2002/03, UK

Percentages

Type of account	
Current account	88
Post Office account	7
Tax Exempt Special Savings Account (TESSA)	8
Individual Savings Account (ISA)	32
Other bank or building society accounts (excluding current accounts, ISAs and TESSAs)	55
Stocks and shares/member of a share club	24
Personal Equity Plans	9
Unit trusts or investment trusts	5
Gilt-edged stock	1
Premium Bonds	23
National Savings Bonds	4
Company share scheme/profit-sharing scheme	5
Save as you earn	1
Any type of account	92

Source: Family Resources Survey, Department for Work and Pensions

The universal banking programme, giving access to basic bank accounts and a Post Office card account, became available through post offices in 2003. These services are intended to tackle financial exclusion and bring those people without bank accounts into the financial mainstream, while ensuring that benefit recipients and pensioners can continue to receive their money in cash at their local post office when such payments are automated. Automated payment arrangements commenced in April 2003 and will be completed by October 2005. The major financial institutions have agreed to contribute by making their own basic bank accounts accessible at post offices and by making a contribution of £182 million to the cost of running the Post Office card account.

By the end of 2003, 1.38 million of the 5.04 million basic bank accounts in the United Kingdom were accessible at the Post Office.

The major retail banks have traditionally operated through local branches, but technological developments are having a major impact on the way in which banking is conducted. Between 1993 and 2003, the number of branches in the United Kingdom fell by one-quarter to 11,100. Electronic delivery channels, including automated teller machines (ATMs), Internet banking, corporate electronic banking, interactive TV and mobile phone banking, have all gained in importance in recent years. The number of ATMs has more than doubled over the past decade (see page 465). The United Kingdom is the largest market for online banking in Europe, with over 8 million adults accessing online banking websites in 2002.

Supervision

The FSA (see page 471) is responsible for regulating banks. Banks are required to meet minimum standards on the integrity and competence of directors and management, the adequacy of capital and cash flow, and the systems and controls to deal with the risks they experience. Should a bank fail to meet these criteria, its activities may be restricted, or it may be closed. These arrangements are intended to strengthen, but not guarantee, the protection of bank depositors, thereby increasing confidence in the banking system as a whole.

The Banking Code is an additional, voluntary arrangement, setting out the relationship between banks and building societies and their customers. The independent Banking Code Standards Board assesses compliance with the Code. A review of the Code began in January 2004 and will continue until autumn 2004, with a new version coming into effect from March 2005.

Investment and private banking

London is a major international financial centre for investment banking, accounting for an estimated 50 per cent of such activity in Europe. Although the United Kingdom is the source of around a quarter of European investment banking fee revenue, around half of European banking activity is conducted through London, and the majority of investment banks have either a headquarters or a major office in the City.

Global investment banking revenue increased by a fifth in 2003 to reach US$40.7 billion but this was still over a quarter below the 2000 peak. In 2003, the United Kingdom accounted for 27 per cent of the US$11.4 billion earned by the investment banking industry in Europe.

Investment banks offer a range of professional financial services, including corporate finance and asset management. Advice on mergers and acquisitions accounted for 59 per cent of

investment banking revenue originating in the United Kingdom in 2003.

Building societies

Building societies are mutual institutions, owned by, and run for, their members. As well as their retail deposit-taking services, they specialise in housing finance, making long-term mortgage loans against the security of property – usually private dwellings purchased for owner-occupation. In recent years, a number of building societies have diversified and now offer a wide range of personal financial services. The chief requirements for societies are that:

- their principal purpose is making loans which are secured on residential property and are funded substantially by their members;
- at least 75 per cent of lending has to be on the security of housing; and
- a minimum of 50 per cent of funds must be in the form of deposits made by individual members.

In May 2004 there were 63 building societies in the United Kingdom, all of which were members of the Building Societies Association (BSA). The number of societies has fallen from 273 in 1980 as a result of mergers. In addition, several large societies have given up their mutual status and become banks. Many of the remaining societies have taken steps to defend their mutual status, for example by requiring new members to assign to charity any 'windfall' payments arising from a conversion.

Total assets at the end of 2003 amounted to over £205 billion. Building societies employed over 43,000 staff in head offices and had 2,081 branches. They had almost 21 million savings accounts issued to around 15 million savers, and had issued approximately 2.7 million mortgages to about 2.5 million borrowers.

The largest society is the Nationwide, with group assets of £101 billion in April 2004, followed by the Britannia and Yorkshire (£21 billion and £14 billion respectively at end-2003).

National Savings and Investments

National Savings and Investments (NS&I) is an executive agency reporting to the Chancellor of the Exchequer. It is a source of finance for government borrowing, offering personal savers a range of savings and investments. The *Finance Act 2003* included a number of provisions in respect of NS&I. For example, it can issue plastic cards so that customers can make cash withdrawals from ATM machines (see box).

Closure of NS&I Ordinary Account

On 31 July 2004 the NS&I Ordinary Account was closed after more than 140 years. It was originally introduced in 1861, the year National Savings (then known as the Post Office Savings Bank) was founded by the Government to encourage workers to 'provide for themselves against adversity and ill health'. The account has been replaced by the Easy Access Savings Account, launched in January 2004, in response to changing customer needs, offering increased access and consistent and competitive interest rates. The new account comes with an ATM card for cash machines.

Gross sales of NS&I products (including accrued interest) were £12.7 billion in 2003/04 and £66.5 billion was invested in NS&I products at March 2004. Savings products include Premium Bonds, which offer tax-free prizes instead of interest in a monthly draw, Savings Certificates (both Fixed Interest and Index-linked), Pensioners Guaranteed Income Bonds, Capital Bonds, Children's Bonus Bonds, cash mini ISAs (see page 469), Investment Accounts (where deposits can be made at post offices) and Guaranteed Equity Bonds, where the investor's return is linked to the performance of the FTSE 100 index (see page 470).

Friendly societies

Friendly societies are mutual organisations – set up and owned by their members and run for their benefit – providing a wide range of savings, assurance, insurance and healthcare products, often tax-free. The representative trade body for the United Kingdom is the Association of Friendly Societies. In March 2004, 2,377 societies (including branches) were registered under the *Friendly Societies Acts 1974 and 1992*, according to the Mutual Societies Registrar.

Credit unions

Credit unions are financial co-operatives, established under the *Credit Unions Act 1979*,

owned and controlled by their members, who save in a common fund. The money saved is used to make low-interest loans to other credit union members. The Association of British Credit Unions Ltd is the main trade association in Great Britain. In the year ending September 2003, 444 credit unions were registered, with membership of about 365,000 and savings balances of around £293 million. In Northern Ireland credit unions are served by the Irish League of Credit Unions, which covers the whole of Ireland.

Responsibility for registration and supervision of credit unions lies with the FSA (see page 471). Credit unions must meet a basic test of solvency and maintain a level of initial capital and a minimum liquidity ratio. Members have protection for their deposits through the Financial Services Compensation Scheme (see page 472).

Private equity/venture capital

Private equity/venture capital companies offer medium- and long-term equity financing for new and developing businesses, management buy-outs and buy-ins, and company rescues. The British Venture Capital Association (BVCA) represents private equity and venture capital sources in the United Kingdom. According to its report on investment activity (based on data provided by 165 firms that were then members), worldwide investment by UK private equity and venture capital firms increased by 16 per cent in 2003 to £6.4 billion. Of this, £4.1 billion (64 per cent) was in the United Kingdom. The Government has encouraged the development of venture capital, including Regional Venture Capital Funds.

Other credit and financial services

Finance houses and leasing companies provide consumer credit, business finance and leasing, and motor finance. There are 107 full and 75 associate members of the Finance and Leasing Association, achieving new business worth £90 billion in 2003, of which £65 billion was credit granted to private individuals. Factoring and invoice discounting companies offer a range of financial services, including credit management and finance against a company's outstanding invoices. Member companies of the Factors & Discounters Association handled business worth £117 billion in 2003, 13 per cent higher than in 2002, of which £95 billion was domestic invoice discounting.

Payment systems

Apart from credit and debit card arrangements, three companies manage the major UK payment clearing systems:

- Cheque and Credit Clearing Company, responsible for the bulk clearing of cheques and paper credits throughout Great Britain – cheque and credit payments in Northern Ireland are processed locally;

- CHAPS (Clearing House Automated Payment System), an electronic transfer system for same-day payments from bank to bank; and

- BACS Payment Schemes Ltd, managing the schemes under which bulk payments are made.

The UK trade association for payments is the Association for Payment Clearing Services (APACS). A total of 33 banks and building societies belonged to APACS at the end of June 2004, while several hundred others obtain access to one or all of the clearings through agency arrangements with one of the members.

In March 2004, the Office of Fair Trading (OFT) announced the establishment of a new Banking Payment System Task Force to consider competition, efficiency and incentive issues relating to payment systems. The creation of the Task Force followed the publication of the Government's Pre-Budget report in December 2003, which said that the OFT would take on an enhanced role on payments systems for four years. The Government would review competition in the industry at the end of the four-year period and would legislate unless there had been a significant improvement.

Trends in financial transactions

The nature of financial transactions has undergone major changes since the first plastic cards appeared in 1966. Most small non-regular payments are still made by cash, but there is a trend away from cheques towards greater use of plastic cards (Table 29.3).

Consumers now acquire more than half their cash through withdrawals from ATMs, which in 2003 dispensed £144 billion in 2.4 billion transactions. About two-thirds of adults use ATMs regularly, making on average 70 withdrawals a year.

In 2003, direct debit and standing order payments accounted for 62 per cent of regular bill payments, and 73 per cent of adults have set up at least one direct debit or standing order. Many mortgage and other loan repayments and life insurance contributions are made by this means, as are the majority of utility and council tax bills. Direct debit payments rose by 6 per cent to reach 2.4 billion in 2003.

Plastic cards

According to APACS, there were 160 million plastic cards in issue in 2003 and 7.8 billion plastic card transactions in the United Kingdom.

Table 29.3 Transaction trends in the UK

	1993	1998	2003
Transaction volumes (million)			
All plastic card purchases	1,488	3,094	5,317
of which:			
Debit card	659	1,736	3,364
Credit and charge card	748	1,224	1,822
Plastic card withdrawals at			
ATMs and counters	1,277	1,917	2,457
Direct debits, standing orders,			
direct credits and CHAPS	2,047	3,056	4,272
Cheques	3,559	2,986	2,251
of which:			
For payment	3,163	2,757	2,110
For cash acquisition	396	229	141
Total non-cash transactions	8,371	11,053	14,297
Cash payments[1]	27,273	25,309	25,859
Post Office Order Book payments			
and passbook withdrawals	1,144	1,017	690
Total transaction volumes	36,788	37,379	40,750
UK ATM network			
Number of ATMs	19,100	24,600	46,500
ATM withdrawals (million)	1,242	1,850	2,373
ATM cards (million)	51	66	88

1 Estimated figures.
Source: Association for Payment Clearing Services

Debit card payments are deducted directly from the purchaser's bank or building society account. The number of transactions grew by over 12 per cent to nearly 3.4 billion in 2003. Less than £18 billion of goods and services were paid for by debit card in 1993. By 2003, this figure had grown to over £130 billion.

At the end of 2003 there were 66.8 million credit cards and 4.4 million charge cards in use in the United Kingdom. They are the most common way for adults to buy goods and services using the Internet. Of the 200 million online transactions, 69 per cent are made by credit card.

According to figures from APACS, UK plastic card fraud fell for the first time in eight years in 2003, to £402 million from £425 million in 2002. However, the fall was entirely due to a reduction in the amount of fraud committed abroad on UK cards, whereas for UK-based transactions there was a very slight increase. Counterfeit card fraud saw the largest reduction in 2003, down by 28 per cent to £107 million. The bulk of the reduction occurred in mainland Europe, where it was down by £26 million on 2002. To combat fraud, banks are investing in new systems, in which information is contained on a microchip embedded in cards. By 2005 the majority of transactions involving credit and debit cards will involve chip and PIN (personal identification number) cards.

Banknotes and coins

The Bank of England is the sole issuer of currency notes in England and Wales, and although banks in Scotland and Northern Ireland[1] issue their own notes, there is a legal framework which stipulates the conditions under which these need to be covered, pound for pound, by Bank of England notes or other assets. Net profits from the Bank of England note issue are paid over to the Government.

The provision of UK coinage is the responsibility of the Royal Mint, based at Llantrisant, south Wales. At the end of 2003 there were an estimated 25.7 billion coins in circulation in the United Kingdom, with a face value of £3.15 billion. The number of coins issued during 2003/04 amounted to 1.8 billion.

Insurance

The UK insurance industry is the largest in Europe and the third largest in the world. It employs 348,000 people, a third of all financial services jobs, and accounts for 17 per cent of investment in the stock market. It pays out £281 million a day in

Table 29.4 Banknotes in circulation, UK

	Value of notes in circulation end-February 2004 (£ billion)	Number of new notes issued in year to end-February 2004 (million)
£5	1.0	313
£10	5.7	345
£20	20.1	245
£50	5.7	11
Other notes[1]	3.5	–
Total	**36.0**	**914**

1 Includes higher value notes used internally in the Bank, for example, as cover for the note issues of banks of issue in Scotland and Northern Ireland in excess of their permitted issues.
Source: Bank of England

pension and life insurance benefits and £47 million a day in general insurance claims.

The UK insurance industry generated net worldwide premiums of £159 billion in 2003, according to the Association of British Insurers (ABI). UK risks were £124 billion and overseas risks £35 billion. The industry has over £1,150 billion invested in company shares and other assets.

Main types of insurance

Insurance can be long-term, such as life insurance, pensions and savings, where contracts may be for many years; and general, such as motor, household and commercial insurance, where contracts are usually for up to one year only. Most insurance companies reinsure their risks; this performs an important function in spreading losses and in helping companies manage their businesses.

UK long-term insurance accounted for £118 billion of net worldwide premiums by the UK industry in 2003, compared with £41 billion of general insurance. Life insurance accounted for 31 per cent of long-term premium income, occupational pensions 39 per cent and individual pensions 27 per cent. About 50 per cent of households have life insurance cover.

Motor insurance accounts for over a third of UK company market general insurance premiums. Other important areas are property insurance, and accident and health insurance. Independent

---

1 In Scotland these comprise the Bank of Scotland, Royal Bank of Scotland and Clydesdale Bank, and in Northern Ireland the Bank of Ireland, First Trust Bank, Northern Bank and Ulster Bank.

intermediaries distributed 55 per cent of general insurance premiums in 2003, direct selling 21 per cent, banks and building societies 8 per cent, and company agents 7 per cent. Direct selling in motor insurance has increased, reflecting the growth of insurers offering telephone-based and Internet-based services.

Structure of the industry

At the end of 2003, 768 companies were authorised to conduct insurance business in the United Kingdom. Nearly three-quarters of these companies carry on general business only. About 400 companies belong to the ABI. The industry includes both public limited companies and mutual institutions (companies owned by their policyholders), although the mutual sector has gradually contracted. The biggest insurance group in the United Kingdom in 2003 was Aviva, with net premium income of around £14 billion.

In March 2004, Standard Life, the biggest mutual insurance company in Europe, announced that it planned to abandon its mutual status and seek a stock market listing. The company has been adversely affected by stock market falls and a declining market for its with-profits policies. The decision to consider listing is part of a strategic review after talks with the FSA over how to meet new solvency requirements.

Insurance firms and markets have been affected by weak equity markets and by events such as the destruction of the New York World Trade Centre in 2001. At the time, the FSA relaxed some of its requirements on solvency to ease the position for insurance companies. Its prime focus now is on introducing a new capital regime requiring companies to hold sufficient financial resources that more adequately reflect the risks they underwrite. This means that life insurance companies are better able to meet their responsibilities to policyholders and absorb any market falls that may occur.

Equitable Life, the world's oldest mutual life assurer, experienced particular problems arising from guarantees offered to a number of its policyholders and closed to new business in December 2000. HM Treasury appointed Lord Penrose to lead an inquiry into the history of the Equitable, and to find out who was to blame, what lessons could be learned and whether there was a failure by the regulatory authorities. The Penrose report, published in March 2004, found that the balance of blame lay more with Equitable than with its regulators. In response to the inquiry, the Government announced an independent review of the actuarial profession, with a wide-ranging remit to examine the profession and the Government Actuary's Department. The review, which will build on the work of the Myners review of institutional investment (see page 468), will report by spring 2005. The Government has also announced a review led by Paul Myners into the corporate governance arrangements applicable to mutual life offices. This review is due to report by the end of 2004.

The London Market

The London Insurance Market (London Market) is a distinct part of the UK insurance and reinsurance industry centred in the City of London. It is the main centre for reinsurance business and for energy, marine, aviation, satellite and other forms of transport insurance. It comprises insurance and reinsurance companies, Lloyd's syndicates, Protection and Indemnity clubs (mutual insurers for shipowners) and brokers who handle most of the business. The business traded is mainly non-life (general) insurance and reinsurance, with an increasing emphasis on high-exposure risks.

Estimated gross premiums of the London Market from reported returns were £24.6 billion in 2002. Virtually all companies participating in the company sector are members of the International Underwriting Association of London (IUA), which in May 2004 had 42 ordinary members. Over three-quarters of companies operating in the London Market are overseas-owned.

Lloyd's of London

Lloyd's of London is the world's leading insurance market, with a capacity to accept premiums of £14.9 billion in 2004. It provides insurance services to businesses and individuals in more than 190 countries. In 2004, 66 syndicates were underwriting insurance at Lloyd's, covering many speciality areas including marine, aviation, catastrophe, professional indemnity and motor. Syndicates, staffed by underwriters, compete for business and cover either all or a portion of the risk. They are run by managing agents who have a franchise to operate within the Lloyd's market.

Lloyd's is administered by the Council of Lloyd's and a Franchise Board. In 2003, it reported a profit of £1.9 billion on an annually accounted basis, and an initial projection of profit of £1.8 billion on a three-year accounted basis for the 2003 underwriting year. In addition, the net resources of the society and its members increased by 35 per cent to £10.1 billion at the end of 2003.

Investment

The United Kingdom has considerable expertise in fund management, which involves managing funds on behalf of investors, or advising them how best to invest their money. The main institutional groups and asset types are shown in Table 29.5. The assets of these institutions were valued at £1,652 billion at the end of 2002, compared with £1,838 billion at the end of the previous year.

Table 29.5 Assets and net investment by UK insurance companies, pension funds and trusts

£ billion

	Holdings at end of 2002 (market values)	Net investment in 2003 (cash values)
Long-term insurance funds	852.8	27.7
General insurance funds	97.9	11.1
Self-administered pension funds	610.5	20.5
Investment trusts	40.6	−0.4
Unit and property unit trusts[1]	202.8	19.5
Consolidation adjustment[2]	−152.2	−10.6
Total	**1,652.5**	**67.8**
of which:		
UK company securities	725.2	22.6
Government sterling securities (gilts)	241.7	21.4
Overseas company and government securities	364.5	8.3

1 Including open-ended investment companies (OEICs).
2 Adjustment to take account of investment of one institutional group in another.
Source: Office for National Statistics

The Myners review of institutional investment was published in 2001 and the Government subsequently confirmed it would take forward all the review's recommendations, including revised Codes of Investment Principles to encourage diversity in investment approaches. Since then:

- the Institutional Shareholders' Committee (ISC) published guidance for fund managers (and their clients) in 2002 on shareholder activism, helping them to maximise the value of their clients' equity holdings and the productivity of the companies they own. The Government is reviewing how successful the ISC's statement of principles has been;
- the Pensions Bill introduced into Parliament in February 2004 (see also page 165) includes a requirement that pension scheme trustees in Great Britain have adequate knowledge and understanding;
- the Government launched a major review of the effectiveness of the Myners principles in driving changes in investment decision-making by occupational pension schemes. The review will inform future decisions on the need for further action; and
- in May 2004, the FSA announced the results of a review of the practice of 'soft commissions' (whereby a broker agrees to pay for the supply of services from a third party to a fund manager in return for an agreed volume of business at an agreed commission rate) and 'bundling' (the provision by brokers of other in-house services, such as research, together with dealing in securities in a single commission charge) of transaction costs by brokers, following discussions of these issues in the Myners report. The FSA agreed with the Myners report that these practices create conflicts of interest for fund managers and said it would seek to limit the scope for both bundling and charging soft commissions.

Pension funds

At the end of 2002, total identified assets of UK self-administered pension funds amounted to £611 billion, compared with £714 billion at the end of 2001. Pension funds are major investors in securities markets, holding around 20 per cent of securities listed on the London Stock Exchange. Funds are managed mainly by the investment management houses.

Unit trusts and open-ended investment companies (OEICs)

Authorised unit trusts pool investors' money in funds divided into units of equal size, enabling people with relatively small amounts of money to benefit from diversified and professionally managed portfolios. Unit trusts can invest in a range of asset classes, such as equities, cash and bonds, and most have a geographical theme, such as the United Kingdom and North America. However, there are also specialist funds with a sector focus such as property or telecommunications. OEICs, set up in 1997, are similar to unit trusts, but investors buy shares in the fund rather than units.

At the end of June 2004 there were 1,925 UK authorised unit trusts and OEICs. There were 124 fund management companies, of which 75 were OEIC providers. Total funds under management were valued at £250 billion in June 2004, 16 per cent higher than in June 2003, including £158 billion of funds in OEICs. In June 2004 Personal Equity Plans accounted for £37 billion and Individual Savings Accounts (ISAs) for £34 billion. The Investment Management Association represents the UK asset management industry.

Investment trusts

Investment trusts are companies that invest in the shares of other companies. They are listed on the London Stock Exchange and their shares can be bought and sold in the same way as for other companies. Assets are purchased mainly out of shareholders' funds, although investment trusts are also allowed to borrow money for investment.

At the end of March 2004, there were 351 investment trusts, forming the largest listed sector of the London Stock Exchange, with assets worth £58 billion and market capitalisation of £44 billion. Members of the Association of Investment Trust Companies accounted for 249 of the total listed trust companies.

Share ownership

Results from the ONS Share Ownership Survey for 2003 (Table 29.6) indicate that nearly half of all ordinary shares listed on the UK Stock Exchange were owned by UK insurance companies, pension funds and other institutional shareholders. About 24 per cent of households in the United Kingdom have at least one adult owning shares (Table 29.2).

Tax-free savings

Tax-free saving is encouraged by Individual Savings Accounts (ISAs), launched in 1999 for an initial ten-year period as the successor to Personal Equity Plans (PEPs) and TESSAs (Tax Exempt Special Savings Accounts). Until April 2006, £7,000

Table 29.6 Ownership of UK ordinary shares[1]

	£ billion		Percentages
	2002	2003	2002
UK shareholders			
Insurance companies	230.1	236.9	*17.3*
Pension funds	180.1	219.8	*16.1*
Individuals	165.5	203.9	*14.9*
Unit trusts	18.9	27.2	*2.0*
Investment trusts	20.6	31.2	*2.3*
Other financial institutions	121.4	151.3	*11.1*
Banks	24.2	30.1	*2.2*
Charities	13.1	15.9	*1.2*
Private non-financial companies	9.1	9.9	*0.7*
Public sector	1.3	0.3	*–*
Total UK shareholders	784.3	926.5	*67.7*
Rest of the world	370.4	441.7	*32.3*
Total	**1,154.6**	**1,368.0**	*100*

1 As at 31 December.
Source: ONS Share Ownership Survey

can be invested every tax year. There are three main elements of an ISA:

- cash – up to £3,000 each year – such as in a bank or building society ISA account;
- stocks and shares – up to £7,000 a year in a maxi ISA and £3,000 in a mini ISA (see below); and
- life insurance – up to £1,000 a year.

In addition, savers can roll over capital from a matured TESSA into a cash ISA or a special TESSA-only ISA.

There are two main types of ISA: a maxi ISA, which can include all three elements in an ISA with a single manager up to the value of £7,000; and a mini ISA, which allows savers to have different managers, for the cash, stocks and shares, and life insurance components up to the value of £7,000. Savers can choose to put money into a mini ISA or a maxi ISA, but not both, in each tax year. Subscriptions are shown in Table 29.7.

Financial markets

London Stock Exchange

The London Stock Exchange is one of the three great financial centres of the world (along with

New York and Tokyo). Founded in 1801, it is the most international market in terms of the equities traded on the exchange and it is the leading provider of equity market services in Europe. A market for smaller, fast-growing companies – AIM, the Alternative Investment Market – opened in 1995. Within the Main Market of the London Stock Exchange, two 'attribute markets' have been launched – in 1999, techMARK, a market for innovative technology companies, followed in 2001 by techMARK mediscience, the world's first international market for healthcare companies. The number of companies operating in these markets and the equity market value of each is shown in Table 29.8.

A range of indices track share price movements on the Stock Exchange. The most widely quoted is the FTSE 100 index (the 'Footsie'), which relates to the 100 largest UK companies, by market capitalisation, listed on the Exchange. Figure 29.9 shows monthly closing levels for the FTSE 100 since its inception in January 1984.

Several other products for raising capital are handled, including Eurobonds, warrants, depositary receipts and gilt-edged stock (see page 370). The London Stock Exchange provides a secondary or trading market where investors can buy or sell UK Government securities (gilts). The Government raised £53 billion through issues of gilts on the Exchange in 2003.

Other equity exchanges

There are three other, relatively small markets in the City of London for trading equities: Virt-x,

Table 29.8 London Stock Exchange selected statistics

	2002	2003
UK – Main Market		
Number of companies	1,701	1,557
Equity market value (£ billion)	1,148	1,356
of which:		
techMARK		
Number of companies	210	178
Equity market value (£ billion)	246	296
techMARK mediscience		
Number of companies	44	40
Equity market value (£ billion)	117	141
International – Main Market		
Number of companies	419	381
Equity market value (£ billion)	1,902	1,975
AIM		
Number of companies	704	754
Equity market value (£ billion)	10	18

Source: London Stock Exchange

Figure 29.9 FTSE 100 index[1]

January 1984=1,000

1 Monthly data.
Source: London Stock Exchange

Table 29.7 Subscriptions to ISAs, UK

	2002/03 (£ million)	2003/04 (£ million)	% 2003/04
Mini ISAs			
Stocks and shares	1,712	1,540	5.7
Cash	18,391	18,642	69.0
Life insurance	190	174	0.6
Total	20,293	20,356	75.4
Maxi ISAs			
Stocks and shares	7,484	6,505	24.1
Cash	167	125	0.5
Life insurance	18	17	0.1
Total	7,669	6,647	24.6
Total invested	27,962	27,004	100

Source: Inland Revenue

OFEX and OM London. A new equities derivatives business, EDX London Ltd, jointly owned by the London Stock Exchange and OM AB, began trading Scandinavian equity derivatives in 2003.

Bond markets

London is at the centre of the Euromarket (a major market in a variety of currencies lent outside their domestic markets) and houses most of the leading international banks and securities firms. According to IFSL, bookrunners based in London are estimated to account for about 60 per cent of the primary and 70 per cent of the secondary market in Eurobonds.

Foreign exchange market

A Bank for International Settlements (BIS) survey in April 2004 showed that daily foreign exchange turnover in the United Kingdom was US$753 billion and that London was the world's biggest trading centre, handling over 31 per cent of global net daily turnover. Dealing is conducted by telephone and electronic links between the banks, other financial institutions and a number of firms of foreign exchange brokers which act as intermediaries. Electronic trading accounts for 55 per cent of foreign exchange activity.

Bullion markets

London is the world's most liquid 'spot' (immediate) market for gold and the global clearing centre for gold and silver. Around 60 banks and other financial trading companies participate in the London gold and silver markets. World gold prices are fixed twice a day and the world silver price once a day in London, through the members of the London Bullion Market Association.

Derivatives

Financial derivatives, including 'futures' and 'options', offer a means of protection against changes in prices, exchange rates and interest rates. Futures and options contracts can be traded on an exchange or over-the-counter (OTC). The United Kingdom is the most important OTC market place, as measured by booking location. According to the BIS, the UK share of world turnover represented average daily turnover of US$643 billion in April 2004, compared with US$275 billion in 2001.

Euronext.liffe is the international derivatives business of Euronext, comprising the Amsterdam, Brussels, LIFFE, Lisbon and Paris derivatives markets. It is the world's leading exchange for euro short-term interest rate derivatives and equity options. Euronext.liffe is creating a single market for derivatives, by bringing all its derivatives products together on a single electronic trading

platform LIFFE CONNECT. The exchange traded 695 million futures and options contracts in 2003, representing an underlying value of €251 trillion. In the first half of 2004, volume was up 24 per cent on the first half of 2003, to 438 million contracts with an underlying value of €157 trillion.

Other exchanges

Other important City exchanges include:

- the London Metal Exchange (LME) – the primary non-ferrous metals market in the world, trading contracts in aluminium, aluminium alloy, copper, lead, nickel, tin and zinc. It traded 72.3 million futures and options lots in 2003;

- the International Petroleum Exchange (IPE), a subsidiary of Intercontinental Exchange Inc of the United States, and Europe's leading energy futures and options exchange. Over US$2 billion in underlying value is traded each day on the IPE; and

- the Baltic Exchange, the world's premier maritime market.

The LCH.Clearnet Group – formed by a merger between the London Clearing House and Clearnet S.A. in December 2003 – clears and settles business at the LSE, EDX London, Euronext.liffe, LME, IPE and Virt-x.

Regulation

Financial Services Authority

The Financial Services Authority (FSA) is the independent body that regulates the UK financial services industry. The Government established the FSA in 1997, and the *Financial Services and Markets Act 2000*, which came into effect in 2001, gave the FSA statutory powers to regulate the industry. A new single Financial Services Compensation Scheme and a single Financial Ombudsman Service were also set up (see page 472). The FSA is the single statutory regulator responsible for the authorisation and supervision of deposit taking (such as by banks), insurance and the investment business. In October 2004 it will become responsible for regulation of mortgages, followed in January 2005 by general insurance regulation.

The FSA's key objectives are to maintain confidence in and promote public understanding of the UK financial system; secure the right degree of protection for consumers; and help to reduce financial crime.

The FSA monitors advertising and marketing of investment products such as pensions, ISAs, bonds, unit trusts and OEICs. Coverage will be extended to mortgages from October 2004. The FSA has set up a hotline for the public and firms to report misleading advertisements for financial products.

The *Freedom of Information Act 2000* (see page 63) gives a general right of access by the public to information held by public authorities, sets out exemptions from that right of access and places a number of obligations on public authorities. The Government has made the FSA a public authority for these purposes. The Independent Information Commissioner confirmed approval of the FSA publication scheme in January 2004.

Compensation

The Financial Services Compensation Scheme (FSCS) pays compensation if an authorised firm is unable, or likely to be unable, to pay claims against it. The Scheme was set up under the terms of the *Financial Services and Markets Act 2000*. It is an independent, non-profit-making organisation and covers deposits, insurance and investments.

Financial Ombudsman Service

The Financial Ombudsman Service provides consumers with a free, independent service for resolving disputes with financial firms. It considers complaints about a wide range of financial matters from firms in the insurance, mortgage, pensions and investments business.

Non-financial services

Non-financial services covered in this chapter include the motor, wholesale and retail trades; hotels, restaurants and catering; travel agents and tour operators; real estate, renting, computer and related activities, such as software consultancy; business services, such as market research, business and management consultancy and advertising; and tourism. See Table 22.5 on page 351 for the contribution these industries make to the UK economy.

Table 29.10 shows turnover for a range of non-financial services. Computer and related activities

and the motor trades showed the greatest increase in 2003. The United Kingdom is one of the world's major tourism destinations and spending on the hotel and restaurant sector is strongly influenced by the number of visitors coming from overseas. The impact of the conflict in Iraq, weak economic growth in Europe and the outbreak of Severe Acute Respiratory Syndrome affected the tourism industry across the world in 2003.

Table 29.10 Turnover in selected non-financial services,[1] Great Britain

£ billion

	2002	2003	% change in 2003
Motor trades	134.9	144.6	7.2
Wholesale trades	383.2	382.9	−0.1
Hotels and restaurants	59.1	62.0	4.9
Travel agents and tour operators	18.2	17.1	−6.1
Renting	19.0	19.4	1.9
Computer and related activities	45.5	51.0	12.0
Business services	158.4	168.4	6.3

1 Annual data derived from short-term turnover inquiries. Retailing is covered by a separate ONS sales inquiry.
Source: Office for National Statistics

Distributive trades

Motor trades

In December 2003 there were 582,000 employee jobs in the United Kingdom in retailing motor vehicles and parts, and in petrol stations. Turnover of the motor trades in Great Britain in 2003 was £145 billion, 7 per cent higher than in 2002. Most businesses selling new vehicles are franchised by the motor manufacturers. Car sales have grown strongly in recent years, with volumes reaching record levels in 2003 for the third successive year.

At the end of 2003 there were 10,535 petrol stations, 890 fewer than a year previously. However, the number of supermarket sites included in this total increased by 59 to 1,126. Many petrol stations offer other retail services, such as shops, car washes and fast-food outlets (there were 708 'quick-serve' restaurants at the end of 2003). Oil company sites accounted for 66 per cent of UK petrol stations in 2003.

Wholesaling and retailing

In 2003 over 106,000 enterprises were engaged in wholesaling in the United Kingdom; 23 per cent were sole proprietors and 14 per cent partnerships. There were 1.1 million employee jobs in the United Kingdom in this sector in December 2003.

Almost all large retailers in the food and drink trade have their own buying and central distribution operations. Many small wholesalers and independent grocery retailers belong to voluntary 'symbol' groups, which provide access to central purchasing facilities and coordinated promotions. This helps smaller retailers to remain relatively competitive; many local and convenience stores and village shops would otherwise not be able to stay in business.

Retailing is the leading private sector service industry in the United Kingdom, employing over 2.85 million people in March 2004 (around 11 per cent of the workforce). In 2003 there were nearly 189,000 retail enterprises in the United Kingdom; 41 per cent were sole proprietors and 32 per cent partnerships. The sector recorded £236 billion in sales, or 34 per cent of total consumer spending.

The volume of retail sales in Great Britain rose by over 16 per cent between 2000 and 2003 (Table 29.11). Growth in non-food stores (21 per cent) was higher than in predominantly food stores (12 per cent), with the greatest increase (29 per cent) in textile, clothing and footwear stores.

Small independent retail businesses and co-operative societies have been in relative decline for some time. To help their competitive position,

Table 29.11 Volume of retail sales, Great Britain

		2000 = 100	
	1993	1998	2003
Predominantly food stores	83.3	95.5	111.8
Predominantly non-food stores			
Non-specialised stores	79.6	91.5	113.6
Textile, clothing and footwear stores	73.2	88.8	129.0
Household goods stores	63.2	85.8	126.2
Other stores	82.9	93.6	114.5
Total	74.0	89.9	121.2
Non-store retailing and repair	87.6	93.2	107.8
All retailing	78.9	92.5	116.4

Source: Office for National Statistics

under the *Sunday Trading Act 1994*, small shops (under 280 square metres) have no restrictions on Sunday opening, while large shops (over 280 square metres) are restricted (except in Scotland) to six hours only between 10.00 am and 6.00 pm. In February 2004, the OFT published a review of the Supermarkets Code of Practice, which found a widespread belief among suppliers that the Code is not working, although the OFT found no hard evidence to support this view. The OFT has commissioned further work to establish how supermarkets deal with suppliers under the Code, which was introduced in 2002 following a Competition Commission report into supermarkets.

In April 2004, supermarket group Morrisons re-opened the first of the stores to be converted following its £3 billion takeover of Safeway in March. The takeover gives Morrisons a greater presence in southern England.

The Co-operative Group (CWS) Limited is the largest UK mutual retail group, with total food sales of £3 billion in 2003. As well as food retailing, the Group's operations include funeral businesses, travel retailing, motor trading and non-food department stores. The Co-operative Group is the principal supplier of goods and services to the Co-operative Movement – comprising 42 independent retail societies and 3,246 stores. Retail co-operative societies are voluntary organisations controlled by their members, membership being open to anyone paying a small deposit on a minimum share.

Franchising is the granting of a licence by one company (the franchiser) to another (the franchisee), usually by means of an initial payment with continuing royalties. Franchised activities operate in many areas, including cleaning services, film processing, print shops, fitness centres, courier delivery, car rental, engine tuning and servicing, and fast-food retailing. About 260 franchisers are members of the British Franchise Association (BFA), which conducts an annual survey of franchising. Its findings for 2004 estimated that there were 695 franchisors, with around 33,800 franchisees, accounting for about 330,000 jobs in the United Kingdom and with annual turnover of £9.7 billion.

Shopping facilities

There are eight regional out-of-town shopping centres in the United Kingdom, located at sites offering good road access and ample parking facilities. Opened between 1985 and 1999, they range in size from 56,000 square metres (Braehead, near Glasgow) to 160,000 square metres (Bluewater, in Kent, which is the largest such development in Europe).

Since 1996, social, economic and environmental considerations have led the Government and local planning authorities to limit new retail developments outside town centres. Out-of-town superstores, retail warehouses and shopping centres were felt to be undermining the vitality and viability of existing town and district centres. Government policy is now to focus new retail development in existing centres and so revitalise them. This is to ensure that everyone has easy access to a range of shops and services, whether or not they have a car; and to enable businesses of all types and sizes to prosper.

All new retail development requires planning permission from the local planning authority, which must consult central government before granting permission for most developments of 2,500 square metres or more.

Home shopping

Traditionally, all kinds of goods and services are purchased through mail-order catalogues. The largest-selling items are clothing, footwear, furniture, household textiles and domestic electrical appliances. Internet sales (see page 253) and electronic home shopping have grown rapidly. In 2002, 71 per cent of online sales of goods and services by UK businesses in the non-financial sector were in the wholesale, retail, catering, travel and telecommunications sectors.

Hotels, restaurants and catering

There were 1.8 million employee jobs in the hotel and restaurant trades in the United Kingdom in December 2003. This includes pubs, wine bars and other licensed bars, in addition to businesses offering accommodation and prepared food. Turnover in 2003 in Great Britain, at £62.0 billion, was 4.9 per cent higher than in 2002.

In 2002 there were 54,340 enterprises in the United Kingdom in the licensed restaurant industry (including fast-food and takeaway outlets), an increase of 3.2 per cent on 2001. Total turnover in 2003 in Great Britain amounted to £20.3 billion, 6.2 per cent higher than in 2002.

Real estate, renting and business activities

Exhibition and conference centres

The United Kingdom is one of the world's leading centres for international conferences. Many UK towns and cities have conference and exhibition facilities, including several traditional seaside resorts which have adapted to the growing business tourism market.

Key exhibition venues include the National Exhibition Centre and International Conference Centre in Birmingham; ExCeL in London's Docklands; Earls Court and Olympia Exhibition Centres and Wembley Exhibition Centre in London; the Scottish Exhibition & Conference Centre in Glasgow; and King's Hall Exhibition Centre in Belfast.

The Exhibition Venues Association represents most of the leading exhibition complexes across the United Kingdom and Ireland. The Association of Exhibition Organisers represents many trade and consumer event organisers, while the British Exhibition Contractors Association represents the interests of contractors. These three bodies tackle issues of common concern through the Exhibition Association Forum.

Total visitor attendance at exhibitions in 2003 fell by 16 per cent, but was only 4 per cent lower than in 2001. Including multiple exhibitions, there were 856 events in 2003, attracting 9.6 million visitors.

UK Trade & Investment (see page 385) provides key funding towards development and maintenance of the United Kingdom's official listing of all consumer, trade, public and industrial exhibitions held in major UK venues.

Renting

A varied range of rental services, many of which are franchised, are available across the United Kingdom. These include hire of cars and other vehicles; televisions, video recorders and camcorders; household appliances such as washing machines; tools and heavy decorating equipment such as ladders and floor sanders; and videos, DVDs and computer games. In the business sector these services include renting of agricultural or civil engineering machinery. Retailing of many types of service is dominated by chains, although independent operators are still to be found in most fields. In December 2003 there were 165,000 employee jobs in the United Kingdom in the rental sector. Turnover in 2003 in Great Britain amounted to £19.4 billion, 1.9 per cent higher than in 2002.

Computing and related activities

The computing software and services industry comprises businesses engaged in software development; systems integration; IT consultancy; IT 'outsourcing'; processing services; and the provision of complete computer systems. It also includes companies that provide IT education and training; independent maintenance; support, contingency planning and recruitment; and contract staff. Intellect is the trade body for the UK-based IT, telecommunications and electronics industry.

In December 2003 there were 490,000 employee jobs in computer and related activities in the United Kingdom. Turnover of companies in this sector in Great Britain amounted to £51.0 billion in 2003, 12.0 per cent higher than in 2002. UK firms and universities have established strong reputations in software R&D and a number of international IT conglomerates, such as Microsoft, have set up R&D operations in the United Kingdom. Academic expertise is especially evident in such areas as artificial intelligence (AI), neural networks, grid computing, formal programming for safety-critical systems, and parallel programming systems.

Software firms have developed strengths in sector-specific applications, including systems for retailing, banking, finance and accounting, the medical and dental industries, and the travel and entertainment industries. Specialist 'niche' markets in which UK software producers are active include AI, scientific and engineering software (especially computer-aided design), mathematical software, geographical information systems, and data visualisation packages. Some firms specialise in devising multimedia software. Distance learning, 'virtual reality' and computer animation all benefit from a large pool of creative talent.

One of the biggest users of software is the telecommunications industry (see page 252). The provision of almost all new telecommunications services, including switching and transmission, is dependent on software.

Many IT jobs have been outsourced to lower cost bases overseas. In December 2003, for example, the largest UK insurance group, Aviva, announced the transfer of 2,350 administrative and IT jobs to India.

Business services

In December 2003 the other business activities sector accounted for 2.8 million employee jobs in the United Kingdom. The sector includes market research, business and management consultancy activities and advertising. Turnover in 2003 in Great Britain amounted to £168.4 billion, 6.3 per cent higher than in 2002.

Market research

The British Market Research Association aims to promote good practice in market research in the United Kingdom and to cater for the professional and trade needs of UK market research companies. Its members' turnover grew by 2.8 per cent in 2003 to an estimated £1.22 billion. UK-owned market research companies include the largest international customised market research specialists. The top ten companies by turnover are shown in Table 29.12.

Table 29.12 Top ten UK market research companies[1] by turnover

£ million

Company	2002	2003
TNS	160	159
NOP World	77	76
Ipsos (UK)	44	47
MORI	36	39
Information Resources	35	34
Maritz/TRBI	25	27
Incepta Marketing Intelligence[2]	.	20
Martin Hamblin GfK	19	17
Synovate	16	16
ORC International	13	13

1 BMRA members only.
2 Not included in 2002 data.
Source: British Market Research Association

Management consultancy

The United Kingdom's 70,000 management consultants supply technical assistance and advice to business and government clients. In 2003 revenues for the industry were estimated at

£10 billion, with exports worth £1 billion. The 45 member firms of the Management Consultancies Association, which accounts for roughly 60 per cent of UK revenues, generated £5.8 billion in fee income in 2003, nearly 23 per cent more than in 2002 (Table 29.13). Income from outsourcing activities increased by 64 per cent and accounted for 40 per cent of all UK fee income.

Table 29.13 Management consultancy income,[1] UK

	2002	2003
		£ million
Outsourcing	1,273	2,090
Strategy	289	358
IT consultancy	1,069	1,163
Financial systems	200	93
Production management	239	139
Human resources	398	529
Project management	622	654
Marketing	55	31
Economic/environmental	2	15
E-business	17	20
Change management	33	60
Business process re-engineering	19	97
Total UK fee income	4,216	5,248
Overseas fee income	528	563
Total	**4,743**	**5,811**

1 MCA firms only.
Source: Management Consultancies Association

Advertising and public relations

The United Kingdom is a major centre for creative advertising, and multinational companies often use UK-created advertising for marketing their products globally. UK agencies have strong foreign links through overseas ownership and associate networks. UK television advertising has received many international awards. According to the Advertising Association, total UK advertising expenditure rose by 2.4 per cent in 2003 to £17.2 billion (Table 29.14).

There were around 1,480 advertising agencies in 2003. As well as their creative, production and media-buying roles, some offer integrated marketing services, including consumer research and public relations. Many agencies have sponsorship departments, which arrange for

Table 29.14 UK advertising expenditure by medium

	£ million		Percentages
Medium	2002	2003	2003
Press	8,333	8,382	48.7
of which:			
National newspapers	1,933	1,902	11.0
Regional newspapers	2,894	2,986	17.3
Consumer magazines	785	784	4.6
Business and professional magazines	1,088	1,048	6.1
Directories	990	1,029	6.0
Press production costs	643	634	3.7
Television	4,332	4,374	25.4
Direct mail	2,378	2,431	14.1
Outdoor and transport	816	901	5.2
Radio	545	582	3.4
Cinema	180	180	1.0
Internet	233	376	2.2
Total all media	**16,817**	**17,227**	**100**

Source: *Advertising Statistics Yearbook 2004* – World Advertising Research Center

businesses to sponsor products and events, including artistic, sporting and charitable events.

The UK public relations industry has developed rapidly, and there are now a wide variety of consultancy firms with different specialisms and sizes. The Public Relations Consultants Association membership accounts for 70 per cent of UK fee income. It has over 130 members generating more than £400 million each year in fees from clients.

Travel and tourism

Overseas travel

Spain and France were the top countries visited by UK residents in 2003 (Table 29.15). Long-haul holidays have remained popular, despite recent global events. The United States is still the top long-haul destination, with the Caribbean, Canada, Australia, India, South Africa and New Zealand maintaining their popularity. A survey carried out by the Association of British Travel Agents (ABTA) in February 2004 found that consumer confidence had returned to holiday

Table 29.15 Number of visits abroad by UK residents, by country visited

Millions

	2001	2002	2003
Spain	11.8	12.5	13.8
France	12.0	12.1	12.0
Republic of Ireland	3.9	4.0	3.9
United States	4.0	3.6	3.6
Italy	2.5	2.7	2.9
Greece	3.2	3.0	2.9
Netherlands	2.1	2.1	2.1
Germany	2.2	2.3	2.1
Belgium	1.7	1.8	2.0
Portugal	1.6	1.8	1.9
Other countries	13.3	13.6	14.3
Total world	**58.3**	**59.4**	**61.4**

Source: Overseas travel and tourism, Office for National Statistics

bookings, with only 3 per cent saying the threat of terrorism would lead them to delay booking until nearer the time they travelled, compared with 15 per cent in 2003.

In 2003 total turnover in the travel agency and tour operator businesses in Great Britain amounted to £17.1 billion, 6.1 per cent lower than in 2002. Around 6,500 high street travel agents belonged to ABTA in January 2004 and 85 per cent

of UK-sold package holidays are handled by ABTA members. Although most are small businesses, a few large firms have hundreds of branches.

ABTA operates financial protection schemes to safeguard customers and maintains a code of conduct drawn up with the Office of Fair Trading. It also offers a free consumer affairs service to help resolve complaints against its members, and a low-cost independent arbitration scheme for customers.

Tourism in the UK

The total value of tourism in 2000 was estimated to be nearly £90 billion (Table 29.16). Figures for subsequent years will be available following completion of the UK Tourism Satellite Account.[2] The bulk of tourism services are provided by 131,000 mainly independent small businesses such as hotels and guest houses, restaurants, holiday homes, caravan and camping parks.

The British Incoming Tour Operators Association represents the commercial and political interests of incoming tour operators and suppliers to the British inbound tourism industry.

Nearly 25 million overseas visitors came to the United Kingdom in 2003 (Table 29.18), an increase

2 A set of data tables based around analyses of data on both expenditure by tourists, and business sectors that serve tourists.

Table 29.16 Value of tourism,[1] UK

£ billion

	2000	2001	2002	2003
Spending by:				
Overseas residents				
Visits to the UK	12.8	11.3	11.7	11.9
Overseas fares to UK carriers less overseas agents' margins	3.3	n/a	n/a	n/a
Domestic tourists				
Trips of one night or more	26.1	26.1	26.7	26.5
Day trips	31.8	31.5	31.3	31.3
Outbound spend pre/post trip	14.7	n/a	n/a	n/a
Second homes (estimate)	0.9	n/a	n/a	n/a
Total	**89.6**	**n/a**	**n/a**	**n/a**

1 Figures for 2001 to 2003 are not fully available pending completion of the UK Tourism Satellite Account.
Source: Overseas travel and tourism, Office for National Statistics; National Tourist Boards; Department for Culture, Media and Sport

Table 29.17 Employment in tourism-related industries, June 2003, Great Britain[1]

	Thousands
Hotels and other tourist accommodation	393
Restaurants, cafés, etc	590
Bars, public houses and nightclubs	568
Travel agencies/tour operators	117
Libraries/museums and other cultural activities	87
Sport and other recreation activities	413
Total	**2,168**
of which: Self-employment jobs	156

1 These data will be superseded by estimates based on the Tourism Satellite Account.
Source: Department for Culture, Media and Sport

Table 29.18 Overseas visits to the UK

Millions

	2001	2002	2003
By area			
North America	4.2	4.3	4.0
EU-15	12.9	14.1	14.8
Other Europe	2.0	2.1	2.4
Other countries	3.8	3.7	3.5
By purpose			
Holiday	7.6	7.7	8.0
Business	6.8	7.2	7.0
Visiting friends or relatives	5.9	6.4	7.0
Miscellaneous	2.6	2.9	2.8
All visits	**22.8**	**24.2**	**24.7**

Source: Overseas travel and tourism, Office for National Statistics

of 2.2 per cent on the previous year. The earnings they generated increased by 1.1 per cent to £11.9 billion (Table 29.16). These figures are still below 2000 levels, but they suggest a continuing recovery from the effects of the foot-and-mouth outbreak and 11 September 2001. Holiday visits by overseas visitors to the United Kingdom increased by 3.1 per cent in 2003. However, the number of arrivals from North America fell, declining by 6.4 per cent in 2003 to 4.0 million, nearly 1 million below the levels recorded in 2000. Arrivals from the EU continued to rise, by 4.7 per cent to 14.8 million in 2003.

Business travel, which includes attendance at conferences, exhibitions, trade fairs and other business sites, accounted for 28 per cent of all overseas visits in 2003. The numbers of business visitors declined slightly during the year, reflecting the continuing weak state of the global economy and in particular the economic slowdown in the rest of the EU, which accounted for 60 per cent of visitors. Around 71 per cent of visitors arrived by air.

Domestic tourism expenditure was estimated to be nearly £58 billion in 2003, with day visits accounting for over half of this expenditure.

Historic towns and cities and the scenic rural and coastal areas of the United Kingdom continue to have great appeal for domestic and overseas tourists alike. Their popularity reflects the interest in UK heritage, arts and culture. Tourism plays an increasingly important role in supporting the UK national heritage and creative arts, in addition to the large financial contribution it makes to hotels, restaurants, cafés and bars, and public transport.

Activity holidays are often based on walking, cycling, canoeing, mountain climbing, or artistic activities. The Youth Hostel Association operates a network of 225 hostels in England and Wales offering a range of facilities, including self-catering, to families and people of all ages. The Scottish Youth Hostels Association operates over 60 hostels, including purpose-built premises, historic buildings and country cottages. Hostelling International Northern Ireland operates a further six hostels. The British Airways London Eye was the most popular UK attraction charging admission in 2002. With the abolition of admission charges to several museums and galleries, London's Natural History, Victoria & Albert and Science Museums recorded sharp increases in visitor numbers.

Tourism promotion

The Department for Culture, Media and Sport (DCMS) and the devolved administrations are responsible for policy on UK tourism. VisitBritain promotes the United Kingdom to an international audience and England domestically. It is sponsored by DCMS and has a network of 31 overseas offices, located in markets that offer the best potential return and covering 88 per cent of all visitors to the United Kingdom. There are separate national tourist boards in Scotland, Wales and Northern Ireland that support domestic tourism and work with VisitBritain to promote their products overseas. Since April 2003, the Regional

Table 29.19 Number of overseas visits to the UK, by country of residence

Millions

	2001	2002	2003
United States	3.6	3.6	3.3
France	2.9	3.1	3.1
Germany	2.3	2.6	2.6
Republic of Ireland	2.0	2.4	2.5
Netherlands	1.4	1.4	1.5
Spain	0.9	1.0	1.2
Italy	0.9	1.0	1.2
Belgium	0.9	1.0	0.9
Australia	0.7	0.7	0.7
Canada	0.6	0.7	0.7
Other countries	6.7	6.8	7.0
Total world	**22.8**	**24.2**	**24.7**

Source: Overseas travel and tourism, Office for National Statistics

Development Agencies in England have been playing a stronger role and are required to develop and implement regional sustainable tourism strategies, working with regional and local partners as well as with VisitBritain on marketing.

VisitBritain and the national tourist boards inform and advise the Government on issues of concern to the industry. They also research and publicise trends affecting the industry and work closely with regional tourist boards, on which local government and business interests are represented. There are several hundred local Tourist Information Centres in the United Kingdom. The national tourist boards, in conjunction with the Automobile Association and the Royal Automobile Club, administer the National Quality Assurance Standards schemes for accommodation.

Consumer protection

The Government aims to maintain and develop a clear and fair regulatory framework that gives confidence to consumers and contributes to business competitiveness. It works closely with outside bodies that have expert knowledge of consumer issues in order to develop policies and legislation. The DTI is responsible for the Government's consumer policy and in July 2004 launched a consultation on a consumer strategy for the next five to ten years. The consultation

document, *Extending Competitive Markets: Empowered Consumers, Successful Business*, sets out the practical actions required to bring the United Kingdom up to world-class standards.

The DTI is currently working with the free debt advice sector and the credit industry to increase capacity and improve access to free debt advice. As part of this work, the Government continues to provide a substantial part of the funding for National Debtline, a telephone helpline for people with debt problems in Great Britain.

The EU consumer programme covers activities such as health and safety, protection of the consumer's economic interests, promotion of consumer education and strengthening of consumer representation. The interests of UK consumers on EU matters are represented by a number of organisations, including the Consumers' Association and the National Consumer Council.

Consumer legislation

Purchasers of goods, services or credit are protected by the following legislation:

- the *Trade Descriptions Act 1968*;
- the *Consumer Credit Act 1974*;
- the *Sale of Goods Act 1979*;
- the *Weights and Measures Act 1985*;
- the *Consumer Protection Act 1987*;
- the Doorstep Selling Regulations (1987 and 1998);
- the Control of Misleading Advertisements Regulations 1988;
- the Unfair Terms in Consumer Contracts Regulations 1999;
- the Distance Selling Regulations 2000; and
- the *Enterprise Act 2002* (see page 358).

Consumer advice and information

The Citizens Advice service delivers advice from over 3,200 locations across England, Wales and Northern Ireland and handled 5.7 million enquiries, including consumer issues, in 2002/03 (Table 29.20). Their work is coordinated by a national association – Citizens Advice, formerly known as the National Association of Citizens Advice Bureaux – linked to individual locations by local and regional committees. In 2002/03,

Citizens Advice Scotland handled an additional 396,000 enquiries. Assistance is provided by trading standards and consumer protection departments of local authorities in Great Britain and, in some areas, by specialist consumer advice centres.

Table 29.20 Citizens Advice new enquiries, England, Wales and Northern Ireland

Thousands

Category	2001/02	2002/03	% change
Benefits	1,629	1,668	2.4
Consumer and utilities	1,194	1,190	−0.3
Employment	601	574	−4.5
Housing	573	560	−2.2
Legal	460	452	−1.8
Relationships	390	371	−4.8
Tax	150	149	−0.4
Other	721	708	−1.9
Total	**5,718**	**5,672**	**−0.8**

Source: Citizens Advice

The National Consumer Council is a consumer policy and research organisation with a special focus on the needs of disadvantaged consumers. It is a non-profit-making company limited by guarantee and most of its funding is from the DTI. It works with associate organisations in England, Wales and Scotland and the General Consumer Council of Northern Ireland to represent all consumer interests to policy makers, regulators and suppliers in the United Kingdom and in the EU.

Consumer bodies for privatised utilities, such as electricity and gas, investigate questions of concern to the consumer. Some trade associations have set up codes of practice. In addition, several organisations work to further consumer interests by representing the consumer's view to government, industry and other bodies. The largest is the Consumers' Association (www.which.co.uk), with over 700,000 members in August 2004, funded largely by subscriptions to Which? magazine. Around 103,000 subscribers have online access to the complete range of Which? publications.

Consumer Direct

The DTI is launching a new national telephone and online consumer advice and information service, Consumer Direct (www.consumerdirect.gov.uk). Consumers will be able to access clear, practical consumer advice through a single national telephone number. The service was introduced in Yorkshire and the Humber, Wales and Scotland during summer 2004 and will be available throughout the United Kingdom by spring 2007.

Further reading

Department for Culture, Media and Sport Annual Report 2004. Cm 6220. The Stationery Office, 2004.

Bank of England Annual Report. Bank of England.

Financial Services Authority Annual Report. FSA.

Websites

Bank of England
www.bankofengland.co.uk

British Bankers' Association
www.bba.org.uk

Department for Culture, Media and Sport
www.culture.gov.uk

Financial Services Authority
www.fsa.gov.uk

London Stock Exchange
www.londonstockexchange.com

National Statistics
www.statistics.gov.uk

www.

Appendix A UK Parliament and devolved administrations, government departments and agencies

This appendix gives contact details for the main government departments and describes their principal functions. It is divided into the following sections:

- non-devolved functions (including matters 'reserved' to the UK Government); and
- devolved administrations – Wales, Scotland and Northern Ireland.

The entries for departments responsible for non-devolved functions give a broad indication of their geographical remit, but details may vary.

Executive agencies are listed at the end of the entry for their sponsor department. Those marked with an asterisk* also have an entry in their own right.

Following the entry for the UK Parliament, the listing within each section is alphabetical, except that words like 'the' 'and' 'of' and 'for' are ignored, as is the 'HM' before Customs and Excise, Land Registry and Treasury.

A complete listing of government departments, executive agencies, non-departmental public bodies, and a range of related organisations, such as museums, galleries and research establishments, is published in the *Civil Service Year Book*; and there is further information in *Public Bodies 2003*, published by HMSO.

Houses of Parliament
House of Commons and House of Lords

Westminster
London SW1A 0AA (Commons) and
SW1A 0PW (Lords)
Tel: 020 7219 3000
Website: *www.parliament.uk*

Responsible for examining the work of Government (see chapter 6) and for all legislation for England, primary legislation for Wales, and legislation for the whole of the United Kingdom on areas not devolved to the National Assembly for Wales, Scottish Parliament and Northern Ireland Assembly (when it is sitting). This includes constitutional affairs; the franchise (including at local government elections, and the conduct and funding of parliamentary elections); defence, national security and official secrets; foreign policy; overall economic, fiscal and monetary policy; competition policy; international trade policy; consumer safety and protection; some elements of health; home affairs including the police (except Scotland); asylum, immigration and extradition; misuse of drugs and firearms; the legal system (except Scotland); human rights, anti-discrimination, equal opportunities and data protection; the Post Office; energy; telecommunications; control over broadcasting and the National Lottery; and power over the regulation and safety of aviation and shipping.

The House of Commons also decides what taxes should be collected and in broad terms how the money should be spent.

Non-devolved functions and England

Cabinet Office (CO)

70 Whitehall
London SW1A 2AS
Tel: 020 7276 3000
Website: *www.cabinetoffice.gov.uk*
Status: Ministerial department

Supports the Prime Minister in leading the Government and coordinates policy and operations across government (see also page 56).

Executive agencies
COI Communications*
Government Car and Despatch Agency

Charity Commission

Harmsworth House
13–15 Bouverie Street
London EC4Y 8DP
Tel: 0870 333 0123

Website: *www.charitycommission.gov.uk*
Status: Non-ministerial department

Responsible for registering bodies qualifying for charitable status in England and Wales, advising charities and their trustees, monitoring the activities of charities and investigating maladministration and abuse.

Child Support Agency (CSA)

Benton Park View
Benton Park Road
Newcastle upon Tyne NE98 1YX
Tel: 08457 133 133
Website: *www.csa.gov.uk*
Status: Executive agency of the Department for Work and Pensions

Calculates the financial support required for children in Great Britain whose parents do not live together, and ensures that this is paid.

COI Communications

Hercules Road
London SE1 7DU
Tel: 020 7928 2345
Website: *www.coi.gov.uk*
Status: Non-ministerial department and executive agency of the Cabinet Office. Operates as a trading fund.

Consultancy, procurement and project management of marketing and communications activity on behalf of government departments, agencies and other public sector clients across the UK.

Companies House

Crown Way
Cardiff CF14 3UZ
Tel: 0870 33 33 636
Website: *www.companieshouse.gov.uk*
Status: Executive agency of the Department of Trade and Industry

Incorporates and dissolves companies, registers the information they are required to supply under companies and related legislation, and makes that information available to the public.

Court Service

7th Floor
Southside
105 Victoria Street
London SW1E 6QT
Tel: 020 7210 2266
Website: *www.courtservice.gov.uk*
Status: Executive agency of the Department for Constitutional Affairs

Provides administrative support to most of the courts and tribunals in England and Wales. In April 2005 it will be replaced by a new agency, HM Courts Service, which will also be responsible for magistrates' courts.

Crown Prosecution Service (CPS)

50 Ludgate Hill
London EC4M 7EX
Tel: 020 7796 8000
Website: *www.cps.gov.uk*
Status: Non-ministerial department

Prosecutes people in England and Wales who have been charged by the police with a criminal offence. The CPS is headed by the Director of Public Prosecutions, who is accountable to Parliament through the Attorney General.

HM Customs and Excise (HMCE)

New King's Beam House
22 Upper Ground
London SE1 9PJ
Tel: 0845 010 9000 (UK local rate)
+44 (0) 20 8929 0152 (international)
Website: *www.hmce.gov.uk*
Status: Non-ministerial department responsible to the Chancellor of the Exchequer.

Collects and accounts for UK customs and excise duties (including value added tax). Also responsible for the prevention of smuggling and of the import or export of illegal goods; and for compiling overseas trade statistics. HMCE is to merge with Inland Revenue to form a new department, HM Revenue and Customs.

Department for Constitutional Affairs (DCA)

Selborne House
54–60 Victoria Street
London SW1E 6QW
Tel: 020 7210 8500
Website: *www.dca.gov.uk*
Status: Ministerial department

UK-wide: reform of the constitution; freedom of information; privacy, data protection and data sharing; human rights; reform of the House of Lords; the constitutional relationship with the Channel Islands and the Isle of Man; royal, church and hereditary issues; electoral law and policy; referendums; and party funding.

In England and Wales: the administration of justice; reform of civil law; appointment and training of the judiciary; provision of legal aid and legal services.

For administrative purposes only, the DCA is also responsible for the staff of the Scotland Office and the Wales Office – both of which retain their separate identities and continue to report to their respective Secretaries of State – and for the Office of the Advocate General for Scotland, which is an independent legal office.

Executive agencies
Court Service*
HM Land Registry*
The National Archives*
Public Guardianship Office

Department for Culture, Media and Sport (DCMS)

2–4 Cockspur Street
London SW1Y 5DH
Tel: 020 7211 6000
Website: *www.culture.gov.uk*
Status: Ministerial department

In England, responsibility for the arts, public libraries and archives, museums and galleries, tourism, sport and the built heritage. In England and Wales, responsibility for the film industry, and alcohol and public entertainment licensing.

UK-wide responsibility for broadcasting, press regulation, creative industries, public lending rights, gambling and the National Lottery, censorship and video classification. However, the devolved administrations also have some operational responsibilities in these areas.

Executive agency
Royal Parks Agency

Department for Education and Skills (DfES)

Sanctuary Buildings
Great Smith Street
London SW1P 3BT
Tel: 0870 000 2288
Website: *www.dfes.gov.uk*
Status: Ministerial department

In England, policies relating to children, young people and families; school, college and university education; youth and adult training and programmes. In England and Wales, student support and teachers' pay and conditions.

Department for Environment, Food and Rural Affairs (Defra)

Nobel House
17 Smith Square
London SW1P 3JR
Tel: 08459 33 55 77
Website: *www.defra.gov.uk*
Status: Ministerial department

Sustainable development and the environment; agriculture, horticulture, fisheries and food; rural development; the countryside; animal welfare and hunting. This remit is broadly confined to England, but Defra also has a UK coordinating role on some aspects of environmental affairs.

Executive agencies
Central Science Laboratory
Centre for Environment, Fisheries and
  Aquaculture Science
Pesticides Safety Directorate
Rural Payments Agency
Veterinary Laboratories Agency
Veterinary Medicines Directorate

Department of Health (DH)

Richmond House, 79 Whitehall
London SW1A 2NS
Tel: 020 7210 4850
Website: *www.doh.gov.uk*
Status: Ministerial department

Responsible for the National Health Service, adult personal social services provided by local authorities and all other health issues in England, including public health matters and the health consequences of environmental and food issues. Represents UK health policy interests in the EU and the World Health Organisation.

Executive agencies
Medicines and Healthcare products Regulatory
  Agency
NHS Estates
NHS Purchasing and Supply Agency

Department for International Development (DFID)

1 Palace Street
London SW1E 5HE
Tel: 0845 300 4100
Website: *www.dfid.gov.uk*
Status: Ministerial department

Responsible for promoting sustainable international development and the reduction of global poverty; managing the UK programme of assistance to developing countries; and for ensuring that government policies affecting developing countries, including environment, trade, investment and agricultural policies, take account of those countries' concerns.

Department of Trade and Industry (DTI)

1 Victoria Street
London SW1H 0ET
Tel: 020 7215 5000
Website: *www.dti.gov.uk*
Status: Ministerial department

Competitiveness; enterprise, innovation and productivity; science, engineering and technology; markets; the legal and regulatory framework for business and consumers. Specific responsibilities in England include innovation policy; regional industrial policy and the Regional Development Agencies; small businesses; spread of management best practice; and business/education links.

UK-wide responsibilities include employment relations, consumer and competition policy, international trade policy, energy policy, company law, insolvency, patents and copyright protection, import and export licensing, Research Councils, and relations with specific business sectors. See also Office of Science and Technology and UK Trade & Investment.

Executive agencies

Advisory, Conciliation and Arbitration Service (ACAS)
Companies House*
Employment Tribunals Service
Insolvency Service
National Weights and Measures Laboratory
Patent Office*
Small Business Service*

Department for Transport (DfT)

Great Minster House
76 Marsham Street
London SW1P 4DR
Tel: 020 7944 8300
Website: *www.dft.gov.uk*
Status: Ministerial department

Policies on roads, local transport and shipping in England; railways in Great Britain; and aviation, including the Civil Aviation Authority, across the UK.

Executive agencies

Driver and Vehicle Licensing Agency*
Driving Standards Agency*
Highways Agency*
Maritime and Coastguard Agency
Vehicle Certification Agency
Vehicle and Operator Services Agency

Department for Work and Pensions (DWP)

The Adelphi
1–11 John Adam Street
London WC2N 6HT
Tel: 020 7712 2171
Website: *www.dwp.gov.uk*
Status: Ministerial department

Welfare, pensions, employment and disability issues in Great Britain.

Executive agencies

Appeals Service
Child Support Agency*
Disability and Carers' Service
Jobcentre Plus*
The Pension Service*
The Rent Service*

Driver and Vehicle Licensing Agency (DVLA)

Longview Road
Morriston
Swansea SA6 7JL
Tel: 0870 240 0009 (drivers) or
0870 240 0010 (vehicles)
Website: *www.dvla.gov.uk*
Status: Executive agency of the Department for Transport

Registration of drivers and vehicles; collection of vehicle excise duty (Great Britain).

Driving Standards Agency (DSA)

Stanley House
56 Talbot Street
Nottingham NG1 5GU
Tel: 0115 901 2500
Website: *www.dsa.gov.uk*
Status: Executive agency of the Department for
Transport

Testing of drivers, motorcyclists and driving
instructors; maintaining registers of approved
driving instructors and large goods vehicle
instructors; supervising training of learner
motorcyclists (Great Britain).

Export Credits Guarantee Department (ECGD)

PO Box 2200, 2 Exchange Tower
Harbour Exchange Square
London E14 9GS
Tel: 020 7512 7000
Website: *www.ecgd.gov.uk*
Status: Non-ministerial department

The official UK export credit agency. Insures UK
exporters of capital goods against non-payment;
guarantees bank loans for buyers of UK goods;
provides insurance for UK investors against
political risks overseas.

Food Standards Agency

Aviation House
125 Kingsway
London WC2B 6NH
Tel: 020 7276 8000
Website: *www.food.gov.uk*
Status: Non-ministerial department

Protection of health and consumer interests in
relation to food, UK-wide.

Executive agency
Meat Hygiene Service

Foreign & Commonwealth Office (FCO)

King Charles Street
London SW1A 2AH
Tel: 020 7008 1500
Website: *www.fco.gov.uk*
Status: Ministerial department

The means of communication between the UK
Government and other governments and
international governmental organisations on all
matters of international relations. Alerts the UK
Government to the implications of developments
overseas; promotes UK interests and protects
British citizens abroad; explains UK policies
to, and cultivates relationships with, overseas
governments; and discharges UK responsibilities
to the Overseas Territories. Also responsible for
entry clearance (through UK visas, with the Home
Office) and for promoting UK business overseas
(with the Department of Trade and Industry
through UK Trade & Investment).

Executive agency
Wilton Park (conferences)

Forestry Commission

Silvan House
231 Corstorphine Road
Edinburgh EH12 7AT
Tel: 0131 334 0303
Website: *www.forestry.gov.uk*
Status: Non-ministerial department reporting
directly to forestry ministers in England, Wales
and Scotland.

Forestry policy in England, Wales and Scotland,
including grant-aid for stewardship of existing
woodlands and woodland expansion in the private
sector. Manages nearly 1 million hectares of public
forests.

Executive agencies
Forest Enterprise England
Forest Enterprise Scotland
Forest Enterprise Wales
Forest Research

Highways Agency

5th Floor, 123 Buckingham Palace Road
London SW1W 9HA
Tel: 08459 556575
Website: *www.highways.gov.uk*
Status: Executive agency of the Department for
Transport

Manages, maintains and improves the motorway
and trunk road network in England.

Home Office

50 Queen Anne's Gate
London SW1H 9AT
Tel: 0870 000 1585
Website: *www.homeoffice.gov.uk*
Status: Ministerial department

England and Wales: crime and policing; aspects of the criminal justice system, including the prison and offender management services; race equality and diversity policies; active communities and volunteering.

UK-wide: combating terrorism and other threats to national security; drugs policy; regulation of entry to and settlement in the UK (see also entry for the Immigration and Nationality Directorate).

Great Britain: licensing of the use of animals in scientific procedures.

Executive agencies
Criminal Records Bureau (England and Wales)
Forensic Science Service (England and Wales)
HM Prison Service (England and Wales)
UK Passport Service*

Immigration and Nationality Directorate (IND)
Lunar House
40 Wellesley Road
Croydon CR9 2BY
Tel: 0870 606 7766
Website: *www.ind.homeoffice.gov.uk*
Status: A directorate of the Home Office

Regulation of entry to, and settlement in, the UK, including policies on asylum and managed migration.

Inland Revenue
Somerset House
London WC2R 1LB
Tel: 020 7438 6622
Website: *www.inlandrevenue.gov.uk*
Status: Non-ministerial department and executive agency, reporting to the Chancellor of the Exchequer

Administration and collection of direct taxes in the UK and valuation of property in Great Britain. Income tax, corporation tax, capital gains tax, petroleum revenue tax, inheritance tax, stamp duties, tax credits, National Insurance contributions and advice on tax and National Insurance contributions policy. Also enforces the national minimum wage on behalf of the Department of Trade and Industry. The Inland Revenue is to merge with HM Customs and Excise to form a new department, HM Revenue and Customs.

Executive agency
Valuation Office Agency (Great Britain)

Jobcentre Plus
Caxton House
Tothill Street
London SW1H 9NA
Tel: 020 7272 3000
Website: *www.jobcentreplus.gov.uk*
Status: Executive agency of the Department for Work and Pensions

Helping people into work and employers to fill vacancies; payment of benefits to people of working age (Great Britain).

HM Land Registry
Lincoln's Inn Fields
London WC2A 3PH
Tel: 020 7917 8888
Website: *www.landregistry.gov.uk*
Status: Government department, executive agency and trading fund reporting to the Secretary of State for Constitutional Affairs.

Guarantees the title to, and records the ownership of, interests in registered land in England and Wales.

Legal Secretariat to the Law Officers (LSLO)
9 Buckingham Gate
London SW1E 6JP
Tel: 020 7271 2400
Website: *www.lslo.gov.uk*
Status: Ministerial department

Supports the Attorney General who (assisted by the Solicitor General) is a government minister and the chief legal adviser to the Government in England, Wales and Northern Ireland. The Attorney General is also ultimately responsible for all Crown litigation and is the legal adviser to the UK Parliament. The Law Officers' Departments are the Treasury Solicitor's Department (TSol), Crown Prosecution Service, HM Crown Prosecution Service Inspectorate, Serious Fraud Office and LSLO. The Attorney General also oversees the work of the Customs and Excise Prosecution Office and the Director of Public Prosecutions for Northern Ireland.

Executive agency
TSol*

Met Office

FitzRoy Road
Exeter EX1 3PB
Tel: 0870 900 0100
Website: *www.metoffice.gov.uk*
Status: Executive agency of the Ministry of
Defence

Provides meteorological services (including
climate advice) to the Armed Forces, government
departments, the public, civil aviation, shipping,
and others.

Ministry of Defence (MoD)

Main Building
Whitehall
London SW1A 2HB
Tel: 020 7218 9000 or 0870 607 4455
Website: *www.mod.uk*
Status: Ministerial department

Defending the UK and its interests. Strengthening
international peace and security.

Executive agencies
The MoD has 33 agencies, including:

British Forces Post Office
Defence Analytical Services Agency
Defence Estates
Defence Procurement Agency
Defence Science and Technology Laboratory
Met Office*
Ministry of Defence Police
Veterans Agency*

The National Archives (TNA)

Ruskin Avenue
Kew
Richmond
Surrey TW9 4DU
Tel: 020 8876 3444
Website: *www.nationalarchives.gov.uk*
Status: Non-ministerial department and executive
agency, reporting to the Secretary of State for
Constitutional Affairs

Responsible for the public records and national
archives of England, Wales and the United
Kingdom; and for historical manuscripts relating
to British history. Brings together the work of the
Public Record Office and the Historical
Manuscripts Commission.

National Savings and Investments (NS&I)

Charles House
375 Kensington High Street
London W14 8SD
Tel: 020 7348 9200
Website: *www.nsandi.com*
Status: Executive agency reporting to the
Chancellor of the Exchequer

Raises funds for the Government by selling a range
of investments to personal savers across the UK.

Office of Communications (Ofcom)

Riverside House
2A Southwark Bridge Road
London SE1 9HA
Tel: 020 7981 3000
Website: *www.ofcom.org.uk*

Independent regulator and competition authority
for the UK communications industries, with
responsibilities across television, radio,
telecommunications and wireless communications
services.

Ofcom has assumed the duties and powers of the
Broadcasting Standards Commission, the
Independent Television Commission, Oftel, the
Radio Authority and the Radiocommunications
Agency.

Office of the Deputy Prime Minister (ODPM)

26 Whitehall
London SW1A 2WH
Tel: 020 7944 4400
Website: *www.odpm.gov.uk*
Status: Ministerial department

Policy in England on housing, planning, regional
and local government and the fire service. Includes
the Social Exclusion Unit, the Neighbourhood
Renewal Unit and the Government Offices for
the Regions.

Executive agencies
Fire Service College
Ordnance Survey*
Planning Inspectorate*
Queen Elizabeth II Conference Centre

Office of Fair Trading (OFT)
Fleetbank House
2–6 Salisbury Square
London EC4Y 8JX
Tel: 020 7211 8000 or 08457 224499
Website: *www.oft.gov.uk*
Status: Non-ministerial department

Administers and enforces legislation relating to competition and consumer protection; promotes competition and consumer awareness (UK).

Office of Gas and Electricity Markets (Ofgem)
9 Millbank
London SWIP 3GE
Tel: 020 7901 7000
Website: *www.ofgem.gov.uk*
Status: Non-ministerial department

Regulates the gas and electricity industries across England, Wales and Scotland.

Office for National Statistics (ONS)
1 Drummond Gate
London SW1V 2QQ
Tel: 0845 601 3034
Website: *www.statistics.gov.uk*
Status: Executive agency and non-ministerial department reporting to the Chancellor of the Exchequer

Collects, compiles and provides a wide range of statistical information, including the UK National Accounts, UK Census of Population, and population estimates and projections. Also carries out research studies on behalf of other government departments concerned with social and economic issues. The Director of ONS is the National Statistician and Registrar General of England and Wales.

Office of Rail Regulation (ORR)
1 Waterhouse Square
138–142 Holborn
London EC1N 2TQ
Tel: 020 7282 2000
Website: *www.rail-reg.gov.uk*
Status: Non-ministerial department

Independent regulation of Network Rail's stewardship of the national rail network infrastructure (track, signalling, bridges, tunnels, stations and depots); economic regulation of the monopoly and dominant elements of the rail industry (Great Britain).

Office of Science and Technology (OST)
1 Victoria Street
London SW1H 0ET
Tel: 020 7215 5000
Website: *www.ost.gov.uk*
Status: Department of the Department of Trade and Industry

Supports the Secretary of State for Trade and Industry and the Minister for Science on issues relating to science, engineering and technology (SET). Headed by the Government's Chief Scientific Adviser (who reports directly to the Prime Minister), the OST is responsible for policy on SET, both nationally and internationally, and coordinates SET policy across government departments. Through the Director General of Research Councils, the OST also has responsibility for the science budget and for the government-financed Research Councils.

Office for Standards in Education (Ofsted)
Alexandra House
33 Kingsway
London WC2B 6SE
Tel: 020 7421 6800
Website: *www.ofsted.gov.uk*
Status: Non-ministerial department

Inspection of schools, 16–19 education, teacher training institutions, local education authorities and youth work in England; also regulation of early years childcare, including childminders.

Office of Water Services (OFWAT)
Centre City Tower
7 Hill Street
Birmingham B5 4UA
Tel: 0121 625 1300
Website: *www.ofwat.gov.uk*
Status: Non-ministerial department

Economic regulator of the water and sewerage industry in England and Wales.

Ordnance Survey
Romsey Road
Southampton SO16 4GU
Tel: 08456 05 05 05
Website: *www.ordnancesurvey.co.uk*

Status: Executive agency and non-ministerial department reporting to the Office of the Deputy Prime Minister

The national mapping agency of Great Britain.

Patent Office

Concept House
Cardiff Road
Newport
Gwent NP10 8QQ
Tel: 08459 500505
Website: *www.patent.gov.uk*
Status: Executive agency of the Department of Trade and Industry

Administers patents, trade marks, registered designs and copyright (UK).

The Pension Service

PO Box 50101
London SW1P 2WU
Tel: 0845 60 60 265
Website: *www.thepensionservice.gov.uk*
Status: Executive agency of the Department for Work and Pensions

Payment of state retirement pensions, Pension Credit and winter fuel payments (Great Britain).

Planning Inspectorate

Temple Quay House
2 The Square
Temple Quay
Bristol BS1 6PN
Tel: 0117 372 6372
Website: *www.planning-inspectorate.gov.uk*
Status: Executive agency of the Office of the Deputy Prime Minister and the National Assembly for Wales

Appeals and other casework under planning and environmental legislation relating to England and Wales.

Prime Minister's Office (No 10)

10 Downing Street
London SW1A 2AA
Tel: 020 7930 4433
Website: *www.pm.gov.uk*
Status: Part of the Cabinet Office, which is a ministerial department

Provides support to the Prime Minister and works with the Cabinet Office to provide central

direction for the development, implementation and presentation of government policy.

The Rent Service

5 Welbeck Street
London W1G 9YQ
Tel: 020 7023 6000
Website: *www.therentservice.gov.uk*
Status: Executive agency of the Department for Work and Pensions

Makes fair rent evaluations for regulated and secure tenancies, and determines whether Housing Benefit claimants (and prospective claimants) are being asked to pay more rent than their landlords might reasonably expect in open market conditions (England).

Royal Mint

Llantrisant
Pontyclun
Mid-Glamorgan CF72 8YT
Tel: 01443 623061
Website: *www.royalmint.com*
Status: Executive agency of HM Treasury

Production of coins for the United Kingdom and for overseas customers. Also manufactures military and civilian decorations and medals; commemorative medals; and royal and official seals.

Scotland Office

Dover House
Whitehall
London SW1A 2AU
Tel: 020 7270 6754
Website: *www.scottishsecretary.gov.uk*
Status: Office within the Department for Constitutional Affairs

Supports the Secretary of State for Scotland who represents Scottish interests within the UK Government in matters that are reserved to the UK Parliament under the terms of the *Scotland Act 1998*.

Small Business Service (SBS)

66–74 Victoria Street
London SW1E 6SW
Tel: 0845 001 0031
Website: *www.sbs.gov.uk*
Status: Executive agency of the Department of Trade and Industry

Provides guidance and services for small and medium-sized enterprises (SMEs) in England, and works in partnership with similar organisations in the rest of the UK.

HM Treasury (HMT)

1 Horse Guards Road
London SW1A 2HQ
Tel: 020 7270 5000
Website: *www.hm-treasury.gov.uk*
Status: Ministerial department

Financial and economic policy; overseeing the framework for monetary policy; tax policy; planning and control of public spending; government accounting; the quality and cost-effectiveness of public services; increasing productivity and expanding economic and employment opportunities; promoting international financial stability and UK economic interests; the regime for supervision of financial services; management of central government debt; and supply of notes and coins across the UK. The Office of Government Commerce (OGC) is an independent office of the Treasury.

Executive agencies
UK Debt Management Office
National Savings and Investments*
Office for National Statistics*
OGCbuying.solutions
Royal Mint*

TSol (formerly Treasury Solicitor's Department)

Queen Anne's Chambers
28 Broadway
London SW1H 9JS
Tel: 020 7210 3000
Website: *www.treasury-solicitor.gov.uk*
Status: Government department and executive agency, reporting to the Attorney General.

Provides litigation and advisory services to government departments and other publicly funded bodies in England and Wales, and collects and manages *bona vacantia* in England, Wales and Northern Ireland, on behalf of the Crown. (*Bona vacantia* include the estates of people who die intestate with no entitled relatives, and the assets of dissolved companies).

UK Trade & Investment

Kingsgate House
66–74 Victoria Street

London SW1E 6SW
Tel: 020 7215 8000
Website: *www.uktradeinvest.gov.uk*
Status: Non-ministerial department

The UK Government's lead organisation for supporting UK companies in overseas markets, and attracting inward investment. Reports jointly to the Foreign & Commonwealth Office and the Department of Trade and Industry.

United Kingdom Passport Service (UKPS)

Globe House
89 Eccleston Square
London SW1V 1PN
Tel: 0845 521 0410
Website: *www.ukpa.gov.uk*
Status: Executive agency of the Home Office

Issues new, replacement and amended passports to British nationals living in the United Kingdom.

Veterans Agency

Tomlinson House
Government Buildings
Norcross
Blackpool FY5 3WP
Tel: 0800 169 2277
Website: *www.veteransagency.mod.uk*
Status: Executive agency of the Ministry of Defence

Information and advice for veterans and their families; administration of the War Pension Scheme; and welfare support to war pensioners and war widow(er)s.

Wales Office

Gwydyr House
Whitehall
London SW1A 2ER
Tel: 020 7270 0583
Website: *www.walesoffice.gov.uk*
www.swyddfa.cymru.gov.uk (yn Gymraeg)
Status: Office within the Department for Constitutional Affairs

Supports the Secretary of State for Wales, who represents Welsh interests within the UK Government and takes the lead in matters connected with the *Government of Wales Act 1998*.

Wales

Welsh Assembly Government
Llywodraeth Cynulliad Cymru

Cathays Park
Cardiff CF10 3NQ
Tel: 029 20 825111
Website: *www.wales.gov.uk*
www.cymru.gov.uk (yn Gymraeg)

The Welsh Assembly Government is accountable to the National Assembly for Wales and develops and implements policy on issues that have been devolved: most aspects of agriculture, forestry, fisheries and food, including animal health and welfare, the Forestry Commission in Wales, payments to Welsh farmers, and a role in the negotiations and implementation of EU policy in Wales; culture, including the arts, ancient monuments and historic buildings, sport and the Welsh language; economic development, including running the Welsh Development Agency and Wales Tourist Board, and administering European Structural Funds; education and training, including setting and monitoring school standards, the content of the National Curriculum, funding further and higher education, and overseeing and funding training; the environment, including controlling water quality and flood defence, and determining policies on town and country planning; some areas of health, including running the National Health Service in Wales; local government and housing, including deciding on overall funds for local authorities, and overseeing the council tax system in Wales; social services, including care in the community, social services for children, and adoption; the promotion of trade and inward investment; and some aspects of transport.

National Assembly for Wales
Cynulliad Cenedlaethol Cymru

Cardiff Bay
Cardiff CF99 1NA
Tel: 029 20 825111
Website: *www.wales.gov.uk*
www.cymru.gov.uk (yn Gymraeg)

The National Assembly for Wales has powers to make secondary legislation to meet distinctive Welsh needs in areas that have been devolved, sets the budget for those areas, and holds the Welsh Assembly Government to account for its policies

and operational decisions. It approves the overall policy framework within which the Welsh Assembly Government operates, and its committees work collaboratively with Welsh Assembly Government ministers to develop new policies.

Agencies

The National Assembly is responsible for over 50 public bodies including:
Higher Education Funding Council for Wales
Sports Council for Wales
Welsh Development Agency
Welsh Language Board

Scotland

Scottish Parliament

Edinburgh EH99 1SP
Tel: 0131 348 5000
Website: *www.scottish.parliament.uk*

The Scottish Parliament is responsible for most health issues; education and training; local government, social services, housing and planning; inward investment and promotion of trade; economic development and tourism; most aspects of law and home affairs, including prisons, the prosecution system and the courts; the police and the fire services; the road network, bus policy, ports and harbours; agriculture, the environment, fisheries, forestry and food; the natural and built heritage; sport, culture, the arts and language; and statistics, public registers and records.

Scottish Executive

St Andrew's House
Edinburgh EH1 3DG
Tel: 0131 556 8400
Website: *www.scotland.gov.uk*

The Scottish ministers and Scottish Executive are responsible in Scotland for a wide range of statutory functions. These are administered by six main departments (see pages 492–93). Along with Change and Corporate Services, Finance and Central Services Department, Legal and Parliamentary Services, and the Crown Office and Procurator Fiscal Service, these departments are collectively known as the Scottish Executive. In addition, there are a number of other Scottish departments for which Scottish ministers have some degree of responsibility: the department of the Registrar General for Scotland (the General Register Office), the National Archives of Scotland and the department of the Registers of Scotland. Other government departments with significant Scottish responsibilities have offices in Scotland and work closely with the Scottish Executive.

Scottish Executive Development Department

Victoria Quay
Edinburgh EH6 6QQ

Housing and area regeneration, social justice (including equality, voluntary and social inclusion issues); land-use planning; building control.

Executive agency
Communities Scotland

Scottish Executive Education Department

Victoria Quay
Edinburgh EH6 6QQ

Administration of school education; services for children, families and young people; social care; the arts, libraries, museums and galleries; Gaelic; broadcasting, sport and tourism; protection and presentation to the public of historic buildings and ancient monuments.

Executive agencies
Historic Scotland
HM Inspectorate of Education

Scottish Executive Enterprise, Transport and Lifelong Learning Department

Meridian Court
5 Cadogan Street
Glasgow G2 7AB
and
Europa Building
450 Argyle Street
Glasgow G2 8LG
Tel: 0141 242 5703
and
Victoria Quay
Edinburgh EH6 6QQ

Industrial and economic development: selective financial and regional development grant assistance to industry; promotion of industrial development; urban regeneration and training policy; administration of European Structural Funds programmes for Scotland; and matters relating to energy policy, including renewables.

Sponsorship of Scottish Enterprise and Highlands and Islands Enterprise.

Transport: public transport, cycling and walking; trunk road construction and maintenance; Clyde Hebrides and Northern Isles ferry services; devolved aspects of rail; Highlands and Islands Airports Ltd.

Lifelong learning and skills: further and higher education; science; student support; youth and adult training; workforce development; transitions to work; Modern Apprenticeships; Careers Scotland; sponsorship of the Scottish Further and Higher Education Funding Councils and development of the Scottish Credit and Qualifications Framework; labour market information; adult literacy and numeracy; Individual Learning Account Scotland, Enterprise in Education; Scottish University for Industry/learndirect scotland.

Scottish Executive Environment and Rural Affairs Department

Pentland House
47 Robb's Loan
Edinburgh EH14 1TY

Agriculture and food; safeguarding of plant, animal health and welfare; land use and forestry; CAP subsidies and commodities; farm inspections. Coordination of the Executive's policy on the promotion of rural development and overall responsibility for land reform. Environment, including environmental protection, nature conservation and the countryside; water and sewerage services; waste management; sustainable development, biodiversity, and climate change. Fisheries and aquaculture; control of sea fishing under the CFP; protection of the marine environment. Agricultural and biological research; support of the agricultural and biological science base and funding of related research.

Executive agencies
Fisheries Research Service
Scottish Agricultural Science Agency
Scottish Fisheries Protection Agency

Scottish Executive Health Department

St Andrew's House, Regent Road
Edinburgh EH1 3DG

Executive leadership of NHSScotland and the development and implementation of health and community care policy, in particular: improving, protecting and monitoring the health of the people of Scotland, implementing policies that address health inequalities, prevent disease, prolong life and promote and protect health; developing and delivering modern primary care and community care services; providing hospital and specialist services; encouraging collaboration and joint working between health and other partner organisations; and promoting and monitoring consistent standards of performance throughout NHSScotland.

Scottish Executive Justice Department

St Andrew's House, Regent Road
Edinburgh EH1 3DG

Law and order issues; police, fire and emergency planning; criminal law and criminal justice; community justice services and parole; victims and witnesses; civil law, and jurisdiction and procedure; access to justice, legal aid and the legal system; human rights; courts and judicial appointments; EU justice and home affairs issues.

Executive agencies
Accountant in Bankruptcy
Registers of Scotland
Scottish Court Service
Scottish Prison Service

Crown Office and Procurator Fiscal Service

25 Chambers Street
Edinburgh EH1 1LA
Tel: 0131 226 2626
Website: *www.crownoffice.gov.uk*

Provides Scotland's independent public prosecution and deaths investigation service. Although it is a department of the Scottish Executive, the independent position of the Lord Advocate as head of the systems of criminal prosecution and investigation of deaths in Scotland is protected by the *Scotland Act 1998*.

Change and Corporate Services

S1/5 Saughton House
Broomhouse Drive
Edinburgh EH11 3XD

Human resources, including personnel policy, propriety, recruitment, staff appraisal and interchange, pay, employee relations, training and

development, equal opportunities and welfare; change management; estate management; accommodation services; internal communications; IT facilities and security matters.

Finance and Central Services Department

St Andrew's House, Regent Road
Edinburgh EH1 3DG

Local government; finance; public service delivery; Europe and external relations; media and communications; public bodies and public appointments; and development of Scotland's cities.

Legal and Parliamentary Services

25 Chambers Street
Edinburgh EH1 1LA

Policy on constitutional issues, devolution settlement and electoral matters; the Scottish Parliament's powers and procedures; coordination of the Scottish Executive's legislative programme; liaison with the Scottish Parliamentary Ombudsman; freedom of information policy and legislation; legal advice and services for the Scottish Executive (through the Office of the Solicitor to the Scottish Executive). Also responsible for drafting Bills to be put before Parliament by the Executive and handling associated work.

Executive agency
National Archives of Scotland

Office of the Permanent Secretary (OPS)

St Andrew's House, Regent Road
Edinburgh EH1 3DG

OPS consists of the Ministerial Support Group; Analytical Services Group; the Performance and Innovation Unit; and Changing to Deliver Division.

Northern Ireland

Northern Ireland Office

Stormont Castle
Stormont
Belfast BT4 3TT
Tel: 028 9052 0700
Website: *www.nio.gov.uk*

11 Millbank
London SW1P 4PN
Tel: 020 7210 3000

Supports the Secretary of State for Northern
Ireland, who has direct responsibility for matters
not devolved to the Northern Ireland Assembly,
including political and constitutional matters, law
and order, security, criminal justice and electoral
matters. If the Northern Ireland Assembly is
suspended, the Secretary of State for Northern
Ireland also assumes responsibility for the
direction of the Northern Ireland
departments.

Executive agencies
Compensation Agency for Northern Ireland
Forensic Science Northern Ireland
Northern Ireland Prison Service
Youth Justice Agency

The Northern Ireland Court Service is an
executive agency reporting to the Secretary of State
for Constitutional Affairs.

Northern Ireland Assembly
Parliament Buildings
Stormont
Belfast BT4 3XX
Tel: 028 9052 1133
Website: *www.niassembly.gov.uk*
When it is sitting, the Northern Ireland Assembly
has the power to make laws on all domestic
matters that have been devolved by the
Westminster Parliament: agriculture, forestry,
fisheries and food; culture, media and sport;
economic development; education and training;
most areas of employment legislation;
environment; making agreements for cross-border
co-operation with the Republic of Ireland through
the North-South Ministerial Council; the National
Health Service; local government; social security;
social services; some areas of trade and industry,
including inward investment, promotion of trade,
exports and tourism, and some elements of
company regulation; and most areas of transport.

Northern Ireland Executive and Departments

Website: *www.northernireland.gov.uk*

Department of Agriculture and Rural Development
Dundonald House
Upper Newtownards Road
Belfast BT4 3SB
Tel: 028 9052 0100

Food; farming and environment policy; agri-food
development; veterinary matters; Science Service;
rural development; forestry; sea fisheries; rivers.

Executive agencies
Forest Service
Rivers Agency

Department of Culture, Arts and Leisure
Interpoint, 20–24 York Street
Belfast BT15 1AQ
Tel: 028 9025 8825

Arts, culture, sport, museums, public libraries,
inland waterways, inland fisheries, language
diversity, visitor amenities and matters relating
to the National Lottery and the Northern Ireland
Events Company. Also responsible for two agencies
and two cross-border implementation bodies that
deal with inland waterways and language issues.

Executive agencies
Ordnance Survey
Public Record Office

Department of Education
Rathgael House
Balloo Road
Bangor BT19 7PR
Tel: 028 9127 9279

Control of the five Education and Library Boards
and education from nursery to secondary
education; youth services; and the development of
community relations within and between schools.

Department for Employment and Learning
39–49 Adelaide House
Adelaide Street
Belfast BT2 8FD
Tel: 028 9025 7777

Higher education; further education; vocational
training; employment services; employment law
and labour relations; teacher training and teacher

education; student support and postgraduate awards; training grants.

Department of Enterprise, Trade and Investment

Netherleigh House
Massey Avenue
Belfast BT4 2JP
Tel: 028 9052 9900

Economic policy development, energy, tourism, mineral development, health and safety at work, Companies Registry, Insolvency Service, consumer affairs, labour market and economic statistics services. It also has a role in ensuring the provision of the infrastructure for a modern economy.

Executive agencies
General Consumer Council for Northern Ireland
Health and Safety Executive for Northern Ireland
Invest NI
Northern Ireland Tourist Board

Department of the Environment

Clarence Court
10–18 Adelaide Street
Belfast BT2 8GB
Tel: 028 9054 0540

Most of the Department's functions are carried out by executive agencies. These include: planning; protection and conservation of the natural and built environment; and driver and vehicle testing and licensing. Core departmental functions include the improvement and promotion of road safety; and supporting the system of local government.

Executive agencies
Driver and Vehicle Licensing (Northern Ireland)
Driver and Vehicle Testing Agency
Environment and Heritage Service
Planning Service

Department of Finance and Personnel

Rathgael House
Balloo Road
Bangor BT19 7NA
Tel: 028 9185 8111

Control of public expenditure; personnel management of the Northern Ireland Civil Service; provision of central services and advice.

Executive agencies
Business Development Service
Construction Service
Government Purchasing Agency
Land Registers of Northern Ireland
Northern Ireland Statistics and Research Agency
Office of Law Reform
Rates Collection Agency
Valuation and Lands Agency

Department of Health, Social Services and Public Safety

Castle Buildings
Stormont
Belfast BT4 3SJ
Tel: 028 9052 0500

Health and personal social services; public health and public safety; health promotion; Fire Authority.

Executive agency
Health Estates

Department for Regional Development

Clarence Court
10–18 Adelaide Street
Belfast BT2 8GB
Tel: 028 9054 0540
Strategic planning; transport strategy; transport policy and support, including rail and bus services, ports and airports policy; provision and maintenance of roads; and water and sewerage services.

Executive agencies
Roads Service
Water Service

Department for Social Development

Lighthouse Building
1 Cromac Place
Gasworks Business Park
Ormeau Road
Belfast BT7 2JB
Tel: 028 9082 9000

Urban regeneration; voluntary and community sector; housing; social policy and legislation; child support; state, occupational and personal pensions; social security policy and legislation.

Executive agencies
Northern Ireland Child Support Agency
Northern Ireland Social Security Agency

Appendix B Significant dates in UK history

55 and 54 BC: Julius Caesar's expeditions to Britain

AD 43: Roman conquest begins under Claudius

122–38: Hadrian's Wall built

***c.*409:** Roman army withdraws from Britain

450s onwards: foundation of the Anglo-Saxon kingdoms

597: arrival of St Augustine to preach Christianity to the Anglo-Saxons

664: Synod of Whitby opts for Roman Catholic rather than Celtic church

789–95: first Viking raids

832–60: Scots and Picts merge under Kenneth Macalpin to form what is to become the kingdom of Scotland

860s: Danes overrun East Anglia, Northumbria and eastern Mercia

871–99: reign of Alfred the Great in Wessex

1066: William the Conqueror defeats Harold Godwinson at Hastings and takes the throne

1086: *Domesday Book* completed: a survey of English landholdings undertaken on the orders of William I

1215: King John signs *Magna Carta* to protect feudal rights against royal abuse

13th century: first Oxford and Cambridge colleges founded

1301: Edward of Caernarvon (later Edward II) created Prince of Wales

1314: Battle of Bannockburn ensures survival of separate Scottish kingdom

1337: Hundred Years War between England and France begins

1348–49: Black Death (bubonic plague) wipes out a third of England's population

1381: Peasants' Revolt in England, the most significant popular rebellion in English history

1400–*c.*1406: Owain Glyndŵr (Owen Glendower) leads the last major Welsh revolt against English rule

1411: St Andrews University founded, the first university in Scotland

1455–87: Wars of the Roses between Yorkists and Lancastrians

1477: first book to be printed in England, by William Caxton

1534–40: English Reformation; Henry VIII breaks with the Papacy

1536–42: Acts of Union integrate England and Wales administratively and legally, and give Wales representation in Parliament

1547–53: Protestantism becomes official religion in England under Edward VI

1553–58: Catholicism restored by Mary I

1558: loss of Calais, last English possession in France

1558–1603: reign of Elizabeth I; moderate Protestantism established

1588: defeat of Spanish Armada

1603: union of the crowns of Scotland and England under James VI of Scotland

1642–51: Civil Wars between King and Parliament

1649: execution of Charles I

1653–58: Oliver Cromwell rules as Lord Protector

1660: monarchy restored under Charles II

1660: founding of the Royal Society for the Promotion of Natural Knowledge

1665: the Great Plague, the last major epidemic of plague in England

1666: the Great Fire of London

1686: Isaac Newton sets out his laws of motion and the idea of universal gravitation

1688: Glorious Revolution; accession of William and Mary

1707: Acts of Union unite the English and Scottish Parliaments

1721–42: Robert Walpole, first British Prime Minister

1745–46: Bonnie Prince Charlie's failed attempt to retake the British throne for the Stuarts

***c.*1750–*c.*1850:** Industrial Revolution

1761: opening of the Bridgewater Canal ushers in Canal Age

1775–83: American War of Independence leads to loss of the Thirteen Colonies

1800: Act of Union unites Great Britain and Ireland

1805: Battle of Trafalgar, the decisive naval battle of the Napoleonic Wars

1815: Battle of Waterloo, the final defeat of Napoleon

1825: opening of the Stockton and Darlington Railway, the world's first passenger railway

1829: Catholic emancipation

1832: first Reform Act extends the franchise (increasing the number of those entitled to vote by about 50 per cent)

1833: abolition of slavery in the British Empire (the slave trade having been abolished in 1807)

1837–1901: reign of Queen Victoria

1868: founding of the Trades Union Congress (TUC)

1910–36: during the reign of George V, the British Empire reaches its territorial zenith

1914–18: First World War

1918: the vote given to women over 30

1921: Anglo-Irish Treaty establishes the Irish Free State; Northern Ireland remains part of the United Kingdom

1928: voting age for women reduced to 21, on equal terms with men

1936: King Edward VIII abdicates

1936: Jarrow Crusade, the most famous of the hunger marches in the 1930s

1939–45: Second World War

1947: independence for India and Pakistan: the United Kingdom begins to dismantle its imperial structure

1948: the National Health Service begins to offer free medical care to the whole population

1952: accession of Elizabeth II

1965: first commercial natural gas discovery in the North Sea

1969: first notable discovery of offshore oil in the North Sea

1969: the vote is extended to all over the age of 18

1971: decimal currency is introduced

1973: the United Kingdom enters the European Community (now the European Union)

1979–90: Margaret Thatcher is the first UK woman Prime Minister

1994: Channel Tunnel opens to rail traffic

1999: Scottish Parliament, National Assembly for Wales and Northern Ireland Assembly assume devolved powers

Appendix C Obituaries

Joan Aiken
Writer
Born 1924, died January 2004

Sir Alan Bates, CBE
Actor
Born 1934, died December 2003

Christabel Bielenberg (née Burton)
Author of *The Past is Myself* (1968), her life as an
Englishwoman in Germany during 1934–45
Born 1909, died November 2003

John Bingham
Pianist
Born 1942, died December 2003

Professor Peter Birks
Regius Professor of Civil Law, Oxford, 1989–2004
Born 1941, died July 2004

Lord Blake, FBA (Robert Norman William Blake)
Historian
Born 1916, died September 2003

Professor David Blow, FRS
Biophysicist
Born 1931, died June 2004

Ernest Bond, OBE, QPM
Founder member of the SAS and counter-
terrorism expert
Born 1919, died November 2003

Professor Sir Robert Boyd, CBE, FRS
Space scientist
Born 1922, died February 2004

Fenton Bresler
Journalist and author
Born 1929, died December 2003

Baroness Brigstocke (Heather Renwick Brown)
High Mistress of St Paul's Girls' School, 1974–89
Born 1929, died April 2004

Jack Brymer, OBE
Clarinettist
Born 1915, died September 2003

Anthony Buckeridge, OBE
Author and playwright
Born 1912, died June 2004

Lord Bullock (Alan Louis Charles Bullock)
Historian and founding Master of St Catherine's
College, Oxford
Born 1914, died February 2004

Robert William Burchfield, CBE
Lexicographer, chief editor of Oxford English
Dictionaries, 1971–84
Born 1923, died July 2004

Judy Campbell
Actress
Born 1916, died June 2004

Charles Causley
Poet
Born 1917, died November 2003

John Charles, OBE
Welsh international footballer
Born 1931, died February 2004

Susan Chilcott
Operatic soprano
Born 1963, died September 2003

Don Concannon
Miner and former Labour minister
Born 1930, died December 2003

Sir Alan Cook, FRS
Geophysicist
Born 1922, died July 2004

Judith Cook
Journalist and playwright
Born 1933, died May 2004

Alistair Cooke (Hon. KBE)
Journalist and broadcaster
Born 1908, died March 2004

Dame Felicitas Corrigan, OSB
Benedictine nun and writer
Born 1908, died October 2003

Francis Crick, OM, FRS
Biologist and co-discoverer of the structure of
DNA
Born 1916, died July 2004

David Davies, OBE, DSC
Test pilot
Born 1920, died December 2003

Duke of Devonshire, KG, MC (Andrew Robert
Buxton Cavendish; 11th duke)
Owner, restorer and promoter of Chatsworth
Born 1920, died May 2004

Lord Diamond (John [Jack])
Former Labour minister and SDP politician
Born 1907, died April 2004

Nicholas Evans
Painter of Wales
Born 1907, died February 2004

Nigel Fannin
Marine geologist and pioneer explorer of the
UKCS
Born 1943, died November 2003

Harold Fielding
Impresario
Born 1917, died September 2003

John Flemming, CBE, FBA
Economist and Warden of Wadham College,
Oxford
Born 1941, died August 2003

Paul Foot
Journalist and author
Born 1937, died July 2004

Air Chief Marshal Sir Christopher Foxley-Norris,
GCB, DSO, OBE
Pilot
Born 1917, died September 2003

Sir Terry Frost, RA
Artist
Born 1915, died September 2003

Lord Geraint (Geraint Howells)
Former Liberal Democrat MP and leader of Welsh
Liberal Party
Born 1925, died April 2004

Lord Gibson (Richard Patrick Tallentyre Gibson)
Chairman of Arts Council, 1972–77 and Chairman
of National Trust, 1977–86
Born 1916, died April 2004

Stanley Gilliam
Librarian, the London Library, 1956–80
Born 1915, died April 2004

Sir Alexander Glen, KBE, DSC and Bar
Explorer, sailor and businessman
Born 1912, died March 2004

Ram Gopal
Dancer and choreographer
Born 1920, died October 2003

Nick Gordon
Wildlife film-maker
Born 1952, died April 2004

Sir John Gray, KBE, CMG
Diplomat
Born 1936, died September 2003

Dame Mary Green, DBE
Pioneer of comprehensive schools
Born 1913, died April 2004

Lord Greene of Harrow Weald (Sidney Greene)
General Secretary, National Union of Railwaymen,
1957–75
Born 1910, died July 2004

Thom Gunn (Thomson William Gunn)
Poet
Born 1929, died April 2004

Paul Hamburger
Pianist
Born 1920, died April 2004

Professor Sir Stuart Hampshire
Philosopher
Born 1914, died June 2004

George Hardwick
Footballer and former captain of England
Born 1920, died April 2004

Ray Harford
Football coach and manager
Born 1945, died August 2003

David Hemmings
Actor and director
Born 1941, died December 2003

Madeleine Henrey (Mrs Robert Henrey)
Writer
Born 1906, died April 2004

Admiral of the Fleet Lord Hill-Norton, GCB
(Peter John Hill-Norton)
Chief of the Defence Staff, 1971–73 and Chairman
of NATO Military Committee, 1974–77
Born 1915, died May 2004

David Hobman, CBE
Director of Age Concern, 1970–87
Born 1927, died December 2003

Mary Holland
Journalist
Born 1936, died June 2004

Sir Ian Hunter, MBE
Impresario
Born 1919, died September 2003

Lord Islwyn (Royston John Hughes)
Labour politician
Born 1925, died December 2003

Molly Izzard
Writer
Born 1919, died February 2004

Lord Jenkins of Putney (Hugh Jenkins)
Labour politician
Born 1908, died January 2004

Vivian Jenkins
Welsh international rugby player and journalist
Born 1911, died January 2004

M.M. Kaye (Mary Margaret – Mollie)
Author
Born 1908, died January 2004

Caron Keating
Television presenter
Born 1962, died April 2004

Sir John Killick, GCMG
Diplomat
Born 1919, died February 2004

Right Reverend Donal Lamont
Bishop of Umtali
Born 1911, died August 2003

Dinsdale Landen
Actor
Born 1932, died December 2003

Melvin Lasky
Editor of *Encounter,* 1958–90
Born 1920, died May 2004

Nicholas Luard
1960s satirist, writer and environmentalist
Born 1937, died May 2004

Robert David MacDonald
Playwright and co-director of Glasgow Citizens'
Theatre, 1970–2003
Born 1929, died May 2004

Sir Donald MacDougall, CBE
Economist
Born 1912, died March 2004

Ally MacLeod
Football manager
Born 1931, died February 2004

Lord Manton (Joseph Robert Rupert Eric Watson;
3rd baron)
Jockey, owner and breeder; former senior steward
of the Jockey Club
Born 1924, died August 2003

Dame Jean Maxwell-Scott, DCVO
Preserver of Abbotsford, home of her ancestor Sir
Walter Scott
Born 1923, died May 2004

Dame Sheila McKechnie, DBE
Director of housing charity Shelter, 1985–94 and
of the Consumers' Association, 1995–2004
Born 1948, died January 2004

Norris McWhirter, CBE
Author, broadcaster and founder editor of
Guinness Book of Records
Born 1925, died April 2004

Bob (Robert Alan) **Monkhouse,** OBE
Comedian
Born 1928, died December 2003

Helen Montagu
Theatre producer
Born 1928, died January 2004

Peter Morgan
Sports car manufacturer
Born 1919, died October 2003

The Hon. Lady Mosley (Hon. Diana
Freeman-Mitford)
Writer, third of the Mitford sisters, widow of Sir
Oswald Mosley
Born 1910, died August 2003

Lord Murray of Epping Forest, OBE (Lionel [Len]
Murray)
General Secretary of the TUC, 1973–84
Born 1922, died May 2004

Patrick Nuttgens
Architect, writer and broadcaster
Born 1930, died March 2004

Julia Trevelyan Oman (Lady Strong)
Designer and author
Born 1930, died October 2003

Robert Palmer
Rock and soul singer
Born 1949, died September 2003

Frances Partridge, CBE
Writer and member of Bloomsbury set
Born 1900, died February 2004

Sir Edward Pickering
Journalist
Born 1912, died August 2003

Professor Ben Pimlott
Historian and writer
Born 1945, died April 2004

Norman Platt, OBE
Founder of Kent Opera
Born 1920, died January 2004

Professor Sir John Pople, KBE, FRS
Quantum chemist and Nobel prizewinner (1998)
Born 1925, died March 2004

Patrick Procktor, RA
Artist
Born 1936, died August 2003

Denis Quilley, OBE
Actor
Born 1927, died October 2003

Lord Rayne (Max Rayne)
Property developer, philanthropist; chairman,
National Theatre Board, 1971–88
Born 1918, died October 2003

Jack Rosenthal, CBE
Television dramatist
Born 1931, died May 2004

Cosmo Russell
Campaigner for European integration
Born 1911, died October 2003

Robert Sangster
Racehorse owner
Born 1936, died April 2004

Lord Scanlon (Hugh Scanlon)
President of Amalgamated Engineering Union,
1968–78
Born 1913, died January 2004

The Hon. Mrs Shand Kydd (Hon. Frances Ruth
Burke Roche)
Daughter of 4th Baron Fermoy and mother of the
late Diana, Princess of Wales
Born 1936, died June 2004

Milton Shulman
Drama critic
Born 1913, died May 2004

Ronnie Simpson
Scotland international goalkeeper
Born 1930, died April 2004

C.H. (Charles Hubert) **Sisson,** CH
Writer
Born 1914, died September 2003

Professor John Maynard Smith, FRS
Biologist
Born 1920, died April 2004

Professor Sir Roland Smith
Businessman
Born 1928, died November 2003

Ivor Stanbrook
Former Conservative MP
Born 1924, died February 2004

John Stephen
Fashion designer who made Carnaby Street famous
Born 1934, died February 2004

Stewart Steven
Journalist and newspaper editor
Born 1925, died January 2004

Sir Noel Stockdale
Founding chairman of Asda
Born 1920, died February 2004

Peter Stockham
Bookseller
Born 1925, died September 2003

John Tanner, CBE
Director, RAF Museum, 1963–88
Born 1927, died May 2004

John Terraine
Historian
Born 1921, died December 2003

Norman Thelwell
Cartoonist
Born 1923, died February 2004

Sir Wilfred Thesiger, KBE, DSO
Explorer, soldier and writer
Born 1910, died August 2003

Rt Rev. Jim (James Lawton) **Thompson**
Bishop of Stepney, 1978–91 and of Bath and Wells, 1991–2003
Born 1936, died September 2003

Sir Stephen Tumim
Chief Inspector of Prisons for England and Wales, 1987–95
Born 1930, died December 2003

Sir Peter Ustinov, CBE
Actor, writer, wit, raconteur, stage and film director
Born 1921, died March 2004

Professor Sir William Wade, QC
Jurist
Born 1918, died March 2004

Lord Walker of Doncaster (Sir Harold Walker)
Chairman of Ways and Means and Deputy Speaker of the House of Commons, 1983–92
Born 1927, died November 2003

Willie Watson
Yorkshire, Leicestershire and England cricketer, and England international footballer
Born 1920, died April 2004

Harry West
Leader of Ulster Unionist Party 1974–79
Born 1917, died February 2004

Peter West
Broadcaster
Born 1920, died September 2003

Anne, Duchess of Westminster
Racehorse owner and owner of Arkle, the most successful of all steeplechasers
Born 1915, died August 2003

Con Whalen
Last survivor of the 1936 Jarrow March
Born 1909, died September 2003

Lord Williams of Mostyn, QC (Gareth Wyn Williams)
Leader of the House of Lords, 2001–03
Born 1941, died September 2003

Fred Winter, CBE
Champion National Hunt jockey and trainer
Born 1926, died April 2004

Richard Wollheim
Philosopher
Born 1923, died November 2003

Professor Esmond Wright
Academic and Conservative politician
Born 1915, died August 2003

Hugo Young
Journalist
Born 1938, died September 2003

Percy M. Young
Musicologist
Born 1912, died May 2004

Anne Ziegler
Singer and actress
Born 1910, died October 2003

Appendix D Abbreviations

AIDS Acquired Immune Deficiency Syndrome

AONB Area of Outstanding Natural Beauty

ATMs Automated teller machines

BAP Biodiversity Action Plan

BBC British Broadcasting Corporation

BBSRC Biotechnology and Biological Sciences
Research Council

BCS British Crime Survey

BNFL British Nuclear Fuels

BNSC British National Space Centre

BOA British Olympic Association

BSE Bovine spongiform encephalopathy

CAA Civil Aviation Authority

CAP Common Agricultural Policy

CBI Confederation of British Industry

CCGT Combined cycle gas turbine

CCLRC Council for the Central Laboratory of the
Research Councils

CCW Countryside Council for Wales

CFCs Chlorofluorocarbons

CFP Common Fisheries Policy

CFSP Common Foreign and Security Policy

CHAI Commission for Healthcare Audit and
Inspection

CITES Convention on International Trade in
Endangered Species

CO Carbon monoxide

CO_2 Carbon dioxide

CPI Consumer Prices Index

CPS Crown Prosecution Service

CRE Commission for Racial Equality

CSA Child Support Agency

CSCI Commission for Social Care Inspection

CSIW Care Standards Inspectorate for Wales

CTC Child Tax Credit

DARD Department of Agriculture and Rural
Development (Northern Ireland)

DCA Department for Constitutional Affairs

DCAL Department of Culture, Arts and Leisure
(Northern Ireland)

DCMS Department for Culture, Media and Sport

Defra Department for Environment, Food and
Rural Affairs

DEL Department for Employment and Learning
(Northern Ireland); Departmental Expenditure
Limits

DETI Department of Enterprise, Trade and
Investment (Northern Ireland)

DfES Department for Education and Skills

DFID Department for International Development

DfT Department for Transport

DH Department of Health

DHSSPS Department of Health, Social Services
and Public Safety (Northern Ireland)

DNA Deoxyribonucleic acid

DoE Department of the Environment (Northern
Ireland)

DPP Director of Public Prosecutions

DRC Disability Rights Commission

DRD Department for Regional Development
(Northern Ireland)

DSD Department for Social Development
(Northern Ireland)

DTI Department of Trade and Industry

DTTO Drug treatment and testing order

DVD Digital Versatile Disc

DWP Department for Work and Pensions

EC European Community

ECGD Export Credits Guarantee Department

EEA European Economic Area

EHS Environment and Heritage Service (Northern Ireland)

ELWa National Council for Education and Training for Wales

EMU Economic and monetary union

EOC Equal Opportunities Commission

EPSRC Engineering and Physical Sciences Research Council

ERDF European Regional Development Fund

ERDP England Rural Development Programme

ESA Environmentally sensitive area; European Space Agency

ESRC Economic and Social Research Council

EU European Union

EU-15 The EU of 15 members before enlargement in May 2004

EU-25 The EU of 25 members after enlargement in May 2004

Europol European Police Office

FCO Foreign & Commonwealth Office

FSA Financial Services Authority; Food Standards Agency

G7 Group of seven leading industrial countries

G8 Group of eight leading industrial countries (the G7 members plus Russia)

GCE General Certificate of Education

GCSE General Certificate of Secondary Education

GDP Gross domestic product

GM Genetically modified

GNVQ General National Vocational Qualification

GOs Government Offices (for the Regions)

GP General practitioner

GVA Gross value added

HICP Harmonised Index of Consumer Prices

HIV Human Immuno-deficiency Virus

HND Higher National Diploma

HPA Health Protection Agency

HSC Health and Safety Commission

HSE Health and Safety Executive

ICT Information and communications technology

IEA International Energy Agency

ILO International Labour Organisation

IMF International Monetary Fund

ISA Individual Savings Account

ISP Internet Service Provider

IT Information technology

JNCC Joint Nature Conservation Committee

JSA Jobseeker's Allowance

km/h Kilometres per hour

kW Kilowatt

LEA Local Education Authority

LFS Labour Force Survey

LSC Learning and Skills Council

LTPs Local Transport Plans

MEP Member of the European Parliament

MHRA Medicines and Healthcare products Regulatory Agency

Ml Megalitre

MMR Measles, mumps and rubella

MoD Ministry of Defence

MP Member of Parliament

mph Miles per hour

MRC Medical Research Council

MRSA Methicillin-resistant *Staphylococcus aureus*

MSP Member of the Scottish Parliament

mtc million tonnes of carbon

MW Megawatt

NAO National Audit Office

NATO North Atlantic Treaty Organisation

NATS National Air Traffic Services Ltd

NAW National Assembly for Wales

NCIS National Criminal Intelligence Service

NDPBs Non-departmental public bodies

NERC Natural Environment Research Council

NHS National Health Service

NI Northern Ireland; National Insurance

NICE National Institute for Clinical Excellence

NICS Northern Ireland Civil Service

NICs National Insurance contributions

NIHE Northern Ireland Housing Executive

NITHC Northern Ireland Transport Holding Company

NO$_x$ Oxides of nitrogen

NQ National Qualification

NRU Neighbourhood Renewal Unit

NS&I National Savings and Investments

NSF National Service Framework

NVQ National Vocational Qualification

ODPM Office of the Deputy Prime Minister

OECD Organisation for Economic Co-operation and Development

Ofcom Office of Communications

Ofgem Office of Gas and Electricity Markets

Ofsted Office for Standards in Education

OFT Office of Fair Trading

OFWAT Office of Water Services

OGC Office of Government Commerce

ONS Office for National Statistics

Opra Occupational Pensions Regulatory Authority

ORR Office of Rail Regulation

OSCE Organisation for Security and Co-operation in Europe

OSPAR Oslo and Paris Convention on the Protection of the Marine Environment of the North East Atlantic

OST Office of Science and Technology

OTs Overseas Territories

PAYE Pay-As-You-Earn

PCT Primary Care Trust

PFI Private finance initiative

plc Public limited company

PM$_{10}$ Particulate matter

PPARC Particle Physics and Astronomy Research Council

PPG Planning Policy Guidance

PPP Public-private partnership

PSA Public Service Agreement

PSNI Police Service of Northern Ireland

R&D Research and development

RAF Royal Air Force

RCUK Research Councils UK

RDAs Regional Development Agencies

RDPs Rural Development Programmes

RPG Regional Planning Guidance

RPI Retail Prices Index

RPIX Retail Prices Index (*excluding* mortgage interest payments)

RSL Registered social landlord

SAC Scottish Agricultural College

SBS Small Business Service

SCRC Scottish Commission for the Regulation of Care

SDR Strategic Defence Review

SE Scottish Executive

SEERAD Scottish Executive Environment and Rural Affairs Department

SEN Special educational needs

SEPA Scottish Environment Protection Agency

SET Science, engineering and technology

SIC Standard Industrial Classification

SMEs Small and medium-sized enterprises

SNH Scottish Natural Heritage

SO_2 Sulphur dioxide

SRA Strategic Rail Authority

SSI Social Services Inspectorate

SSSI Site of Special Scientific Interest

SVQ Scottish Vocational Qualification

TB Tuberculosis

TME Total Managed Expenditure

UDP Unitary development plan

UK United Kingdom of Great Britain and Northern Ireland

UKCS United Kingdom Continental Shelf

UKSI United Kingdom Sports Institute

UN United Nations

UNCTAD United Nations Conference on Trade and Development

US United States

VAT Value added tax

VED Vehicle excise duty

VOCs Volatile organic compounds

WDA Welsh Development Agency

WTO World Trade Organisation

Appendix E Bank and public holidays in 2005

Saturday 1 January	New Year's Day	UK
Monday 3 January	Substitute Bank Holiday in lieu of New Year's Day	UK
Tuesday 4 January	Bank Holiday in lieu of 2 January	Scotland
Thursday 17 March	St Patrick's Day	Northern Ireland
Friday 25 March	Good Friday	UK
Monday 28 March	Easter Monday	England, Wales and Northern Ireland
Monday 2 May	Early May Bank Holiday	UK
Monday 30 May	Spring Bank Holiday	UK
Tuesday 12 July	Orangemen's Day	Northern Ireland
Monday 1 August	Summer Bank Holiday	Scotland
Monday 29 August	Summer Bank Holiday	England, Wales and Northern Ireland
Sunday 25 December	Christmas Day	UK
Monday 26 December	Boxing Day	UK
Tuesday 27 December	Substitute Bank Holiday in lieu of Christmas Day	UK

Note: In addition, there are various traditional local holidays in Scotland that are determined by the local authorities there.

Glossary

Additional Member System

Used in elections for the Scottish Parliament and the Welsh and London assemblies, this system combines the election of constituency members on a first-past-the-post basis with additional members elected from a party list in each electoral region. In the United Kingdom, the additional members are elected using the **d'Hondt** system.

Adoption Order

Gives parental responsibility for a child to the adoptive parent(s). The Order is made on application to an authorised court.

Alcohol-related deaths

Includes only those causes regarded as being most directly due to alcohol consumption. Does not include other diseases where alcohol may be a contributory factor, such as cancer of the liver. Also excludes road traffic deaths and other accidents.

Balance of payments basis

Refers to data on exports and imports that have been adjusted in coverage and valuation to make them consistent with international standards for national accounting.

Basic prices

Prices excluding taxes and subsidies on products.

Biodiversity

This covers the whole variety of living things, including the habitats that support them, the different arrays of species and the genetic variation within species.

Carers

In the 2001 Census, unpaid care was defined as unpaid help, looking after or supporting family members, friends, neighbours or others because of long-term physical or mental ill-health or disability or problems related to old age.

Chained volume measures

These are time series that measure **gross domestic product** in real terms (that is, excluding price effects). They are produced by a method known as annual chain-linking. This means that the figures

for 2002 and 2003 quoted in this book are based on 2001 prices (the reference year), figures for 2001 on 2000 prices, and so on.

Children

In surveys, children are never-married people of any age who live with one or both parents. The category also includes step-children, adopted children (but not foster children) and grandchildren (where the parents are absent).

Class A, B and C drugs

In the United Kingdom, illegal drugs are classified under the *Misuse of Drugs Act 1971* into:

- Class A drugs, which include opiates (such as heroin and morphine); hallucinogens (such as LSD and magic mushrooms); ecstasy and cocaine;

- Class B drugs, which include amphetamines and barbiturates; and

- Class C drugs, which include cannabis, most anabolic steroids and benzodiazepine tranquillisers.

Current account

In the Balance of Payments, this is an account of transactions in respect of trade in goods and services, income, and current transfers.

Current prices

Actual prices for the time period in question, without adjusting for inflation.

Decent home standard

This is measured against the following criteria:

- whether the home meets the current statutory minimum for housing, which at present is the **fitness standard;**

- whether it is in a reasonable state of repair;

- whether it has reasonably modern facilities; and

- whether it provides a reasonable degree of thermal comfort through effective insulation and efficient heating.

Dependent children

In the Labour Force Survey and the General Household Survey, dependent children are childless never-married children in families who are aged under 16, or aged 16 to 18 and in full-time education.

DERV

Diesel-engined road vehicle fuel used in internal combustion engines that are compression-ignited.

Detection of crime

A crime is 'detected' (or in Scotland 'cleared up') if a suspect has been identified and interviewed and there is sufficient evidence to bring a charge. There does not have to be a prosecution: for example, the offender may accept a caution or ask for the crime to be taken into consideration by the court, or the victim may not wish to give evidence.

d'Hondt system

A form of proportional representation used in England, Wales and Scotland for elections to the European Parliament and, as part of the **Additional Member System,** used in elections to the Welsh Assembly, Scottish Parliament, and London Assembly.

The party with the most votes in an electoral region receives the first seat. The votes for that party are then divided by two and this new figure compared with votes for the other parties. The party that now has the most votes receives the next seat. Each time a party wins a seat, its total vote is divided by a number equal to the number of seats it has already been allocated, plus one, and the process is repeated until all seats are allocated.

Downstream

Used in oil and gas processes to refer to the part of the industry after the production of the oil and gas. For example, it covers refining, supply and trading, marketing and exporting.

Economically active

Those in **employment** plus those who are **unemployed**.

Employment

Those in employment include employees, self-employed people, participants in government employment and training programmes, and people doing unpaid family work.

Energy use of fuel

Energy use of fuel mainly comprises use for lighting, heating or cooling, motive power and power for appliances.

EU-15

The EU of 15 members before enlargement in May 2004.

EU-25

The EU of 25 members after enlargement in May 2004.

Family

In household surveys, this is a married or cohabiting couple, with or without any of their never-married children (of any age) or a lone parent with his or her never-married children. A family could also consist of grandparent(s) and grandchildren if the parents of the children are not usually resident in the household.

Feedstock

In the refining industry, this is a product or a combination of products derived from crude oil, destined for further processing (other than blending).

Final consumption expenditure

Spending on goods and services that are used for the direct satisfaction of individual or collective needs, as distinct from purchases for use in a productive process.

Final energy consumption

Energy consumed by the final user, as opposed to energy which is being used for transformation into other forms of energy.

Financial account

In the Balance of Payments, this records transactions in external assets and liabilities of the United Kingdom. It consists of direct investment, portfolio investment, financial derivatives, other investment and reserve assets.

Fitness standard

The fitness standard in England and Wales is set out in the *Local Government and Housing Act 1989* and in guidance issued to local authorities. A property is fit for human habitation if it meets all of the following requirements:

- it is structurally stable;
- it is free from serious disrepair;
- it is free from dampness prejudicial to the health of any occupants;

- it has adequate provision for lighting, heating and ventilation;
- it has an adequate supply of wholesome, piped water;
- it has satisfactory facilities for preparing and cooking food, including a sink with supplies of hot and cold water;
- it has a suitably located WC;
- it has a bath or shower and basin, each with supplies of hot and cold water; and
- it has an effective system for draining foul, waste and surface water.

There is a separate fitness standard for houses in multiple occupation.

Fuel poverty

A fuel poor household is one that needs to spend more than 10 per cent of household income to achieve a satisfactory heating regime (21°C in the living room and 18°C in the other occupied rooms).

Gigawatt hour (GWh)

A 1 Gigawatt power station running for one hour produces 1 GWh of electrical energy.

Gross domestic product (GDP)

The total value of economic activity in a region. It is measured in either **current prices** or as **chained volume measures**.

Gross fixed capital formation

Investment in assets, primarily by businesses, which are used repeatedly or continuously over a number of years to produce goods, such as machinery used to create a product.

Gross value added (GVA)

The difference between the value of the output of goods and services produced by an industry or sector, and its **intermediate consumption**.

Household

A person living alone or a group of people who have the address as their only or main residence and who either share one meal a day or share the living accommodation.

Household final expenditure

Spending by the household sector on products or services to satisfy immediate needs or wants.

Household reference person (HRP)

The person who owns the household accommodation, is legally responsible for the rent or has the accommodation by virtue of some relationship to the owner, where the latter is not a member of the household. If this should apply to more than one person in the household, then the HRP is taken to be the person with the highest income.

Household sector

This covers all residents of the United Kingdom as receivers of income and consumers of products. It includes families, residential homes and one-person businesses where the household and business accounts cannot be separated.

Incidence

The frequency of occurrence in a specific period, for example the number of notifications of an infectious disease in a calendar year.

Index

A number giving the value of a quantity relative to a base year, where the value in the base year is set at 100. Index numbers are used to indicate trends in prices, production and other economic variables.

Indigenous production

For oil this includes production from the UK Continental Shelf, both onshore and offshore.

Intermediate consumption

The cost of raw materials and other inputs which are used up in the production process.

Life expectancy

This is the average total number of years that a person of a given age would be expected to live if the rates of mortality at each age were those experienced in that year. 'Healthy life expectancy' is defined as the expected number of years of life in good or fairly good self-assessed general health.

Limiting long-term illness

A self assessment of whether or not a person has a long-term illness, health problem or disability that limits their daily activities or the work they can do, including problems that are due to old age.

Lone parent family

In the Labour Force Survey, a lone parent family consists of a lone parent living with his or her never-married children, provided these children have no children of their own living with them.

Low income

Households living below 60 per cent of median equivalised household disposable income. This can be calculated before or after deducting housing costs – both are equally valid. Household incomes are equivalised in order to adjust for variations in household size and composition.

Magnox

A type of gas-cooled nuclear fission reactor developed in the United Kingdom, so called because of the magnesium alloy used to clad the uranium fuel.

Market prices

The prices actually paid by the purchaser for goods and services, including transport costs, trade margins and taxes.

Owner-occupied property

Includes accommodation that is owned outright, owned with a mortgage or loan, or on a shared ownership basis (paying part rent and part mortgage).

Pensionable age

State pension age is currently 65 for men, 60 for women.

Prevalence

The total number of cases of a disease in a given population at a specific time.

Primary fuels

Fuels obtained directly from natural sources – for example coal, oil and natural gas.

Real household disposable income

The amount of money the household sector has available to spend after taxes and other deductions.

Single transferable vote

A system in which voters rank candidates in order of preference. If the candidate who is a voter's first choice does not need the vote (because they can be elected without it, or because they have too few votes to be elected) then the vote is transferred to the voter's second choice.

Social rented accommodation

Accommodation that is rented from a council or registered social landlord, such as a housing association, housing co-operative, charitable trust, or non-profit housing company.

Trade in services

The provision of services between UK residents and non-residents, and transactions in goods that are not freighted out of the country in which they take place – for example, purchases by tourists.

Unemployed

Those aged 16 and over who are without a job, are available to start work in the next two weeks, who have been seeking a job in the previous four weeks, or are out of work and have accepted a job that they are willing to start in the next two weeks. This definition is recommended by the International Labour Organisation and is used in the Labour Force Survey.

Unemployment rate

Percentage of the **economically active** who are unemployed.

Index

H

M

Q

R

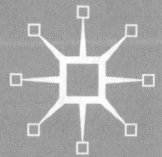